Herrn Sprich,

mit herzlichen Grüßen

[Signature]

3/VIII/10

THE FREE MOVEMENT OF CAPITAL AND FOREIGN DIRECT INVESTMENT

The Free Movement of Capital and Foreign Direct Investment

The Scope of Protection in EU Law

STEFFEN HINDELANG

OXFORD
UNIVERSITY PRESS

Great Clarendon Street, Oxford OX2 6DP

Oxford University Press is a department of the University of Oxford.
It furthers the University's objective of excellence in research, scholarship,
and education by publishing worldwide in

Oxford New York

Auckland Cape Town Dar es Salaam Hong Kong Karachi
Kuala Lumpur Madrid Melbourne Mexico City Nairobi
New Delhi Shanghai Taipei Toronto

With offices in

Argentina Austria Brazil Chile Czech Republic France Greece
Guatemala Hungary Italy Japan Poland Portugal Singapore
South Korea Switzerland Thailand Turkey Ukraine Vietnam

Oxford is a registered trade mark of Oxford University Press
in the UK and in certain other countries

Published in the United States
by Oxford University Press Inc., New York

© Steffen Hindelang, 2009

The moral rights of the author have been asserted

Crown copyright material is reproduced under Class Licence
Number C01P0000148 with the permission of OPSI
and the Queen's Printer for Scotland

Database right Oxford University Press (maker)

First published 2009

All rights reserved. No part of this publication may be reproduced,
stored in a retrieval system, or transmitted, in any form or by any means,
without the prior permission in writing of Oxford University Press,
or as expressly permitted by law, or under terms agreed with the appropriate
reprographics rights organization. Enquiries concerning reproduction
outside the scope of the above should be sent to the Rights Department,
Oxford University Press, at the address above

You must not circulate this book in any other binding or cover
and you must impose the same condition on any acquirer

D21
Zugl. Diss. Univ. Tübingen

British Library Cataloguing in Publication Data

Data available

Library of Congress Cataloging in Publication Data

Hindelang, Steffen.
 The free movement of capital and foreign direct investment : the scope of protection
in EU law / Steffen Hindelang.
  p. cm.
  ISBN 978–0–19–957265–6
 1. Capital movements—Law and legislation—European Union countries. 2.
Investments, Foreign—Law and legislation—European Union countries. I. Title.
 KJE5175.H56   2009
 343.24'03—dc22
                                                                                                                   2009016644

Typeset by Newgen Imaging Systems (P) Ltd., Chennai, India
Printed in Great Britain
on acid-free paper by
CPI Antony Rowe, Chippenham, Wiltshire

ISBN 978–0–19–957265–6

1 3 5 7 9 10 8 6 4 2

Meiner Familie

Preface

This study presents a doctrinal construction of the EC Treaty provisions on free movement of capital in a third country context. There is a particular focus on direct investment. The legal regime applicable to intra-Community capital movement serves as a point of reference and a benchmark and, thus, is also part of a substantial review. The central question of the study is: What rights does a private market participant, engaged in cross-border direct investment originating from or directed to a non-EC Member State, enjoy by virtue of Art 56 EC *et seq?* The study—probably somewhat challenging the contemporary *Zeitgeist* and the resulting reading of economic liberties—argues that in principle, the provisions on free movement of capital apply the *same* liberal standards irrespective of whether intra-Community or third country direct investment is involved. Hence, those who participate in third country direct investment enjoy essentially the same guarantees by virtue of the provisions on free movement of capital as those active in intra-Community direct investment.

Besides aiming at filling a research gap in one of the key areas of EC law, the book's subject matter has lately become very topical and of considerable practical relevance as neo-protectionist ideas are on the rise within the Member States of the EC. The Member States have faced considerable problems in acclimatizing themselves to increasing inward direct investment originating from developing and emerging market countries. Scepticism increases, at times bordering on irrational blunt hostility, if an investment is placed by a so-called sovereign wealth fund headquartered in an emerging market. Political opinion, after a very emotional debate, has been strong enough that some Member States have started tightening their regulatory framework on foreign direct investment. However, such protectionist regulatory measures restricting the admission and treatment of foreign direct investment cannot be imposed *ad libitum*. They must be measured against the freedom of capital movement. This study wishes to provide the relevant evaluation tools to scholars, advanced students, and practitioners alike by offering topical research as well as in-depth analysis of the jurisprudence of the European Court of Justice in the respective area. Due to a large number of reference sources, current issues which are the subject of intense discussion can be identified, the argumentative 'battle lines' and underlying political questions being outlined.

This study reviews German scholarship *in extenso*. In addition to the relevant English literature on the subject, it might help to counteract 'isolation', which vitiates legal scholarship, especially in a discipline such as EC law, when it is confined within linguistic and political frontiers.

Any comments, suggestions, or critiques are welcome and may be sent to the following email address: st.hi@gmx.de.

Steffen Hindelang

Acknowledgements

This study, developed from my doctoral thesis accepted by the Eberhard Karls University Tübingen in 2008, would have never seen the light of day without the support of so many people whom I had the pleasure to meet and the chance to exchange fruitful thoughts and information with over the last three years, not only at the Faculty in Tübingen, but also at international conferences, summer schools, or elsewhere. I am greatly indebted to them.

Thanks are particularly owed to my academic teacher and *Doktorvater* at the Faculty of Law of the University of Tübingen, Professor Martin Nettesheim; not only for providing a stimulating and thought-provoking scholarly environment but also for granting enormous freedom to develop and pursue my own academic projects in the area of EC law and international and European investment law and arbitration. To Professor Wolfgang Graf Vitzthum, the second rapporteur on my doctoral thesis besides Professor Martin Nettesheim, thanks are due not only for the speedy preparation of the examiner's report but also for his guidance and support in preparing a draft study jointly with other colleagues of the School on the interrelation of the law of the sea and international investment law.

To the team of Professor Nettesheim's Chair of Public, European and International Law and Foreign Politics, which I have had the pleasure to be part of as researcher and lecturer since 2004, I would like to express my gratitude for the cooperative working relationship.

The annual participation in the interdisciplinary joint doctoral seminar of the Universities of St. Gallen and Tübingen, headed by Advocate General Juliane Kokott, Professor Heinz Hauser, and Professor Martin Nettesheim, provided a valuable scholarly discussion forum from which I personally greatly benefited. The fruitful, pleasant exchange of thought with Dr Max Gutbrod of Baker & McKenzie Moscow, which culminated in two jointly published papers on international investment law and Russian reality, helped towards a better understanding of the broader context of the subject matter covered by this study. Likewise, the generous invitation of the late Professor Thomas Wälde of the University of Dundee to assist in drafting two of his expert opinions on certain issues in international investment arbitration provided a most valuable insight into economic realities from which my work benefited.

I gratefully acknowledge the support of the *Stiftung der Deutschen Wirtschaft— Studienförderwerk Klaus Murmann* ('Foundation of German Business—Klaus Murmann Fellowship Programme') for providing me with a merit doctoral scholarship. I am also very grateful to the Reinhold und Maria Teufel-Foundation for awarding to my thesis its 'Reinhold und Maria Teufel-Foundation Prize' in 2009.

Thanks are also due to Professor Gerhard Wegen and Dr. Stephan Wilske, both of Gleiss Lutz Stuttgart, Professor Martha O'Brien of the University of Victoria Faculty of Law, and Professor August Reinisch of the University of Vienna Faculty of Law, for their valuable feedback on this study.

Thanks are also due to the team of Oxford University Press. Alex Flach, assisted by Chris Champion, saw the project through to the production stage with great skill and patience. Thereafter, I am indebted to Lucy Ford, the production editor, and Caroline Quinnell, the copy editor, for steering me through the final stages as smoothly and painlessly as could be imagined.

Nicht vergessen werden sollen all die Freunde und Bekannten, die über die Jahre die Entstehung dieser Arbeit verfolgen konnten. Ihnen sei gedankt für all die schönen gemeinsamen Stunden, die die eine oder andere Widrigkeit im Leben eines Doktoranden schnell verblassen ließen.

Gar nicht genug danken kann ich schließlich meiner Familie, die mich von meinen ersten zögerlichen wissenschaftlichen Gehversuchen an stets mit Ermunterung, Wohlwollen, gutem Rat und Unterstützung begleiteten. Ihr sei in den Worten Giuseppe Mazzinis an dieser Stelle zugerufen: La famiglia è la patria del cuore.

Steffen Hindelang

Summary Contents

Preface	vii
Acknowledgements	ix
Summary Contents	xi
Contents	xiii
Table of Cases	xxiii
Table of Treaties, European Legislative Instruments, and National Legislation	xxxv
List of Abbreviations	xliii

	Introduction	1
I	Preparing the Foundation: Economic Rationale for the Liberalization of Capital Movements and the Art of Political Compromise	17
II	Foreign Direct Investment and the Material Scope of Application of Article 56(1) EC	42
III	The Influence of Competing Freedoms on the Scope of Application—Direct Investment between Free Movement of Capital and the Freedom of Establishment	81
IV	Which Level of Protection?—The Scope of the Prohibition of Restriction: Equal Treatment and Market Access	115
V	Personal Scope of Application	201
VI	Exceptions to the Freedom Applicable to Intra-Community and Third Country Situations	214
VII	Exceptions to the Freedom Exclusively Applicable to Third Country Contexts	275
	Perspectives—'Anxiety is the Dizziness of Freedom'	327
	Annex: Summary: Position Statements	332

Bibliography	353
Index	391

Contents

Preface	vii
Acknowledgements	ix
Summary Contents	xi
Contents	xiii
Table of Cases	xxiii
Table of Treaties, European Legislative Instruments, and National Legislation	xxxv
List of Abbreviations	xliii

Introduction   1

1. Subject of this Work and Statement of the Question to Be Investigated   1
2. Available Sources and References   8
3. The Purpose of this Study   13
4. Areas Excluded from this Work   15
5. The Course of this Study   15

I Preparing the Foundation: Economic Rationale for the Liberalization of Capital Movements and the Art of Political Compromise   17

1. Introduction   17
2. The Contribution of Free Movement of Capital to the Attainment of the Aims of the EC Treaty   18
   a. Liberalized Capital Movement within the EC   19
      (1) Free Movement of Capital and the Attainment of the Economic Aims of Price Stability, Equalization of the Balance of Payments, and Economic Growth   19
      (2) Free Movement of Capital and the Attainment of the Aim of an Economic and Monetary Union   21
      (3) Free Movement of Capital and the Attainment of the Aim of Free Movement of Goods, Services, and Persons   23
      (4) Free Movement of Capital and the Attainment of the Aim of Free and Fair Competition   23
      (5) Free Movement of Capital and the Economic Constitution of the Common Market   24
   b. Unilateral Liberalization of Third Country Capital Movement: Lack of Aims?   24
   c. Conclusion   31

3 The Art of Political Compromise: The Way from Coordination of
   Currency Policy to Free Movement of Capital *Erga Omnes*   31
   a Starting with a Clean Sheet—The 1957 Treaty establishing the
     European Economic Community and the 1960 and 1962 Directives   32
   b Lost Momentum—Capital Control on the Rise in the
     Mid-1960s and 1970s   34
   c Liberalization Back on Track—The Single European
     Act and the 1988 Directive   35
   d Seizing the Moment—Free Movement of Capital *Erga Omnes*
     Enshrined in the Maastricht Treaty   37
   e From a Clean Sheet to One of the Strictest, Most Comprehensive and
     Most Effectively Enforceable Multinational Agreements Governing
     Capital Movement   39

II Foreign Direct Investment and the Material Scope of Application of Article 56(1) EC   42

1 Introduction   42
2 What Constitutes a 'Movement of Capital'?   43
   a Wording, Context, Genesis and 'Economic Teaching'   43
   b The Meaning of 'Capital'   45
      (1) 'Capital' in Economic Terms   45
      (2) From Economics to Law   46
   c The Meaning of 'Movement of Capital'   48
      (1) Unilateral Transaction   49
      (2) Financial Transfer   52
      (3) Investment Character   53
   d Summary so Far   57
3 Capital Movements Beyond National Boundaries   58
   a Localizing Capital   58
   b Cross-Border Element   60
4 The Notions of 'Direct Investment' and 'Foreign Direct
   Investment' within the Ambit of Free Movement of Capital   63
   a Economic Impregnation   64
   b The Notion of 'Direct Investment' within the Ambit of
     Free Movement of Capital   66
      (1) EC Capital Movements Directive and the Breadth of the Notion of
          'Direct Investment'—Application 'in its Widest Sense'?   66
      (2) The 'Lasting and Direct Links'   70
   c The Third Country Context: The Notion of 'Foreign Direct
     Investment' within the Ambit of Free Movement of Capital   74
      (1) What Are 'Third Countries'?   74
      (2) Third-Country Capital Movement—A 'Sufficient Link' to a
          Member State of the European Community   75

		(3) Delineating Intra-Community and Foreign Direct Investment	76
	d	Summary so Far 79	

III	The Influence of Competing Freedoms on the Scope of Application—Direct Investment between Free Movement of Capital and the Freedom of Establishment	81
	1 Introduction	81
	2 Direct Investment as an Economic Cross-sectional Activity	82
	3 Parallelism or Exclusivity of Free Movement of Capital and the Freedom of Establishment	88

    a The Provisions of the Treaty—Article 43(2) EC and Article 58(2) EC 88
    b The European Court of Justice: Half-hearted Parallelism 89
        (1) The 'Not Knowing' Strand of Case Law 90
        (2) The 'Not Necessary' Strand of Case Law 92
        (3) The 'Centre of Gravity' Approach 96
    c The Views in the Literature 108
        (1) Exclusivity 108
        (2) Parallelism 110
        (3) Appraisal 110

	4 Summary so Far	113

IV	Which Level of Protection?—The Scope of the Prohibition of Restriction: Equal Treatment and Market Access	115
	1 Introduction	115
	2 The Situation within the Internal Market	116

    a Non-Hindrance Test 116
        (1) Beyond Non-Discrimination 117
        (2) Non-hindrance Test for Inbound and Outbound Capital Movements 119
        (3) Readjusting the Scope of Protection of Free Movement of Capital—*Commission v Kingdom of Spain* and *Commission v United Kingdom* 122
            (a) Shifting to a Test based on 'Substantial Impediment' 123
            (b) A Need for a Substantial Impediment Test?—The Seemingly Non-exhaustive Character of Article 58(1) lit. b EC 128
        (4) Conclusion 129
    b The Non-Discrimination Test in an Intra-Community Context 129
        (1) Comparison Groups 131
        (2) Direct and Indirect Discrimination—Relevant Distinguishing Criteria 135
            (a) Terminology 135

- (b) Direct Discrimination—Expressly Prohibited
  Distinguishing Criteria   137
  - i The Origin/Destination of Capital Movements   137
  - ii Nationality and Residence as Additional Autonomous
    Prohibited Distinguishing Criteria?   140
- (3) Distinguishing Criteria, Direct and Indirect Discrimination, and
  the Delineation of the 'Non-discrimination' and 'Non-hindrance'
  Tests within the Case Law of the Court   140
- (4) The Issue of Comparability   143
  - (a) Comparability Questions with respect to the Regulation of
    Ongoing Businesses—The Issue of Direct Taxation   145
    - i International Tax Law and the EC Treaty   146
    - ii Non-resident Taxpayers Facing Different Treatment by the
      Source (Host) State Compared to Resident Taxpayers   147
      - (i) Article 293 EC, the Distribution of Tax Jurisdiction,
        Double Taxation Relief, and Most-favoured-nation
        Treatment   149
    - iii Different Treatment of a Fully Taxable Resident Depending
      on the Place Where the Capital Was Invested   152
    - iv Article 58(1) lit. a EC—A General Exception to the
      Prohibition of Discrimination?   154
  - (b) Comparability Questions with Respect to Market Access/
    Exit Regulations for Direct Investments   157
- (5) Summary and Appraisal   160

3 The Scope of Prohibition of Article 56(1) EC in a
Third Country Context—Any Modification?   162
- a The Scope of Prohibition in a Third Country Context as
  reflected in the Emerging Case Law of the Court   163
- b Making the Case for a Parallel Understanding of the Scope of
  Prohibition in a Third Country Context: A Critical Appraisal of
  Voices in the Literature   168
  - (1) The Clear and Unambiguous Wording of Article 56(1) EC   170
  - (2) Keeping the Promise of Free Capital Movement *Erga Omnes*?
    Teleological and Contextual Arguments to Restrict the Scope of
    Prohibition in a Third Country Context   170
    - (a) 'One Provision—Two Meanings? How to Split
      what Belongs together'   170
    - (b) A Factual 'Domaine Réservé'?   171
      - i Aiming at Optimized Global Capital Allocation
        per se as a Precondition for Liberalizing Capital
        Movements *Erga Omnes*?   172
      - ii Free Capital Movement *Erga Omnes* as a Mere
        'Auxiliary Function'?   178

    (c) Does the Greater Number of Permissible Restrictions
     Lead to a Restricted *Telos* in a Third Country Context? 180
    (d) The 'Channel Phenomenon' Remedied by Evaporating the
     Scope of Prohibition of Article 56(1) EC to a Mere Ban of
     Exchange Controls? 181
   (3) The Operation of the Non-discrimination Test in a
    Third Country Context 183
    (a) General Exceptions from the Non-Discrimination Test?—
     Article 58(1) lit. a EC 184
    (b) Comparability of Capital Movements in a
     Third Country Context 184
     i Comparability and Direct Taxation in a Third
      Country Context: Taking Differences in the Levels of
      Taxation into Account? 186
     ii Comparability and Market Access and Exit Regulation 190
      (i) Comparability and Market Access Regulation: Taking
       Community Harmonization into Account? 190
      (ii) Comparability and Market Exit Regulation for
       Direct Investment Directed to Third Countries 194
    (c) Appraising 'Comparability'—A Hardly Effective
     Interpretative Parameter to Limit the Freedom's Scope 196
  c Putting Together the Pieces: No Principal Differences in Construing
   the Scope of Protection in a Third Country Context 197

V Personal Scope of Application 201

1 Introduction 201
2 Vertical Direct Effect 201
3 The Irrelevance of Nationality and Habitual Residence for the
  Personal Scope of Application 204
4 The Beneficiaries of the Freedom in Detail 206
5 The Addressees of the Corresponding Obligations 208
  a Member States 208
  b European Community 209
  c Private Persons—Horizontal Direct Effect 210
6 Summary so Far 212

VI Exceptions to the Freedom Applicable to Intra-Community and Third Country Situations 214

1 Introduction 214
2 Exceptions by virtue of Article 58 EC: Grounds of
  Justification and Reference Provision 215
  a Exceptions based on Article 58(1) lit. b EC:
   Intra-Community Context 216

        (1) Preventing Infringements of National Law and Regulations   218
            (a) National Measures in the Field of Taxation   218
            (b) National Measures in the Field of Prudential
                Supervision of Financial Institutions   221
            (c) National Measures in other Fields—A Gradual
                Changeover to the Rule of Reason   222
        (2) Procedures for the Declaration of Capital Movements for the
            Purpose of Administrative or Statistical Information   225
        (3) Public Policy and Public Security—The *Ordre Public*
            Exception   225
        (4) The Proportionality Test   228
        (5) Summary so Far   234
    b Exceptions based on Article 58(1) lit. b EC: Third Country Context   236
        (1) National Measures to Prevent Infringements of National
            Laws and Regulations   237
        (2) National Measures that Establish Procedures for the Gathering of
            Administrative and Statistical Information and the
            Ordre Public Exception   241
        (3) Appraisal: No Fundamental Differences   242
    c The Relationship of Free Movement of Capital and Freedom of
       Establishment on the Level of Grounds of Justification:
       Article 58(2) EC   243
3 'The System of Property Ownership' as a Ground of
   Justification?: Article 295 EC   248
4 The '*Ultima Ratio*' Defence and Security Exception:
   Article 297 EC   253
5 Transitional Periods and Permanent Derogations from the
   Duty to Liberalize Capital Movements   254
    a Transitional Periods Granted to Accession Countries   254
    b Permanent Derogations Granted to Individual Member States   254
6 The 'Rule of Reason' within the Ambit of Free
   Movement of Capital   255
    a The Scope of the 'Rule of Reason': Applicability to
       Discriminatory National Measures   257
    b Mandatory Requirements Established by the Court
       in an Intra-Community Context   261
    c Mandatory Requirements Rejected by the Court in an
       Intra-Community Context   266
    d Summary so Far   268
    e The Operation of the 'Rule of Reason' in a
       Third Country Context   268
        (1) The Mandatory Requirement of 'Fiscal Cohesion'—Reloaded?   269
        (2) The Mandatory Requirement of Securing the Tax
            Base and Preventing the Loss of Tax Revenue—Rebuilt?   271

		(3) Appraisal: No Across-the-board Judgements but Careful Balancing on a Case-by-case Basis 274	

VII Exceptions to the Freedom Exclusively Applicable to Third Country Contexts — 275

1. Introduction 275
2. The True Blind Spot on the Mirror of Free Movement of Capital *Erga Omnes*: The Grandfathering Clause of Article 57(1) EC 276
   a. International Treaties and Article 57(1) EC 279
   b. The Notion of 'Restrictions' 280
   c. The Notion of 'Foreign Direct Investment' within the Scope of Article 57(1) EC: Less is More! 280
   d. The Notion of 'National or Community Law': Don't Break the Link! 283
   e. Determining the Crucial Date: Effectiveness of a Law 286
   f. Appraisal and Summary: A Gateway for Unreasonable Restriction of Intra-Community and Third Country Capital Movement? 290
   g. Incursus: National and Community Laws Restricting Third Country Capital 291
      (1) Identifying National Laws Restricting Third Country Capital Movements 291
         (a) OECD Code of Liberalisation of Capital Movements 292
         (b) WTO GATS: Annex on Article II Exemptions and Schedules of Specific Commitments 293
      (2) Selected Examples for Restrictive Laws 294
         (a) Credit Institutions ('Banks'), Investment Firms, Management and Investment Companies 294
         (b) Non-Life and Life Insurers 297
         (c) Transport 298
3. A Liberalization and Bargaining Tool: Article 57(2) EC 299
   a. Underlying Liberal Notion 299
   b. Competence 301
   c. Limits on the Competence 303
   d. Means of Action 304
   e. Appraisal: The Sleeping Beauty yet to be Woken? 304
4. Managing Situations of Economic Emergency: Article 59 EC 305
   a. Preconditions for Resorting to Safeguard Measures 306
   b. Which Form of 'Safeguard Measures'? 308
   c. Voting in a 'Diminished Council'? 309
   d. Appraisal: Setback in the Standard of Liberalization? 310
5. Responding to Situations of Political Crisis: Article 60 EC 311
   a. Community Measures: Article 60(1) EC 311

            (1) Admissibility of Restrictive Measures Taken by the
                EC under International Law: A Brief Overview   313
            (2) Procedure   317
            (3) Sanction Addressees—'As Regards the
                Third Countries Concerned'   319
        b Member State Measures: Article 60(2) EC   322
            (1) The Relationship of Article 297 EC and Article 60(2) EC   323
            (2) 'Serious Political Reasons'   324
            (3) 'Council Intervention': Community Sanctions on the Basis of
                Article 60(1) EC and Amendment or Abolishment of
                Autonomous Member State Measures by virtue of Article 60(2)
                Subparagraph 2 EC   324
        c Appraisal: Too much Leeway for the Member States?   325

Perspectives—'Anxiety is the Dizziness of Freedom'   327

Annex: Summary: Position Statements   332
    1 Preparing the Ground: Economic Rationale of the Liberalization
       of Capital Movements and the Art of Political Compromise   332
    2 Material Scope of Application of Article 56(1) EC   333
        a What Constitutes a 'Movement of Capital'   333
        b Capital Movements beyond National Boundaries   334
        c The Notions of 'Direct Investment' and 'Foreign Direct Investment'
           within the Ambit of Free Movement of Capital   334
        d The Influence of Competing Freedoms: The Relationship of
           Free Movement of Capital and the Freedom of Establishment   336
        e Which Level of Protection?—The Scope of the Prohibition of
           Restriction: Equal Treatment and Market Access   337
            (1) Intra-Community Context   338
                (a) Non-hindrance Test   338
                (b) Non-discrimination Test   338
            (2) Third Country Context   340
    3 Direct Effect and Personal Scope   342
    4 Exceptions to Free Movement of Capital   343
        a Exceptions Applicable to Intra-Community and
           Third Country Situations   343
            (1) Article 58(1) lit. b EC   343
                (a) Intra-Community Context   343
                    i The Proportionality Test   344
                (b) Third Country Context   345
            (2) Article 58(2) EC—The Relationship of Free Movement of
                Capital and Freedom of Establishment on the Level of
                Grounds of Justification   346

    (3) Article 295 EC—The System of Property Ownership as Ground of Justification?   347
    (4) Article 297 EC—The *Ultima Ratio* Defence and Security Exception   347
    (5) Transitional Periods and Permanent Derogations from the Duty to Liberalize Capital Movements   347
    (6) Rule of Reason   348
        (a) Intra-Community Context   348
        (b) Third Country Context   349
  b Exceptions Applicable Exclusively to Third Countries   349
    (1) Article 57(1) EC   349
    (2) Article 57(2) EC   350
    (3) Article 59 EC   351
    (4) Article 60 EC   351

Bibliography   353
Index   391

Table of Cases

EUROPEAN COURT OF JUSTICE (CHRONOLOGICAL)

Case 1/54 *French Republic v High Authority of the European Coal and Steel Community* [1954] ECR (Spec Ed) 1 144
Joined Cases 7–54 and 9–54 'Sidérurgiques' *Groupement des Industries Sidérurgiques Luxembourgeoises v High Authority of the European Coal and Steel Community* [1956] ECR (Spec Ed) 175. 144
Joined Cases 3–58 to 18–58, 25–58, and 26–58 *Barbara Erzbergbau AG and others v High Authority of the European Coal and Steel Community* [1960] ECR (Spec Ed) 173 143
Case 26/62 *NV Algemene Transport- en Expeditie Onderneming van Gend & Loos v Netherlands Inland Revenue Administration* [1963] ECR (Spec Ed) 1 . . . . . . 201, 202
Case 13/63 *Italian Republic v Commission* [1963] ECR (Spec Ed) 165. 132
Case 6/64 *Flaminio Costa v E.N.E.L.* [1964] ECR (Spec Ed) 585. 202
Joined Cases 56 and 58/64 *Établissements Consten S.à.R.L. and Grundig-Verkaufs-GmbH v Commission* [1966] ECR (Spec Ed) 299 23
Case 32/65 *Italian Republic v Council and Commission* [1966] ECR (Spec Ed) 389 17
Case 57/65 *Alfons Lütticke GmbH v Hauptzollamt Sarrelouis* [1966] ECR (Spec Ed) 205 . . . 202
Case 22/70 *Commission v Council (Re European Agreement on Road Transport: 'AETR')* [1971] ECR 263 . . . . 302, 303
Case 6/71 *Rheinmühlen Düsseldorf v Einfuhr- und Vorratsstelle für Getreide und Futtermittel* [1971] ECR 823 144
Case 6/72 *Europemballage Corporation and Continental Can Company Inc. v Commission* [1973] ECR 215. 23
Joined Cases 6 and 7/73 *Istituto Chemioterapico Italiano S.p.A. and Commercial Solvents Corporation v Commission* [1974] ECR 223 17
Case 152/73 *Giovanni Maria Sotgiu v Deutsche Bundespost* [1974] ECR 153 . . . . . . 136, 137
Case 8/74 *Procureur du Roi v Benoît and Gustave Dassonville* [1974] ECR 837 . . . . 117, 122, 132, 255
Case 33/74 *Johannes Henricus Maria van Binsbergen v Bestuur van de Bedrijfsvereniging voor de Metaalnijverheid* [1974] ECR 1299 118
Case 36/74 *B.N.O. Walrave and L.J.N. Koch v Association Union cycliste internationale, Koninklijke Nederlandsche Wielren Unie et Federación Española Ciclismo* [1974] ECR 1405 211
Case 41/74 *Yvonne van Duyn v Home Office* [1974] ECR 1337 226
Case 4/75 *Rewe-Zentralfinanz eGmbH v Landwirtschaftskammer* [1975] ECR 843 157
Joined Cases 3, 4, and 6/76 *Cornelis Kramer and others* [1976] ECR 1279 302
Case 13/76 *Gaetano Donà v Mario Mantero* [1976] ECR 1333 211
Case 46/76 *W. J. G. Bauhuis v The Netherlands State* [1977] ECR 5. 128
Case 85/76 *Hoffmann-La Roche & Co. AG v Commission* [1979] ECR 461 17
Case 30/77 *R v Pierre Bouchereau* [1977] ECR 1999 226
Case 106/77 *Amministrazione delle Finanze dello Stato v Simmenthal SpA* [1978] ECR 629. 202

Joined Cases 110 and 111/78 *Ministère public and 'Chambre syndicale des agents artistiques et impresarii de Belgique' ASBL v Willy van Wesemael and others* [1979] ECR 35 258
Case 120/78 *Rewe-Zentral AG v Bundesmonopolverwaltung für Branntwein ('Cassis de Dijon')* [1979] ECR 649 .... 160, 191, 222, 224, 243, 255, 265, 266
Case 15/79 *P.B. Groenveld BV v Produktschap voor Vee en Vlees* [1979] ECR 3409 .... 117, 120
Case 22/80 *Boussac Saint-Frères SA v Brigitte Gerstenmeier* [1980] ECR 3427 130
Case 58/80 *Dansk Supermarked A/S v A/S Imerco* [1981] ECR 181 211
Case 113/80 *Commission v Ireland (Re Irish Souvenirs)* [1981] ECR 1625. .... 128, 257, 259
Case 155/80 *Summary proceedings against Sergius Oebel* [1981] ECR 1993. .... 117, 118, 120
Case 203/80 *Criminal proceedings against Guerrino Casati* [1981] ECR 2595 .... 23, 33, 51, 201
Case 270/80 *Polydor Limited and RSO Records Inc. v Harlequin Records Shops Limited and Simons Records Limited* [1982] ECR 329 170
Case 15/81 *Gaston Schul Douane Expediteur BV v Inspecteur der Invoerrechten en Accijnzen, Roosendaal* [1982] ECR 1409 17
Joined Cases 62 and 63/81 *Société anonyme de droit français Seco et Société anonyme de droit français Desquenne & Giral v Etablissement d'assurance contre la vieillesse et l'invalidité* [1982] ECR 223 258
Case 59/82 *Schutzverband gegen Unwesen in der Wirtschaft v Weinvertriebs-GmbH* [1983] ECR 1217. 257
Case 77/82 *Anastasia Peskeloglou v Bundesanstalt für Arbeit* [1983] ECR 1085 287
Joined Cases 177 and 178/82 *Criminal proceedings against Jan van de Haar and Kaveka de Meern BV* [1984] ECR 1797 211
Joined Cases 286/82 and 26/83 *Graziana Luisi and Giuseppe Carbone v Ministero del Tesoro* [1984] ECR 377. .... 47, 49, 50, 53, 54, 306
Case 15/83 *Denkavit Nederland BV v Hoofdproduktschap voor Akkerbouwprodukten* [1984] ECR 2171 304
Case 36/83 *Mabanaft GmbH v Hauptzollamt Emmerich* [1984] ECR 2497. 35
Case 72/83 *Campus Oil Limited and others v Minister for Industry and Energy and others* [1984] ECR 2727 .... 226, 227
Case 182/83 *Robert Fearon & Company Limited v Irish Land Commission* [1984] ECR 3677 .... 248, 249, 251
Case 229/83 *Association des Centres distributeurs Édouard Leclerc and others v SARL 'Au blé vert' and others* [1985] ECR 1. .... 212, 257
Case 270/83 *Commission v French Republic (Re Corporation Tax and Shareholders' Tax Credits: 'avoir fiscal'* [1986] ECR 273 .... 27, 130, 148, 152, 214 258, 266, 267
Case 222/84 *Marguerite Johnston v Chief Constable of the Royal Ulster Constabulary* [1986] ECJ 1651 253
Case 157/85 *Luigi Brugnoni and Roberto Ruffinengo v Cassa di risparmio di Genova e Imperia* [1986] ECR 2013 139
Case 311/85 *ASBL Vereniging van Vlaamse Reisbureaus v ASBL Sociale Dienst van de Plaatselijke en Gewestelijke Overheidsdiensten* [1987] ECR 3801 211

Case 352/85 *Bond van Adverteerders and others v The Netherlands State* [1988]
ECR 2085... 257
Case 12/86 *Meryem Demirel v Stadt Schwäbisch Gmünd* [1987]
ECR 3719... 280
Case 302/86 *Commission v Kingdom of Denmark* [19988]
ECR 4607...224, 266
Case 81/87 *R v H.M. Treasury and Commissioners of Inland Revenue, ex p
Daily Mail and General Trust plc* [1988] ECR 5483 118
Case 81/87 (Opinion of AG Darmon) *R v H. M. Treasury and Commissioners of
Inland Revenue, ex p Daily Mail and General Trust plc* [1988] ECR 5483........ 220
Case 305/87 *Commission v Hellenic Republic* [1989] ECR 1461................. 73, 87
Case 145/88 (Opinion of AG van Gerven) *Torfaen Borough Council v B & Q plc*
[1989] ECR 3851.. 124
Case 175/88 *Klaus Biehl v Administration des contributions du grand-duché de
Luxembourg* [1990] ECR I-1779...148, 258
Case C-188/89 (Opinion of AG Van Gerven) *A. Foster and others v British Gas plc*
[1990] ECR I-3313.. 208
Case C-192/89 *S. Z. Sevince v Staatssecretaris van Justitie* [1990] ECR I-3461........ 280
Case C-360/89 *Commission v Italian Republic (Re Award of Public Works Contracts)*
[1992] ECR I-3401.. 258
Case C-2/90 *Commission v Kingdom of Belgium (Re Prohibition of Tipping Waste
Originating in Another Member State)* [1992] ECR I-4431 259
Case C-76/90 *Manfred Säger v Dennemeyer & Co Ltd* [1991] ECR I-4221 ..... 118, 123, 255
Case C-204/90 *Hanns-Martin Bachmann v The Belgian State* [1992]
ECR I-249 .... 99, 136, 224, 233, 258, 262, 263, 265
Case C-300/90 *Commission v Kingdom of Belgium (Re Deduction of Insurance
Contributions)* [1992] ECR I-305 .... 224, 233, 258, 259, 262, 265
Case C-148/91 *Vereniging Veronica Omroep Organisatie v Commissariaat voor de Media*
[1993] ECR I-487 ....224, 256, 262
Case C-237/91 *Kazim Kus v Landeshauptstadt Wiesbaden* [1992] ECR I-6781 280
Joined Cases C-267/91 and C-268/91 *Criminal proceedings against Bernard
Keck and Daniel Mithouard* [1993] ECR I-6097 122
Case C-312/91 *Procedural Issue relating to a Seizure of Goods belonging to Metalsa Srl*
[1993] ECR I-3751.. 170
Case C-330/91 *R v Inland Revenue Commissioners, ex p Commerzbank AG*
[1993] ECR I-4017..148, 266
Case C-19/92 *Dieter Kraus v Land Baden-Württemberg* [1993] ECR I-1663........ 255, 258
Case C-130/92 *OTO SpA v Ministero delle Finanze* [1994] ECR I-3281 179
Case C-275/92 *H.M. Customs and Excise v Gerhart Schindler and Jörg Schindler*
[1994] ECR I-1039.. 98
Case C-292/92 *Ruth Hünermund and others v Landesapothekerkammer
Baden-Württemberg* [1993] ECR I-6787 122
Case C-391/92 *Commission v Greece (Re Processed Milk for Infants)* [1995] ECR I-1621 137
Case C-391/92 (Opinion of AG Lenz) *Commission v Greece (Re Processed Milk for
Infants)* [1995] ECR I-1621 137
Case C-1/93 (Opinion of AG Lenz) *Halliburton Services BV v Staatssecretaris van
Financiën* [1994] ECR I-1137 144
Case C-51/93 *Meyhui NV v Schott Zwiesel Glaswerke AG* [1994] ECR I-3879 304
Case C-279/93 'Schumacker' *Finanzamt Köln-Altstadt v Roland Schumacker*
[1995] ECR I-225 ....145, 147, 156, 167, 258

Joined Cases C-358/93 and C-416/93 *Criminal proceedings against Aldo Bordessa and Vicente Marí Mellado and Concepción Barbero Maestre* [1995]
ECR I-361 . . . . 8, 37, 50, 51, 119, 139, 142, 163, 201, 202, 222, 230, 236, 375

Joined Cases C-367/93 to C-377/93 *F. G. Roders BV and others v Inspecteur der Invoerrechten en Accijnzen* [1995] ECR I-2229 132

Case C-384/93 *Alpine Investments BV v Minister van Financiën* [1995]
ECR I-1141 . . . . 52, 118, 127, 221, 266

Case C-412/93 (Opinion of AG Jacobs) *Société d'Importation Edouard Leclerc-Siplec v TF1 Publicité SA and M6 Publicité SA* [1995] ECR I-179. . . . . 123, 124, 125, 127

Case C-415/93 (Opinion of AG Lenz) *Union royale belge des sociétés de football association ASBL v Jean-Marc Bosman, Royal club liégeois SA v Jean-Marc Bosman and others and Union des associations européennes de football (UEFA) v Jean-Marc Bosman* [1995] ECR I-4921 259

Case C-415/93 *Union royale belge des sociétés de football association ASBL v Jean-Marc Bosman, Royal club liégeois SA v Jean-Marc Bosman and others and Union des associations européennes de football (UEFA) v Jean-Marc Bosman)*
[1995] ECR I-4921. . . . . 118, 123, 211, 259

Case C-484/93 *Peter Svensson et Lena Gustavsson v Ministre du Logement et de l'Urbanisme* [1995] ECR I-3955 . . . . 98, 120, 139, 259, 264, 267

Case C-55/94 *Reinhard Gebhard v Consiglio dell'Ordine degli Avvocati e Procuratori di Milano* [1995] ECR I-4165. . . . . 82, 118, 123, 255

Case C-80/94 *G. H. E. J. Wielockx v Inspecteur der Directe Belastingen*
[1995] ECR I-2493. 145, 147, 156, 258, 265

Case C-83/94 *Criminal proceedings against Peter Leifer, Reinhold Otto Krauskopf and Otto Holzer* [1995] ECR I-3231 253

Case C-101/94 *Commission v Italian Republic (Re Dealing in Transferable Securities)*
[1996] ECR I-2691 259

Case C-107/94 *P. H. Asscher v Staatssecretaris van Financiën*
[1996] ECR I-3089 . . . . 145, 147, 148, 156, 258, 262

Joined Cases C-163/94, C-165/94, and C-250/94 *Criminal proceedings against Lucas Emilio Sanz de Lera, Raimundo Díaz Jiménez and Figen Kapanoglu*
[1995] ECR I-4821. . . . . 9, 38, 45, 50, 51, 55, 67, 139, 142, 162, 163, 164, 202, 203, 222, 230, 277, 280, 281

Joined Cases C-163/94, C-165/94, and C-250/94 (Opinion of AG Tesauro)
Criminal proceedings against Lucas Emilio Sanz de Lera, Raimundo Díaz Jiménez and Figen Kapanoglu [1995] ECR I-4821. . . . . 163, 202, 284

Case C-233/94 *Federal Republic of Germany v European Parliament and Council (Re Directive on Deposit-guarantee Schemes)* [1997] ECR I-2405 210

Case C-237/94 *John O'Flynn v Adjudication Officer* [1996] ECR I-2617 258

Case C-28/95 *A. Leur-Bloem v Inspecteur der Belastingdienst/Ondernemingen Amsterdam 2* [1997]
ECR I-4161 229

Joined Cases C-34/95, C-35/95, and C-36/95 *Konsumentombudsmannen (KO) v De Agostini (Svenska) Förlag AB and TV-Shop i Sverige AB* [1997] ECR I-3843. . . . . 257, 259

Case C-222/95 *Société civile immobilière Parodi v Banque H. Albert de Bary et Cie*
[1999] ECR I-3899 98

Case C-250/95 *Futura Participations SA and Singer v Administration des contributions*
[1997] ECR I-2471. . . . . 130, 149, 234

Table of Cases

Case C-265/95 *Commission v French Republic (Re Trade Barriers Resulting from Actions by Private Individuals)* [1997] ECR I-6959 209
Case C-299/95 *Friedrich Kremzow v Republic of Austria* [1995] ECR I-2629 60
Case C-368/95 *Vereinigte Familiapress Zeitungsverlags- und vertriebs GmbH v Heinrich Bauer Verlag* [1997] ECR I-3689. . . . . 60, 257
Joined Cases C-51/96 and C-191/97 *Christelle Deliège v Ligue francophone de judo et disciplines associées ASBL, Ligue belge de judo ASBL, Union européenne de judo and François Pacquée* [2000] ECR I-2549. 118
Case C-114/96 *Criminal proceedings against René Kieffer and Romain Thill* [1997] ECR I-3629 304
Case C-118/96 *Jessica Safir v Skattemyndigheten i Dalarnas Län, formerly Skattemyndigheten i Kopparbergs Län* [1998] ECR I-1897. 139
Case C-203/96 (Opinion of AG Jacobs) *Chemische Afvalstoffen Dusseldorp BV and Others v Minister van Volkshuisvesting, Ruimtelijke Ordening en Milieubeheer* [1998] ECR I-4075 259
Case C-264/96 *Imperial Chemical Industries plc (ICI) v Kenneth Hall Colmer (H.M. Inspector of Taxes)* [1998] ECR I-4695 . . . . 219, 229, 267
Case C-266/96 *Corsica Ferries France SA v Gruppo Antichi Ormeggiatori del porto di Genova Coop. arl, Gruppo Ormeggiatori del Golfo di La Spezia Coop. arl and Ministero dei Trasporti e della Navigazione* [1998] ECR I-3949. 118
Case C-336/96 *Mr and Mrs Robert Gilly v Directeur des services fiscaux du Bas-Rhin* [1998] ECR I-2793. . . . . 130, 150
Case C-389/96 *Aher-Waggon GmbH v Federal Republic of Germany* [1998] ECR I-4473 259
Case C-222/97 *Manfred Trummer and Peter Mayer* [1999] ECR I-1661. . . . . 44, 45, 53, 54, 120, 139, 142, 224, 256, 262
Case C-224/97 *Erich Ciola v Land Vorarlberg* [1999] ECR I-2517 259
Case C-254/97 *Société Baxter, B. Braun Médical SA, Société Fresenius France and Laboratoires Bristol-Myers-Squibb SA v Premier Ministre, Ministère du Travail et des Affaires sociales, Ministère de l'Economie et des Finances and Ministère de l'Agriculture, de la Pêche et de l'Alimentation* [1999] ECR I-4809 . . . . . 221, 229, 233, 258
Case C-273/97 *Angela Maria Sirdar v The Army Board and Secretary of State for Defence* [1999] ECR I-7403. 253
Case C-294/97 (Opinion of AG Mischo) *Eurowings Luftverkehrs AG v Finanzamt Dortmund-Unna* [1999] ECR I-7447 . . . . 159, 188
Case C-302/97 *Klaus Konle v Republik Österreich* [1999] ECR I-3099 . . . . 46, 73, 88, 92, 127, 131, 137, 140, 145, 219, 222, 224, 230, 231, 249, 256, 260, 262, 289, 290
Case C-302/97 (Opinion of AG La Pergola) *Klaus Konle v Republik Österreich* [1999] ECR I-3099 . . . . .126, 249
Case C-307/97 *Compagnie de Saint-Gobain, Zweigniederlassung Deutschland v Finanzamt Aachen-Innenstadt* [1999] ECR I-6161 . . . . 133, 148, 149, 150, 151, 187, 266, 267
Case C-311/97 *Royal Bank of Scotland plc v Elliniko Dimosio (Greek State)* [1999] ECR I-2651. . . . . 145, 148, 149
Case C-412/97 *ED Srl v Italo Fenocchio* [1999] ECR I-3845 125
Case C-412/97 (Opinion of AG Cosmas) *ED Srl v Italo Fenocchio* [1999] ECR I-3845. 121

Case C-439/97 *Sandoz GmbH v Finanzlandesdirektion für Wien, Niederösterreich und Burgenland* [1999] ECR I-7041 . . . . 72, 87, 119, 142, 205, 219, 220, 229
Case C-439/97 (Opinion of AG Léger) *Sandoz GmbH v Finanzlandesdirektion für Wien, Niederösterreich und Burgenland* [1999] ECR I-7041 . . . . 72, 87
Case C-35/98 *Staatssecretaris van Financiën v B.G.M. Verkooijen* [2000] ECR I-4071 . . . . 51, 54, 90, 120, 121, 139, 141, 153, 156, 157, 224, 228, 256, 260, 264, 267, 282
Case C-35/98 (First Opinion of AG La Pergola) *Staatssecretaris van Financiën v B.G.M. Verkooijen* [2000] ECR I-4071 . . . . 90, 260
Case C-35/98 (Second Opinion of AG La Pergola) *Staatssecretaris van Financiën v B.G.M. Verkooijen* [2000] ECR I-4071 90
Case C-44/98 *BASF AG v Präsident des Deutschen Patentamts* [1999] ECR I-6269 125
Case C-55/98 *Skatteministeriet v Bent Vestergaard* [1999] ECR I-7641 . . . . 233, 258
Case C-200/98 *X AB and Y AB v Riksskatteverket* [1999] ECR I-8261 139
Case C-251/98 *C. Baars v Inspecteur der Belastingen Particulieren/Ondernemingen Gorinchem* [2000] ECR I-2787 . . . . 48, 71, 83, 84, 85, 86, 93, 97, 107, 139, 263, 265
Case C-251/98 (Opinion of AG Alber) *C. Baars v Inspecteur der Belastingen Particulieren/Ondernemingen Gorinchem* [2000] ECR I-2787 . . . . 73, 83, 84, 85, 87, 93, 109
Case C-254/98 *Schutzverband gegen unlauteren Wettbewerb v TK-Heimdienst Sass GmbH* [2000] ECR I-151 124
Case C-281/98 *Roman Angonese v Cassa di Risparmio di Bolzano SpA* [2000] ECR I-4139 . . . . 60, 211, 212
Case C-367/98, C-483/99, and C-503/99 (Joined Opinion of AG Colomer) *Commission v Portuguese Republic, French Republic and Kingdom of Belgium (Re Golden Shares I-III)* [2002] ECR I-4731 . . . . 94, 248, 250, 251
Case C-367/98 *Commission v Portuguese Republic (Re Golden Shares I)* [2002] ECR I-4731 . . . . 54, 66, 94, 95, 119, 131, 140, 145, 158, 219, 223, 230, 232, 249, 256, 257, 258, 260
Case C-379/98 *PreussenElektra AG v Schhleswag AG, in the presence of Windpark Reußenköge III GmbH and Land Schleswig-Holstein* [2001] ECR I-2099 259
Case C-379/98 (Opinion of AG Jacobs) *PreussenElektra AG v Schhleswag AG, in the presence of Windpark Reußenköge III GmbH and Land Schleswig-Holstein* [2001] ECR I-2099 . . . . 259, 260
Joined Cases C-397/98 and C-410/98 *Metallgesellschaft Ltd and Others, Hoechst AG and Hoechst (UK) Ltd v Commissioners of Inland Revenue and H.M. Attorney General* [2001] ECR I-1727 . . . . 94, 139, 149, 263, 267
Case C-405/98 *Konsumentombudsmannen v Gourmet International Products AB* [2001] ECR I-1795 124
Case C-423/98 *Alfredo Albore* [2000] ECR I-5965 . . . . 46, 112, 131, 139, 140, 226, 253
Case C-423/98 (Opinion of AG Cosmas) *Alfredo Albore* [2000] ECR I-5965 . . . . 92, 145, 226, 253

Case C-476/98 *Commission v Federal Republik of Germany (Re 'Open Skies' Agreement)* [2002] ECR I-9855 303
Case C-478/98 *Commission v Kingdom of Belgium (Re Loans issued abroad)* [2000] ECR I-7587 . . . . 54, 60, 120, 139, 207, 218, 219, 223, 224, 228, 229, 260
Case C-54/99 *Association Eglise de Scientologie de Paris and Scientology International Reserves Trust v The Prime Minister* [2000] ECR I-1335 . . . . 54, 66, 91, 139, 141, 225, 226, 228, 230, 231
Case C-58/99 *Commission v Italian Republic (Re Grant of Special Powers in Privatised Publik Undertakings)* [2000] ECR I-3811 93
Case C-205/99 *Asociación Profesional de Empresas Navieras de Líneas Regulares (Analir) and Others v Administración General del Estado* [2001] ECR I-1271 *et seq.* 230
Case C-221/89 *R v Secretary of State for Transport, ex p Factortame Ltd and others* [ECR] ECR I-3908 . . . . .82, 83, 182
Case C-260/89 *Elliniki Radiophonia Tiléorassi AE and Panellinia Omospondia Syllogon Prossopikou v Dimotiki Etairia Pliroforissis and Sotirios Kouvelas and Nicolaos Avdellas and others* [1991] ECR I-2925 60
Case C-353/89 *Commission v Kingdom of the Netherlands (Re Television Advertising)* [1991] ECR I-4069. 257
Case C-390/99 *Canal Satélite Digital SL v Adminstración General del Estado, and Distribuidora de Televisión Digital SA (DTS)* [2002] ECR I-607. . . . . 98, 100
Case C-483/99 *Commission v French Republic (Re Golden Shares II)* [2002] ECR I-4781 . . . . 53, 66, 94, 95, 119, 120, 226, 227, 230, 232, 248, 249, 250, 251
Case C-503/99 *Commission v Kingdom of Belgium (Re Golden Shares III)* [2002] ECR I-4809 . . . . 53, 66, 94, 95, 226, 227, 231, 232, 245, 248, 249, 250, 251
Joined Cases C-515/99 and C-527/99 to C-540/99 and Joined Cases C-519/99 to C-524/99 and C-526/99 *Hans Reisch and Others v Bürgermeister der Landeshauptstadt Salzburg and Grundverkehrsbeauftragter des Landes Salzburg and Anton Lassacher and Others v Grundverkehrsbeauftragter des Landes Salzburg and Grundverkehrslandeskommission des Landes Salzburg* [2002] ECR I-2157. . . . . 53, 121, 127, 224, 231
Joined Cases C-515/99 and C-527/99 to C-540/99 and Joined Cases C-519/99 to C-524/99 and C-526/99 (Opinion of AG Geelhoed) *Hans Reisch and Others v Bürgermeister der Landeshauptstadt Salzburg and Grundverkehrsbeauftragter des Landes Salzburg and Anton Lassacher and Others v Grundverkehrsbeauftragter des Landes Salzburg and Grundverkehrslandeskommission des Landes Salzburg* [2002] ECR I-2157. 60
Case C-55/00 *Elide Gottardo v Istituto nazionale della previdenza sociale (INPS)* [2002] ECR I-413. . . . . 133, 151, 187
Case C-60/00 *Mary Carpenter v Secretary of State for the Home Department* [2002] ECR I-6279 . . . . 60, 122
Case C-112/00 *Eugen Schmidberger, Internationale Transporte und Planzüge v Republik Österreich* [2003] ECR I-5659 209
Case C-136/00 *Rolf Dieter Danner* [2002] ECR I-8147. . . . . .233, 267
Case C-208/00 *Überseering BV v Nordic Construction Company Baumanagement GmbH (NCC)* [2002] ECR I-9919. 83
Case C-279/00 *Commission v Italian Republic (Re Italian Recruitment Agencies)* [2002] ECR I-1425 139
Case C-324/00 *Lankhorst-Hohorst GmbH v Finanzamt Steinfurt* [2002] ECR I-11779 . . 241, 267
Case C-436/00 *X and Y v Riksskatteverket* [2002] ECR I-10829 . . . . 84, 94, 97, 141, 218, 219, 223, 224, 229, 241, 263, 264, 267

Case C-463/00 *Commission v Kingdom of Spain (Re Golden Shares IV)*
[2003] ECR I-4581 . . . . 53, 66, 120, 123, 125, 126, 227, 230, 232, 249
Case C-463/00 and C-98/01 (Opinion of AG Colomer) *Commission v Kingdom of Spain and United Kingdom (Re Golden Shares IV and V)*
[2003] ECR I-4581 . . . . 45, 94, 95, 232, 250
Case C-98/01 *Commission v United Kingdom (Re Golden Shares V)*
[2003] ECR I-4641 . . . . .53, 94, 95, 125, 127, 249
Case C-322/01 *Deutscher Apothekerverband eV v 0800 DocMorris NV and Jacques Waterval* [2003] ECR I-14887. . . . . 60, 122
Case C-361/01 *The Heirs of H. Barbier v Inspecteur van de Belastingdienst Particulieren/Ondernemingen buitenland te Heerlen* [2003] ECR I-15013 . . . . . . .50, 55, 139
Case C-431/01 *Philippe Mertens v Belgian State* [2002] ECR I-7073 . . . . 144, 149
Case C-452/01 (Opinion of AG Geelhoed) *Margarethe Ospelt and Schlössle Weissenberg Familienstiftung* [2003] ECR I-9743. . . . . 26, 27, 28, 75, 138, 142, 164,
203, 247, 278, 279,
289, 290
Case C-452/01 *Margarethe Ospelt and Schlössle Weissenberg Familienstiftung*
[2003] ECR I-9743 . . . . .162, 164, 224, 266, 279, 283, 289
Case C-9/02 *Hughes de Lasteyrie du Saillant v Ministère de l'Économie, des Finances et de l'Industrie* [2004] ECR I-2409. . . . . .264, 267
Case C-12/02 *Criminal Proceedings against Marco Grilli* [2003] ECR I-11585 117
Case C-36/02 *Omega Spielhallen- und Automatenaufstellungs-GmbH v Oberbürgermeisterin der Bundesstadt Bonn* [2004] ECR I-9609 . . . . 97, 98
Case C-71/02 *Herbert Karner Industrie-Auktionen GmbH v Troostwijk GmbH*
[2004] ECR I-3025 98
Case C-293/02 *Jersey Produce Marketing Organisation Ltd v States of Jersey and Jersey Potato Export Marketing Board* [2005] ECR I-9543 117
Case C-315/02 *Anneliese Lenz v Finanzlandesdirektion für Tirol*
[2004] ECR I-7063 . . . . 54, 91, 105, 141, 153, 218, 219,
223, 224, 233, 260, 263, 284
Case C-315/02 (Opinion of AG Tizzano) *Anneliese Lenz v Finanzlandesdirektion für Tirol* [2004] ECR I-7063 141
Case C-319/02 *Petri Manninen* [2004] ECR I-7477 . . . . 54, 91, 139, 153, 167,
185, 224, 233, 263
Case C-319/02 (Opinion of AG Kokott) *Petri Manninen* [2004]
ECR I-7477 . . . . .48, 54, 91, 139, 141,
153, 162, 164, 167,
185, 187, 224, 233,
260, 263, 265, 270
Case C-334/02 *Commission v French Republic (Re Tax on Income Arising from Investment)* [2004] ECR I-2229 . . . . 54, 139, 219, 233
Case C-442/02 *CaixaBank France v Ministère de l'Économie, des Finances et de l'Industrie* [2004] ECR I-8961 139
Case C-20/03 *Criminal proceedings against Marcel Burmanjer, René Alexander Van Der Linden and Anthony De Jong* [2005] ECR I-4133 98
Case C-169/03 *Florian W. Wallentin v Riksskatteverket* [2004] ECR I-6443 147
Case C-205/03 P (Opinion of AG Maduro) *Federación Española de Empresas de Tecnología Sanitaria (FENIN), formerly Federación Nacional de Empresas, Instrumentación Científica, Médica, Técnica y Dental* [2006] ECR I-6295 252

Case C-242/03 *Ministre des Finances v Jean-Claude Weidert
and Élisabeth Paulus* [2004] ECR I-7379. . . . . 54, 91, 139, 224, 260
Case C-242/03 (Opinion of AG Kokott) *Ministre des Finances v Jean-Claude Weidert
and Élisabeth Paulus* [2004] ECR I-7379. . . . . 47, 205, 260
Case C-268/03 *Jean-Claude De Baeck v Kingdom of Belgium*
[2004] ECR I-5961 . . . . 94, 141
Case C-376/03 *D v Inspecteur van de Belastingdienst/Particulieren/Ondernemingen
buitenland te Heerlen* [2005] ECR I-5821 . . . . 54, 132, 142, 145, 147, 150, 151
Case C-376/03 (Opinion AG Colomer) *D v Inspecteur van de Belastingdienst/
Particulieren/Ondernemingen buitenland te Heerlen*
[2005] ECR I-5821 . . . . .129, 132, 133, 138, 141, 150
Case C-411/03 *SEVIC Systems AG* [2005] ECR I-10805 . . . . 83, 139
Case C-446/03 *Marks & Spencer plc v David Halsey (H.M. Inspector of Taxes)*
[2005] ECR I-10837. 91, 145, 150, 229, 233, 234, 263, 268
Case C-446/03 (Opinion of AG Maduro) *Marks & Spencer plc v David Halsey
(H.M. Inspector of Taxes)* [2005] ECR I-10837. . . . . 149, 229, 234
Case C-512/03 *J.E.J. Blanckaert v Inspecteur van de Belastingdienst/Particulieren/
Ondernemingen buitenland te Heerlen* [2005] ECR I-7685. 53
Case C-513/03 *Heirs of M. E. A. van Hilten-van der Heijden v Inspecteur van de
Belastingdienst/Particulieren/Ondernemingen buitenland te Heerlen*
[2006] ECR I-1957 . . . . .52, 55, 62, 133, 165, 187
Case C-513/03 (Opinion of AG Léger) *Heirs of M. E. A. van Hilten-van der Heijden v Inspecteur
van de Belastingdienst/Particulieren/Ondernemingen buitenland te Heerlen*
[2006] ECR I-1957 . . . . .52, 62, 133, 157, 165
Joined Cases C-94/04 and C-202/04 'Cipolla' (Opinion of AG Maduro)
*Federico Cipolla v Rosaria Fazari, née Portolese and Stefano Macrino
et Claudia Capoparte v Roberto Meloni* [2006] ECR I-11421 252
Case C-174/04 *Commission v Italian Republic (Re Automatic Suspension of Voting
Rights in Privatised Undertaking)* [2005] ECR I-4933 . . . . 54, 92, 119, 256
Case C-174/04 (Opinion of AG Kokott) *Commission v Italian Republic (Re Automatic
Suspension of Voting Rights in Privatised Undertaking)*
[2005] ECR I-4933 92
Case C-196/04) *Cadbury Schweppes and Cadbury Schweppes Overseas Ltd v
Commissioners of Inland Revenue* [2006]
ECR I-7995 . . . . .84, 96, 97, 98, 104, 105, 106, 145, 188, 220, 229, 239
Case C-196/04 (Opinion of AG Léger) *Cadbury Schweppes and Cadbury Schweppes
Overseas Ltd v Commissioners of Inland Revenue* [2006] ECR I-7995. 97
Case C-265/04 *Margaretha Bouanich v Skatteverket* [2006] ECR I-923 . . . . .91, 139, 141, 265
Case C-265/04 (Opinion of AG Kokott) *Margaretha Bouanich v Skatteverket*
[2006] ECR I-923. . . . . 91, 123, 141
Joined Cases C-282/04 and C-283/04 *Commission v Kingdom of the Netherlands
(Re Golden Shares VI)* [2006] ECR I-9141 . . . . 53, 232, 249
Joined Cases C-282/04 and C-283/04 (Opinion of AG Maduro) *Commission v
Kingdom of the Netherlands (Re Golden Shares VI)* [2006] ECR I-9141 . . . . . . 208, 250, 252
Case C-292/04 *Wienand Meilicke, Heidi Christa Weyde, Marina Stöffler v
Finanzamt Bonn-Innenstadt* [2007] ECR I-1835. 139
Case C-292/04 (Opinion of AG Tizzano) *Wienand Meilicke, Heidi Christa Weyde, Marina Stöffler
v Finanzamt Bonn-Innenstadt* [2007] ECR I-1835. 153
Case C-347/04 *Rewe Zentralfinanz eG, as Universal Legal Successor of
ITS Reisen GmbH v Finanzamt Koln-Mitte* [2007] ECR I-2647 102

xxxii *Table of Cases*

Case C-347/04 (Opinion of AG Maduro) *Rewe Zentralfinanz eG, as Universal Legal Successor of ITS Reisen GmbH v Finanzamt Köln-Mitte* [2007] ECR I-2647 .... 86, 101, 102, 150
Case C-374/04 *Test Claimants in Class IV of the ACT Group Litigation (Pirelli, Essilor and Sony), Test Claimants in Class IV of the ACT Group Litigation (BMW) v Commissioners of Inland Revenue* [2006] ECR I-11673 .... 101, 102, 105, 133, 139, 151, 152, 162, 166, 187
Case C-374/04 (Opinion of AG Geelhoed) *Test Claimants in Class IV of the ACT Group Litigation (Pirelli, Essilor and Sony), Test Claimants in Class IV of the ACT Group Litigation (BMW) v Commissioners of Inland Revenue* [2006] ECR I-11673 .... 150, 151, 153, 166, 186, 187
Case C-446/04 *Test Claimants in the FII Group Litigation v Commissioners of Inland Revenue* [2006] ECR I-11753 .... 9, 38, 51, 52, 67, 84, 85, 101, 102, 104, 105, 139, 162, 168, 182, 189, 203, 246, 281, 284, 290
Case C-446/04 (Opinion of AG Geelhoed) *Test Claimants in the FII Group Litigation v Commissioners of Inland Revenue* [2006] ECR I-11753 .... 86, 87, 101, 102, 167, 185, 187, 197, 289, 290
Case C-452/04 *Fidium Finanz AG* [2006] ECR I-9521 .... 9, 38, 95, 97, 98, 100, 105, 162, 166, 203
Case C-452/04 (Opinion of AG Stix-Hackl) *Fidium Finanz AG* [2006] ECR I-9521 .... 9, 38, 95, 97, 98, 99, 100, 105, 162, 166, 203
Case C-470/04 *N v Inspecteur van de Belastingdienst Oost/kantoor Almelo* [2006] ECR I-7409 150
Case C-492/04 *Lasertec Gesellschaft für Stanzformen mbH (formerly Riess Laser Bandstahlschnitte GmbH) v Finanzamt Emmendingen* [2007] ECR I-3775 .... 10, 104, 105, 162, 186, 286, 287
Case C-513/04 (Opinion of AG Geelhoed) *Mark Kerckhaert, Bernadette Morres v The Belgian State* [2006] ECR I-10967 .... 152, 153
Case C-524/04 *Test Claimants in the Thin Cap Group Litigation* [2007] ECR I-2107 .... 9, 38, 77, 78, 103, 104, 106, 139, 162, 186, 203
Case C-524/04 (Opinion of AG Geelhoed) *Test Claimants in the Thin Cap Group Litigation* [2007] ECR I-2107 109
Case C-101/05 *Skatteverket v A* [2007] ECR I-11531 .... 27, 28, 162, 168, 170, 175, 176, 181, 186, 196, 197, 203, 238, 240, 289
Case C-101/05 (Opinion of AG Bot) *Skatteverket v A* [2007] ECR I-11531 .... 27, 28, 30, 168, 170, 180, 181, 239, 240
Case C-102/05 *Skatteverket v A and B* [2007] ECR I-3871 .... 104, 106, 162
Case C-112/05 *Commission v Germany (Re Golden Shares VII 'Volkswagengesetz')* [2007] ECR I-8995 .... 119, 120
Case C-112/05 (Opinion AG Colomer) *Commission v Germany (Re Golden Shares VII 'Volkswagengesetz')* [2007] ECR I-8995 .... 95, 111, 249, 250
Case C-157/05 *Winfried Holböck v Finanzamt Salzburg-Land* [2007] ECR I-4051 .... 10, 38, 66, 105, 106, 162, 166, 187, 203, 281, 282, 284, 289, 290
Case C-201/05 *The Test Claimants in the CFC and Dividend Group Litigation v Commissioners of Inland Revenue* [2008] ECR I-2875 .... 101, 162
Case C-231/05 *Oy AA* [2007] ECR I-6373 104

Case C-298/05 *Columbus Container Services BVBA & Co. v Finanzamt Bielefeld-Innenstadt*
  [2007] ECR I-10451 105
Joint Cases C-402/05 P and C-415/05 P *Yassin Abdullah Kadi and Al Barakaat
  International Foundation v Council and Commission* [2008] ECR nyp 319, 320, 321, 322
Case C-194/06 *Staatssecretaris von Financiën v Orange European Smallcap Fund NV*
  [2008] ECR I-3747. . . . . 86, 162
Case C-205/06 *Commission v Republic of Austria (Re Provisions on the Free Transfer of
  Investment Related Payments in Bilateral Investment Agreements)* [nyd] 12, 40
Case C-249/06 *Commission v Kingdom of Sweden (Re Provisions on the Free Transfer of
  Investment Related Payments in Bilateral Investment Agreements)* [nyd] 12, 40
Case C-274/06 *Commission v Kingdom of Spain (Re Golden Shares VIII)*
  [2008] ECR I-26. 249
Case C-414/06 *Lidl Belgium GmbH & Co. KG v Finanzamt Heilbronn*
  [2008] ECR I-3601. 104
Case C-415/06 *Stahlwerk Ergste Westig GmbH v Finanzamt Düsseldorf-Mettmann*
  [2007] ECR I-151 RJ.Pub_Somm 104, 286
Case C-118/07 *Commission v Republic of Finland (Re Provisions on the Free Transfer of
  Investment Related Payments in Bilateral Investment Agreements)* [nyd] 12, 41
Opinion 1/76 *Draft Agreement Establishing a European Laying-up Fund for Inland
  Waterway Vessels* [1977] ECR 741 302
Opinion 1/91 *Draft Agreement between the Community, on the one Hand, and the
  Countries of the European Free Trade Association, on the other, Relating to the Creation
  of the European Economic Area* [1991] ECR I-6079 . . . . 170, 171
Opinion 2/91 *Convention No 170 of the International Labour Organization concerning
  Safety in the Use of Chemicals at Work* [1993] ECR I-1061 302
Opinion 2/92 *Competence of the Community or one of its Institutions to
  Participate in the Third Revised Decision of the OECD on National Treatment:
  'OECD'* [1995] ECR I-521 303
Opinion 1/94 *Competence of the Community to Conclude International Agreements
  Concerning Services and the Protection of Intellectual Property*
  [1994] ECR I-5267. . . . . 176, 302, 303

COURT OF FIRST INSTANCE (CHRONOLOGICAL)

CFI, Case T-306/01 *Ahmed Ali Yusuf and Al Barakaat International Foundation v
  Council and Commission* [2005] ECR II-3533 . . . . 277, 313, 314, 319, 320, 321
CFI, Case T-315/01 *Yassin Abdullah Kadi v Council and Commission)*
  [2005] ECR II-3649 . . . . 319, 320, 321
CFI, Case T-253/02 'Ayadi' *Chafiq Ayadi v Council* [2006] ECR II-2139. 320
CFI, Case T-362/04 *Leonid Minin v Commission* [2007] ECR II-2003 320

OTHER COURTS (CHRONOLOGICAL)

ICJ, *Advisory Opinion on Legality of the Use by a State of Nuclear Weapons in
  Armed Conflict* adopted on 08.07.1996. 316
EFTA Court, *Case E-1/00 State Debt Management Agency v Íslandsbanki-FBA
  hf* adopted on 14.07.2000 119
Unabhängiger Finanzsenat Außenstelle Linz (Austria), *GZ. RV/0279-L/04* adopted
  on 13.01.2005. . . . . .237, 269

Table of Treaties, European Legislative Instruments, and National Legislation

INTERNATIONAL TREATIES (CHRONOLOGICAL)

1944 Agreement of the International Monetary Fund (as amended effective 1969, 1978, 1992) (adopted 22.7.1944, entered into force 27.12.1945) <http://www.imf.org/external/pubs/ft/aa/index.htm> accessed 12.12.2005 . . . . 40, 309

1950 Convention for the Protection of Human Rights and Fundamental Freedoms (adopted 04.11.1950, entered into force 03.09.1953) <http://www.echr.coe.int/NR/rdonlyres/D5CC24A7-DC13-4318-B457-5C9014916D7A/0/EnglishAnglais.pdf> accessed 07.04.2007 48

1952 Protocol No. 1 to the Convention for the Protection of Human Rights and Fundamental Freedoms (adopted 20.3.1952, entered into force 18.05.1954) <http://www.echr.coe.int/NR/rdonlyres/D5CC24A7-DC13-4318-B457-5C9014916D7A/0/EnglishAnglais.pdf> accessed 07.04.2007 48

1961 OECD Code of Liberalisation of Current Invisible Operations (as amended 19.02.2008) <http://www.oecd.org/dataoecd/41/21/2030182.pdf> accessed 23.12.2008 309

1961 OECD Code of Liberalisation of Capital Movements (as amended 01.11.2007) <http://www.oecd.org/dataoecd/10/62/39664826.pdf> accessed 23.12.2008 . . . . 40, 67, 292, 309

1969 Vienna Convention on the Law of Treaties (adopted 23.05.1969, entered into force 27.01.1980) United Nations, 1155 UNTS 331 207

1970 Agreement Establishing an Association between the European Economic Community and Malta OJ [Not Included in the Spec Ed] L61 of 14.03.1971, 2, date enacted: 15.12.1970, date in force: 01.04.1971 280

1972 Agreement Establishing an Association between the European Economic Community and the Republic of Cyprus, OJ L133 of 21.5.1973, 2, date enacted: 19.12.1972, date in force: 01.06.1973 280

1986 Single European Act, OJ L169 of 29.06.1987, 1, date enacted: 17.02./28.02.1986, date in force: 01.07.1987 35

1990 Convention on the Elimination of Double Taxation in Connection with the Adjustment of Transfers of Profits between Associated Undertakings (90/436/EEC), OJ L225 of 20.08.1990, 10, date enacted: 23.07.1990, date in force: 01.01.1995 [ceased to have effect in 2000] 150

1992 Final Act of the Intergovernmental Conference adopting the Maastricht Treaty, date enacted: 07.02.1992 180

1992 Agreement on the European Economic Area – Final Act (as amended), OJ L001 of 03.01.1994, 3, date enacted: 02.05.1992, date in force: 01.01.1994 . . . . 40, 283

1992 Treaty on European Union – Protocol (No 1) on the Acquisition of Property in Denmark, OJ C191 of 29.07.1992, 68, date enacted: 07.02.1992, date in force: 01.11.1993 . . . . 254, 289

1994 WTO General Agreement on Trade in Services (adopted 15.04.1994, entered into force
  01.01.1995) <http://www.wto.org/english/docs_e/legal_e/26-gats_01_e.htm>
  accessed 22.8.2006 . . . . .40, 292, 309
1994 EC-Russia Agreement on Partnership and Cooperation, OJ L327 of 28.11.1997, 1,
  date enacted: 24.06.1994, date in force: 01.12.1997 239
1997 Treaty of Amsterdam amending the Treaty on European Union, the Treaties
  establishing the European Communities and Related Acts, OJ C340 of 10.11.1997, 1,
  date enacted: 02.10.1997, date in force: 01.05.1999 38
2000 Treaty of Nice amending the Treaty on European Union, the Treaties establishing
  the European Communities and Certain Related Acts, OJ C80 of 10.03.2001, 1,
  date enacted: 11.12.2000, date in force: 01.02.2003 39
2003 Understanding concerning certain U.S. Bilateral Investment Treaties
  (adopted 22.09.2003) Digest of United States Practice in International Law
  Chapter 11, No 40 <http://www.state.gov/s/l/2003/44366.htm>
  accessed 12.12.2007. . . . . 12, 40
2003 Treaty of Accession of the Czech Republic, Estonia, Cyprus, Latvia, Lithuania,
  Hungary, Malta, Poland, Slovenia and Slovakia – Annexes V to XIV,
  OJ L236 of 23.09.2003, 803, date enacted: 16.04.2003 254
2007 Treaty of Lisbon amending the Treaty on European Union and the
  Treaty establishing the European Community, OJ C306 of 17.12.2007, 1,
  date enacted: 13.12.2007 . . . . .276, 330

EC DIRECTIVES (CHRONOLOGICAL)

First Directive for the Implementation of Article 67 of the Treaty, Spec Ed Series I
  Chapter 1959–1962, 49, date enacted: 11.05.1960, date in force:
  11.05.1960 [Repealed]. 33
Second Directive of Adding to and Amending the First Directive for the
  Implementation of Article 67 of the Treaty (63/21/EEC), Spec Ed Series I
  Chapter 1963–1964, 5, date enacted: 18.12.1962, date in force: 18.12.1962 [Repealed] . . . 33
Directive concerning Indirect Taxes on the Raising of Capital (69/335/EEC), OJ L249 of
  03.10.1969, 25, date enacted: 17.07.1969. 178
First Directive on the Coordination of Laws, Regulations and Administrative
  Provisions Relating to the Taking-up and Pursuit of the Business of Direct
  Insurance other than Life Assurance (73/239/EEC), OJ L228 of 16.08.1973,
  3, date enacted: 24.07.1973, date in force: 27.07.1973 . . . . 297, 298, 301
Directive on Mutual Assistance for the Recovery of Claims Resulting from Operations
  Forming Part of the System of Financing the European Agricultural Guidance and
  Guarantee Fund, and of the Agricultural Levies and Customs Duties
  (76/308/EEC), OJ L73 of 19.03.1976, 18, date enacted: 15.03.1976,
  date in force: 19.03.1976. 195
First Directive on the Coordination of the Laws, Regulations and Administrative Provisions
  Relating to the Taking up and Pursuit of the Business of Credit Institutions (77/780/EEC),
  OJ L322 of 17.12.1977, 30, date enacted: 12.12.1977, date in force: 22.12.1989 [Repealed
  15.06.2000] 295, 296
Directive Concerning Mutual Assistance by the Competent Authorities of the Member
  States in the Field of Direct Taxation and Taxation of Insurance Premiums
  (77/799/EEC), OJ L336 of 27.12.1977, 15, date enacted: 19.12.1977,
  date in force: 23.12.1977. . . . . 189, 195, 220, 233, 238, 240

Fourth Directive based on Article 54(3)(g) of the Treaty on the Annual Accounts of
  Certain Types of Companies (78/660/EEC), OJ L222 of 14.08.1978, 11, date enacted:
  25.07.1978, date in force: 31.07.1978 . . . . 71, 84
First Directive on the Coordination of Laws, Regulations and Administrative Provisions
  Relating to the Taking up and Pursuit of the Business of Direct Life Assurance
  (79/267/EEC), OJ L63 of 13.03.1979, 1, date enacted: 05.03.1979, date in force:
  15.03.1979 [Repealed] 298
Seventh Directive based on the Article 54(3)(g) of the Treaty on Consolidated
  Accounts (83/349/EEC), OJ L193 of 18.07.1983, 1, date enacted: 13.06.1983,
  date in force: 29.06.1983 . . . . 71, 84
Directive on the Coordination of Laws, Regulations and Administrative Provisions
  Relating to Undertakings for Collective Investment in Transferable Securities
  (UCITS) (85/611/ECC), OJ L375 of 31.12.1985, 3, date enacted: 20.12.1985,
  date in force: 24.12.1985 . . . . 294, 295, 297, 301
Directive amending the First Directive of 11 May 1960 for the Implementation of Article 67
  of the Treaty (86/566/EEC), OJ L332 of 26.11.1986, date enacted: 17.11.1986,
  date in force: 26.11.1986 [Repealed] 36
Directive for the Implementation of Article 67 of the Treaty ('EC Capital Movements
  Directive') (88/361/EEC), OJ L178 of 08.07.1988, 5, date enacted: 24.06.1988,
  date in force: 01.07.1990 . . . . 8, 21, 36, 37, 44, 47, 49, 52, 53, 55, 62,
                                                  66, 67, 68, 70, 72, 84, 87, 98, 108, 111, 155,
                                                  173, 201, 216, 218, 221, 222, 272, 281, 335
Second Directive on the Coordination of Laws, Regulations and Administrative
  Provisions Relating to the Taking up and Pursuit of the Business of Credit
  Institutions and amending Directive 77/780/EEC (89/646/EEC), OJ L386 of
  30.12.1989, 1, date enacted: 15.12.1989, date in force: 22.12.1989
  [Repealed 15.06.2000] 295, 296
Directive on the Common System of Taxation Applicable to Mergers, Divisions,
  Transfers of Assets and Exchanges of Shares Concerning Companies of Different
  Member States (90/434/EEC), OJ L225 of 20.08.1990, 1 *et seq*, date enacted:
  23.07.1990, date in force: 30.07.1990 272
Directive on the Common System of Taxation Applicable in the Case of Parent Companies and
  Subsidiaries of Different Member States (90/435/EEC), OJ L225 of
  20.08.1990, 6, date enacted: 23.07.1990, date in force: 30.07.1990 . . . . 71, 84, 272
Directive Amending, Particularly as Regards Motor Vehicle Liability Insurance, Directive
  73/239/EEC and Directive 88/357/EEC which Concern the Coordination of Laws,
  Regulations and Administrative Provisions Relating to Direct Insurance other than Life
  Assurance (90/618/EEC), OJ L330 of 29.11.1990, 44, date in force: 08.11.1990 298
Directive on the Coordination of Laws, Regulations and Administrative Provisions
  Relating to Direct Life Assurance, Laying down Provisions to Facilitate the Effective
  Exercise of Freedom to Provide Services and Amending Directive 79/267/EEC
  (90/619/EEC), OJ L330 of 29.11.1990, 50, date enacted: 08.11.1990, date in force:
  20.11.1990 [Repealed] 298
Directive on Investment Services in the Securities Field (93/22/EEC),
  OJ L141 of 11.06.1993, 27, date enacted: 10.05.1993, date in force: 24.05.1993
  [Repealed] 297
Directive amending Directives 77/780/EEC and 89/646/EEC in the Field of Credit Institutions,
  Directives 73/239/EEC and 92/49/EEC in the Field of Non-life Insurance, Directives 79/267/
  EEC and 92/96/EEC in the Field of Life Assurance, Directive 93/22/EEC in the Field of
  Investment firms and Directive 85/611/EEC in the Field of Undertakings for Collective

Investment in Transferable Securities (UCITS), with a View to Reinforcing Prudential
  Supervision (95/26/EC), OJ L168 of 18.07.1995, 7, date enacted: 29.06.1995,
  date in force: 07.08.1995. . . . . 295, 298
Directive Relating to the Taking up and Pursuit of the Business of Credit Institutions
  (2000/12/EC), OJ L126 of 26.05.2000, 1, date enacted: 20.05.2000, date in force:
  15.06.2000 [19.07.2006 [Repealed]]. 174, 221, 294, 295, 296, 300
Directive on Markets in Financial Instruments (2000/39/EC), OJ L145 of 30.04.2004,
  1, date enacted: 21.04.2004, date in force: 30.04.2004 . . . . 294, 297, 301
Directive amending Council Directive 85/611/EEC on the Coordination of Laws, Regulations
  and Administrative Provisions Relating to Undertakings for Collective Investment in
  Transferable Securities (UCITS) with a View to Regulating Management Companies
  and Simplified Prospectuses (2001/107/EC), OJ L41 of 13.02.2002, 20, date enacted:
  21.01.2002, date in force: 13.02.2002. . . . . 295, 297
Directive concerning Life Assurance (2002/83/EC), OJ L345 of 19.12.2002, 1, date enacted:
  05.11.2002, date in force: 19.12.2002 . . . . 297, 298, 301
Directive on Taxation of Savings Income in the Form of Interest Payments
  (2003/48/EC), OJ L157 of 26.06.2003, 38, date enacted: 03.06.2003,
  date in force: 01.07.2005 272
Directive on a Common System of Taxation Applicable to Interest and Royalty Payments Made
  Between Associated Companies of Different Member States (2003/49/EC), OJ L157 of
  26.06.2003, 49, date enacted: 03.06.2003, date in force: 01.01.2004 272
Directive on Markets in Financial Instruments amending Council Directives
  85/611/EEC and 93/6/EEC and Directive 2000/12/EC and repealing
  Directive 93/22/EEC (2004/39/EC), OJ L145 of 30.04.2004, 1, date enacted:
  21.04.2004, date in force: 30.04.2004. . . . . 221, 295
Directive Relating to the Taking up and Pursuit of the Business of Credit Institutions
  (Recast) (2006/48/EC), OJ L177 of 30.06.2006, 1, date enacted: 14.06.2006,
  date in force: 20.07.2006 . . . . 12, 221, 295

EC REGULATIONS (CHRONOLOGICAL)

Regulation Laying down the Conditions under which Non-resident Carriers
  May Transport Goods or Passengers by Inland Waterway within a Member State
  (3921/91/EEC), OJ L373 of 31.12.1991, 1, date enacted: 16.12.1991,
  date in force: 05.01.1994. 299
Regulation on Licensing of Air Carriers (2407/92/EEC), OJ L240 of 24.08.1992, 1, date enacted:
  23.07.1992, date in force: 01.01.1993 298
Regulation Specifying Definitions for the Application of the Prohibition of Privileged
  Access referred to in Article 104a of the Treaty [now, after amendment, Art 102]
  (3604/93/EC), OJ L332 of 31.12.1993, 4, date enacted: 13.12.1993,
  date in force: 01.01.1994 221
Regulation on Common Rules Applicable to the Transport of Goods or Passengers by Inland
  Waterway between Member States with a View to Establishing Freedom to Provide such
  Transport Services (1356/96/EC), OJ L175 of 13.07.1996, 7, date enacted: 08.07.1996,
  date in force: 02.08.1996. 299
Regulation Protecting against the Effects of the Extra-territorial Application of
  Legislation Adopted by a Third Country, and Actions Based thereon or Resulting
  therefrom (2271/96/EC), OJ L309 of 29.11.1996, 1, date enacted: 22.11.1996, date in force:
  29.11.1996. 301

Regulation on the Strengthening of the Surveillance of Budgetary Positions and the Surveillance
 and Coordination of Economic Policies (1466/97/EC), OJ L209 of 02.08.1997, 1, date enacted:
 07.07.1997 22
Regulation on Speeding up and Clarifying the Implementation of the Excessive Deficit Procedure
 (1467/97/EC), OJ L209 of 02.08.1997, 6, date enacted: 07.07.1997 22
Regulation on Specific Restrictive Measures Directed against Certain Persons and
 Entities with a View to Combating Terrorism (2580/2001/EC), OJ L344 of 28.12.2001,
 70, date enacted: 27.12.2001, date in force: 28.12.2001 312
Regulation establishing a Facility Providing Medium-term Financial Assistance for Member
 States' Balances of Payments (332/2002/EC), OJ L53 of 23.02.2002, 1, date enacted:
 18.02.2002, date in force: 24.02.2002. 309
Regulation amending Regulation (EC) No 1466/97 on the Strengthening of the Surveillance of
 Budgetary Positions and the Surveillance and Coordination of Economic Policies
 (1055/2005/EC), OJ L174 of 07.07.2005 1, date enacted: 27.06.2005 22
Regulation amending Regulation (EC) No 1467/97 on Speeding up and Clarifying the
 Implementation of the Excessive Deficit Procedure (1056/2005/EC),
 OJ L174 of 07.07.2005, 5, date enacted: 27.06.2005. 22

EC DECISIONS (CHRONOLOGICAL)

Decision on the Provisional Application of the Energy Charter Treaty by the European
 Community (94/998/EC), OJ L380 of 31.12.1994, 1, date enacted: 15.12.1994,
 date in force: 15.12.1999 [22.09.1997 [Repealed]] 301
Decision concerning the Conclusion on behalf of the European Community, as Regards
 Matters within its Competence, of the Results of the World Trade Organization Negotiations
 on Financial Services and on the Movement of Natural Persons (96/412/EC), OJ L167 of
 06.07.1996, 23, date enacted: 25.06.1996, date in force: 25.06.1996. 301
Decision on the Conclusion of the Partnership and Cooperation Agreement between the
 European Communities and their Member States, of the One Part, and the Russian
 Federation, of the Other Part (97/800/EC, ECSC, Euratom), OJ L327 of 28.11.1997,
 date enacted: 30.10.1997, date in force: 30.10.1997 301
Decision on the Conclusion of the Partnership and Cooperation Agreement between the
 European Communities and their Member States, of the One Part, and Ukraine, of the
 Other Part (98/149/EC, ECSC, Euratom), OJ L49 of 19.02.1998, 1, date enacted:
 26.01.1998, date in force: 26.01.1998 301
Decision on the Conclusion, by the European Communities, of the Energy Charter
 Treaty and the Energy Charter Protocol on Energy Efficiency and Related Environmental
 Aspects (98/181/EC, ECSC, Euratom), OJ L69 of 9.03.1998, 1, date enacted: 23.09.1997,
 date in force: 23.09.1997. 301
Decision on the Conclusion of the Partnership and Cooperation Agreement between the
 European Communities and Their Member States, of the One Part, and the Republic
 of Moldova, of the Other Part (98/401/EC, ECSC, Euratom), OJ L181 of 24.06.1998,
 1, date enacted: 28.05.1998, date in force: 28.05.1998. 301
Decision Concerning the Conclusion on behalf of the European Community, as Regards Matters
 within its Competence, of the Results of the World Trade Organisation Negotiations on
 Financial Services (1999/61/EC), OJ L20 of 27.01.1999, 38, date enacted: 14.12.1998, date in
 force: 14.12.1998. 301
Decision on the Conclusion of the Partnership and Cooperation Agreement between the
 European Communities and their Member States, of the One Part, and the Republic of

Kazakhstan, of the Other Part (1999/490/EC, ECSC, Euratom), OJ L196 of 28.07.1999, 1, date enacted: 12.05.1999, date in force: 12.05.1999 301

Decision on the Conclusion of the Partnership and Cooperation Agreement between the European Communities and their Member States, of the One Part, and the Kyrgyz Republic, of the Other Part (1999/491/EC, ECSC, Euratom), OJ L196 of 28.07.1999, 46, date enacted: 12.05.1999, date in force: 12.05.1999 301

Decision on the Signing and Provisional Application of a Protocol to the Partnership and Cooperation Agreement (PCA) between the European Communities and their Member States, of the One Part, and Ukraine, of the Other Part, on the Accession of the Republic of Bulgaria and Romania to the PCA (2007/251/EC), OJ L110 of 27.04.2007, 28, date enacted: 22.03.2007, date in force: 22.03.2007 301

Decision on the Signing and Provisional Application of a Protocol to the Partnership and Cooperation Agreement, Establishing a Partnership between the European Communities and their Member States, of the One Part, and the Russian Federation, of the Other Part, to Take Account of the Accession of the Republic of Bulgaria and Romania to the European Union (2007/318/EC), OJ L119 of 9.05.2007, 31, date enacted: 23.04.2007, date in force: 23.04.2007 301

Decision on the Conclusion of the Protocol to the Partnership and Cooperation Agreement Establishing a Partnership between the European Communities and their Member States, of the One Part, and the Russian Federation, of the Other Part, to Take Account of the Accession of the Republic of Bulgaria and Romania to the European Union (2007/541/EC, Euratom), OJ L200 of 01.08.2007, 44, date enacted: 28.06.2007, date in force: 28.06.2007 301

Decision on the Signing and Provisional Application of a Protocol to the Partnership and Cooperation Agreement (PCA) between the European Communities and their Member States, of the One Part, and the Republic of Moldova, of the Other Part, on Accession of the Republic of Bulgaria and Romania to the PCA (2007/546/EC), OJ L202 of 03.08.2007, 19, date enacted: 22.03.2007, date in force: 22.03.2007 301

Decision on the Signing and Provisional Application of a Protocol to the Partnership and Cooperation Agreement between the European Communities and their Member States, of the One Part, and the Republic of Armenia, of the Other Part, to Take Account of the Accession of the Republic of Bulgaria and Romania to the European Union (2007/547/EC), OJ L202 of 03.08.2007, 25, date enacted: 05.06.2007, date in force: 05.06.2007 301

Decision on the Signing and Provisional Application of a Protocol to the Partnership and Cooperation Agreement between the European Communities and their Member States, of the One Part, and Georgia, of the Other Part, to Take Account of the Accession of the Republic of Bulgaria and Romania to the European Union (2007/548/EC), OJ L202 of 03.08.2007, 30, date enacted: 05.06.2007, date in force: 05.06.2007 301

EC ACTS (CHRONOLOGICAL)

Act concerning the Conditions of Accession of the Kingdom of Norway, the Republic of Austria, the Republic of Finland and the Kingdom of Sweden and the Adjustments to the Treaties on which the European Union is Founded – Protocol No 2 on the Åland Islands, OJ C241 of 29.08.1994, 352, date enacted: 24.06.1994, date in force: 01.01.1995 255

Act concerning the Conditions of Accession of the Czech Republic, the Republic of Estonia, the Republic of Cyprus, the Republic of Latvia, the Republic of Lithuania, the Republic of Hungary, the Republic of Malta, the Republic of Poland, the Republic of Slovenia and the Slovak Republic and the Adjustments to the Treaties on which the European Union is

Table of Treaties

Founded – Protocol No 6 on the Acquisition of Secondary Residences in Malta, OJ L236 of 23.09.2003, 947, date enacted: 16.04.2003 254

Act concerning the Conditions of Accession of the Republic of Bulgaria and Romania and the Adjustments to the Treaties on which the European Union is Founded – Annex VII: List Referred to in Article 23 of the Act of Accession: Transitional Measures, Romania, OJ L157 of 21.06.2005, 311, date enacted: 25.04.2005 254

Act concerning the Conditions of Accession of the Republic of Bulgaria and Romania and the Adjustments to the Treaties on which the European Union is Founded – Annex VI – List Referred to in Article 23 of the Act of Accession: Transitional Measures, Bulgaria, OJ L157 of 21.06.2005, 278, date enacted: 25.04.2005 254

EU COMMON POSITIONS

Common Position on the Application of Specific Measures to Combat Terrorism (2001/931/CFSP), OJ L344 of 28.12.2001, 93, date enacted: 27.12.2001, date in force: 27.12.2001 312

RESOLUTIONS OF THE EUROPEAN COUNCIL (CHRONOLOGICAL)

Resolution of the European Council on the Establishment of an Exchange-rate Mechanism in the Third Stage of Economic and Monetary Union, Amsterdam, 16.06.1997, OJ C236 of 02.08.1997, 5, date enacted: 16.06.1997 26

Resolution of the European Council on the Stability and Growth Pact, OJ C236 of 02.08.1997, 1, date enacted: 17.06.1997 22

EC LEGISLATIVE PROPOSALS (CHRONOLOGICAL)

European Commission, 'Proposal for a Directive amending Regulation (EC) No 1775/2005 on Conditions for Access to the Natural Gas Transmission Networks – Explanatory Memorandum' (Explanatory Memorandum of the 3rd Energy Package II, Brussels 19.09.2007) 12, 305

—— 'Proposal for a Directive amending Directive 2003/54/EC of 26 June 2003 concerning Common Rules for the Internal Market in Electricity, for a Directive amending Directive 2003/55/EC of 26 June 2003 concerning Common Rules for the Internal Market in Natural Gas, for a Regulation establishing an Agency for the Cooperation of Energy Regulators, for a Regulation amending Regulation (EC) No 1228/2003 and for a Regulation amending Regulation (EC) No 1775/2005 – Explanatory Memorandum' (Explanatory Memorandum of the 3rd Energy Package, Brussels 19.09.2007) 12, 305

NATIONAL LAWS, REGULATIONS, AND BILLS (ALPHABETICAL)

Germany

Außenwirtschaftsgesetz ('1961 German Foreign Trade and Payments Act' (AWG)), BGBl. I 1961, 481, 495, 1555 .... 132, 225, 227

Außenwirtschaftsverordnung ('1986 German Degree on the Execution of the
   Foreign Trade and Payments Act' (AWO)), BGBl. I 1986, 2671 227
Bundesministerium für Wirtschaft und Technologie, Entwurf eines Dreizehnten Gesetzes zur
   Änderung des Außenwirtschaftsgesetzes und der Außenwirtschaftsverordnung' (2007), Status:
   Referentenentwurf <http://www.bmwi.de/BMWi/Redaktion/PDF/Gesetz/
   entwurf-eines-dreizehnten-gesetzes-zur-aenderung-aussenwirtschaft,property=pdf,
   bereich=bmwi,sprache=de,rwb=true.pdf> accessed 22.12.2007. 328
Bürgerliches Gesetzbuch ('2002 German Civil Code' (BGB)), BGBl. I 2002, 2909 71
Deutscher Bundestag, Entwurf eines Dreizehnten Gesetzes zur Änderung des
   Außenwirtschaftsgesetzes und der Außenwirtschaftsverordnung,
   Deutscher Bundestag Drucksache 16/10730, <http://dip21.bundestag.de/
   dip21/btd/16/107/1610730.pdf> accessed 23.12.2008. 6
Gesetz über das Kreditwesen ('1961 German Banking Act' (KWG)),
   BGBl. I 1961, 881 . . . . 192, 193, 296
Handelsgesetzbuch ('1897 German Commercial Code' (HGB)), BGBl. III,
   Gliederungsnummer 4100–1 72
Körperschaftssteuergesetz ('2002 German Law on Corporation Tax' (KStG)),
   BGBl. I, 4144 . . . . 107, 286

France

Code monétaire et financier ('French Monetary and Financial Code') 5, 132
Décret n° 2005–1739 réglementant les relations financières avec l'étranger et portant
   application de l'article L. 151–3 du code monétaire et financier ('2005 French
   Degree on the application of Art. L. 151–3 of the Monetary and Financial Code on Foreign
   Investment Activities'), J.O. n° 304 du 31 décembre 2005, 20779 . . . . 5, 132

Others

2001 UN General Assembly Resolution A/RES/56/83 of 12.12.2001 on ILC Draft
   Articles on Responsibility of States for Internationally Wrongful Acts,
   United Nations, Fifty-sixth Session, Official Records of the General Assembly,
   <http://daccessdds.un.org/doc/UNDOC/GEN/N01/477/97/PDF/N0147797.
   pdf?OpenElement> accessed 05.03.2007 315

List of Abbreviations

ACT	Advanced corporation tax
AG	*Die Aktiengesellschaft*
AG	Advocate General
AöR	*Archiv des öffentlichen Rechts*
AP	Associated Press
AVR	*Archiv des Völkerrechts*
AWG	*Außenwirtschaftsgesetz* 1961 (German Foreign Trade and Payments Act)
AWO	*Außenwirtschaftsverordnung* 1986 (German Decree on the Execution of the Foreign Trade and Payments Act)
BaFin	*Bundesanstalt für Finanzdienstleistungsaufsicht* (German) Federal Financial Supervisory Authority
BB	*Betriebsberater*
BGB	*Bürgerliches Gesetzbuch* 2002 (German Civil Code)
BIFD	Bulletin for International Fiscal Documentation
Bn	Billion
C.D.E	*Cahiers de droit européen*
CFI	Court of First Instance
CFS	Controlled foreign company
CLB	Commonwealth Law Bulletin
CMLR	Common Market Law Review
Columbia J. Transnat'l L	Columbia Journal of Transnational Law
Court	European Court of Justice also referred to in this Study as 'ECJ'
DB	*Der Betrieb*
Dr.pratique. comm.int	*Droit et Pratique du Commerce International*
DStR	*Deutsches Steuerrecht*
DStZ	*Deutsche Steuer-Zeitung*
DVBl	*Deutsches Verwaltungsblatt*
€	Euro; 1 € ≈ 1.43 US$
EC	European Community, or Treaty establishing the European Community as amended by subsequent treaties
ECB	European Central Bank
ECJ	European Court of Justice also referred to in this Study as 'the Court'
EC Treaty	Treaty establishing the European Community as amended by subsequent treaties
EEC	European Economic Community
EFTA	European Free Trade Association
EHRLR	European Human Rights Law Review

EJIL	European Journal of International Law
ELJ	European Law Journal
ELR	European Law Review
ELRep.	European Law Reporter
EMU	Economic and Monetary Union
ET	European Taxation
EU	European Union
EuGRZ	*Europäische Grundrechte-Zeitschrift*
EuR	*Europarecht* (Journal)
EurUP	*Zeitschrift für Europäisches Umwelt- und Planungsrecht*
EuZW	*Europäische Zeitschrift für Wirtschaftsrecht*
EWiR	*Entscheidungen zum Wirtschaftsrecht*
EWS	*Europäisches Wirtschafts- & Steuerrecht*
FDI	Foreign direct investment
FET	Fair and Equitable Treatment
FGR	Future Generations Fund
FII	Franked investment income
FJ	*Finanz-Journal*
Fordham Int'l L. J	Fordham International Law Journal
FR	*Finanz-Rundschau Ertragssteuerrecht*
GATS	General Agreement on Trade in Services
GesRZ	*Der Gesellschafter*
GmbHR	*GmbH-Rundschau*
GRF	General Reserve Fund
Harv. Int'l. L. J	Harvard International Law Journal
Hastings Int'l & Comp. L. Rev	Hastings International and Comparative Law Review
HGB	*Handelsgesetzbuch* 1897 (German Commercial Code)
Hous. J. Int'l L	Houston Journal of International Law
ICLQ	International and Comparative Law Quarterly
ICSID Rev	ICSID Review—Foreign Investment Law Journal
IFLR	International Financial Law Review
ILC	International Law Commission
IMF	International Monetary Fund
Int. A. L. R	International Arbitration Law Review
Int'l	International
Int'l Lawyer	International Lawyer
INVEST-SD	Investment Law and Policy News Bulletin
IStR	*Internationales Steuerrecht*
ITN	Investment Treaty News
J. Air L. & Com	Journal of Air Law and Commerce
JAL	Journal of African Law
JbUmweltTechnR	*Jahrbuch des Umwelt- und Technikrechts*
JCMS	Journal of Common Market Studies
JRP	*Journal für Rechtspolitik*

JWIT	Journal of World Investment and Trade
JWT	Journal of World Trade
JWTL	Journal of World Trade Law
JZ	*Juristenzeitung*
Kreditwesen	*Zeitschrift für das gesamte Kreditwesen*
KStG	*Körperschaftssteuergesetz* 2002 (German Law on Corporation Tax)
KWG	*Gesetz über das Kreditwesen* 1961 (German Banking Act)
Law & Contemp. Probs	Law and Contemporary Problems
Law & Pol'y Int'l Bus	Law and Policy in International Business
LIEI	Legal Issues of Economic Integration
L. & Bus. Rev. Am	Law and Business Review of the Americas
MFC	*Code monétaire et financier* (French Monetary and Financial Code)
MFN	Most-favoured-nation (treatment)
mn	Margin number, margin numbers
NJW	*Neue Juristische Wochenschrift*
NT	National Treatment
NvWZ	*Neue Zeitschrift für Verwaltungsrecht*
Nw. J. Int'l. L. & Bus	Northwestern Journal of International Law and Business
nyd	Not yet decided
nyp	Not yet published
NZG	*Neue Zeitschrift für Gesellschaftsrecht*
OECD	Organisation for Economic Co-operation and Development
OGEL	Oil-Gas-Energy Law
ÖJZ	*Österreichische Juristen-Zeitung*
ÖStZ	*Österreichische Steuer-Zeitung*
para/paras	Paragraph(s) also referred to in this study as '§, §§'
R	Rex/Regina
RabelsZ	*Rabels Zeitschrift für ausländisches und internationales Privatrecht*
RDAI	*Revue de Droit des Affaires Internationales*
RDW	*Österreichisches Recht der Wirtschaft*
RIS	Review of International Studies
RIW	*Recht der internationalen Wirtschaft*
RMCUE	*Revue du Marché Commun et de l'Union européenne*
Rs	*Rechtssache*
SchiedsVZ	*Zeitschrift für Schiedsverfahren*—German Arbitration Journal
SIAR	Stockholm International Arbitration Review
Spec Ed	English Special Edition
StuB	*Steuern und Bilanzen*
StuW	*Steuer und Wirtschaft*
SWI	*Steuer- und Wirtschaft International*
TCJ	Transnational Corporations Journal

TeC	Treaty Establishing a Constitution for Europe
TNI	Tax Notes International
ToA	EC Treaty as amended by the Treaty of Amsterdam
ToL	EC Treaty as amended by the Treaty of Lisbon
ToM	EC Treaty as amended by the Treaty of Maastricht
ToN	EC Treaty as amended by the Treaty of Nice
Treaty	Treaty establishing the European Community as amended by subsequent treaties
trn	Trillion
UN	United Nations
UN-Charter	Charter of the United Nations
UNCTAD	United Nations Conference on Trade and Development
UNSC	United Nations Security Council
UNTS	United Nations Treaty Series
US$	United States Dollar, 1 US$ ≈ 0.69 €
VCLT	Vienna Convention on the Law of Treaties
Vol	Volume
WBl	*Wirtschaftsrechtliche Blätter—Zeitschrift für österreichisches und europäisches Wirtschaftsrecht*
WiRO	*Wirtschaft und Recht in Osteuropa*
WM	*Wertpapier-Mitteilungen*
WRP	*Wettbewerb in Recht und Praxis*
Ybk	Yearbook
YEL	Yearbook of European Law
ZaöRV	*Zeitschrift für ausländisches öffentliches Recht und Völkerrecht*
ZBB	*Zeitschrift für Bankrecht und Bankwirtschaft*
ZeuS	*Zeitschrift für europarechtliche Studien*
ZGesStW	*Zeitschrift für die gesamte Staatswissenschaft*
ZglRWiss	*Zeitschrift für vergleichende Rechtswissenschaft*
ZGR	*Zeitschrift für Unternehmens- und Gesellschaftsrecht*
ZHR	*Zeitschrift für das gesamte Handelsrecht und Wirtschaftsrecht*
ZRP	*Zeitschrift für Rechtspolitik*
ZRph	*Zeitschrift für Rechtsphilosophie*
§, §§	Paragraph, paragraphs also referred to in this study as 'para'

Introduction

1. Subject of this Work and Statement of the Question to Be Investigated

'Basically unagitated'—this is how one could sketch the view formerly predominant in the Member States with respect to direct investment originating from or directed to non-EC countries (third countries). For many decades, policymakers had adopted a steadily increasing *laissez-faire* regulatory approach. Direct investment, the business of acquiring a controlling interest in an undertaking,[1] was in the end basically left to the private market participants. Only a very limited number of 'high profile' transactions have been greeted with scepticism by Member States' governments. Luxembourg's ultimately unsuccessful 'emergency legislative' effort to prevent the takeover of steel producer *Arcelor* of Luxembourg by the Indian steel maker *Mittal*[2] provides a case in point for such rare ad hoc government interference.[3]

The restraint exercised in terms of governmental interference[4] was due to the fact that, in general, third country direct investment—irrespective of its origin or destination—was perceived altogether as having positive effects on the respective Member State's economy. During this time, the overall interests of the key players in cross-border direct investment—investor, host, and home country—were largely aligned. The investors undertook such investments to enhance their international competitiveness, inter alia, by 'slicing' the production chain, by allocating different parts to those countries in which production costs are low, and/or by 'duplicating' the production chain in order to place production closer to a foreign market. In the latter case, the investor gains strategic market access and reduces

---

[1] This is an abbreviated definition of the notion of direct investment. For a detailed account of the concept in the context of free movement of capital, see Chapter II.4.
[2] M Hennes, 'Luxemburg hilft Arcelor im Kampf gegen Mittal' *Handelsblatt* (16.03.2006).
[3] Other Member States' governments did not let things 'slide' that far in the first place. In 2005, the mere rumour that *PepsiCo* of the United States of America might consider a hostile takeover of the French *Groupe Danone* sufficed to let the French establishment go 'into overdrive to declare its hostility to the hypothetical bid from what the Le Figaro...described as the "American ogre"'. [T Fuller, 'French Fear Eye of "Ogre" is on Danone' *International Herald Tribune* (21.07.2005); see also M Lynn, 'Investing: France's "Don't Do that Here" Folly' *International Herald Tribune* (10.01.2006)]
[4] In fact, the restrictiveness of Member State economies significantly decreased between 1980 and 2000. *Cf* SS Golub, 'Measures of Restrictions on Inward Foreign Direct Investment for OECD Countries' (Online Working Paper, OECD, Paris 2003), 22.

delivery time.[5] Host countries sought inward direct investment to further their economic development in multiple ways. It is believed that free movement of capital contributes to economic growth by increasing the production base, by creating employment and through so-called multiplier effects. The term 'multiplier effects' refers to the idea that new players usually intensify competition in the host State's market. Domestic firms might have to improve efficiency and product quality in order to resist the challenge, and non-competitive local firms could be crowded out. Furthermore, cross-border direct investment can act as a catalyst for domestic investment and technological progress through the transfer of technology.[6] Home countries also benefit in several ways; primarily, though, they supported outward direct investment in order to promote the international competitiveness of their firms.[7]

It was this alignment, developed over the years,[8] that allowed the EC to emerge as today's largest worldwide recipient and source of cross-border direct investment.[9] It accounted for about 41 per cent of all cross-border direct investment inflows, including intra-EC flows, and 55 per cent of all outflows worldwide in the period 2003–2005.[10] Even though the vast majority of those investments occurred within the EC,[11] the in- and outflows from or to non-EC countries are by no means negligible. The EC received 19 per cent of world cross-border direct investment inflows[12] and accounted for 49 per cent of world outflows[13]

---

[5] This is a much abbreviated depiction of the view of the so-called mainstream economists, cf, eg, PR Krugman and M Obstfeld, *Economics*, 157 *et seq*. There are plenty more elaborated explanations offered in economic science with respect to why cross-border direct investment takes place. For an excellent account of the different approaches in economic science, refer to R Gilpin, *Economy*, 278 *et seq*.

[6] *Cf* R Gilpin, *Economy*, 303; Critical on a fundamental basis: SH Hymer, *International Operations*; W Greider, *Global Capitalism*; see also M Sornarajah, *Int'l Law on Foreign Investment*, 50 *et seq*.

[7] For a more detailed discussion of the depicted alignment of investor, host, and home State, refer to KP Sauvant, 'Regulatory Risk', 67 *et seq*.

[8] For an account of the long-term process of liberalization of capital movements by the EC and its Member States, see Chapter I. 3.

[9] L Kekic, 'Global FDI to 2011', 33; UNCTAD, *World Investment Report 2006*, xxii.

[10] UNCTAD, *World Investment Report 2006*, 7.

[11] Direct Investment occurs mainly within the Community. The percentage of intra-EC flows out of the total cross-border direct investment inflows reached 80 per cent for the period 2004–05. [EUROSTAT, *EU FDI Ybk 2007*, 11 *et seq*]

[12] Ibid, 11. Most inward investment from non-Member States originates from developed countries. Within the group of extra-EC investors, the USA has been the largest, with an 18 per cent share of total extra-EC inflows (€ 94 bn = US$ 134 bn) in 2005 equalling € 17 bn = US$ 24 bn, followed by Switzerland with 17 per cent (€ 16 bn = US$ 23 bn) and Canada with 8 per cent (€ 8 bn = US$ 11 bn). In terms of inward FDI stocks held by extra-EC investors, in 2005 the USA led the group with a total of € 769 bn = US$ 1100 bn, Switzerland came in second with € 237 bn = US$ 339 bn, and Japan third with € 90 bn = US$ 129 bn. [EUROSTAT, *EU FDI Ybk 2007*, 44.] Together they own 62 per cent of the total extra-EC inward FDI stocks.

[13] EUROSTAT, *EU FDI Ybk 2007*, 14.

in 2005.[14] This translates into about € 94 bn[15] = US$ 134 bn[16] in inflows and € 172 bn = US$ 246 bn in outflows from or to non-EC countries. In the same year, investors from third countries held assets worth € 1.7 trn = US$ 2.4 trn within the EC. Assets of EC investors in third countries amounted to € 2.4 trn = US$ 3.4 trn.[17]

For some years, however, the alignment depicted above has become more and more fragile and governmental interferences more frequent,[18] such that one must doubt whether the EC can assert its position as the world's largest recipient and source of cross-border direct investment. The respective political sentiments towards cross-border direct investment in general, and third country direct investment in particular, have become more critical in some major Member States.[19] This rising criticism coincides with a changing environment for national security, increased challenges to protect technologies considered vital for national sovereignty and competitiveness, growing concerns about jobs in the aftermath of cross-border mergers and acquisitions, and intensified efforts by developing countries to secure access to energy and rare raw materials.[20]

In particular, some Member States face considerable problems in acclimatizing themselves to inward direct investment from developing countries. As a consequence of their growth and advancement in recent decades, corporations headquartered in those markets have started pursuing internationalization strategies. Developing countries therefore increasingly become sources of outward

---

[14] In 2006, the EC accounted for 20 per cent of world cross-border direct investment inflows and 34 per cent of outflows, totalling € 157 bn = US$ 225 bn and € 260 bn = US$ 372 bn respectively. A relative drop of the EC's share in world cross-border direct investment outflows in 2006 compared to 2005 was recorded due to an atypical decrease of the US share and consequential increase of the EC share in world cross-border direct investment outflows in 2005. [EUROSTAT—European Commission, *EU FDI Ybk 2008*, 11, 13 *et seq*]

[15] 1 € ≈ 1,43 US$.   [16] 1 US$ ≈ 0,69 €.

[17] EUROSTAT, *EU FDI Ybk 2007*, 21.

[18] KP Sauvant, 'Regulatory Risk', 71; UNCTAD, *World Investment Report 2006*, 24; OECD, *Int'l Investment Perspectives 2007*, 141 *et seq*; see also T Koyama and SS Golub, 'OECD's FDI Regulatory Restrictiveness Index: Revision and Extension to More Economies' (Online Working Paper, OECD, Paris 2006).

[19] *Cf*, eg, T Fuller, 'French Fear Eye of "Ogre" is on Danone' *International Herald Tribune* (21.07.2005); N Buckley et al, 'Gazprom Warned on Centrica Interest' *Financial Times.com* (03.02.2006); H Williamson, 'EU "Should Vet State-funded Bids"' *Financial Times.com* (18.07.2007); D Drewes, 'Prosche ja, Gasprom nein' *Spiegel Online* (23.10.2007); M Streitz, et al, 'Union schmiedet Abwehrwaffen gegen Firmenaufkäufer' *Spiegel Online* (16.10.2007); A Mihm, 'Investoren sollen Regierung informieren' *Frankfurter Allgemeine Zeitung* (30.10.2007); C Dougherty, 'Europe Looks at Controls on State-owned Investors' *International Herald Tribune* (13.07.2007).

[20] OECD, *Int'l Investment Perspectives 2007*, 54, 70 *et seq*; see for a summary of the discussion in Germany: Sachverständigenrat zur Begutachtung der gesamtwirtschaftlichen Entwicklung, *Jahresgutachten 2007/08*, para 583 *et seq*; In this connection it should be noted that the depicted developments began well before the 2007/8 world financial crisis. It is too early to evaluate the impact of the effects of the crisis on the *political* and *regulatory* path currently pursued in respect of cross-border direct investment. For a first economic appreciation of the effects on world cross-border direct investment flows and stocks see: KP Sauvant, 'The FDI Recession Has Begun' (Pdf-file, The Vale Columbia Center on Sustainable International Investment, New York 2008).

direct investment.[21] In terms of total numbers, though, the cross-border direct investment inflows into the EC[22] (as well as stocks) today are still rather small compared with those from the USA, Switzerland, Canada, Japan, or Australia. However, if one considers the growth rates in the period 2001 to 2004—inward direct investment stocks from China increased by over 150 per cent and those from Russia by 40 per cent[23]—then this suggests that direct investment from China and Russia is soon likely to play a more significant role within the European Community (EC)[24] than it does today.[25]

While the unfamiliar origin of the direct investment leads to considerable unease in some Member States, scepticism increases—at times bordering on irrational blunt hostility—if the relevant emerging-market firm is State-owned.[26] An investment placed by a so-called 'sovereign investment agency' or 'sovereign wealth fund' (SWFs)[27] headquartered in an emerging market creates even more concerns.[28] Such investment vehicles of governments are actually not new. One

---

[21] UNCTAD, *World Investment Report 2006*, 103 *et seq*; The Economist Intelligence Unit (ed) *World Investment Prospects to 2011*, 28; OECD, *Int'l Investment Perspectives 2007*, 54.

[22] By way of example, in 2005 the EC received from Russia inflows worth € 4 bn = US$ 8 bn, which equals four per cent of total inward flow from extra-EC countries. Among the group of non-EC European countries, Russia has emerged the second largest investor after Switzerland. [EUROSTAT, *EU FDI Ybk 2007*, 45] From China (ex. Hong-Kong [The inflows from Hong-Kong account for over € 1 bn in 2005]), inflows in 2005 amounted to € 0.4 bn = US$ 0.6 bn. [EUROSTAT, *EU FDI Ybk 2007*, 46]

[23] EUROSTAT, *EU FDI Ybk 2007*, 49.

[24] In this study, the term Community is used synonymously with European Community (EC).

[25] It is projected that China's global outward direct investment stock will have sextupled from 2004 to 2011 from € 37 bn = US$ 53 bn in 2004 to € 233 bn = US$ 330 bn. [*Cf* The Economist Intelligence Unit (ed) *World Investment Prospects to 2011*, 128] It should be noted, though, that most of the cross-border direct investments will not be directed to the EC but to resource rich countries in Africa, Central Asia, and Latin America. [The Economist Intelligence Unit (ed) *World Investment Prospects to 2011*, 128; UNCTAD, *World Investment Report 2006*, 58] Russia's global outward direct investment stock will have quadrupled in the same period of time from € 31 bn = US$ 44.4 bn in 2004 to € 136 bn = US$ 194.7 bn in 2011. [*Cf* The Economist Intelligence Unit (ed) *World Investment Prospects to 2011*, 172]

[26] KP Sauvant, 'Regulatory Risk', 73; In 2006, the United Kingdom government—generally considered not to be hostile to cross-border direct investment—in an initial statement warned energy giant *Gazprom* of Russia that any attempt to take over British energy supplier *Centrica* would face 'robust scrutiny'. It should be mentioned, though, that the resistance was subsequently—at least on the face of it—given up. [*Cf* N Buckley, et al, 'Gazprom Warned on Centrica Interest' *Financial Times.com* (03.02.2006); J Blitz and S Wagstyl, 'Gazprom Block over Centrica Ruled out' *Financial Times* (26.04.2006)]; see also Sachverständigenrat zur Begutachtung der gesamtwirtschaftlichen Entwicklung, *Jahresgutachten 2007/08*, para 634 *et seq* as well as A Jung, et al, 'Märchenhafter Reichtum' *Der Spiegel*, 176 *et seq* (31.03.2008).

[27] There is no generally agreed-upon definition. The IMF attempted to define SWFs as follows 'SWFs can generally be defined as special investment funds created or owned by governments to hold foreign assets for long-term purposes'. [International Monetary Fund, *Global Financial Stability Report*, 45.]

[28] The discussion within Germany can be mentioned by way of example in this respect. See, eg, C Dougherty, 'Europe Looks at Controls on State-owned Investors' *International Herald Tribune* (13.07.2007); B Benoit, 'German Call to Curb Foreign Buyers' *Financial Times.com* (12.07.2007); B Benoit and M Schieritz, 'Berlin Looks to Vet Foreign Funds Deals' *Financial Times.com* (26.06.2007); M Streitz, et al, 'Union schmiedet Abwehrwaffen gegen Firmenaufkäufer' *Spiegel*

of the oldest is the Kuwait Investment Authority, established in the early 1950s.[29] The growing number and size of these funds over the years has certainly contributed to current increased attention.[30] However, first and foremost, it is the mere fact that most of them are controlled by developing countries or countries in transition, such as China, Russia, and certain Gulf States, that prompts policymakers in Europe to act.[31] Although systematic evidence is still lacking, it is nevertheless widely feared that these funds—which are not a prime example of transparency in terms of publishing their strategic objectives,[32] investment portfolios, and returns[33]—are instruments of government policy, meant not only to advance the economic welfare of a country, but to support political power goals.[34]

While most of the arguments recently advanced in favour of a restrictive policy on cross-border direct investment do not stand up to close economic examination,[35] political opinion after a very emotional debate has been strong enough that some Member States have adjusted or have started adjusting their regulatory frameworks. It is not surprising that those adjustments have not been guided by a liberal sentiment. France, for example, tightened its regulations on cross-border direct investment in 2005. *Décret n°2005-1739*[36] makes cross-border direct investment in sectors that are perceived to be sensitive to public

---

Online (16.10.2007); D Drewes, 'Prosche ja, Gasprom nein' *Spiegel Online* (23.10.2007); M Kröger and AP, 'Ausländische Investoren sollen um Genehmigung bitten' *Spiegel Online* (30.10.2007); P Steinbrück, 'Staatsfonds'; H Haasis, 'Staatsfonds'.

[29] The Kuwait Investment Authority [*cf* Kuwait Investment Authority, 'Kuwait Investment Authority' (Website, Kuwait City 2007)] 'is an autonomous government body responsible for the management of the GRF [(General Reserve Fund)] and FGF [(Future Generations Fund)], as well as any other funds entrusted to it on behalf of the government of Kuwait'. [International Monetary Fund, *Global Financial Stability Report*, 18]; see also KP Sauvant, 'Regulatory Risk', 69 *et seq*.

[30] According to Jen of *Morgan Stanley*, total assets of SWFs could grow from € 1,75 trn = US$ 2.5 trn today to nearly € 8,4 trn = US$ 12 trn by 2015. *Cf* S Jen, 'How Big Could Sovereign Wealth Funds Be by 2015?'; concurring: International Monetary Fund, *Global Financial Stability Report*, 45.

[31] KP Sauvant, 'Regulatory Risk', 73; for a list of the different investment vehicles refer to: International Monetary Fund, *Global Financial Stability Report*, 48 *et seq*; KP Sauvant, 'Regulatory Risk', 70; for an analysis of the largest 22 SWFs note: G Lyons, 'State Capitalism'.

[32] The policy objectives of SWFs include inter alia the insulation of the budget and economy from volatile commodity prices, the spreading of wealth across generations, reduction of the negative cost-of-carry of holding reserves, the generation of a higher return, and funding of socioeconomic projects managing pensions. Those objectives usually multiply in practice and change gradually over time. [International Monetary Fund, *Global Financial Stability Report*, 46]

[33] A positive exception is the 'Norwegian Government Pension Fund Global' that, once a year, discloses its portfolio and returns. *Cf* Norges Bank, 'Statens pensjonsfond—Utland' (Website, Oslo 2007); see also 'The World's Most Expensive Club' *The Economist* (24.05.2007).

[34] KP Sauvant, 'Regulatory Risk', 73; see for a critical account of the discussion on SWFs: Sachverständigenrat zur Begutachtung der gesamtwirtschaftlichen Entwicklung, *Jahresgutachten 2007/08*, para 600 *et seq*; OECD, 'Sovereign Wealth Funds and Recipient Country Policies'.

[35] *Cf* Sachverständigenrat zur Begutachtung der gesamtwirtschaftlichen Entwicklung, *Jahresgutachten 2007/08*, para 583 *et seq*; OECD, *Int'l Investment Perspectives 2007*, 70 *et seq*.

[36] Décret n° 2005–1739 (France) based on Art 151-3 of MFC (France); see W Maxwell, 'France' for a brief account of the French regulation, misstating though the situation under EC law. Note also M Lynn, 'Investing: France's "Don't Do that Here" Folly' *International Herald Tribune* (10.01.2006).

order, public security, or public health subject to an authorization regime. In late 2008, a bill became law in Germany that might herald a change in the paradigm of cross-border direct investment regulation. While Germany, a capital-exporting country,[37] has traditionally favoured open markets,[38] the law displays a different spirit, aiming at an across-the-board restriction of cross-border direct investment. Any cross-border acquisition by a non-EC investor, irrespective of the economic sector, exceeding 25 per cent of the capital of an undertaking would become subject to ministerial veto in case it was found to be a(n unspecified) threat to public order or security.[39]

Those regulatory adjustments—outlined as examples above[40]—are likely to remain for some time; despite the 2007/8 world financial crisis.[41] It is clear that the regulatory adjustments have or will have a chilling effect on cross-border direct investment originating from or directed to third countries. The new regulations

---

[37] Germany is a capital exporting country in terms of the balance on capital account. [*Cf* Statistisches Bundesamt, *Datenreport 2006*, 258 *et seq*]

[38] *Cf* P Wruuck, 'Economic Patriotism: New Game in Industrial Policy' (Online Research Paper, Deutsche Bank, Frankfurt 2006), 10; Sachverständigenrat zur Begutachtung der gesamtwirtschaftlichen Entwicklung, *Jahresgutachten 2007/08*, para 590 *et seq*, 599.

[39] (2008) Entwurf eines Dreizehnten Gesetzes zur Änderung des Außenwirtschaftsgesetzes und der Außenwirtschaftsverordnung, Deutscher Bundestag Drucksache 16/10730; For an evaluation of conformity with EC law see: C Tietje, *Staatsfonds*; M Nettesheim, 'Unternehmensübernahmen'; K Krolop, 'Staatliche Einlasskontrolle bei Staatsfonds und anderen ausländischen Investoren im Gefüge von Kapitalmarktregulierung, nationalem und internationalem Wirtschaftsrecht'; K Krolop, 'Staatsfonds'; Bundesverband der deutschen Industrie e.V. and Freshfields Bruckhaus Deringer, *Beschränkung ausländischer Beteiligungen*, 28 *et seq*; see for an economic and political account: Sachverständigenrat zur Begutachtung der gesamtwirtschaftlichen Entwicklung, *Jahresgutachten 2007/08*, para 675 *et seq*; Note also 'Staatsfonds: Politiker verlangen Schutz vor Ausverkauf' *Manager Magazin.de* (08.07.2007); 'Regierungspläne: Schutz vor ausländischen Käufern' *Manager-Magazin.de* (30.06.2007); A Mihm, 'Investoren sollen Regierung informieren' *Frankfurter Allgemeine Zeitung* (30.10.2007); P Steinbrück, 'Staatsfonds'; H Haasis, 'Staatsfonds'.

[40] There is no comprehensive list of Member States' restrictive measures on direct investment in existence. Some guidance is offered by United States Trade Representative, '2007 National Trade Estimate Report on Foreign Trade Barriers' 244 *et seq*; OECD, *Int'l Investment Perspectives 2007*, 61 *et seq*; existing restrictive measures and legislative changes are reported to exist or are currently under discussion in Great Britain, Spain, Italy, Belgium, Poland, Lithuania, Hungary, and Greece. *Cf* Deutscher Bundestag, 'Europarechtliche Beurteilung der geplanten Änderungen des Außenwirtschaftsgesetzes: Antwort der Bundesregierung auf eine Kleine Anfrage der Abgeordneten Rainer Brüderle, Frank Schäffler, Dr. Karl Addicks, weiterer Abgeordneter und der Fraktion der FDP', 5; For recent legislative initiatives in Hungary see: M Pießkalla, 'Lex Mol'; see also Chapter VII. 2. g.

[41] The world financial crisis of 2007/8—most likely temporarily leading to a significant decrease of world cross-border direct investment flows [*Cf* KP Sauvant, 'The FDI Recession Has Begun' (Pdf-file, The Vale Columbia Center on Sustainable International Investment, New York 2008)]—has yet not had an impact on the predominant *regulatory* approaches currently pursued in the Member States. While it is too early to predict the long-term consequences of the crisis on those restrictive regulatory regimes, what is interesting to note is the fact that private businesses in Europe publicly compete for direct investments by sovereign wealth funds from countries like China without causing much adverse reactions in the *political* arena. [*Cf*, eg, 'Siemens: Staatsfonds willkommen' *manager-magazin.de* (28.08.2008); 'Industrie will keinen Schutzzaun gegen Investoren—Verstoß gegen EU-Recht beklagt/"Die jetzigen Regeln reichen aus"' *Frankfurter Allgemeine Zeitung* (05.08.2008)]

already implemented or proposed clearly favour investments occurring within a Member State over those undertaken across the border. They severely restrict the autonomous decision-making of private market participants. The latter suddenly have to, or will have to, justify entrepreneurial investment decisions that a free basic order, in principle, leaves to the discretion of the private market actor.

Apart from this topical issue, and putting it into more abstract terms, any kind of fetter triggers the question of whether it can be imposed *ad libitum* by the respective Member State. Can a Member State, for example, exercise discretion over the degree of openness of its capital market by completely or partly excluding third country direct investment in certain sectors,[42] industries, or regions, or in certain kinds of property or with regard to certain activities? May a Member State decide to admit foreign direct investment only on a case-by-case basis, implementing screening or authorization schemes[43] based, eg, on the assessment of the investment's benefits to the national economy or environmental compatibility or the general concordance with local standards related to national security, policy, customs, or public morals?[44] Can Member States prescribe at will a certain legal form[45] of incorporation, or restrictive measures that relate to control over ownership,[46] to control based on limitation of shareholder powers,[47] or to control based on the possibility of governmental intervention in their management?[48] Is a

---

[42] These are usually the sectors perceived by the host State as 'key sectors', ieie, sectors decisive for national security and defence or culturally significant industries. [P Muchlinski, *Multinational Enterprises*, 175] For an overview of the policies employed by major cross-border direct investment players refer to CD Wallace, *Multinational Enterprise*, 192 *et seq*.

[43] *Cf* M Sornarajah, *Int'l Law on Foreign Investment*, 116 *et seq*; P Muchlinski, *Multinational Enterprises*, 194 *et seq*; for a detailed account of the policies of Japan, France, and Canada, refer to CD Wallace, *Multinational Enterprise*, with further references at 213 *et seq*. The successful completion of the screening process (inclusive of the acceptance of certain conditions) can either be a precondition for entry or a precondition for the granting of some sort of preferential treatment or both. All screening schemes usually have in common a high degree of discretion on the part of the authority entrusted with the task of selecting beneficial cross-border direct investment projects for approval. [P Muchlinski, *Multinational Enterprises*, 203]

[44] UNCTAD, *Admission and Establishment*, 8 *et seq*.

[45] eg, the investor can be prompted to incorporate its business venture in accordance with local laws and regulations, thus operating through the legal forms available under the legal order of the host State. Or the investor might be forced to enter into joint ventures with either the host State or local investors. See also M Sornarajah, *Int'l Law on Foreign Investment*, 120 *et seq*, 128 *et seq*, 133 *et seq*; CD Wallace, *Multinational Enterprise*, 314 *et seq*.

[46] These can, eg, take the form of restrictions on third country ownership (eg, no more than 50 per cent foreign-owned capital).

[47] Restrictions might be imposed upon entry on the type of shares or bonds held by foreign investors (eg, shares with non-voting rights) or on the free transfer of shares or other proprietary rights over the company held by investors (eg, shares cannot be transferred without permission). Equally possible are restrictions on shareholders' rights (eg, on payment of dividends, reimbursement of capital upon liquidation, voting rights, denial of information disclosure on certain aspects of the running of the investment). [UNCTAD, *Admission and Establishment*, 10]

[48] A government may reserve the right to appoint members of the board of directors, may impose restrictions on the nationality of directors, or limitations on the number of expatriates in top managerial positions. A government could reserve the right to veto certain decisions or require that important board decisions be unanimous. 'Golden' shares to be held by the host government

Member State free to tax direct investments differently or to provide for different administrative procedures depending on their origins?

Any such hurdle erected by a Member State for third country direct investment almost inevitably compels a market participant to assure himself of the rights he possesses in the (potential) host Member State if he does not want to risk suffering a competitive disadvantage, ie, falling victim to discriminatory or any other kind of protectionist measure.

Whereas protection of an investor in such a situation may arise from a number of legal sources,[49] this study places its focus on the fundamental freedom of capital movement. While all other fundamental freedoms are restricted in their scope of application to the Common Market, free movement of capital occupies an exceptional position. Article 56(1) EC states in simple terms that 'all restrictions on the movement of capital…between Member States and third countries shall be prohibited'.

This provision is quite remarkable, even astonishing. Prima facie, the Community appears to have given a unilateral promise not to interfere with—neither to discriminate nor to hinder—the access and operation of direct investments, a subcategory of capital, originating from non-EC countries. The same seems to apply *mutatis mutandis* to investment directed to non-EC countries, so-called outbound investment. It is this extraordinary scope that inevitably prompts the question of how sustainable this promise is. This study, therefore, poses and seeks to answer the following question: What rights does a private market participant, engaged in cross-border direct investment originating from or directed to a non-EC Member State, enjoy by virtue of the EC Treaty provisions on free movement of capital?

2. Available Sources and References

It was not until the 1990s—coinciding with the coming into force of Council Directive 88/361/EEC[50] and the subsequent ECJ[51] decision on the direct effect of free movement of capital[52]—that this freedom started to move from the outside

---

could be introduced in order to allow it to intervene if, for example, the foreign investor captures more than a certain percentage of the investment. The least interventionist requirement within this group would be mandatory consultation with the host State government before a certain decision is adopted. [Ibid]

[49] Protection may flow from national law, in particular from fundamental rights enshrined in the constitutions of the Member States, or from public international law, in particular from bilateral investment treaties concluded by the Member States.

[50] Directive 88/361/EEC.

[51] The abbreviation 'ECJ' for European Court of Justice and the term 'the Court' are used interchangeably in this study.

[52] With respect to the Directive: Joined Cases C-358/93 and C-416/93 *Criminal proceedings against Aldo Bordessa and Vicente Marí Mellado and Concepción Barbero Maestre*; on the Maastricht

margin to the centre of academic attention.[53] Even if one limits oneself—which this study does—to contributions in the German and English languages, then by now, one can safely establish that the EC Treaty provisions on free movement of capital have been the subject of academic elaboration in a more substantial way. They have, however, certainly not yet reached the degree of 'saturation' in terms of scholarly examination that can be found in the ambits of the other freedoms. So far, the main focus of debate has been on the operation of free movement of capital (hereafter also referred to as 'the freedom') in an intra-Community context. In this discussion, free movement of capital has largely been explained against the background of the converging tendencies among the fundamental freedoms.[54] Aside from the insightful but older works of Bakker[55] and Mohamed[56] and the tax law-related study of Dahlberg,[57] all three drawn up in English, the vast majority of the monographic writings appear to be penned in German. While the contributions of Backer and Mohamed aim to explain the provisions on free movement of capital more in terms of their historical development and political contexts, German authors approach the topic by summarizing, explaining, and clarifying the current state of the law, offering thoughtful constructions of the freedom in a doctrinal fashion with varying focus.[58]

The application of Art 56 EC *et seq* in a third country context has only been examined either briefly and/or very selectively in interaction with certain specific areas of national law. Most of these academic contributions with a narrow focus are in the area of direct taxation law, discussing the compatibility of certain specific national provisions with the Court's jurisprudence. Direct taxation is also the area of law from which all but one[59] of the third country situations before the Court have stemmed to date.[60] A small number of contributions adopted an

---

provisions: Joined Cases C-163/94, C-165/94, and C-250/94 *Criminal proceedings against Lucas Emilio Sanz de Lera, Raimundo Díaz Jiménez and Figen Kapanoglu*.

[53] For early accounts of the freedom refer to, eg, U Everling, Art. 67 EEC (1960); JT Lang, 'Right of Establishment'; P Oliver, 'Free Movement of Capital'; P Oliver and J-P Baché, 'Free Movement of Capital'; A Harz, *Schutzklauseln*; W Groß, *Direktinvestitionen*.

[54] *Cf*, eg, A Cordewener, et al, 'Emerging Issues', 108 for further references.

[55] AFP Bakker, *Capital Movements*.   [56] S Mohamed, *Free Movement of Capital*.

[57] M Dahlberg, *Direct Taxation*.

[58] *Cf*, eg, for rather general accounts: F Kimms, *Kapitalverkehrsfreiheit*; A Rohde, *Kapitalverkehr*; JCW Müller, *Kapitalverkehrsfreiheit*; U Haferkamp, *Kapitalverkehrsfreiheit*; AC Digel, 'Europäischer Finanzmarkt', Inaugural-Dissertation, Eberhard-Karls-Universität. For an account of the interdependences of free movement of capital, foreign exchange policy, and monetary union, *cf* Z Bognar, *Währungsintegration*; A Honrath, *Kapitalverkehr*; R Molzahn, *Kapitalverkehrsfreiheit und Währungsunion*. Exploring the interrelation between free movement of capital and the freedom of establishment: D Trüten, *Mobilität*; J Lübke, *Kapitalverkehrs- und Niederlassungsfreiheit*. For a discussion of the admissibility of special rights in an undertaking, on the basis of private and public law, in the light of free movement of capital: Kleinschmit, *Volkswagengesetz*; M Pießkalla, *Goldene Aktien*.

[59] Case C-452/04 *Fidium Finanz AG*.

[60] *Cf* Case C-446/04 *Test Claimants in the FII Group Litigation v Commissioners of Inland Revenue*; Case C-524/04 *Test Claimants in the Thin Cap Group Litigation*; Case C-157/05 *Winfried*

international investment law perspective.[61] Of a more seminal nature, though also with a tax law background, are the articles of Ståhl,[62] Schön,[63] Peters/Gooijer,[64] Schwenke,[65] and Cordewener/Kofler/Schindler.[66]

However, a comprehensive examination of the provisions on free movement of capital in a third country context is still missing. Part of this gap will be filled by this study, which places the focus on direct investment. The perspective from which the freedom will be scrutinized is that of a potential beneficiary. This study will do so by applying a classic doctrinal approach explaining, clarifying, and reviewing the current state of the law. To a great extent the applicability of the freedom in a third country context must be developed by building on the existing writing on intra-Community capital movement, which is largely drawn up in German. The positive ancillary effect of this is that German scholarship in the subject area is made accessible to the English-speaking world.

Apart from the topical layout, analytical approach, comprehensiveness, and language of existing literature, it is remarkable that many authors who favour a restrictive interpretation of the freedom in a third country context rely heavily on teleological considerations. Allegedly the spirit and purpose of the freedom in a third country context is limited; liberalized capital movement does not contribute in the same way as in an intra-Community context to the attainment of the aims[67] of the EC Treaty, but supposedly performs only ancillary functions. Unfortunately, those assumptions are only rarely backed up by an analysis of the functions which the freedom in a third country context might possibly perform. This study intends to follow another path by first setting out its view of the aims which may be pursued by free movement of capital in intra-Community and third country contexts before entering into a discussion of the scope of the freedom.

So far I have not referred to documents drawn up by European institutions, aside from judgments of the Court and legislative acts, as sources of interpretive guidance. A cursory look at the officially publicly available material reveals that those documents are almost exclusively concerned with intra-Community capital movement. In this respect, the Commission has made a considerable effort to explain (and shape) the law in a more transparent and systematic fashion by clarifying its overall strategy. Several communications were issued over the last

---

Holböck v Finanzamt Salzburg-Land; Case C-492/04 *Lasertec Gesellschaft für Stanzformen mbH (formerly Riess Laser Bandstahlschnitte GmbH) v Finanzamt Emmendingen).*

[61] *Cf*, eg, S Young and N Hood, 'Inward Investment Policy'; A Young, 'Foreign Economic Policy'; CD Wallace, *Multinational Enterprise*, 212 *et seq*, 267 *et seq*, 309 *et seq*, 423 *et seq*; A-S Georgiadou, *Foreign Direct Investments*; J Karl, 'Competence'; W Shan, 'EU Enlargement'; S Hindelang, 'Competing Freedoms'; S Hindelang, 'Kapitalverkehrs- und Niederlassungsfreiheit'.

[62] K Ståhl, 'Movement of Capital'. [63] W Schön, 'Kapitalverkehr mit Drittstaaten'.

[64] C Peters and J Gooijer, 'Movement of Capital'.

[65] M Schwenke, 'Kapitalverkehrsfreiheit'.

[66] A Cordewener, et al, 'Emerging Issues'. [67] *Cf* Art 2 EC.

few years, in particular the 1997 Communication on intra-EU Investment,[68] the 2003 Communication on Dividend Taxation of Individuals in the Internal Market[69] and the 2005 Communication on Intra-EU Investment in the Financial Services Sector,[70] as well as studies such as those on Capital Movements in the Legal Framework of the Community[71] and on Special Rights in Privatised Companies in the Enlarged Union—A Decade Full of Developments.[72]

If, however, one turns to third country capital movement, although studies and legal comments exist,[73] one will notice that hardly anything that would allow for conclusions in terms of a coherent overall position taken on the interpretation of Art 56 EC *et seq* has been made officially publicly available.[74] Rather, third countries, notably the United States of America, expend considerable effort to explain to their businesses the rights enjoyed by virtue of Art 56 EC *et seq*.[75]

The Commission, it appears, has simply chosen not to commit itself to a particular overall strategy. Only occasional indications surface, which certainly do not justify any conclusive inference of the Commission's overall view on third country capital movement. While, for example, it states in a recent working document on its strategy on the Single Market for twenty-first century Europe that '[t]he single market remains the EU's main competitive advantage in attracting foreign direct investment (FDI), which benefits European citizens and the economy through more growth and jobs',[76] at the same time it sends contradictory signals when

---

[68] European Commission, 'Communication on "Certain Legal Aspects concerning Intra-EU Investment"'.

[69] European Commission, 'Communication to the Council, The European Parliament and the European Economic and Social Committee: Dividend Taxation of Individuals in the Internal Market' (COM (2003) 810 final).

[70] European Commission, 'Communication on Intra-EU Investment in the Financial Services' Sector'.

[71] European Commission, 'European Economy No. 6/2003: The EU Economy: 2003 Review' 320 *et seq*.

[72] European Commission, 'Commission Staff Working Document on "Special Rights in Privatised Companies in the Enlarged Union—A Decade Full of Developments"'.

[73] *Cf*, eg, European Council, 'CLS no 6554/97 "Contribution of the Council's Legal Service to the Proceedings of the Ad Hoc Working Party on the Multinational Investment Agreement with regard to the On-going OECD Negotiations for the Conclusion of a Multilateral Investment Agreement (MAI)"' (CLS no 6554/96); European Commission, 'Commission Staff Working Paper on CLS no 6393/96 "Opinion of the Council's Legal Service as regards the Provisions of the EC Treaty applicable to Foreign Direct Investment and to Freedom of Establishment of Companies or Firms Owned or Controlled by Third-Country Natural or Legal Persons" [Title varying]' (SEC (97) 1428) whereby access was denied to the former document, *cf* Statement by H Brunmayr (Letter on 'Confirmatory Application to the Council for Access to Documents 6393/96 and 65554/97', 19.01.2006).

[74] For the sake of fairness, I must also mention that some European officials obligingly provided valuable background information. To them warm thanks are owed.

[75] US Foreign Commercial Service and US Department of State, 'Doing Business in the European Union: A Commercial Guide for the U.S. Companies' (US State Department, Washington, DC 2007); United States Trade Representative, '2007 National Trade Estimate Report on Foreign Trade Barriers' 244 *et seq*.

[76] European Commission, 'Commission Staff Working Document on "The External Dimension of the Single Market Review—Accompanying Document to the Communication

putting forward legislative proposals that suggest that the Commission might not see free movement of capital *erga omnes* as desirable in every economic sector. With regard to natural gas transmission systems or transmission system operators, for instance, 'the Commission proposes a requirement that third country individuals and countries cannot acquire control... unless this is permitted by an agreement between the EU and the third country'.[77]

One possible reason for the self-restraint of the Commission might be seen in the unresolved issue of competence for investment relations with third countries under the current Treaty.[78] The mere existence of two documents is evidence that there actually is or was a serious debate on this topic between the

from the Commission to the European Parliament, the Council, the European Economic and Social Committee and the Committee of the Regions"' (SEC (2007) 1519), 5. See also European Commission, 'Sovereign Wealth Funds—Frequently Asked Questions' (MEMO/08/126); European Commission, 'A Common European Approach to Sovereign Wealth Funds' (COM (2008) 115 final).

[77] European Commission, 'Proposal for a Directive amending Regulation (EC) No 1775/2005 on Conditions for Access to the Natural Gas Transmission Networks—Explanatory Memorandum' (Explanatory Memorandum of the 3rd Energy Package II), 5. See also European Commission, 'Proposal for a Directive amending Directive 2003/54/EC of 26 June 2003 concerning Common Rules for the Internal Market in Electricity, for a Directive amending Directive 2003/55/EC of 26 June 2003 concerning Common Rules for the Internal Market in Natural Gas, for a Regulation establishing an Agency for the Cooperation of Energy Regulators, for a Regulation amending Regulation (EC) No 1228/2003 and for a Regulation amending Regulation (EC) No 1775/2005—Explanatory Memorandum' (Explanatory Memorandum of the 3rd Energy Package), 7; Art 38(3) of Directive 2006/48/EC 'Bank Directive (Recast)'.

[78] For a discussion of a treaty making competence of the Community see, eg, J Karl, 'Competence'; N Maydell, 'Minimum Platform on Investment'; N Maydell, 'Competence', PhD Dissertation, University of Vienna Law School; partially unconvincing A Radu, 'Interactions'. See also European Commission, 'Issues Paper: Upgrading the EU Investment Policy'. Note also the recent infringement proceedings initiated by the Commission in regard to provisions on free transfer of funds in pre-accession bilateral investment treaties with third countries as well as the US–EC Investment Understanding for Accession Countries: European Commission, 'Internal Market: infringement proceedings against Austria, Finland, France, Italy, Greece, Portugal and Sweden' (IP/05/1288); European Commission, 'Internal Market: infringement cases against the UK, Portugal, Denmark, Austria, Sweden and Finland' (IP/05/352); Case C-205/06 *Commission v Republic of Austria (Re Provisions on the Free Transfer of Investment Related Payments in Bilateral Investment Agreements)*; Case C-249/06 *Commission v Kingdom of Sweden (Re Provisions on the Free Transfer of Investment Related Payments in Bilateral Investment Agreements)*; Case C-118/07 *Commission v Republic of Finland (Re Provisions on the Free Transfer of Investment Related Payments in Bilateral Investment Agreements)*; 2003 Understanding concerning certain US Bilateral Investment Treaties. For available but older communications predominantly dealing with a treaty making competence of the EC, *cf*, eg, European Commission, 'Investment Promotion and Protection Clauses in Agreements between the Community and Various Categories of Developing Countries: Achievements to Date and Guidelines for Joint Action' (COM (80) 204 final); European Commission, 'Need for Community Action to Encourage European Investment in Developing Countries and Guidelines for such Action' (COM (78) 23 final); European Commission, 'Communication on "A Level Playing Field for Direct Investment World Wide"' (COM (95) 42 final); European Parliament, 'Resolution on the Communication from the Commission Entitled: "A Level Playing Field for Direct Investment World Wide"' (COM (95) 42); European Economic and Social Committee, 'Opinion of the Economic and Social Committee on the "Global Harmonisation of Direct Investment Regulations"' (96/C 153/16).

Council and the Commission.[79] However, access to those documents was partly denied.[80]

3. The Purpose of this Study

This study will present a coherent construction of the provisions on free movement of capital in a third country context with a focus on direct investment. By depicting, explaining, and reviewing the current state of the law, it seeks to develop and advance a deeper understanding of the rights enjoyed by private market participants engaged in cross-border direct investment originating from or directed to non-EC Member States by virtue of the EC Treaty provisions on free movement of capital. The respective regime applicable to intra-Community capital movement serves as a point of reference and a benchmark. Choosing the market participant's perspective furthers and promotes a view that recognizes that the provisions of the EC Treaty on capital movement also form part of the body of international investment law.[81] The rights conferred (unilaterally) on non-EC investors *vis-à-vis* (predominantly) the Member States of the Community are a most remarkable, if seldom noted, aspect of EC law. Bringing those rights to the attention of third country investors seeking entrance to the Common Market and to EC investors wishing to invest outside the Community could even encourage investment by the mere fact of knowing that the investors in principle can expect—by virtue of the freedom of capital movement—to carry out their economic activity on a level playing field.

Giving a thorough reply to the central question of this study posed above and presenting a construction of Art 56 EC *et seq* as a 'coherent whole' presupposes taking a stand on a number of sub-questions that I have chosen to call 'interpretative parameters', the answers to which will largely decide the breadth and depth of the freedom's scope. To begin with, an analysis of the EC Treaty aims, *cf* Art 2 EC, will show that a preferably complete liberalization of cross-border direct

---

[79] *Cf* European Council, 'CLS no. 6393/96 "Opinion of the Council's Legal Service as regards the Provisions of the EC Treaty applicable to Foreign Direct Investment and to Freedom of Establishment of Companies or Firms Owned or Controlled by Third-Country Natural or Legal Persons" [Title varying]' (CLS no 6393/96); European Commission, 'Commission Staff Working Paper on CLS no. 6393/96 "Opinion of the Council's Legal Service as regards the Provisions of the EC Treaty applicable to Foreign Direct Investment and to Freedom of Establishment of Companies or Firms Owned or Controlled by Third-Country Natural or Legal Persons" [Title varying]' (SEC (97) 1428). Note also in this respect European Commission, 'Communication on "A Level Playing Field for Direct Investment World Wide"' (COM (95) 42 final), 13.

[80] Statement by H Brunmayr (Letter on 'Confirmatory Application to the Council for Access to Documents 6393/96 and 65554/97', 19.01.2006).

[81] See for a similar approach: eg, J Karl, 'Competence'; W Shan, 'Community Policy'; W Shan, *EU-China Investment Relations*; S Hindelang, 'Competing Freedoms'; note also US Foreign Commercial Service and US Department of State, 'Doing Business in the European Union: A Commercial Guide for the U.S. Companies' (US State Department, Washington, DC 2007).

investment in an intra-Community as well as a third country context not only facilitates but partially constitutes a precondition for the successful attainment of a multitude of predominantly (socio-)economic Treaty aims. A restrictive interpretation of the freedom in a third country context cannot be based on the argument that unilateral liberalization *vis-à-vis* third countries would not, or not to the extent that it does in an intra-Community context, serve the attainment of the Treaty aims. Second, it will be demonstrated, in partial deviation from the position of the ECJ, that with respect to direct investment, the relationship of free movement of capital and the freedom of establishment is a parallel one at the level of the scope of application. Direct investment is, hence, an economic activity constituting 'movement of capital' within the meaning of Art 56(1) EC, as well as 'establishment' as defined for the purposes of Art 43 EC. In a third country context, Art 56(1) EC is not superseded by any other freedom. Third, it will be highlighted that Art 56(1) EC is also directly effective in a third country context. Thus, it transfers individual rights to its potential beneficiaries that are enforceable by national courts. Fourth, it will be stressed that neither the wording nor systematic nor teleological arguments would justify a different construction of the non-hindrance or non-discrimination tests in a third country context as compared to the one applied in the context of intra-Community capital movements. In particular, intra-Community and third country direct investments are in principle comparable. Fifth, an examination of those expressly stated grounds of justification—as such construed narrowly—applying to intra-Community and third country capital movement alike[82] will reveal that they must be applied in the same way in both situations. The interpretation of 'rule of reason' in a third country context follows the lines drawn by the Court for intra-Community capital movements. No additional valid mandatory requirements can be identified with respect to third country direct investment. In particular, mandatory requirements related to budgetary purposes are equally not admissible in a third country context. Moreover, this study will show that those expressly stated exceptions to Art 56(1) EC that apply exclusively to third country capital movement[83]—in sharp contrast to the Court's approach—must be interpreted narrowly. This is in particular true for Art 57(1) EC, the true blind spot on the mirror of free movement of capital *erga omnes*.

In a nutshell, I put forward the hypothesis that in principle, the provisions on free movement of capital apply the same liberal standards irrespective of whether intra-Community or third country direct investment is involved. Those provisions that provide for exceptions applicable only in a third country context must be interpreted in the narrowest and most restrictive sense possible in order to make the freedom as effective as possible. Hence, those who participate in third country direct investment enjoy essentially the same guarantees by virtue of the provisions on free movement of capital as those active in intra-Community direct investment. The existence of Arts 57(1) EC, 59 EC, and 60 EC does not

---

[82] *Cf* Art 58(1) lit. b EC. [83] *Cf* Art 57(1) EC, 59 EC, 60 EC, 119 EC, and 120 EC.

fundamentally alter these findings. The restrictive effects flowing from Art 57(1) EC—if one is prepared to accept the interpretation of the provision suggested in this study—are increasingly fading away. Articles 59 EC and 60 EC do not affect the scope of the freedom in the absence of an economic or security crisis.[84]

4. Areas Excluded from this Work

This work is essentially limited in three ways. Even though some considerations and arguments put forward in the course of the study might be of a more general nature and are also true with respect to other categories of capital movement within the meaning of Art 56(1) EC, the focus of the study is exclusively on cross-border direct investment. Hence, I will not endeavour to make statements on any other kinds of capital movement, as they partly occur against a different economic and legal background.

I have chosen in this study to take the perspective of a potential beneficiary of the freedom of capital movement facing restrictions on its economic activity by national regulatory measures. In assessing the beneficiary's rights, I will consider only those that are granted directly by virtue of the Treaty provisions on free movement of capital. While I shall explain Art 56 EC *et seq* in context and refer, if necessary, to interdependencies with other provisions of national, European, and international law, possible rights flowing from other EC Treaty provisions, secondary Community law including international treaties, or possible rights under national law are not considered.

By reason of the chosen perspective, questions of internal and external competences of the European Community with respect to the regulation of third country direct investment will receive no specific attention.

5. The Course of this Study

This study will run as follows: the interpretation of any provision of the EC Treaty must be guided by its aims referred to in Art 2 EC. In order to prepare the foundation for a doctrinal analysis, I shall therefore begin in Chapter I by setting out in which sense free, ie, unrestricted, movement of capital within the Community helps in attaining the Treaty aims (Ch I. 2. a). I shall then assess whether the findings just made apply equally in a third country context (Ch I. 2. b). An outline of the genesis of the EC Treaty rules on free movement of capital (Ch I. 3) will facilitate an understanding of the current provisions in their historical context. The

---

[84] It goes without saying that rights correspond to duties. By exposing the rights enjoyed by third country investment, this study implicitly prescribes the Member States' limits set by the provisions on free movement of capital on their regulatory autonomy with respect to such investment and identifies those overriding public interests that might justify a restriction of the freedom.

respective results reached will guide my interpretation of the freedom throughout this study.

In Chapters II to IV, I will turn to the material scope of Art 56(1) EC. Here, I will first develop my understanding of the notions of 'capital' (Ch II. 2. b) and 'movement of capital' (Ch II. 2. c), two legal concepts that are heavily infused with economic content. Characterizing free movement of capital as an 'object-related production factor freedom'—hence it is the cross-border movement of capital itself, not that of its holder, which is liberalized by virtue of Art 56(1) EC—I attend to the issue of how to localize capital (Ch II. 3. a) and the related problem of construction of the cross-border element within the ambit of the freedom of capital movement (Ch II. 3. b). Second, arriving at the 'object of investigation' of this study, I shall build up and form a definition of the concepts of 'direct investment' (Ch II. 4. b) and 'foreign direct investment' (Ch II. 4. c), the latter referring to such 'direct investment' originating from or directed towards non-EC countries. Third, moreover, I shall demonstrate that direct investment constitutes a classic cross-sectional activity falling, prima facie, within the ambit of free movement of capital and the freedom of establishment. The configuration of the relationship of those two competing freedoms can have a significant impact on the scope of Art 56(1) EC in a third country context and will therefore be brought into focus (Ch III). Subsequently, I shall map at length the scope of the 'prohibition of restriction' enshrined in Art 56(1) EC—comprising two tests, the non-hindrance and the non-discrimination tests—in both intra-Community and third country contexts (Ch IV).

The personal scope of application will be reviewed in Chapter V of this study. As Art 56(1) EC is directly effective in intra-Community and third country contexts (section 2), beneficiaries (section 4) can rely on it, in particular, in the courts of the Member States (section 5. a). The group of addressees, however, also extends to the Community itself (section 5. b) and, under certain conditions, to private persons (section 5. c).

Chapters VI and VII are devoted to the exceptions to the freedom. Those exceptions that apply in intra-Community and third country contexts alike are addressed first, ie, basically Art 58(1) lit. b EC and the 'rule of reason' (Ch VI). Within this context, I also address by way of example the operation of the proportionality test (Ch VI. 2. a. (4)). Second, I shall address at length the exceptions that apply exclusively to third country direct investment, ie, Arts 57(1) EC, 59 EC, and 60 EC (Ch VII).

The study ends by placing the findings of the doctrinal analysis into a broader legal and political context, thereby pointing out areas for future research.

A summary of the findings of the thesis, in which all the conclusions previously drawn in the discussions are recapitulated and presented, is annexed.

This study has been written on the basis of the law as it stood on 31 October 2008.

I

Preparing the Foundation: Economic Rationale for the Liberalization of Capital Movements and the Art of Political Compromise

1. Introduction

Why liberalize cross-border capital movements? In order to comprehend a country 's motivation in subjecting itself to the task of tearing down restrictions on cross-border capital movement, including those on direct investment,[1] a basic understanding of the economic effects of liberalized capital movement is first desirable. By having recourse to the teachings of 'mainstream economists',[2] which proceed basically from the assumption that economic activity around the world is determined by the theory of location and the principle of comparative advantage,[3] the first section of this chapter will outline the main effects of free capital movement on the economy of the European Community.[4]

As an abstract sketch in economic terms is of only limited value for the purposes of this study, the discussion will be framed as the analysis of how the economic effects of free movement of capital can help to attain the aims (also called tasks) of the Treaty contained in Art 2 EC. These aims guide the interpretation of any provision of the Treaty. They shed light on the *telos* of a provision and, at the same time, they provide the boundaries of a possible construction.[5]

---

[1] See Chapter II. 4. [2] For a definition of the term, refer to R Gilpin, *Economy*, 279.
[3] *Cf* PR Krugman and M Obstfeld, *Economics*, 160, 25 *et seq*.
[4] See for an appraisal of the economic motives of liberalization of capital movements against a legal background: JCW Müller, *Kapitalverkehrsfreiheit*, 12 *et seq*; J Lübke, *Kapitalverkehrs- und Niederlassungsfreiheit*, 115 *et seq*; see in general from a economic perspective: M Borchert, *Außenwirtschaftslehre*, 165 *et seq*, 388 *et seq*; PR Krugman and M Obstfeld, *Economics*, 172 *et seq*; R Gilpin, *Economy*, 278 *et seq*; CP Kindleberger, 'Int'l Capital Market'; M Borchert, *Monetary Economics*.
[5] R Streinz, Art. 2 EC (2003), mn 18 *et seq*; JCW Müller, *Kapitalverkehrsfreiheit*, 76 *et seq*; see in this respect also Case 32/65 *Italian Republic v Council and Commission*; Joined Cases 6 and 7/73 *Istituto Chemioterapico Italiano S.p.A. and Commercial Solvents Corporation v Commission*, para 32; Case 85/76 *Hoffmann-La Roche & Co. AG v Commission*, para 125; Case 15/81 *Gaston*

It goes without saying that this applies equally to the provisions on free movement of capital (*cf* Arts 56–60 EC).

As will be demonstrated further below, the (socio-)economic aims, in particular those described by the 'magic square' through the establishment of a Common Market and Economic and Monetary Union (EMU),[6] are served best if cross-border movement of capital is as unrestricted as possible. This, in consequence, would suggest a broad interpretation of Art 56(1) EC. However, the EC Treaty itself as well as the case law of the Court show that liberalization is not embraced unconditionally; interests that might run counter to the precept of liberalization[7] flowing from an economic rationale and the (socio-)economic Treaty aims are also recognized. It is therefore conceivable that in an individual case, in a process of balancing competing objectives,[8] free movement of capital must give priority to another legitimate interest.

Preparing the foundation for a doctrinal analysis of the current provisions on free movement of capital requires not only a certain understanding of economic realities, but also an appreciation of the historical processes that ultimately culminated in the adoption of the current provisions in the course of the Maastricht amendments. The genesis of the rules on free movement of capital demonstrates that the present provisions are the result of a successful struggle, lasting for over 50 years, for liberalization of capital movements on the national, European, and international levels.

In the second section of this chapter, I will characterize this process. If one seeks to draw any conclusion from such a historical perspective, it should be that in the present EC Treaty provisions, a liberal political undercurrent has solidified.

2. The Contribution of Free Movement of Capital to the Attainment of the Aims of the EC Treaty

Free movement of capital as one of the four fundamental freedoms, as part of the Common Market and Internal Market, as part of Economic and Monetary Union, and as an element of a market order based on competition, is part of the matrix of aims of the EC Treaty (as well as the EU Treaty[9]).[10]

Schul Douane Expediteur BV v Inspecteur der Invoerrechten en Accijnzen, Roosendaal, para 33; more cautious: M Nettesheim, 'Einleitung III', mn 8.

[6] JCW Müller, *Kapitalverkehrsfreiheit*, 70 *et seq*.

[7] *Cf* R Streinz, Art. 2 EC (2003), mn 40, who wishes to attribute pre-eminence to the economic aims of the establishment of the Common Market or Internal Market, respectively. More cautious: M Nettesheim, 'Einleitung III', mn 8; A Hatje, 'Wirtschaftsverfassung', 724.

[8] Both competing interests are to be balanced so that in the long run both are optimized. In the style of German constitutional law, one would speak of the establishment of a '*praktische Konkordanz*'.

[9] By virtue of Art 2, first dash EU together with Art 1(3) EU, free movement of capital also serves the attainment of the aims of the EU. See JCW Müller, *Kapitalverkehrsfreiheit*, 68 *et seq*.

[10] *Cf* Ibid, 69.

This freedom, as one of the policies of the Community mentioned in Art 3(1) lit. c EC, contributes in particular to the attainment of the (socio-)economic aims described by the 'magic square' through the establishment of a Common Market and of Economic and Monetary Union (EMU).[11]

Free movement of capital is not only a means but also a (subordinate) aim within the EC Treaty. Free movement of capital substantiates the tasks contained in Art 2 EC, in particular the establishment of the Common Market and Economic and Monetary Union, and in this way it turns from an instrument into an aim to be achieved.[12]

The subsequent discussion will proceed in two steps. First, I shall analyse the way in which free movement of capital, which includes cross-border direct investment,[13] helps to attain the aims of the Treaty in an intra-Community context. In a second step, the question of whether the previous analysis must be re-assessed when it comes to third country capital movements is posed.

a. Liberalized Capital Movement within the EC

(1) Free Movement of Capital and the Attainment of the Economic Aims of Price Stability, Equalization of the Balance of Payments, and Economic Growth

In this section, I will sketch out the reasons why free, ie, unrestricted, capital movement can—if certain institutional preconditions, first and foremost a stable banking and supervision system, free competition, and a functioning tax and legal system,[14] are met—especially contribute to the Treaty aims of price stability, equalization of the balance of payments, and economic growth.[15]

To begin with, optimal allocation of capital furthers prosperity: if the flow of capital is unrestricted, capital can be directed to the places where it can be used most efficiently to generate the best returns, and it is thereby capable of contributing to an efficient squaring of demand and supply of capital within the Community. Funds can be transferred from countries with high savings quotas to countries with low ones, thus fuelling economic growth[16] in the latter. In doing so, the inflowing capital helps to reduce the deficit in savings and foreign exchange. Capital taking the form of cross-border direct investment is seen as an especially important instrument for long-term economic

---

[11] Ibid, 70 *et seq*.
[12] In principle: M Zuleeg, Art. 2 EC (2003), mn 13; R Streinz, Art. 3 EC (2003), mn 1.
[13] See Chapter II. 4.
[14] B Fischer and H Reisen, *Kapitalverkehrskontrollen*, 15 *et seq*, 30 *et seq*; G Ress and J Ukrow, Art. 56 EC (2002), mn 59. It can be assumed that such preconditions are present within the Community: *cf* AC Digel, 'Europäischer Finanzmarkt', Inaugural-Dissertation, Eberhard-Karls-Universität, 14 *et seq*.
[15] JCW Müller, *Kapitalverkehrsfreiheit*, 78.
[16] Economic growth is an explicit aim contained in Art 2 EC. See also R Streinz, Art. 2 EC (2003), mn 24.

growth.¹⁷ It is believed that cross-border direct investment contributes to economic growth in the host country by increasing the production base, by creating employment, and through multiplier effects; that is, new players intensify competition in the host State's market, forcing domestic firms to improve efficiency and product quality in order to resist the challenge and squeezing non-competitive local firms out of the market.¹⁸ Furthermore, if less developed economies experience robust growth, they might narrow the gap between themselves and more developed economies in the Community. Hence, free capital movement helps to reduce regional differences.¹⁹ Capital controls, in contrast, would endanger the attainment of these aims.²⁰

Moreover, the free movement of capital overcomes the problem of financing import and export surpluses by means of public foreign exchange reserves, which creates an advantage for those economies that are less developed and usually lack large foreign exchange reserves. In the case of free movement of capital, those reserves are set free and can be used for investment. Liberalized capital movements therefore further the aims of a harmonious development of economic activities and a convergent expansion of economic performance throughout the Community.²¹

Eventually, liberalized capital movements in general and unrestricted cross-border direct investment in particular will intensify competition within the Common Market. Just a few positive effects of such intensification will be mentioned here: investment opportunities will increase, and a growing number of financial instruments will offer both investors and capital recipients a greater freedom of choice. Intensified competition breaks up and prevents oligopolistic or monopolistic structures; it reduces transaction costs and opens up the possibility of higher profits. The higher productivity of capital will ultimately attract more (foreign) capital, which increases the size of the financial market. These effects serve most of the (socio-)economic aims contained in Art 2 EC.²² Capital control, however, would not only violate the principles of an open market economy and free competition in general,²³ but is ineffective in regard to the prevention of speculation, an argument often put forward to justify restrictive measures.²⁴

---

¹⁷ JCW Müller, *Kapitalverkehrsfreiheit*, 79 *et seq*.
¹⁸ R Gilpin, *Economy*, 303; Critical on a fundamental basis: SH Hymer, *International Operations*; W Greider, *Global Capitalism*; see also M Sornarajah, *Int'l Law on Foreign Investment*, 50 *et seq*.
¹⁹ Article 2 EC demands a '*harmonious, balanced and sustainable* development of economic activities' [emphasis added] and 'convergence of economic performance'. *Cf* R Streinz, Art. 2 EC (2003), mn 23, 28.
²⁰ JCW Müller, *Kapitalverkehrsfreiheit*, 80 *et seq*.
²¹ Ibid, 81 *et seq*.   ²² Ibid, 82 *et seq*.
²³ The principles of an open market economy and free competition explicitly mentioned in Art 4(1) EC are implicitly, via the aim of economic growth, also part of Art 2 EC. See on this R Streinz, Art. 2 EC (2003), mn 24.
²⁴ Speculations usually occur in situations in which a fixed exchange rate does not correspond to the 'real' exchange rate in which the actual economic relations between two countries are expressed. Capital controls only delay the necessary adjustments of economic policy. Even if

Finally, optimized capital allocation and intensified competition as mentioned above increase the pressure on national economic and collective bargaining policy to maintain fiscal and tariffs discipline. This has an overall stabilizing effect on the economy, which is one of the aims of Art 2 EC.[25] Of course, capital movements are not only directed by expected returns but, as mentioned earlier, are also influenced by the environment in which they are placed, eg the security of an investment, national politics, tax regimes, financial market, and consumer protection regulations, to mention only a few.[26] Thus, the positive effects which may be reached via liberalized capital movement can be adversely affected by poor 'general' political and regulatory conditions. However, this should not be abused as an argument for restricting free movement of capital; on the contrary, steps should be taken to ensure that those 'general' conditions are upheld or set in such a way that they actually contribute to giving full effect to the benefits of free movement of capital.

(2) Free Movement of Capital and the Attainment of the Aim of an Economic and Monetary Union

Special attention is warranted by the 'symbiotic' relationship between free movement of capital and the attainment of the aim of Economic and Monetary Union (Art 4 EC). It was not by chance that the first step of the EMU and the (internal) liberalization of capital movements (Directive 88/361/EEC) entered into force at the same time.[27] When capital is freed from any constraints, its flow is directed, as mentioned above, by the return it can possibly generate and the general political conditions found in the host and to a lesser extent in the home country. This free flow will sooner or later make existing economic and regulatory differences between States obvious. In the absence of any coordination of economic and monetary policies across borders, it can force a State to adjust—probably more drastically than if it had chosen to coordinate with other States—its policies to the realities of the market. This pressure to adjust constrains autonomous agenda setting in the policy fields just mentioned.[28] Until the late 1980s, the abandonment of such political power was unpopular among the Member States of the Community.[29] The adoption of Directive 88/361/EEC marked a political turn.[30] In order to clear a path for

---

a speculative capital movement happens to be undertaken for another reason besides the difference between 'real' and fixed exchange rates, capital control measures usually cure only the symptoms and prevent not only the unwanted speculative transactions but also the desired capital movements. See JCW Müller, *Kapitalverkehrsfreiheit*, 88. See also H-P Fröhlich, *Kapitalverkehr*, 16 *et seq*; CP Kindleberger, 'Int'l Capital Market', 615; M Neumann, *Volkswirtschaftslehre*, 302 *et seq*; L Weniger, *Kapitalverkehrskontrollen*, 67 *et seq*; H Werner, *Kontrolle*, 20 *et seq*.

[25] JCW Müller, *Kapitalverkehrsfreiheit*, 84 *et seq*.   [26] Ibid, 88 *et seq*.
[27] See in general S Mohamed, *Free Movement of Capital*, 82; A Rohde, 'Freier Kapitalverkehr'.
[28] *Cf* M Seidel, 'Kapitalmarkt', 581.   [29] AFP Bakker, *Capital Movements*, 189 *et seq*.
[30] Ibid, 211 *et seq*. Directive 88/361/EEC was adopted on 24.6.1988; the Commission under the chairmanship of *Delors*, which was to study and propose suggestions for the establishment

the successful establishment of Economic and Monetary Union, the Member States relinquished their respective powers and liberalized capital movements.[31] Free movement of capital constituted an important prerequisite for the successful implementation of Economic and Monetary Union.[32] A common currency that is supposed to fulfil the function of a international investment, trade, and reserve currency alongside the US Dollar, the Japanese Yen, and the British Pound requires free capital movement within the currency area but—equally importantly—also with respect to third countries.[33] Moreover, stability of the currency, especially price stability, is of paramount importance for general welfare and the protection of individual property.[34] In this respect, the market forces delivered due to the free flow of capital act as important indicators and guardians—much better than any political declarations of intent or Stability and Growth Pact[35]—for the stability of the common currency.[36] Free capital movement enables the markets to judge the stability of monetary union in the most efficient way: money is simply withdrawn from an unstable currency area. The implementation of any capital restrictions as a reaction instead of tackling the fundamental economic issues would simply reinforce the judgement of the markets that the currency area is sailing in stormy waters. However, capital restrictions would by no means lead to (re-)stabilization.[37]

A stable currency does not only require liberalized capital movements; additionally, a stable monetary union is advantageous for a liberalized capital market.[38] An unstable currency could prompt investors to move capital out of the currency area to safer harbours. This in turn could lead to the introduction of capital restrictions towards countries not part of the monetary union. This, however, is most likely to lead only to a further increase in distrust in, and instability of, the currency. It is therefore far better to remove the internal economic cause and leave the capital flow unrestricted instead of covering up economic difficulties by means of capital restrictions.[39]

---

of Economic and Monetary Union, was mandated on 27/28.6.1988 at the European Council in Hanover, Germany.

[31] M Seidel, 'Kapitalmarkt', 763; H Tietmeyer, 'Europäische Währung', 103; M Seidel, 'Kapitalmarkt', 584, 589; AFP Bakker, *Capital Movements*, 212 *et seq*. See also European Commission, *Europäischer Kapitalmarkt*, 15, 45 *et seq*.

[32] For a different view: N Horn, 'Kapitalverkehr', 66.

[33] M Seidel, 'Kapitalmarkt', 764.

[34] Free movement of capital also serves as an element for safeguarding fundamental rights, especially those rights which guarantee economic and professional freedom. See on this: JCW Müller, *Kapitalverkehrsfreiheit*, 92 *et seq*. and J Schwarze, *Europäisches Verwaltungsrecht*, 703 *et seq*.

[35] Resolution of the European Council on the Stability and Growth Pact; Regulation 1466/97/EC; Regulation 1055/2005/EC; Regulation 1467/97/EC; Regulation 1056/2005/EC.

[36] R Hasse and J Starbatty, 'Währungsunion', 128 *et seq*.

[37] Ibid. Reinforcing the above stated with respect to third countries: C Watrin, 'Währungsunion', 38 *et seq*. See also JCW Müller, *Kapitalverkehrsfreiheit*, 258 *et seq*.

[38] H Tietmeyer, 'Europäische Währung', 102.

[39] JCW Müller, *Kapitalverkehrsfreiheit*, 257.

(3) Free Movement of Capital and the Attainment of the Aim of Free Movement of Goods, Services, and Persons

The free movement of capital as the fourth freedom is a constituting element of both the Internal Market (*cf* Art 3(1) lit. c. EC and Art 14(2) EC) and the Common Market.[40] A complete liberalization of capital movements is a precondition of, and thus serves the aim of, the implementation of the other freedoms.[41] Indeed, in practice it is a precondition for the effective exercise of the other freedoms since, generally speaking, it enables entrepreneurs to locate production where it is most efficient, it guarantees that financial transactions related to the provision of banking and insurance services are free from any national interference, and last but not least, it makes possible the financing of cross-border trade in terms of, eg, credits on goods.[42]

(4) Free Movement of Capital and the Attainment of the Aim of Free and Fair Competition

Free movement of capital makes possible and furthers the aim of undistorted competition[43] as an essential element of the Common Market.[44] Article 3(1) lit. g EC refers to 'a system ensuring that competition in the internal market is not distorted'. Article 4(1), 98, 2rd sentence EC and 105(1) 3rd sentence EC commit the Community to the 'principle of an open market economy with free competition'. Free movement of capital removes the major obstacles to free competition, ie, the constriction of investment opportunities on one hand and the limitation of sources to finance business ventures on the other. Free flow of capital, therefore, furthers free competition within and between the national markets.[45]

---

[40] For my purposes the way in which the concepts of internal and common market are to be delineated is not central. It suffices to note that free movement of capital is part of both concepts. See for a discussion of delineation of both concepts: S Leible, Art. 14 EC (2003), mn 10–15; J Pipkorn, et al, Art. 14 EC (2003), mn 10 *et seq*. See also M Schweitzer and W Hummer, *Europarecht*, mn 1066 *et seq*.

[41] JCW Müller, *Kapitalverkehrsfreiheit*, 97; H Tietmeyer, 'Europäische Währung', 104; European Commission, *Vollendung des Binnenmarktes*, mn 125.

[42] Case 203/80 *Criminal proceedings against Guerrino Casati*, para 8; W Kiemel, Vorbem. zu den Artikeln 56 bis 60 EC (2003), mn 2.

[43] *Cf* Joined Cases 56 and 58/64 *Établissements Consten S.à.R.L. and Grundig-Verkaufs-GmbH v Commission*; Case 6/72 *Europemballage Corporation and Continental Can Company Inc. v Commission*. Once freed, competition is protected against public and private interferences by the Treaty provisions on competition and state aid, ie, Arts 81–89 EC.

[44] The Common Market is characterized by the four market freedoms, by equal opportunities for market participants, and by the prohibition of restrictions on free competition.

[45] JCW Müller, *Kapitalverkehrsfreiheit*, 108 *et seq*.

(5) Free Movement of Capital and the Economic Constitution of the Common Market

Moreover, free movement of capital is a constituting element of the economic constitution[46] of the Common Market, which is characterized by the competing principles of 'market' (*cf* Art 4(1), 98, 2nd sentence EC and 105(1) 3rd sentence EC) and 'planning' (*cf*, eg, industry policy (Art 157 EC), research and technology policy (Art 163 *et seq*.), and regional policy (Art 158 EC *et seq*)). Free capital movement is a major pillar of the first principle.[47] Limiting free capital movement by way of interventionist policy would mean no less than to apply the axe to the roots of the aforementioned principle.[48]

b. Unilateral Liberalization of Third Country Capital Movement: Lack of Aims?

While hardly any dispute evolves today around the aims pursued by free capital movement in an intra-Community context, the situation quickly becomes more heterogeneous and complex when one turns to the external perspective.

For some commentators, it is difficult to envisage any 'specific reason which can be attributed to the shift in the Community policy in unilaterally opening its capital markets to third countries'.[49] For example, Mohamed, who concurs with the conclusions that free movement of capital between the Member States constitutes a prerequisite for the completion and functioning of the Common Market and of Economic and Monetary Union, on the other hand hardly speculates at all as to which aims are possibly pursued by a unilateral liberalization of capital movements with respect to third countries. Such an alleged 'lack of aims' possibly pursued together with the liberalization of third country capital movement is, as a second step, employed to reduce dramatically the scope of application of Art 56(1) EC by means of teleological construction.[50]

The stumbling block and the centrepiece of their incomprehension, it appears, can be identified in the 'outrageous' act of unilateralism in which capital

---

[46] See with respect to the term 'economic constitution' (*Wirtschaftsverfassung*) for further references: J Basedow, *Wirtschaftsverfassung*, 6 *et seq* and T Oppermann, 'Wirtschaftsverfassung'; and more recently: P Behrens, 'Konventsentwurf'; E-J Mestmäcker, 'Wirtschaftsverfassung'; J Baquero Cruz, *Economic Constitutional Law*.

[47] Free capital movement enjoys a paramount position in a market-oriented model: HH Rupp, *Grundgesetz und 'Wirtschaftsverfassung'*, 16.

[48] JCW Müller, *Kapitalverkehrsfreiheit*, 120 *et seq*.

[49] S Mohamed, *Free Movement of Capital*, 216.

[50] An interpretation, in order not to be viewed as a subjective value judgement, needs to pay due attention to the relationship of the different methods of construction to one another. It appears that the view advanced above attributes supremacy to the teleological construction over the literal interpretation. This study proceeds from the assumption, shared by the ECJ, that the wording of a provision provides both the starting point and also the outer limits of any valid legal interpretation. For a more detailed account of the different methods of construction, see F Müller and R Christensen, *Methodik*, 75.

movements were liberalized in EC–third country relations. In the eyes of those commentators, this *'generous unilateral move'*[51]—indicated by the clear wording of Art 56(1) EC—is at best an editorial mistake of the Treaty drafters or at worst a huge political and economic mistake.

It is argued that the benefits of the Common Market and of Economic and Monetary Union are not extended to third countries and, consequently, there is no need for unilateral liberalization of capital movements towards third countries. In a nutshell, with no Common Market or Economic and Monetary Union, there is no free movement of capital. The only function one of these commentators can therefore imagine for Art 56(1) EC in a third country context is the facilitation of foreign trade and international financial operations.[52]

Another somewhat more moderate view structures its argument as follows: it asks whether the EC aims for the creation of a 'liberalized capital market' on a world scale.[53] Only if answered in the affirmative would it be justified in taking seriously the wording of Art 56(1) EC, ie, the unilateral liberalization of capital movements *erga omnes*. Asking the question in this way, the commentator cannot help but conclude that the Treaty does not pursue such an aim due to the fact that, in principle, the Treaty focuses on the development of the EC and its Common Market by abolition of internal borders.[54] The commentator therefore wants to attribute a mere *'ancillary function'* to the *erga omes* rule in Art 56(1) EC, which is meant only to drive the creation of a common border regime for capital, comparable to the Customs Union.[55] Without endeavouring to enter into an in-depth discussion of this view at this point in the study, it is nevertheless worth mentioning that I think that the answer proposed falls short in two ways. First, this view discounts that the realization of complete[56] unilateral liberalization of capital movement *erga omnes* beyond the implementation of a common border regime can indeed significantly further the development of the Common Market, as I will show further below. Second, the Treaty also contains aims that do not exclusively focus on the EC, but, for example, on the harmonious development of world trade at large (*cf* Art 131(1) EC) by means of intensified global competition, even if this could lead to higher adaptation costs within the EC than elsewhere.[57] Thus, an aim of the Community that seeks an

---

[51] S Mohamed, *Free Movement of Capital*, 219.
[52] Ibid, 216. Having attributed such a function, Mohamed seeks to reduce the right contained in Art 56(1) EC in third country relations to pure physical transport of money across borders. [*Cf* S Mohamed, *Free Movement of Capital*, 219] See also K Ståhl, 'Movement of Capital', 51.
[53] Posing such a question, eg: W Kiemel, Art. 56 EC (2003), mn 26; G Ress and J Ukrow, Art. 56 EC (2002), mn 53.
[54] W Schön, 'Kapitalverkehr mit Drittstaaten', 503 *et seq*.
[55] Ibid, 506. Thus, Art 56(1) EC would only guarantee the technical access and exit of capital, ie, the act of the actual transfer, but not non-discrimination or non-hindrance of third country capital within the Community.
[56] Of course, a regulatory framework ensuring in particular a strong supervision of the financial market to prevent abusive practices remains indispensable.
[57] *Cf* M Nettesheim and JL Duvigneau, 'Art. 131 EC', mn 3 *et seq*.

EC contribution to the establishment of a global capital market at large is at least debatable.[58]

Before entering into a debate, another argument will be introduced into the discussion that is advanced in favour of a restrictive understanding of the aims pursued by Art 56(1) EC. It is feared that by unilaterally liberalizing capital movement *erga omnes* in the absence of a level playing field, the harmonious development of the Community's internal financial market could be distorted.[59] The argument runs as follows: '[A]s all Member States are bound by the same set of rules and regulations'[60]—ie, a level playing field exists—there is no need for any reciprocity within the internal market due to the fact that it exists by virtue of the EC Treaty itself. This regulatory convergence, however, is missing towards third countries.[61] In order to avoid alleged distortions, the EC capital market should only be opened up to third countries on the condition of

---

[58] *Cf* G Ress and J Ukrow, Art. 56 EC (2002), mn 54. Such an interpretation appears plausible if one considers the notion behind Art 57(2) EC. This provision renders any attempt to depart from liberalization already achieved more difficult than further liberalization by requiring a unanimous vote. One could deduce from this provision that the EC is not only pursuing an agenda with a strong tendency towards further liberalization, but also that it is willing to make a contribution to the capital liberalization efforts on a global scale.

In reference to the Common Commercial Policy, of course, the situation is slightly different from the one in which the freedom of capital movement is placed. The former contains explicit special aims to be pursued by the relevant policy (*cf* Art 131 EC). In the latter case, in order to identify the aims pursued, one has to have recourse to the general Treaty aims. Yet the unconditional wording of Art 56(1) EC in connection with the notion of an open market economy (Arts 4(1), 98, 2nd sentence EC, and 105 (1) 3rd sentence EC), at least, does not rule out the drawing of such a parallel.

This study, however, tends to give priority to the more persuasive arguments that do not place a liberalized global capital market at large at the centre of the aims to be pursued by Art 56(1) EC, but rather an EC capital market open to the world. Thus, unilaterally allowing for free capital flow *erga omnes* is favoured not because it contributes to a liberalized world capital market, but because it furthers the development of the Common Market. In this sense, a liberalized global capital market can be a means but is not necessarily seen as an end.

[59] S Mohamed, *Free Movement of Capital*, 219. See also W Schön, 'Kapitalverkehr mit Drittstaaten', 504 *et seq.*

[60] S Mohamed, *Free Movement of Capital*, 218.

[61] In this respect, Advocate General Geelhoed in *Ospelt* noted the following: '[W]ithin a completed Monetary Union the Member States have renounced their monetary sovereignty.' [Case C-452/01 (Opinion of AG Geelhoed) *Margarethe Ospelt and Schlössle Weissenberg Familienstiftung*, para 37] Thus, in reference to Art 119(4) EC and Art 120(4) EC, they are no longer allowed to apply protective measures. Member States that are not part of the Euro-zone are obliged to coordinate their exchange rate policies (*cf* Art 124 in connection with the Second European Monetary System outlined in the Resolution of the European Council on the Establishment of an Exchange-rate Mechanism in the Third Stage of Economic and Monetary Union, Amsterdam, 16.6.1997). None of these requirements apply towards third countries. '[T]hese differences in the level of monetary integration have a bearing on the interpretation of Art. 56 EC...' [Case C-452/01 (Opinion of AG Geelhoed) *Margarethe Ospelt and Schlössle Weissenberg Familienstiftung*, para 40], ie, exceptions based on monetary considerations to the freedom of capital movements may be only applied to third countries.

The statement of the Advocate General is to be concurred with in the sense that externally more exceptions to the freedom, ie, Arts 57–60 EC, are allowed. However, his analysis is not to be read as suggesting that the *erga omnes* liberalization runs counter to any Treaty aim.

reciprocity,[62] ie, EC investors abroad should be granted similar rights to the ones enjoyed by foreign investors within the EC. Thus, what is required is first and foremost a certain degree of regulatory convergence. With a unilateral opening of the EC capital market, presumably, the Community gives away its bargaining powers to press for this.[63]

If one strips this argument down to its essentials, what is suggested here is that Art 56(1) EC, if one were to take its wording seriously, not only does not further the attainment of any legitimate Treaty aim, but actually endangers the Treaty aim of 'harmonious development' contained in Art 2 EC. The Treaty makers, others seemingly want us to believe, must have acted profoundly carelessly while compiling the Treaty, not realizing what a dangerous thing they had actually written in the final text. If one were to follow such argumentation, the reasonable conclusion would be to interpret Art 56(1) EC in a third country context as a programmatic statement in order to avoid any distorting effects on the Common Market. The actual liberalization would be based on Art 57(2) EC, contingent on reciprocity.

Above I have outlined the reasoning of those who doubt that liberalized capital movement *erga omnes* significantly facilitates the attainment of the Treaty aims. This study does not share these views. Ultimately the question that must be answered in the following is whether any Treaty aim can reasonably be pursued by a unilateral liberalization of capital movements *erga omes* in the absence of three things: first, in the absence of a 'common market' with third countries; second, in the absence of an 'economic and monetary union' with third countries; and last but not least, in the absence of any precondition (eg, reciprocity) for the opening of the EC market.

If one is prepared to perceive the Community as a non-protectionist, open market economy (*cf* Arts 4(1), 98, 2nd sentence EC and 105(1) 3rd sentence EC),[64] disapproving of the notion of a 'Fortress Europe',[65] then those arguments that speak in favour of a complete liberalization of capital movements within the Community can also be utilized in a third country context.[66] As discussed

---

[62] Note that in an intra-Community context it was explicitly stated by the Court that the rights contained in the Treaty are not subject to the condition of reciprocity. [*Cf* Case 270/83 *Commission v French Republic (Re Corporation Tax and Shareholders' Tax Credits: 'avoir fiscal'*, para 26]

[63] S Mohamed, *Free Movement of Capital*, 217 *et seq*. See also W Schön, 'Kapitalverkehr mit Drittstaaten', 504 *et seq*. For the opposite view: Case C-101/05 *Skatteverket v A*, para 38.

[64] The *erga omnes* applicability of the provisions of free movement of capital constitutes one of the purest means for realization of the commitment of the Community to the 'principle of an open market economy with free competition'. See JCW Müller, *Kapitalverkehrsfreiheit*, 110; Case C-452/01 (Opinion of AG Geelhoed) *Margarethe Ospelt and Schlössle Weissenberg Familienstiftung*, para 34; in older literature: E-J Mestmäcker, 'Offene Märkte'; E Grabitz, 'Marktzugang'. For a critical view: G Ress and J Ukrow, Art. 56 EC (2002), mn 54 who argue that this principle relates only to the Internal Market. See also HJ Abs, 'Capital Movements', 508 *et seq*.

[65] A Rohde, 'Freier Kapitalverkehr', 457. For the notion of a 'Fortress Europe' see W Kirchhoff, 'Festung Europa'.

[66] Partially concurring: Case C-101/05 (Opinion of AG Bot) *Skatteverket v A*, para 72 *et seq*.

above, if certain institutional preconditions are met,[67] free movement of capital extending beyond the Common Market leads to increasingly optimized capital allocation[68] and to intensified competition fuelling economic growth. It increases the freedom of choice, especially for European capital recipients but also for European investors not hindered by Member States or the EC in moving capital out of the Common Market.[69] Due to intensified competition, the Community—or rather, its businesses—are rendered even more competitive on a world level. This will certainly add to the pressure on Member States to maintain fiscal and tariffs discipline, but this in turn can have an overall stabilizing effect on the European economy, which is one of the aims of Art 2 EC. Thus, even in the absence of a 'common market' or an 'economic and monetary union' with third countries, the complete liberalization of capital movement *erga omnes* contributes to the attainment of those Treaty aims that, in their perspective, point to the Common Market.[70] None of the benefits from liberalized capital movement mentioned above depend on reciprocal access of EU capital to third country markets.[71]

Moreover, as also stated in the previous section, free movement of capital towards third countries is the best watchdog for the stability of the common currency.[72] Free capital movement enables the markets to judge the stability of

---

[67] In this respect one has to think, inter alia, of an effective anti-trust and subsidy control, a functioning tax and legal system, or a stable banking system. All of that can be found within the EC.
[68] See on the aim of 'optimal allocation of capital on a world scale': C Ohler, Art. 56 EC (2002), mn 4, 214; G Ress and J Ukrow, Art. 56 EC (2002), mn 54; W Kiemel, Vorbem. zu den Artikeln 56 bis 60 EC (2003), mn 31; F Kimms, *Kapitalverkehrsfreiheit*, 173; A Rohde, *Kapitalverkehr*, 181. See also the very interesting argument of A Baines, 'Capital Mobility', 344 *et seq*, which states that deregulation of capital flows is primarily reactive and triggered by increased international competition.
[69] An open market approach also builds up trust in the investment area since an investor does not have to fear that once he has placed his investment he will be taken hostage by a sudden change to a restrictive national capital movements policy.
[70] For example, confining the scope of application of Art 56(1) EC to the mere physical transfer of money across borders (Mohamed) or, somewhat more broadly, to the act of the actual transfer (Schön) would imperil the attainment of those aims due to the fact that, for one thing, such confinement would leave an enormous amount of room for regulatory measures that, in turn, could severely distort the process of capital allocation. The ECJ—without giving a reason—appears to be of a different view stating that 'the liberalisation of the movement of capital with third countries may pursue objectives other than that of establishing the internal market'. [Case C-101/05 *Skatteverket v A*, para 31] It seeks to confine the aims pursued by a liberalized third country capital movement to aims 'such as, in particular, that of ensuring the credibility of the single Community currency on world financial markets and maintaining financial centres with a world-wide dimension within the Member States'. [Case C-101/05 *Skatteverket v A*, para 31] See also Case C-101/05 (Opinion of AG Bot) *Skatteverket v A*, para 74 *et seq*; L Pappers, 'National Report Netherlands', 396.
[71] OECD, *Int'l Investment Perspectives 2007*, 73.
[72] R Hasse and J Starbatty, 'Währungsunion', 128 *et seq*; W Kiemel, Art. 56 EC (2003), mn 79. Advocate General Geelhoed in *Ospelt* states 'The free movement of capital must be regarded as a constituent element of an economic and monetary union' [Case C-452/01 (Opinion of AG Geelhoed) *Margarethe Ospelt and Schlössle Weissenberg Familienstiftung*, para 36]. See also Case C-101/05 *Skatteverket v A*, para 31. Schön asks sceptically and incredulously why only free movement of capital in its scope of application was extended 'in a revolutionary act' beyond the borders

monetary union in the most reliable way and thus increases the trust of market participants in a freely convertible currency, which is supposed to aspire to be an international investment, financing, trade, and reserve currency.[73]

Any capital control measure would endanger the attainment of the abovementioned aims due to its distorting effects.[74] A restrictive interpretation, such as the one referred to above, that intends to reverse the rule–exception relationship laid out in the Treaty (Art 56(1) EC and Arts 57–60 EC) would further imperil the realization of the Treaty aims and must for this reason alone be disapproved.[75]

Furthermore, the contention that due to a lack of regulatory convergence between the European market and third country economies, free movement of capital would not only be undesirable but could even endanger the attainment of Treaty aims is open to question. From an economic viewpoint:

> while there is no doubt that financial integration means that domestic policy-makers must pay more attention to international economic developments and policy spillovers when setting policy, it does not follow that formal policy coordination is actually required[76]

to allow for free capital movement. The European Community, due to the large size of its market, can absorb external shocks by interest and exchange rate adjustments and, hence, the harmonious development of the internal market would not be put at risk with capital movement being liberalized.[77] Moreover, it can be argued that prioritizing liberalization over harmonization builds up the necessary pressure on the Member States to actively seek compromises with respect to the establishment of a common regime towards third countries.[78] Thus, the assertion that a level playing field, in the sense of regulatory convergence, is a necessary precondition for capital liberalization *erga omnes* must be disregarded as a spurious argument.[79]

---

of the Common Market. [W Schön, 'Kapitalverkehr mit Drittstaaten', 504] In reply to his question, it is especially, but not exclusively, the interconnection of the common currency and free movement of capital that explains and justifies the elevation of free movement of capital to the only freedom that extends beyond the borders of the Common Market.

[73] M Seidel, 'Kapitalmarkt', 763 *et seq*, 772; G Ress and J Ukrow, Art. 56 EC (2002), mn 54; A Rohde, 'Freier Kapitalverkehr', 457; C Ohler, Art. 56 EC (2002), mn 4, 8; JCW Müller, *Kapitalverkehrsfreiheit*, 84 *et seq*; RH Weber, Vorb. Art. 56–60 EC (2003), mn 2 *et seq*.

[74] W Kiemel, Vorbem. zu den Artikeln 56 bis 60 EC (2003), mn 30. This, however, should by no means be understood as ruling out a regulatory framework, first and foremost guaranteeing effective banking supervision and adherence to financial security standards. See G Ress and J Ukrow, Art. 56 EC (2002), mn 59.

[75] 'The European currency can only fulfil its function if capital movement is entirely free both within the Community and from and towards third countries …' [translation by the author; W Kiemel, Vorb. zu den Art. 67 bis 73 EEC (1991), mn 31]. See also G Ress and J Ukrow, Art. 56 EC (2002), mn 54; C Ohler, Art. 56 EC (2002), mn 4.

[76] European Commission, 'European Economy No. 6/2003: The EU Economy: 2003 Review' 283.

[77] AFP Bakker, *Capital Movements*, 230.

[78] See H Tietmeyer, 'Europäische Währung', 108, though, in an intra-Community context.

[79] Of the same opinion is A Rohde, 'Freier Kapitalverkehr', 457 who notes that the Community is prepared to respond to economic turbulence by means of Art 59 EC.

In addition, it is difficult to comprehend that the Community, in the case of a liberal interpretation of Art 56(1) EC, would lack bargaining power in negotiations with third countries, thereby endangering the attainment of their Treaty aims.[80] Rather, the pessimistic outlook provided by those who oppose a liberal interpretation of Art 56(1) EC appears as an attempt to reverse the results reached by the Treaty of Maastricht.

The negotiation history of the Maastricht Treaty reveals that Member States which favoured the *erga omnes* principle, ie, unconditional unilateral liberalization with respect to any country as opposed to liberalization based on reciprocity, finally succeeded in defending it as the axiom of the regulations on capital movements. However, they had to accept certain exceptions to it.[81] These exceptions, Arts 57(1) EC, 59 EC, and 60 EC, met some of the reservations of those countries that were sceptical of the *erga omnes* principle; at the same time, these provisions implicitly confirm that the *erga omnes* precept is to be seen as the principle, not the exception.[82] Having the *erga omnes* principle as the basic rule—instead of making any concession of liberalization towards third countries conditional upon reciprocity—does not mean that the bargaining powers of the Community were significantly weakened with the introduction of Art 56(1) EC (or Art 73b(1) ToM, which it then was).[83] Especially by virtue of Art 57(2) EC (but also, for example, on the basis of Arts 94 and 95 EC),[84] the Community was given the means to fight off abusive and impairing practices of third countries, for example, by means of demanding reciprocity.[85] Although the Community was equipped with the necessary 'managing tools', which could be turned into razor-sharp blades if need be, the Treaty makers seemed to be optimistic that the Community could resist any third country challenge without restricting capital movements by reason of its economic strength and stability. Due to this view, they chose to implant the seed of liberalization in Art 57(2) EC, providing for the power to enact capital control measures. Not without reason is it stated that the powers contained must be exercised with a view to achieving *'the objective of free movement of capital between Member States and third countries to the greatest extent possible'*. Moreover, for restrictive measures the provision requires unanimity, which is seen as a rather high threshold to overcome.[86]

---

[80] Of the same view: Case C-101/05 (Opinion of AG Bot) *Skatteverket v A*, para 84 *et seq*.
[81] AFP Bakker, *Capital Movements*, 244 *et seq*.
[82] See for an account of these provisions: Chapter VII. 2, Chapter VII. 4, and Chapter VII. 5.
[83] JCW Müller, *Kapitalverkehrsfreiheit*, 107; G Ress and J Ukrow, Art. 56 EC (2002), mn 52.
[84] *Cf* Chapter IV. 3. b. (2) (b) and Chapter VII. 3.
[85] However, secondary Community legislation should operate carefully with such means. Demanding reciprocity on a regular basis would be at odds with the rule–exception relationship in Art 56 EC *et seq* and would endanger the openness of the system, which is of particular importance for the common currency. [*Cf* W Kiemel, Art. 56 EC (2003), mn 79; W Kiemel, Art. 57 EC (2003), mn 13. See also P Eeckhout, *External Relations*, 124]
[86] W Kiemel, Art. 57 EC (2003), mn 20; Art 57 (2) EC provides the Community with the opportunity to develop a common regime on cross-border direct investment; see TL Brewer and S Young, 'Multinational Enterprises', 44.

c. Conclusion

Free movement of capital in an intra-Community context contributes in particular to the attainment of the (socio-)economic aims described by the 'magic square' through the establishment of a Common Market and of Economic and Monetary Union. Consequentially, in order to attain those aims prima facie, a broad interpretation of the freedom of capital movement would be indicated.

Liberalized capital movement from and towards third countries, implemented on a unilateral basis, does not only facilitate but also partially constitutes a precondition for the successful attainment of a multitude of predominantly (socio-)economic Treaty aims (first and foremost, economic growth, overall stabilization of the European economy, and the implementation of Economic and Monetary Union) by serving as an important indicator for the stability of the common currency. In short, keeping the doors open—even on a unilateral basis—serves the overall economic development of the EC with its Common Market. Returning to the introductory question in light of the above, this study cannot envisage sufficient reason why the analysis that (socio-)economic aims are best served when the freedom of capital movement is construed in a liberal and wide understanding must be re-assessed when it comes to third country capital movements.

However, the EC Treaty also recognizes a diversity of other interests that might run counter to the precept of liberalization flowing from economic rationales and the (socio-)economic Treaty aims. It is therefore conceivable that, in the individual case, measures which, for example, aim to guarantee public security, defence of the consumer, protection of the environment, or the preservation of small-scale agriculture are permissible even though they restrict free movement of capital. Even different economic aims can conflict with each other; one may recall that free movement of capital—in order to produce all the positive effects for the European economy mentioned above—requires in particular a mature and stable banking system and a functioning legal order, the latter comprising, inter alia, an effective banking and competition supervisory system, as well as a working tax and insolvency regime.

The doctrinal analysis of the Treaty provisions on free movement of capital later on in this study will provide detailed guidance on how to resolve these conflicts.

3. The Art of Political Compromise: The Way from Coordination of Currency Policy to Free Movement of Capital *Erga Omnes*

The provisions on capital movement have experienced significant change over the years, not only in numbering but also substantively.[87] While for a long time 'free

---

[87] For the genesis of the provisions on free movement of capital, see first and foremost: AFP Bakker, *Capital Movements*; F Kimms, *Kapitalverkehrsfreiheit*; A Rohde, *Kapitalverkehr*, 39 *et seq*;

movements of capital' were treated like the 'poor cousin'[88] of the other market freedoms, it now takes the lead—at least if one dares to trust the promise of Art 56(1) EC—by being the only freedom that in its scope of application extends beyond the outer borders of the Community, liberalizing capital movements from and towards third countries.

a. Starting with a Clean Sheet—The 1957 Treaty establishing the European Economic Community and the 1960 and 1962 Directives

The initial 1957 Treaty establishing the European Economic Community (EEC) *'started with a clean sheet'*[89] with respect to the liberalization of capital movements. Besides a weak stand-still clause in Art 71 EEC prohibiting the introduction of new restrictions on non-trade-related capital movements, the Member States committed themselves in Art 67 EEC only to progressively abolishing between themselves all restrictions on the movement of capital belonging to persons resident in Member States and any discrimination based on nationality, the place of residence of the parties, or the place where the capital is invested to the extent necessary to ensure the proper functioning of the Common Market. The conditionality (*'to the extent necessary...'*) and gradualism (*'progressively abolish...'*) of this provision had the consequence that liberalization had to be brought about by secondary legislation, for which the Community was empowered in Arts 69 and 70 EEC.[90] Article 69 EEC provided for the implementation of Art 67 EEC, which in effect was limited to the Common Market.[91] With respect to third countries, the EEC Treaty allowed in Art 70 only for Commission proposals on the progressive coordination of currency policy with a view toward reaching an increasing degree of liberalization.[92]

All in all, the initial provisions on capital movement mirrored a cautious approach towards liberalization that was given relatively low priority. The EEC Treaty clearly focused on the establishment of a customs union[93] that, it was feared, could be endangered by destabilizing capital flows. Given these fears, and in the situation of fixed exchange rates under the Bretton Woods system at this time, Member States were unwilling to agree on surrender of competences

---

A Honrath, *Kapitalverkehr*, 51 *et seq* and S Mohamed, *Free Movement of Capital*, 39 *et seq*. For a concise account refer, eg, to U Haferkamp, *Kapitalverkehrsfreiheit*, 18 *et seq*; C Barnard, *Substantive Law*, 462 *et seq*; W Kiemel, Vorbem. zu den Artikeln 56 bis 60 EC (2003), mn 7 *et seq* or JA Usher, 'Capital Movements', 35 *et seq*. For a very comprehensive discussion, see S Mohamed, *Free Movement of Capital*, 39 *et seq*. See also J Story and I Walter, *Financial Integration*.

[88] W Schön, 'Kapitalverkehr mit Drittstaaten', 491.
[89] AFP Bakker, *Capital Movements*, 41.
[90] W Kiemel, Vorbem. zu den Artikeln 56 bis 60 EC (2003), mn 7.
[91] Unanimous vote was required.
[92] W Kiemel, Vorbem. zu den Artikeln 56 bis 60 EC (2003), mn 13; AFP Bakker, *Capital Movements*, 41.
[93] AFP Bakker, *Capital Movements*, 42 *et seq*.

in the financial field.[94] This strong tendency to the preservation of autonomy is underlined by a number of escape clauses in case of disturbances on the domestic capital market (Art 73 EEC) and balance of payments problems (Arts 108 and 109 EEC).

The Court exercised an equally cautious approach and chose to read the freedom in a rather restrictive way, which might have been influenced by the currency unrest at the time of the judgment in the early 1980s.[95] In *Casati*,[96] probably the most important case on capital movement at this time, it was held that Art 67 EEC would not be directly effective due to the escape clauses. By doing so, it barred individual market participants from using the freedom as an instrument of liberalization.[97] The Court remained true to itself in the years to follow, as the case law reflects a tendency 'to merely follow the political agreement reached elsewhere on the pace of liberalisation in the Community'.[98] It denied itself a proactive role in the area of the free movement of capital, quite in contrast to its activities in the areas of the other freedoms.[99]

Shortly after the adoption of the EEC Treaty, the first steps to liberalize capital movements within the Community were initiated. A first Directive of 1960[100] obliged the Member States, inter alia, to liberalize short and medium-term trade-related credits, direct investment flows, and transactions in listed shares, all transactions viewed as having direct influence on the establishment of the Common Market. While the Commission fought for full liberalization of all capital movements, the Member States in turn could merely agree on those types of capital movements to be included in the Directive, which had already been liberalized autonomously by some Member States. In this sense, the first Directive is a consolidation of the steps previously undertaken by the Member States on their own.[101] The issue of liberalizing capital movements with respect to third countries was not touched upon in the Directive. However, liberalized categories of capital movement in fact enjoyed the same treatment in intra-Community and third country contexts.[102]

In the aftermath, the Commission was eager to maintain momentum and proposed a second Directive[103] on the liberalization of capital movements aiming at medium-term and long-term credit by banks in 1962. However, the Member States—due to varying economic situations and differing political views[104]—were unwilling to accept further major common obligations at that time. Rather, they wanted to pursue further liberalization steps on their own. 'Apparently the political and economic limits to unconditional liberalisation

---

[94] Ibid, 53.　[95] Ibid, 47.
[96] Case 203/80 *Criminal proceedings against Guerrino Casati*, para 8 *et seq*.
[97] Along similar lines: W Schön, 'Kapitalverkehrsfreiheit', 744; U Haferkamp, *Kapitalverkehrsfreiheit*, 19.
[98] AFP Bakker, *Capital Movements*, 47.　[99] Ibid.
[100] First Capital Movement Directive.
[101] AFP Bakker, *Capital Movements*, 88 *et seq*.　[102] Ibid, 88.
[103] Directive 63/21/EEC.　[104] *Cf* AFP Bakker, *Capital Movements*, 92 *et seq*.

had been reached.'[105] Hence, the second Directive in the end emerged merely as *'a supplement to the 1960 Directive'*.[106] Short-term and medium-term credits were de-linked from trade-related transactions and liberalized unconditionally for services as well.

b. Lost Momentum—Capital Control on the Rise in the Mid-1960s and 1970s

Further attempts by the Commission in the subsequent decade to push forward with and broaden the liberalization of capital movements within the Community were doomed to failure. The Member States at that time were not prepared to open up their domestic capital markets, as this was perceived as a particularly sensitive political issue. The differing monetary philosophies among the Member States made it even harder to agree on further liberalization, as some of them needed capital restrictions as a complement to domestic monetary instruments. The fear of speculative capital movements, which hit France hard in 1968 and 1969,[107] additionally discouraged the taking up of common obligations.

'By the mid-1970s the momentum had been completely lost.'[108] The Member States had to deal with enormous capital inflows originating from the United States of America, which forced even traditionally liberal-minded Germany to introduce capital controls. The Commission turned from an advocate for the free movement of capital to a supporter of capital control measures in order to prevent further inflow of speculative capital.[109] The worsening international environment—highlighted by the collapse of the Bretton Woods system and the first oil price shock—led each major Member State to formulate significantly different policy approaches, which made compromise on further integration in the area of capital movement extremely difficult. Germany and the Netherlands, although traditionally in the 'economist camp', acquiesced into capital control measures as long as they prevented or hindered capital movements into the Deutsche Mark and the guilder. France and Italy, partisans of the 'monetarist camp,' perceived *'capital control as a useful safety valve as long as economic convergence was lacking'*,[110] and thus made extensive use of it. All in all—although the *acquis communautaire* was not changed—the European capital market was less integrated in the 1970s than it was in the 1960s.[111] This not being enough, at the end of the 1970s it became apparent that capital control measures were actually of very limited effectiveness under the economic conditions of the time. However, '[a]lthough the limited effectiveness was generally recognised, Member States did not draw the same conclusions'[112] in policy terms. Only Germany in 1977 and 1978, and

---

[105] Ibid, 93.   [106] Ibid.
[107] Described by the French authorities as '*les événements*' of May 1968.
[108] AFP Bakker, *Capital Movements*, 140.   [109] Ibid.
[110] Ibid, 141.   [111] Ibid.   [112] Ibid, 142.

later the United Kingdom, which had originally championed monetarist ideas, abolished (the latter in a radical move in 1979) all their restrictions on capital movement. Although driven purely by national motivation, this shift should not be viewed as being without significance for the whole of the European Economic Community.

c. Liberalization Back on Track—The Single European Act and the 1988 Directive

It was the shift of two major European economies that would herald a new twist in policy on the European level. Germany and the United Kingdom, jointly with the Netherlands, proposed to the Commission the taking up of the nearly forgotten issue of liberalization of capital movements. However, the Commission gave this a cold reception. In previous years, it tolerated the unilateral extension and intensification of capital control measures in France and Italy without even examining whether the two Member States were entitled to do so by the respective safeguard clauses of the EEC Treaty. Only massive external criticism in the early 1980s by the European Parliament and the Court,[113] calling upon the Commission to observe the procedures of the EEC Treaty strictly, initiated a process of reconsideration.[114] After France, shifting from the monetarist camp closer to the economist one, successfully managed to stabilize its financial market, momentum was regained for further liberalization of capital movements. Backed by an improved economic climate in Europe, the Commission under Delors could take the lead. In its famous White Paper[115] of 1985 entitled *'Completing the Internal Market',* the full liberalization of capital movements was defined as an essential part of this process. Notable in this respect is that no positive discrimination of capital movements on the Internal Market compared to the ones with third countries—continuously advocated by France—was proposed.[116]

For the subsequent negotiations of the Single European Act,[117] however, the Commission's position of complete liberalization proved to be too bold. The Member States resisted a suggestion of the Commission to get rid of the conditionality clause (*'to the extent necessary…'*) in Art 67 EEC. A direct effect of the provisions on free movement of capital was still unacceptable at this point in time. However, the Commission succeeded in defining the notion of 'Internal

---

[113] *Cf* Case 36/83 *Mabanaft GmbH v Hauptzollamt Emmerich*, para 34. See for a resolution of the European Parliament of 18.6.1982 on the lax attitude of the Commission *vis-à-vis* Italy with respect to the application of Art 108(3) 3 EEC: European Parliament, 'Resolution on the Deposit on Imports into Italy', paras 5, 7.
[114] AFP Bakker, *Capital Movements*, 154 *et seq*.
[115] European Commission, 'Completing the Internal Market. White Paper from the Commission to the European Council (Milan, 28–29 June 1985)' (COM (85) 310 final), para 124 *et seq*.
[116] AFP Bakker, *Capital Movements*, 161.
[117] Single European Act.

Market' as encompassing free movement of capital.[118] Even more importantly, the Single European Act changed the decision-making process. Qualified majority voting was introduced for measures that further liberalized capital movements; unanimity would be required for any step back. While in this way a veto of one Member State could be overcome, the introduction of the principle of 'mutual recognition'[119] made compromise among Member States easier by requiring Member States only to agree on a minimum standard of harmonization to be recognized throughout the Community; each Member State could still individually set an elevated standard at home.[120]

Shortly after the adoption of the Single European Act, the Commission initiated a capital movement liberalization programme based on two phases. Within the first phase the Commission set expiry dates on the safeguard measures taken by France, Italy, and Ireland, and it proposed a new directive intended to enlarge the liberalization obligations. The 1986 Directive[121]—while not bringing about full liberalization—provided evidence that the arguments in favour of liberalization had gained ground among Member States.[122]

The second phase brought about the complete liberalization of capital movements within the Community.[123] Even the politically sensitive group of short-term capital movements—thus far left outside of any liberalization commitment due to its supposed interrelation with undesired speculative capital movements—was now included in the new 1988 Directive for the Implementation of Art 67 EEC ('EC Capital Movements Directive').[124] *'The adoption of the 1988 Directive was a landmark in the history of the Community.'*[125] A favourable cyclical situation, relative calm within the European Monetary System, and the agreement among Member States to negotiate without preconditions opened up a window of opportunity. The Commission's three major arguments—that the European economy required a well-functioning integrated capital market, that liberalization of capital movement was a precondition for any economic and monetary union,[126] and that economic convergence among the Member States could be reached through the disciplinary effect of free movement of capital—met with approval among the Member States.[127] The driving forces behind the Directive—alongside the Commission—were Germany, the United Kingdom, the Netherlands, and France. Those countries formed a liberal-minded alliance

---

[118] AFP Bakker, *Capital Movements*, 162.
[119] See for a brief description of this concept: Chapter IV. 3. b. (3) (b) ii. (i).
[120] AFP Bakker, *Capital Movements*, 165.
[121] Directive 86/566/EEC.   [122] AFP Bakker, *Capital Movements*, 180.
[123] Art 1 of Directive 88/361/EEC reads as follows: 'Member States shall abolish restrictions on movements of capital taking place between persons resident in Member States.'
[124] Ibid.
[125] AFP Bakker, *Capital Movements*, 212.
[126] Liberalization of capital movement was a precondition for entry into the first phase of the Monetary Union. *Cf*, eg, C Barnard, *Substantive Law*, 461.
[127] AFP Bakker, *Capital Movements*, 212.

that could not be resisted by the monetarist camp led by Italy. The consent of more hesitant Member States was gained by including in the Directive longer transition periods for some Member States, by the postponement of the date of transposition and by the incorporation of a monetary safeguard clause.[128]

With its subsequent judgment in *Bordessa*[129] declaring the Directive directly effective, the Court opened up the possibility for market participants to use it as an instrument of liberalization.[130] In this way, the ECJ removed the 'congenital defect' of the freedom, lifting it to the level of the free movement of goods, the freedom to provide services, and the freedom of establishment.

Concerning third country capital movement, the 1988 Directive introduced the '*erga omnes* principle' into the regulation of free movement of capital. Although the principle not to distinguish between the liberalization of capital movement within the Community and with respect to third countries was at that time only phrased as a political commitment,[131] its inclusion in the Directive can nevertheless be seen as a major achievement. The majority of Member States could resist a Commission proposal, backed by France and Italy, to leave third countries in doubt as to whether the Community was actually embracing the principle, which would have indirectly shielded the European capital market.[132]

d. Seizing the Moment—Free Movement of Capital *Erga Omnes* Enshrined in the Maastricht Treaty

After adoption of the 1988 Directive, the Member States removed existing restrictions on capital movement well in advance of the formal date of transposition, which was taken by the markets as a sign of strength. At the beginning of the 1990s, '[c]apital liberalisation, decreasing inflation differentials and satisfactory cyclical circumstances all provided a virtuous circle, mutually reinforcing each other.'[133] Under such conditions the transfer of the standard of liberalization achieved from secondary Community law to the EC Treaty[134] in 1992 faced no major obstacle.[135] The Maastricht Treaty (ToM) went even beyond this point. The '*erga omnes* principle', subject to certain exceptions and safeguard clauses,[136]

---

[128] Ibid, 212 *et seq*.
[129] Joined Cases C-358/93 and C-416/93 *Criminal proceedings against Aldo Bordessa and Vicente Marí Mellado and Concepción Barbero Maestre*, paras 17, 33 *et seq*.
[130] See also Chapter V. 2.
[131] Art. 7(1) of the Directive reads as follows: 'In their treatment of transfers with respect to movements of capital to or from third countries, the Member States *shall endeavour to attain* the same degree of liberalisation as that which applies to operations with residents of other Member States, subject to the other provisions of this Directive.' [Emphasis added] Directive 88/361/EEC.
[132] AFP Bakker, *Capital Movements*, 198 *et seq*.
[133] Ibid, 244.
[134] Art 73 lit. b–g ToM (now, after amendment, Arts 56(1) EC–60 EC).
[135] In this way it became even more difficult to reduce the standard of liberalization already achieved. [U Haferkamp, *Kapitalverkehrsfreiheit*, 25]
[136] Art 73 lit. c, 73 lit. f, 73 lit. g ToM (now, after amendment, Arts 57 EC, 59 EC, and 60 EC).

turned from a political commitment into a legally binding, directly effective[137] obligation.

Although it was not easy to hold up the principle during the Maastricht Treaty negotiations, the minutes reveal that the Member States[138] that favoured the *erga omnes* principle finally succeeded in defending it as the axiom of the regulations on capital movements; however, they had to accept certain exceptions to it.[139] These exceptions, Arts 57(1) EC, 59 EC, and 60 EC, met some of the reservations of those countries that were sceptical of the principle, but at the same time these provisions implicitly confirm that the *erga omnes* rule is to be seen as the principle, not the exception.[140]

Shortly after signing the Maastricht Treaty, the European Monetary System again slid into a crisis. In 1992 strong pressure on the weak currencies, in particular the Italian lira, the Spanish peseta, and the Portuguese escudo, led to the introduction of temporary capital restrictions, which had only a very limited effect. The respective governments quickly lifted restrictions as they realized that they were not only fruitless but also perceived by the markets as a negative confidence signal leading to an exodus of capital, which only worsened the overall situation.[141]

The second crisis of the European Monetary System in 1993—mainly hitting the French and Belgian franc—again led to calls for the reintroduction of capital restrictions. Ironically, the former champion of liberalization, the President of the Commission Jacques Delors, suddenly demanded the regulation of capital movements.[142] Fortunately, the wail of the sirens was resisted by the other Member States.[143] This episode, however, demonstrates that governments easily '*mis[take] the symptom for the disease*'[144] and are vulnerable to resorting to capital controls in times of turbulence despite economic rationales and (painful) empirical evidence.

Regardless of occasional calls for reviving capital control, the Treaty of Amsterdam (ToA)[145] did not bring about substantive but only technical changes to the Treaty provisions.[146] Basically, redundant articles were eliminated from

---

[137] For the first time: Joined Cases C-163/94, C-165/94, and C-250/94 *Criminal proceedings against Lucas Emilio Sanz de Lera, Raimundo Díaz Jiménez and Figen Kapanoglu*, para 40 *et seq*; confirmed, eg, in Case C-452/04 *Fidium Finanz AG*; Case C-446/04 *Test Claimants in the FII Group Litigation v Commissioners of Inland Revenue*; Case C-524/04 *Test Claimants in the Thin Cap Group Litigation*; Case C-157/05 *Winfried Holböck v Finanzamt Salzburg-Land*.

[138] In particular Germany and the Netherlands, and to a lesser extent also the United Kingdom.

[139] AFP Bakker, *Capital Movements*, 244 *et seq*.

[140] Ibid, 230 *et seq*, 232 *et seq*.   [141] Ibid, 237 *et seq*.

[142] Ibid, 239.   [143] Ibid, 236 *et seq*.

[144] Eddie George, Governor of the Bank of England, in a statement at the Frankfurt European Banking Congress on 19.11.1993; cited in ibid, 239.

[145] Treaty of Amsterdam.

[146] For more detail refer to W Kiemel, Vorbem. zu den Artikeln 56 bis 60 EC (2003), mn 33 *et seq*.

the Treaty text and Articles 73 lit. b–g ToM were renumbered Articles 56–60 ToA. The Treaty of Nice (ToN)[147] did not alter the provisions on free movement of capital at all.

e. From a Clean Sheet to One of the Strictest, Most Comprehensive and Most Effectively Enforceable Multinational Agreements Governing Capital Movement

Although temporal setbacks had to be overcome, the genesis of the rules on free movement of capital demonstrates a drive to (almost) complete liberalization of capital movement. It can hardly be doubted that the current provisions bear the hallmarks of the 'economist camp' and embrace a liberal undercurrent in both intra-Community and third country contexts. Achieving this end was only possible under several advantageous concomitant circumstances. A favourable economic climate provided the famous 'window of opportunity'. The alliance of Germany, the Netherlands, and Great Britain reanimated the project at a moment when it was in danger of being forgotten. It was France, however, that played the pivotal role. 'The evolution in French thinking provides an important clue to the question of why this attempt to liberalise succeeded where others failed.'[148] Only the shift from the 'monetarist' to the 'economist camp' added the necessary weight to the course of liberalization and motivated the Commission to move on, which it did with the right strategic choices and the necessary enthusiasm.[149]

In the aftermath of the adoption of the 1988 Directive and the Maastricht amendments on capital movement, the Community experienced a decade of dramatic liberalization. In relation to direct investment, the subject matter of this study, by the year 2000 the Member States could present economies which were among the most open worldwide.[150] With those liberalization measures the Member States aligned themselves with a global trend to free cross-border direct investment of its fetters.[151] It was a decade, as explained above, in which host and home countries perceived economic activity as overwhelmingly beneficial to their interests[152] and, consequently, they opened up their doors, which inevitably resulted in a deregulation spiral.

After over 50 years of continuing struggle for capital market integration and liberalization, the EC Treaty has emerged as the strictest, most comprehensive, and most effectively enforceable multinational agreement governing capital movement between its members. Although the EC Member States are party

---

[147] Treaty of Nice.   [148] AFP Bakker, *Capital Movements*, 256.
[149] Ibid.
[150] *Cf*, eg, SS Golub, 'Measures of Restrictions on Inward Foreign Direct Investment for OECD Countries' (Online Working Paper, OECD, Paris 2003), paras 3, 28, and 37. See also the Introduction to this Study.
[151] *Cf*, eg, Ibid; The Economist Intelligence Unit (ed) *World Investment Prospects to 2011*, 12.
[152] See also the Introduction this Study.

to other multinational agreements that touch upon or partly regulate capital movement—in particular, the 1944 Agreement of the International Monetary Fund,[153] the 1961 OECD Code of Liberalisation of Capital Movements,[154] the 1961 OECD Code of Liberalisation of Current Invisible Operations,[155] and the 1994 WTO General Agreement on Trade in Services (GATS)[156]—de facto intra-Community capital movements are exclusively governed by the EC Treaty.[157]

Concerning the movement of capital between the Member States and third countries, in addition to the aforementioned multinational agreements, association agreements concluded by the Community and the Member States on one side and a wide range of third countries on the other must be taken into account.[158] The most prominent example is the 1992 Agreement on the European Economic Area.[159] While the EC Treaty, relative to the already mentioned IMF, OECD, and WTO/GATS Agreements, contains stricter rules on capital movement, and thus later agreements have in principle no factual impact on the Member States with respect to regulation of third country capital movement, the EEA-Agreement in its ambit in turn does not provide for the application of Art 57(1) EC and Art 60 EC exceptions. Equally prohibited in an EEA context are Community measures that 'constitute a step back in Community law as regards the liberalisation of the movement of capital to or from third countries' (*cf* Art 57(2) EC). Hence, owing to the circumstances, certain Member State measures—although in accord with the EC Treaty—could infringe upon the EEA Agreement.[160]

---

[153] 1944 Agreement of the International Monetary Fund (as amended effective 1969, 1978, 1992).
[154] 1961 OECD Code of Liberalisation of Capital Movements (as amended 01.11.2007).
[155] Ibid.   [156] 1994 WTO General Agreement on Trade in Services.
[157] JCW Müller, *Kapitalverkehrsfreiheit*, 311, 313; W Kiemel, Vorbem. zu den Artikeln 56 bis 60 EC (2003), mn 48.
[158] *Cf* European Commission—Directorate General Internal Market and Services, 'Provisions on Capital Movements in Multilateral & Bilateral Agreements of the European Union with Third Countries' (Pdf-file, European Commission, 2005).
[159] EEA Agreement.
[160] JCW Müller, *Kapitalverkehrsfreiheit*, 311 *et seq*; W Kiemel, Vorbem. zu den Artikeln 56 bis 60 EC (2003), mn 49 *et seq*. A similar situation can be found with respect to certain bilateral agreements between Member States and third countries covering specific types of capital movement such as direct investment (so-called bilateral investment treaties). They occasionally provide for fewer exceptions than the EC Treaty. The Commission is currently endeavouring to bring those agreements in line with the EC Treaty provisions on free movement of capital. *Cf* European Commission, 'European Commission, Eight Acceding Countries and US Sign Bilateral Investment Understanding' (Website, Brussels 2003); United States Mission to the European Union, 'U.S., EC Sign Bilateral Investment Understanding for Accession Countries'; United States Mission to the European Union, 'U.S. Welcomes Bilateral Investment Treaty Understanding'; 2003 Understanding concerning certain US Bilateral Investment Treaties; OGEL, 'Free Movement of Capital'; European Commission, 'Internal Market: infringement proceedings against Austria, Finland, France, Italy, Greece, Portugal and Sweden' (IP/05/1288); European Commission, 'Internal Market: infringement cases against the UK, Portugal, Denmark, Austria, Sweden and Finland' (IP/05/352); Case C-205/06 *Commission v Republic of Austria (Re Provisions on the Free Transfer of Investment Related Payments in Bilateral Investment Agreements)*; Case C-249/06

While the EC Treaty provisions are to a certain degree static, the political appreciation of free movement of capital is far more volatile. While today the EC Member States and the institutions of the European Community by and large still perceive free movement of capital as beneficial overall, recently—as already explained in the Introduction to this study[161]—critical voices, in particular with respect to third country capital movement, can increasingly be noticed. In some cases, the partial political rethinking has already resulted in legislative adaptations on the Member State level. At what point the EC Treaty sets limits on proposed restrictive adaptations—or those already undertaken—will be answered by subsequent doctrinal analysis of the current provisions on free movement of capital.

Commission v Kingdom of Sweden (Re Provisions on the Free Transfer of Investment Related Payments in Bilateral Investment Agreements); Case C-118/07 *Commission v Republic of Finland (Re Provisions on the Free Transfer of Investment Related Payments in Bilateral Investment Agreements)*; See also A Radu, 'Interactions'.

[161] See the Introduction to this Study.

II

Foreign Direct Investment and the Material Scope of Application of Article 56(1) EC

1. Introduction

This and the subsequent two chapters will set out the material scope of application of the freedom of capital movement with respect to cross-border direct investment originating from or directed to non-EC countries (foreign direct investment).

To what extent foreign direct investment is covered by the notion of 'movement of capital', the subject of liberalization of Art 56(1) EC, will be the overarching issue of this chapter. Answering this question presupposes a series of answers on sub-issues.

Article 56(1) EC liberalizes the flow of a factor of production.[1] It frees the 'movement of capital'. The EC Treaty, however, is silent as to what precisely is meant by the notion of 'movement of capital'. I will consequently start off my deliberations by defining this concept (section 2).

Although in each case the beneficiaries of the fundamental freedoms are persons, their guarantees are partially tied up in the cross-border movement of objects[2] and partially committed to the movement of persons[3] across borders.

---

[1] In economic terms, the fundamental freedoms protect different aspects of economic activity. They can be differentiated according to whether they liberalize the flow of products or the flow of factors of production, ie, labour, land, and capital. [P-C Müller-Graff, 'Einflußregulierungen', 937; P-C Müller-Graff, Art. 43 EC (2003), mn 5; see also E Dichtl and O Issing (eds), *Vahlens Großes Wirtschaftslexikon*, 1084] Free movement of workers (Art 39 EC) and the freedom of establishment (Art 43 EC) liberalize the 'labour', factor the former with respect to employment, the latter in regard to self-employed occupations. In contrast, free movement of goods (Art 28 EC *et seq*) and the freedom to provide services (Art 49(1) EC) aim, respectively, at the liberalization of tangible and intangible products of gainful occupation. [J Lübke, *Kapitalverkehrs- und Niederlassungsfreiheit*, 158]

[2] *Cf*, eg, free movement of goods.

[3] The fundamental freedoms can not only be categorized by the type of economic activity they liberalize, but also by the legal subject of their protection. In the case of person-related freedoms, they are characterized by the liberalization of a personal economic activity; it is the person who moves across a border. Free movement of workers (Art 39 EC) as well as the freedom

Free movement of capital belongs to the former category. Object-related freedoms liberalize certain economic activities due to their object, not by reason of the characteristics of the persons who take part therein; this is because the object amounts to more than the sheer personal activity. Free movement of capital is hence guaranteed irrespective of whether those who are involved hold the nationality of a Member State or reside within the territory of one of the Member States. It suffices, but at the same time it also constitutes an indispensable precondition for benefiting from the protection of Art 56(1) EC, that capital movement occurs in a cross-border context, ie, that the respective movement extends beyond the borders of a Member State.[4] Consequentially, those criteria that a capital movement must meet in order to qualify as a 'cross-border' capital movement must be set out (section 3).

After having developed a construction in EC law of the notion of 'foreign direct investment' (section 4), I will finally be able to demonstrate to what extent this concept is covered by 'movement of capital', the subject of liberalization of the object-related production factor freedom of free movement of capital.[5]

2. What Constitutes a 'Movement of Capital'?

a. Wording, Context, Genesis, and 'Economic Teaching'

The content and meaning of the term 'movement of capital' in Art 56(1) EC can only be developed out of a holistic view of the EC Treaty, drawing in particular on the system and aims, as well as the flow of the genesis of the chapter on the free movement of capital.[6] In contrast to other basic notions of fundamental freedom, such as establishment,[7] the term 'movements of capital' is not defined by the EC Treaty. The wording was intentionally openly phrased by the Treaty drafters in order to endow the freedom with the necessary flexibility to cover the different facets of economic reality and render the freedom capable of accommodating

---

of establishment (Art 43 EC) can be grouped into this category. They predominantly seek to erase discrimination of Member States' nationals on the basis of nationality, which also forms in this group the 'expressly prohibited distinguishing criterion' within the non-discrimination test. The freedom to provide services (Art 49(1) EC) is difficult to group, constituting a hybrid within this matrix. It extends in its guarantee only to EC nationals who must, as service provider and recipient, be resident in different Member States. On the other hand, however, the freedom also covers the case in which only the service crosses the border, exemplifying the object-related side of the freedom. Thus, the freedom to provide services contains both person as well as object-related elements, whereby traditionally the view through the lens of a person-related freedom predominates. [J Lübke, *Kapitalverkehrs- und Niederlassungsfreiheit*, 161 with further references]

[4] See also ibid, 159.
[5] The fundamental freedoms can be categorized by the type of economic activity they liberalize and also by the legal subject of their protection.
[6] J Bröhmer, Art. 56 EC (2007), mn; C Ohler, Art. 56 EC (2002), mn 15.
[7] *Cf* Art 43(2) EC.

future developments of the capital markets.[8] Only individual aspects of the notion can be deduced from provisions scattered throughout the EC Treaty,[9] of which Art 57(1) EC provides an example: capital movement, inter alia, must comprise so-called 'direct investments'.

Having just learned that the Treaty itself does not contain a general definition of 'movement of capital', the EC legislator and the Court are called upon to specify the content and meaning of the term. The most detailed specifications are found in secondary Community law[10] in the nomenclature annexed to Council Directive 88/361 EEC on the Liberalisation of Capital Movements.[11] While this list does not constitute an exhaustive enumeration of financial operations falling under the Articles on free movements of capital,[12] and thus is not capable of providing a general and conclusive definition, it reveals, by way of example, the scope of the freedom.[13] Despite the repealing of the legal foundation of the Directive[14] with the coming into force of the Treaty of Maastricht, in principle it continues to be in force to the extent that it is reconcilable with the provisions of the present Treaty.[15]

The Court in its case law, which expanded considerably after the major liberalization which took effect in 1990,[16] has refrained from offering the guidance hoped for in order to compile a definition of general scope.[17] Rather, the ECJ, for the purpose of defining the scope of the term 'movements of capital' in more detail, has regularly consulted the nomenclature annexed to the Directive as an

---

[8] G Ress and J Ukrow, Art. 56 EC (2002), mn 13; C Ohler, Art. 56 EC (2002), mn 15; JCW Müller, *Kapitalverkehrsfreiheit*, 84.

[9] *Cf* Arts 3 lit. c EC, 14(2) EC, 57 EC, 43(2) EC, 58(2) EC, and 51(2) EC.

[10] See for the issue of whether and to what extent primary EC law can be interpreted in the light of secondary EC law: F Müller and R Christensen, *Methodik*, 328 *et seq*; J Anweiler, *Auslegungsmethoden*, 195 *et seq*. See with respect to Directive 88/361/EEC: J Lübke, *Kapitalverkehrs- und Niederlassungsfreiheit*, 173.

[11] Directive 88/361/EEC.

[12] *Cf* Introduction to Annex I of ibid. Note Case C-222/97 *Manfred Trummer and Peter Mayer*, para 12; see also C Barnard, *Substantive Law*, 465.

[13] G Ress and J Ukrow, Art. 56 EC (2002), mn 15.

[14] Directive 88/361/EEC. The Directive was based on Arts 69 EC and 70(1) EEC, which were replaced with effect from 01.01.1994. At least regarding movements of capital within the Single European Market, no new legal basis was reintroduced within the ToM.

[15] For an account of the legal status and continuing importance of the Directive refer to S Mohamed, *Free Movement of Capital*, 111 *et seq*; U Haferkamp, *Kapitalverkehrsfreiheit*, 29 *et seq*; see also W Kiemel, Art. 56 EC (2003), mn 3; G Ress and J Ukrow, Art. 56 EC (2002), mn 17; C Ohler, 'Kapitalverkehrsfreiheit', 1801; C Ohler, Art. 56 EC (2002), mn 19 *et seq*; J Glöckner, 'Grundverkehrsbeschränkungen', 605. For a different view: eg, FC de la Torre, 'Case Note Jointed Cases C-163/94, C-165/94 and C-250/94', 1069; A Honrath, *Kapitalverkehr*, 24 *et seq*. On the issue of compatibility of the Directive and Art. 73 b ToM *et seq* see S Mohamed, *Free Movement of Capital*, 114 *et seq*.

[16] The Directive 88/361/EEC entered into force on 01.07.1990; Art 6 of Directive 88/361/EEC.

[17] A Landsmeer, 'Movement of Capital', 58 *et seq*; the Court has, however, made a contribution to the interpretation of the term 'movement of capital' by way of distinguishing the freedom of capital movements from the other freedoms. [*Cf* G Ress and J Ukrow, Art. 56 EC (2002), mn 18; A Fischer, 'Kapitalverkehrsfreiheit', 398]

'ancilla of construction'.[18] With regard to its continuing validity, the Court held explicitly in *Trummer* that the Directive has 'the same indicative value, for the purpose of defining the notion of capital movements, as it did before the entry into force of Art 73 lit. b et seq. [ToM; now Art 56 EC *et seq*].'[19]

Teachings in macro- and microeconomics come within the ambit not only of free movement of capital but of all fundamental freedoms of importance due to the fact that the freedoms aim to protect economic activity in its various forms. However, the existing multitude of definitions of the terms 'capital' and 'capital movement' in macro- and microeconomics certainly adds another challenge for clarification of the EC term 'movement of capital'.[20] This, however, does not mean that an understanding of the economic realities of a certain transaction shall be disregarded or neglected. Without knowing the economic purpose behind it, it might be impossible to 'assign' a transaction to the different ambits of the fundamental freedoms contained in the Treaty.[21] However, besides the terminological problems, the economic purpose pursued by a certain transaction is not necessarily obvious. In this respect, it could also prove helpful to take into consideration the intended legal consequences in private law that form the basis of the transaction at issue in order to attribute a given transaction to a certain fundamental freedom.[22]

In the following section, I shall proceed in two stages. First, I shall set out my understanding of the term 'capital.' Second, building upon that, the meaning that this study will attribute to the phrase 'movement of capital' in Art 56(1) EC will be developed.

b. The Meaning of 'Capital'

(1) 'Capital' in Economic Terms

The process of developing an understanding of the term 'capital' in EC law should, in the first instance, begin by looking at the economic understanding of the term 'capital'.[23] In economic terms—although the precise meaning of the

---

[18] The Court referred to the Directive for the first time in connection with the Maastricht rules on free movements of capital in Joined Cases C-163/94, C-165/94 and C-250/94 *Criminal proceedings against Lucas Emilio Sanz de Lera, Raimundo Díaz Jiménez and Figen Kapanoglu*, para 34.
[19] Case C-222/97 *Manfred Trummer and Peter Mayer*, para 21. Note, however, the recent strong opposition of Advocate General Colomer voiced in Case C-463/00 and C-98/01 (Opinion of AG Colomer) *Commission v Kingdom of Spain and United Kingdom (Re Golden Shares IV and V)*, para 36.
[20] Note for such a characterization: J Lübke, *Kapitalverkehrs- und Niederlassungsfreiheit*, 108.
[21] C Ohler, Art. 56 EC (2002), mn 23.
[22] Ibid.
[23] See with respect to the term 'capital' in economic literature: eg, A Woll, *Volkswirtschaftslehre*, 63; W Henrichsmeyer, et al, *Volkswirtschaftslehre*, 163. See also Samuelson and Nordhaus, who understand 'capital' as meaning 'real capital' and refer to those means that are used to acquire 'real capital' as 'money'. [PA Samuelson and WD Nordhaus, *Economics*, 33; in legal literature: eg,

term has never been conclusively settled and depends very much on the theoretical perspective of the beholder, as mentioned above—one can characterize 'capital' as follows: The term 'capital' in modern economic theory refers, on one hand, to the ('produced'[24]) factors of production, namely real capital, that can be used directly as durable productive inputs for further production, such as machinery, factory workshops, or intermediate goods.[25] On the other hand, it denotes financial capital, consisting of, eg, non-invested or non-consumed savings or bank loans, which may be employed to acquire other factors of production, land, and labour, but can also be converted into real capital.[26] In this sense, financial capital constitutes an indirect or potential input for further production. Moreover, financial capital refers also to the rights of disposal over capital goods that have a monetary value of their own and are freely, ie, independently of the real capital, transferable. The prime example of this would be stocks.

(2) From Economics to Law

While economic systematization facilitates understanding, it goes without saying that the economic usage of the term, which itself is burdened with uncertainties, will not be completely congruent with the legal appreciation of the term 'capital' in EC law.[27]

The first example that should be mentioned in this respect is the legal treatment of the purchase of real property. It is beyond controversy[28] that real property ownership and related rights *in rem*,[29] though not usage rights based on the law of obligations such as rental,[30] constitute capital within the meaning of Art 56(1) EC. In an economic sense, the land itself does not constitute capital, but a factor of production in its own right. However, buildings employed for productive purposes, such as a factory workshop, make up real capital. In the legal sense this distinction is not drawn. Real property, irrespective of its usage, comes within Art 56(1) EC.[31]

J Lübke, *Kapitalverkehrs- und Niederlassungsfreiheit*, 112; C Ohler, Art. 56 EC (2002), mn 21; JCW Müller, *Kapitalverkehrsfreiheit*, 19.

[24] In contrast to the 'primary' factors of production, land, and labour.
[25] *Cf* PA Samuelson and WD Nordhaus, *Economics*, 9, 33, 267; J Altmann, *Volkswirtschaftslehre*, 34.
[26] The conversion of financial capital into real capital is called 'investment'. [A Woll, *Volkswirtschaftslehre*, 303]
[27] J Lübke, *Kapitalverkehrs- und Niederlassungsfreiheit*, 162; for a different view: JCW Müller, *Kapitalverkehrsfreiheit*, 158.
[28] eg, confirmed in Case C-302/97 *Klaus Konle v Republik Österreich*, para 22; Case C-423/98 *Alfredo Albore*, para 14. See also, for further references, C Ohler, Art. 56 EC (2002), mn 126 *et seq*; J Glöckner, 'Grundverkehrsbeschränkungen'.
[29] In regard to the rights *in rem* see C Ohler, Art. 56 EC (2002), mn 42.
[30] *Cf* Ibid, mn 43. Rights based on the law of obligations, such as rental or lease of real property, are in general governed by the freedom applicable to the relevant type of legal act that brings them into existence, alters, or terminates them.
[31] Free movement of capital in this respect functions as a 'catchall element'. The purchase of real property, due to its character as immovable goods, cannot come within the ambit of free movement of goods. [U Haferkamp, *Kapitalverkehrsfreiheit*, 163]

Another contentious case in which economic and legal understandings of the term 'capital' might diverge involves the treatment of capital goods, ie, real capital, within the ambit of free movement of capital.

The great majority of commentators state, often without further explanation, that 'capital' within the meaning of Art 56(1) EC refers to both financial capital and real capital.[32] Others, however, want to restrict the scope of the term 'capital' to financial capital only.[33]

Approaching this issue from a functional perspective, it may be recalled that the spirit and purpose of Art 56(1) EC are in particular to guarantee the optimal allocation of capital.[34] Optimal allocation of capital means that capital is placed where it generates the best returns, ie, where the capital recipient can afford to pay the highest interest because he can use the capital most efficiently in production. The leading thought in defining capital for the purpose of Art 56(1) EC is therefore its usage for productive purposes, an understanding that was in essence also confirmed by the Court in *Luisi and Carbone*.[35]

Both real capital and financial capital can be put to such productive usage. The former can be employed for such purposes directly. The latter can be used indirectly because it either represents real capital (eg, shares) or it can be converted into real capital or one of the factors of production.[36] There is, moreover, no difference between movable and immovable real capital in terms of productive usage. Thus, excluding real capital from the notion of 'capital' in Art 56(1) EC would contradict its guiding idea.

Furthermore, the exclusion of real capital from the scope of Art 56(1) EC would also certainly lead to unsatisfactory results. Consider an investment in kind, taking the form of a movable capital good like machinery, and on the other hand, financial capital introduced into a firm. It would hardly be comprehensible if, although both contributions pursue the same economic purpose of using capital in a productive manner, the former were treated differently from the latter in terms of applicable freedoms.[37]

---

[32] Of this opinion are J Lübke, *Kapitalverkehrs- und Niederlassungsfreiheit*, 177 *et seq*; W Schön, 'Kapitalverkehrsfreiheit', 743 *et seq*, 747, 749; C Ohler, Art. 56 EC (2002), mn 29 *et seq*, 125; concurring, without going into detail: R Freitag, 'Kapitalverkehr', 187; A Glaesner, Art. 56 EC (2000), mn 7; J Bröhmer, Art. 56 EC (2007), mn 8; M Sedlaczek, Art. 56 EC (2003), mn 5; T Schürmann, Art. 56 EC (2006), mn 5; A Harz, *Schutzklauseln*, 21.

[33] S Mohamed, *Free Movement of Capital*, 47 *et seq*; JCW Müller, *Kapitalverkehrsfreiheit*, 156 *et seq*; U Haferkamp, *Kapitalverkehrsfreiheit*, 35 *et seq*.

[34] See Chapter I. 2.

[35] Joined Cases 286/82 and 26/83 *Graziana Luisi and Giuseppe Carbone v Ministero del Tesoro*, para 21. In this connection it should however be added that the capital movements of a personal character mentioned under Point XI of Annex I of Directive 88/361/EEC have only a very indirect link to a productive usage. It is more its potential to eventually be put to such usage. See Chapter II. 2. c. (3).

[36] J Lübke, *Kapitalverkehrs- und Niederlassungsfreiheit*, 177 *et seq*; W Schön, 'Kapitalverkehrsfreiheit', 743 *et seq*, 747, 749; C Ohler, Art. 56 EC (2002), mn 29 *et seq*.

[37] J Lübke, *Kapitalverkehrs- und Niederlassungsfreiheit*, 178, 198 *et seq*; C Ohler, Art. 56 EC (2002), mn 32; W Schön, 'Kapitalverkehrsfreiheit', 749; Case C-242/03 (Opinion of AG Kokott)

However, at this point it should be noted that not every transaction that qualifies as 'capital' within the meaning of Art 56(1) EC also constitutes 'movement of capital'. With respect to movable capital goods, a careful analysis will be necessary in order to clearly delineate goods that are subject to free movement of goods and those that must be considered in the light of free movement of capital.[38]

For the moment, though, I can conclude that in principle, both financial capital and real capital, the latter either movable or immovable, would qualify as capital under the meaning of Art 56(1) EC.

c. The Meaning of 'Movement of Capital'

Article 56(1) EC does not protect 'capital' *per se* like a fundamental right contained in a national constitution or in Art 1 of Protocol No 1[39] of the Convention for the Protection of Human Rights and Fundamental Freedoms.[40] It is the movement, *der Verkehr, les mouvements* thereof, between the Member States or a Member State and a third country, that must be kept free of restrictions. The focus on movement, however, does not mean that only those transactions come into the range of Art 56(1) EC which lead to a change in the national balance of payments.[41] Although reflections through the lens of shifts in the balance of

---

Ministre des Finances v Jean-Claude Weidert and Élisabeth Paulus, 21 *et seq*; Case C-319/02 (Opinion of AG Kokott) *Petri Manninen*, para 32 *et seq*.

An investment in kind would not fall within the ambit of free movement of goods (Art 28 EC) due to the fact that it does not constitute a commercial transaction. [*Cf* C Ohler, Art. 56 EC (2002), mn 32; for a different view: J Lübke, *Kapitalverkehrs- und Niederlassungsfreiheit*, 178, 184] It should be noted, however, that the transaction of introducing investment in kind into a firm would not necessarily be without any protection by the fundamental freedoms. Even if one is of the opinion that investment in kind neither constitutes capital nor qualifies as movement of goods, then the acquisition of shares in the firm in return for the contribution qualifies as acquisition of capital. If the investment, moreover, grants the possibility of exercise of control over the acquired participation in the company [*cf*, eg, Case C-251/98 *C. Baars v Inspecteur der Belastingen Particulieren/Ondernemingen Gorinchem*, para 20; see also J Lübke, *Kapitalverkehrs- und Niederlassungsfreiheit*, 211], it also constitutes establishment within the meaning of Art 43 EC.

[38] See Chapter II. 2. c. (3).

[39] 1952 Protocol No 1 to the Convention for the Protection of Human Rights and Fundamental Freedoms.

[40] 1950 Convention for the Protection of Human Rights and Fundamental Freedoms.

[41] Speaking in economic terms, if capital is transferred then it is either real capital or financial capital that moves. The transfer of real capital is not considered to be different from the transfer of consumer goods; the former just serves a different purpose. These transactions are thus both recorded in the current account of the balance of payments of a national economy [K Rose and K Sauernheimer, *Außenwirtschaft*, 4 *et seq*] and are—from a balance of payments perspective—considered trade of goods. In economic terms, therefore, 'capital transfer'—recorded in the capital account of the balance of payments of an economy—refers to the transfer of financial capital only. [J Lübke, *Kapitalverkehrs- und Niederlassungsfreiheit*, 112]

An international capital transfer occurs if the capital is transferred across national borders. A capital export is the acquisition of foreign claims or reduction of foreign debts by domestic subjects and, *mutatis mutandis*, one speaks of capital import if foreign subjects acquire domestic claims or reduce domestic debts. [K Rose and K Sauernheimer, *Außenwirtschaft*, 9]

payments are not unknown to the Treaty (*cf* Art 59 EC) and might help to regiment a given transaction into the system of fundamental freedoms, such a focus would be both too narrow and too wide. It would be too narrow because the right contained in Art 56(1) EC also extends, for example, to instances in advance of the actual transaction, such as registrations, permissions, or authorizations undertaken in order to effectively employ the capital later on. It would be too wide due to the fact that instances such as depreciations in the values of goods or changes in the balancing rules can lead to changes in the balance of payments that do not constitute movements of capital within the meaning of Art 56(1) EC.[42]

I should begin my examination with the prevailing view to be found in the literature,[43] drawing heavily on Council Directive 88/361 EEC,[44] which defines 'movements of capital' as comprising all unilateral 'financial operations [between two Member States or one Member State and a third country] essentially concerned with the investment of the funds in question rather than remuneration for service',[45] goods and the provision of capital.

Having such a definition must not cloud the fact that it is nothing more than a weak crutch when establishing the meaning of 'movement of capital'. While it certainly conveys the characteristics of 'typical capital movement', in the individual case, the definition requires modification in order to give sufficient consideration to the great diversity of possible financial transactions that—although not fully matching the definition—are subject to the provisions on free movement of capital. The individual criteria mentioned in the definition set out above are hence more indicative than clearly delineating or limiting in character. Formulating a 'general definition', one must admit, has remained[46] an illusion.

(1) Unilateral Transaction

The criterion of a unilateral financial transaction is mistakable in the sense that typically a capital movement is a synallagmatic transaction in which a certain asset, such as bonds, partner's interest shares, or land, is given in return for money

---

[42] C Ohler, Art. 56 EC (2002), 47.
[43] eg, U Everling, Art. 67 EEC (1960), mn 2; HP Ipsen, *Europäisches Gemeinschaftsrecht*, § 36 remark 3 (at 649); R Eckhoff, 'Kapital- und Zahlungsverkehr', mn 1702; G Ress and J Ukrow, *Kapitalverkehrsfreiheit und Steuergerechtigkeit*, 23 *et seq*; A Pajunk, *Mobiliarkreditsicherheiten*, 35; F Roy, *Niederlassungsrecht und Kapitalverkehrsfreiheit*, 27 *et seq*; MA Dauses, *Wirtschafts- und Währungsunion*, 76 *et seq*; M Sedlaczek, Art. 56 EC (2003), mn 5; W Kiemel, Art. 56 EC (2003), mn 1; K-D Borchardt, *Grundlagen*, para 1034 *et seq*; for a more cautious view: G Ress and J Ukrow, Art. 56 EC (2002), mn 32.
[44] Directive 88/361/EEC.
[45] Joined Cases 286/82 and 26/83 *Graziana Luisi and Giuseppe Carbone v Ministero del Tesoro*, para 21.
[46] Already during the negotiations of the EEA Treaty the idea of formulating a definition of general value was quickly dropped. [A Harz, *Schutzklauseln*, 15 *et seq*; G Ress and J Ukrow, Art. 56 EC (2002), mn 13] See for an account of the drafting process of the present provisions on capital movement: AFP Bakker, *Capital Movements*, 218 *et seq*.

or other assets (*quid pro quo*).⁴⁷ The criterion of being 'unilateral' relates to the idea that remuneration in cases of capital movement is typically not rendered instantly—in contrast to the movement of goods or the provision of services—but is stretched over a longer period of time.⁴⁸

The criterion gains significance insofar as it helps to articulate the fact that remunerations in return for goods and services, but also, in principle,⁴⁹ for capital, are subject to the provisions on free movement of payments.⁵⁰ Movement of capital and movement of payments are mutually exclusive.⁵¹ A financial transaction that presents itself from an economic perspective as 'induced' instead of 'autonomous',⁵² ie, it does not itself have the character of an economic activity but constitutes a consideration for it, forms remuneration and is therefore exclusively subject to the ancillary freedom⁵³ of free movement of payments.

While this test is certainly useful in abstract terms when it comes to the classification of a certain transaction as movement of capital or movement of payments in an individual case, a straightforward answer often proves to be difficult,

---

⁴⁷ The use of the term 'unilateral' does not meet with criticism in the event of a genuine unilateral transaction [U Haferkamp, *Kapitalverkehrsfreiheit*, 36; C Ohler, Art. 56 EC (2002), mn 25], eg, the increase of the equity capital in one's own firm [*cf* J Lübke, *Kapitalverkehrs- und Niederlassungsfreiheit*, 180], a donation, or an inheritance [for the latter, see Case C-361/01 *The Heirs of H. Barbier v Inspecteur van de Belastingdienst Particulieren/Ondernemingen buitenland te Heerlen*, para 58]. Note also JCW Müller, *Kapitalverkehrsfreiheit*, 157, who holds the view that the criterion of a 'unilateral' transaction is 'inappropriate' and, therefore, redundant. Of the same view are: M Seidel, 'Kapitalmarkt', 578; C Ohler, 'Kapitalverkehrsfreiheit', 1805; A Honrath, *Kapitalverkehr*, 50.
⁴⁸ B Börner, 'Zahlungsverkehr', 22; W Schön, 'Kapitalverkehrsfreiheit', 747; U Everling, Art. 67 EEC (1960), mn 2.
⁴⁹ Some commentators [*cf* W Kiemel, Art. 56 EC (2003), mn 6; J Glöckner, 'Grundverkehrsbeschränkungen', 606] are of the opinion that all financial transactions in some way related to the free movement of capital fall within the ambit of the aforementioned. Thus, the freedom of capital movements would not have its own freedom of transfer of payments within the meaning of Art 56 (2) EC. This view must be rejected. In *Luisi and Carbone* the Court held explicitly that '... movements of capital may themselves give rise to current payments ...'. [Joined Cases 286/82 and 26/83 *Graziana Luisi and Giuseppe Carbone v Ministero del Tesoro*, para 21] See also C Ohler, 'Kapitalverkehrsfreiheit', 1802; C Ohler, 'Zweitwohnungserwerb', 252; A Rohde, *Kapitalverkehr*, 106 *et seq*; W Schön, 'Kapitalverkehrsfreiheit', 749.
⁵⁰ C Ohler, Art. 56 EC (2002), mn 25; S Lütke, *CFC-Legislation*, 76; see also JCW Müller, *Kapitalverkehrsfreiheit*, 157; M Seidel, 'Kapitalmarkt', 578; for a very strict view: J Lübke, *Kapitalverkehrs- und Niederlassungsfreiheit*, 180 *et seq*; for the relevant case law refer to Joined Cases 286/82 and 26/83 *Graziana Luisi and Giuseppe Carbone v Ministero del Tesoro*; Joined Cases C-358/93 and C-416/93 *Criminal proceedings against Aldo Bordessa and Vicente Marí Mellado and Concepción Barbero Maestre*; Joined Cases C-163/94, C-165/94, and C-250/94 *Criminal proceedings against Lucas Emilio Sanz de Lera, Raimundo Díaz Jiménez and Figen Kapanoglu*.
⁵¹ See for a delineation of the two freedoms, eg, A Rohde, *Kapitalverkehr*, 106 *et seq*; U Haferkamp, *Kapitalverkehrsfreiheit*, 38 *et seq*; for a summary of the discussion of the nature of free movement of payments ('fifth freedom' vs 'annex freedom'), note A Rohde, *Kapitalverkehr*, 104.
⁵² B Börner, 'Zahlungsverkehr', 22; J Lübke, *Kapitalverkehrs- und Niederlassungsfreiheit*, 182.
⁵³ eg, R Streinz, *Europarecht*, mn 895; P Steinberg, 'Konvergenz', 14; T Kingreen, *Struktur der Grundfreiheiten*, 20; T Oppermann, *Europarecht*, § 23, mn 12; J Lübke, *Kapitalverkehrs- und Niederlassungsfreiheit*, 181 *et seq*.

What Constitutes a 'Movement of Capital'? 51

as in the case of dividend payments.[54] The Court, in case of uncertainties with respect to the use of the objects of transactions as payments, tends to apply Art 56(1) EC,[55] which delineated both freedoms negatively: everything that does not undoubtedly qualify as payment constitutes capital movement.[56]

The necessity of delineating both freedoms has lost some of its significance since the time when capital movements were fully liberalized.[57] Some differences, however, continue to exist. Certain restrictions and safeguard measures with respect to third countries[58] can only be adopted in the ambit of free movement of capital.[59] An example in relation to a situation in which the demarcation of the two freedoms is still of significance is again the qualification of dividend payments. Depending on whether they are perceived as capital (direct investment)

---

[54] The Court, in *Verkooijen*, stated: 'Although the Treaty does not define the term capital movements, Annex I to Directive 88/361 contains a non-exhaustive list of the operations which constitute capital movements within the meaning of Article 1 of the Directive. Although receipt of dividends is not expressly mentioned in the nomenclature annexed to Directive 88/361 as capital movements, *it necessarily presupposes participation in new or existing undertakings* referred to in Heading I (2) of the nomenclature. Moreover, since in the main proceedings, the company distributing dividends has its seat in a Member State other than the Kingdom of the Netherlands and is quoted on the stock exchange, receipt of dividends on shares in that company by a Netherlands national *may also be linked to acquisition by residents of foreign securities dealt on a stock exchange* as referred to in Heading III. A (2) of the nomenclature annexed to Directive 88/361, as Mr Verkooijen, the United Kingdom Government and the Commission contend. *Such an operation is thus indissociable from a capital movement.*' [Emphases added; Case C-35/98 *Staatssecretaris van Financiën v B.G.M. Verkooijen*, para 27 *et seq*, confirmed, eg, in Case C-446/04 *Test Claimants in the FII Group Litigation v Commissioners of Inland Revenue*, para 183. See also N Dautzenberg, 'Verkooijen', 723] Thus, the Court applies a global view to the initial transaction and considers the transfer of shares and the entitlement to participate in expected profits of the public company (dividends) as a unit. The shares, including the holding out of the prospect of future dividend payments, appear as an initial transfer (performance) for which a certain amount of money was paid (counter performance). Others qualify dividends as being payments (as consideration in an economic sense) for the entrepreneurial risk inherent in participation in an undertaking. [*Cf*, eg, A Glaesner, Art. 56 EC (2000), mn 9; U Haferkamp, *Kapitalverkehrsfreiheit*, 44 *et seq*; J Lübke, *Kapitalverkehrs- und Niederlassungsfreiheit*, 2006]

[55] *Cf* Joined Cases C-358/93 and C-416/93 *Criminal proceedings against Aldo Bordessa and Vicente Marí Mellado and Concepción Barbero Maestre*, which concerned the physical transfer of means of payments. Initially, the Court asked whether the physical transfer of means of payment for a certain transaction was usual and necessary in order to effect it: Case 203/80 *Criminal proceedings against Guerrino Casati*. This jurisprudence, dating back to a time in which free movement of capital and free movement of payments significantly diverged, can be considered outdated. [*Cf*, eg, A Rohde, *Kapitalverkehr*, 111; W Kiemel, Art. 56 EC (2003), mn 6; U Haferkamp, *Kapitalverkehrsfreiheit*, 49]

[56] *Cf* Joined Cases C-163/94, C-165/94, and C-250/94 *Criminal proceedings against Lucas Emilio Sanz de Lera, Raimundo Díaz Jiménez and Figen Kapanoglu*, para 17. See also A Rohde, *Kapitalverkehr*, 113; J Lübke, *Kapitalverkehrs- und Niederlassungsfreiheit*, 182 *et seq*, and also H-K Ress, 'Anmerkung zu Verb. Rs. C-358/93 and C-416/93', 1010.

[57] A Fischer, 'Kapitalverkehrsfreiheit', 399.

[58] With respect to safeguard measures, this study proceeds from the assumption that Art 59 EC allows for restrictive measures in the ambit of both free movement of capital and the freedom of payments. See Chapter VII. 4. b.

[59] eg, W Kiemel, Art. 56 EC (2003), mn 6; S Lütke, *CFC-Legislation*, 73.

(2) Financial Transfer

Financial operations between two Member States or one Member State and a non-Member State do not only comprise the initial transfer of capital from one economy to another, but also, for example, the alteration of the contract on which the initial transfer was based; however, a transfer of capital in economic terms might not be involved.[61] This relates to what was previously said: an understanding of movement of capital as mere changes in the national balances of payments would be too narrowly defined.

Annex I of the EC Capital Movements Directive[62] confirms this reading when stating that

[t]he capital movements listed in [the] Nomenclature are taken to cover:
- all the operations *necessary* for the purpose of capital movements: conclusion and performance of the transaction and related transfers.[63]

Thus, in the run-up to the actual financial operation, preparatory activities, such as effective access to information or expert advice in the respective Member State, the conduct of due diligence necessary to arrange for the financial transaction, the submission of an offer to conclude the necessary contracts on which the financial transaction will be based,[64] the obtaining of required official permissions, concessions or authorizations,[65] access to all legal forms of organization, or even advertising campaigns[66] to influence public sentiment, must be covered by the scope of application in order to render the freedom effectively.

Due to the fact that free movement of capital does not only seek to exact the opening-up of the Member States' markets but also to ensure their continuing openness, the factors discussed above must also be true for follow-up activities subsequent to the 'actual' financial transaction, such as the completion of any registration procedure and the subsequent unimpaired operation of the investment

---

[60] The Court, for example, perceives dividends as capital movements (direct investment). [Case C-446/04 *Test Claimants in the FII Group Litigation v Commissioners of Inland Revenue*, para 183.] See Chapter VII. 2.

[61] C Ohler, Art. 56 EC (2002), mn 27. No transfer takes place with the mere change of the place of residence: *cf* Case C-513/03 (Opinion of AG Léger) *Heirs of M. E. A. van Hilten-van der Heijden v Inspecteur van de Belastingdienst/Particulieren/Ondernemingen buitenland te Heerlen*, paras 45, 57; Case C-513/03 *Heirs of M. E. A. van Hilten-van der Heijden v Inspecteur van de Belastingdienst/Particulieren/Ondernemingen buitenland te Heerlen,* para 49 *et seq.*

[62] Directive 88/361/EEC.

[63] [Emphasis added] *Cf* D Trüten, *Mobilität*, 28; GC Schwarz, *Europäisches Gesellschaftsrecht*, mn 112.

[64] *Cf,* though decided within the ambit of the freedom to provide services: Case C-384/93 *Alpine Investments BV v Minister van Financiën*, para 19.

[65] C Ohler, Art. 56 EC (2002), mn 47.

[66] *Cf* P-C Müller-Graff, Art. 28 EC (2003), mn 117 *et seq* for the corresponding issue in the ambit of free movement of goods.

on the host Member State market.⁶⁷ In cases of a direct investment, unimpaired operation in particular comprises effective participation in the management or control of the investment, which was expressly confirmed—with reference to the Explanatory Notes to Annex I of the EC Capital Movement Directive⁶⁸—by the Court in its *'Golden Shares'* judgments.⁶⁹

Having spoken of follow-up activities, I should clarify that the mere having and holding of the investment in the aftermath of the transfer is comprised by the guarantee of Art 56(1) EC.⁷⁰

(3) Investment Character

The definition provided above states that the financial operation must essentially be concerned with *'investment'*, ie, it must possess 'investment character'.⁷¹ This 'investment character' is conceptualized in the Treaty by Art 57 EC, which speaks of 'direct investment', and 58 (1) lit. a EC, which refers to 'the place where their capital is invested'. Additionally, the Court—often in the process of delineating free movement of capital and payments—alluded to the movement of capital as 'financial operations essentially concerned with the investment of... funds'.⁷²

---

⁶⁷ By virtue of Art 56(1) EC, the third country investor cannot bring the goods, workers, and services he needs for effective employment of his capital from his home country. He is not entitled to 'home country' treatment but effective employment of capital, ie, the third country investor is entitled to the same treatment as a national investor or an investor from another Member State on the host market. This, however, does not open up the Common Market to third countries with respect to anything other than capital. *Cf* W Frenz, *Europarecht*, mn 1959, 1962, 1963.

⁶⁸ Directive 88/361/EEC.

⁶⁹ Case C-483/99 *Commission v French Republic (Re Golden Shares II)*, para 37 *et seq*; Case C-503/99 *Commission v Kingdom of Belgium (Re Golden Shares III)*, para 38 *et seq*; Case C-463/00 *Commission v Kingdom of Spain (Re Golden Shares IV)*, para 53 *et seq*; Case C-98/01 *Commission v United Kingdom (Re Golden Shares V)*, para 40 *et seq*; Joined Cases C-282/04 and C-283/04 *Commission v Kingdom of the Netherlands (Re Golden Shares VI)*, para 24 *et seq*; Ohler holds the view—albeit without any compelling argument—that all national measures referring to the entrepreneur as a person (as well as those measures that are aimed at his employees) are subject to the freedom of establishment only. [C Ohler, Art. 56 EC (2002), mn 119; probably also U Everling, Art. 67 EEC (1960), mn 4]

⁷⁰ eg, U Haferkamp, *Kapitalverkehrsfreiheit*, 36.

⁷¹ Note JCW Müller, *Kapitalverkehrsfreiheit*, 157 *et seq*; T von Hippel, 'Fremdnützige Vermögenstransfers', 9 *et seq*; J Lübke, *Kapitalverkehrs- und Niederlassungsfreiheit*, 182 *et seq*, who state that this attribute is redundant, at least in case of financial capital.

⁷² Joined Cases 286/82 and 26/83 *Graziana Luisi and Giuseppe Carbone v Ministero del Tesoro*, para 21.

See by way of example ECJ judgments in which the Court mentioned the 'investment nature': Case C-512/03 *J.E.J. Blanckaert v Inspecteur van de Belastingdienst/Particulieren/Ondernemingen buitenland te Heerlen*, para 34 *et seq*, where the ECJ stated that '... it is important to note that Mr. Blanckaert, who is resident in Belgium, has invested in property in the Netherlands. In accordance with Articles 2.3 and 5.2 of the IB Law, that investment provides him with notional income which is taxed in the Netherlands as income from savings and investments. It is settled case-law that capital movements within the meaning of Article 56 EC include investments in property on the territory of a Member State by non-residents'; citing, inter alia, Case C-222/97 *Manfred Trummer and Peter Mayer*, para 21 *et seq*; Joined Cases C-515/99 and C-527/99 to C-540/99 and Joined Cases C-519/99 to C-524/99 and C-526/99 *Hans Reisch and Others v Bürgermeister der Landeshauptstadt Salzburg und Grundverkehrsbeauftragter des Landes Salzburg and Anton Lassacher*

What is meant by 'investment character' is that the transfer will present itself, from the perspective of an objective, reasonable, and understanding person, as the acquisition of cross-border claims to income in the hope of getting a return from it in the future.[73]

However, in the same way as for the other criteria of the definition of capital movement, the attribute of 'investment character' also performs in most cases only a typifying function in the way that it paraphrases the gist of Art 56(1) EC.[74] As mentioned above, the Court employed it to highlight the difference between free movement of payments (remuneration) and capital (investment) in regard to financial capital.[75] In this respect, however, the criterion hardly goes beyond this highlighting function, as it essentially restates that a transaction that appears 'autonomous'—ie, it constitutes the economic activity itself instead of

---

and Others v Grundverkehrsbeauftragter des Landes Salzburg and Grundverkehrslandeskommission des Landes Salzburg, para 30. Also: Case C-376/03 *D v Inspecteur van de Belastingdienst/ Particulieren/Ondernemingen buitenland te Heerlen*, para 24; Case C-222/97 *Manfred Trummer and Peter Mayer*, para 22 *et seq*. In Case C-174/04 *Commission v Italian Republic (Re Automatic Suspension of Voting Rights in Privatised Undertaking)*, para 28 the Court explains: 'Points I and III of the nomenclature annexed to Directive 88/361 and the explanatory notes which it contains indicate that direct investment in the form of shareholding in an undertaking and the acquisition of securities on the capital market constitute capital movements within the meaning of Article 56 EC. By virtue of those explanatory notes, direct investment, in particular, is characterised by the possibility of participating effectively in the management and control of a company.' Also: Case C-367/98 *Commission v Portuguese Republic (Re Golden Shares I)*, para 38; Case C-478/98 *Commission v Kingdom of Belgium (Re Loans issued abroad)*, 18; Case C-54/99 *Association Eglise de Scientologie de Paris and Scientology International Reserves Trust v The Prime Minister*, para 14. In Case C-319/02 *Petri Manninen*, para 22 *et seq* the ECJ has recourse to the investment character of movement of capital as follows: '[T]he Finnish tax legislation has the effect of deterring fully taxable persons in Finland from investing their capital in companies established in another Member State. Such a provision also has a restrictive effect as regards companies established in other Member States, in that it constitutes an obstacle to their raising capital in Finland. Since revenue from capital of non-Finnish origin receives less favourable tax treatment than dividends distributed by companies established in Finland, the shares of companies established in other Member States are less attractive to investors residing in Finland than shares in companies which have their seat in that Member State.' Citing Case C-35/98 *Staatssecretaris van Financiën v B.G.M. Verkooijen*, para 35; Case C-334/02 *Commission v French Republic (Re Tax on Income Arising from Investment)*, para 24. See also Case C-242/03 *Ministre des Finances v Jean-Claude Weidert and Élisabeth Paulus*, para 13 *et seq*; Case C-315/02 *Anneliese Lenz v Finanzlandesdirektion für Tirol*, para 32 *et seq*.

[73] Ohler defines the notion of 'investment character' as the intention to realize profits with a certain transaction. This, however, appears to be too broad due to the fact that—and this he expressly acknowledges—it applies to any transaction within the ambit of the fundamental freedoms. [*Cf* C Ohler, Art 56 EC (2002), mn 28] Note, furthermore, that the given definition clearly deviates from the macroeconomic meaning of investment, which refers merely to the output used by private firms to produce future output. [*Cf* PR Krugman and M Obstfeld, *Economics*, 283]

[74] eg, U Haferkamp, *Kapitalverkehrsfreiheit*, 37; AC Digel, 'Europäischer Finanzmarkt', Inaugural-Dissertation, Eberhard-Karls-Universität, 108 *et seq*.

[75] *Cf* Joined Cases 286/82 and 26/83 *Graziana Luisi and Giuseppe Carbone v Ministero del Tesoro*, para 21.

a consideration for it—comes within the ambit of capital movement, whilst an induced transaction is subject to the provisions on payments.[76]

Also, with respect to transfers with a personal character, such as inheritances[77] and legacies, gifts and endowments, dowries, etc, the criterion of 'investment character' fades into the background.[78] Although such transfers do not present themselves as investments,[79] the spirit and purpose of Art 56(1) EC nevertheless speaks in favour of their inclusion within the scope of application: As mentioned previously, free movement of capital seeks to guarantee the optimal factor allocation. Indeed, an inheritance, for example, neither constitutes an economic activity nor does it directly optimize capital allocation.[80] Its protection is nonetheless essential. The guarantee that capital can be kept and freely disposed of, eg, bequeathed and inherited, generates the necessary incentive to save income and use it for productive purposes at a later point in time instead of consuming it right away.[81] In this sense, protecting a legacy inherently carries the idea of preserving it for potential productive purposes at a later point in time.[82]

In exceptional cases, the criterion of 'investment character' can, however, gain a certain degree of constitutive function. Above, while discussing the term 'capital', I stated that it comprises both financial and real capital. With respect to the latter, I argued that it does not make a difference whether real capital comes in the form of an immovable or a movable capital good. However, the inclusion of movable capital goods, like machinery, in this notion leads to the necessity of delineating free movement of goods and the freedom of capital movement, the two being mutually exclusive.[83]

The question of whether a given transaction falls within the scope of Art 56(1) EC must be answered with a view to its character. Consequently, free movement of capital applies if the transfer exhibits an investment character. The provisions on free movement of goods are to be consulted if the transfer constitutes a trading transaction.

---

[76] *Cf* Joined Cases C-163/94, C-165/94, and C-250/94 *Criminal proceedings against Lucas Emilio Sanz de Lera, Raimundo Díaz Jiménez and Figen Kapanoglu*, para 17. See also A Rohde, *Kapitalverkehr*, 121 and above Chapter II. 2. c. (1).
[77] For inheritance see Case C-361/01 *The Heirs of H. Barbier v Inspecteur van de Belastingdienst Particulieren/Ondernemingen buitenland te Heerlen*, para 58; Case C-513/03 *Heirs of M. E. A. van Hilten-van der Heijden v Inspecteur de Belastingdienst/Particulieren/Ondernemingen buitenland te Heerlen*.
[78] To the best of my knowledge, nobody denies that capital movements of a personal character fall within the ambit of free movement of capital.
[79] *Cf*, eg, A Honrath, *Kapitalverkehr*, 40; C Ohler, Art. 56 EC (2002), mn 28; T von Hippel, 'Fremdnützige Vermögenstransfers', 8; for a different view: J Kaass, *Erbschaftsteuer*, 66 *et seq*.
[80] J Lübke, *Kapitalverkehrs- und Niederlassungsfreiheit*, 183; probably of a different view: D Müller-Etienne, *Europarechtswidrigkeit des Erbschaftsteuerrechts*, 134.
[81] J Lübke, *Kapitalverkehrs- und Niederlassungsfreiheit*, 183.
[82] Inheritance as a subcategory of personal movements of capital is also mentioned in the Annex to the EC Capital Movements Directive. [Directive 88/361/EEC]
[83] eg, W Frenz, *Europarecht*, mn 717; J Lübke, *Kapitalverkehrs- und Niederlassungsfreiheit*, 184.

The suggestion to consider a cross-border investment in kind, taking the form of a movable capital good, in the light of Art 56(1) EC will probably lead to very little opposition.[84] The categorization of the purchase of movable capital goods abroad, however, seems to be more challenging.

The purchase of movable capital goods abroad and subsequent transfer to the place of productive employment by an entrepreneur for the purpose of pursuing its own entrepreneurial aims constitutes movement of goods.[85] In support of this view, one can argue that by virtue of the transaction, no cross-border claim to income is acquired. The purchase merely increases the productive potential of the acquirer itself at its own location but lacks a cross-border claim to income due to the fact that the purchase itself is not synonymous with productive employment. The subsequent import and productive employment at the place of the acquirer of the capital good does not give rise to a cross-border claim to income. Thus, the purchase is deficient in 'investment character'.[86] In this respect, it is important to stress that the meaning of 'investment character' within the meaning of Art 56(1) EC deviates from the understanding of 'investment' in macroeconomics, where it describes '[t]he part of the output used by private firms to produce future output'.[87] Hence, in a macroeconomic reading, the purchase would qualify as investment; it does not, however, with respect to Art 56(1) EC.

In contrast, the purchase of movable capital goods in the context of a cross-border takeover must be considered in the light of movement of capital. Ohler argues that in this context the capital goods serve productive purposes, and are thus within the range of Art 56(1) EC.[88] Although the result he reached seems to be correct, the argument voiced in its support appears to be vulnerable. In both cases—and also in the case in which the good is imported—the capital good is or will clearly be employed for productive purposes. In order to defend his outcome, one could take a 'global view' arguing that the acquirer is not interested economically in the single capital good but in the sum of all goods: the undertaking, which is the true (economic) object of acquisition. Instead of acquiring the shares of the undertaking (share deal)—a transfer clearly subject to Art 56(1) EC—the investor can also choose to purchase the assets of an undertaking (asset deal). There is no apparent reason, though, why share and asset deals should be treated differently. Moreover, a 'micro perspective' also seems to speak in favour of applying free movement of capital in the situation at hand. By acquiring the capital good for the purpose of pursuing entrepreneurial aims, the purchaser at the same time acquires a claim to income that extends across the border. If the

---

[84] The contribution leads to the acquisition of claims to income in the hope of getting a return from it in the future. [*Cf* J Lübke, *Kapitalverkehrs- und Niederlassungsfreiheit*, 184]

[85] Of the same opinion: C Ohler, Art. 56 EC (2002), mn 31; J Lübke, *Kapitalverkehrs- und Niederlassungsfreiheit*, 184.

[86] Arguing in the same direction: J Lübke, *Kapitalverkehrs- und Niederlassungsfreiheit*, 184.

[87] PR Krugman and M Obstfeld, *Economics*, 283.

[88] C Ohler, Art. 56 EC (2002), mn 31, 125.

capital good were to be imported, as in the first example, this cross-border link would be missing.

d. Summary so Far

Summarizing the above, this study concludes that the notion of *'capital'* employed in Art 56(1) EC comprises both financial and real capital as understood in economics. However, not all of what qualifies as capital also amounts to a 'movement of capital'. Especially with respect to movable capital goods (real capital), at the crossroads of free movement of capital and goods, a careful analysis is indicated.

'Movements of capital' as referred to in Art 56(1) EC encompasses all unilateral financial operations between two Member States or one Member State and a third country essentially concerned with the investment of the funds in question rather than remuneration for services, goods, and the provision of capital.

This definition, widely used in legal literature for the notion of 'movement of capital' but in fact nothing more then a weak crutch, provides us with an understanding of its typical kinds or forms of appearance. However, it does not constitute a conclusive and exhaustive general explanation of the term. While the definition lacks exclusionary and delineating effects, it nevertheless forms a useful basis from which the evaluation of a transaction in the individual case can start.

The EC Capital Movements Directive—still of indicative value—reveals the scope of the freedom by way of example. The Court, using this directive as an 'ancilla of construction', has so far refrained from providing a general definition. It regularly limits itself to a general statement that a certain transaction constitutes 'movement of capital', which leaves us with a fragmented picture of the Court's understanding of the notion.[89]

A given transaction must therefore be judged against the background of all available factual and legal circumstances on an individual basis. In particular, the economic purpose pursued by the transaction, the intended legal consequence in private law, the Treaty aims and system as well as the function of the fundamental freedoms will guide the evaluation. In order to achieve the aim of an optimized capital allocation to the greatest extent possible, and hence, to endow the freedom with the greatest effectiveness (*'effet utile'*), a broad understanding of the term 'movement of capital' is indicated.[90] Thus, the notion of 'movement of capital' comprises not only the 'actual transfer', but also activities in the run-up to it, as well as follow-up activities.

---

[89] See for an enumeration of types of capital movement that are confirmed by the Court as constituting movement of capital: P von Wilmowsky, 'Kapital- und Zahlungsverkehr', mn 2; J Bröhmer, Art. 56 EC (2007), mn 39 *et seq.*
[90] *Cf* T Oppermann, *Europarecht*, § 23, mn 13; S Lütke, *CFC-Legislation*, 75 *et seq.*

Regarding the relationship of free movement of capital and payments, both freedoms being mutually exclusive, in case of doubt as to whether a certain transaction constitutes remuneration for goods, etc, or indeed capital, free movement of capital applies.

3. Capital Movements Beyond National Boundaries

Free movement of capital, like all fundamental freedoms, protects 'movement of capital' only insofar as it occurs in a so-called 'cross-border context,' ie, that the movement in question extends beyond the national borders of a Member State. Article 56(1) EC speaks in this respect from the prohibition of restrictions on 'the movement of capital between Member States and between Member States and third countries'. In this section I shall set out those criteria that a capital movement must meet in order to qualify as a 'cross-border' capital movement. As capital does not always have a physical location, I must first answer the question of how to localize capital in order to be able to spot later on its movement across a national border.

a. Localizing Capital

Localizing capital in order to be in a position to determine from where and to where it has moved is not always an easy task, as it sometimes lacks a physical location. The original provision on the free movement of capital in the old EEC Treaty linked its guarantee to residence within the Community.

By selecting residence, the problem of 'localizing' intangible capital was overcome; intangible capital, by virtue of a legal fiction, was placed where its holder resided. In order to benefit from the freedom as a holder of intangible capital, one had to reside within the Community.[91]

In the course of the substantial changes[92] brought about by the Treaty of Maastricht, the residence criterion was dropped and free movement of capital *per se* was liberalized. However, this shift has not relieved the burden of localizing capital. Article 56(1) EC liberalizes only cross-border economic activities. Economic activities within a Member State have remained outside the scope of

---

[91] J Lübke, *Kapitalverkehrs- und Niederlassungsfreiheit*, 160.
[92] The drop of the 'residence requirement' in the Treaty of Maastricht is sometimes described as a shift in paradigm, which it actually was not. Right from the beginning, free movement of capital carried inherently the characteristics of an object-related production factor freedom. [W Kiemel, Art. 67 EEC (1991), mn 11] Already in its initial version (Art 67(1) EEC) it did not presuppose nationality, as would have been characteristic for a person-related freedom. Thus, alleged economic activity in a Member State rather than legal affiliation to a Member State by nationality, which could reasonably be assumed if one was resident within a Member State, was chosen as the centre of reference.

the Treaty.⁹³ Although free movement of capital has been liberalized *erga omnes*, third country capital movement is still subject to additional restrictions, in particular on the basis of Art 57 EC. Thus, it is still necessary to draw a distinction between internal, intra-Community, and third country capital movements.

The location of capital depends on its type. Real property, drawing from the principles of private international law, is located where it is situated. The same applies to movable capital goods,⁹⁴ which are located at the storage location.⁹⁵ Difficulties are caused by intangible capital. A (tangible) good has just one defined physical location, from which it may be moved to another defined physical location. Locating intangible capital requires having recourse to the holder of that capital.⁹⁶ Only by taking the old and new holder into consideration can one make a transaction of intangible rights visible. This necessary recourse also makes explicit that the free movements of capital and goods do not run fully in parallel.⁹⁷ Thus, assessing whether the free movement of capital applies with respect to its *ratione materiae* is only 'on the first level' object-related, but requires with respect to intangible capital, so to speak, 'on the second level' recourse to the person who holds the capital.

Having said that intangible capital is to be localized where its holder is, I must now localize the holder: he is placed where his habitual residence is to be found.⁹⁸ With regard to the content and meaning of (habitual) residence for the purpose of Art 56(1) EC—no definition is provided by the EC Treaty—one can find a source of inspiration in private international law.⁹⁹ Hence, the residence of natural persons is where they ordinarily stay.¹⁰⁰ One can assume that this is also the place where their centre of gravity with respect to their economic activity is located. With respect to the residence of legal persons, it is suggested that it be determined along the lines of Art 43(1), 2nd sentence EC.¹⁰¹ A legal person is resident in a certain State if the person shows an effective and continuous link to the economy of that State.¹⁰²

---

⁹³ C Ohler, Art. 56 EC (2002), mn 207 for further references.
⁹⁴ *Cf* B von Hoffmann, *Internationales Privatrecht*, § 5, mn 95.
⁹⁵ The origin of a good refers to the place of its physical location, where it is situated before the actual movement, but not to the place where it was produced or extracted. This makes sense since free movement of goods aims to secure the free flow of goods across national borders. See S Plötscher, *Diskriminierung*, 169 *et seq*.
⁹⁶ J Lübke, *Kapitalverkehrs- und Niederlassungsfreiheit*, 161.
⁹⁷ Kiemel seems to argue in favour of 'strict parallelism' in the sense that the holder of the capital is without any importance for the purposes of Art 56(1) EC: W Kiemel, Art. 56 EC (2003), mn 24 *et seq*.
⁹⁸ J Lübke, *Kapitalverkehrs- und Niederlassungsfreiheit*, 160.
⁹⁹ Of the same opinion: C Ohler, Art. 56 EC (2002), mn 219.
¹⁰⁰ B von Hoffmann, *Internationales Privatrecht*, § 5, mn 72 *et seq*; C Ohler, Art. 56 EC (2002), mn. 219; see also C Bond, Art. 67 EEC (1999), § 67.06.
¹⁰¹ C Ohler, Art. 56 EC (2002), mn 219.
¹⁰² Ibid. See also A Randelzhofer and U Forsthoff, Art. 43 EC (2001), mn 53 *et seq*; European Commission, 'Allgemeines Programm zur Aufhebung der Beschränkungen der Niederlassungsfreiheit', Section I, 4. Indent.

b. Cross-Border Element

The fundamental freedoms aim to protect an economic activity only if it occurs in a cross-border context, ie, the movement extends beyond the borders of a Member State.[103] Article 56(1) EC speaks in this respect from the prohibition of restriction on 'the movement of capital between Member States and between Member States and third countries'.[104]

This cross-border link or element, as it may also be termed, is to be understood in the broadest sense. Even a remote linkage to another national economy suffices, as the Court made clear in *Commission v Belgium*. It stated that:

> although the contested measure imposed by the Kingdom of Belgium is addressed to its own residents, it cannot in any event be regarded as a purely internal measure, since the loan in question was issued in German marks on the Eurobond market, was subscribed by an international syndicate of banks and financial institutions, is listed on the Frankfurt stock exchange, and is governed by German law.[105]

Consequently, a given transaction[106] lacks a cross-border element only in cases where it extends in no way beyond the borders of a Member State.[107] A view that seeks to go even further, suggesting that the cross-border element within the ambit of free movement of capital is superfluous,[108] must be met with scepticism. The concept of the Internal Market, at least if one perceives the Court's[109]

---

[103] *Cf*, eg, P Oliver, 'Free Movement of Capital', 413; HD Jarass, 'Dogmatik I', 204; HD Jarass, 'Dogmatik II', 706; JCW Müller, *Kapitalverkehrsfreiheit*, 161, 164; G Ress and J Ukrow, Art. 56 EC (2002), mn 51; C Ohler, Art. 56 EC (2002), mn 205; C Ohler, 'Zweitwohnungserwerb', 252; A Schnitger, 'Geltung', 712; U Haferkamp, *Kapitalverkehrsfreiheit*, 50 *et seq*; W Frenz, *Europarecht*, mn 372 *et seq*; J Lübke, *Kapitalverkehrs- und Niederlassungsfreiheit*, 185 *et seq*; J Bröhmer, Art. 56 EC (2007), mn 38 The non-application of the freedoms to internal transfers leads to the issue of reverse discrimination. [*Cf* A Epiney, *Umgekehrte Diskriminierungen*]

[104] [Emphasis added].

[105] Case C-478/98 *Commission v Kingdom of Belgium (Re Loans issued abroad)*, para 16.

[106] The subsequent considerations focus on the cross-border element with respect to direct investment. For other types of capital movement different considerations may apply.

[107] C Ohler, Art. 56 EC (2002), mn 205.

[108] A Honrath, *Kapitalverkehr*, 42 with reference to reinvested earnings; also AC Digel, 'Europäischer Finanzmarkt', Inaugural-Dissertation, Eberhard-Karls-Universität, 110, 127 *et seq*. See also the Opinion of Advocate General Geelhoed, who argues that after completion of Economic and Monetary Union any national regulation has cross-border effects. [Joined Cases C-515/99 and C-527/99 to C-540/99 and Joined Cases C-519/99 to C-524/99 and C-526/99 (Opinion of AG Geelhoed) *Hans Reisch and Others v Bürgermeister der Landeshauptstadt Salzburg and Grundverkehrsbeauftragter des Landes Salzburg and Anton Lassacher and Others v Grundverkehrsbeauftragter des Landes Salzburg and Grundverkehrslandeskommission des Landes Salzburg*, para 107]

[109] *Cf*, eg, Case C-260/89 *Elliniki Radiophonia Tileorassi AE and Panellinia Omospondia Syllogon Prossopikou v Dimotiki Etairia Pliroforissis and Sotirios Kouvelas and Nicolaos Avdellas and others*; Case C-299/95 *Friedrich Kremzow v Republic of Austria*; Case C-368/95 *Vereinigte Familiapress Zeitungsverlags- und vertriebs GmbH v Heinrich Bauer Verlag*; Case C-281/98 *Roman Angonese v Cassa di Risparmio di Bolzano SpA*; Case C-322/01 *Deutscher Apothekerverband eV v 0800 DocMorris NV and Jacques Waterval*; Case C-60/00 *Mary Carpenter v Secretary of State for the Home Department*. See for a discussion of the Court's approach: eg, MP Maduro, *We the*

'deontological remodelling'[110] of the fundamental freedoms as critical, is based on the idea that the fundamental freedoms perform only the basic function of removing discriminations and hindrances as a result of border crossing with a view to securing a level playing field. For the harmonization of the national legal orders within the Internal Market, the Treaty provides for Community competences, particularly in Art 95 EC. The fundamental freedoms predominantly do not intend to harmonize the Member States' national economic orders, but rather must preserve neutrality towards them. The Member States continue to be competent to regulate their purely internal affairs.[111] Therefore, purely internal capital movements remain outside the material scope[112] of Art 56(1) EC.[113]

Free movement of capital as an object-related freedom, like free movement of goods,[114] does not link to the nationality or residence of the persons who take part in a given capital transfer; rather, it is the 'location of capital' that one must examine.[115] A cross-border element is therefore the first thing to be searched for in the actual capital transfer. The import or export of money or rights of disposal over capital probably constitutes the case in which the cross-border element becomes most visible. The purchase of shares in a company situated in State A by a resident of Member State B from a resident of State A clearly exemplifies a cross-border transaction. The intangible capital is, as explained above, located at the place where its holder resides. Thus, in the case at hand, the intangible rights (shares) are 'transferred across the border from State A to Member State B'.[116]

Court; M Nettesheim, *Grundfreiheiten und Grundrechte*; T Kingreen, 'Fundamental Freedoms'; U Haltern, 'Constitutionalism'; all with further references.

[110] The term 'deontological remodelling' means that the function of the fundamental freedoms is not restricted to market integration but is extended to deregulation of the general internal economic and social order of the Member States without the latter having a protectionist or market access restricting effect. The fundamental freedoms would be given an additional human rights component, which is naturally based on deontological considerations. *Cf* M Nettesheim, *Grundfreiheiten und Grundrechte*, 21 *et seq*.

[111] In detail W Frenz, *Europarecht*, mn 22 *et seq.* with further references. See also J Lübke, *Kapitalverkehrs- und Niederlassungsfreiheit*, 185 *et seq*. For an opposite view see, eg, V Heydt, 'Funktionswandel', 105; for a balancing view: M Nettesheim, *Grundfreiheiten und Grundrechte*.

[112] For a discussion of the doctrinal issue of whether the prerequisite of a 'cross-border element' relates to the level of the material scope of protection or to the level of interference with this scope of protection, refer to W Frenz, *Europarecht*, mn 373 *et seq*; T Kingreen, *Struktur der Grundfreiheiten*, 84 *et seq*.

[113] C Ohler, Art. 56 EC (2002), mn 205; U Haferkamp, *Kapitalverkehrsfreiheit*, 52; J Lübke, *Kapitalverkehrs- und Niederlassungsfreiheit*, 186.

[114] J Lübke, *Kapitalverkehrs- und Niederlassungsfreiheit*, 160 *et seq*; A Rohde, *Kapitalverkehr*, 133 *et seq*; see also M Hintersteininger, *Diskriminierungsverbot*, 75.

[115] For example, it does not suffice for the establishment of a cross-border element that a national of Member State B, resident in Member State A, purchases real property in his Member State of residency. The cross-border element within the ambit of free movement of capital as an object-related freedom is not established by reference to nationality. *Cf* J Lübke, *Kapitalverkehrs- und Niederlassungsfreiheit*, 188.

[116] With respect to the transfer of movable capital goods—as long as they qualify as capital movement within the meaning of Art 56(1) EC—the cross-border element in such a transfer can be established in a similar way as within the ambit of free movement of goods.

Also, the mere transfer of residence from one State to another would—by consequence of the approach taken in this study—display a cross-border element.[117]

However, free movement of capital is not limited to actual import or export of money and rights of disposal over capital. Recalling the spirit and purpose of Art 56(1) EC, ie, the unrestricted optimal allocation of capital,[118] a cross-border capital movement also takes place if it qualifies in economic terms as an investment in another country. This is the case when the return on investment is determined by the conditions present in this other country. For example, this relates to the transfer of shares in a company situated in State A by residents who are both situated in Member State B. While the location of the capital does not change in this example, the old and new holders being residents of Member State B and, thus, the actual transfer occurring within that Member State, the capital movement nevertheless contains—for the reasons mentioned above—a cross-border element. The profit of the investment is determined by the efficiency of the capital employment abroad.[119]

In this context, one could critically ask whether one can still speak of a cross-border transfer with respect to the example above if the company mentioned invested the capital it collected in its own branch or in a third company in the State of residence of both parties to the transaction.[120] The capital would ultimately be employed in a productive manner in the same place in which both the transferor and transferee reside. This example shows that the suggested economic perspective in evaluating whether a certain transaction occurs across a border is not truly economic, but is qualified by a formalistic component. It does

---

[117] Concurring: N Dautzenberg, 'Wegzugsbesteuerung', 181; N Dautzenberg, '2. Anmerkung zu BFH, Beschluß v. 17.12.1997', 306 *et seq*; N Dautzenberg, 'Erbschaftssteuer', 87, 89 *et seq*; B Matzka, *Freiheit des Kapitalverkehrs*, 120 *et seq*; G Sass, 'EuGH und Deutsches Steuerrecht', 7; H Schaumburg, *Internationales Steuerrecht*, 284 *et seq*; J Lübke, *Kapitalverkehrs- und Niederlassungsfreiheit*, 187; probably also D Hohenwarter and P Plansky, 'Anmerkung Schlussanträge Rs. van Hilten', 420 *et seq*. Disagreeing: Case C-513/03 (Opinion of AG Léger) *Heirs of M. E. A. van Hilten-van der Heijden v Inspecteur van de Belastingdienst/Particulieren/Ondernemingen buitenland te Heerlen*, para 57 *et seq*; Case C-513/03 *Heirs of M. E. A. van Hilten-van der Heijden v Inspecteur van de Belastingdienst/Particulieren/Ondernemingen buitenland te Heerlen*, para 49 *et seq*; H Hahn, 'Von Spartanern und Athenern', 18; H Hahn, *Vereinbarkeit*, 71 *et seq*; G Kofler, 'Hughes de Lasteyrie Du Saillant', 264; A Schnitger, 'Kapitalverkehrsfreiheit', 497; probably also E Reimer, 'Ertragssteuerrecht', 98.

[118] For a different argumentative approach based on the demarcation of jurisdictional ambits *cf* U Haferkamp, *Kapitalverkehrsfreiheit*, 50 *et seq*; convincingly criticizing and rebutting this argumentation: J Lübke, *Kapitalverkehrs- und Niederlassungsfreiheit*, 187 *et seq*.

[119] J Lübke, *Kapitalverkehrs- und Niederlassungsfreiheit*, 188; Art 56(1) EC equally includes those profits generated abroad that are reinvested there. [*Cf* Annex I, Heading I. 4. of Directive 88/361/EEC; see also C Ohler, Art. 56 EC (2002), mn 205] Although the capital does not cross the border, the holder of the claim resides abroad. The profit of the reinvestment is determined by the efficiency of the capital employment at the place of reinvestment, which constitutes a sufficient cross-border link.

[120] Lübke asks the question slightly differently, but ultimately she touches upon the same issue: what if only the statutory seat is placed abroad but the economic activity takes place within the State of residence of the transferor and transferee? [J Lübke, *Kapitalverkehrs- und Niederlassungsfreiheit*, 187]

not look at the transfer as an economic whole; it splits it into its component parts, each of which usually constitutes a single legal transaction. Such an approach appears reasonable. While it is true that in economic terms, it is the ultimate location of productive employment that largely determines the effectiveness of the capital usage, establishing this location is hardly feasible. Moreover, again drawing from the *telos* of Art 56(1) EC, free movement of capital must also protect the economic activity of mere 'channelling' of capital through different (Member) States.[121]

If a certain transaction extends across a national border, both parties to this transaction can rely on Art 56(1) EC. In this respect, it is without significance that the transaction appears for one participant in the transaction as only (Member) State-internal because the freedom protects on an equal footing both investment (acquisition) and de-investment (liquidation). By way of example, the purchase of real property by someone present in the same (Member) State in which the property is situated from somebody else residing in another (Member) State appears to the purchaser as an investment in his own State of residence. However, to the seller it is the liquidation of a cross-border investment.[122] Thus, the transaction as a whole possesses a cross-border element.

Consequently, a cross-border element is present in a given capital movement if either the capital is actually crossing the border or, seen from an economic perspective, if a capital movement appears as a cross-border investment.

4. The Notions of 'Direct Investment' and 'Foreign Direct Investment' within the Ambit of Free Movement of Capital

This section will set out the content and meaning of the notion of 'foreign direct investment', the 'object of investigation' of this study. In approaching the topic, the economic roots of the notion are first briefly examined. Second, the legal understating of the notion of 'direct investment' as applicable in the chapter on free movement of capital will be elaborated, a notion which is rather new to the EC Treaty.[123] It was introduced via Art 73c ToM [now, after further amendment, Art 57 EC] in the course of the adoption of the Treaty of Maastricht; before that,

---

[121] A Haratsch, et al, *Europarecht*, mn 904.
[122] J Lübke, *Kapitalverkehrs- und Niederlassungsfreiheit*, 189.
[123] The notion (and term) 'investment' in general has emerged relatively recently in the language of international agreements and international legal practice. 'Customary international law and earlier international agreements did not generally utilize this notion. They relied instead on the notion of "foreign property".' UNCTAD, *Key Issues*, 116; for an account of the evolution of the term 'investment' refer to M Sornarajah, *Int'l Law on Foreign Investment*, 9 *et seq*.

it could be found in secondary law, in Annex I to the EC Capital Movements Directive.

In a third step, the relevant criteria to distinguish 'direct investment' from 'foreign direct investment' will be identified. This categorization is crucial, as only the latter is subject to the additional restrictions on free movement provided for especially in Art 57(1) EC.

As already mentioned in the introduction to this study, all attempts to spot this precise phrase in the text of the Treaty will be in vain. When the Treaty is referring to 'foreign direct investment', it speaks of 'movement of capital to or from third countries involving direct investment'.[124] Thus, in terms of terminology, 'foreign' in this study, except where otherwise stated, refers to transactions that occur between a Member State and a non-Member State, ie, a third country. By attributing such meaning to 'foreign,' I deviate from the common understanding, which denotes somebody or something situated outside the national economy or nation State, respectively.

a. Economic Impregnation

Approaching 'direct investment' in conceptual terms, one should visualize that—in the same way as the term 'capital'—it has its origin in economic teaching. This also has implications for the legal construction in the way that it befalls an economic impregnation.[125]

Speaking in economic terms, a direct investment occurs when an investor acquires managing control over economic activities, for example, by way of acquisition of a controlling stake in a public company. The distinctive feature is that the investor is placed in a position to pursue entrepreneurial aims. In contrast, if the investor does not acquire control over decision-making at the microeconomic level, one speaks of portfolio investment,[126] which constitutes the antonym to direct investment.

If those investments involve more than one national economy, one speaks of foreign[127] direct investment and foreign portfolio investment, respectively. Applying this to the definitions provided above translates this into the following:

[f]oreign direct investment (FDI) occurs when citizens of one nation (the 'home' nation) acquire managing control over economic activities in some other nation (the

---

[124] *Cf* Art 57 EC.
[125] Refer to J Lübke, *Kapitalverkehrs- und Niederlassungsfreiheit*, 102 *et seq* for further references.
[126] M Kuczynski, 'Foreign Investment', 167.
[127] The term 'foreign' is here used as 'commonly' understood, which denotes an investment outside one's own national economy.

'host' nation).'[128] Consequently, foreign portfolio investment (FPI) is described as 'the purchase by one country's...citizens...of non-controlling positions in foreign equity, debt and cash securities issued by other countries' private citizens, corporations, banks and governments'.[129]

Previously, I have explained that the distinctive feature of direct investment is that the investor acquires managing control over economic activities. This is to be determined objectively, ie, the mere possibility of control over economic activities suffices. The opposite view, which requires, in addition to the factual possibility, the investor's actual intention to exercise control, is hardly feasible. The intention of the investor at the moment of transaction is very difficult to ascertain. Therefore, the subjective approach must also take into account objective criteria, which then constitute evidence of the investor's intention.[130]

Having found that it is better to establish control objectively, one must next ask by what criteria the possibility of exercising control will be determined. The possibility of influencing economic activities usually comes with the acquisition of a holding in an undertaking by way of provision of equity capital. However, the provision of credit capital, taking the form of loans or the reinvestment of earnings,[131] among companies affiliated by shareholding or even among companies not affiliated by any equity holding at all can also lead to the possibility of entrepreneurial influence. In the latter case, ie, the provision of credit capital to an undertaking not affiliated with any equity holding, the possibility of exercising entrepreneurial influence will usually flow from a profit participating loan or other special arrangements such as subcontracting, management contracts, turnkey arrangements, or franchising. Also, the integration of two undertakings by way of transfer of technical or commercial know-know, immaterial goods, and/or intellectual property can be of importance for the exercise of managing control.[132]

---

[128] EM Graham, 'FDI', 147 *et seq*; see also M Borchert, *Außenwirtschaftslehre*, 389; *Gabler Wirtschaftslexikon*, 746 *et seq*; Redaktion der 'Zeitschrift für das gesamte Kreditwesen' and JE Cramer (eds), *Lexikon des Geld-, Bank- und Börsenwesens*, 393; PR Krugman and M Obstfeld, *Economics*, 169 *et seq*.

[129] M Adler and P Jorion, 'Foreign Portfolio Investment', 172; See also M Borchert, *Außenwirtschaftslehre*, 389; *Gabler Wirtschaftslexikon*, 2437 *et seq*; Redaktion der 'Zeitschrift für das gesamte Kreditwesen' and JE Cramer (eds), *Lexikon des Geld-, Bank- und Börsenwesens*, 1445.

[130] Refer to J Lübke, *Kapitalverkehrs- und Niederlassungsfreiheit*, 103 *et seq* for further references. In this connection it is worth mentioning that the preference for the objective view is also generally shared by international organizations when defining direct investment for their purposes. [*Cf*, eg, OECD, *OECD Benchmark Definition of Foreign Direct Investment*, 7 *et seq*; International Monetary Fund, *Balance of Payments Manual*, §§ 359, 362]

[131] Reinvestment of earnings of direct investments refers to income retained within the enterprise from after-tax profits that is attributable to direct investors.

[132] *Cf* UNCTAD, *World Investment Report 2003*, 232.

The criteria identified by way of example above, when present in the person of the investor, do not in any case place him automatically in the actual position to exercise control over an undertaking. The question of when an investment will turn from a portfolio into a direct investment cannot be answered in abstract terms, but must be assessed in the individual case, taking into account in particular the conditions under company law in which the undertaking is embedded.[133] Arbitrarily setting certain thresholds, such as the one found in the OECD Benchmark Definition of Foreign Direct Investment requiring a holding of '10 percent or more of the ordinary shares or voting power'[134] in the investment, might suffice for statistical purposes, eg, for the compilation of a balance of payments, which requires clear cut and easily revisable criteria. However, they do not necessarily justify the conclusion that in the individual case the investor is in the actual position to exercise control over the entrepreneurial activities of the investment.

b. The Notion of 'Direct Investment' within the Ambit of Free Movement of Capital

(1) EC Capital Movements Directive and the Breadth of the Notion of 'Direct Investment'—Application 'in its Widest Sense'?

Article 56(1) EC declares all movements of capital free of restrictions. Although not mentioned expressly, it can hardly be doubted that 'direct investment' comes into the range of the material scope of application of the aforementioned provision, forming a (sub-)category of 'capital movement'.[135] This can already be drawn from Art 57(1) EC, which provides for exceptions to the freedom for, inter alia, national measures concerned with direct investment with respect to third countries. Such a provision would make no sense if the (sub-)category of direct investment was not covered by Art 56(1) EC. Furthermore, the EC Capital Movements Directive,[136] which still carries indicative value[137] for the interpretation of the notion of 'capital movement,' mentions 'direct investment' in its Annex I under Heading I.

---

[133] J Lübke, *Kapitalverkehrs- und Niederlassungsfreiheit*, 104 *et seq*.

[134] OECD, *OECD Benchmark Definition of Foreign Direct Investment*, 7 *et seq*.

[135] *Cf* C Ohler, Art. 56 EC (2002), para 120; similarly the Court, eg Case C-54/99 *Association Eglise de Scientologie de Paris and Scientology International Reserves Trust v The Prime Minister*, para 14; Case C-367/98 *Commission v Portuguese Republic (Re Golden Shares I)*, para 38; Case C-483/99 *Commission v French Republic (Re Golden Shares II)*, para 37; Case C-503/99 *Commission v Kingdom of Belgium (Re Golden Shares III)*, para 38; Case C-463/00 *Commission v Kingdom of Spain (Re Golden Shares IV)*, para 53; recently Case C-157/05 *Winfried Holböck v Finanzamt Salzburg-Land*, para 33 *et seq*.

[136] Directive 88/361/EEC.

[137] See Chapter II. 22a. Note in this respect, inter alia, also the following judgments of the Court: Case C-367/98 *Commission v Portuguese Republic (Re Golden Shares I)*, para 38; Case C-483/99 *Commission v French Republic (Re Golden Shares II)*, para 37; Case C-503/99 *Commission v Kingdom of Belgium (Re Golden Shares III)*, para 38; Case C-463/00 *Commission v Kingdom of Spain (Re Golden Shares IV)*, para 53.

The Notions of 'Direct Investment' and 'Foreign Direct Investment' 67

While the notion of 'direct investment' is not defined in the Treaty, interpretive guidance[138] is offered by the Directive just mentioned,[139] which describes 'direct investment' as comprising:

1. Establishment and extension of branches or new undertakings belonging solely to the person providing the capital, and the acquisition in full of existing undertakings.
2. Participation in new or existing undertakings with a view to establishing or maintaining lasting economic links.
3. Long-term loans with a view to establishing or maintaining lasting economic links.
4. Reinvestment of profits with a view to maintaining lasting economic links.[140]

The Exemplary Note at the end of Annex I, as well as the introductory sentences to the Nomenclature of the Directive, make it explicit that the categories mentioned under Heading I are merely to be understood as referring to common varieties of 'direct investment'. In more abstract terms, the notion of 'direct investment' must therefore be understood as covering:

[i]nvestments of all kinds by natural persons or commercial, industrial or financial undertakings, and which serve to establish or to maintain lasting and direct links between the person providing the capital and the entrepreneur to whom or the undertaking to which the capital is made available in order to carry on an economic activity.[141]

The Exemplary Notes proceed further, stating that the 'concept must...be understood in its widest sense'. This call for an application of the notion of 'direct investment' 'in its widest sense',[142] often reproduced in the literature *sans* further comment,[143] is not without problems, and hence deserves critical attention

---

[138] Concerning the methodology of construction, in a different context, with respect to Art 57 EC, it has been stated that the notions mentioned therein are all to be interpreted autonomously from the perspective of EC law [G Ress and J Ukrow, Art. 56 EC (2002), mn 6; for a different view: A Rohde, *Kapitalverkehr*, 190, who pleads with respect to the definitions employed by the Member States for mere control of the absence of arbitrariness by the ECJ]; consequently also the notion of 'direct investment.' The Court made clear in this respect that '[t]he exception provided for in Article 73c (1) of the Treaty [now, after amendment, Art. 57 (1)]...is precisely worded, with the result that no latitude is granted to the Member States or the Community legislature regarding...the categories of capital movements which may be subject to restrictions.' [Emphasis added. Joined Cases C-163/94, C-165/94, and C-250/94 *Criminal proceedings against Lucas Emilio Sanz de Lera, Raimundo Díaz Jiménez and Figen Kapanoglu*, para 44] The same is true for the notion of direct investment in the ambit of Art 56(1) EC.
[139] See also, eg, the approach of the Court in Case C-446/04 *Test Claimants in the FII Group Litigation v Commissioners of Inland Revenue*, para 178 *et seq* within the context of Art 57(1) EC.
[140] Annex I, Heading I of Directive 88/361/EEC The definition—with a slight difference—is modelled on the definition contained in Annex A, List A, Heading I-III of the 1961 OECD Code of Liberalisation of Capital Movements (as amended 01.11.2007).
[141] Annex I, Explanatory Notes of Directive 88/361/EEC.
[142] Annex I, Explanatory Notes, ibid.
[143] *Cf*, eg, U Haferkamp, *Kapitalverkehrsfreiheit*, 171; C Bond is pleasantly critical, Art. 68 EEC (1999), § 68.02 [1], pointing towards the issue but refraining from suggesting a solution. Taking note of the conflict: A Rohde, *Kapitalverkehr*, 190; arguing in favour of a strict reading of Art 57 EC, though not mentioning the conflict: G Ress and J Ukrow, Art. 57 EC (2002), mn 6; W Kiemel, Art. 57 EC (2003), mn 4. Completely uncritical, however, is PR Vergano, Art. 57 EC

here. This study suggests that the phrase *'in its widest sense'*—at least after the Maastricht Treaty amendments—must be understood in the way that the varieties of direct investment mentioned explicitly under Heading I do not represent a conclusive enumeration. However, any call for a wide understanding of the notion of 'direct investment' in the EC Capital Movements Directive should not be utilized to lower the required threshold necessary to identify the 'lasting and direct links between the person providing the capital and the entrepreneur to whom or the undertaking to which the capital is made available in order to carry on an economic activity'. Quite to the contrary, the link must be interpreted strictly; essentially in parallel terms to the 'definite influence test' required in Art 43 EC for the finding of an 'establishment'.[144]

To begin with, the definitions in the EC Capital Movements Directive,[145] which implemented Art 67 EEC, were adopted with a view to liberalizing capital movements within the Community, *cf* Art 1(1) 1st sentence of the Directive. The Nomenclature in Annex I was used to specify and illustrate the diversity of the different transactions in order 'to facilitate application of this Directive'.[146] However, no categories of capital movements were singled out from the list contained in Annex I in order to restrict the scope of liberalization in respect to them.[147]

The current provisions on free movement of capital have created a completely different situation, with the consequence that a wide interpretation (in the sense of a low threshold) of the notion of 'direct investment' would lead to a very different result from the one initially intended at the time of adoption of the EC Capital Movements Directive.

(2005), § 137.03 [1]; AC Digel, 'Europäischer Finanzmarkt', Inaugural-Dissertation, Eberhard-Karls-Universität, 154 *et seq*. Expressly arguing in favour of a broad interpretation of the notion of 'direct investment' with the consequence of a maximum of restriction on the freedom by virtue of Art 57(1) EC: A Honrath, *Kapitalverkehr*, 137 *et seq*.

[144] See Chapter III. 2. for a detailed discussion of whether the required 'link' present between the investor and the investment within the notion of 'direct investment' ('effective participation test') requires the same threshold as the 'definite influence test' for the finding of an 'establishment' within the meaning of Art 43 EC.

[145] Directive 88/361/EEC.

[146] *Cf* S Mohamed, *Free Movement of Capital*, 83.

[147] Although Art 7(1) of the Directive states that:

'In their treatment of transfers with respect to movements of capital to or from third countries, the Member States shall endeavour to attain the same degree of liberalisation as that which applies to operations with residents of other Member States, subject to the other provisions of this Directive.

The provisions of the preceding subparagraph [of the Directive] shall not prejudice the application to third countries of domestic rules or Community law, particularly any reciprocal conditions, concerning operations involving *establishment, the provisions of financial services and the admission of securities to capital markets* [emphasis added].' The categories have no constitutive effect, ie, their content and meaning is not of importance for the determination of the breadth of the exception from the (legal) duty to liberalize due to the fact that generally all domestic rules or Community laws restricting third country capital movement are exempted. With respect to third countries, the 'duty' is only a political one.

Within the ambit of Art 56(1) EC, the grouping of a transaction into one or the other category of capital movement in accordance with the Nomenclature has no impact on the applicability of the freedom, which safeguards the free flow of capital movements at large. By way of example, it is without significance for Art 56(1) EC where the 'demarcation line' between direct and portfolio investment actually runs. If the degree of control that an investor can possibly exercise over an investment is below a certain threshold—in whichever way this threshold is defined—then the investment is protected not as 'direct investment' but as 'portfolio investment'. Both categories are covered on an equal footing by the scope of application of Art 56(1) EC.

The categorization of capital movement, however, becomes of sudden relevance when turning to Art 57(1) EC. It represents an exception to the duty to liberalize all capital movements *erga omnes* for certain categories of capital movement, inter alia, for direct investments. It is apparent that the thrust of Art 57(1) EC is diametrically opposed to that of Art 56(1) EC.

If one were now to take the Explanatory Notes of the Directive seriously, in a non-reflective manner, then one could also think of interpreting the notion of 'direct investment' in the context of Art 57(1) EC broadly (in the sense of a low threshold). In consequence, this would mean giving a wide understanding to Art 57(1) EC. At this point, if not earlier, one should pause for a minute to consider, in essence, what one would do if one were to follow the path just depicted and turn a definition drafted with a view to liberalizing to the greatest possible extent into the very opposite. One would, in fact, be restricting the freedom to the greatest possible extent. It is, however, clear that such a construction is at odds with the basic axiom of construction to interpret exceptions strictly. If one considers, moreover, that the Nomenclature of the Directive is of an indicative and non-binding nature and should, therefore, not be capable of overriding fundamental rules of construction, the interpretation portrayed appears even more doubtful.

In order to avoid the consequence just depicted, this study suggests interpreting the notion of 'direct investment' in the context of free movement of capital with respect to the 'lasting and direct link' in a strict sense. Such an interpretation does not have the effect of reducing the protective scope of Art 56(1) EC due to the fact that the 'demarcation line' is simply 'internally' shifted between direct and portfolio investment, which has no impact on the overall material scope of the freedom. On the other hand, a strict reading of the notion of 'direct investment' ensures that the exception to the freedom contained in Art 57 (1) EC is construed narrowly, which gives the freedom a broad scope of application as the Treaty aims suggest. A narrow reading of the notion of 'direct investment', of course, also leads to a narrow understanding of the competence of adopting Community measures with respect to the movement of capital to or from third countries involving direct investment, etc, found in Art 57(2) EC. This effect appears to be acceptable, as this study perceives Art 57(2) EC primarily as a means to remove existing restrictions on third country capital movement by virtue of Art 57(1) EC.

In sum, with Art 57(1) EC in view, the notion of 'direct investment' must be interpreted in a strict sense, in particular with respect to the 'lasting and direct link', within the whole ambit of free movement of capital.[148]

(2) The 'Lasting and Direct Links'

Having established that the notion of 'direct investment' must be interpreted strictly, in particular with respect to the link present between the investor and the investment, I shall now consider the configuration of this link.

It is stated[149] that participation in a new or existing undertaking and the grant of a long-term loan as well as the reinvestment of profits must be undertaken with a view to establishing or maintaining a lasting economic link. The Explanatory Notes add—in the context of their general definition of 'direct investment'— that the investment must serve to establish or to maintain lasting and also '*direct links*'.[150] With respect to the varieties of direct investment mentioned under Heading I of the Nomenclature, the Explanatory Notes specify the meaning of the link at any one time.

As regards shareholding within the meaning of Heading I.2 of the Nomenclature, the Exemplary Note states that the objective of establishing or maintaining a lasting (and direct) economic link presupposes that:

> the block of shares held by a natural person of another undertaking[151] or any other holder enables the shareholder, either pursuant to the provisions of national laws relating to companies limited by shares or otherwise, *to participate effectively in the management of the company or in its control*.[152]

I stated above, when speaking in economic terms, that the distinctive feature of direct investment is that the investor must be placed in a position to pursue his entrepreneurial aims. The definition just cited seems to indicate two ways in which this can be done: either by participation in the management or by control of the investment. However, the two terms are not to be understood antithetically, but the former as merely a somewhat 'more active' variety of the latter: the investor who participates in the management of the undertaking is actively taking part in the day-to-day exercise of executive, administrative, and supervisory direction. Control is the broader, more general term denoting the exercise of restraining or directing influence over the undertaking, which can take many forms. The question of whether an investor acquires the necessary

---

[148] For the opposite view: A Honrath, *Kapitalverkehr*, 137 *et seq*.
[149] *Cf* Annex I, Heading I of Directive 88/361/EEC.
[150] [Emphasis added] Ibid.
[151] [Footnote added] 'The undertakings mentioned under I-1 of the Nomenclature include legally independent undertakings (wholly-owned subsidiaries) and branches.'
[152] [Emphasis added] Annex I, Explanatory Notes Directive 88/361/EEC.

control over economic activities—as already conceptually explained[153]—is to be determined objectively. The Exemplary Notes take up this approach by stating that the shareholder must be 'enabled' to participate in the control of the undertaking.

Turning to the 'necessary quantum' for saying that an investor effectively participates in the management or control of an investment, one could think of requiring the majority of the voting rights and/or stocks if one is looking for a fixed threshold. Along similar lines would be a suggestion to look at secondary Community law using the thresholds provided therein.[154] International standards, such as the one found in the Balance of Payments Manual of the International Monetary Fund,[155] also offer such a threshold. However, all those 'magic numbers'[156] do not provide an answer to whether an investor is in fact in a position to exercise control over his investment; rather, such fixed thresholds are used for specific statistical purposes, for example, those that require clear cut and easily revisable criteria.[157]

The decisive test in this respect appears to be that of whether major or important entrepreneurial decisions cannot be reached without the consent of the investor.[158] It is not necessary that the investor be the only person in the undertaking who is in a position to control the entrepreneurial activities, as with a sole trader; the very idea of setting up partnerships, societies, associations, and companies is to pursue entrepreneurial aims together with others.[159] It is only an assessment on an individual basis, taking into account in particular—but not exclusively[160]—the conditions under company law in which the undertaking is placed that can reliably inform us whether the investor is in the actual position to exercise his influence in the aforementioned fashion. This does not necessarily presuppose a majority holding. Also, minority stakes coupled with veto rights[161]

---

[153] See Chapter II. 4. a above.
[154] eg, Art 1(2) lit. a in connection with Art 1(1) lit. d of Directive 83/349/EEC: 20%; Art 3 (1) of Directive 90/435/EEC: 15%, from 01.01.2009 onwards 10%; Art 17 of Directive 78/660/EEC: 20%.
[155] International Monetary Fund, *Balance of Payments Manual*, §§ 359, 362, see also OECD, *OECD Benchmark Definition of Foreign Direct Investment*, 7 et seq.
[156] The expression is borrowed from A Rohde, *Kapitalverkehr*, 187 citing H Fleischer, 'Haftung', 853.
[157] eg, A Rohde, *Kapitalverkehr*, 186 *et seq*; U Haferkamp, *Kapitalverkehrsfreiheit*, 175; J Lübke, *Kapitalverkehrs- und Niederlassungsfreiheit*, 107; note also Case C-251/98 *C Baars v Inspecteur der Belastingen Particulieren/Ondernemingen Gorinchem*, para 20, though in the context of Art 43 EC.
[158] *Cf* C Ohler, Art. 56 EC (2002), mn 121.
[159] J Lübke, *Kapitalverkehrs- und Niederlassungsfreiheit*, 212 *et seq*.
[160] Case C-251/98 *C Baars v Inspecteur der Belastingen Particulieren/Ondernemingen Gorinchem*, para 20; for a different view see Case C-251/98 *C Baars v Inspecteur der Belastingen Particulieren/Ondernemingen Gorinchem*, para 33. Both quotes relate to Art 43 EC though.
[161] *Cf*, eg, with respect to the '*Gesellschaft bürgerlichen Rechts*' (non-trading partnership) § 709 of the BGB (Germany) entitled '*Gemeinschaftliche Geschäftsführung*' (joint management) reads in its first section: 'Die Führung der Geschäfte der Gesellschaft steht den Gesellschaftern gemeinschaftlich zu; für jedes Geschäft ist die Zustimmung aller Gesellschafter erforderlich': each decision requires the

or other similar arrangements such as management contracts can grant the investor the necessary influence for participation in the control of the undertaking.

Proceeding to the next variety of direct investment, long-term loans, which are referred to under Heading I.3 of the Nomenclature, must be 'of a participating nature', 'for a period of more than five years', and they have to be 'made for the purpose of establishing or maintaining lasting economic links'. Examples are:

> loans granted by a company to its subsidiaries or to companies in which it has a share and loans linked with a profit-sharing arrangement. Loans granted by financial institutions with a view to establishing or maintaining lasting economic links are also included under this heading.

The definition makes clear ('...of a participating nature...') that the link between the borrower and the lender must go beyond the mere provision of credit capital.[162] In order to characterize a loan as direct investment, the conditions under which the loan is advanced must place the lender in a position in which major or important entrepreneurial decisions in the linked undertaking cannot be reached without his approval; in principle, the same as was argued above with respect to the link between investor and investment in the context of shareholdings applies *mutatis mutandis* here as well. The period of more than five years mentioned in the definition appears not to be an exclusionary criterion if undercut. There is no reason why a loan that must be paid back after four years, but that is granted in such a way that it secures a certain degree of directly substantial influence over an undertaking, should not be considered a 'direct investment'. Also, in this context, the essential test is whether the lender can exercise control over the borrower's undertaking, which is most appropriately assessed on an individual basis.

The Nomenclature mentions under Heading I.4 the reinvestment of earnings with a view to maintaining lasting economic links. In such a case, the investor is already in a position to exercise control over the entrepreneurial activities of the undertaking that generates the profits he later reinvests. The reinvestment consolidates his position. The express reference probably hearkens back to the desire of the Drafters to make clear that reinvestments of profits—even though they themselves are not transferred across borders—were also covered by the

---

consent of all partners. See also §§ 114 *et seq* of HGB (Germany) on the '*Offene Handelsgesellschaft*' (ordinary partnership) and §§ 161, 164 of HGB (Germany) on the '*Kommanditgesellschaft*' (limited commercial partnership).

[162] Along similar lines: A Rohde, *Kapitalverkehr*, 188. Note in this context also: Case C-439/97 *Sandoz GmbH v Finanzlandesdirektion für Wien, Niederösterreich und Burgenland*, para 12, 19. Note in particular Case C-439/97 (Opinion of AG Léger) *Sandoz GmbH v Finanzlandesdirektion für Wien, Niederösterreich und Burgenland* which clearly qualified the loan taken out by Austrian Sandoz GmbH as 'a financial transaction which enables funds to be obtained generally for investment purposes' within the meaning of Heading B of Annex I (VIII) of Directive 88/361/EEC.

Directive.¹⁶³ In essence, the inclusion of reinvestments of profits indicates a balance of payments perspective taken while drafting the Directive because they are recorded as direct investments in the national balance of payments.

Although not mentioned explicitly under Heading I of the Nomenclature, the acquisition of real property with which entrepreneurial purposes can be pursued constitutes 'direct investment'.¹⁶⁴ This can be taken from the headline to Heading II of the Nomenclature, which speaks of 'Investment in Real Estate (*not included under I.*)',¹⁶⁵ thus—'*argumentum e contrario*'—real property for entrepreneurial purposes is covered by Heading I of the Nomenclature. The phrase 'direct investment—including in real estate' in Art 57(1) EC must be read in the same way: real estate with which entrepreneurial aims can be pursued constitutes a subcategory of 'direct investment'.¹⁶⁶

So far I have not discussed the '[e]stablishment and extension of branches or new undertakings belonging solely to the person providing the capital, and the acquisition in full of existing undertakings'. The holding of all shares in the hands of a single person constitutes the most unambiguous variety of direct investment:

since all the shares are owned by one person. The sole owner of all of a company's shares can make decisions about that company's activities on his own: there is no-one else entitled to a say whose views he must heed. Only the legal form of the undertaking distinguishes him from a sole trader; like the latter, he is in a position to direct the activities of the business in question.¹⁶⁷

The situation just described should, however, not be confused with that of 'emigration', ie, complete relocation from one country into another. By way of example, the establishment of a self-employed (foreign) person in a Member State who finances his establishment in the host country by money brought along with him does not constitute direct investment due to the fact that there is no separate

---

¹⁶³ A Honrath, *Kapitalverkehr*, 42 See for a discussion of the meaning of the 'cross-border element' within the ambit of free movement of capital:0.
¹⁶⁴ C Bond, Art. 68 EEC (1999), § 68.02 [1]; C Ohler, Art. 56 EC (2002), mn 129; G Ress and J Ukrow, Art. 56 EC (2002), mn 7; P-C Müller-Graff, Art. 43 EC (2003), mn 15; Case 305/87 *Commission v Hellenic Republic*, para 21 *et seq*; Case C-302/97 *Klaus Konle v Republik Österreich*, 21 *et seq*.
¹⁶⁵ [Emphasis added] The German text, which reads '*soweit* nicht unter I. erfasst' [emphasis added] makes the point even clearer.
¹⁶⁶ For a probably different view: C Bond, Art. 68 EEC (1999), § 68.02 [2], who is of the opinion that the categories under Headings I and II are merged into one concept with respect to Art 57 EC. This would extend the provision's scope of restriction to real estate investments by private persons for personal use as well as to portfolio investments in real estate. Neither constitutes a subcategory of direct investment. The wording of Art 57 EC ('*including*') seems, however, to suggest that only those real estate investments with which entrepreneurial aims can be pursued are included in its scope.
¹⁶⁷ Case C-251/98 (Opinion of AG Alber) *C Baars v Inspecteur der Belastingen Particulieren/ Ondernemingen Gorinchem*, para 34. The above-cited statement was made in the context of Art 43 EC. It has, however, the same validity in the present context.

financier in another country who exercises entrepreneurial control over the venture. The movement of financial means could, however, still qualify as capital movement. The EC Capital Movements Directive mentions in Annex I, Heading XI.F the '[t]ransfers of assets constituted by residents, in the event of emigration, at the time of their installation or during their period of stay abroad' as constituting capital movement.[168]

In summary so far, the distinctive feature of the notion of 'direct investment' is that the investor is placed in a position to exercise control over entrepreneurial activities in such a way that major or important entrepreneurial decisions cannot be reached without his consent. In order to assess whether the investor is in such a position, recourse must be taken to the actual circumstances in the individual case.

c. The Third Country Context: The Notion of 'Foreign Direct Investment' within the Ambit of Free Movement of Capital

I explained above that although Art 56(1) EC 'extends its guarantee to the world at large' and liberalizes capital movements, including direct investments, irrespective of their origin or destination, it is nevertheless necessary to differentiate between intra-Community and third country capital movement, as in particular Art 57 EC but also Arts 59 and 60 EC establish a special regime for the latter.

Additionally, it is necessary to carefully single out such capital movements that display no connection at all to the Community. Article 56(1) EC aims to cover only 'movement of capital between Member States and between Member States and third countries' but not that occurring between third countries exclusively.[169]

In the following, I will first set out which countries qualify as 'third' within the meaning of the EC Treaty. Secondly, I will depict the necessary linkage of a given direct investment to the Community in order to qualify for coverage by the freedom of capital movement. Last, I will explain how to distinguish between intra-Community and foreign direct investment. At this point, it should be recalled that this study uses the term 'foreign', except where otherwise stated, as referring to transactions that occur between a Member State and non-EC Country.

(1) What Are 'Third Countries'?

Third countries are those States to which the EC Treaty does not apply.[170] These are in the first instance all States that are not Members of the EC (*cf* Art 299(1)

---

[168] P Troberg, Art. 52 ToM (1997), mn 12 and relating fn 15; J Tiedje and P Troberg, Art. 43 EC (2003), mn 26 and fn 42.
[169] A special position is occupied by Art 60 EC, which seems to be broader in its scope. See Chapter II. 4 and Chapter VII. 5. a. (3).
[170] C Ohler, Art. 56 EC (2002), mn. 210; C Ohler, Art. 57 EC (2002), mn 2.

EC).¹⁷¹ States with which the Community has concluded agreements establishing an association (*cf* Art 310 EC), including those non-Member States party to the EEA Agreement,¹⁷² are also third countries.¹⁷³

The French overseas departments, the Azores, Madeira, and the Canary Islands, however, are not 'third countries' (*cf* Art 299(2) EC). By virtue of Art 299(4) EC, the EC Treaty, including the provision on free movement of capital, also applies to Gibraltar; hence, it does not qualify as a 'third country' within the meaning of the EC Treaty.¹⁷⁴ However, contrary to the wording of Art 299(4) EC, the States of Andorra, Monaco, San Marino, and the State of Vatican City are 'third countries'.¹⁷⁵ Equally considered 'third countries' are those overseas countries and territories mentioned in Annex II to the EC Treaty¹⁷⁶ (*cf* Art 299(3) subparagraph (1) EC). The aforementioned are subject to the association provisions set out in Art 182 EC *et seq*, which do not call for application of Art 56 EC *et seq* in these countries and territories. In pursuance of Art 299(6) lit. a, b, c EC, the authorities of the Faeroe Islands, of the sovereign base areas of Great Britain in Cyprus, and of the Channel Islands and the Isle of Man, are not bound to apply the provisions on free movement of capital and are therefore also considered 'third countries'.¹⁷⁷

(2) Third-Country Capital Movement—A 'Sufficient Link' to a Member State of the European Community

The freedom's scope does not extend to capital movements, including direct investments, that display no connection at all to the Community. What is therefore required is a 'sufficient link' of the respective capital movement to at least one Member State (*cf* Art 299(1) EC).¹⁷⁸ On the basis of the findings with respect to the cross-border element¹⁷⁹ and with a view to giving the freedom a broad reading, such a 'sufficient link' is present if either of the two parties to the transaction

---

¹⁷¹ Advocate General Geelhoed put it in this way: 'Any State which is not a Member State of the European Union is a third country.' [Case C-452/01 (Opinion of AG Geelhoed) *Margarethe Ospelt and Schlössle Weissenberg Familienstiftung*, para 51]

¹⁷² EEA Agreement; for another view: K Ståhl, 'Movement of Capital', 49, fn 21.

¹⁷³ C Ohler, Art. 57 EC (2002), mn 2; Case C-452/01 (Opinion of AG Geelhoed) *Margarethe Ospelt and Schlössle Weissenberg Familienstiftung*, para 51; for a different view: R Geiger, *EUV, EGV*, Art. 57, mn 1; T Schürmann, Art. 57 EC (2006), mn 2.

¹⁷⁴ J Kokott, Art. 299 EC (2003), mn 13.

¹⁷⁵ C Ohler, Art. 56 EC (2002), mn 210.

¹⁷⁶ Greenland, New Caledonia and Dependencies, French Polynesia, French Southern and Antarctic Territories, Wallis and Futuna Islands, Mayotte, Saint Pierre and Miquelon, Aruba, Netherlands Antilles (Bonaire, Curaçao, Saba, Sint Eustatius, Sint Maarten), Anguilla, Cayman Islands, Falkland Islands, South Georgia and the South Sandwich Islands, Montserrat, Pitcairn, Saint Helena and Dependencies, British Antarctic Territory, British Indian Ocean Territory, Turks and Caicos Islands, British Virgin Islands, Bermuda.

¹⁷⁷ W Kiemel, Vorbem. zu den Artikeln 56 bis 60 EC (2003), mn 38 C Ohler, Art. 56 EC (2002), mn 211 *et seq*.

¹⁷⁸ C Ohler, Art. 56 EC (2002), mn 208.   ¹⁷⁹ *Cf* Chapter II. 3. b.

is resident within the Community[180] or, from an economic perspective, if the return on investment is determined by the economic conditions found in at least one Member State.[181]

(3) Delineating Intra-Community and Foreign Direct Investment

It is not the freedom itself but its restrictions in Arts 57(1) and 59 EC that require a clear delineation of foreign and intra-Community direct investment.

Today, a great number of direct investments, although they originate from and are ultimately directed to a Member State, probably possess at some point in the chain of transactions a link to a third country. Not just any remote link to a third country, however, can turn an intra-Community direct investment into a third country, ie, foreign, direct investment. If one were to attribute a wide understanding to the notion of 'foreign', ie, subjecting direct investments that have only a remote link to a third country to Arts 57 and 59 EC, then this could result in an impermissible restriction of intra-Community direct investment.

Hence, while the criterion of 'foreign' may not be construed too narrowly in a way that the legitimate purposes pursued by Arts 57 and 59 EC cannot be preserved, those Articles may not turn into a gateway for unreasonable restriction of Art 56(1) EC, which—in accordance with its spirit and purpose, developed earlier in this study—must be interpreted in a broad sense in order to endow the freedom with the greatest possible effectiveness.

Article 57(1) contains grandfathered Member State restrictions for certain categories of capital movements that are viewed as economically very important. Their liberalization will be carried out under the particular consideration of general welfare. They are thus burdened with a high political sentiment. Article 57(2) contains a mirror-inverted Community competence, which is predominantly to be exercised with a view to removing existing national restrictions.[182]

With respect to the subject matter of this study, the category of foreign direct investment,[183] the regulatory idea behind the grandfathering clause in Art 57(1) EC is chiefly to maintain Member State control over the system of property ownership in the respective territory.[184] The Member State shall

---

[180] C Ohler, Art. 56 EC (2002), mn 18 *et seq.*
[181] Ohler, however, does not wish to have recourse to an economic perspective but differentiates with respect to the type of investment: real property and related rights *in rem* and movable capital goods must be situated within the Community; with respect to intangible rights, the debtor must be resident within the Community. [Ibid, mn 220]
[182] See Chapter VII. 3.
[183] This includes direct investments in real estate.
[184] The same purpose is pursued by the inclusion of the category of establishment. Concerning the other categories of capital movements mentioned in Art 57 EC, the provision of financial services and the admission of securities to capital markets, the protection of investors and the risks for stability of the financial system are the main concerns. [*Cf* C Ohler, Art. 57 EC (2002), mn 1] With respect to the two latter categories, different considerations with respect to the third country link may apply.

have the opportunity to prevent or restrict controlling holdings by residents of non-Member States.[185] Hence, it is the cross-border capital movement which establishes (or perpetuates) control of the undertaking that must possess the third country link. As with respect to the cross-border element, the third country link is to be examined in the individual transaction. Any 'global perspective' inherently carries the threat of unduly restricting intra-Community direct investment. For example, if an investor resident in Member State A grants a participating loan to an undertaking in Member State B, and the guarantor of the credit is resident in a third country, then any defence by Member State B on the basis of Art 57(1) EC of any restrictive national measure with respect to the loan must fail. The control over the undertaking is acquired by virtue of the 'intra-Community loan', not by way of the 'third country guarantee'. The same is true, *mutatis mutandis,* if an undertaking resident in Member State A and controlled by a company resident in a third country[186] acquires a controlling share in an undertaking resident in Member State B. Here as well, Member State B cannot employ Art 57(1) EC in order to restrict the acquisition of shares.[187]

Article 59 EC is designed to empower the Community to interrupt or restrict third country capital movements, including foreign direct investment, in case of serious difficulties or the threat thereof for the operation of Economic and Monetary Union (EMU). The nature of the provision as an economic emergency safeguard clause is evidenced and stressed by several criteria, such as the seriousness of a threat, the maximum period of time, and the limitation to measures strictly necessary. Hence this suggests that measures must be precisely targeted at third county capital movements instead of applying 'broadband measures' affecting all sorts of capital movements, including those that have only remote or no linkage to third countries.[188] Again, with respect to foreign direct investment, the third country link must be present in the transaction that establishes (or perpetuates) control of the undertaking.

While it is also true that Art 60 EC—containing a Community and Member State competence to resort to financial sanctions—applies exclusively to third countries, due to its particular nature, it should be discounted in this context. In contrast to the two aforementioned provisions, it does not presuppose 'movement of capital to or from third countries' but targets 'movement of capital . . . as regards the third countries concerned'. Article 60 EC is hence not based on

---

[185] For the notion of 'non-Member State' see Chapter II. 4. c. (1).
[186] See the Court's judgment in Case C-524/04 *Test Claimants in the Thin Cap Group Litigation*, para 98 *et seq*, which might evidence a different understanding.
[187] If such a constellation were to be perceived as a 'third country' transaction, then such a view would readily amount to the introduction by the backdoor of the theory seeking to determine the nationality of a company by the nationality of its shareholders ('control theory'). This theory, however, is not compatible with EC law. *Cf*, eg, J Tiedje and P Troberg, Art. 48 EC (2003), mn 38 *et seq*.
[188] See Chapter VII. 4.

a cross-border movement perspective, but employs a broader view looking at reducing, in part or completely, economic relations with third countries. Article 60 EC presupposes a *'political link'* between the person involved in the capital movement and a third country.[189] The capital movement affected by a measure must neither necessarily possess a cross-border link nor occur between a Member State and a third country.[190] In this sense, the measures taken by virtue of Art 60 EC can extend their scope beyond Art 56(1) EC, which is in its guarantee limited to 'movement of capital between Member States and between Member States and third countries'. Due to this different perspective, nothing can be drawn from Art 60 EC on the question of how to delineate intra-Community and foreign direct investment.

From the above, it can be taken that the foreign link is to be sought in the actual transfer that establishes (or perpetuates) control over the investment. Taking any wide 'economic perspective' with respect to the link would impermissibly restrict intra-Community direct investment.[191] Having said all of this, this study submits that a *foreign* direct investment is on hand if either of the two parties to the transaction is resident in a third country or, although the two parties involved are resident within the Community, from an economic perspective, the return on investment is determined by the economic conditions present in a third country or vice versa. In this connection, it should once again be stressed that due to the character of free movement of capital as an object-related freedom, the nationality of the transferee or transferor is of no relevance.

---

[189] This was held by the Court of First Instance in a case in which so-called smart sanctions, ie, those that target a particular person or group of people instead of a country as a whole, were at issue. [See Chapter VII. 5. a. (3)]

[190] See Chapter VII. 5. a (3).

[191] The Court, however, seems to have taken the opposite view, ie, applying a broad economic understanding. Otherwise, the solution it adopted in Case C-524/04 *Test Claimants in the Thin Cap Group Litigation*, para 98 *et seq* would hardly be comprehensible. In 'a situation in which a [Member State] *resident* company is granted a loan by a company which is resident *in another Member State* and which does not itself have a controlling shareholding in the borrowing company and where each of those companies is directly or indirectly controlled by a common parent company which is resident, for its part, in a non-member country', the Court chose not to consider the transaction between the borrower and lender company on the basis of Art 56(1) EC but applied a 'global view' on the constellation, opting for Art 43 EC. The ECJ justified its choice by stating that '[w]here, in such a situation, the Member State which has adopted that legislation treats interest paid by the borrowing company as a distribution, that measure affects freedom of establishment, not as regards the lending company, but only as regards the parent company, which enjoys a level of control over each of the other companies concerned, allowing it to influence the funding decisions of those companies.' Due to the limited territorial scope of Art 43 EC, however, the economic activity was completely outside the guarantees of the EC Treaty. This example shows how an unambiguous intra-Community transaction can be re-interpreted in a third country constellation. See also J Schönfeld, 'Anmerkung zu C-524/04'.

d. Summary so Far

An economic understanding constitutes the starting point for any meaningful evaluation of the notion of 'direct investment'. In the same way as with respect to the term 'capital', its legal construction is strongly influenced by economic thinking. Speaking in economic terms, a direct investment occurs when an investor acquires managing control over economic activities. The distinctive feature is that the investor is placed in a position to pursue entrepreneurial aims. In contrast, if the investor does not acquire such control over decision-making at the microeconomic level, one speaks of portfolio investment, which is the antonym to direct investment.

In legal terms, 'direct investment' constitutes a subcategory of 'capital' within the meaning of Art 56(1) EC. This can be drawn from both Art 57 EC and the Nomenclature of the EC Capital Movement Directive.

The Directive just mentioned also offers interpretive guidance with respect to the content of the term. The notion of 'direct investment' refers to:

[i]nvestments of all kinds by natural persons or commercial, industrial or financial undertakings, and which serve to establish or to maintain lasting and direct links between the person providing the capital and the entrepreneur to whom or the undertaking to which the capital is made available in order to carry on an economic activity.

With the potential for restrictions of the freedom flowing from Art 57(1) EC in view, the notion of 'direct investment' must be strictly interpreted in particular with respect to the 'lasting and direct link' within the whole ambit of free movement of capital.

The distinctive feature of the notion of 'direct investment'—not just in economics but also in law—is that the investor is placed in a position to exercise control over entrepreneurial activities in such a way that major or important entrepreneurial decisions cannot be reached without his consent. In order to assess whether the investor is in such a position, recourse must be taken to the actual circumstances in the individual case. The EC Capital Movement Directive paraphrased this by referring to the establishment or maintenance of 'lasting and direct links' between investor and entrepreneur.

The scope of the freedom does not extend to direct investments displaying no connection at all to the Community. What is required is a 'sufficient link' to the Community, which is present if either of the two parties to the transaction is resident within the Community or the return on investment is determined by the economic conditions found in at least one Member State.

The Treaty requires the drawing of a distinction between intra-Community direct investment and foreign direct investment; the latter term refers in this study to transactions that occur between a Member State and a non-Member State. This is to be sought in the actual transfer that establishes (or perpetuates) control over the investment. Taking any wide 'global perspective' with respect to assessing the link of a transaction to a third country is not indicated in this situation due to the fact that it would impermissibly restrict intra-Community direct investment. A foreign direct investment is thus on hand if either of the two parties to the transaction resides in a third country or, despite the two parties involved being resident within the Community, the return on investment is determined by the economic conditions present in a third country or vice versa.

Third countries within the meaning of the EC Treaty are all those States to which the Treaty does not apply.

III

The Influence of Competing Freedoms on the Scope of Application—Direct Investment between Free Movement of Capital and the Freedom of Establishment

1. Introduction

In this chapter,[1] I shall discuss the influence of the freedom of establishment on the scope of application of free movement of capital. The debate on the doctrinal relationship of the two freedoms is one of the most controversial disputes in EC Law. As I shall show in more detail further below,[2] direct investment constitutes a classical cross-sectional activity. It usually constitutes 'capital movement' within the meaning of Art 56(1) EC, and it amounts to an establishment to be considered in the light of Art 43 EC.

Suggestions of how to deal with this 'double topical relevance' display great diversity. The two main positions diametrically oppose each other. One view seeks to subject a relevant national measure encroaching upon direct investment to both freedoms.[3] The opposite view suggests dealing with it only in the light of the freedom of establishment.[4]

The object of investigation of this study being foreign direct investment, at first sight, one might think that the issue just described is of no relevance to us. Foreign direct investment refers to capital that either originates from or is directed to third countries. Due to the fact that the the territorial scope of the provisions on the freedom of establishment, in contrast to those on free movement of capital, do not extend to third countries, one could—*arguendo*—take the (ostensible) position that there is no conflict between the two freedoms. Hence, is there much ado about nothing?

Far from it! One could consider resolving the conflict of the competing freedoms—'one step earlier,' so to speak—on the level of the material scope. It

---

[1] This section is closely modelled on S Hindelang, 'Competing Freedoms'; see also S Hindelang, 'Kapitalverkehrs- und Niederlassungsfreiheit'.
[2] See Chapter III. 2.   [3] See Chapter III. 3. c. (2).   [4] See Chapter III. 3. c. (1).

may possibly be argued that as soon as a given transaction qualifies as both direct investment within the meaning of Art 56(1) EC in connection with the EC Capital Movements Directive and establishment as defined for the purposes of Art 43 EC, it *per se* falls within the ambit of the freedom of establishment; in consequence, with regard to third countries, direct investment—or foreign direct investment, as it would then properly be called—falls outside the ambit of the Treaty.[5]

One might also take the view, which will also be explained in detail further below,[6] that a transaction that constitutes both direct investment and establishment is covered by both freedoms, but with the addition that foreign direct investment happens to fall outside the scope of any freedom due to an alleged limiting effect of the scope of application of the freedom of establishment on that of free movement of capital in a third country context.

Thus, as these two examples show, it is anything but superfluous to consider the doctrinal relationship of the abovementioned freedoms and their bearing on the applicability of the freedom of capital movements to foreign direct investment.[7] In consideration of the very recent judgments of the Court specifically dealing with this question,[8] the depiction of the importance of this issue as 'anything but superfluous' appears almost as a *litotes* not just in a linguistic sense. Rather, this interpretative question appears to amount to one of the most important—maybe even the most important—parameters for the effectiveness of the freedom when it comes to third country transactions.

This study will suggest in the following sections, first, that both freedoms are to be applied in parallel with respect to direct investment and, secondly, that the relationship of the two freedoms does not have a bearing on the applicability of the provisions on free movement of capital to foreign direct investment in such a way that it would be excluded from the freedom's scope of protection.

2. Direct Investment as an Economic Cross-sectional Activity

It was explained above,[9] that direct investment forms a (sub-)category of the notion of 'capital movement' within the meaning of Art 56(1) EC. The economic activity of direct investment does not, however, constitute only 'capital movement', but can also qualify as establishment for the purpose of Art 43 EC.

The Court construed establishment as 'the actual pursuit of an economic activity through a fixed establishment in another Member State for an indefinite period'.[10]

---

[5] See Chapter III. 3. c. (1).   [6] See ibid.
[7] *Cf* J Lübke, *Kapitalverkehrs- und Niederlassungsfreiheit*, 216.
[8] See Chapter III. 3. b.   [9] See Chapter II. 4. b.
[10] Case C-221/89 *R v Secretary of State for Transport, ex p Factortame Ltd and others*, para 20; Case C-55/94 *Reinhard Gebhard v Consiglio dell'Ordine degli Avvocati e Procuratori di Milano*, para 25.

Although Art 43(2) EC provides only that the '[f]reedom of establishment shall include the right to...set up and manage undertakings', this does not mean that the provision is limited to the establishment and management of 'new' undertakings; flowing from the telos of Art 43 EC, the freedom extends equally to the purchase of shares in an 'already existing' undertaking11 or a cross-border merger.[12] Not every share purchase, though, is covered by Art 43 EC, but only those that form the basis for a prospective entrepreneurial activity.[13] Putting it in the words of Schön, the freedom of establishment protects the active 'entrepreneurial stockholder', but not the 'portfolio investor'.[14] The former premises a certain degree of influence within the undertaking in order to have the option to implement his own entrepreneurial aims by way of 'control or management of the company'.[15] The objective possibility—in contrast to the objective possibility plus the subjective intention—of exercising influence within the undertaking suffices.[16] In this sense, one might also speak of the potential 'entrepreneurial stockholder', who is protected by Art 43 EC.

Having learnt that the entrepreneurial activity can be pursued either by setting up new undertakings or by participating in existing ones, this prompts, as a next step, the question of what degree of influence the *founder* or acquirer must be able to exert in order to refer to him as a '(potential) entrepreneurial stockholder'. The Court replied as follows: a holding must 'confer on the holder *definite*[17]

---

[11] Case C-208/00 *Überseering BV v Nordic Construction Company Baumanagement GmbH (NCC)*, para 77. See also W Schön, 'Gesellschafter', 11; GC Schwarz, *Europäisches Gesellschaftsrecht*, mn 146; A Glaesner, Art. 56 EC (2000), mn 11; U Haferkamp, *Kapitalverkehrsfreiheit*, 170.

[12] 'Cross-border merger operations, like other company transformation operations, respond to the needs for cooperation and consolidation between companies established in different Member States. They constitute particular methods of exercise of the freedom of establishment, important for the proper functioning of the internal market, and are therefore amongst those economic activities with respect to which Member States are required to comply with the freedom of establishment laid down by Article 43 EC.' [Case C-411/03 *SEVIC Systems AG*, para 19]

[13] W Schön, 'Kapitalverkehrsfreiheit', 750 *et seq*; J Tiedje and P Troberg, Art. 43 EC (2003), mn 26.

[14] W Schön, 'Gesellschafter', 11 *et seq*, in the same direction: J Tiedje and P Troberg, Art. 43 EC (2003), mn 28; note also A Randelzhofer and U Forsthoff, Art. 43 EC (2001), mn 115, who proceed from the assumption that free movement of capital and the freedom of establishment are mutually exclusive in cases in which the direct investment also constitutes an 'establishment' within the meaning of Art 43 EC.

[15] Case C-251/98 *C Baars v Inspecteur der Belastingen Particulieren/Ondernemingen Gorinchem*, para 20; see also Chapter II. 4.

[16] Ibid, para 22, Case C-251/98 (Opinion of AG Alber) *C Baars v Inspecteur der Belastingen Particulieren/Ondernemingen Gorinchem*, para 33, confirmed in Case C-208/00 *Überseering BV v Nordic Construction Company Baumanagement GmbH (NCC)*, para 77; concurring J Lübke, *Kapitalverkehrs- und Niederlassungsfreiheit*, 208 *et seq*; C Ohler, Art. 56 EC (2002), mn 120; P-C Müller-Graff, Art. 43 EC (2003), mn 15; P-C Müller-Graff, 'Einflußregulierungen', 935 *et seq*; A Randelzhofer and U Forsthoff, Art. 43 EC (2001), mn 115. For a different view: the Court in its earlier judgment Case C-221/89 *R v Secretary of State for Transport, ex p Factortame Ltd and others*, para 20 *et seq*; GC Schwarz, *Europäisches Gesellschaftsrecht*, mn 123; F Kainer, *Unternehmensübernahmen*, 62. Unclear: M Pannier, *Harmonisierung*, 45.

[17] [Emphasis added] [German] '*sicher,*' [French] '*certaine*'.

influence over the company's decisions and allow it to determine the company's activities'.[18]

'Direct investments' by way of the '[e]stablishment and extension of branches or new undertakings belonging solely to the person providing the capital, and the acquisition in full of existing undertakings'[19] will surely pass this test and, thus, constitute establishment within the meaning of Art 43 EC.[20]

More contentious appears to be the accommodation of '[p]articipation[s] in new or existing undertakings with a view to establishing or maintaining lasting economic links,'[21] ie, 'to participate effectively in the management of the company or in its control',[22] within the notion of establishment.

It is obvious; in this case, that the investor cannot conduct his business in the manner of a 'sole trader'. Within the ambit of the freedom of establishment, the exposure to a situation in which someone else might be entitled to a say is contentious. The crucial question is where to set the threshold above which one can still assume that the investor is in a position to act as entrepreneur. One could require the majority of the voting rights and/or stocks. It is also possible to have recourse to secondary Community legislation, which offers a range of differing thresholds for specific situations, in order to judge whether two companies are in some way affiliated with each other.[23] If one is not looking for some sort of fixed threshold, but proceeds from the purpose of the freedom, then it could also be argued that one can speak of an establishment within the meaning of Art 43 EC as long as the stockholder exercises its influence over the company's decisions in all important matters[24] that, for example, apply not only to majority holdings but also to 50 per cent holdings or minority holdings coupled with veto rights.[25]

---

[18] [Emphasis added] Case C-446/04 *Test Claimants in the FII Group Litigation v Commissioners of Inland Revenue,* para 37 citing Case C-251/98 *C Baars v Inspecteur der Belastingen Particulieren/Ondernemingen Gorinchem,* para 21 *et seq;* Case C-436/00 *X and Y v Riksskatteverket,* para 37, 66 *et seq; Case C-196/04 Cadbury Schweppes and Cadbury Schweppes Overseas Ltd v Commissioners of Inland Revenue,* para 31.

[19] Annex I, Heading I.1 of Directive 88/361/EEC.

[20] *Cf,* eg, Case C-251/98 (Opinion of AG Alber) *C Baars v Inspecteur der Belastingen Particulieren/Ondernemingen Gorinchem,* para 34; Case C-251/98 *C Baars v Inspecteur der Belastingen Particulieren/Ondernemingen Gorinchem,* para 21 *et seq*; J Tiedje and P Troberg, Art. 43 EC (2003), mn 29; GC Schwarz, *Europäisches Gesellschaftsrecht,* mn 123; P-C Müller-Graff, 'Einflußregulierungen', 935.

[21] Annex I, Heading I.2 of Directive 88/361/EEC.

[22] Annex I, Explanatory Notes of Directive 88/361/EEC.

[23] eg, Art 1(2) lit. a in connection with Art 1(1) lit. d of Directive 83/349/EEC: 20%; Art 3(1) of Directive 90/435/EEC: 15%, from 01.01.2009 onwards 10%; Art 17 of Directive 78/660/EEC: 20%.

[24] J Lübke, *Kapitalverkehrs- und Niederlassungsfreiheit,* 212 *et seq;* of the same opinion: M Geurts, 'Konkurrenzverhältnis', 573; M Pannier, *Harmonisierung,* 45; Schön also concurs with this reading by referring to the definition of 'direct investment' in the EC Capital Movements Directive. He, however, wants to substantiate the former by way of utilizing the threshold contained in Directive 90/435/EEC. [W Schön, 'Kapitalverkehrsfreiheit', 751]

[25] W Schön, 'Gesellschafter', 11. This view is based on the argument that the inherent idea of setting up a company is the association with somebody else in order to achieve a common entrepreneurial purpose. [*Cf.* J Lübke, *Kapitalverkehrs- und Niederlassungsfreiheit,* 213 with further references]

In accordance with my view set forth with respect to the notion of direct investment,[26] this study regards as the most appropriate approach a comprehensive overall view of the factual conditions under particular consideration of the applicable company law[27] in the individual case. The decisive test for finding 'definite influence' is whether major or important entrepreneurial decisions (eg, influence on the composition of the management body[28])—in consideration of the conditions just mentioned—cannot be reached without the approval of the respective stockholder.[29] In this regard, the number of voting rights or stocks has an indicative but not conclusive value.[30] As explained analogously with respect to direct investment,[31]'fixed thresholds' do not constitute reliable criteria for an evaluation of whether a market participant is in a real position to exercise 'definite influence' over the entrepreneurial activities of an undertaking.[32]

If one now wants to compare the test just outlined with respect to identifying an establishment with the one developed for the identification of direct investment with respect to holdings mentioned in Annex I, Heading I.2 of the EC Capital Movements Directive ('effective participation test'), then one notices that the notions of establishment and direct investment are perceived by this study as overlapping to a very great extent.[33] The 'effective participation test' requires essentially the same threshold as the Court's 'definite influence test'.[34]

The opposite view refers in particular to the wording of Art 57(1) EC, which mentions restrictions adopted with respect to the movement of capital to or from third countries involving direct investment alongside those restrictions involving

---

[26] See Chapter II. 4.
[27] Advocate General Alber in Case C-251/98 (Opinion of AG Alber) *C Baars v Inspecteur der Belastingen Particulieren/Ondernemingen Gorinchem*, para 33 suggests having recourse to the company law of the respective Member State in order to determine whether the market participant can influence the entrepreneurial aims of the undertaking so that it can be said that it is in a position to control it. Of the same opinion: U Haferkamp, *Kapitalverkehrsfreiheit*, 172 *et seq*. A broader position seems to be taken up by the ECJ, which attributes only indicative value to national company law. [*Cf.* Case C-251/98 *C Baars v Inspecteur der Belastingen Particulieren/Ondernemingen Gorinchem*, para 20]
[28] J Tiedje and P Troberg, Art. 43 EC (2003), mn 29.
[29] C Ohler, Art. 56 EC (2002), mn 121; GC Schwarz, *Europäisches Gesellschaftsrecht*, mn 123; J Tiedje and P Troberg, Art. 43 EC (2003), mn 30. The ECJ held that it is for the national Courts to determine whether the holder can exercise the necessary degree of influence. [*Cf.* Case C-446/04 *Test Claimants in the FII Group Litigation v Commissioners of Inland Revenue*, para 30]
[30] Case C-251/98 (Opinion of AG Alber) *C Baars v Inspecteur der Belastingen Particulieren/ Ondernemingen Gorinchem*, para 33; C Ohler, Art. 56 EC (2002), mn 121; P-C Müller-Graff, 'Einflußregulierungen', 936.
[31] See Chapter II. 4.
[32] eg, P Troberg, Art. 52 ToM (1997), mn 12; A Rohde, *Kapitalverkehr*, 186 *et seq*; U Haferkamp, *Kapitalverkehrsfreiheit*, 175.
[33] Of the same opinion: P Troberg, Art. 52 ToM (1997), mn 11 *et seq*.
[34] C Ohler, Art. 56 EC (2002), mn 121; J Lübke, *Kapitalverkehrs- und Niederlassungsfreiheit*, 210 *et seq*. Implicitly: W-H Roth, 'Niederlassungsfreiheit', 751.

establishment. If the two notions were completely identical, so it is argued, then the separate mention would be superfluous.[35]

While this study agrees that there can be capital movements that qualify as establishment but not at the same time as direct investment, it has considerable problems following propositions such as that of Advocate General Geelhoed in *Test Claimants in the FII Group Litigation*,[36] which puts forward the thesis that the threshold for the detection of direct investment within the 'effective participation test' is clearly lower than in the 'decisive influence test', as he termed it, in the context of identifying establishment.

An example for the situation in which a capital movement qualifies as establishment but not—at the same time—as direct investment would relate to the establishment of a self-employed person in a Member State who finances himself in the host country by money brought along with him. While it can be said that an establishment within the meaning of Art 43 EC has taken place, the movement does not constitute direct investment due to the fact that there is not a separate financier in another country who exercises entrepreneurial control. The movement of financial means, though, could qualify as capital movement within the meaning of EC Capital Movements Directive, Annex I, Heading XI.F, which extends the notion of capital movement also to '[t]ransfers of assets constituted by residents, in the event of emigration, at the time of their installation or during their period of stay abroad'.[37]

For such (rare) cases, an independent significance is inherent in the term 'establishment' in Art 57(1) EC. Other than that mentioned, the term enjoys—alongside the notion of direct investment—only a residual scope of application, as direct investments including those in real estate are essentially the main forms of establishment. Thus, it may be said that the term 'establishment' in Art 57(1) EC does not go beyond a backup functionality.[38]

Turning from the abstract argument to the very real proposition of Advocate General Geelhoed, he suggests that the threshold in the 'effective participation test' is clearly lower than the one applied for the identification of establishment. Seen in particular against the background of the strict interpretation of the notion

---

[35] U Haferkamp, *Kapitalverkehrsfreiheit*, 171 *et seq.*
[36] Case C-446/04 (Opinion of AG Geelhoed) *Test Claimants in the FII Group Litigation v Commissioners of Inland Revenue*, para 119, note also para 30 *et seq*; along similar lines: Case C-347/04 (Opinion of AG Maduro) *Rewe Zentralfinanz eG, as Universal Legal Successor of ITS Reisen GmbH v Finanzamt Köln-Mitte*, para 62 together with para 64; U Haferkamp, *Kapitalverkehrsfreiheit*, 209; probably also J Schönfeld, 'Anmerkung zu C-452/04', 81 citing Case C-251/98 *C Baars v Inspecteur der Belastingen Particulieren/Ondernemingen Gorinchem*, para 20. I must admit, however, that I have difficulties in drawing this conclusion from this passage of the judgment. Note also Case C-194/06 *Staatssecretaris von Financiën v Orange European Smallcap Fund NV*.
[37] P Troberg, Art. 52 ToM (1997), mn 12 and relating fn 15; J Tiedje and P Troberg, Art. 43 EC (2003), mn 26 and fn 42.
[38] C Ohler, Art. 57 EC (2002), mn 11; and along similar lines A Schnitger, 'Kapitalverkehrsfreiheit', 503.

of direct investment advocated in this study,[39] I encounter difficulties embracing such an assertion. To start with, comparing the statement of Advocate General Geelhoed[40] cited above and the respective judgments of the Court, one notices that the Court used different language from the Advocate General to describe the necessary threshold, speaking of a '*definite* influence'. The ordinary meaning of this phrase does not relate to 'sole', 'definitive', or 'decisive' influence, but rather to influence that is 'free of all ambiguity, uncertainty, or obscurity'.[41] The Advocate General, it appears, 'slightly' narrows the test within the ambit of Art 43 EC and re-construes 'definite' into 'decisive'. Moreover, quite in contrast to the opinion of Advocate General Geelhoed, his colleague Advocate General Alber in *Baars* explicitly referred to the distinction between direct investment and 'portfolio investment' as mentioned in Annex I to the EC Capital Movements Directive for the purpose of identifying establishment.[42]

Direct investment taking the form of the provision of '[l]ong-term loans with a view to establishing or maintaining lasting economic links' follows basically and essentially the same reasoning advanced above. Thus, loans that do not have any other function but to provide credit capital neither constitute direct investment within the meaning of the Nomenclature of the EC Capital Movements Directive nor establishment as required for the applicability of Art 43 EC.[43] However, if the conditions under which the loan is advanced are such as to grant to the lender definite influence over major or important entrepreneurial decisions so that they cannot be reached without him, then the loan must be considered direct investment, as a (sub-)category of 'capital movement', as well as establishment.[44] It could be said that in this situation, the lender pursues entrepreneurial activities in another (Member) State.

The acquisition of real property with which entrepreneurial purposes can be pursued also constitutes both direct investment and establishment.[45] The former is indicated in the heading to Point II. of the Nomenclature, which speaks of

---

[39] See Chapter II. 4. b. (2).
[40] Case C-446/04 (Opinion of AG Geelhoed) *Test Claimants in the FII Group Litigation v Commissioners of Inland Revenue*, para 119; note also para 30 *et seq*.
[41] B Kirkpatrick, *Thesaurus*; C Soanes and A Stevenson, *English Dictionary*.
[42] Case C-251/98 (Opinion of AG Alber) *C Baars v Inspecteur der Belastingen Particulieren/ Ondernemingen Gorinchem*, para 33, endnote 17.
[43] *Cf* Case C-439/97 *Sandoz GmbH v Finanzlandesdirektion für Wien, Niederösterreich und Burgenland*, para 12, 19. See, in particular, Case C-439/97 (Opinion of AG Léger) *Sandoz GmbH v Finanzlandesdirektion für Wien, Niederösterreich und Burgenland*, para 35, who clearly qualified the loan taken out by Austrian Sandoz GmbH as 'a financial transaction which enables funds to be obtained generally for investment purposes' within the meaning of Heading B of Annex I (VIII) of Directive 88/361/EEC.
[44] C Ohler, Art. 56 EC (2002), mn 129; not differentiating with respect to loans but subjecting them to the provisions on free movement of capital only: J Tiedje and P Troberg, Art. 43 EC (2003), mn 30.
[45] C Ohler, Art. 56 EC (2002), mn 129; G Ress and J Ukrow, Art. 56 EC (2002), mn 7; P-C Müller-Graff, Art. 43 EC (2003), mn 15; Case 305/87 *Commission v Hellenic Republic*, para 21 *et seq*; Case C-302/97 *Klaus Konle v Republik Österreich*, 21 *et seq*.

'Investment in Real Estate (*not included under I.*);'[46] thus—'*argumentum e contrario*'—real property for entrepreneurial purposes is covered by Point I. of the Nomenclature on direct investment.[47] The latter, with respect to establishment, can in particular be drawn from Art 44(2) lit. e EC.

In sum, against the backdrop of the above, it can be concluded that the notions of establishment and direct investment are not antonyms, but overlap to a very great extent.[48]

3. Parallelism or Exclusivity of Free Movement of Capital and the Freedom of Establishment

Having established that the economic activity of direct investment falls in principle into the ambit of both freedoms, in the following section it will be discussed how the Treaty, the Court, and the literature deal with this 'double topical relevance'.

a. The Provisions of the Treaty—Article 43(2) EC and Article 58(2) EC

Before entering into a thorough review of what the Court and the literature have said on the relationship between both freedoms, I should start my examination by first examining the Treaty. It contains two provisions, Art 43(2) EC and Art 58(2) EC, each with a reference to the other: The freedom of establishment is '... subject to the provisions of the chapter relating to capital,' and the provisions on

---

[46] [Emphasis added] The German text, which reads '*soweit* nicht unter I. erfasst' [emphasis added] makes the point even clearer.

[47] See also above: Chapter II. 4.

[48] C Ohler, Art. 56 EC (2002), mn 120 *et seq*; somewhat more cautious than this study: J Tiedje and P Troberg, Art. 43 EC (2003), mn 26; with respect to shareholdings: J Lübke, *Kapitalverkehrs- und Niederlassungsfreiheit*, 210 *et seq*. Concerning the personal scope of application, the freedom of establishment differentiates between primary and secondary establishment. [*Cf* C Tietje, 'Niederlassungsfreiheit', mn 32 *et seq*] The right of primary establishment (Art 43(1) 1st sentence EC)—ie, taking up and pursuing completely new activities as a self-employed person, taking part in the incorporation of a company in another Member State [C Barnard, *Substantive Law*, 312], or transferring a company's seat—entitles nationals of a Member State, as well as the companies or firms formed in accordance with the law of a Member State that have their registered office, central administration, or principal place of business within the Community. [*Cf* Art. 48 EC] Secondary establishment, ie, establishment by way of setting up additional dependent bases in other Member States taking the form of, eg, agencies, branches, or subsidiaries, requires—in addition to the aforesaid—that the market participant is already resident within the Community, *cf* Art 43 (1) 2nd sentence EC.

Free movement of capital, being an object-oriented freedom, applies to any cross-border capital movement irrespective of nationality or residency of the transferor or transferee. See Chapter V.

Hence, when an activity falls within the personal scope of the freedom of establishment, it is also automatically within the range of the 'personal' scope of free movement of capital due to the fact that the latter is without any limitations. [*Cf* J Lübke, *Kapitalverkehrs- und Niederlassungsfreiheit*, 203]

free movement of capital 'shall be without prejudice to the applicability of restrictions on the right of establishment which are compatible with this Treaty'.

However, neither Art 43(2) EC nor Art 58(2) EC are to be read as establishing a primacy of one or the other freedom on the level of their scope of application.[49] If the two freedoms were to be seen in a relationship of exclusivity, then a mutual reference would be neither necessary nor logical.[50]

Furthermore, it is not convincing to view Art 43(2) EC as applicable to the respective scope of application and Art 58(2) EC as referring to the grounds of justification.[51] If a conflict between freedoms has been resolved on the level of their scopes of application, then the question of conflict on the level of grounds of justification would not arise.[52]

They rather apply only to the level of grounds of justification, which will be elaborated in more detail further below.[53] Concerning the level of the scope of application, however, the provisions lack any meaningful regulatory content.[54]

b. The European Court of Justice: Half-hearted Parallelism

The Court's understanding of the doctrinal relationship of the freedom of establishment and free movement of capital, in both intra-Community and third country contexts, can hardly be described as a prime example of clarity. In fact, in an intra-Community context, the Court had tried to avoid taking up an unambiguous stance. Concerning the relationship of the two freedoms in a third country context, for a long time there was no decision that explicitly touched upon this issue. Just recently, the situation partially changed. In order to make accessible and to evaluate the recent changes in jurisprudence, it is necessary to bring to mind first the case law that refers to economic activities pursued within the Community.

Within the older case law, it can be demonstrated that there are two strands. One strand comprises situations in which the Court is ignorant of whether, in addition to capital movements, there is an element of definite control over an undertaking, either because the facts of the case did not hint at this or because the parties concerned simply did not refer to the freedom of establishment. The

---

[49] U Haferkamp, *Kapitalverkehrsfreiheit*, 193 *et seq*; P-C Müller-Graff, 'Einflußregulierungen', 929, 935 *et seq*; P-C Müller-Graff, Art. 43 EC (2003), para 102. For a different view: F Kimms, *Kapitalverkehrsfreiheit*, 141; M Schlag, Art. 43 EC (2000), mn 10; T Scherer, *Doppelbesteuerung*, 160 *et seq*; B Matzka, *Freiheit des Kapitalverkehrs*, 50; probably also: European Commission, 'Commission Staff Working Paper on CLS no. 6393/96 "Opinion of the Council's Legal Service as regards the Provisions of the EC Treaty applicable to Foreign Direct Investment and to Freedom of Establishment of Companies or Firms Owned or Controlled by Third-Country Natural or Legal Persons" [Title varying]' (SEC (97) 1428), para 3, fn 2.
[50] U Haferkamp, *Kapitalverkehrsfreiheit*, 193 *et seq*; J Tiedje and P Troberg, Art. 43 EC (2003), mn 8.
[51] So probably F Kimms, *Kapitalverkehrsfreiheit*, 139 *et seq*.
[52] R Freitag, 'Kapitalverkehr', 190.   [53] See Chapter VI. 2. c.
[54] U Haferkamp, *Kapitalverkehrsfreiheit*, 194; see also W Kessler, et al, 'Gesellschafter-Fremdfinanzierung', 326.

second strand of judgments implicitly proceeds from the assumption that both freedoms are to be applied in parallel with respect to direct investment.

The recent change in the jurisprudence of the Court—adopting a 'centre of gravity' approach—partially broke with these 'traditions'. This 'centre of gravity' approach, already known from cases in which the freedom to provide services and free movement of goods were competing with each other, leads under certain circumstances to an exclusivity of the freedom of establishment. In a third country context, this has the consequence that a market participant is deprived of any protection that could potentially flow from Art 56(1) EC.

Before beginning the task of tracing the different strands of case law, one general comment should be made. Caution should be exercised: occasionally the wording of a judgment is misleading in the sense that it conveys the impression that in the respective case two freedoms were competing with each other, but in fact they were not. Such a situation is exemplified by the *Verkooijen* case.[55] The case—a dispute that arose before the coming into force of the Maastricht Treaty—refers to a situation in which dividends paid to a shareholder (Mr Verkooijen) who is not in a position to exercise any control or definite influence whatsoever over the company in which he has his holdings[56] are taxed differently depending on the place of establishment of the distributing company. The Court decided that the case should be measured against the provisions of free movement of capital and felt that it was 'unnecessary' to provide an answer to the question of whether the provisions of freedom of establishment were equally concerned.[57] What the Court probably meant to say is that in the case at hand, the two aforementioned freedoms were not competing with each other with respect to Mr Verkooijen.[58]

It is, therefore, worth stressing that one can only refer to a 'situation of competing freedoms' in a proper sense if the applicability of two freedoms to the same person and the same circumstances is being debated.

(1) The 'Not Knowing' Strand of Case Law

The strand of case law that I have termed here the 'not knowing' strand refers to the situation, as mentioned above, in which the Court is ignorant of whether—in addition to capital movements—there is an element of definite control over an undertaking or *vice versa*. Due to this construction, no meaningful conclusions with respect to the relationship of the two freedoms can be drawn from this strand of case law.

---

[55] Case C-35/98 *Staatssecretaris van Financiën v B.G.M. Verkooijen*.
[56] Ibid, para 13. [57] Ibid, para 63.
[58] A different view is, of course, formed when one looks at the case from the perspective of the companies that distribute dividends. The national tax provision at hand—according to Advocate General La Pergola—constitutes a hindrance, albeit a justified one, to the freedom of establishment. [Case C-35/98 (First Opinion of AG La Pergola) *Staatssecretaris van Financiën v B.G.M. Verkooijen*, para 38, 40–43; see also Case C-35/98 (Second Opinion of AG La Pergola) *Staatssecretaris van Financiën v B.G.M. Verkooijen*, para 8]

Cases that can be grouped into this strand are, for example, *Lenz*,[59] and *Manninen*[60]—dealing with different taxation of dividends paid to shareholders depending on the place of establishment (residence, head office, seat) of the distributing company. No mention is made of the freedom of establishment, but they are decided on the basis of the provisions of free movement of capital, probably due to the fact that the Court was not aware of any element of entrepreneurial influence or control over the undertaking in which the shares are held.[61] Equally in *Bouanich*, a case concerned with the taxation of the resale of shares to the issuing company in connection with the reduction of its share capital, which is taxed differently depending on the domicile/permanent residence of the shareholder,[62] the freedom of establishment is not touched upon.[63] In the same proceedings, Advocate General Kokott, in principle of the opinion that freedom of establishment and the free movement of capital can apply in parallel, delivers an explanation—quasi in advance—for why the Court would not consider the provisions on the freedom of establishment. The Court did not have any indication of whether Ms Bouanich had a dominant influence in the undertaking in which she held the shares.[64]

In C-54/99 (*Re Association Eglise de Scientologie de Paris and Scientology International Reserves Trust v The Prime Minister*), a complete takeover of the assets and extinction of the debts of the *Eglise de Scientologie de Paris* through the UK-based Scientology International Reserves Trust with funds originating from the American Church of Scientology and the English Church of Scientology[65] in which French rules requiring prior authorization of direct investment were scrutinized, the Court did not touch upon Art 43 EC *et seq*, but based its finding on the provisions of free movement of capital.[66] This, it is suggested here, is not necessarily a statement on the relationship of the two freedoms. The question of applicability of the provisions on freedom of establishment was simply not raised in front of the Court.[67]

---

[59] Case C-315/02 *Anneliese Lenz v Finanzlandesdirektion für Tirol*.
[60] Case C-319/02 *Petri Manninen*.
[61] See also Case C-242/03 *Ministre des Finances v Jean-Claude Weidert and Élisabeth Paulus*.
[62] Case C-265/04 *Margaretha Bouanich v Skatteverket*, para 3.
[63] '…not necessary to answer [the question of whether Art. 43 EC applies to the situation at hand]'. [Ibid, para 57]
[64] Case C-265/04 (Opinion of AG Kokott) *Margaretha Bouanich v Skatteverket*, paras 71–73.
[65] Case C-54/99 (Opinion of AG Saggio) *Association Eglise de Scientologie de Paris and Scientology International Reserves Trust v The Prime Minister*, para 8. Not mentioned in the Court's judgment: Case C-54/99 *Association Eglise de Scientologie de Paris and Scientology International Reserves Trust v The Prime Minister*, para 2.
[66] Case C-54/99 *Association Eglise de Scientologie de Paris and Scientology International Reserves Trust v The Prime Minister*, para 14.
[67] See also Case C-446/03 *Marks & Spencer plc v David Halsey (H.M. Inspector of Taxes)*, which can also be grouped into this strand. In this case, no reference to free movement of capital was made.

A case that in principle also belongs to this strand of case law is the recent one of *Commission v Italian Republic (Re Automatic Suspension of Voting Rights in Privatised Undertaking)*.[68] The Court dealt with an Italian law suspending 'voting rights attached to holdings in excess of 2% where those holdings are acquired by public undertakings'.[69] The ECJ established that a regulation that precludes public undertakings of other Member States 'from participating effectively in the management and control of Italian undertakings'[70] restricts free movement of capital.[71] Contrary to Advocate General Kokott, who correctly suggested that the economic activity described above falls within both the ambits of freedom of establishment and free movement of capital,[72] the Court did not address the issue of freedom of establishment. The way chosen by the Court, however, does not contain an implicit statement on the relationship of the freedoms, but the silence of the Court might originate from the failure of the Commission to raise this question in the proceedings.[73]

(2) The 'Not Necessary' Strand of Case Law

If one turns to the second strand of case law, one will quickly notice that the Court drew a more indicative picture that promises to be more fruitful in terms of new insights than the one to which I referred in the previous section.

I shall start off my review with the *Konle* judgment, where the Court held that the acquisition of real property with a view to transferring principal residence and carrying on business activities within the framework of an undertaking that was already running in another Member State falls within both the ambit of free movement of capital and the freedom of establishment.[74] Since an infringement of the rules on free movement of capital was established, there was 'no need to examine' Art 43 EC *et seq*.[75] For the ECJ, it seems to suffice that a national measure is contrary to either of the two freedoms, implicitly suggesting that both rules can apply in parallel.

In *Baars*, the Court was asked to rule on the compatibility of The Netherlands' wealth tax rules, which provide for different taxation of natural persons' substantial holdings in an undertaking depending on where the company is domiciled. Mr Baars, a resident of The Netherlands, held 100 per cent of the capital of a

---

[68] Case C-174/04 *Commission v Italian Republic (Re Automatic Suspension of Voting Rights in Privatised Undertaking)*.
[69] Ibid, para 9.   [70] Ibid, para 30.   [71] Ibid, paras 26–33.
[72] Case C-174/04 (Opinion of AG Kokott) *Commission v Italian Republic (Re Automatic Suspension of Voting Rights in Privatised Undertaking)*, para 22.
[73] Ibid, para 22.
[74] Case C-302/97 *Klaus Konle v Republik Österreich*, para 22.
[75] Ibid, para 55. Advocate General *La Pergola* started from the opposite end. Being also of the opinion that the circumstances in question were subject to both freedoms [Case C-302/97 (Opinion of AG La Pergola) *Klaus Konle v Republik Österreich*, para 14 *et seq*] he began to examine them on the basis of Art 43 EC *et seq*. In light of the answers given, he found that there was no need to address the provisions on free movement of capital. [Case C-302/97 (Opinion of AG La Pergola) *Klaus Konle v Republik Österreich*, para 22] See also in respect to the acquisition of real property Case C-423/98 (Opinion of AG Cosmas) *Alfredo Albore*.

company incorporated and seated in the Republic of Ireland. The Court concluded that at least a:

> 100% holding in the capital of a company having its seat in another Member State undoubtedly brings such a taxpayer within the scope of application of the Treaty provisions on the right of establishment.[76]

Thus, the ECJ examined the Dutch wealth tax in the light of Art 43 EC *et seq.* Concerning Art 56(1) EC *et seq.*, the Court merely stated that it is '*unnecessary*' to consider the aforementioned freedom.[77]

Shortly after *Baars*, the judgment in *Commission v Italian Republic*[78] was handed down. At first glance, one might have thought that the Court had delivered a remarkable judgment, finally explicitly embracing the parallel application of the two freedoms. It declared a national measure providing for special governmental powers in privatized public undertakings, contrary to both the freedom of establishment and the free movement of capital. However, taking a closer look, one can notice that the Court did not deal with the 'typical situation'. In the case at hand, the defendant admitted the violation of the aforementioned provisions right from the beginning, and it was obvious that national measures taken in order to comply with the requirements of the Treaty were delayed. Although the case is atypical, it nevertheless provides us with an indication that the Court was willing to perceive the relationship of the two freedoms as parallel in nature.

---

[76] Case C-251/98 *C Baars v Inspecteur der Belastingen Particulieren/Ondernemingen Gorinchem*, para 21.

[77] Ibid, para 42 Advocate General Alber, in his Opinion, developed his own approach on how to deal with the relationship of Arts 43 EC and 56 EC. He stated: 'These observations on the respective ambits of the free movement of capital and the right of establishment may be summarised as follows: 1. Where the free movement of capital is *directly* restricted such that only an *indirect* obstacle to establishment is created, only the rules on capital movements apply. 2. Where the right of establishment is *directly* restricted such that the ensuing obstacle to establishment leads *indirectly* to a reduction of capital flows between Member States, only the rules on the right of establishment apply. [Case C-251/98 (Opinion of AG Alber) *C Baars v Inspecteur der Belastingen Particulieren/Ondernemingen Gorinchem*, para 26] … 3. Where there is *direct* intervention affecting both the free movement of capital and the right of establishment, both fundamental freedoms apply, and the national measure must satisfy the requirements of both.' [Emphases added, Case C-251/98 (Opinion of AG Alber) *C Baars v Inspecteur der Belastingen Particulieren/Ondernemingen Gorinchem*, para 30]

In *Baars,* Advocate General Alber came to the conclusion that: '[C]ontrary to the position in regard to the right of establishment, the size of the shareholding acquired is immaterial [in the ambit of free movement of capital]. The provisions in question afford protection even when all a company's shares are held or acquired, since otherwise the protection enjoyed by an investor would be inversely proportional to the size of his shareholding. However, if the holding in a company reaches a size which enables the investor to exercise a decisive influence over the undertaking's decision-making, the right of establishment will *supplement* free movement of capital. Such an investment would then additionally fulfil the criteria set out in Article 52(2) [EC], and would be protected by the EC Treaty under *two* separate heads.' [Emphasis added; Case C-251/98 (Opinion of AG Alber) *C Baars v Inspecteur der Belastingen Particulieren/Ondernemingen Gorinchem*, para 50]

[78] Case C-58/99 *Commission v Italian Republic (Re Grant of Special Powers in Privatised Publik Undertakings).*

The Court resumed the 'not necessary' language in its *X and Y* [79] judgment. The ECJ dealt with the tax implications of a transfer of shares without consideration or at undervalue to a company that the transferor either directly or indirectly held. The Swedish tax provision applied two different tax regimes, one demanding the imminent payment of taxes due on the transfer, and the other deferring taxation until a later point. The former regime shall apply if the transferee is a foreign legal person or a Swedish legal person controlled directly or indirectly by a foreign legal person; the latter applies to the situation in which the transferee is a Swedish legal person.[80] This creates a cash-flow advantage for the transferee without any foreign participation.[81] Having found that the Swedish tax regime was contrary to the freedom of establishment, the Court proceeded to examine the national rules against the background of free movement of capital only to the extent that they were not already contrary to the rules of freedom of establishment.[82]

What can be drawn from the abovementioned judgments is that, for the Court, the subjecting a national rule to one freedom did not rule out the applicability of the other, but it is the finding that a national measure is contrary to one of the two freedoms that rendered it needless also to measure it against the other freedom, whereby 'needless' seemed to mean nothing more than that it was 'not worth spending the time' to consider the case in the light of another freedom when it does not alter the result.[83]

The so-called *'Golden Shares'* judgments[84] also belong to the 'not necessary' strand of case law, although a change in language is looming. In each of the

---

[79] Case C-436/00 *X and Y v Riksskatteverket*.
[80] Case C-436/00 (Opinion of AG Mischo) *X and Y v Riksskatteverket*, para 3 *et seq*.
[81] Ibid, para 25.
[82] Case C-436/00 *X and Y v Riksskatteverket*, para 66 *et seq*; applying the same reasoning Case C-268/03 *Jean-Claude De Baeck v Kingdom of Belgium*; see also Joined Cases C-397/98 and C-410/98 *Metallgesellschaft Ltd and Others, Hoechst AG and Hoechst (UK) Ltd v Commissioners of Inland Revenue and H.M. Attorney General*.
[83] See also Case C-436/00 (Opinion of AG Mischo) *X and Y v Riksskatteverket*.
[84] Case C-367/98 *Commission v Portuguese Republic (Re Golden Shares I)*; Case C-483/99 *Commission v French Republic (Re Golden Shares II)*; Case C-503/99 *Commission v Kingdom of Belgium (Re Golden Shares III)*; Case C-98/01 *Commission v United Kingdom (Re Golden Shares V)*. See also the Opinion of Advocate General Colomer, who used to be of the opinion that both freedoms apply in parallel. [Case C-367/98, C-483/99, and C-503/99 (Joined Opinion of AG Colomer) *Commission v Portuguese Republic, French Republic and Kingdom of Belgium (Re Golden Shares I-III)*, paras 28, 30] The same Advocate General, however, stated in one of his subsequent opinions [Case C-463/00 and C-98/01 (Opinion of AG Colomer) *Commission v Kingdom of Spain and United Kingdom (Re Golden Shares IV and V)*, para 36] the following: 'First, I continue to hold the view that the natural and appropriate framework within which to consider the various restrictions deriving from what can, very imprecisely, be described as golden shares is *freedom of establishment*. In each case, what the defendant Member State is seeking to control, using powers of intervention as regards share structure, transfer of assets or certain management decisions, is the formation of the privatised company's corporate will (either by intervening in the composition of the membership or by influencing specific management decisions), *an aspect which has little to do with the free movement of capital* referred to in Article 56 EC. Such powers may affect the right to freedom of establishment and make it less attractive, either directly where they impinge on access to share capital, or indirectly, where they reduce its allure by restricting the powers of the board

Parallelism or Exclusivity

cases, national legislation that reserved certain rights for national governments to approve or disapprove investments in formerly state-owned companies or to intervene in the event of undesired managerial decisions was scrutinized. The Court chose to examine this national legislation against the background of Art 56(1) EC. When turning to the freedom of establishment, this time the ECJ did not content itself with a simple statement that the examination of the national provisions in the light of Art 43 EC was not necessary in consideration of the result reached with respect to free movement of capital. In each case except for one,[85] in almost identical wording, it stated in regard to the freedom of establishment that:

> it is appropriate to point out that insofar as the rules in question entail restrictions on freedom of establishment, such restrictions are a direct consequence of the obstacles to the free movement of capital considered above, to which they are inextricably linked. Consequently, since an infringement of Article 56 EC has been established, there is no need for a separate examination of the measures at issue in the light of the Treaty rules concerning freedom of establishment.[86]

Although this formulation now contains the 'forerunners' of a 'centre of gravity' approach—discussed in more detail further below—it can be still taken as reflecting the spirit of the 'not necessary' strand of case law. In contrast to later judgments, it speaks of 'direct' instead of 'unavoidable'[87] consequences, and it merely explains that there is 'no need for separate examination'; later on, the Court will hold that there is no justification for an independent examination of the respective other freedom. Thus, the *Golden Shares* judgments can still be read as a confirmation of parallel application of the freedoms on the level of their scope of application.

If one wants to look for a particular case in which the shift in the doctrinal approach of the Court is well exemplified, then one must refer to *Fidium Finanz AG*,[88] the first case in which free movement of capital competed with another

---

of directors relating to the ownership or management of the company. Contrary to the Court of Justice's finding, *the resulting restriction of the free movement of capital is incidental, rather than inevitable*. If that is the case as regards measures affecting the composition of the membership, it is even more true as regards measures restricting the adoption of company resolutions (change of company object, disposal of assets). In the latter cases, *the link with the free movement of capital is hypothetical or very tenuous*.' [Footnotes omitted, emphasis added].

[85] Case C-503/99 *Commission v Kingdom of Belgium (Re Golden Shares III)*; see also JA Usher, 'Financial Services', 255 *et seq*.

[86] Case C-367/98 *Commission v Portuguese Republic (Re Golden Shares I)*, para 56; Case C-483/99 *Commission v French Republic (Re Golden Shares II)*, para 56; Case C-98/01 *Commission v United Kingdom (Re Golden Shares V)*, para 52.

[87] Note in this respect the Opinion of Advocate General Colomer, which—before the Court adopted its 'centre of gravity approach' within the relationship of free movement of capital and freedom of establishment—already suggested applying such an approach. [Case C-463/00 and C-98/01 (Opinion of AG Colomer) *Commission v Kingdom of Spain and United Kingdom (Re Golden Shares IV and V)*, para 36 reproduced above in footnote 84 of this Chapter]. Note also his opinion on Case C-112/05 (Opinion AG Colomer) *Commission v Germany (Re Golden Shares VII 'Volkswagengesetz')*, para 58 *et seq*.

[88] Case C-452/04 *Fidium Finanz AG*; for an excellent account of the decision see: M O'Brien, 'Case Note C-452/04'.

freedom in a third country context. The Advocate General and Court found themselves on opposite sides of the trench separating the different opinions of how to solve the issue of competing freedoms.

In *Fidium Finanz AG,* a company limited by shares, established under Swiss law and registered in and administered from Switzerland, granted small-scale loans entirely to German consumers. The company was not subject to Swiss banking supervision.[89] The competent German authority (*BaFin*) ordered it to cease operations due to the fact that the company's activities were not authorized, authorization being subject to the condition that the central administration or at least a branch be physically present in the national territory.[90]

Even though the conflict in *Fidium Finanz AG* was essentially about the relationship of free movement of capital and the freedom to provide services, the opinion of Advocate General Stix-Hackl seems to go beyond this point. Her statements are repeatedly phrased in a very general form, ie, apparently also describing the relationship of free movement of capital to other freedoms. Her submissions are particularly noteworthy with respect to one point. The Advocate General spelled out in clear words what the result of a displacement of free movement of capital in a third country context would be:

If reliance on Art. 56 EC in relation to undertakings in third countries were automatically to be ruled out whenever another fundamental freedom is involved because of the subject-matter in question, the guarantees provided by the free movement of capital would be meaningless.[91]

(3) The 'Centre of Gravity' Approach

While the Court was still deliberating on *Fidium Finanz AG*, the judgment in the *Cadbury Schweppes*[92] case was delivered. In *Cadbury Schweppes*, in an intra-Community context, national legislation on controlled foreign companies ('CFCs') that 'involves a difference in the treatment of resident companies on the basis of the level of taxation imposed on the company in which they have a controlling holding' was challenged.[93] In a nutshell, where the controlled company has been incorporated and taxed in the United Kingdom or in a State in which it is not subject to a lower level of taxation within the meaning of the UK's CFCs legislation, the controlling resident company enjoys a tax advantage compared to those resident companies that have a controlling interest in a company resident in another Member State with a lower level of taxation than the one foreseen in the CFCs legislation.[94]

---

[89] Case C-452/04 (Opinion of AG Stix-Hackl) *Fidium Finanz AG*, para 26.
[90] Ibid, para 28 *et seq*.   [91] Ibid, para 74.
[92] Case C-196/04 *Cadbury Schweppes and Cadbury Schweppes Overseas Ltd v Commissioners of Inland Revenue*.
[93] Ibid, para 43.
[94] Ibid, para 43 *et seq*.

The Court—when it came to the question of the applicable freedoms—headed for Art 43 EC. It explained that 'the legislation on CFCs concerns the taxation, under certain conditions, of the profits of subsidiaries established outside the United Kingdom in which a resident company has *a controlling holding*'.[95]

Thus, due to the fact that the aforementioned legislation applied only to holdings that give the holder definite influence over the holding's activities, in accordance with the settled case law,[96] such legislation had to be examined in the light of the freedom of establishment.

When turning to other potentially applicable freedoms, renouncing its original 'not necessary' language, the Court succinctly noted that if:

legislation has restrictive effects on…the free movement of capital, such effects are an *unavoidable consequence* of any restriction on freedom of establishment and do not justify, *in any event*, an independent examination of that legislation in the light of…[Art.] 56 EC.[97]

Without further explanation on this statement, the Court left its audience behind with not much more than a sense of foreboding that the rising tide was about to flow in, bringing to pass major change. The ones who might have taken comfort in the fact that in the case at issue—being an intra-Community case—it did not really matter, in the spirit of the 'not necessary' strand of case law, which freedom was applicable and perhaps in the hope that only a change in rhetoric had to be coped with, did not need to wait for long to be disabused of their comfort.

Only a few weeks after the judgment in *Cadbury Schweppes* was handed down, the Court ruled on *Fidium Finanz AG*.[98]

I have already examined Advocate General Stix-Hackl's Opinion[99] on *Fidium Finanz AG*, which argued in favour of parallel applicability of the relevant freedoms. Although the case concerns the relationship of free movement of capital and the freedom to provide services, it appears that general lessons can also be learned from the judgment. In retrospect, the tide was actually starting to flow in. The case foreshadowed an argumentative approach to the solution of the issue of competing freedoms in a third country context that was subsequently applied to the relationship of the freedom of establishment and free movement of capital.[100]

---

[95] [Emphasis added] Ibid, para 32.
[96] Ibid., para 31 citing Case C-251/98 *C. Baars v Inspecteur der Belastingen Particulieren/Ondernemingen Gorinchem*, para 22; Case C-436/00 *X and Y v Riksskatteverket*, para 37.
[97] [Emphasis added] Case C-196/04 (Opinion of AG Léger) *Cadbury Schweppes and Cadbury Schweppes Overseas Ltd v Commissioners of Inland Revenue*, para 33 citing Case C-36/02 *Omega Spielhallen- und Automatenaufstellungs-GmbH v Oberbürgermeisterin der Bundesstadt Bonn*, 27; note also Case C-196/04 *Cadbury Schweppes and Cadbury Schweppes Overseas Ltd v Commissioners of Inland Revenue*, para 31 *et seq*.
[98] Case C-452/04 *Fidium Finanz AG*.
[99] Case C-452/04 (Opinion of AG Stix-Hackl) *Fidium Finanz AG*.
[100] Already predicted by C Ohler, 'Anmerkung zu EuGH C-452/04', 693; discussing the effects on tax law: J Schönfeld, 'Anmerkung zu C-452/04', 81 *et seq*.

In the case at hand, the ECJ opened up the discussion on the relationship of the freedom to provide services and free movement of capital by stating that it

will in principle examine the measure in dispute in relation to *only one* of those two freedoms *if* it appears, *in the circumstances of the case, that one of them is entirely secondary* in relation to the other and may be considered together with it.[101]

Having at first found that 'the activity of granting credit on a commercial basis concerns, in principle, both the freedom to provide services within the meaning of Art. 49 EC *et seq.* and the free movement of capital within the meaning of Art. 56 EC *et seq.*'[102]—hence confirming in principle that both freedoms are to be applied in parallel[103]—the Court did not pause there for a moment. The Court continued its line of argument by attempting to create the illusion that the two aspects of the economic activity of granting credit on a commercial basis are distinguishable and 'quantifiable' on a rational basis, with the consequence that one freedom takes precedence over the other because the latter 'is entirely secondary in relation to the other and may be considered together with it'.[104] For this purpose it chose a 'centre of gravity' approach.

The Court observed that the purpose of the applicable national rules is to authorize and supervise the provision of services.[105] The requirement of a permanent establishment for a service provider, stipulated by the national regulation, prevented the market participant from rendering their services on the German market. If the service provider were not established in Switzerland but within the Community, the national measure would undoubtedly amount to a restriction on the freedom to provide services. The reduction of 'cross-border financial traffic relating to those services'[106] is of secondary importance. The restrictions on financial transfers are 'merely an unavoidable consequence of the restriction on the freedom to provide services.'[107]

---

[101] [Emphasis added] Case C-452/04 *Fidium Finanz AG*, para 34 citing (by analogy) Case C-275/92 *H.M. Customs and Excise v Gerhart Schindler and Jörg Schindler*, para 22; Case C-390/99 *Canal Satélite Digital SL v Administración General del Estado, and Distribuidora de Televisión Digital SA (DTS)*, para 31; Case C-71/02 *Herbert Karner Industrie-Auktionen GmbH v Troostwijk GmbH*, para 46; Case C-36/02 *Omega Spielhallen- und Automatenaufstellungs-GmbH v Oberbürgermeisterin der Bundesstadt Bonn*, para 26; Case C-20/03 *Criminal proceedings against Marcel Burmanjer, René Alexander Van Der Linden and Anthony De Jong*, para 35 all on the relationship of free movement of goods and the freedom to provide services.

[102] [Emphases added] Case C-452/04 *Fidium Finanz AG*, para 43 citing with respect to the freedom to provide services: Case C-484/93 *Peter Svensson et Lena Gustavsson v Ministre du Logement et de l'Urbanisme*, para 11; Case C-222/95 *Société civile immobilière Parodi v Banque H. Albert de Bary et Cie*; with regard to free movement of capital: Annex I, Heading VIII of Directive 88/361/EEC.

[103] So also M Dreher and A Görner, 'Art. 49 EG 1/07', 43.

[104] Case C-452/04 *Fidium Finanz AG*, para 34.

[105] Ibid, para 45.   [106] Ibid, para 48.

[107] Ibid citing Case C-36/02 *Omega Spielhallen- und Automatenaufstellungs-GmbH v Oberbürgermeisterin der Bundesstadt Bonn*, para 27; Case C-196/04 *Cadbury Schweppes and*

Looking at the argumentative structure, the Court first reasons from the purposes of the national rules (or better, from their intended regulatory ambit) the (alleged) effect on the economic activities of the market participant. Second, from the latter it extrapolates back to the applicable freedom.[108] This led the Court in the case at hand to the conclusion that the provisions of free movement of capital were not primarily affected and that, therefore, it did not deserve to be considered independently.[109]

It goes without saying that such an interpretation has severe consequences for third country market participants; one could perhaps call them 'third country wannabe market participants'. The supersession in such a context of the only freedom that also applies to third countries leads to the result that the scope of protection of the Treaty is strictly limited to intra-Community movements.[110] In the words of one commentator, the ECJ wanted to silence the 'third country debate'.[111] The way the Court chose to do so, however, is more than merely questionable.[112]

The Court—most likely out of political considerations[113]—engaged in a vague and fuzzy delineation test. The result of this test is that market participants placed in a third country context and involved in a cross-sectional activity do not have their cases considered in the light of free movement of capital—which had involved, inter alia, a balancing process of differing interests within the proportionality test—and are deprived of any protection potentially offered by the Treaty.

To start with, how would the Court have responded if the national regulation had not been aimed at the service provider but at the capital, for example, by requiring a 'declaration of no objection' in the individual case where the capital, which is used for granting a loan, does not originate from illegal activities? Is it still so clear that a restriction on financial transfer is 'merely an unavoidable consequence of the restriction on the freedom to provide services'? Could it not reasonably be argued that restrictions on the service of granting loans are merely an unavoidable consequence of the controls on transfer of capital?

While the economic activity and the effect on the market participant in both situations, ie, the one at issue in *Fidium Finanz AG* and the other chosen for the sake of argument, is the same, the applicable freedom would differ, with the outcome for the market participant being rather accidental. By extrapolating from the purpose of the national measure (ie, the intended regulatory ambit) to

---

Cadbury Schweppes Overseas Ltd v Commissioners of Inland Revenue, para 33 and by analogy Case C-204/90 *Hanns-Martin Bachmann v The Belgian State*, para 34.

[108] Case C-452/04 (Opinion of AG Stix-Hackl) *Fidium Finanz AG*, para 45, 49.
[109] Ibid, 49.   [110] *Cf* J Sedemund, 'Grundfreiheiten', 2784.
[111] C Ohler, 'Anmerkung zu EuGH C-452/04', 692.
[112] J Sedemund, 'Grundfreiheiten', 2784; M Dreher and A Görner, 'Art. 49 EG 1/07', 44.
[113] J Sedemund, 'Grundfreiheiten', 2784.

the effect on the economic activity (and back again to the applicable freedom), the Court places emphasis on the final encroachments intended by the national measure on the movement, characterizing factual effects as 'unavoidable consequences' and thus masking them out; however, it reserved itself a loophole by defining the purpose of the national measure and what constitutes an 'unavoidable consequence'.[114] Regardless, it appears that the Court's approach allows the Member State to decide implicitly on the applicable freedom simply by choosing a certain regulatory approach.[115]

In addition, the argumentative structure of the Court appears debatable on fundamental grounds. The characteristics of a certain kind of economic activity of the market participant—not the regulatory purpose, regulatory ambit, and ultimately the intended encroachments flowing from the national measure—must decide the opening up of the scope of application of a certain freedom. An encroachment cannot inform its own object, but presupposes its existence.[116]

From the perspective of *Fidium Finanz AG*, its economic activity can be understood as the provision of services as well as the allocation of capital to the place where it generates the highest return. The services rendered in the case at hand, besides some advice and account-keeping, mainly consist of the acceptance of a risk for a certain return, which is also the main determinant when it comes to the allocation of capital.[117] Seen from this perspective, it is difficult to comprehend why the economic activity relates predominantly to the freedom to provide services rather than to free movement of capital. It appears, rather, that not only the Court's doctrinal approach but also its view of the freedom of movement of capital as in essence protecting merely 'cross border financial traffic'[118] is a skewed and biased understanding.

The Court could and should instead have chosen to approach the issue of third country market participants by means of giving particular attention to the question of comparability of intra-Community and third country circumstances or by way of giving sufficient consideration to the situation on the level of grounds of justification.[119] Such an approach would not have deprived the market participant

---

[114] *Cf* in this respect, eg, Case C-390/99 *Canal Satélite Digital SL v Administración General del Estado, and Distribuidora de Televisión Digital SA (DTS)*, para 31 *et seq*.

[115] In the same direction: A Dölker and M Ribbrock, 'Kapitalverkehrsfreiheit', 1931.

[116] In the same direction: Case C-452/04 (Opinion of AG Stix-Hackl) *Fidium Finanz AG*, para 72; RM Cadosch, et al, 'Cross-Border Dividends', 634; in fundamental terms: M Sachs, 'Gewährleistungsgehalt', III.1 b) ß); implicitly along similar lines: T Kingreen, *Struktur der Grundfreiheiten*, 76 *et seq*, 78, 82 *et seq*; note also R Alexy, *Grundrechte*, 273 *et seq*; embracing the Court's construction: R Lyal, *Free Movement of Capital*, 3 *et seq*.

[117] Concurring M Dreher and A Görner, 'Art. 49 EG 1/07', 44; J Sedemund, 'Grundfreiheiten', 2784. Also mentioning this, but ultimately arguing along lines similar to the ECJ: C Ohler, 'Anmerkung zu EuGH C-452/04', 692.

[118] Case C-452/04 *Fidium Finanz AG*, para 48.

[119] See for a discussion of such approaches: Chapter IV. 2. b. (4), Chapter VI. 2. b, and Chapter VII.

in a third country context of any protection, and on the other hand, it would have provided the ECJ with considerably more room to manoeuvre without having to invent scarcely convincing delineation tests.

While *Fidium Finanz AG* concerned the relation of free movement of capital and the freedom to provide services, the English Group Litigation cases, in particular *Test Claimants in the FII Group Litigation* and *Test Claimants in the Thin Cap Group Litigation*, dealt specifically with the freedom of establishment and its relation to free movement of capital.

The Test Claimants in the FII Group Litigation case, broadly speaking, was concerned with franked investment income (FII) of companies resident in the United Kingdom that held shares in companies resident in other Member States or in third countries. The test claimants alleged that in each of the various situations presented to the Court, nationally sourced dividends, ie, dividends received by a resident company from a company that is also resident in this State, are treated more favourably than foreign-sourced dividends, which relate to dividends paid by a non-resident to a resident company.[120]

The first question dealt with by the Court was whether it is, in an intra-Community context, compatible with Community law to apply 'an exception system in the case of nationally-sourced dividends and an imputation system in the case of foreign-sourced dividends'.[121] The resident companies selected as test claimants and receiving foreign-sourced dividends either held 100 per cent of the shares in the distributing company[122] or the nature of their holding was unknown.[123]

As a preliminary statement on the applicable freedoms in the case at hand, the Court explained that, in principle, national legislation that makes the receipt of dividends liable to tax, as well as the tax base and the possibility of deductions depending on the residence of the source, may fall into both the freedom of establishment and free movement of capital.[124] However, in case the receiving company's holding puts it in a position to exercise definite influence over the holding's decisions and allows it to determine its activities, which is undoubtedly so in the case of a 100 per cent stake, the freedom of establishment will apply.[125] With respect to a holding that 'does not give them definite influence over the decisions

---

[120] Note also Case C-201/05 *The Test Claimants in the CFC and Dividend Group Litigation v Commissioners of Inland Revenue*.

[121] Case C-446/04 *Test Claimants in the FII Group Litigation v Commissioners of Inland Revenue*, paras 33, 42, 61.

[122] Ibid, para 37. [123] Ibid, para 38. [124] Ibid, para 36.

[125] Ibid, para 37; note also Case C-446/04 (Opinion of AG Geelhoed) *Test Claimants in the FII Group Litigation v Commissioners of Inland Revenue*, para 31; a similar configuration can be found in Case C-374/04 *Test Claimants in Class IV of the ACT Group Litigation (Pirelli, Essilor and Sony), Test Claimants in Class IV of the ACT Group Litigation (BMW) v Commissioners of Inland Revenue*, para 39; Case C-347/04 (Opinion of AG Maduro) *Rewe Zentralfinanz eG, as Universal Legal Successor of ITS Reisen GmbH v Finanzamt Köln-Mitte*, para 22.

of the company making the distribution and does not allow them to determine its activities',[126] free movement of capital may apply.[127]

Having considered the above, one could think that the Court wanted to suggest that the freedom of establishment shall apply exclusively to (dividends flowing from) direct investments, as understood in this study, and free movement of capital to (such flowing from) portfolio investments. Since, however, ultimately it did not make a difference with respect to the findings of which freedom was to apply in an intra-Community context—the ECJ itself referred in its discussion on Art 56(1) EC to its findings with respect to Art 43 EC[128]—with some goodwill, one could argue that at this stage in the judgment, the Court merely stated the obvious. Free movement of capital is the only freedom applicable to dividend payments out of portfolio investments, and due to the lack of difference in results, the discussion of dividend payments flowing from direct investment in the light of Art 43 EC rendered it unnecessary to refer in this respect again to Art 56(1) EC. The Court did not rule out the possibility that direct investment could also be considered within the ambit of free movement of capital.[129]

In the second part of the fourth question,[130] the Court turned to the consideration of third country contexts. The respective national legislation applied irrespective of the size of the holding by the resident company.[131] The test claimants, as already mentioned above, comprised both resident companies that exercised definite control over their holdings and others that—it must be assumed—did not.[132] Finally, the Court had to take a clear stand on the question of whether free movement of capital applies not only to portfolio but also to direct investments; Art 43 EC, due to its limited territorial scope, is not applicable.

---

[126] Case C-446/04 *Test Claimants in the FII Group Litigation v Commissioners of Inland Revenue*, para 38; note also Case C-446/04 (Opinion of AG Geelhoed) *Test Claimants in the FII Group Litigation v Commissioners of Inland Revenue*, para 32. A similar configuration can be found in Case C-374/04 *Test Claimants in Class IV of the ACT Group Litigation (Pirelli, Essilor and Sony), Test Claimants in Class IV of the ACT Group Litigation (BMW) v Commissioners of Inland Revenue*, para 40. In Case C-347/04 *Rewe Zentralfinanz eG, as Universal Legal Successor of ITS Reisen GmbH v Finanzamt Köln-Mitte*, para 71 the Court stated that it was 'not necessary to consider whether the provisions of the Treaty relating to free movement of capital also preclude that legislation' due to the fact that the legislation at issue was already precluded by virtue of Art 43 EC.

[127] The answers provided by the Court to questions two, three, and the first part of question four, all intra-Community questions, did not vary in substance on the issue of the applicable freedom but only diverged slightly in their wording. [Case C-446/04 *Test Claimants in the FII Group Litigation v Commissioners of Inland Revenue*, paras 80, 81, 95, 117 *et seq*, 131, 142 *et seq*, 165]

[128] Ibid, para 60.

[129] This interpretation seems to be confirmed by Case C-347/04 *Rewe Zentralfinanz eG, as Universal Legal Successor of ITS Reisen GmbH v Finanzamt Köln-Mitte*, para 22 *et seq*, 71, where the Court delivered a judgment in the classic style of the 'not necessary' strand of case law. Note also Case C-347/04 (Opinion of AG Maduro) *Rewe Zentralfinanz eG, as Universal Legal Successor of ITS Reisen GmbH v Finanzamt Köln-Mitte*, para 13 *et seq*, 61 *et seq*.

[130] Case C-446/04 *Test Claimants in the FII Group Litigation v Commissioners of Inland Revenue*, para 165 *et seq*.

[131] Ibid, para 142.   [132] Ibid, para 142 *et seq*.

The Court held:

Insofar as, according to the national court, that question also concerns companies established in non-member countries which, accordingly, do not fall within the scope of Art. 43 EC on freedom of establishment,..., the question arises whether national measures such as those at issue in the main proceedings also contravene Art. 56 EC on the free movement of capital.[133]

Having posed this question, the ECJ entered into a discussion of the legislation in the light of free movement of capital in substantive terms, referencing its statements made with respect to Art 43 EC in an intra-Community context.

It seemed—recalling that the group of test claimants also comprised dividends received from wholly owned subsidiaries in third counties—that the ECJ wanted to consider portfolio and direct investment—at least in third country contexts—in the light of free movement of capital. This conclusion could rest on the application of Art 57(1) EC to the case at hand—the provision constituting a grandfathering clause, inter alia, for national measures encroaching upon third country direct investments[134]—which otherwise would hardly make any sense.[135]

After this ruling, one might have thought the 'worst-case-scenario', as envisaged after the ruling in *Fidium Finanz AG*, did not actually materialize in the relationship of free movement of capital and the freedom of establishment. It took the Court only another three months to turn this view upside down.

In *Test Claimants in the Thin Cap Group Litigation*, the British provisions regarding thin capitalization were at issue. These provided:

that, in some circumstances, interest paid by a company to another company belonging to the same group with respect to a loan granted by the latter is to be treated as a distribution, thereby prohibiting the borrowing company from deducting the interest paid from its taxable profits.[136]

The re-characterisation of interest payments as distributions can increase the liability of the borrowing company to tax. The national legislation distinguished borrowing companies according to whether or not the related lending company is established in the United Kingdom.

Considering first the intra-Community context, the ECJ analysed the scope of application of the national tax legislation.[137] Having found that it applied only to

---

[133] Ibid, para 165.   [134] Ibid, para 174 *et seq*.
[135] Although the Court, when examining Art 57(1) EC, confined its statements to the national provisions, 'to the extent to which they also constitute restrictions on capital movements prohibited in principle by Art. 56 EC,' [Ibid, para 174] this reference must be read in conjunction with the aforesaid on the applicability of Art 56(1) EC with respect to third countries.
[136] Case C-524/04 *Test Claimants in the Thin Cap Group Litigation*, para 38.
[137] Ibid, para 27 *et seq*. As a 'moreover argument', the Court also pointed to the selected test claimants, which all had direct or indirect holdings of 75% and more in the borrowing companies. [Case C-524/04 *Test Claimants in the Thin Cap Group Litigation*, para 32]

the situation in which the lending company has definite influence on the borrowing company or is itself controlled by a company that has such influence, the Court concluded that such legislation '*primarily* affects freedom of establishment'.[138]

If the ECJ had stopped there, its conclusion would not have been particularly worrisome; it would still leave sufficient room for an interpretation in the spirit of the 'not necessary' strand of case law. However, this time the ECJ wanted to 'rub it in'. Borrowing from *Fidium Finanz AG* it held:

> If... it were to be accepted that that legislation has restrictive effects on ... the free movement of capital, such effects must be seen as an unavoidable consequence of any restriction on freedom of establishment and do not justify an independent examination of that legislation in the light of [Art.] 56 EC The questions referred to should therefore be answered in the light of Art. 43 EC *alone*.[139]

For those who still met the Court with some disbelief, it put the rule to the test and applied its 'centre of gravity' approach to the third country context in the case at hand. First, the Court explained the obvious, ie, that for Art 43 EC to apply, the lending company must either be identical to an established EC parent company controlling the borrowing company, or the borrowing company and the lending company must both be controlled directly or indirectly by an EC-established parent company. Insofar as the company that either directly or indirectly controls the funding decisions is not established in a Member State for the purposes of Art 48 EC, Art 43 EC is not applicable.[140]

Continuing with the examination of the other freedoms, similar to the ruling in *Fidium Finanz AG*,[141] the Court limited itself to the predictable statement that the legislation at issue is targeted only at relations within a group of companies. Hence, it would primarily affect freedom of establishment. Possible effects on the free movement of capital 'must be seen as an unavoidable consequence of any restriction on freedom of establishment and do not justify an independent examination of that legislation in the light of... [Art.] 56 EC'.[142]

---

[138] [Emphasis added] Case C-524/04 *Test Claimants in the Thin Cap Group Litigation*, para 33 citing Case C-196/04 *Cadbury Schweppes and Cadbury Schweppes Overseas Ltd v Commissioners of Inland Revenue*, para 32; Case C-446/04 *Test Claimants in the FII Group Litigation v Commissioners of Inland Revenue*, para 118.

[139] [Emphasis added] Case C-524/04 *Test Claimants in the Thin Cap Group Litigation*, para 34 *et seq*.

[140] Ibid, para 97 *et seq*.

[141] *Cf* J Schönfeld, 'Anmerkung zu C-524/04', 260.

[142] Case C-524/04 *Test Claimants in the Thin Cap Group Litigation*, para 101; confirmed in: Case C-492/04 *Lasertec Gesellschaft für Stanzformen mbH (formerly Riess Laser Bandstahlschnitte GmbH) v Finanzamt Emmendingen)*, para 25; Case C-102/05 *Skatteverket v A and B*, para 27; in an intra-community context: Case C-415/06 *Stahlwerk Ergste Westig GmbH v Finanzamt Düsseldorf-Mettmann*, para 15 *et seq*; Case C-414/06 *Lidl Belgium GmbH & Co. KG v Finanzamt Heilbronn*, para 2, 15 *et seq*; Case C-231/05 *Oy AA*, para 21 *et seq*; astonished: W Müller, 'EU-Grundfreiheiten', 119; critical: A Rainer, 'Anmerkung zu EuGH C-524/04', 259; J Schönfeld, 'Anmerkung zu C-524/04'. Note also J Schönfeld, 'Anmerkung zu C-157/05 (Holböck)', 443 who is of the opinion

If one tries to draw a conclusion from the above statement, one might think—at first sight reversing the result reached in the *Test Claimants in the FII Group Litigation* case—that the Court now wanted to tell us that direct investment, as understood in this study, in third country contexts is not protected by the Treaty due to the exclusivity of Art 43 EC.

However, such a conclusion was proven to be premature. The Court in the Austrian case *Holböck*[143] added another not necessarily surprising but doctrinally hardly comprehensible facet to its evolving case law on the relationship of free movement of capital to the other freedoms in third country contexts.

The Austrian case *Holböck*[144] dealt with the same national tax rules on revenue from capital—'dividends distributed to natural persons by companies which are established in Austria are subject to tax at a rate of half the average rate, while foreign dividends are subject to full taxation'[145]—that were already held contrary to Community law in *Lenz*.[146] While *Holböck* concerns the applicability of those rules to a third country context, the judgment in *Lenz* is confined to revenue from capital from other Member States.

For my purposes an interesting fact is that Mr Holböck received the dividends from a public company established in Switzerland in which he held two thirds of the share capital.[147] Having noted that, it does not come as a surprise that the argument concerning which freedom(s) should govern the decision arose before the Court. While the French and Netherlands governments suggested treating the case in the light of the freedom of establishment alone, Mr Holböck and the Commission claimed that the national legislation constitutes a restriction on free movement of capital.

The Court in its judgment—declaring the following to be well established case law—noted that 'it is clear...that the purpose of the legislation concerned must be taken into consideration in order to determine the applicable freedoms'.[148] It

---

that the Court refined its jurisprudence in Case C-492/04 *Lasertec Gesellschaft für Stanzformen mbH (formerly Riess Laser Bandstahlschnitte GmbH) v Finanzamt Emmendingen*) in such a way that in the event that the national measure accidentally also covers portfolio investments the Court has (in a second analytical step) recourse to the actual economic activity undertaken by the market participant in order to verify whether the market participant is in a position to exercise control. I, however, have problems in drawing this from the aforementioned judgment. Further clarification by the Court is necessary.

[143] Case C-157/05 *Winfried Holböck v Finanzamt Salzburg-Land*. See for a similar factual situation, treated along the same lines as *Holböck*, but in an intra-Community context: Case C-298/05 *Columbus Container Services BVBA & Co. v Finanzamt Bielefeld-Innenstadt*, paras 29 *et seq*, 55 *et seq*.
[144] Case C-157/05 *Winfried Holböck v Finanzamt Salzburg-Land*.
[145] Ibid, para 12.
[146] Case C-315/02 *Anneliese Lenz v Finanzlandesdirektion für Tirol*.
[147] Case C-157/05 *Winfried Holböck v Finanzamt Salzburg-Land*, para 9.
[148] Ibid, para 22 citing in support Case C-196/04 *Cadbury Schweppes and Cadbury Schweppes Overseas Ltd v Commissioners of Inland Revenue*, para 31 *et seq*; Case C-452/04 *Fidium Finanz AG*, paras 34, 44 *et seq*; Case C-374/04 *Test Claimants in Class IV of the ACT Group Litigation (Pirelli, Essilor and Sony), Test Claimants in Class IV of the ACT Group Litigation (BMW) v Commissioners of Inland Revenue*, para 37 *et seq*; Case C-446/04 *Test Claimants in the FII Group*

continued, unlike the situations in *Cadbury Schweppes*[149] and *Claimants in the Thin Cap Group Litigation*[150]

the Austrian legislation in the present case is not intended to apply *only* to those shareholdings which enable the holder to have a definite influence on a company's decisions and to determine its activities.[151]

Hence, such national legislation as applies irrespective of the extent of the holding may fall under Art 43 EC as well as Art 56(1) EC.[152]

With respect to Art 43 EC, the Court explained that although the provision, inter alia, 'prohibit[s] the Member State of origin from hindering the establishment in another Member State of one of its nationals or a company incorporated under its legislation',[153] the freedom does not extend to establishment in a third country, and therefore does not apply to the case at hand.[154] The actual size of the market participant's holding in the case at hand was not deemed necessary to be considered in this relationship.

Turning to the discussion of the facts in the light of free movement of capital, the ECJ relied on its ruling in *Lenz,* stating that 'such legislation constitutes a restriction on the free movement of capital that is, in principle, prohibited by Art. 56(1) EC'.[155] Most noteworthy is the pronouncement that:

a Member State national who holds two thirds of the share capital of a company established in a non-member country is justified in invoking the prohibition of restrictions on the movement of capital between Member States and non-member countries set out in Art. 56(1) EC.

Although the freedom of establishment, with its substantive scope, was applicable to the facts of the case at hand, this did not rule out the application of free movement of capital; this time, apparently, the restriction on free movement of capital was not merely an unavoidable consequence of any restriction on the freedom of establishment. The fact that in the present case the market participant was in the end not successful due to the legislation being caught by the exception laid down in Art 57(1) EC is of no relevance for this discussion.[156]

If one compares the respective third country contexts in the judgments on *Test Claimants in the FII Group Litigation, Claimants in the Thin Cap Group Litigation,*

Litigation v Commissioners of Inland Revenue, para 36; Case C-524/04 *Test Claimants in the Thin Cap Group Litigation*, para 26 *et seq.*

[149] Case C-196/04 *Cadbury Schweppes and Cadbury Schweppes Overseas Ltd v Commissioners of Inland Revenue*, para 31 *et seq.*
[150] Case C-524/04 *Test Claimants in the Thin Cap Group Litigation*, para 28 *et seq.*
[151] [Emphasis added] Case C-157/05 *Winfried Holböck v Finanzamt Salzburg-Land*, para 23.
[152] Ibid, para 24.   [153] Ibid, para 27.
[154] Ibid, para 28 citing Case C-102/05 *Skatteverket v A and B*, para 29.
[155] Case C-157/05 *Winfried Holböck v Finanzamt Salzburg-Land*, para 30.
[156] For a different view: N Wunderlich and C Blaschke, 'Kapitalverkehrsfreiheit in Bezug auf Drittstaaten', 758 *et seq.*

and *Holböck*, then one would indeed wonder why the Court has reached diametrically opposing results. In all cases, the market participant was in a position to exercise definite influence over the decisions of the company in which it had a holding and, on the other hand, to participate effectively in the management or control of its holding. In principle, the activity could be subjected to both free movement of capital and the freedom of establishment.

The *Claimants in the Thin Cap Group Litigation* case—the case in which the reliance on free movement of capital was denied—differed from the other two cases with respect to one obvious point in particular.[157] The national legislation at issue applied only to those market participants that were in a position to exercise definite influence over their holdings. In contrast, the legislation in the other two cases applied independently of the size of the holding.

It appears that, for the Court, the '*purpose of the national legislation*' (the intended regulatory ambit or scope of application of the national rule), and not the actual economic activity pursued by the market participant, predominantly determines the applicable freedom.[158]

It can be said that the Court's reasoning is perfectly correct when it states that a given economic activity, such as the receipt of dividends by a person resident in a Member State from a public company established in a third country, covered by national legislation that applies irrespective of the extent of the holding, may fall in the ambits of both Art 43 EC and Art 56(1) EC. The Court, however, has yet to come forward with a comprehensible answer to the question of why one and the same economic activity, this time subject to national legislation applying only to holdings that allow for definite influence, shall only be subject to Art 43 EC.

The artificial distinction drawn by the Court has the effect that 'the protection enjoyed by an investor [is in certain situations] inversely proportionate to the size of his shareholdings'.[159] Depending on the national legislation, it may happen that in a third country context a 'substantial holding' is deprived of any protection, while a holding in a company that remains below the threshold of 'definite influence' would be covered. In an intra-Community context—the effect of the Court's approach being less devastating—the protection of a holding would in certain situations not be strengthened by a second freedom at the point at which the holding turns from a portfolio into a direct investment.[160]

---

[157] It might also be interesting to note that the *Claimants in the Thin Cap Group Litigation* case is the only one of the three cases that concerns inbound investment.

[158] N Wunderlich and C Blaschke, 'Kapitalverkehrsfreiheit in Bezug auf Drittstaaten', are of the view that the 'purpose of the national legislation' and the actual economic activity pursued determines the applicable freedom.

[159] Case C-251/98 *C Baars v Inspecteur der Belastingen Particulieren/Ondernemingen Gorinchem*, para 50; see also H Rehm and J Nagler, 'Anmerkungen zum BFH-Urteil vom 9. 8. 2006', 861; A Cordewener, et al, 'Outer Boundaries', 374; DS Smit, 'Relationship'.

[160] *Cf* J Schönfeld, 'Anmerkung zu C-452/04', 81; M Schraufl, 'Lasertec', 606; note also A Wellens, 'Drittlandsdividenden', 1855; S Köhler and M Tippelhofer, 'Kapitalverkehrsfreiheit', 647 *et seq*; embracing the Court's reasoning and conclusion: R Freitag, '§ 8a KStG 1/07', 572.

Not wanting to be redundant, for an appraisal of such a 'centre of gravity' approach chosen by the Court, I refer the reader to my observations on the *Fidium Finanz AG* case above.

In summary, it appears so far that the Court, in principle, accepts parallel applicability of the provisions on free movement of capital and freedom of establishment with respect to direct investment on the level of scope of application. However, this affirmation of parallel applicability is only half-hearted, subjecting exclusively to the freedom of establishment only cases in which the market participant is restricted in his economic activity by national measures applying only to undertakings over which definite control is exercised. This has fatal consequences for third country capital movements in general and foreign direct investment in particular. As soon as the national measure relates only to undertakings over which definite control is exercised, it is exempted from any scrutiny in the light of the fundamental freedoms.

c. The Views in the Literature

The literature presents itself in a very fragmented state. Nevertheless, two main views can be differentiated: one favouring exclusivity and another pleading parallel applicability of the two freedoms.

(1) Exclusivity

Those who advocate a strict exclusivity of the different freedoms do so basically in order to avoid contradictions on the level of the scope of application and with respect to the differences in the legally recognized justifications of restrictive national measures.[161]

One view, delineating the freedoms from each other by examining the facts of the case from an economic perspective (purpose and substance of the activity), suggests that free movements of capital will govern portfolio investments, while the freedom of establishment would relate to direct investments. The distinguishing criterion is the effective exercise of '*control*' over the business venture. Such an opinion is supposedly 'supported' by the arguments that, first, the Capital Movements Directive—which clearly describes direct investment as being 'capital movement'[162]—due to its secondary law character, would not oppose such an interpretation, and secondly, that Arts 43(2) EC and 58(2) EC would demand a strict delimitation of the freedoms on the level of their scopes of application.[163] If one were to apply this view to foreign direct investment, this would mean that it

---

[161] C Ohler, 'Kapitalverkehrsfreiheit', 1803; R Freitag, 'Kapitalverkehr', 190; W Schön, 'Kapitalverkehrsfreiheit', 750 *et seq*; A Schnitger, 'Geltung', 712; see also R Torrent, *Regional Integration*.
[162] Annex I, Heading I of Directive 88/361/EEC.
[163] C Ohler, 'Kapitalverkehrsfreiheit', 1804 *et seq*.

would be deprived of any protection in the absence of an international treaty or secondary legislation[164] due to the simple fact that there is no other freedom that applies *erga omnes*.

Others, also favouring strict exclusivity, suggest applying the distinguishing criterion of 'direct and indirect impairment'.[165] They proceed from the assumption that both Art 43(2) and Art 58(2) EC are to be applied to the scope of application.[166] In order to avoid an infinite reference loop, Art 58(2) EC points back to the provisions on freedom of establishment if free movement of capital is indirectly impaired.[167] Free movement of capital is impaired indirectly if the market participant gains definite influence over the business concerned.[168] Thus, direct investment would fall outside the ambit of free movement of capital and would be governed solely by the freedom of establishment. This view would therefore also exclude foreign direct investment from the protection of the Treaty.

Still others have recourse to the hypothetical intention of an average investor as a distinguishing criterion.[169] If a given economic activity would primarily serve a (portfolio) investment purpose, the market participant would have to base his claims on free movement of capital; if he intends to pursue entrepreneurial aims, the activity would be subjected to the rules on freedom of establishment. This would equally lead to the exclusion of the economic activity of foreign direct investment from any protection by the fundamental freedoms due to the fact that the inherent idea of placing a (foreign) direct investment is to pursue entrepreneurial aims.[170]

Also worth mentioning is the view of Ohler. Originally a follower of a 'strict exclusivity theory,'[171] he reversed his point of view and now seems to follow the teaching that both freedoms are to be applied in parallel with respect to direct investments.[172] However, as regards direct investments directed to or originating from third countries, the guarantee of Art 56(1) EC will not apply because the chapter on free movement of capital and payments 'shall be without prejudice to the applicability of restrictions on the right of establishment which are compatible with this Treaty' (*cf* Art 58(2) EC). Since the freedom of establishment

---

[164] See also W Kessler, et al, 'Gesellschafter-Fremdfinanzierung', 326.
[165] PO Mülbert, 'Kapitalmarktrecht', 2089; P-C Müller-Graff, 'Einflußregulierungen', 933 *et seq*; A Glaesner, Art. 58 EC (2000), mn 8. But see also Advocate General Alber, who does not preclude parallel application within his test of 'direct and indirect restriction': Case C-251/98 (Opinion of AG Alber) *C Baars v Inspecteur der Belastingen Particulieren/Ondernemingen Gorinchem*, para 10 *et seq*, 26, 30. In the same line in a third country context Case C-524/04 (Opinion of AG Geelhoed) *Test Claimants in the Thin Cap Group Litigation*, para 31 *et seq*, esp. 35.
[166] P-C Müller-Graff, 'Einflußregulierungen', 933 *et seq*.
[167] PO Mülbert, 'Kapitalmarktrecht', 2089.
[168] P-C Müller-Graff, 'Einflußregulierungen', 935 *et seq*.
[169] M Bachlechner, 'Liegenschafterwerb', 528 *et seq*; A Fischer, 'Kapitalverkehrsfreiheit', 402; See also A Glaesner, Art. 58 EC (2000), mn 8, who wants to apply this test to the level of grounds of justification.
[170] See Chapter II. 4.
[171] For this see C Ohler, 'Kapitalverkehrsfreiheit'.
[172] C Ohler, Art. 56 EC (2002), mn 111.

does not apply to third country relationships—he views this as a restriction on the scope of application—Art 56(1) EC can equally not apply to third country relationships.[173] Thus, once again, foreign direct investment would be outside the protective scope of the fundamental freedoms.

(2) Parallelism

The likely prevailing view in the literature suggests accepting that free movement of capital and the freedom of establishment are inextricably linked to each other with respect to the cross-sectional activity of direct investment. Following this insight—without endeavouring to separate artificially what cannot be separated in a comprehensible and clear-cut fashion—the facts of a given case must be measured against the background of both freedoms.[174]

Turning to a third country context and applying this view to foreign direct investment, in contrast to the exclusionary approach, it would not preclude the applicability of the provisions on free movement of capital to the aforementioned economic activity.

(3) Appraisal

In this section, I shall critically review the aforementioned views. I shall demonstrate that a plea for an exclusive relationship of the two freedoms cannot be upheld, but both run parallel on the level of the scope of application. Furthermore, it will be shown that an opinion, already mentioned above, that seeks to exclude foreign direct investment from the scope of application of Art 56(1) EC cannot be reconciled with the Treaty. Rather, as the words of Art 56(1) EC suggest, foreign direct investment as a (sub-)category of 'movement of capital' is comprised and protected by the aforementioned provision.

All 'exclusivity theories' encounter, to begin with, one fundamental criticism. Each freedom uniquely covers and protects an aspect of a certain economic activity. Especially with respect to cross-sectional economic activities that cannot be detangled into single components,[175] preventing the application of one of the freedoms would mean refusing to see the uniquely covered economic aspect

---

[173] Ibid, mn 130; See also A Dölker and M Ribbrock, 'Kapitalverkehrsfreiheit', 1931 *et seq*.

[174] A Rohde, *Kapitalverkehr*, 97; of the same opinion: JCW Müller, *Kapitalverkehrsfreiheit*, 193; A Honrath, *Kapitalverkehr*, 109; U Haferkamp, *Kapitalverkehrsfreiheit*, 197; J Glöckner, 'Grundverkehrsbeschränkungen', 608; P von Wilmowsky, 'Kapital- und Zahlungsverkehr', § 12 mn 3; J Brinkmann, *Unternehmensbesteuerung*, 59 *et seq*; JM Mössner and D Kellersmann, 'Kapitalverkehrsfreiheit', 508; M Sedlaczek, 'Kapitalverkehrsfreiheit', 46 *et seq*; J Tiedje and P Troberg, Art. 43 EC (2003), mn 26; probably also W Kiemel, Art. 56 EC (2003), para 22; A Glaesner, Art. 56 EC (2000), mn 11. Of the opinion that a 'tendency' towards parallelism can be shown: J Bröhmer, Art. 56 EC (2002), mn 16 *et seq*; speaking of a 'complementary function' of the provisions on free movement of capital in regards to the freedom of establishment: W Kessler, et al, 'Gesellschafter-Fremdfinanzierung', 326. For a differentiated approach: M Nettesheim, 'Unternehmensübernahmen'.

[175] S Weber, 'Kapitalverkehr', 564; P Oliver, 'Free Movement of Capital', 417.

(optimal capital allocation[176] and entrepreneurial activity[177]) and potentially exposing it to unjustified discrimination or hindrance. Only the simultaneous application of the freedoms can prevent such a result and further the effectiveness of Community law.[178] Of course, it could be argued that due to the converging tendencies in the interpretation of the fundamental freedoms it does not really matter to which freedom a certain economic activity is subjected.[179] While this argument might—in practical, but not doctrinal terms—not be dismissed right away, the outcome of the 'exclusivity theory' would be devastating when it comes to third country capital movements. In the event that the freedom of capital movements was to become second to the freedom of establishment, third country transfers would be without any protection. Accepting such a result would be contrary to the words and intent of the Treaty,[180] which explicitly provides in Art 56(1) EC for capital movement liberalization *erga omnes* without any exceptions from the scope of application with respect to certain categories of capital movements.[181] The expansion of the protective scope of the provision introduced by the Treaty of Maastricht would be nullified for the economic cross-sectional activity of foreign direct investment, and thus, the effectiveness of the fundamental freedom would be clearly limited.

Moreover, the opinions that favour a strict exclusivity are difficult to reconcile with the words of the Treaty, which confirm in Art 57 EC that direct investment—largely, as regards the content of the term, overlapping with the notion of establishment found in Art 43 EC—constitutes a (sub-)category of 'capital movement'.[182] Also, the nomenclature of the EC Capital Movements Directive,[183] having an indicative character under 'post-Maastricht law', expressly refers to direct investment as a (sub-)category of capital movement.[184]

Apart from that, the suggested 'distinguishing criteria' are largely unfeasible. To delineate the freedoms according to the *hypothetical intention* of an average investor is unsatisfactory due to the fact that such an intention is difficult to ascertain and would simply lead to unacceptable uncertainties.[185]

---

[176] Object-related facet.
[177] Personal-related facet.
[178] W Schön, 'Kapitalverkehrsfreiheit', 749; U Haferkamp, *Kapitalverkehrsfreiheit*, 197; J Lübke, *Kapitalverkehrs- und Niederlassungsfreiheit*, 232 *et seq*.
[179] *Cf*, eg, Case C-112/05 (Opinion of AG Colomer) *Commission v Germany (Re Golden Shares VII 'Volkswagengesetz')*, para 60.
[180] See: Chapter I. 2. a. (1) and Chapter IV. 3.
[181] U Haferkamp, *Kapitalverkehrsfreiheit*, 196 *et seq*.
[182] A Rohde, *Kapitalverkehr*, 97; JCW Müller, *Kapitalverkehrsfreiheit*, 193; U Haferkamp, *Kapitalverkehrsfreiheit*, 195.
[183] Annex I, Heading I of Directive 88/361/EEC.
[184] Ibid, Annex I (I). See also W Kiemel, Art. 56 EC (2003), para 21; A Honrath, *Kapitalverkehr*, 110 *et seq*; U Haferkamp, *Kapitalverkehrsfreiheit*, 195.
[185] U Haferkamp, *Kapitalverkehrsfreiheit*, 196; J Glöckner, 'Grundverkehrsbeschränkungen', 608. The Court in *C-423/98 (Re Alfredo Albore)* held that irrespective of the ends pursued by the investor, a purchase of real property falls (at least) within the ambit of Art 56(1) EC. Thus, the

To delineate the two freedoms by way of establishing whether a State measure directly or indirectly impairs one of the freedoms, or adopting—as the Court did—a 'centre of gravity' approach, which is essentially the same, is of little practical value, but helps to create the illusion of resolving delineation problems on a rational basis. This view basically encounters the dilemma of failing to determine clearly what constitutes a direct or indirect impairment of a given freedom when it comes to cross-sectional activities such as direct investment. The problem of delineation is not resolved, but is just 'relocated'.[186]

More attention should be paid to the argument that Art 56(1) EC does not comprise the liberalization of direct investment flow with respect to third country relationships. The argument runs as follows. The scope of application of Art 43 EC, which has no external component, serves as a restriction within the meaning of Art 58(2) EC. Since foreign direct investment is not covered by Art 43 EC, and the chapter on the free movement of capital and payments 'shall be without prejudice to the applicability of restrictions on the right of establishment which are compatible with this Treaty', foreign direct investment would also fall outside the ambit of Art 56(1) EC. This finding is allegedly confirmed by Art 57(1) EC. Moreover, only this construction would explain the existence of Art 57(2) EC, which grants the competence to the Council to regulate—ie, predominantly to liberalize but also to restrict—foreign direct investment.[187]

This interpretation, however, meets strong reservations in regard to several points. In a nutshell, it is not only that it overstretches the meaning of 'restrictions' in Art 58(2) EC, but it is also contrary to the words and *telos* of the provisions of free movements of capital.[188]

The first criticism is aimed at the construction of Art 58(2) EC. This study submitted that Art 58(2) EC applies only to the level of grounds of justification and has no referencing effects with respect to the scope of application. While a literal interpretation of the term 'restrictions', though hinting towards the applicability of Art 58(2) EC only to the grounds of justification, does not provide us with a conclusive answer, the systematic placement of the provision supports the finding put forward here: the referencing provision of Art 58(2) EC follows an enumeration of grounds of justification in the first section of the Article.[189] Thus, the placement of Art 58(2) EC after a provision that contains grounds of justification indicates that it applies only to this level.[190]

Court implicitly rejected the view that competing freedoms are to be delineated by having recourse to the hypothetical intention of an average investor. [Case C-423/98 *Alfredo Albore*, para 14]

[186] C Ohler, Art. 56 EC (2002), mn 117; S Weber, 'Kapitalverkehr', 564; note also Case C-452/04 (Opinion of AG Stix-Hackl) *Fidium Finanz AG*, para 62.
[187] C Ohler, Art. 56 EC (2002), mn 130.
[188] W Schön, 'Kapitalverkehr mit Drittstaaten', 501 *et seq*; also concurring AC Digel, 'Europäischer Finanzmarkt', Inaugural-Dissertation, Eberhard-Karls-Universität, 189.
[189] U Haferkamp, *Kapitalverkehrsfreiheit*, 194, 202.
[190] Ibid, 194.

The restrictive construction of Ohler is further called into question by the words and *telos* of Art 56(1) EC, which shall be touched on only very briefly in this context.[191] This study takes the view that the message relayed by the words of the provision is clear and unambiguous: '*complete* liberalization' of all capital movements as the fundamental principle on which Art 56 EC *et seq* is based. This principle applies irrespective of whether capital movements are directed to or originating from another Member State or a third country. It is true that, in the case of third countries, there are more exceptions that can lead to a restriction on free capital movements.[192] However, this does not change or even reverse the basic decision of the drafters of the Treaty.[193]

Furthermore, a liberal interpretation is presupposed by the Treaty aims, informing the *telos* of a provision, which suggests—also with respect to third countries—that unconditional free movement of capital not only facilitates but also constitutes a partial precondition for their attainment.[194] Turning to the opinion of Ohler, by excluding foreign direct investment from the guarantee of Art 56(1) EC by means of a broad interpretation of Art 58(2) EC, the rule–exception relationship of Art 56 EC *et seq.* would simply be reversed in this respect. Moreover, it creates implicitly two different meanings of 'capital movements' depending on whether *intra*-Community or third country capital movements are concerned.

A third argument, referring to Art 57(1) EC, also speaks in favour of the opinion advocated in this study. Article 57 EC contains in its first section a grandfathering clause for national provisions imposing restrictions on, inter alia, foreign direct investment. Why then, one must ask, should one include such a clause in the Treaty if foreign direct investment were to be excluded from the guarantee of Art 56(1) EC anyway? Obviously, the provision would be superfluous in such a situation.[195]

4. Summary so Far

Direct investment constitutes an economic cross-sectional activity, potentially falling within the scope of both the freedom of establishment and free movement of capital. It forms a (sub-)category of 'movement of capital' within the meaning of Art 56(1) EC, and it qualifies as 'establishment' for the purposes of Art 43 EC.

Articles 43(2) EC and 58(2) EC do not apply to the scope of application, but only to the level of grounds of justification, and therefore do not have the effect of

---

[191] For a detailed discussion refer to Chapter IV. 3. b.
[192] See Chapter IV. 3. b. (2) (c).
[193] M Sedlaczek, Art. 58 EC (2003), mn 17; M Sedlaczek, 'Kapitalverkehrsfreiheit', 50 *et seq.*; for a more cautious view: JCW Müller, *Kapitalverkehrsfreiheit*, 187.
[194] See Chapter I. 2. b.
[195] Concurring: M Schraufl, 'Lasertec', 605.

establishing the primacy of one freedom over the other on the level of the scope of application.

The Court, in principle, accepts the parallel applicability of the provisions on free movement of capital and freedom of establishment with respect to direct investment. However, this affirmation is only half-hearted: cases in which the market participant is restricted in his economic activity by national measures applying only to undertakings over which definite control is exercised are subjected exclusively to the freedom of establishment. This has fatal consequences for foreign direct investment. As soon as the national measure is phrased in the aforementioned fashion, it is completely exempted from scrutiny in the light of the fundamental freedoms. However, neither the way in which the Court delineates the freedoms from each other nor the achieved outcome is convincing.

After having also discussed the different views in the literature, it appears that the more convincing arguments speak in favour of a parallel application of Arts 43 EC and 56(1) EC. Otherwise, the freedom of capital movement would be deprived of any effectiveness in the situation in which an economic activity falls potentially into the ambit of more than one freedom.

All in all, the relationship between free movement of capital and freedom of establishment on the level of the scope of application is of a parallel nature. Thus, due to the fact that the freedom of establishment does not supersede free movement of capital, foreign direct investment is not excluded from the scope of Art 56(1) EC.

IV

Which Level of Protection?—The Scope of the Prohibition of Restriction: Equal Treatment and Market Access

1. Introduction

Article 56(1) EC prohibits 'all restrictions on the movement of capital'. This prohibition breaks up into two complementary guarantees: equal treatment in the market, enforced by the prohibition of discrimination, and access to the market, assured by the prohibition of hindrance.[1] The former relates to national distinctly applicable measures, the latter to such measures operating indistinctly.

Both tests will be the subject of substantial review in this chapter. I shall first analyse the operation of the non-hindrance and non-discrimination tests in an intra-Community context.[2] With respect to the 'non-hindrance test' I shall in particular address the issue of whether and to what extent the doctrinal concepts developed by the Court in the context of other freedoms can be translated into the ambit of free movement of capital. Turning to the 'non-discrimination' test, although Art 56(1) EC does not explicitly mention the 'prohibition of discrimination', this omission is not to be understood as saying that within the ambit of free movement of capital, discriminatory conduct would not in principle be prohibited.[3] One can draw from Art 58(3) EC, which bans 'arbitrary

---

[1] See on the converging tendencies among all fundamental freedoms with a view to creating a common doctrinal approach with respect to direct effect, the co-existence of the two tests of non-discrimination and the prohibition of all hindrances: D Ehlers, 'Allgemeine Lehren', § 7, mn 16; P Steinberg, 'Konvergenz'; C Barnard, 'Remaining Pieces'; HD Jarass, 'Dogmatik II'; W Pfeil, 'Freier Kapitalverkehr', 789; HD Jarass, 'Dogmatik I'; K Lenaerts and P Van Nuffel, *Constitutional Law*, mn 5–083; M Sedlaczek, 'Kapitalverkehrsfreiheit', 38 *et seq*; M Sedlaczek, Art. 58 EC (2003), mn 1 *et seq*; S Weatherill, 'After Keck', 906; see also CD Classen, 'Dogmatik'; M Eberhartinger, 'Konvergenz'; N Schleper, *Dogmatik der Grundfreiheiten*; M Nettesheim, *Grundfreiheiten und Grundrechte*. Of the opinion that two tests, ie, a 'non-discrimination test' and a 'non-hindrance test,' also co-exist within the ambit of free movement of capital: eg, U Haferkamp, *Kapitalverkehrsfreiheit*, 54; C Ohler, Art. 56 EC (2002), mn 255; W Kiemel, Art. 56 EC (2003), mn 27.

[2] See Chapter IV. 2.

[3] A Haratsch, et al, *Europarecht*, mn 904, 728; A Honrath, *Kapitalverkehr*, 64; S Mohamed, *Free Movement of Capital*, 102 *et seq*; G Ress and J Ukrow, *Kapitalverkehrsfreiheit und Steuergerechtigkeit*, 33.

discrimination', the conclusion that discriminatory conduct must be included in the scope of application of Art 56(1) EC.[4] With regard to the operation of the non-discrimination test in an intra-Community context, in particular the challenges of forming comparison groups, of selecting the expressly prohibited distinguishing criterion, as well as the issue of comparability, are brought into focus.

In the second part of the discussion,[5] I shall assess whether the construction set forth for an intra-Community context needs to be revised when it comes to third country capital movement. The discussion will largely evolve around two points. I shall first critically review the persuasiveness of teleological considerations based on the argument that free capital movement in a third country context allegedly serves the Treaty aims to a lesser extent than it does in an intra-Community context. Secondly, within the context of the non-discrimination test, the question of 'comparability in principle' of domestic/intra-Community and third country direct investment will be examined.

2. The Situation within the Internal Market

a. Non-Hindrance Test

A general tendency towards a converging doctrinal approach in interpreting the freedoms[6] and the similarity of free movements of capital and goods[7] cannot hide from view the fact that considerable uncertainty still exists with respect to the interpretation of the scope of the non-hindrance test, both in general and also within the ambit of free movement of capital.

The majority view in the literature, emphasizing this convergence of the fundamental freedoms and the similarity between free movement of capital and free movement of goods,[8] seeks to transport the concepts developed in the context of the other freedoms into the ambit of free movement of capital.[9] However, caution should be exercised when operating with great constructs of ideas. A strict

---

[4] U Haferkamp, *Kapitalverkehrsfreiheit*, 54.

[5] See Chapter IV. 3.

[6] For an account of the converging tendencies among the fundamental freedoms see footnote 1 of this Chapter above.

[7] Both freedoms are 'object-related' freedoms, ie, their guarantees are tied to the cross-border movement of objects. Moreover, the wording of Arts 56 EC and 58 EC appears to be closely modelled on Arts 28 and 30 EC. [J Glöckner, 'Grundverkehrsbeschränkungen', 592; A Rohde, *Kapitalverkehr*, 130; A Honrath, *Kapitalverkehr*, 67; U Haferkamp, *Kapitalverkehrsfreiheit*, 82; G Ress and J Ukrow, Art. 56 EC (2002), mn 35; J Lübke, *Kapitalverkehrs- und Niederlassungsfreiheit*, 157 *et seq*] Of the opinion that although the aforementioned similarities are not disputed, the likeness of both freedoms is not sufficient to transfer the principles developed in the context of free movement of goods to the freedom of capital movements: U Haferkamp, *Kapitalverkehrsfreiheit*, 82 *et seq*.

[8] See footnote 7 of this Chapter above.

[9] eg, J Bröhmer, Art. 56 EC (2002), mn 50 *et seq*; W Kiemel, Art. 56 EC (2003), mn 11 *et seq*; G Ress and J Ukrow, Art. 56 EC (2002), mn 35 *et seq*; A Rohde, *Kapitalverkehr*, 130 *et seq*; more

standard of doctrinal consistency cultivated especially by some German EC law scholars is hardly echoed by the Court's jurisprudence. Rather, the Court exercises a pragmatic approach, at times literally feeling its way forward.[10] This seems to be just as true in the ambit of Art 56(1) EC as with respect to the other freedoms. Although the Court's case law on free movement of capital, after decades of a shadowy existence, has experienced rapid development in recent years, so far the increased number of judgments has not necessarily led to a simultaneous improvement in clarity. What can reasonably be said, though, is that the Court seems to approach Art 56(1) EC in a manner broadly convergent with the other freedoms.

(1) Beyond Non-Discrimination

At an early stage of development of EC law, the Court had already realized that the mere prohibition of discrimination in cross-border movements was not enough to significantly reduce the existing national restrictions in order to integrate the different European economies into one Common Market. A prohibition of discrimination is simply ineffective in cases where there is nothing in the host State to which one can compare a certain cross-border transaction. Of equally little help will be the prohibition of discrimination if the laws and regulations of the host State, while not discriminatory, render it unattractive for a non-national market participant to enter the market, due to the additional costs he will incur in order to comply with the standards of both the home and potential host countries. It is not the existence of such laws and regulations that causes the problem, but rather their indifferent application to national and cross-border situations that results in real barriers for the latter.[11]

The Court hence broadened the scope of protection of the fundamental freedoms. With respect to free movement of goods, the ECJ established in *Dassonville* that '[a]ll trading rules enacted by Member States which are capable of hindering, directly or indirectly, actually or potentially, intra-Community trade are to be considered'[12] in the light of Art 28 EC, which covers only imports. With respect to national measures restricting exports, the ECJ seems in principle to subject them only to the non-discrimination test, being apparently of the opinion that in such situations the risk of dual burden is normally not present.[13]

---

critical, especially with respect to the *Keck* formula: JCW Müller, *Kapitalverkehrsfreiheit*, 161 *et seq*; P von Wilmowsky, 'Kapital- und Zahlungsverkehr', mn 7.

[10] M Nettesheim, *Grundfreiheiten und Grundrechte*, 18 *et seq*.
[11] PP Craig and G de Búrca, *EU Law*, 677; U Haferkamp, *Kapitalverkehrsfreiheit*, 64 for further references.
[12] Case 8/74 *Procureur du Roi v Benoît and Gustave Dassonville*, para 5.
[13] Case 15/79 *P.B. Groenveld BV v Produktschap voor Vee en Vlees*, para 9; Case 155/80 *Summary proceedings against Sergius Oebel*, para 15; recently: Case C-12/02 *Criminal Proceedings against Marco Grilli*, para 41 *et seq*; Case C-293/02 *Jersey Produce Marketing Organisation Ltd v States of Jersey and Jersey Potato Export Marketing Board*, para 73; *cf* J Steiner and L Woods, *EC Law*, 236 *et*

In the area of the freedom to provide services, the non-discrimination test was equally perceived as insufficient for integrating national markets. In a series of judgments starting with *van Binsbergen*,[14] through *Säger*[15] and up to *Corsica Ferries II*,[16] the Court firmly established a non-hindrance test. Hence, Art 49 EC:

> requires not only the elimination of all discrimination against a person providing services on the ground of his nationality but also the abolition of any restriction, even if it applies without distinction to national providers of services and to those of other Member States, when it is liable to prohibit or otherwise impede the activities of a provider of services established in another Member State where he lawfully provides similar services.[17]

There are signs in the case law—*cf Alpine Investments*[18]—that this might apply in principle to import and export situations alike.[19]

In *Bosman*,[20] the principle of application of the non-hindrance test in entrance and exit situations was established for free movement of workers.[21] With some delay, the non-hindrance test was also introduced to the ambit of the freedom of establishment.[22] The *Gebhard*[23] ruling provides us with the clearest indication in this respect. As in the ambit of the freedom to provide services, the non-hindrance test applies to restrictive entrance and exit measures.[24]

Despite the Court's effort to extend the protective scope of the freedoms, it should be noted that not every restrictive national measure would be subjected to the non-hindrance test. Rules that are insufficiently direct or significant are perceived as not having the effect of restricting cross-border transactions.[25]

---

seq; PP Craig and G de Búrca, *EU Law*, 680 *et seq*; critical: C Ohler, Art. 56 EC (2002), mn 253 for further references; see also P von Wilmowsky, *Europäisches Kreditsicherungsrecht*, 21 *et seq*.

[14] Case 33/74 *Johannes Henricus Maria van Binsbergen v Bestuur van de Bedrijfsvereniging voor de Metaalnijverheid*.

[15] Case C-76/90 *Manfred Säger v Dennemeyer & Co Ltd*.

[16] Case C-266/96 *Corsica Ferries France SA v Gruppo Antichi Ormeggiatori del porto di Genova Coop. arl, Gruppo Ormeggiatori del Golfo di La Spezia Coop. arl and Ministero dei Trasporti e della Navigazione*.

[17] Case C-76/90 *Manfred Säger v Dennemeyer & Co Ltd*, para 12.

[18] Case C-384/93 *Alpine Investments BV v Minister van Financiën*, paras 28, 35 *et seq*.

[19] P-C Müller-Graff, Art. 49 EC (2003), mn 85 *et seq*, esp. 88; PP Craig and G de Búrca, *EU Law*, 681, 832 *et seq*.

[20] Case C-415/93 *Union royale belge des sociétés de football association ASBL v Jean-Marc Bosman, Royal club liégeois SA v. Jean-Marc Bosman and others and Union des associations européennes de football (UEFA) v Jean-Marc Bosman)*, para 98 *et seq*.

[21] See also PP Craig and G de Búrca, *EU Law*, 760 *et seq* for further references.

[22] Ibid, 801 *et seq*.

[23] Case C-55/94 *Reinhard Gebhard v Consiglio dell'Ordine degli Avvocati e Procuratori di Milano*, para 37.

[24] *Cf*, eg, Case 81/87 *R v H.M. Treasury and Commissioners of Inland Revenue, ex p Daily Mail and General Trust plc*.

[25] *Cf*, eg, Case 155/80 *Summary proceedings against Sergius Oebel*, para 20; Joined Cases C-51/96 and C-191/97 *Christelle Deliège v Ligue francophone de judo et disciplines associées ASBL, Ligue belge de judo ASBL, Union européenne de judo and François Pacquée*; See also PP Craig and G de Búrca, *EU Law*, 833, fn 212.

(2) Non-hindrance Test for Inbound and Outbound Capital Movements

The fundamental idea behind the expansion of the protective scope of the freedoms is that the prohibition of discrimination in cross-border movements is insufficient to reduce and ultimately abolish the existing national restrictions in order to integrate the different European economies into one Common Market. This idea carries equal weight with respect to free movement of capital, which can be illustrated by the example of legislative limitations or suspensions of voting rights to or beyond a certain percentage of capital held in companies in a certain sector of economy. Although such national measures usually apply indistinctly to domestic and cross-border investments, they nevertheless dissuade cross-border investors from acquiring shares in a company subject to such provisions.[26]

The prohibition of restrictions to which Art 56(1) EC refers must therefore, borrowing from the Court's judgment in *Commission v Portuguese Republic (Re Golden Shares I)*, go 'beyond the mere elimination of unequal treatment, on grounds of nationality, as between operators on the financial markets'.[27] It was this judgment in which the Court made it reasonably clear that it was also prepared to apply a non-hindrance test in the ambit of free movement of capital. The Court found that a national measure is subject to Art 56(1) EC—'[e]ven though the rules in issue may not give rise to unequal treatment'—if it is capable of impeding capital movements and dissuading investors in other Member States from investing and, thus, capable of rendering the free movement of capital illusory.[28]

The language used by the Court in *Commission v Portuguese Republic*[29] can hardly be described as a prime example of clarity and precision. The Court, however, cannot be criticized for not remaining true to itself in the way it drew up its judgment. It is merely the consequent continuation of its earlier jurisprudence, characterized by rather pragmatic handling of doctrinal concepts in the area of free movement of capital:[30] in *Bordessa*,[31] the Court stated that the national measure would impede capital movements; in *Sandoz*,[32] the ECJ talked, inter alia,

---

[26] *Cf* D Chalmers, et al, *EU Law*, 509 *et seq*; Case C-174/04 *Commission v Italian Republic (Re Automatic Suspension of Voting Rights in Privatised Undertaking)*, 29 *et seq*; note also Case C-112/05 *Commission v Germany (Re Golden Shares VII 'Volkswagengesetz')*; M Weiss, 'VW-Gesetz'; For a specific account of the issues surrounding so-called 'Golden Shares' and the relevant jurisprudence of the Court refer to: M Pießkalla, *Goldene Aktien*; J Bröhmer, 'Golden Shares'; S Pläster, 'Kapitalverkehrsfreiheit'.
[27] Case C-367/98 *Commission v Portuguese Republic (Re Golden Shares I)*, para 44 *et seq*; see also EFTA Court, Case E-1/00 *State Debt Management Agency v Íslandsbanki-FBA hf*.
[28] Case C-367/98 *Commission v Portuguese Republic (Re Golden Shares I)*, para 45; confirmed in Case C-483/99 *Commission v French Republic (Re Golden Shares II)*, para 41.
[29] Case C-367/98 *Commission v Portuguese Republic (Re Golden Shares I)*.
[30] D Chalmers, et al, *EU Law*, 511.
[31] Joined Cases C-358/93 and C-416/93 *Criminal proceedings against Aldo Bordessa and Vicente Marí Mellado and Concepción Barbero Maestre*, para 25.
[32] Case C-439/97 *Sandoz GmbH v Finanzlandesdirektion für Wien, Niederösterreich und Burgenland*, para 19.

about obstacles to the movement of capital; and in other cases, such as *Svensson*,[33] *Trummer*,[34] *Commission v Belgium*,[35] *Verkooijen*,[36] *Commission v France*,[37] and *Commission v Spain*,[38] the Court found national measures liable to dissuade the parties from exercising the freedom of capital movement. In *Trummer*, in addition to the Court's 'liable to dissuade' formulation, the ECJ also focused on the question of whether the national measure would cause additional costs to the foreign market participant.[39] Having adopted a broad understanding of the 'non-hindrance test' in all of the cases mentioned above, it appears that the variations in speech do not mark a difference in substance. The principle of subjection of non-discriminatory national measures to the freedom can be regarded as firmly established.[40]

It is furthermore worth drawing attention to a significant difference in the interpretation of the non-hindrance tests within the ambits of Arts 28 and 30 EC and Art 56(1) EC. According to the case law of the ECJ, the *Dassonville* formula in the ambit of free movement of goods shall only apply to the freedom to import goods (Art 28 EC), but not to the freedom to export (Art 30 EC).[41] In the ambits of other freedoms, it is not always clear whether export situations are equally covered by the non-hindrance test.[42] For free movement of capital, it is suggested that a distinction between import and export situations not be drawn. Such a distinction neither finds any support in the wording of Art 56(1) EC, nor would it be justified on the basis of teleological considerations. Restrictive measures of the capital-exporting country can cause similar hindrances to cross-border movement as measures of the (potential) capital importing country.[43] The guarantee

---

[33] Case C-484/93 *Peter Svensson et Lena Gustavsson v Ministre du Logement et de l'Urbanisme*, para 10.

[34] Case C-222/97 *Manfred Trummer and Peter Mayer*, para 26.

[35] Case C-478/98 *Commission v Kingdom of Belgium (Re Loans issued abroad)*, para 18 *et seq*.

[36] Case C-35/98 *Staatssecretaris van Financiën v B.G.M. Verkooijen*, para 34 *et seq*. In *Verkooijen*, the Court stressed that possible countervailing advantages open only with respect to foreign capital movements would not remedy any other violation of Art 56(1) EC. [*Cf* Case C-35/98 *Staatssecretaris van Financiën v B.G.M. Verkooijen*, para 61; see also L Flynn, 'Coming of Age', 781 *et seq*]

[37] Case C-483/99 *Commission v French Republic (Re Golden Shares II)*. The Court uses in addition the expression 'liable to impede'.

[38] Case C-463/00 *Commission v Kingdom of Spain (Re Golden Shares IV)*, para 61; see also Case C-112/05 *Commission v Germany (Re Golden Shares VII 'Volkswagengesetz')*, para 52 *et seq*; F Sander, 'VW-Gesetz-Entscheidung'.

[39] Case C-222/97 *Manfred Trummer and Peter Mayer*, para 27.

[40] C Barnard, *Substantive Law*, 471 *et seq*.; see also S Peers, 'Movement of Capital', 341

[41] Case 15/79 *P.B. Groenveld BV v Produktschap voor Vee en Vlees*, para 9; Case 155/80 *Summary proceedings against Sergius Oebel*, para 15; *cf* J Steiner and L Woods, *EC Law*, 236 *et seq*; PP Craig and G de Búrca, *EU Law*, 680 *et seq*; for a critical view: C Ohler, Art. 56 EC (2002), mn 253 with further references; see also P von Wilmowsky, *Europäisches Kreditsicherungsrecht*, 21 *et seq*.

[42] Especially with respect to the freedom to provide services: PP Craig and G de Búrca, *EU Law*, 681.

[43] P von Wilmowsky, 'Kapital- und Zahlungsverkehr', mn 7; P von Wilmowsky, 'EG-Grundfreiheiten', 364; C Ohler, Art. 56 EC (2002), mn 254; for a different view: J Glöckner,

of being able to withdraw capital at any time is in many cases an important determinant of the decision to invest in the first place.

Turning to academia, the Court's expansion of the protective scope of free movement of capital has generally been viewed favourably. The inclusion within the ambit of Art 56(1) EC, not only of the prohibition of national measures that discriminate in law and/or in fact, but also of those applied without distinction that have a potential deterrent effect ('chilling effect'[44]) on the use of the freedom is deemed necessary in order to successfully integrate European capital markets.[45] However, commentators also point out that this move is not completely without problems. By virtue of a broad reading, the freedom suddenly runs the risk of overreach, a phenomenon already known from other freedoms.[46] By interpreting the fundamental freedoms as prohibiting any hindrance to cross-border movement, they potentially not only subject protectionist national measures to the need for justification (market integration), but a prohibition understood in such a broad sense can also be used to attack the general economic and social order of the Member States (deregulation). While the former application can be explained by the ordoliberal idea of social welfare maximization through opening up and integrating national markets,[47] the latter application means adding a new quality to the fundamental freedoms. They acquire a fundamental rights component in the sense that they would tear down national regulations which, while not impeding access to the market, restrict individual economic autonomy.[48]

It came as no surprise that those deontological tendencies in interpreting the fundamental freedoms sparked off a lively academic debate.[49] Depending on the view taken of the function of the freedoms, ie, either serving market integration or, in addition also bringing about deregulation, the appreciation of judgments rendered subsequently to *Dassonville* and its respective offspring within the ambits of the other freedoms naturally varies. Rulings that limit the scope of

---

'Grundverkehrsbeschränkungen', 619; see also Case C-412/97 (Opinion of AG Cosmas) *ED Srl v Italo Fenocchio*, para 57 *et seq*; the Court, however, refused to follow the Advocate General.

[44] See on the development of the notion 'chilling effect', with further references: G Ress and J Ukrow, Art. 56 EC (2002), mn 36.

[45] The purpose behind a measure is irrelevant, although sometimes it is employed by the Court to highlight the protectionist intentions underlying the relevant measure. *Cf* Case C-35/98 *Staatssecretaris van Financiën v B.G.M. Verkooijen*, para 34; Joined Cases C-515/99 and C-527/99 to C-540/99 and Joined Cases C-519/99 to C-524/99 and C-526/99 *Hans Reisch and Others v Bürgermeister der Landeshauptstadt Salzburg and Grundverkehrsbeauftragter des Landes Salzburg and Anton Lassacher and Others v Grundverkehrsbeauftragter des Landes Salzburg and Grundverkehrslandeskommission des Landes Salzburg*, para 32. See also A Haratsch, et al, *Europarecht*, 904 *et seq*; J Steiner, et al, *EU Law*, 347 *et seq*.

[46] D Chalmers, et al, *EU Law*, 511.

[47] M Nettesheim, *Grundfreiheiten und Grundrechte*, 7 *et seq*.

[48] Ibid, 17 *et seq*.

[49] Those tendencies can be found on both the level of the scope of application as and the level of grounds of justification of the freedoms: ibid., 21 *et seq*, 25 *et seq*.

the non-hindrance test—like *Keck*[50]—are either welcomed as doctrinally necessary and consequential or are played down, for example, as merely responding to the practical challenges of handling the huge caseload the ECJ faced after *Dassonville*.[51] Conversely, rulings that possibly display a deontological understanding of the freedoms—such as *DocMorris*[52] and *Carpenter*[53]—are either interpreted as detrimental to the system or celebrated as another milestone on the path to the amalgamation of fundamental freedoms and rights in EC law.[54]

Although this study is sceptical towards a deontological construction for several reasons,[55] it will not enter into a debate on the overall structure and function(s) of the freedoms,[56] as this would detract from the focus of the study.

(3) Readjusting the Scope of Protection of Free Movement of Capital—Commission v Kingdom of Spain *and* Commission v United Kingdom

Whether it is perceived as an attempt to respond to the criticism on its (overly) broad reading of the scope of protection of the fundamental freedoms or simply a move to reduce workload and readjust the relationship between the ECJ and national courts,[57] the Court has attempted to readjust its interpretative approach. The first move was again made within the ambit of free movement of goods, where the Court put forward the so-called *Keck* formula, which states that:

the application to products from other Member States of national provisions restricting or prohibiting certain selling arrangements is not such as to hinder directly or indirectly, actually or potentially, trade between Member States within the meaning of the Dassonville judgment, so long as those provisions apply to all relevant traders operating within the national territory and so long as they affect in the same manner, in law and in fact, the marketing of domestic products and of those from other Member States.[58]

---

[50] Joined Cases C-267/91 and C-268/91 *Criminal proceedings against Bernard Keck and Daniel Mithouard*; see also in this respect N Reich, 'November Revolution'; T Jestaedt and F Kästle, 'Keck-Urteil'; MP Maduro, *We the Court*; C Barnard, 'Remaining Pieces'; S Weatherill, 'After Keck'.
[51] Case 8/74 *Procureur du Roi v Benoit and Gustave Dassonville*.
[52] Case C-322/01 *Deutscher Apothekerverband eV v 0800 DocMorris NV and Jacques Waterval*.
[53] Case C-60/00 *Mary Carpenter v Secretary of State for the Home Department*.
[54] *Cf* for an outline of the debate M Nettesheim, *Grundfreiheiten und Grundrechte*.
[55] eg, fundamental freedoms and fundamental rights perform different functions, and this difference must be preserved. A decision that cannot be justified by economic-functional reasoning must not be overruled by deontological considerations, whereas, with respect to the latter, considerable uncertainties exist as to the meaning and content. *Cf* Ibid, 66 *et seq*.
[56] *Cf*, eg, ibid; N Schleper, *Dogmatik der Grundfreiheiten*; T Kingreen, *Struktur der Grundfreiheiten*; MP Maduro, *We the Court*; M Eberhartinger, 'Konvergenz'; HD Jarass, 'Dogmatik I'; CD Classen, 'Dogmatik'; V Heydt, 'Funktionswandel'; all with further references.
[57] M Nettesheim, *Grundfreiheiten und Grundrechte*, 18.
[58] Joined Cases C-267/91 and C-268/91 *Criminal proceedings against Bernard Keck and Daniel Mithouard*, para 16; affirmed in *Hünermund* Case C-292/92 *Ruth Hünermund and others v Landesapothekerkammer Baden-Württemberg*, para 21.

Leaving aside for the moment the constructive weaknesses of this formula, what the Court in essence attempted was to reduce the scope of judicial review by subjecting certain areas of national law—ie, those that restrict or prohibit 'certain selling arrangements'—henceforth only to the non-discrimination test.

While not formalistically transposing its original *Keck* formula, the Court has also gradually relieved the pressure on the Member States in the ambits of the freedom to provide services, the free movement of workers, and the freedom of establishment. It introduced formulae modifying the original non-hindrance test set out in *Säger*,[59] *Bosman*,[60] and *Gebhard*,[61] taking into account the characteristics of the individual freedom.[62] Concerning free movement of capital, the Court, for some time, had left us in uncertainty on the question of whether it was willing to readjust the scope of protection. More recently it provided us with clear signs[63] that it intends to do so, albeit not by a formalistic 100 per cent transfer of its original *Keck* judgment, which might be viewed as a response to the fundamental criticism it has been facing.

(a) Shifting to a Test based on 'Substantial Impediment'

Probably the most commonly voiced argument in the literature against a simple copying of the *Keck* formula to the ambits of the other freedoms is that the weaknesses of *Keck*, both in terminological and teleological terms, are merely transferred into the ambit of another freedom.[64] The criticism in regard to *Keck* is aimed in particular at the uncertainty with respect to the ambit of the phrase 'certain selling arrangements' and at the difficulties in assessing the undercutting effects of the requirement that selling arrangements shall apply non-discriminatorily in law and in fact.[65] However, also from a teleological point of view, the *Keck* formula meets with strong reservations:

---

[59] Case C-76/90 *Manfred Säger v Dennemeyer & Co Ltd*.
[60] Case C-415/93 *Union royale belge des sociétés de football association ASBL v Jean-Marc Bosman, Royal club liégeois SA v. Jean-Marc Bosman and others and Union des associations européennes de football (UEFA) v Jean-Marc Bosman*, para 98 *et seq*.
[61] Case C-55/94 *Reinhard Gebhard v Consiglio dell'Ordine degli Avvocati e Procuratori di Milano*, para 37.
[62] *Cf*, inter alia, U Haferkamp, *Kapitalverkehrsfreiheit*, 71 *et seq*, 78 *et seq* for further references.
[63] *Cf* Case C-463/00 *Commission v Kingdom of Spain (Re Golden Shares IV)*, para 58 *et seq*.
[64] P von Wilmowsky, 'Kapital- und Zahlungsverkehr', mn 7; A Fischer, 'Kapitalverkehrsfreiheit', 404; Case C-412/93 (Opinion of AG Jacobs) *Société d'Importation Edouard Leclerc-Siplec v TF1 Publicité SA and M6 Publicité SA*, para 38; along similar lines: S Peers, 'Movement of Capital', 344. Also against the application based on the argument—in the mean time rebutted—that the *Keck* formula is specific to free movements of goods ('selling arrangements'): F Kimms, *Kapitalverkehrsfreiheit*, 183;. See also F Sander, 'Volkswagen', 108, who wants to introduce a test looking at the 'symmetry of capital invested and control exercisable over the investment', thereby misconceiving of the freedom as a mere freedom of direct investment. Obviously, the aforementioned test was modelled on direct investment but it already fails when it comes to portfolio investment or to situations in which nothing is known about the control exercisable, *cf* Case C-265/04 (Opinion of AG Kokott) *Margaretha Bouanich v Skatteverket*, para 73. If one does not wish to develop a different notion of 'hindrance' for each type of capital movement, then such a test must be disapproved.
[65] N Reich, 'November Revolution', 470.

the exclusion from the scope of Article 30 [now, after amendment, Art. 28 EC] of measures which 'affect in the same manner, in law and in fact, the marketing of domestic products and those from other Member States' amounts to introducing, in relation to restrictions on selling arrangements, a test of discrimination. That test, however, seems inappropriate. The central concern of the Treaty provisions on the free movement of goods is to prevent unjustified obstacles to trade between Member States. If an obstacle to inter-State trade exists, it cannot cease to exist simply because an identical obstacle affects domestic trade. [It is difficult to accept]...the proposition that a Member State may arbitrarily restrict the marketing of goods from another Member State, provided only that it imposes the same arbitrary restriction on the marketing of domestic goods.[66]

In consideration of the criticism outlined above, inter alia, it was suggested that a more principled approach be applied, focusing on the question of 'whether there is a substantial restriction on that access'[67] to the market.

Not endeavouring to enter into an in-depth analysis of the *Keck* judgment, for my purposes it will suffice to direct attention to some more recent judgments of the Court in the context of free movement of goods which demonstrate a tendency towards a test that comes closer to the one focusing on a substantial impediment to market access. In cases such as *TK Heimdienst*[68] and *Gourmet International Products*,[69] while still formally elaborating on the question of whether certain 'selling arrangements' operate equally in fact, the Court seems to focus (although not entirely clearly) on the impact/effect of a national measure on access to the market. Such an approach has at its heart the idea that with regard to market entry all barriers to trade shall be removed, ie, liberalization with a view to fostering and maintaining market integration. Once the respective good has entered the market, it is (only) necessary to establish and perpetuate a level playing field (fair competition).[70] With respect to the 'classic *Keck* approach', a test that is designed to compare the obstacles faced by a foreign product to those of a domestic product does not serve the purpose of creating and maintaining a Common Market. What is necessary in order to integrate markets is to look at the possible obstacles that the foreign good alone faces when entering the market of a Member State.

Furthermore, in the Court's case law on free movement of goods, a strand that implicitly accommodates the idea of a *de minimis* test can be evidenced. In *BASF*

---

[66] Case C-412/93 (Opinion of AG Jacobs) *Société d'Importation Edouard Leclerc-Siplec v TF1 Publicité SA and M6 Publicité SA*, para 39.

[67] Ibid., para 42; *cf* also W-H Roth, 'Keck and Hünermund', 853; for an even stricter view: P von Wilmowsky, 'EG-Grundfreiheiten', 374; for a test based upon the criterion of whether a measure partitions the market see Case 145/88 (Opinion of AG van Gerven) *Torfaen Borough Council v B & Q plc*, para 21 *et seq*.

[68] Case C-254/98 *Schutzverband gegen unlauteren Wettbewerb v TK-Heimdienst Sass GmbH*, para 25 *et seq*.

[69] Case C-405/98 *Konsumentombudsmannen v Gourmet International Products AB*, para 21.

[70] *Cf* W-H Roth, 'Niederlassungsfreiheit', 740 *et seq*; for a different view: M Nettesheim, *Grundfreiheiten und Grundrechte*, 65.

AG v Präsident des Deutschen Patentamtes[71] and ED *Srl v Fenocchio*,[72] the Court held that the 'repercussions [on intra-Community trade] *are too uncertain and too indirect* to be considered to be an obstacle within the meaning of Article 30 [now, after amendment, Art. 28 EC].'[73]

The Court's shift in accentuation—accommodating both elements, ie, a focus on impediments to market access coupled with some sort of *de minimis* test—can be assessed as a rapprochement towards a more principled test similar to the one suggested by Advocate General Jacobs in *Leclerc-Siplec*.[74] While it is admitted that a focus on 'substantial impediment' is also burdened with imperfections, it can be submitted that this shift in stress steals the thunder from the critics of the *Keck* formula to a considerable extent.[75]

Acknowledging the need to restrict the overstretched scope of the *Dassonville* formula and its respective variations in the ambit of the other freedoms, and with a view to interpreting the four freedoms in a convergent manner,[76] it is hence suggested that the weaknesses of a *Keck*-style formula are not of such a nature as to object to its application to free movement of capital. This presumes, however, that one is prepared to follow a sensible understanding of the meaning of a 'substantial impediment test' as advanced in this study.[77]

If one now wishes to direct one's attention to free movement of capital, then it appears that the Court indeed conducts its readjustment of the protective scope in such a way as to focus on whether a national measure restricts 'access to the market'. In two cases, *Commission v Kingdom of Spain*[78] and *Commission v United Kingdom*,[79] the United Kingdom government argued that the national measures at issue in the proceedings were not of such a nature as to restrict access to the

---

[71] Case C-44/98 *BASF AG v Präsident des Deutschen Patentamts*, para 21.
[72] Case C-412/97 *ED Srl v Italo Fenocchio*, para 11.
[73] [Emphasis added] Case C-44/98 *BASF AG v Präsident des Deutschen Patentamts*, para 21.
[74] This shift would probably not have come as a surprise to Advocate General *Jacobs*, who had already stated in *Leclerc-Siplec*: '[T]he underlying principle [to determine whether a measure falls within the scope of Art. 28 EC] which has inspired the Court's approach from Dassonville through 'Cassis de Dijon' to Keck' is such that 'all undertakings which engage in a legitimate economic activity in a Member State should have unfettered access to the whole of the Community market, unless there is a valid reason for denying them full access to a part of that market'. [Case C-412/93 (Opinion of AG Jacobs) *Société d'Importation Edouard Leclerc-Siplec v TF1 Publicité SA and M6 Publicité SA*, para 31]
[75] The Court has not yet embraced a *de minimis* exception within the ambit of free movement of capital, although it has been suggested by the parties to the dispute. *Cf* Case C-98/01 *Commission v United Kingdom (Re Golden Shares V)*, para 36.
[76] C Ohler, 'Kapitalverkehrsfreiheit', 1806.
[77] Also in favour of an application of a *Keck*-style formula: J Bröhmer, Art. 56 EC (2002), mn 51; G Ress and J Ukrow, Art. 56 EC (2002), mn 37; G Ress and J Ukrow, *Kapitalverkehrsfreiheit und Steuergerechtigkeit*, 31; A Rohde, *Kapitalverkehr*, 131 *et seq*; W-H Roth, 'Niederlassungsfreiheit', 740 *et seq*; C Koenig and A Haratsch, *Europarecht*, mn 697 *et seq*; A Haratsch, et al, *Europarecht*, mn 905 *et seq*; J Glöckner, 'Grundverkehrsbeschränkungen', 616 *et seq*. Undecided: P-C Müller-Graff, 'Einflußregulierungen', 940; JCW Müller, *Kapitalverkehrsfreiheit*, 165 *et seq*; W Kiemel, Art. 56 EC (2003), mn 27 *et seq*; C Ohler, Art. 56 EC (2002), mn 251 *et seq*.
[78] Case C-463/00 *Commission v Kingdom of Spain (Re Golden Shares IV)*, para 58 *et seq*.
[79] Case C-98/01 *Commission v United Kingdom (Re Golden Shares V)*, para 45 *et seq*.

market and and, thus, would not be subject to Art 56(1) EC. The Court did not reject such considerations outright,[80] but actually entered into a substantive examination of the effects of the national measures. The ECJ's finding that in the two individual cases the national provisions did indeed affect access to the market and therefore did not give rise to exceptions is only of minor importance. What is of interest is the general approach the Court chose, ie, it engaged in an analysis of whether the national measures which were indistinctly applicable would restrict access to the market. The Court would not have done so had it proceeded from the assumption that such a consideration would be inadmissible with respect to free movement of capital.

In principle, any national regulatory measure ultimately affects access of capital to a market; some do so directly and significantly, while others might produce only remote or negligible effects. Hence, as a next step, the question of when a measure substantially impedes market access has to be posed. Paraphrasing the Court's judgment in *Golden Shares IV*,[81] one could answer that a national measure substantially impedes market access when it affects 'the position of a person acquiring a shareholding as such'. Although the underlying notion to exempt the 'general regulatory framework', such as land register regulations, from the scope of Art 56(1) EC[82] is to be welcomed for the reasons mentioned above, the statement must be viewed—if it is intended to be of general value—as imperfect in at least three ways.

First, the recourse to 'person' within the scope of an object-oriented freedom[83] is, to say the least, unfortunate.[84]

Second, focusing on the impediment of '*access*' is not without problems. Peers rightly points out that an investor is not only concerned with gaining access to a market, but equally 'with the ability to repatriate or otherwise transfer profits or some or all of the original capital' out of the market.[85] Having established above that import ('access') and export ('exit') of capital is—in contrast to free movement of goods—subject to a single regime under Art 56(1) EC,[86] a national measure, in order to benefit from the *Keck*-style formula as understood here, must neither substantially impede access to nor exit from the market.[87]

Finally, while the acquisition of a shareholding is certainly one of the most relevant forms of the notion of 'movement of capital', one should not forget that this mirrors only a portion of the material scope of Art 56(1) EC.

---

[80] Also the judgment in Case C-302/97 (Opinion of AG La Pergola) *Klaus Konle v Republik Österreich* cannot be viewed as a rejection. See for a discussion: J Glöckner, 'Grundverkehrsbeschränkungen', 614 *et seq*. See *Oechsler* [J Oechsler, 'Golden Shares VI', 163] for a different view of the Court's 'Golden Share' case law.

[81] Case C-463/00 *Commission v Kingdom of Spain (Re Golden Shares IV)*, para 61.

[82] *Cf* J Bröhmer, Art. 56 EC (2002), mn 51; A Haratsch, et al, *Europarecht*, mn 905.

[83] PO Mülbert, 'Kapitalmarktrecht', 2090.

[84] See Chapter V.   [85] S Peers, 'Movement of Capital', 345.

[86] See Chapter IV. 2. a. (2).

[87] The transit of capital is nothing other than the summation of access and exit.

If one considers all of the above, it becomes reasonably clear that the ECJ's ruling is only conditionally capable of generalization. If one seeks to sensibly restrict the broad non-hindrance test à la *Commission v Portuguese Republic (Re Golden Shares I)* without sliding into a disguised discrimination test[88] of the kind criticized by Advocate General Jacobs in his opinion on *Leclerc-Siplec*,[89] the ultimate question of whether an indistinctly applicable measure should benefit from a *Keck*-style formula is one of the degree of impediment of capital movements into or out of the market. However, at what point this degree amounts to a 'substantial impediment' is a question that cannot be answered in abstract terms, but must be left to clarification—in a casuistic way—by the Court.[90] So far, the Court has not indicated in its case law that it would apply some sort of *de minimis* rule.[91] This, however, does not necessarily mean that such a rule does not exist or is not desirable, but simply that the facts presented before the Court have not given rise to an application of a *de minimus* rule.

---

[88] Peers, for example, suggests an 'adverse effect test'. 'Where it can be shown that a national rule is inherently likely to deter movement of capital from outside the country more than it would deter movements inside the country, then it should fall within the scope of the capital rules.' [S Peers, 'Movement of Capital', 345; leaning in the same direction J Glöckner, 'Grundverkehrsbeschränkungen', 619, G Ress and J Ukrow, Art. 56 EC (2002), mn 37] However, this interpretation, it is submitted, misconceives of the basic notion behind the non-hindrance test, which is liberalization. If one were to follow Peers's suggestion, then a Member State may arbitrarily restrict capital flow across its border provided only that it imposes the same arbitrary restriction on capital flows within the State. [*Cf* Case C-412/93 (Opinion of AG Jacobs) *Société d'Importation Edouard Leclerc-Siplec v TF1 Publicité SA and M6 Publicité SA*, para 39] This certainly does not lead to liberalization and market integration.

[89] Case C-412/93 (Opinion of AG Jacobs) *Société d'Importation Edouard Leclerc-Siplec v TF1 Publicité SA and M6 Publicité SA*, para 39. A shift away from the 'disguised discrimination test' within the *Keck* formula can be seen in Case C-384/93 *Alpine Investments BV v Minister van Financiën*, para 35: 'Although a prohibition such as the one at issue in the main proceedings is general and non-discriminatory and neither its object nor its effect is to put the national market at an advantage over providers of services from other Member States, it can nonetheless . . . constitute a restriction on the freedom to provide cross-border services.'

[90] While, for example, the requirement of prior approval of acquisition of real property amounts by its very nature to a substantial impediment [Case C-302/97 *Klaus Konle v Republik Österreich*, para 39; Joined Cases C-515/99 and C-527/99 to C-540/99 and Joined Cases C-519/99 to C-524/99 and C-526/99 *Hans Reisch and Others v Bürgermeister der Landeshauptstadt Salzburg and Grundverkehrsbeauftragter des Landes Salzburg and Anton Lassacher and Others v Grundverkehrsbeauftragter des Landes Salzburg and Grundverkehrslandeskommission des Landes Salzburg*, para 32], the situation might be a different one if the Court is called to rule upon the question of whether the announcement of a minister to amend certain national legislation in order to prevent the takeover of a public company by a foreign competitor deters capital movement across borders. ['Gazprom kreuzt die Klinge mit Brüssel: Russlands Gasgigant will expandieren und stößt dabei auf Widerstand' *Handelsblatt* (26.4.2006); J Blitz and S Wagstyl, 'Gazprom Block over Centrica Ruled out' *Financial Times* (26.4.2006)]

[91] An application was suggested by the parties to the dispute in *Commission v United Kingdom*, *cf* Case C-98/01 *Commission v United Kingdom (Re Golden Shares V)*, para 36. See also J Steiner, et al, *EU Law*, 347; strictly opposing a *de minimis* rule but embracing the application of the *Keck* formula: G Ress and J Ukrow, Art. 56 EC (2002), mn 50, 37; see also W Schön, 'Kapitalverkehrsfreiheit', 755; L Flynn, 'Coming of Age', 783.

Recalling my finding above that only a broad interpretation of the scope of application of Art 56(1) EC gives sufficient consideration to the achievement of the economic aims pursued by the freedom,[92] the threshold for subjecting a measure which is indistinctly applicable to review should not be set too high. One must also keep in mind that a very narrow construction of a *Keck*-style formula could cause a drastic levelling of differences in the legal orders of the Member States. Levelling dissimilarities among legal orders of the Member States means hampering competition for the best regulatory solution. In the end, when considering the question of whether a national measure substantially impedes the access/exit of capital to/from a national market, it is necessary to strike a balance between the instruction given by Art 56(1) EC, ie, to liberalize capital flows to the greatest extent possible in order to maximize general welfare effects, and the preservation of a coherent general legal framework within the Member State.

(b) A Need for a Substantial Impediment Test?—The Seemingly Non-exhaustive Character of Article 58(1) lit. b EC

Even if the critics of an application of a *Keck*-style formula were prepared to accept that the inherent weaknesses of *Keck* after reconstruction in the way suggested above are not of such a nature as to preclude their application to the ambit of free movement of capital, another argument against the application of such a formula (but also against the application of the rule of reason) is advanced that deserves to be considered. Critics argue that the non-exhaustive character of Art 58 EC ('... in particular...') would render the necessity of an application of a *Keck*-style formula in the context of Art 56 EC doubtful.[93] While Art 30 EC provides an exhaustive list of grounds of justification that are narrowly construed,[94] the—by its wording—seemingly 'open-ended list' of Art 58(1) lit. b EC provides the Member States with sufficient room for political choice. Thus, there would be no need for further exceptions. With respect to the application of the *Cassis de Dijon* formula, this argument is to some extent debatable;[95] however, with respect to the *Keck*-style formula, it is not convincing. Not applying a *Keck*-style formula would ultimately mean subjecting all national measures to the necessity of justification irrespective of whether or not they substantially impede access to or exit from the market. In other words, the opinion mentioned above would subject national measures within the ambit of free movement of capital to a more rigid review than in the context of free movement of goods and other freedoms, for which no

---

[92] See Chapter I. 2.
[93] This argument is mentioned by JCW Müller, *Kapitalverkehrsfreiheit*, 165 *et seq*; however, it appears that ultimately Müller does not subscribe to this view.
[94] Case 46/76 *W. J. G. Bauhuis v The Netherlands State*, para 12; Case 113/80 *Commission v Ireland (Re Irish Souvenirs)*, para 7.
[95] This study proceeds from the assumption that the seemingly 'open-ended' list in Art 58(1) lit. b EC is in fact not at all 'open-ended' in the true sense of the word, and there is thus sufficient room and need for an application of the *Cassis de Dijon* formula. For a discussion refer to Chapter VI. 2. a. (1) (c).

justification can be envisaged if one is prepared to accept that the non-hindrance test is primarily about guaranteeing access to/exit from the market.

(4) Conclusions

Free movement of capital is part of the broader context of converging tendencies of construction among the fundamental freedoms, which means first that Art 56(1) EC contains, besides a prohibition of discrimination, one of hindrance too. The latter can be sketched as follows: A national measure is subject to Art 56(1) EC, even though the rules in issue may not give rise to unequal treatment, if they are capable of impeding cross-border capital movements and dissuading investors from investing.

It is worth noting that in the context of free movement of capital, no distinction is drawn between import and export of capital.

In order to prevent a potential overreach of the non-hindrance test as well as to remain true to 'market integration' as the central idea inherent in the fundamental freedoms, a *Keck*-style formula is also applied to the freedom of capital movement and can be summarized as follows: A national measure is not subject to Art 56(1) EC if it does not substantially impede capital movements across borders and, at the same time, if it applies indistinctly in law and in fact.

The seemingly non-exhaustive character of Art 58(1) lit. b EC does not render the application of a *Keck*-style formula unnecessary. The degree of impediment required in order to amount to a substantial one is a question that can ultimately not be answered in abstract terms, but must be left to clarification by the Court. It requires striking a balance between the gist of Art 56(1) EC, ie, to liberalize the movement of capital to the greatest extent possible in order to maximize general welfare effects, and the preservation of a coherent general legal framework within the Member State.

b. The Non-Discrimination Test in an Intra-Community Context

As discussed above, the 'prohibition of restrictions' of Art 56(1) EC also contains a 'prohibition of discrimination', which itself is *lex specialis* to Art 12 EC.[96] While the 'prohibition of hindrance' establishes an absolute legal position operating 'vertically', the prohibition of discrimination constitutes a relative legal position with a horizontal character.[97] Thus, if someone makes a claim of discrimination, then this must be done 'against' someone else or 'between' two situations. With respect to Art 56(1) EC, this means that one capital movement must always

---

[96] *Cf* S Mohamed, *Free Movement of Capital*, 58 *et seq*; C Ohler, Art. 56 EC (2002), mn 258; note also: Case C-376/03 (Opinion of AG Colomer) *D v Inspecteur van de Belastingdienst/Particulieren/Ondernemingen buitenland te Heerlen*, mn 97, endnote 52.

[97] T Kingreen and R Störmer, 'Subjetiv-öffentlichen Rechte', 268.

be seen in comparison to another one.[98] The groups of capital movement to be contrasted, cross-border[99] and domestic and cross-border and cross-border, will be referred to in this study as comparison groups. If cross-border and domestic situations are compared, then this corresponds to the international economic law principle of 'national treatment' (NT).[100] Comparing two cross-border situations to one other resembles in structure the international economic law principle of most-favoured-nation (MFN)[101] treatment.

In general parlance, discrimination (unequal treatment) is said to exist if either similar or comparable ('issue of comparability') situations are treated differently or if situations differing from each other are treated alike.[102] Transferred to the ambit of Art 56(1) EC, this denotes that if cross-border and domestic capital movement, although comparable, are treated differently, or if cross-border and domestic capital movement, although not comparable, are treated alike, discrimination can be established. The same applies, *mutatis mutandis*, to the situation in which different cross-border capital movements are involved.

As a result of the discrimination, the capital movement that was discriminated against must be placed in a less favourable position by the measure at issue.[103]

Furthermore, discriminatory treatment must originate from one and the same Member State authority (or any other person who is bound by Art 56(1) EC[104]). Thus, differences in treatment resulting from differences between the legal orders of two or more Member States cannot give rise to a discrimination claim. The alleged discriminatory conduct must always be attributable to one source.[105]

---

[98] As I shall discuss further, in principle, different cross-border capital movements can also be contrasted. See Chapter IV. 2. b. (1).

[99] In the ambit of free movement of capital, 'cross-border' means both capital movement that links two different Member States and that linking a Member State and a third country.

[100] R Dolzer, 'Wirtschaft und Kultur im Völkerrecht (4th edn)', mn 23 *et seq.*

[101] Ibid, mn 19 *et seq.*

[102] S Plötscher, *Diskriminierung*, 33 *et seq.* It is worth mentioning that the latter case does not play a significant practical role due to the fact that the Court deals with such a situation by means of the non-hindrance test. See for example, though not decided on the basis of the rules on free movement of capital: Case C-250/95 *Futura Participations SA and Singer v Administration des contributions*, para 23 *et seq ; Cf* also C Ohler, Art. 56 EC (2002), mn 256. Moreover, an equal treatment of unequal situations can often be re-phrased as an unequal treatment of equal situations.

[103] Case 22/80 *Boussac Saint-Frères SA v Brigitte Gerstenmeier*, paras 10, 13; Case C-336/96 *Mr and Mrs Robert Gilly v Directeur des services fiscaux du Bas-Rhin*, para 33 *et seq ;* see for a more principled account S Plötscher, *Diskriminierung*, 49 *et seq.* It is not sufficient that disadvantages are counterbalanced by advantages flowing from measures other than the one at issue. *Cf* Case 270/83 *Commission v French Republic (Re Corporation Tax and Shareholders' Tax Credits: 'avoir fiscal'*, para 21.

[104] For the issue of horizontal direct effect of Art 56(1) EC, See Chapter V. 5. c.

[105] A Epiney, Art. 12 EC (2002), mn 5; U Haferkamp, *Kapitalverkehrsfreiheit*, 92 *et seq*; R Streinz, Art. 12 EC (2003), mn 45; R Wernsmann, 'Steuerliche Diskriminierung', 757; M Zuleeg, Art. 12 EC (2003), mn 6; Differentiating: W Schön, 'Kapitalverkehrsfreiheit', 761 *et seq.*

However, even if all of the conditions above are fulfilled, this has not necessarily led to the conclusion that such discrimination is prohibited by virtue of Art 56(1) EC. In certain situations, such unequal treatment may be justified.[106]

So-called reverse discrimination is generally outside the scope of Community law. In this study, I refer to reverse discrimination if a national measure operates solely to the detriment of domestic capital movement. Due to the fact that EC law applies only to cross-border situations and, on the other hand, that the competence of the Community is limited, Member States are *per se* free to put their own nationals, who do not wish to make use of the fundamental freedoms or products that are produced and will remain within the Member State, in a less favourable position than nationals or products taking part in cross-border movements.[107]

This having been said, in the following subsections I shall now set out my understanding of the non-discrimination test embodied in Art 56(1) EC in more detail. I shall first explain the formation of comparison groups, which relates, simply speaking, to the question of what is compared with what. Secondly, I shall explain what I deem to be the relevant distinguishing criteria and how direct and indirect discrimination may be delineated. Before I turn to a discussion of the issue of comparability, I will, in an excursion, contrast the doctrinal framework developed in the previous section with that of the Court with respect to distinguishing criteria, direct and indirect discrimination, and the delineation of the non-discrimination and non-hindrance tests.

(1) Comparison Groups

In the normal case, cross-border capital movements[108] and domestic capital movements are compared.[109] Unless a discriminatory national measure is justified by overriding public interests,[110] free movement of capital grants to their beneficiaries, pursuing cross-border economic activity, the individual right not to be treated differently from comparable domestic situations.[111] Such a comparison, as mentioned above, corresponds to the international economic law principle of national treatment.

It is, however, also conceivable that cross-border capital movements originating from or directed to different Member States or third countries are treated

---

[106] See Chapter VI and Chapter VII.
[107] D Ehlers, 'Allgemeine Lehren', § 7, mn 20 *et seq*; G More, 'Equal Treatment', 528 *et seq*; S Plötscher, *Diskriminierung*, 74 *et seq*; J Steiner and L Woods, *EC Law*, 223, 266 *et seq*; all with further references.
[108] Either originating from or directed to another Member State or from or to a third country.
[109] eg, Case C-302/97 *Klaus Konle v Republik Österreich*, 23; Case C-423/98 *Alfredo Albore*, para 16; Case C-367/98 *Commission v Portuguese Republic (Re Golden Shares I)*, para 40.
[110] See Chapter VI and Chapter VII.
[111] This right is to be understood as a ('negative') right to be protected from the State. *Cf* C Tietje, 'Meistbegünstigungspflicht', 398 *et seq*.

differently amongst themselves.[112] The comparison of different cross-border capital movements resembles in its structure the international economic law principle of most-favoured-nation treatment and suggests the formation of additional comparison groups within the non-discrimination test contained in Art 56(1) EC;[113] ie, first, cross-border capital movement originating from or directed to two different Member States compared to each other, second, cross-border capital movements originating from or directed to another Member State compared with a third country capital movement, and third, capital movements directed to or originating from third countries compared to one other.

The comparison of different cross-border movements is in principle not alien to the Court's case law. In *Dassonville*, examining the question of whether the national measure at issue constitutes arbitrary discrimination within the meaning of Art 30, 2nd sentence EC, the Court compared the treatment of imports of goods originating from different Member States.[114] In *Roders*, a case concerned with tax discrimination (Art 90 EC), the Court held that the Benelux countries were 'not at liberty to favour fruit wines produced in one of the three Benelux countries, to the detriment of beverages which might be similar, coming from another Member State of the Community.'[115] Thus, what was compared was the treatment of goods originating from different Member States.

In the ambit of free movement of capital, the issue featured prominently in the so-called 'D' case.[116] A German resident, Mr D, challenged tax treatment by the Netherlands under the Dutch-German tax treaty on the grounds that it treated him less favourably than Belgian residents under the Dutch-Belgian tax treaty.[117]

---

[112] That all of this is not just of academic interest is demonstrated best—with respect to the subject matter of this study—by the French foreign investment rules, which differentiate between domestic, EC, and non-EC capital movements: see Art L 151–1 to Art L 151–6 of the MFC (France) and Décret n° 2005–1739 (France); see also, for a brief account of the new French legislation, W Maxwell, 'France'. Note, though, that the aforementioned author proceeds—I think erroneously—from the assumption that '[t]he European rules on the free movement of capital do *not* apply to non-EU investments…' [emphasis added]. The situation in Germany is informed by § 7(1) and (2) No 5 of the AWG (Germany) and § 52 of the AWV (Germany). The respective provisions establish different treatment for residents and for non-residents.

[113] The wording of Art 56(1) EC—in the same way as Arts 39 EC and 12 EC—would clearly cover MFN-style comparison groups. [N Herzig and N Dautzenberg, 'Doppelbesteuerungsabkommen', 2522; along similar lines Case C-376/03 (Opinion of AG Colomer) *D v Inspecteur van de Belastingdienst/Particulieren/Ondernemingen buitenland te Heerlen*, para 97, endnote 52] However, given the converging tendency in interpreting the fundamental freedoms—embedding MFN treatment in the wording of Arts 43 EC and 49 EC causes problems—it is open to debate whether one would not do better to choose Art 12 EC as the legal foundation of an MFN treatment standard. However, this seems to face even more difficulties. *Cf* G Kofler, 'MFN Treatment', 63 *et seq*.

[114] Case 8/74 *Procureur du Roi v Benoît and Gustave Dassonville*, para 9. See also Case 13/63 *Italian Republic v Commission*; *cf* in this respect: S Plötscher, *Diskriminierung*, 109.

[115] Joined Cases C-367/93 to C-377/93 *F. G. Roders BV and others v Inspecteur der Invoerrechten en Accijnzen*, para 23.

[116] Case C-376/03 *D v Inspecteur van de Belastingdienst/Particulieren/Ondernemingen buitenland te Heerlen*.

[117] *Cf*, eg, G Kofler, 'MFN Treatment', 52 *et seq*; see also G Kofler and CP Schindler, 'MFN Treatment', 531.

Although the Court in '*D*' ultimately denied a violation of Art 56(1) EC, it did not do so on the basis of the argument that the MFN treatment standard is completely alien to EC law in general or free movement of capital in particular. The ECJ came to the conclusion that in the case at hand, the two cross-border capital movements at issue were not comparable.[118] Hence, one could read the ECJ's judgment as stating that the Member States are, by reason of Art 56(1) EC, not at liberty to treat comparable cross-border capital movements in a discriminatory fashion. Such an interpretation also seems to find sufficient support in systematic and teleological considerations.[119]

Article 306 EC provides that the provisions of the EC Treaty 'shall not preclude the existence or completion of regional unions between Belgium, Luxembourg and the Netherlands, to the extent that the objectives of these regional unions are not attained by application of this Treaty'. This provision explicitly reserves special benefits for the beneficiaries of the Belgium-Luxembourg Economic Union and Benelux Customs Union that cannot be extended to other Member State nationals by virtue of EC law. Hence, *argumentum e contrario*, in the absence of a specific permission, a Member State appears not to be entitled to grant specific benefits to a particular Member State or group of Member States.[120]

Furthermore, viewed against the background of the function of the prohibition of discrimination in EC law, it is only consistent to allow for the aforementioned comparison groups.[121] Not only the principle of national treatment but

---

[118] Case C-376/03 (Opinion of AG Colomer) *D v Inspecteur van de Belastingdienst/Particulieren/Ondernemingen buitenland te Heerlen*, para 44 *et seq*. For a discussion of the issue of comparability in such situations, see Chapter IV. 2. b. (4) (a) ii. (i). Within the ambit of taxation the following cases, inter alia, touched upon the issue of most-favoured-nation treatment with regard to double taxation treaties: Case C-376/03 (Opinion of AG Colomer) *D v Inspecteur van de Belastingdienst/Particulieren/Ondernemingen buitenland te Heerlen* (double taxation treaty between Member States); Case C-307/97 *Compagnie de Saint-Gobain, Zweigniederlassung Deutschland v Finanzamt Aachen-Innenstadt*; Case C-374/04 *Test Claimants in Class IV of the ACT Group Litigation (Pirelli, Essilor and Sony), Test Claimants in Class IV of the ACT Group Litigation (BMW) v Commissioners of Inland Revenue* (third country double taxation treaty); for social security convention concluded with a third country see: Case C-55/00 *Elide Gottardo v Istituto nazionale della previdenza sociale (INPS)*. See also the *van Hilten* case: Case C-513/03 *Heirs of M. E. A. van Hilten-van der Heijden v Inspecteur van de Belastingdienst/Particulieren/Ondernemingen buitenland te Heerlen*—although not the 'classical' situation of infringement of the most-favoured-nation treatment standard, at least from a systematic viewpoint, possibly to be placed in this group. See for a more detailed discussion of the issue of selecting the comparison groups in this case: A Schnitger, 'Kapitalverkehrsfreiheit', 499. However, both the Advocate General as well as the Court refused—in the special situation—to treat the case in terms of a most-favoured-nation situation. See Case C-513/03 (Opinion of AG Léger) *Heirs of M. E. A. van Hilten-van der Heijden v Inspecteur van de Belastingdienst/Particulieren/Ondernemingen buitenland te Heerlen*, para 71 *et seq*.

[119] See in this respect also the very instructive Case C-376/03 (Opinion of AG Colomer) *D v Inspecteur van de Belastingdienst/Particulieren/Ondernemingen buitenland te Heerlen*; note KE Sørensen, 'MFN Principle'.

[120] C Tietje, 'Meistbegünstigungspflicht', 406 *et seq*; G Kofler, 'MFN Treatment', 65.

[121] The discussion surrounding MFN treatment in EC law is mainly conducted in the context of bilateral tax treaties. The number of publications dealing with this particular issue—ranging from warmly welcoming to vehemently rejecting MFN treatment—has grown enormously. For a bibliographic account, refer to G Kofler and CP Schindler, 'MFN Treatment', 532, fn 15.

equally the principle of MFN treatment arises from the idea of equal treatment of economic activities and non-discrimination in cross-border situations.[122] Their function is to guarantee that every market participant enjoys the same material rights. This is also precisely what is intended to be reached by the prohibitions of discrimination contained in the fundamental freedoms and in Art 12 EC. The equal endowment with rights (and duties) of the market participants constitutes the indispensable proposition of any economic integration. The functioning of the Internal Market[123] essentially requires a competitive, level playing field and the absence of protectionism.[124] Hence, in short, one could suggest that MFN treatment is, in the same way as national treatment, generally inherent in the concept of a close Community of States.[125]

In the absence of MFN treatment, however, the level playing field just mentioned could be endangered, which can be demonstrated by the following example. Imagine two Member States, A and B, each with a distinct economic sector in which their businesses are very competitive. The respective sector that is strong in one Member State is underdeveloped and with no appreciable economic activity in the other Member State. Assume, moreover, that these two Member States would agree to reciprocally grant advantageous benefits better than national treatment standards to the residents of the other Member State in their respective underdeveloped sectors. As a consequence, the business of Member State A will possibly acquire a strong market position in the underdeveloped sector in B and *vice versa*. If, now, an entrepreneur of Member State C wants to enter into the sector in B in which the entrepreneurs of A enjoy better than national treatment standards, then the former will face problems competing if he is only entitled to national treatment. If the entrepreneur of C were to decide to enter the sector in B through an establishment in A in order to participate in the special benefits, it would still face the costs of an additional establishment, which might render it unattractive to enter the sector of B at all. Moreover, if A were not a Member State but a third country, the entrepreneur of C would not even have the right by virtue of the EC Treaty to enter the sector in B via an establishment in A.

The above makes it clear that without the MFN treatment standard, the Member States could erect—with the help of other Member States or third countries—protectionist hurdles, distorting competition and furthering

---

[122] C Tietje, 'Meistbegünstigungspflicht', 406 *et seq*, esp. 409. Those who hold the view that MFN treatment constitutes a *minus* compared to NT treatment face the problem that the NT treatment standard would then prescribe the outer boundary of the freedom. Hence, the most a market participant would be entitled to would be the NT treatment standard. *Cordewener* correctly points out that in this case, the whole MFN discussion would be 'much ado about nothing'. [A Cordewener, *Grundfreiheiten*, 838 *et seq* for further references]

[123] *Cf* Art 14(2) EC.

[124] C Tietje, 'Meistbegünstigungspflicht', 406 *et seq*, esp. 409; G Kofler and CP Schindler, 'MFN Treatment'; see also A von Bogdandy, Art. 12 EC (2002), mn 1.

[125] S De Ceulaer, 'MFN Treatment', 495; L Hinnekens, 'Bilateral Tax Treaties', 213; opposing: T Rödder and J Schönfeld, 'Anmerkung zu C-376/03 ('D')', 525.

misallocating resources as they coax entrepreneurs to channel their economic activities through certain Member States in order to participate in special benefits. It therefore seems only reasonable to allow for both national treatment as well as MFN treatment-style comparison groups within the ambit of Art 56(1) EC.

However, MFN treatment-style comparison groups will probably not play an overly decisive role. Following the rules of logic, the different treatment of capital movements originating from or directed to two third countries, or two other Member States, or a third country and another Member State compellingly also means different treatment for the third country/other Member State capital movement in comparison to domestic capital movement. If capital movement from country A is treated differently from capital movement from country B, then there are three opinions with respect to the domestic capital movement D: if A is treated like D, then B is treated differently from D; if B is treated like D, then A is treated differently from D or A, B, and D are all treated differently. In each case, there is a difference between the cross-border and domestic capital movements.

An MFN treatment-style comparison will play an independent role, though, in cases in which MFN treatment is simply more advantageous than national treatment. Different lines of argument apply depending on whether one is defending different treatments of cross-border and domestic capital movements or different treatments of two cross-border capital movements.[126]

(2) Direct and Indirect Discrimination—Relevant Distinguishing Criteria

(a) Terminology

Concurrently with the converging system of interpretation of the fundamental freedoms,[127] two types of discrimination can be distinguished. For these types no coherent terminology exists. This study will differentiate between these two types by referring to direct and indirect discrimination.[128]

'Direct discrimination' refers to a national measure containing an expressly prohibited distinguishing criterion (eg, 'nationality' in Art 12(1) EC or Art 39(2) EC) as one of its elements. 'Indirect discrimination' will be referred to if the prohibited distinguishing criterion is replaced by a 'neutral' surrogate criterion that

---

[126] S Plötscher, *Diskriminierung*, 168 *et seq*. It could, for example, occur that domestic and foreign capital movements are not in comparable situations but two foreign capital movements are. Moreover, different grounds of justification could also apply depending on whether one looks at the issue from the perspective of national treatment or from that of most-favoured-nation treatment.

[127] See, for a brief account of the prohibition of discrimination in other freedoms, U Haferkamp, *Kapitalverkehrsfreiheit*, 61 *et seq*.

[128] CO Lenz, Art. 12 EC (2003), mn 4 *et seq*; formal and material discrimination: *cf*, eg, A Epiney, Art. 12 EC (2002), mn 11 *et seq*; U Haferkamp, *Kapitalverkehrsfreiheit*, 61 *et seq*; W Kiemel, Art. 56 EC (2003), mn 7; overt and covert discrimination: *cf*, eg, R Eckhoff, 'Kapital- und Zahlungsverkehr', mn 1705; C Ohler, Art. 56 EC (2002), mn 255; P-C Müller-Graff, Art. 43 EC (2003), mn 43.

'in fact leads to the same result' ('*Satgiu* jurisprudence')[129] as if the distinction had been based on the prohibited distinguishing criterion.[130]

There can be hardly any doubt that both categories of discrimination are part of the EC Treaty's notion of discrimination. Even though the distinction between direct and indirect discrimination is of no relevance on the level of the scope of application and both categories are increasingly dealt with by the Court in similar terms on the level of grounds of justification, delineating both categories remains necessary until the case law of the Court has become sufficiently clear on the problem of whether unwritten grounds of justification ('rule of reason') equally apply to direct discrimination.[131]

While the issue within the concept of indirect discrimination revolves around the question of which degree of equivalence between the prohibited distinguishing criterion and the 'neutral' surrogate criterion must exist,[132] a different discussion, which must be strictly distinguished from the aforementioned, has been spinning around the ambiguous heading of 'effect based discrimination',[133] ie, discrimination in substance, or *'materielle Diskriminierung'*.[134] It relates to the question of whether it suffices to locate the discrimination exclusively in the effect of a national measure (discrimination in fact; causal discrimination), or whether one should demand that discrimination originate in some way from the form of the norm (discrimination in form; final discrimination[135]). The

---

[129] Case 152/73 *Giovanni Maria Sotgiu v Deutsche Bundespost*, para 11. A considerable lack of clarity exists with respect to the precise content of the criteria employed by the ECJ in order to define the phrase 'in fact leads to the same result'. Instead of specifying the aforementioned criteria, the Court operates with certain categories of precedents. [*Cf* S Plötscher, *Diskriminierung*, 55] Doctrinally, the question of which requirements the connection between the prohibited distinguishing criterion and the surrogate criterion must meet is asked. With all necessary brevity, this study proceeds from the assumption that, first, a factual (ie, the same effects in fact, having some statistical significance) or at least a normative (risk of the same effects, *cf* Case C-204/90 *Hanns-Martin Bachmann v The Belgian State*, para 9) equivalence between the differentiation based upon the prohibited and the surrogate criterion must exist. Secondly, what is also required is the absence of objective grounds for the use of the surrogate criterion. For an in-depth discussion refer to S Plötscher, *Diskriminierung*, 54 *et seq*; see also N Bernard, 'Discrimination', 97 *et seq*.

[130] S Plötscher, *Diskriminierung*, 54.

[131] See Chapter VI. 6. a.   [132] See footnote 129 of this Chapter.

[133] N Bernard, 'Discrimination', 97 *et seq*.

[134] J Lübke, *Kapitalverkehrs- und Niederlassungsfreiheit*, 272 *et seq*; along similar lines: T Kingreen, *Struktur der Grundfreiheiten*, 121 *et seq*; N Bernard, 'Discrimination', 102.

[135] In case of a final understanding of the concept of discrimination, it is assumed that the national measure serves certain purposes. Therein the issue of whether the discrimination test contains a voluntary element, ie, some sort of intention, is raised. [S Plötscher, *Diskriminierung*, 70] 'A "true" disparate impact theory [, in contrast,] . . . would focus exclusively on the effect and would locate discrimination in the effect itself.' [N Bernard, 'Discrimination', 101] However, even if one were to follow a final understanding of discrimination, a voluntary element can play only an ancillary, dependent role. At most, voluntary elements could have relevance if they refer to the pursued protectionist purpose, which is already implied in the case of direct discrimination. Regarding measures that discriminate indirectly, while a protectionist purpose cannot be said to exist at face value, such a purpose can be deduced from the typical effect. [*Cf.* S Plötscher, *Diskriminierung*, 207] See also C Ohler, Art. 56 EC (2002), 268 *et seq*; A Honrath, *Kapitalverkehr*, 90; JCW Müller, *Kapitalverkehrsfreiheit*, 164 *et seq*; L Flynn, 'Coming of Age', 780. Note also Case C-302/97

former aims more at the eradication of a certain state and the latter of a particular conduct.[136] One could of course argue that the formal design of a measure could not be decisive because, in principle, every element of a rule constitutes a 'neutral' distinguishing criterion. However, this argument is too short-sighted. While it is true that any element of a rule constitutes a 'neutral' distinguishing criterion, the crucial question is whether the required '*same result*'[137] as discrimination based on the prohibited distinguishing criterion must originate in some way from the form of the rule.[138] If one were to abandon the need for such a link, one would face the difficulty that such a concept of discrimination extends also to those cases in which a different effect is coincidental, ie, it originates from the situation but not from the rule that is applied to it.[139] This concept of discrimination blurs considerably the distinction between the non-discrimination test and the non-hindrance test due to the fact that it runs the risk of loosening the link between the respective national measure, its addressee, and the different effects.[140] Therefore, this study seeks to limit the concept of indirect discrimination to those measures that expressly provide for some 'neutral' surrogate distinguishing criterion.[141] Although this might provide some clarity with respect to the delineation of national measures that discriminate indirectly from those that constitute a 'mere' hindrance (ie, such measures that, although operating indistinctly, constitute a barrier to free capital flow), nevertheless, instead of speaking about a sharp dividing line, one can better visualize the situation as a grey area of crossover.[142]

(b) Direct Discrimination—Expressly Prohibited Distinguishing Criteria

i. The Origin/Destination of Capital Movements   As with the provisions on free movement of goods, the wording of Art 56(1) EC also does not expressly mention a prohibited distinguishing criterion. Thus, this criterion—which is essentially also the criterion with which the cross-border element is established[143]—must be

---

(Opinion of AG La Pergola) *Klaus Konle v Republik Österreich*, para 41, Case C-302/97 *Klaus Konle v Republik Österreich*, para 20 *et seq* for an example of how the Court and the Advocate General refer to a voluntary element.

[136] S Plötscher, *Diskriminierung*, 52.
[137] Case 152/73 *Giovanni Maria Sotgiu v Deutsche Bundespost*, para 11.
[138] The relevant distinction is drawn by the distinctly applicable measure, ie, the national measure treats two circumstances differently by virtue of a distinguishing criterion. In other words, the measure expressly distinguishes.
[139] S Plötscher, *Diskriminierung*, 62 *et seq*; *cf.* Case C-391/92 *Commission v Greece (Re Processed Milk for Infants)*, para 17; see also Case C-391/92 (Opinion of AG Lenz) *Commission v Greece (Re Processed Milk for Infants)*; for a different view: J Lübke, *Kapitalverkehrs- und Niederlassungsfreiheit*, 282.
[140] S Plötscher, *Diskriminierung*, 70 *et seq*; Lübke, although not discounting this argument, nevertheless seeks to have recourse to the concept of 'material discrimination', *cf* J Lübke, *Kapitalverkehrs- und Niederlassungsfreiheit*, 282.
[141] Of the same opinion: C Ohler, Art. 56 EC (2002), mn 264.
[142] Ibid.   [143] See Chapter II. 3. b.

extracted by means of the remaining methods of construction, first and foremost by teleological interpretation of Art 56(1) EC.[144]

In reviewing the available literature, it appears that some insecurity still exists as to what amounts to this prohibited distinguishing criterion, which has a direct bearing on what constitutes direct discrimination. In the view of some commentators, direct discrimination refers to the situation in which a national measure differentiates on the basis of nationality (expressly prohibited distinguishing criterion). Indirect discrimination shall allude to a measure that employs a different distinguishing criterion, such as residence or place of investment,[145] which supposedly operates in fact like discrimination based on nationality.[146]

This view, however, appears to be hardly convincing. While the old Art 67 EEC, in its first section, did indeed ask the Member States to progressively abolish any discrimination based, inter alia, on nationality, the aforementioned provision was repealed and replaced by Art 73b(1) ToM (now, after amendment, Art 56(1) EC); any reference to nationality was purposely omitted. The current wording of Art 56(1) EC provides for the prohibition of 'all restrictions on the movement of capital between Member States and between Member States and third countries' and, hence, liberalizes the movement of capital *per se*. As stated earlier in the course of this study, free movement of capital aims at the optimal allocation of the production factor 'capital' and consequently seeks to prevent discrimination against imported or exported capital in comparison to capital transferred within a Member State.[147] Establishing whether capital was imported or exported, ie, whether it crossed a national border, usually requires a comparison of the locations of capital before and after a given transaction.[148] Concerning intangible capital, the location of capital is ascertained with reference to the (habitual) residence of the holder, or if need be by a search for the country where local conditions determine the return on investment.[149] The legal affiliation to a Member State of those participating in a transaction by nationality is—in contrast to the person-oriented freedoms—in this respect of no relevance.

Hence, the origin and destination of the capital movements constitutes the expressly prohibited distinguishing criterion within the ambit of free movement

---

[144] Also along similar lines: J Lübke, *Kapitalverkehrs- und Niederlassungsfreiheit*, 274.

[145] *Cf* Art 58(1) lit. a EC.

[146] *Cf*, eg, C Ohler, Art. 56 EC (2002), mn 261. Ohler wants to transfer the findings made with respect to the person-related freedoms to the ambit of free movement of capital. [C Ohler, Art. 56 EC (2002), mn 256] See also A Honrath, *Kapitalverkehr*, 85; M Sedlaczek, Art. 58 EC (2003), mn 6 *et seq*; A Knapp, 'Diskriminierende Grunderwerbsbeschränkungen', 413; N Dautzenberg, 'Kapitalanlageort', 380; Case C-452/01 (Opinion of AG Geelhoed) *Margarethe Ospelt and Schlössle Weissenberg Familienstiftung*, para 124; Case C-376/03 (Opinion of AG Colomer) *D v Inspecteur van de Belastingdienst/Particulieren/Ondernemingen buitenland te Heerlen*, mn 57, 66.

[147] See Chapter II. 3.

[148] See Chapter II. 3. b for situations in which additional considerations, in particular, recourse to the place of productive employment of the capital, are necessary in order to establish the cross-border element.

[149] See Chapter II. 3. b.

of capital. Direct discrimination exists if the respective national measure treats a cross-border capital movement disadvantageously on the basis of its origin or destination.[150] Discrimination on the basis of the participants' place of residence is functionally equivalent in cases of intangible capital due to the fact that this capital is—normatively speaking—found where its holder resides. Indirect discrimination occurs if a surrogate criterion is employed that 'in fact leads to the same result'[151] as if the distinction had been based on the origin or destination of capital flows. An example for such a surrogate criterion in the ambit of free movement of capital would then be nationality, which only typically leads to discrimination in cross-border capital movements against those occurring within a Member State.[152] In this context, it is worth adding that nationality as a distinguishing criterion[153] does not play a significant practical role within the ambit of free movement of capital, but it is the place of residence of those who participate in a transaction, as well as the place of investment, that is regularly chosen by the Member States as the basis of discrimination.[154]

---

[150] R Eckhoff, 'Kapital- und Zahlungsverkehr', mn 1705; G Ress and J Ukrow, Art. 56 EC (2002), mn 39, who refer explicitly to criteria of the origin of capital and the place of investment as marking direct discrimination. See also W Pfeil, 'Freier Kapitalverkehr', 789 *et seq*; J Lübke, *Kapitalverkehrs- und Niederlassungsfreiheit*, 274 *et seq*.

[151] '*Satgiu* jurisprudence'; see footnote 129 of this Chapter.

[152] J Lübke, *Kapitalverkehrs- und Niederlassungsfreiheit*, 277 *et seq*, 279. See for the question of parallel applicability of Arts 294 EC and 12 EC with respect to discrimination on the basis of nationality: J Lübke, *Kapitalverkehrs- und Niederlassungsfreiheit*, 280 *et seq*. Another example for a surrogate criterion would be 'foreign currency', *cf* Case C-222/97 *Manfred Trummer and Peter Mayer*.

[153] *Cf*, eg, Case C-54/99 *Association Eglise de Scientologie de Paris and Scientology International Reserves Trust v The Prime Minister*; Case C-423/98 *Alfredo Albore*.

[154] eg, Case 157/85 *Luigi Brugnoni and Roberto Ruffinengo v Cassa di risparmio di Genova e Imperia*; Joined Cases C-358/93 and C-416/93 *Criminal proceedings against Aldo Bordessa and Vicente Marí Mellado and Concepción Barbero Maestre*; Joined Cases C-163/94, C-165/94, and C-250/94 *Criminal proceedings against Lucas Emilio Sanz de Lera, Raimundo Díaz Jiménez and Figen Kapanoglu*; Case C-484/93 *Peter Svensson et Lena Gustavsson v Ministre du Logement et de l'Urbanisme*; Case C-118/96 *Jessica Safir v Skattemyndigheten i Dalarnas Län, formerly Skattemyndigheten i Kopparbergs Län*; Case C-200/98 *X AB and Y AB v Riksskatteverket*; Case C-251/98 *C Baars v Inspecteur der Belastingen Particulieren/Ondernemingen Gorinchem*; Case C-478/98 *Commission v Kingdom of Belgium (Re Loans issued abroad)*; Case C-35/98 *Staatssecretaris van Financiën v B.G.M. Verkooijen*; Joined Cases C-397/98 and C-410/98 *Metallgesellschaft Ltd and Others, Hoechst AG and Hoechst (UK) Ltd v Commissioners of Inland Revenue and H.M. Attorney General*; Case C-319/02 *Petri Manninen*; Case C-279/00 *Commission v Italian Republic (Re Italian Recruitment Agencies)*; Case C-361/01 *The Heirs of H. Barbier v Inspecteur van de Belastingdienst Particulieren/Ondernemingen buitenland te Heerlen*; Case C-334/02 *Commission v French Republic (Re Tax on Income Arising from Investment)*; Case C-242/03 *Ministre des Finances v Jean-Claude Weidert and Élisabeth Paulus*; Case C-442/02 *CaixaBank France v Ministère de l'Économie, des Finances et de l'Industrie*; Case C-411/03 *SEVIC Systems AG*; Case C-265/04 *Margaretha Bouanich v Skatteverket*; Case C-374/04 *Test Claimants in Class IV of the ACT Group Litigation (Pirelli, Essilor and Sony), Test Claimants in Class IV of the ACT Group Litigation (BMW) v Commissioners of Inland Revenue*; Case C-446/04 *Test Claimants in the FII Group Litigation v Commissioners of Inland Revenue*; Case C-292/04 *Wienand Meilicke, Heidi Christa Weyde, Marina Stöffler v Finanzamt Bonn-Innenstadt*; Case C-524/04 *Test Claimants in the Thin Cap Group Litigation*.

ii. Nationality and Residence as Additional Autonomous Prohibited Distinguishing Criteria? Another question is that of whether Art 56(1) EC prohibits, on an equal footing with the prohibition of discrimination on the basis of origin/destination of a capital movement, discrimination against the market participant. This would suggest additional comparison groups and expressly prohibited distinguishing criteria, such as nationality or residence.

I explained above that free movement of capital is an object-oriented freedom. If one wishes to be serious about the structural similarities of free capital movement and free movement of goods,[155] then there is no room for an additional prohibited distinguishing criterion alongside the origin/destination of capital movement.[156] Article 56(1) EC does not refer to the free movement of 'capitalists,' but merely to the free movement of capital.

Of course, capital flows can be impaired by discrimination against a person on the basis of nationality or residence. However, nationality or residence does not constitute expressly prohibited distinguishing criteria in their own right. Discrimination on the basis of residence, as shown above, can be functionally equivalent to discrimination on the basis of origin/destination of a capital movement. This, however, relates back to the necessity of locating intangible capital, which is placed wherever its holder habitually resides. Once again, disadvantageous treatment on the basis of nationality constitutes only an indirect discrimination within the ambit of an object-oriented freedom.[157]

(3) Distinguishing Criteria, Direct and Indirect Discrimination, and the Delineation of the 'Non-discrimination' and 'Non-hindrance' Tests within the Case Law of the Court

Above, on the basis of a theoretical analysis of the scope of protection of Art 56(1) EC by means of the ordinary methods of construction against the background of academic writing, I argued that a distinction can be drawn between the prohibition of discrimination and that of hindrance. Furthermore, I explained that the prohibition of discrimination can be further split into the categories of direct and indirect discrimination. Turning to the Court's jurisprudence, however, I must note that the doctrinal categorizations just mentioned are hardly visible.

Although the Court held that discrimination on the basis of nationality is undoubtedly subject to Art 56(1) EC, the language of the 'non-discrimination test' in such situations is seldom used. There are rare examples, such as *Konle*,[158] *Albore*,[159] and *Commission v Portuguese Republic*,[160] where the Court

---

[155] G Ress and J Ukrow, Art. 56 EC (2002), para 34 *et seq*; A Rohde, *Kapitalverkehr*, 133.
[156] *Cf* A Rohde, *Kapitalverkehr*, 133; J Lübke, *Kapitalverkehrs- und Niederlassungsfreiheit*, 277.
[157] J Lübke, *Kapitalverkehrs- und Niederlassungsfreiheit*, 277 *et seq*.
[158] Case C-302/97 *Klaus Konle v Republik Österreich*, para 23 *et seq*, 41.
[159] Case C-423/98 *Alfredo Albore*, para 16 *et seq*.
[160] Case C-367/98 *Commission v Portuguese Republic (Re Golden Shares I)*, para 40.

in its judgments expressly referred to the discriminatory character of national measures. However, no statement was made on the nature of the distinguishing criterion. In *Scientology*,[161] the ECJ proceeded in an even less doctrinal fashion. Although it can be said that the national measure discriminated on the basis of nationality,[162] the Court did not use this language, but referred merely to 'restriction' of capital movements.

There is also no doubt when looking at the Court's case law that national measures which distinguish on the basis of the place of residence or the place of investment, often concerned with direct taxation issues, are subject to Art 56(1) EC. Again, they have rarely been treated by means of the 'non-discrimination test' on the level of examination of the scope of application of Art 56(1) EC.[163] Elements of the discrimination test, especially the question of comparability, are, however, found on the level of grounds of justification within the examination of Art 58(1) lit. a, (3) EC. For example, in *Verkooijen*, although the national provision was clearly discriminating against dividends on shares in a company headquartered in another Member State, the Court used the language of the 'non-hindrance test', finding that the national provisions had a 'dissuading' effect and were thus within the scope of Art 56(1) EC.[164] Questions of comparability of the two situations at issue in the case were treated in connection with an examination of Art 58(1) lit. a, (3) EC.[165] The cases of *Bouanich*,[166] *Lenz*,[167] *D.*,[168] and *Manninen*,[169] inter alia, were dealt with in a similar way. The Court, when considering discrimination issues related to national tax measures, focuses—certainly due to the existence of Art 58(1) lit. a, (3) EC for tax measures—more on the level of grounds of

---

[161] Case C-54/99 *Association Eglise de Scientologie de Paris and Scientology International Reserves Trust v The Prime Minister*, para 14.
[162] The relevant French law distinguished between 'foreign' and 'domestic' direct investment.
[163] Case C-268/03 *Jean-Claude De Baeck v Kingdom of Belgium*, para 22 *et seq*. Note that para 26 appears, at first sight, to be exceptional in this sense. However, the Court speaks (merely) about 'difference in treatment' but not about 'discrimination' or 'discriminatory treatment'; thus, eventually, it has recourse to the non-hindrance test.
[164] Case C-35/98 *Staatssecretaris van Financiën v B.G.M. Verkooijen*, para 31 *et seq*; note, in particular, para 34; see also Case C-436/00 *X and Y v Riksskatteverket*, paras 36, 70.
[165] Case C-35/98 *Staatssecretaris van Financiën v B.G.M. Verkooijen*, para 37 *et seq*.
[166] Case C-265/04 *Margaretha Bouanich v Skatteverket*, paras 32 *et seq*., 36 *et seq*.; see also Case C-265/04 (Opinion of AG Kokott) *Margaretha Bouanich v Skatteverket*, para 32, who clearly used the language of the non-discrimination test.
[167] Case C-315/02 *Anneliese Lenz v Finanzlandesdirektion für Tirol*, paras 18 *et seq*, 23 *et seq*; Case C-315/02 (Opinion of AG Tizzano) *Anneliese Lenz v Finanzlandesdirektion für Tirol*, paras 19 *et seq*, 26 *et seq*.
[168] The Court examines the scope of application and the grounds of justification together: Case C-376/03 (Opinion of AG Colomer) *D v Inspecteur van de Belastingdienst/Particulieren/Ondernemingen buitenland te Heerlen*, para 25 *et seq*.
[169] Case C-319/02 (Opinion of AG Kokott) *Petri Manninen*, paras 20 *et seq*, 28 *et seq*; Case C-319/02 (Opinion of AG Kokott) *Petri Manninen*, paras 37 *et seq*, 34 *et seq*.

justification than on the level of the scope of application of Art 56(1) EC;[170] occasionally it examines both in one step.[171]

In *Sandoz,* a national provision differentiated on the basis of the place of contracting. The Court merely noted that the provision at issue was discriminatory.[172] In *Trummer,* a case in which a national provision discriminated on the basis of currency,[173] the Court again applied the 'non-hindrance test' instead of referring to the non-discrimination test. In *Bordessa,*[174] the national legislation concerned the physical export of coins, banknotes, and bearer cheques, and discriminated on the basis of the country of destination. The Court, however, states that such legislation has the 'effect of impeding capital movements'.[175]

With regard to the distinction between direct and indirect discrimination, this differentiation finds hardly any echo in the case law of the ECJ. In this sense Advocate General Geelhoed's opinion on *Ospelt* is exceptional. He states that:

According to the established case-law, only national provisions which provide for different treatment on the basis of nationality are *formally* discriminatory. Where, on the other hand, legislation is intended to apply to all those who carry on the activity concerned in the territory of a particular Member State, it is regarded as applicable without distinction, even where that legislation expressly lays down a residence or establishment requirement. Furthermore, national measures may have discriminatory effect even though they are applied without distinction.[176]

With reference to the view I advocated above, this study respectfully disagrees with such a stipulation: if one wishes to be serious about the object-related nature of the freedom, then nationality cannot be the prohibited (formal) distinguishing criterion.

To summarize so far, the ECJ has not yet formulated precise criteria concerning when it intends to apply the language of the 'non-discrimination test' and when that of the non-hindrance test within the ambit of Art 56(1) EC.[177] The present

---

[170] For a more detailed consideration of the issue, refer to Chapter IV. 2. b. (4) (a).
[171] An example of such treatment would be Case C-376/03 *D v Inspecteur van de Belastingdienst/Particulieren/Ondernemingen buitenland te Heerlen,* para 25 *et seq.*
[172] Case C-439/97 *Sandoz GmbH v Finanzlandesdirektion für Wien, Niederösterreich und Burgenland,* para 31.
[173] A mortgage securing a debt payable in the currency of another Member State could only be registered in the land register of the relevant Member State if, for the purpose of registration, the value was expressed in the currency of this Member State. *Cf* Case C-222/97 *Manfred Trummer and Peter Mayer.*
[174] Joined Cases C-358/93 and C-416/93 *Criminal proceedings against Aldo Bordessa and Vicente Marí Mellado and Concepción Barbero Maestre*; see with respect to third countries Joined Cases C-163/94, C-165/94, and C-250/94 *Criminal proceedings against Lucas Emilio Sanz de Lera, Raimundo Díaz Jiménez and Figen Kapanoglu.*
[175] Joined Cases C-358/93 and C-416/93 *Criminal proceedings against Aldo Bordessa and Vicente Marí Mellado and Concepción Barbero Maestre,* para 25.
[176] [Emphasis added] Case C-452/01 (Opinion of AG Geelhoed) *Margarethe Ospelt and Schlössle Weissenberg Familienstiftung,* para 124.
[177] Of the same opinion S Peers, 'Movement of Capital', 340 *et seq,* 342; L Flynn, 'Coming of Age', 782; See also M Lang, 'Wohin geht das Internationale Steuerrecht?' 296.

case law shows that the Court quite unsystematically appears to have recourse to the non-discrimination test. A tendency to consider clearly discriminating national measures in terms of the non-hindrance test is detectable. Often, the ECJ also mixes both tests: on the level of scope of application, the Court refers to 'dissuasion', etc, which would indicate the application of the non-hindrance test. Within the grounds of justification, it does not hesitate to consider questions of comparability, which is part of the non-discrimination test. One could surely criticize such an 'unorthodox' doctrinal approach from the Court.[178] In defence of the Court's application of the two tests, one might advance the fact that Art 56(1) EC does not contain an independent and express prohibition of discrimination. The wording of Art 56(1) EC refers to a prohibition of restriction only.[179] Viewed from this perspective, one could question whether the Court 'must' actually spell out the elements and the content out of which the non-discrimination test ultimately arises or more intelligible principles on how to delineate the aforementioned test from the non-hindrance test.[180]

Nevertheless, it is worth noting that the lack of an independent and express prohibition of discrimination did not deter the Court in the ambit of Art 28 EC from (at least) explaining[181] in some detail its approach towards the non-discrimination and non-hindrance tests.[182] It is to be hoped that some clarity will eventually be added once the case law in the ambit of free movement has matured.

Against this background, it might not come as a surprise that the Court has not yet firmly established what it considers to be the prohibited distinguishing criterion within the ambit of Art 56 EC; this renders it impossible to draw a dividing line between direct and indirect discrimination if one chooses to have recourse only to the Court's case law.

(4) The Issue of Comparability

A precondition for the establishment of discrimination is that the capital movement that is affected by the national measure and the capital movement that is not, in objective terms, are both placed in comparable circumstances. But when will this be the case? In principle, two situations or two individuals are never in all aspects equal. The equality and the inequality of two situations or two individuals are always equality and inequality with respect to certain attributes. Equality and inequality must also always relate to a certain treatment of situations or persons. Furthermore, a value-based assessment is required that allows for judging what is equal and unequal.[183]

---

[178] For a more detailed consideration of the issue, refer to Chapter IV. 2. b. (4) (a).
[179] L Flynn, 'Coming of Age', 782.
[180] S Peers, 'Movement of Capital', 341.
[181] With respect to the non-discrimination test, many questions also remain open in the ambit of free movement of goods. See S Plötscher, *Diskriminierung*, 161 *et seq*.
[182] Ibid.
[183] R Alexy, *Grundrechte*, 362 *et seq*. See also for the interpretation of the issue of comparability by the Court: Joined Cases 3–58 to 18–58, 25–58, and 26–58 *Barbara Erzbergbau AG and*

From the above, it is clear that the two capital movements to be compared need not and cannot be identical, but must be comparable in certain essential attributes; the determination of the notion of 'essential' requires, as previously mentioned, a value-based judgement. No general test exists to identify these 'essential attributes', but they are determined on a case-by-case basis.[184] The 'essential attributes' must be deduced primarily from actual circumstances and conditions, against the background of the purpose and content of the respective national measure, and under consideration of the value-based decisions stipulated by the Community legal order in the sense of a value system.[185]

The specific non-discrimination provision applicable to the case at issue sets the outer frame of comparison by means of its scope of application. Sometimes, it expressly stipulates (part of) the 'essential attributes'. The prohibited distinguishing criterion set by the relevant non-discrimination provision always constitutes a 'non-essential attribute'.[186] In this respect, Art 56(1) EC does not prove very indicative, as it does not contain an expressly worded prohibition of discrimination. At the least, as identified above, one can establish that the origin/destination of capital movement constitutes a 'non-essential attribute' within the issue of comparability and at the same time the *tertium comparationis*.

Having previously said that the 'comparability question' has to be answered on a case-by-case basis, I will review two examples in which the issue of comparability has been or could become of prime importance. I will first address the treatment of ongoing investment in terms of direct taxation, where 'comparability' of situations or persons is regularly an issue and, consequently, regularly addressed by the Court. In fact, tax-related cases form the greatest part of the jurisprudence on free movement of capital. Secondly, I look by way of example at national measures that directly regulate access to the market or exit from the market of a Member State. In this area, meaningful case law is virtually nonexistent. The only case

---

others v High Authority of the European Coal and Steel Community, 190 et seq. Refer also to AS Mohn, *Gleichheitssatz*, 47 et seq; M Hintersteininger, *Diskriminierungsverbot*, 9 et seq; S Plötscher, *Diskriminierung*, 41 et seq. For the issue of comparability within the ambit of free movement of capital, see C Ohler, Art. 56 EC (2002), mn 259.

[184] Joined Cases 7–54 and 9–54 'Sidérurgiques' *Groupement des Industries Sidérurgiques Luxembourgeoises v High Authority of the European Coal and Steel Community*, 197 et seq; Case 1/54 *French Republic v High Authority of the European Coal and Steel Community*, 7.

[185] M Hintersteininger, *Diskriminierungsverbot*, 10; AS Mohn, *Gleichheitssatz*, 47 et seq; S Plötscher, *Diskriminierung*, 42 et seq; C Ohler, Art. 56 EC (2002), 259. See Case C-431/01 *Philippe Mertens v Belgian State*, which reads in para 32: '[I]t is settled law that there is unequal treatment when two categories of persons, whose *legal and factual circumstances* are not fundamentally different, are treated differently and when situations which are not comparable are treated in the same way.' [emphasis added] See also Case C-1/93 (Opinion of AG Lenz) *Halliburton Services BV v Staatssecretaris van Financiën*, para 41: 'That constitutes discrimination ... if the companies excluded from the benefit of exemption are on the same footing, from the point of view of the *scheme and purpose of that provision*, as the Netherlands companies qualifying for exemption.' [Emphasis added] See also Case 6/71 *Rheinmühlen Düsseldorf v Einfuhr- und Vorratsstelle für Getreide und Futtermittel*, para 14.

[186] S Plötscher, *Diskriminierung*, 43 et seq.

that deserves mention in this respect is the *'Portuguese Golden Shares Decision'*.[187] It is worth noting that, even if the Court chose to approach cases in terms of the non-discrimination test, frequently it did not elaborate on the 'question of comparability', for example in cases concerning the transfer of real property.[188]

(a) Comparability Questions with respect to the Regulation of Ongoing Businesses—The Issue of Direct Taxation

Chiefly in the area of direct taxation—where, although within the competence of the Member States, respective powers are to be exercised consistently with Community Law[189]—the Court chose to give its detailed opinion on the 'issue of comparability' and to spell out 'essential' and 'non-essential attributes'. The case law has grown tremendously over the years and has formed its own 'discipline' within Community law, which is currently developing extremely quickly. The picture that is presented to us is rarely clear or precise. In this section, not endeavouring to go too far into the details and subtleties of EC tax law,[190] I limit myself to the task of highlighting the broad strands of case law. Complete neglect, however, would not be appropriate due to the fact that direct taxation is one of the most important determinants when it comes to an investment decision. The case law offers insight into how the Court treats national measures encroaching upon ongoing investments, and it will provide us with the basis for answering the question later in the study of whether a different approach is adopted by the Court in a third country context. It is worth stressing that much of the existing case law on the issue was developed within the ambit of free movement of persons and the freedom of establishment. It appears, however, that the reasoning applied in those cases also applies to direct investments within the ambit of free movement of capital.[191]

It is, moreover, worth mentioning again[192] that the Court regularly approaches questions related to the comparability of situations or persons not on the level of the scope of application—quite in contrast to cases dealt with by the provisions on free movement of persons or the freedom of establishment[193]—but within the examination of Art 58(1) lit. a, (3) EC, which relates to the level of grounds

---

[187] Case C-367/98 *Commission v Portuguese Republic (Re Golden Shares I)*.
[188] Case C-302/97 *Klaus Konle v Republik Österreich*; Case C-423/98 (Opinion of AG Cosmas) *Alfredo Albore*.
[189] Settled case law. See recently: Case C-196/04 *Cadbury Schweppes and Cadbury Schweppes Overseas Ltd v Commissioners of Inland Revenue*, para 40; Case C-446/03 *Marks & Spencer plc v David Halsey (H.M. Inspector of Taxes)*, para 29.
[190] For a more detailed review of the ECJ's case law on direct taxation, with further references, see: S Kingston, 'Direct Tax'; C Brown and M O'Brien, 'National Report Canada'; M O'Brien, 'Third Country Dimension'.
[191] See, for example: Case C-376/03 *D v Inspecteur van de Belastingdienst/Particulieren/ Ondernemingen buitenland te Heerlen*; M Lang, 'Kapitalverkehrsfreiheit und Doppelbesteuerungsabkommen', 192.
[192] *Cf* above Chapter IV. 2. b. (3).
[193] eg, Case C-279/93 'Schumacker' *Finanzamt Köln-Altstadt v Roland Schumacker*, para 30; Case C-80/94 *G. H. E. J. Wielockx v Inspecteur der Directe Belastingen*, para 17; Case C-107/94 *P. H. Asscher v Staatssecretaris van Financiën*, para 40; Case C-311/97 *Royal Bank of Scotland plc v Elliniko*

146 *Which Level of Protection?—The Scope of the Prohibition of Restriction*

of justification. Doctrinally, one can cast doubt on such an interpretation; the question of comparability clearly relates to the scope of application of a provision containing a prohibition of discrimination.[194] Having examined the Court's treatment of the issue against the background of its view on Art 58(1) lit. a, (3) EC, it does not change much in essence.[195]

i. International Tax Law and the EC Treaty

One of the basic principles of international tax law is the distinction between taxation based on residents (...) and source taxation (...). Worldwide (total income) taxation is applied to residents, the idea being that all persons resident or established in a certain State, benefiting from economic, social, cultural and physical infrastructure and public expenditure of that State and usually deriving most of their income in that State, should contribute accordingly to their ability to pay. Therefore, their total income and, in the case of individuals, their personal circumstances, should be taken into account. Source taxation, on the other hand, is applied to non-residents, the idea being that the country in which income is earned should have a fair share of that income, wherever the beneficiary may reside... It follows that international tax law fundamentally distinguishes between residents and non-residents.[196, 197]

In examining Art 58(1) lit. a EC, one could be led to believe for a moment that the Treaty has embraced this distinction unconditionally. It would, however, be overly hasty to draw the conclusion from Art 58(1) lit. a EC and the existence of this fundamental distinction in international tax law that EC law as it stands today would follow suit and leave unaffected from the outset national tax measures that distinguish on the basis of residency. The Court, rather, formulated a somewhat more differentiated approach with regard to direct taxation cases concerned with the question of comparability of residents and non-residents, which I will review in the following subsections. The cases will be grouped into two broad strands. The first group—also the first subsection—comprises situations in which

---

Dimosio (Greek State), para 26; Case C-391/97 *Frans Gschwind v Finanzamt Aachen-Außenstadt*, para 21.

[194] The question of comparability of two situations can be viewed as an 'objective' element of justification examined within the scope of application. [For a very critical view of such a doctrinal approach: A Randelzhofer and U Forsthoff, vor Art. 39–55 EC (2001), mn 230] The crucial doctrinal question behind all this is that of whether the non-discrimination test has an independent level of examination of grounds of justification or whether the non-existence of those grounds is already a precondition for the establishment of discrimination at the level of the scope of application. [See S Plötscher, *Diskriminierung*, 64 *et seq*; M Hintersteininger, *Diskriminierungsverbot*, 278 *et seq*] Concerning the free movement of capital, it appears that the Court implicitly operates with two levels of examination. In almost all discrimination cases, the Court notes as the first step that, in principle, a restriction on the free movement exists. It then proceeds to the second level, which refers to grounds of justification. [See generally AS Mohn, *Gleichheitssatz*, 49 *et seq*]

[195] Refer to Chapter IV. 2. b. (4) (a) iv.

[196] See, for example, the 2005 OECD Articles of the Model Convention with respect to Taxes on Income and on Capital which prohibit discrimination on the basis of nationality but do not consider residents and non-residents to be in the same position.

[197] B Terra and PJ Wattel, *European Tax Law*, 45. [footnote added]

non-resident taxpayers faced different treatment by the source State compared to resident taxpayers. The second group—found in the second subsection—relates to the different treatment of (fully taxable) resident taxpayers by their home State depending on the place where the capital was invested. In the third and last subsection, I shall explore the meaning of the previously mentioned Art 58(1) lit. a. EC against the background of the existing case law.

ii. Non-resident Taxpayers Facing Different Treatment by the Source (Host) State Compared to Resident Taxpayers Turning to the first group, in the *Schumacker* case,[198] the ECJ found that:

[i]n relation to direct taxes, the situations of residents and of non-residents are not, as a rule, comparable. Income received in the territory of a Member State by a non-resident is in most cases only a part of his total income, which is concentrated at his place of residence. Moreover, a non-resident's personal ability to pay tax, determined by reference to his aggregate income and his personal and family circumstances, is more easy to assess at the place where his personal and financial interests are centred. In general, that is the place where he has his usual abode. Accordingly, international tax law, and in particular the Model Double Taxation Treaty of the Organization for Economic Cooperation and Development (OECD), recognizes that in principle the overall taxation of taxpayers, taking account of their personal and family circumstances, is a matter for the State of residence.[199]

However, in exceptional cases, the situations of resident and non-resident taxpayers can be objectively comparable. Discrimination is said to exist

where the non-resident receives all or almost all of his worldwide income in that State since the income received in the State in which he resides is insufficient to allow his personal and family circumstances to be taken into account.[200]

What I have just outlined is commonly known as '*Schumacker* jurisprudence'. It does not come as a real surprise that this jurisprudence—essentially saying

---

[198] Case C-279/93 'Schumacker' *Finanzamt Köln-Altstadt v Roland Schumacker*. Note that the *Schumacker* case was decided on the basis of free movement of workers. In Case C-80/94 *G. H. E. J. Wielockx v Inspecteur der Directe Belastingen*, the doctrine was held to apply also under the freedom of establishment. See also, for example, for the application of the '*Schumacker* doctrine' in the ambit of free movement of capital: Case C-376/03 *D v Inspecteur van de Belastingdienst/ Particulieren/Ondernemingen buitenland te Heerlen*.

[199] Case C-279/93 'Schumacker' *Finanzamt Köln-Altstadt v Roland Schumacker*, para 31 *et seq*; Case C-80/94 *G. H. E. J. Wielockx v Inspecteur der Directe Belastingen*, para 18. See also Case C-376/03 *D v Inspecteur van de Belastingdienst/Particulieren/Ondernemingen buitenland te Heerlen*, in which the Court extends the '*Schumacker* jurisprudence' to wealth tax. For a critical review, see M Lang, 'Rechtssache D'.

[200] Case C-107/94 *P. H. Asscher v Staatssecretaris van Financiën*, para 43; Case C-279/93 'Schumacker' *Finanzamt Köln-Altstadt v Roland Schumacker*, para 36 *et seq*. See Case C-391/97 *Frans Gschwind v Finanzamt Aachen-Außenstadt)*, para 32; Case C-169/03 *Florian W. Wallentin v Riksskatteverket*, para 18 for how to determine, for income tax purposes, whether a non-resident taxpayer receives 'all or almost all of his worldwide income' in the source State. A partially different assessment—with a focus on factual instead of taxable wealth—applies in the case of wealth tax. See Case C-376/03 *D v Inspecteur van de Belastingdienst/Particulieren/Ondernemingen buitenland te Heerlen*, para 41.

that residents and non-residents, as a general rule, are not comparable—was greeted not only with applause[201] but also with criticism.[202] The Court in the *Schumacker* case focused very much on personal—in contrast to objective—tax allowances. It therefore seems reasonable to argue that the Court's statement is limited in its effect to those benefits.[203] Indeed, when looking at the case law of the Court, it becomes apparent that one must differentiate between personal tax benefits ('personal circumstances-related tax benefits such as basic tax allowances, splitting of income between spouses and deductions for personal and family circumstances'[204]) and objective tax allowances ('income-related benefits, such as deduction of necessary expenses incurred in earning the income, refund of overpaid wage withholding tax, payment of imputation credits attaching to dividends, etc.'[205]). The former are detached from any specific part of the income of the taxpayer, are usually assessed best by the home State of the taxpayer, and need only to be granted once due to the fact that any taxpayer has only one set of personal circumstances to be taken into account.[206] The latter 'can be attributed to items of income the earning of which they serve or to which they otherwise attach'.[207] It appears that in this case, resident and non-resident taxpayers are in principle in a comparable situation, because those benefits relate to income that is objectively the same for resident and non-resident taxpayers.[208]

Another strand of case law also belonging to this group relates the (un-)equal treatment of branches and subsidiaries of non-resident (parent) companies. The Court held that branches of non-resident companies and resident subsidiaries are in principle in comparable situations with respect to their tax treatment,[209]

---

[201] eg, AJF Jones, 'Carry On Discriminating'; W Vermeend, 'Direct Taxes', 54 *et seq*.
[202] eg, W Schön, 'Kapitalverkehrsfreiheit', 760; M Lang, 'Rechtssache D', 367 *et seq*; J Lüdicke, 'Besteuerung Nichtansässiger', 651; M Lang, 'Schumacker-Rechtsprechung'; PJ Wattel, 'The Schumacker Legacy', 348 *et seq*; PJ Wattel, 'International Tax Law', 229 *et seq*; PJ Wattel, 'Personal Tax Allowances', 210 *et seq*; A Cordewener, *Grundfreiheiten*, 483 *et seq*; N Mattsson, 'Tax Benefits', 186 *et seq*.
[203] Of the same opinion: B Terra and PJ Wattel, *European Tax Law*, 51; implicitly confirmed by the ECR in Case C-107/94 *P. H. Asscher v Staatssecretaris van Financiën*, para 42.
[204] B Terra and PJ Wattel, *European Tax Law*, 48.
[205] Ibid.   [206] Ibid, 50   [207] Ibid.
[208] Case 175/88 *Klaus Biehl v Administration des contributions du grand-duché de Luxembourg*.
[209] Case 270/83 *Commission v French Republic (Re Corporation tax and Shareholders' Tax Credits: 'avoir fiscal'*, para 19 *et seq*. The rule–exception relationship is spelled out quite clearly in para 19 of the aforementioned judgment, where the Court stated that 'the possibility cannot *altogether* be excluded that a distinction based on the location of the registered office of a company or the place of residence of a natural person *may, under certain conditions*, be *justified* in areas such as tax law . . .'. In para 20 the Court set out the indicator for when two situations are comparable: 'By treating the two forms of establishment in the same way for the purposes of taxing their profits, the French legislature has in fact admitted that there is no objective difference between their positions in regard to the detailed rules and conditions relating to that taxation which could justify different treatment' with respect to tax credits. [Emphases added] Refer also to Case C-330/91 *R v Inland Revenue Commissioners, ex p Commerzbank AG*; Case C-307/97 *Compagnie de Saint-Gobain, Zweigniederlassung Deutschland v Finanzamt Aachen-Innenstadt*; Case C-311/97 *Royal Bank of Scotland plc v Elliniko Dimosio (Greek State)*. Note that the taxation

but they are in different positions with regard to their evidential position.[210] Furthermore, subsidiaries of non-resident parent companies and resident companies are in principle, according to the Court, placed in comparable situations concerning group income election schemes.[211]

A general assessment of how the Court conducts the process of comparison in the ambit of the '*Schumacker* jurisprudence' reveals a degree of inconsistency that deserves to be mentioned. The Court regularly compares only the factual situations of resident and non-resident taxpayers.[212] In other cases, such as *Royal Bank of Scotland*[213] and *Saint-Gobain*,[214] the Court compares the legal situation only. Again in others, referring to this interpretation as settled case law, the Court has recourse to the factual and legal situation.[215] Above, I have argued that the 'essential attributes' for conducting the comparison must be deduced primarily from actual circumstances and conditions against the background of the purpose and content of the respective national measure and under consideration of the value-based decisions stipulated by the Community legal order within the meaning of a value system. Indeed, '[c]omparability only exists in the light of a legal rule'[216] and does not depend only on the factual situation.[217] It is, for example, not a question of whether a branch and a subsidiary of a non-resident company in general, ie, irrespective of the specific national legal order, are comparable, but whether those two types of establishments enjoy the same legal position within the national legal order and would, therefore, be comparable.[218]

(i) Article 293 EC, the Distribution of Tax Jurisdiction, Double Taxation Relief, and Most-favoured-nation Treatment The Member States have concluded among themselves and with third countries a great number of double taxation treaties.[219]

---

issues in the aforementioned cases were treated in the context of the freedom of establishment and free movement of workers.

However, such an interpretation is not beyond doubt. Some commentators argue that 'freedom of legal form...does not mean there may not be any differences in taxation of a permanent establishment and of a local subsidiary company, provided such differences are due solely to the fact that a branch is not an independent legal person, whereas a subsidiary company is.... The essential difference in legal (liability) positions of a subsidiary company and a branch will obviously lead to differences in taxation.' [B Terra and PJ Wattel, *European Tax Law*, 88]

[210] Case C-250/95 *Futura Participations SA and Singer v Administration des contributions*.

[211] Joined Cases C-397/98 and C-410/98 *Metallgesellschaft Ltd and Others, Hoechst AG and Hoechst (UK) Ltd v Commissioners of Inland Revenue and H.M. Attorney General*.

[212] M Lang, 'Schumacker-Rechtsprechung', 337.

[213] Case C-311/97 *Royal Bank of Scotland plc v Elliniko Dimosio (Greek State)*, para 24.

[214] Case C-307/97 *Compagnie de Saint-Gobain, Zweigniederlassung Deutschland v Finanzamt Aachen-Innenstadt*, para 48.

[215] Case C-431/01 *Philippe Mertens v Belgian State*, para 32.

[216] D Gutmann, 'Marks & Spencer', 155.

[217] M Lang, 'Rechtssache D', 370; M Lang, 'Marks & Spencer', 259 *et seq*; see also Case C-446/03 (Opinion of AG Maduro) *Marks & Spencer plc v David Halsey (H.M. Inspector of Taxes)*, para 49.

[218] Ibid. See also footnote 209 of this Chapter above.

[219] Among the 25 Member States, in June 2005, 277 double taxation treaties were in existence. See G Kofler, 'Treaty Override', 63, fn 7.

In the absence of unifying or harmonizing measures at the EC level for the division of taxing jurisdiction and double taxation relief mechanisms,[220] the Member States remain—in principle—competent to both determine the allocation of tax powers among themselves by choosing the connecting factors they deem suitable and to decide freely about double taxation relief mechanisms.[221] The second indent of Art 293 EC—the provision not being directly applicable[222]—merely indicates the abolition of double taxation as an objective of any negotiation on double taxation treaties and, thus, neither constitutes the legal basis for any harmonizing measure of the Community, nor does it *per se* preclude such harmonization by the Community.[223] Thus, where different treatment results purely from the co-existence of national tax administrations, disparities between tax systems, or the division of tax jurisdiction between two tax systems, does not fall within the ambit of the freedoms[224] because the difference in treatment does not stem from one authority, but from the simultaneous actions of two or more authorities.[225] Notwithstanding, Art 293 EC does not indemnify the Member States in respect of observing Community law by having recourse to international treaties, but different treatment that goes beyond such resulting inevitably from the coexistence of national tax systems is to be measured against the fundamental freedoms embodied in the Treaty.[226]

One of the questions of particular interest when it comes to the review of double taxation treaties is that of whether and to what extent Community law covers the different treatment of non-residents compared to other non-residents

---

[220] Note also Convention 90/436/EEC in connection with Protocol amending the Convention 90/436/EEC.

[221] Case C-336/96 *Mr and Mrs Robert Gilly v Directeur des services fiscaux du Bas-Rhin*, paras 24, 30, 35, 53; Case C-307/97 *Compagnie de Saint-Gobain, Zweigniederlassung Deutschland v Finanzamt Aachen-Innenstadt*, para 57; Case C-376/03 (Opinion of AG Colomer) *D v Inspecteur van de Belastingdienst/Particulieren/Ondernemingen buitenland te Heerlen*, para 52; Case C-374/04 (Opinion of AG Geelhoed) *Test Claimants in Class IV of the ACT Group Litigation (Pirelli, Essilor and Sony), Test Claimants in Class IV of the ACT Group Litigation (BMW) v Commissioners of Inland Revenue*, para 52; see also B Terra and PJ Wattel, *European Tax Law*, 60 *et seq*.

[222] Case C-336/96 *Mr and Mrs Robert Gilly v Directeur des services fiscaux du Bas-Rhin*, 14 *et seq*.

[223] M Lang, 'Kapitalverkehrsfreiheit und Doppelbesteuerungsabkommen', 183.

[224] Case C-374/04 (Opinion of AG Geelhoed) *Test Claimants in Class IV of the ACT Group Litigation (Pirelli, Essilor and Sony), Test Claimants in Class IV of the ACT Group Litigation (BMW) v Commissioners of Inland Revenue*, para 55. Occasionally, the Court deals with the 'need to allocate taxing powers between the Member States' and the requirements of the 'territoriality principle of international tax law' at the level of grounds of justification. *Cf*, eg, Case C-446/03 *Marks & Spencer plc v David Halsey (H.M. Inspector of Taxes)*; Case C-347/04 (Opinion of AG Maduro) *Rewe Zentralfinanz eG, as Universal Legal Successor of ITS Reisen GmbH v Finanzamt Köln-Mitte*; Case C-470/04 *N v Inspecteur van de Belastingdienst Oost/kantoor Almelo*. See for a discussion and further references: S Kingston, 'Direct Tax', 1352 *et seq*.

[225] Case C-374/04 (Opinion of AG Geelhoed) *Test Claimants in Class IV of the ACT Group Litigation (Pirelli, Essilor and Sony), Test Claimants in Class IV of the ACT Group Litigation (BMW) v Commissioners of Inland Revenue*, para 37 *et seq*.

[226] Case C-376/03 *D v Inspecteur van de Belastingdienst/Particulieren/Ondernemingen buitenland te Heerlen*, para 53; see also M Lang, 'Kapitalverkehrsfreiheit und Doppelbesteuerungsabkommen', 183.

(most-favoured-nation treatment issue). Above I have argued that this situation should in principle also be within the range of the non-discrimination test because such treatment carries the same market-distorting effects as a differentiation between domestic and foreign subjects or situations.[227] In the case of double taxation treaties, however, which in their personal scope are obviously limited to the natural or legal persons referred to in them, the Court is of the opinion that a non-resident taxpayer who is within the scope of a double taxation treaty is not in the same position with respect to a specific taxation regulated by the treaty as a non-resident taxpayer outside the scope of the treaty. This is due to the fact that the rights and obligations contained in a treaty are the result of a '*do ut des*' negotiation process between the two parties to the agreement in which those rights and obligations are reciprocal and, thus, apply only to the persons to which the treaty was intended to apply.[228] In other words, the difference in treatment is a direct consequence of the simultaneous operation of two tax systems and the division of tax jurisdiction agreed upon in the treaty. However, the Court also stated that if a treaty right can 'be regarded as a benefit separable from the remainder of the Convention',[229] ie, not an integral part thereof and not endangering the overall balance, then a taxpayer who is not within the *ratione personae* of the treaty can be in comparable circumstances. When this will be the case was explained in the cases *Saint-Gobain*[230] and *Gottardo*.[231] In *Saint-Gobain,* the ECJ stated that

The balance and the reciprocity of the treaties concluded by the Federal Republic of Germany with those two countries [i.e., the United States of America and the Swiss Confederation] would not be called into question by a unilateral extension, on the part of the Federal Republic of Germany, of the category of recipients in Germany of the tax advantage provided for by those treaties, in this case corporation tax relief for international groups, since such an extension would not in any way affect the rights of the non-member countries which are parties to the treaties and would not impose any new obligation on them.[232]

---

[227] See Chapter IV. 2. b. (1).
[228] Case C-376/03 *D v Inspecteur van de Belastingdienst/Particulieren/Ondernemingen buitenland te Heerlen*, para 61. For an in-depth discussion, see: M Lang, 'Rechtssache D'; see also G Kofler, 'Treaty Override', 64, fn 17 for a compilation of further references. Concurring: Case C-374/04 *Test Claimants in Class IV of the ACT Group Litigation (Pirelli, Essilor and Sony), Test Claimants in Class IV of the ACT Group Litigation (BMW) v Commissioners of Inland Revenue*, para 94 *et seq*; and see also Case C-374/04 (Opinion of AG Geelhoed) *Test Claimants in Class IV of the ACT Group Litigation (Pirelli, Essilor and Sony), Test Claimants in Class IV of the ACT Group Litigation (BMW) v Commissioners of Inland Revenue*, 84 *et seq*.
[229] Case C-376/03 *D v Inspecteur van de Belastingdienst/Particulieren/Ondernemingen buitenland te Heerlen*, para 62.
[230] Case C-307/97 *Compagnie de Saint-Gobain, Zweigniederlassung Deutschland v Finanzamt Aachen-Innenstadt*.
[231] Case C-55/00 *Elide Gottardo v Istituto nazionale della previdenza sociale (INPS)*, para 37.
[232] Case C-307/97 *Compagnie de Saint-Gobain, Zweigniederlassung Deutschland v Finanzamt Aachen-Innenstadt*, para 59.

Irrespective of the question of the persuasiveness of the Court's 'reciprocity qualification',[233] it remains a secret why in *Saint-Gobain* it extended the benefits flowing from the double taxation treaty concluded between Germany and the USA and Switzerland, but refrained from doing so in the *'D'* case.[234] Maybe the Court was afraid of harmonizing all source taxation rates on the basis of the lowest rate, which would amount to the introduction of most-favoured-nation treatment in the ambit of double taxation treaties.[235] Thus, within the ambit of direct taxation, most-favoured nation treatment is rather less likely to be granted.[236]

iii. Different Treatment of a Fully Taxable Resident Depending on the Place Where the Capital Was Invested The approach of the ECJ towards the treatment of national tax rules that differentiate on the basis of where the capital is invested was convincingly summarized by Advocate General Geelhoed in *Kerckhaert and Morres*:

In the case of a Member State exercising worldwide (home State) tax jurisdiction, this principle [(i.e., 'disadvantageous tax treatment should follow from direct or covert discrimination resulting from the rules of one jurisdiction, and not purely from disparities or the division of tax jurisdiction between two or more Member States' tax systems, or from the coexistence of national tax administrations'[237])] means essentially that such a State must treat foreign-source income of its residents consistently with the way it has divided its tax base. Insofar as it has divided its tax base to include this foreign-source income—i.e., by treating it as taxable income—it must not discriminate between foreign-source

---

[233] It appears that the 'reciprocity qualification' of the Court in *Gottardo, Saint-Gobain,* and *'D'* is at odds with its previous case law. In *Avoir fiscal*, it stated: 'The rights conferred by Article 52 of the Treaty are unconditional and a Member State cannot make respect for them subject to the contents of an agreement concluded with another Member State. In particular, that article does not permit those rights to be made subject to a condition of reciprocity imposed for the purpose of obtaining corresponding advantages on other Member States.' [Case 270/83 *Commission v French Republic (Re Corporation Tax and Shareholders' Tax Credits: 'avoir fiscal'*, para 23] See also M Lang, 'Rechtssache D', 371. Moreover, the 'reciprocity qualification' could lead to the rather peculiar result that compliance with EC law suddenly depends on the choice of legal means. If a Member States agrees with another State on certain protective measures within a double taxation treaty, it could be exempted from scrutiny, while the same measures, if unrelated to any international treaty, would have to be justified by mandatory requirements. [See M Lang, 'Rechtssache D', 370 *et seq*]

[234] See for a discussion: M Lang, 'Rechtssache D', 371 *et seq*; see also Case C-374/04 *Test Claimants in Class IV of the ACT Group Litigation (Pirelli, Essilor and Sony), Test Claimants in Class IV of the ACT Group Litigation (BMW) v Commissioners of Inland Revenue.*

[235] M Lang, 'Rechtssache D', 374 *et seq*; M Lang, 'Wohin geht das Internationale Steuerrecht?' 295.

[236] It is worth mentioning that the question of most-favoured-nation treatment can also be discussed from the perspective of the home State: why should a home State be allowed to tax its residents' income earned abroad differently depending on the content of the double taxation agreement concluded with the respective source State?

[237] [footnote omitted] Case C-513/04 (Opinion of AG Geelhoed) *Mark Kerckhaert, Bernadette Morres v The Belgian State*, para 18.

and domestic income.²³⁸ In particular, its legislation should not have the effect that foreign-source income is treated less favourably than domestic-source income. For example, insofar as a home State chooses to relieve economic double taxation on its residents' dividends, it must provide the same relief for incoming foreign-source dividends as for domestic dividends, and must take foreign corporation tax paid into account for this purpose.²³⁹, ²⁴⁰

The Opinion just referred to was preceded, inter alia, by the *Lenz* case²⁴¹ concerned with an Austrian tax rule—applicable only to domestic situations—that was designed to attenuate the effects of double taxation (corporation tax/income tax) of the profits distributed by an undertaking in which a fully taxable shareholder invested his capital. The Court held that a shareholder fully taxable in Austria and receiving profits from an undertaking established in Austria and likewise a fully taxable shareholder who receives revenue from capital from an undertaking established within another Member State are placed in a comparable situation, ie, both are capable of being subject to double taxation.²⁴² This approach was confirmed by the Court in *Manninen*.²⁴³

---

²³⁸ Case C-374/04 (Opinion of AG Geelhoed) *Test Claimants in Class IV of the ACT Group Litigation (Pirelli, Essilor and Sony), Test Claimants in Class IV of the ACT Group Litigation (BMW) v Commissioners of Inland Revenue*, para 58.
²³⁹ Ibid. See Case C-319/02 *Petri Manninen*; Case C-35/98 *Staatssecretaris van Financiën v B.G.M. Verkooijen*, and Case C-315/02 *Anneliese Lenz v Finanzlandesdirektion für Tirol*.
²⁴⁰ Case C-513/04 (Opinion of AG Geelhoed) *Mark Kerckhaert, Bernadette Morres v The Belgian State*, para 19. It is worth noting that, in substance, the Advocate General in the aforementioned case was of the opinion that Community law as it stands today 'does not as such oblige home States to relief of juridical double taxation resulting from the dislocation of tax base between two Member States'. [Case C-513/04 (Opinion of AG Geelhoed) *Mark Kerckhaert, Bernadette Morres v The Belgian State*, para 30] The national measure as such applied without distinction. For a discussion of the issue of juridical double taxation with further references, refer to G Kofler, 'Treaty Override'. See, for the Commission's view on the issue of dividend taxation: European Commission, 'Communication to the Council, The European Parliament and the European Economic and Social Committee: Dividend Taxation of Individuals in the Internal Market' (COM (2003) 810 final).
²⁴¹ Case C-315/02 *Anneliese Lenz v Finanzlandesdirektion für Tirol*.
²⁴² Ibid, para 31 *et seq*. See for a general account of the legal situation in Austria: C Staringer, 'Dividendenbesteuerung'.
²⁴³ Case C-319/02 *Petri Manninen*, para 32 *et seq*; see also Case C-292/04 (Opinion of AG Tizzano) *Wienand Meilicke, Heidi Christa Weyde, Marina Stöffler v Finanzamt Bonn-Innenstadt*, 15 *et seq*. A different route was followed by Advocate General Kokott [*cf* Case C-319/02 (Opinion of AG Kokott) *Petri Manninen*, para 40 *et seq*], who was of the opinion that as regards the avoidance of double taxation of dividends, those distributed by a resident company and those distributed by a non-resident company are not in a comparable situation but are the consequence of a lack of coordination between the two Member States. However, in the end she arrived at the same result as the Court when she stated: 'that differences in treatment of all kinds would [not] be permissible, for different situations may be treated differently only to the extent that is unavoidable because of the differences.' [Case C-319/02 (Opinion of AG Kokott) *Petri Manninen*, para 48] See for an account of the judgment: G Kofler, 'Manninen'; G Kofler, 'Manninen II', esp. 29.

iv. Article 58(1) lit. a EC—A General Exception to the Prohibition of Discrimination? Particular difficulties in interpretation of the non-discrimination test are caused by Art 58(1) lit. a, (3) EC, which provides in its first paragraph, lit. a for the right of the Member States:

to apply the relevant provisions of their tax law which distinguish between taxpayers who are not in the same situation with regard to their place of residence or with regard to the place where their capital is invested.[244]

One view in the literature that Art 58(1) lit. a EC, like Art 45 EC, constitutes a *domaine réservé* of the Member States in the sense that national measures that discriminate on the basis of the place of residence[245] or place of investment[246]

---

[244] Differentiations on the basis of nationality are not covered by Art 58(1) lit. a EC. [M Sedlaczek, 'Kapitalverkehrsfreiheit', 53] In order to fall within the scope of application of Art 58(1) lit. a EC, a national measure must refer expressly to the person liable to tax. [*Cf* W Kiemel, Art. 58 EC (2003), mn 10]

[245] The first 'distinguishing criterion' employed by Art 58(1) lit. a EC refers to the place of residence, for which no definition can be found in the Treaty. The English, French (*'leur résidence'*), Spanish (*'lugar de residencia'*), and Italian (*'luogo di residenza'*) versions of the Treaty all use the term 'residence', an expression known from double taxation treaties pointing to the place with which the taxpayer maintains a special and durable relationship of a personal and economic nature. The German text of Art 58(1) lit. a EC employs the term *'Wohnort'* in the singular form. From this it is obvious that a taxpayer—within the meaning of Art 58(1) lit. a EC—can only have one *'Wohnort'* in the same way as he can only have one residence. The *'Wohnort',* therefore, is not synonymous with the German tax term *'Wohnsitz',* of which a taxpayer can have several. It rather seems that *'Wohnort'* equals *'Ansässigkeit'* (habitual place of abode). *'Ansässigkeit'* is the term used in German translations of double taxation treaties in situations in which other language versions refer to 'residence', *'leur résidence,' 'lugar de residencia'* or *'luogo di residenza'.* [See on the interpretation of the 'place of residence' within the meaning of Art 58(1) lit. a EC N Dautzenberg, 'Steuervorbehalt', 538 *et seq*; U Haferkamp, *Kapitalverkehrsfreiheit*, 121 *et seq*; W Schön, 'Kapitalverkehrsfreiheit', 766 *et seq*; J Lübke, *Kapitalverkehrs- und Niederlassungsfreiheit*, 365 *et seq*]

For legal persons, Arts 43 EC and 48 EC provide us with some guidance. A company can be resident at the place of its central administration or principal place of business due to the fact that at those places the centre of management or the centre of economic activities, respectively, can be found. Also, the statutory seat can be the residence of a legal person as long as a certain economic closeness to this place can be shown. Thus, for a legal person—following the idea of the double taxation treaties—it is the special and durable economic relationship binding it to a certain national economy that constitutes the decisive criterion. [B Matzka, *Freiheit des Kapitalverkehrs*, 83; U Haferkamp, *Kapitalverkehrsfreiheit*, 122]

[246] The second 'distinguishing criterion' referred to in Art 58(1) lit. a EC is the 'place where the capital is invested'. Its meaning is contentious when the location where the capital is initially placed and the place where it is productively employed differ from each other. That is the case, for example, when an investor resident in Germany transfers money to an investment fund resident in France, and this fund again places this money in a corporation resident in the USA. In such a situation, some commentators think the decisive place is the place where the first debtor of the capital resides. [eg, U Haferkamp, *Kapitalverkehrsfreiheit*, 124 *et seq*; K Ståhl, 'Dividend Taxation', 230 *et seq*. Others point towards the ultimate place of productive employment of capital, which is an economic understanding of the connecting factor. [eg, N Dautzenberg, 'Kapitalanlageort', 382 *et seq*; N Dautzenberg, 'Steuervorbehalt', 540; C Staringer, 'Dividendenbesteuerung', 105; note also M Sedlaczek, 'Kapitalverkehrsfreiheit', 54 *et seq*] Still others suggest differentiating on the basis of whether the intermediary can decide, on his sole responsibility, where to transfer the received capital or whether he has to follow the orders of his creditor. [eg, A Rohde, *Kapitalverkehr*, 153; J Bröhmer, Art. 58 EC (2002), mn 4] In the former case, the place of the debtor (mediatory)

fall outside the ambit of the duty to liberalize capital movements contained in Art 56(1) EC.[247] Article 58(1) lit. a. EC was included in the Treaty, it is argued, to allow for the lack of harmonization of direct taxation within the Common Market.[248]

This interpretation, however, is unconvincing. As a preliminary observation, if one were prepared to read Art 58(1) lit. a. EC in the way suggested above, this would mean that the Treaty provisions on free movement of capital with respect to taxation would fall behind the standard of liberalization already achieved by its preceding provisions in Directive 88/361 EEC,[249] which did not contain a respective provision.[250] One can, however, cast doubt on the allegation that the drafters of the Treaty of Maastricht intended to fall short of the *acquis communautaire* already achieved.[251] Be that as it may, recalling that the historical

---

is crucial; in the latter, the place where the capital is ultimately productively employed shall be the relevant one. However, the opinion just mentioned suffers from uncertainty connected to the question of what amounts to an independent decision to transfer the capital. For example, is a fund manager whose fund can only invest in European stocks independent in its decisions? Haferkamp suggests not fully; but, then, where should the dividing line be drawn? [*Cf* U Haferkamp, *Kapitalverkehrsfreiheit*, 123 *et seq*]

In favour of the ultimate place of productive employment of capital is the idea that the alternative opinion, which champions the initial place of investment, could lead to both distortion of competition within the Common Market and allowing for indirect discrimination because the place where the first creditor resides is usually the same as his State of nationality. [N Dautzenberg, 'Kapitalanlageort', 381; N Dautzenberg, 'Steuervorbehalt', 540] Moreover, taking into account that free movement of capital is an object-related freedom, the 'place of residence of the *capital* for taxation purposes' seems to be more decisive than the place of residence for tax purposes of the debtor of the capital. [M Sedlaczek, Art. 58 EC (2003), mn 13]

However, this approach cannot disguise the fact that it faces considerable problems in identifying the ultimate place of productive employment of capital in situations in which the money was transferred through multiple mediators. [U Haferkamp, *Kapitalverkehrsfreiheit*, 124; J Lübke, *Kapitalverkehrs- und Niederlassungsfreiheit*, 366] Instead of a cumbersome quest for the ultimate place of productive employment of capital, Haferkamp correctly suggests splitting the multiple transfers into components and applying to each of them the provisions on free movement of capital. The suggestion of Lübke follows the same reasoning. [*Cf* J Lübke, *Kapitalverkehrs- und Niederlassungsfreiheit*, 366]

Be that as it may, ultimately, due to the fact that Art 58(1) lit. a EC does not constitute a *domaine réservé*, the whole discussion at this point is of a somewhat academic nature. Either two capital movements are comparable or not, and if they are comparable, then different treatment, irrespective of whether the measure differentiates on the basis of the place where the debtor resides or on the basis of where the capital is effectively used or whatever distinguishing criterion might have been used, has to be justified by express or implied mandatory requirements. The treatment, furthermore, must be proportionate.

[247] De Bont reaches this conclusion on the basis of his opinion that Art 58(3) EC does not apply at all to Art 58(1) lit. a EC. [G de Bont, 'Taxation', 138 *et seq*]
[248] A Honrath, *Kapitalverkehr*, 80 *et seq*.
[249] Directive 88/361/EEC.
[250] As to the opinion that Art 58(1) lit. a EC indeed constitutes a step backwards in terms of liberalization: J Bröhmer, Art. 58 EC (2002), mn 2; W Kiemel, Art. 58 EC (2003), mn 9; G Ress and J Ukrow, Art. 58 EC (2002), mn 10.
[251] M Sedlaczek, 'Kapitalverkehrsfreiheit', 52; M Sedlaczek, Art. 58 EC (2003), mn. 11; HG Ruppe, 'Kapitalverkehrsfreiheit', 19.

interpretation of Treaty provisions is only of limited value,[252] it is suggested that an understanding of Art 58(1) lit. a EC in its textual context, especially in its interaction with Art 58(3) EC, be developed.[253]

As a starting point, 'discrimination [within the meaning of Art. 56(1) EC] can arise only through the application of different rules to comparable situations or the application of the same rule to different situations'.[254] In this sense, Art 58(1) lit. a EC has to a large degree only declaratory functions. It merely confirms what the Court had already held in its '*Schumacker* jurisprudence',[255] ie, that for direct taxes 'the situations of residents and of non-residents are not, as a rule, comparable'.[256] If, however, the situations of residents and non-residents, in certain special circumstances, are comparable,[257] then Art 58(3) EC demands that their different treatment 'shall not constitute a means of arbitrary discrimination...on the free movement of capital'.[258] Thus, as a next step, the question of what constitutes 'arbitrariness' must be answered. This might be done best by looking at the similarly worded provision of Art 30, 2nd sentence EC. For this provision, it was held that discrimination is to be conceived as arbitrary if no

---

[252] *Cf* for further references, F Müller and R Christensen, *Methodik*, 256 *et seq*.

[253] The relationship of Arts 58(1) lit. a EC and 58(3) EC constituted one of the most contentious issues discussed when it came to questions of what impact the provisions on free movement of capital actually have on national taxation measures: *cf* for further references, W Schön, 'Kapitalverkehrsfreiheit', 765 *et seq*, arguing with the '*effet utile*'. The dispute was finally settled in Case C-35/98 *Staatssecretaris van Financiën v B.G.M. Verkooijen*, para 44 *et seq*. It was held that Art 58(3) EC also relates to Art 58(1) lit. a EC. See also J Bröhmer, Art. 58 EC (2002), mn 21.

[254] Case C-279/93 'Schumacker' *Finanzamt Köln-Altstadt v Roland Schumacker*, para 30.

[255] Ibid, para 30 *et seq*; Case C-80/94 *G. H. E. J. Wielockx v Inspecteur de Directe Belastingen*, para 18 *et seq*; Case C-107/94 *P. H. Asscher v Staatssecretaris van Financiën*, para 41 *et seq*.

[256] 'Income received in the territory of a Member State by a non-resident is in most cases only a part of his total income, which is concentrated at his place of residence. Moreover, a non-resident's personal ability to pay tax, determined by reference to his aggregate income and his personal and family circumstances, is more easy to assess at the place where his personal and financial interests are centred. In general, that is the place where he has his usual abode. Accordingly, international tax law, and in particular the Model Double Taxation Treaty of the Organization for Economic Cooperation and Development (OECD), recognizes that in principle the overall taxation of taxpayers, taking account of their personal and family circumstances, is a matter for the State of residence.' [Case C-279/93 'Schumacker' *Finanzamt Köln-Altstadt v Roland Schumacker*, para 31 *et seq*]

[257] It is indeed possible that '[t]here is no objective difference between the situations of such a non-resident and a resident engaged in comparable employment, such as to justify different treatment as regards the taking into account for taxation purposes of the taxpayer's personal and family circumstances.' [Ibid, para 37]

[258] National measures may also not constitute a means of disguised restriction. A national measure amounts to a disguised restriction if this measure, although at face value appearing to be in the public interest, actually, in objective terms [see for a discussion of whether a subjective element is required: P-C Müller-Graff, Art. 30 EC (2003), mn 174 *et seq*], constitutes a camouflage of a protectionist act. [*Cf* P-C Müller-Graff, Art. 30 EC (2003), mn 169 *et seq*] While any measure based on Arts 58(1) or (2) EC has to pass both the 'arbitrary discrimination test' and the 'disguised restriction test', in practice the latter is of minimal importance. *Cf* U Haferkamp, *Kapitalverkehrsfreiheit*, 140 *et seq*.

recognized overriding reason in the general interest can be shown.²⁵⁹ Moreover, it does not suffice that the national measure is in the public interest, but the measure must also be proportionate.²⁶⁰

If one is prepared to view Art 58(1) lit. a EC from the angle suggested above, which appears almost mandatory against the background of the threat national tax rules potentially cause for the establishment of a Common Market and free movement of capital, one can reasonably conclude that it has only declaratory functions, neither constituting a *domaine réservé* for tax rules nor an independent ground of justification for restrictive national measures.²⁶¹ This interpretation was embraced by the Court in its *Verkooijen* judgment.²⁶²

(b) Comparability Questions with Respect to Market Access/Exit Regulations for Direct Investments National measures of Member States may not only disadvantage already existing or ongoing direct investments originating from other Member States, but they may also take measures that establish a discriminatory regime for first-time access to their markets. Access might be sought, inter alia, by the acquistion, in part or in full, of an ongoing undertaking by way of a

---

²⁵⁹ *Cf* Case 4/75 *Rewe-Zentralfinanz eGmbH v Landwirtschaftskammer*, para 8 *et seq*. Concurring, eg: A Honrath, *Kapitalverkehr*, 87 *et seq*; JA Usher, *Law of Money*, 57, 236; W Schön, 'Kapitalverkehrsfreiheit', 767; J Bröhmer, Art. 58 EC (2002), mn 21; C Staringer, 'Dividendenbesteuerung', 106 *et seq*.
²⁶⁰ A Honrath, *Kapitalverkehr*, 90 *et seq*; JCW Müller, *Kapitalverkehrsfreiheit*, 177 *et seq*; J Bröhmer, Art. 58 EC (2002), mn 21; U Haferkamp, *Kapitalverkehrsfreiheit*, 144 *et seq*.
²⁶¹ *Cf*, eg, W Schön, 'Kapitalverkehrsfreiheit', 768; JCW Müller, *Kapitalverkehrsfreiheit*, 177 *et seq*; M Sedlaczek, 'Kapitalverkehrsfreiheit', 56; U Haferkamp, *Kapitalverkehrsfreiheit*, 141 *et seq*, 145; HG Ruppe, 'Kapitalverkehrsfreiheit', 21–23; B Terra and PJ Wattel, *European Tax Law*, 18 *et seq*, 40 *et seq*; J Röhrbein and K Eicker, 'Verlustberücksichtigung', 470 *et seq*; C Staringer, 'Dividendenbesteuerung', 107; S Peers, 'Movement of Capital', 348 *et seq*; L Flynn, 'Coming of Age', 793 *et seq*.

Against the background outlined above, the debate surrounding the question of a possible legal effect of the Declaration on Art 73d EC (now, after amendment, Art 58 EC) accompanying the Maastricht Treaty—Final Act is also only of minor importance. [W Schön, 'Kapitalverkehrsfreiheit', 768, fn 113; U Haferkamp, *Kapitalverkehrsfreiheit*, 121, 145] The Declaration reads as follows: 'The Conference affirms that the right of Member States to apply the relevant provisions of their tax law as referred to in Article 73d(1)(a) of this Treaty will apply only with respect to the relevant provisions which exist at the end of 1993. However, this Declaration shall apply only to capital movements between Member States and to payments effected between Member States.' This study is of the opinion that the Declaration possesses only political effects due to the fact that only protocols, not declarations, are annexed to the Treaty. Of the same opinion, inter alia, are: W Kiemel, Art. 58 EC (2003), mn 11; A Rohde, *Kapitalverkehr*, 151; HG Ruppe, 'Kapitalverkehrsfreiheit', 23 *et seq*. Holding a different view, inter alia: G Ress and J Ukrow, Art. 58 EC (2002), mn 11; C Ohler, 'Kapitalverkehrsfreiheit', 1807. Where the question of effect was raised but left open: Case C-513/03 (Opinion of AG Léger) *Heirs of M. E. A. van Hilten-van der Heijden v Inspecteur van de Belastingdienst/Particulieren/Ondernemingen buitenland te Heerlen*, paras 27, 84. For a lengthy discussion, see A Honrath, *Kapitalverkehr*, 82 *et seq*.
²⁶² Case C-35/98 *Staatssecretaris van Financiën v B.G.M. Verkooijen*, para 43 *et seq*.

cross-border merger or by setting up a new subsidiary company, but also by way of the purchase or setting up of a legally dependent office, agency, or branch.[263]

The potential host State might, for several reasons, be tempted to restrict such cross-border direct investments, inter alia, by means of authorization or approval requirements for the setting up or acquisition of its businesses, quantitative limitations on foreign ownership, control-based limitations of shareholder powers, foreclosure of certain legal forms of incorporation or certain forms of establishment, additional requirements or procedures for registration, or the possibility of governmental intervention in management. The policy aims possibly pursued by a host State could relate, for example, to the protection of an infant or non-competitive industry, natural wealth, infrastructure, and strategic industry or cultural heritage, but also to the securing of effective supervision of certain business activities, such as banking, insurance, or trade in securities.[264]

The different treatment of domestic investment and investment originating from another Member State amounts to discrimination if a domestic investment and investment linked to another Member State are made in comparable circumstances with respect to the situation regulated by the respective national market access measure. In the Common Market, it appears to be difficult to envisage any 'essential attribute' that would question *per se* the comparability of a domestic investment and an inward investment coming from another Member State.

The non-domestic origin of a capital movement (an expressly prohibited distinguishing criterion) can never lead to incomparability, being itself a 'non-essential attribute'. The same is true for the seat or nationality of the owner of the capital, which constitutes a surrogate criterion and, hence, also forms a 'non-essential attribute'.

Despite the fact that the aforementioned distinguishing criteria are *per se* 'non-essential attributes', in most cases the regulatory questions that are posed by placing a direct investment do not in any way vary depending on its origin, especially not on the nationality or seat of the owner. Rather, these regulatory questions have their origin in the problem that a particular activity of a private undertaking—especially in areas such as services in the public interest[265] but also beyond—touches upon *Gemeinwohlinteressen* (issues of the public good), and that those *Gemeinwohlinteressen* are—from a Member State's

---

[263] For an even more detailed categorization of the different forms of establishment, refer to J Tiedje and P Troberg, Art. 43 EC (2003), mn 47 *et seq*. Note, however, that the notions of establishment and direct investment are not fully congruent. See Chapter III. 2.

[264] *Cf* UNCTAD, *Admission and Establishment*, 38 *et seq*.

[265] With respect to a measure which, for example, aims at the protection of certain key elements of infrastructure (motorways, railways, airports, water supply, etc) or strategic branches of industry, such as steel and energy, with a view to guaranteeing a stable and sufficient supply, domestic and cross-border direct investment are in comparable situations due to the fact that an ill-managed domestic investment could in the same way as a cross-border investment threaten the aim of a stable and sufficient supply in the given Member State. A stable, sufficient supply has nothing to do with the origin of the direct investment but rather with, eg, the diversity of the ownership structure so that the bankruptcy of one shareholder has no significant impact on the undertaking. *Cf* Case C-367/98 *Commission v Portuguese Republic (Re Golden Shares I)*, para 39 *et seq*.

perspective—insufficiently taken into account by private undertakings under general circumstances of *Privatautonomie* (party autonomy). Insufficient consideration of *Gemeinwohlinteressen* originates in the decision of the Member State to let a private undertaking rather than a public sector undertaking perform the respective activity.[266] The conflict arising exists independent of the nationality or seat of the owner of the private undertaking because there is no reason to believe that a domestically owned private undertaking would be more likely to take into account *Gemeinwohlinteressen* than a non-domestically owned one.[267] Rather, a private undertaking predominantly pursues its own commercial interests.[268]

In this context, the argument could be advanced that it makes a difference whether the cross-border direct investment is owned by a private person or by a State. The latter could exploit its position as owner by pursuing political rather than commercial interests in the host State by means of its direct investment. However, the pursuance of political interests presupposes first and foremost market power, which is derived from a dominant position in a market. If one fears dependency on a certain investor, then this calls for rigorous application of competition law in order to restrict this market power. The State ownership of the direct investment, though, plays no significant role in this respect.[269]

It is, furthermore, settled case law that economic grounds cannot serve as justification for any restriction of the free movement of capital. This means that if those considerations, namely, inter alia, the competitive structure of the market from which the investment originates or the degree of development of this market, are not acceptable as grounds of justification, then they cannot *a fortiori* be regarded as 'essential attributes' leading to the negation of comparability.

Thus, although 'comparability' has to be judged on a case-by-case basis, one can safely establish that domestic investments and investments originating from another Member State are usually made in comparable circumstances as concerns their access to a Member State's market. The fact that the investment originates from another Member State in which different political or economic situations are to be found is no reason to deny 'comparability'. This is the very idea of the Common Market in general and the freedoms in particular.[270]

In the context of the aforesaid, another 'phenomenon' of so-called '*double regulation*' or '*double control*' needs to be mentioned and distinguished. Even if the national measure of the host State operates indistinctly, it could lead to the result that an investment originating from another country needs to provide the same information, or must fulfil certain requirements twice, both in its home State and

---

[266] Sachverständigenrat zur Begutachtung der gesamtwirtschaftlichen Entwicklung, *Jahresgutachten 2007/08*, mn 631, 663.

[267] Even more questionable in terms of the rule of law is the argument that a domestically owned private undertaking is more easily motivated by (arbitrary) pressure or incentives to take into account *Gemeinwohlinteressen*. [Ibid, mn 632 *et seq*, 663]

[268] Ibid, mn 632 *et seq*.   [269] Ibid, mn 634 *et seq*.

[270] Case C-294/97 (Opinion of AG Mischo) *Eurowings Luftverkehrs AG v Finanzamt Dortmund-Unna*, para 59.

in the host State. The so-called *'double regulation'* or *'double control'* issue does not constitute discrimination due to the fact that it is the result of the application of two different legal systems. Consequently, any restriction on free movement of capital resulting from it is only subject to the non-hindrance test, where the phenomenon of double regulation/control will be considered as part of the question of whether the host Member State's measure is proportionate.[271] Under certain conditions, the host Member State can be required to recognize regulatory or control measures of the home Member State as functionally equivalent.[272] The hindering effect of 'double regulation' or 'double control' can, however, also be remedied by means of harmonization.[273]

Moreover, Art 56(1) EC also covers measures of the home Member State that discriminate between domestic investments and investments directed towards other Member States, so-called outward or outbound investments. I have already discussed this issue from the perspective of taxation, ie, the different treatment of fully taxable residents depending on the place where they invested their capital.[274] I concluded that a domestic investment and an investment in another Member State are, in principle, comparable. The scope or application of the non-discrimination test is, of course, not limited to exit-restricting direct taxation issues but extends to any other measure that differentiates between investments placed within the respective Member State and those directed towards other Member States. Again, in the Common Market it is difficult to envisage 'essential attributes' that would *per se* call into question the comparability of domestic and cross-border direct investment.

(5) Summary and Appraisal

I have identified different comparison groups above. Cross-border and domestic capital movements are commonly compared. Such a comparison corresponds to the international economic law principle of national treatment. Moreover, two cross-border capital movements may also be the objects of comparison; they may either originate from or be directed to two different Member States, or they may originate from or be directed to a Member State and a third country. Also, the treatment of two third country capital movements can be compared, which relates to the international economic law principle of most-favoured-nation treatment.

The wording of Art 56(1) EC does not expressly mention the prohibited distinguishing criterion, but it has to be established by construction. In the case of free

---

[271] U Haferkamp, *Kapitalverkehrsfreiheit*, 92 *et seq.*
[272] *Cf* Case 120/78 *Rewe-Zentral AG v Bundesmonopolverwaltung für Branntwein ('Cassis de Dijon')*, para 14; ('so-called second Cassis principle')
[273] For example, Art 26(1) of the old 'Banking Directive,' which attributes the prime competence of control to the home Member State of a bank, implying that the host Member State is in principle obliged to recognize the extraterritorial effect of measures taken by the home Member State without any further examination.
[274] See Chapter IV. 2. b. (4) (a) iii.

movement of capital, an object-oriented freedom, the decisive distinguishing criterion is the place of origin/destination of capital movement. If a national measure expressly refers to the foreign origin or destination of the capital, then under the condition that it puts the cross-border capital movement in a less favourable position than a domestic or another cross-border capital movement, it is referred to as direct discrimination.

Indirect discrimination can be established if the national measure does not expressly refer to the foreign origin/destination but employs a neutral distinguishing criterion that 'in fact leads to the same results' as a distinction based on the expressly prohibited criterion. Nationality and residence do not constitute an additional autonomous prohibited distinguishing criterion alongside the origin/destination of capital.

The Court, while certainly acknowledging that national measures that differentiate on the basis of nationality, residence, etc can constitute discrimination, fails to put forward reasoning of a more doctrinal nature on what constitutes direct and indirect discrimination. Moreover, it appears that the Court does not attempt seriously to delineate clearly the 'non-discrimination' from the 'non-hindrance' test. This might to some extent be understandable when one looks at the wording of Art 56(1) EC, which also does not differentiate between the two tests.

Only comparable capital movements must, in principle, be treated equally. Incomparable capital movements must be dealt with differently. Judging 'comparability' has to be done on a case-by-case basis taking into account actual circumstances against the background of the purpose and content of the respective national measure and under consideration of the value-based decisions stipulated by the Community legal order. The Court, however, does not always adhere to this, occasionally considering only the factual or the legal situation.

Decisions on national direct taxation legislation, ie, legislation that essentially encroaches on ongoing direct investments, form the core of the existing case law on comparability. No consistent picture has so far emerged from those cases concerning comparability. The situation is complicated by the constant process of balancing the desire to preserve the Member States' competences on direct taxation and the necessary selective intervention into this highly politicized area in order to give the fundamental freedoms the meaning they deserve; no general exception to the prohibition of discrimination in the area of taxation can be derived from the Treaty, especially not by reference to Art 58(1) lit. a, (3) EC. However, one should keep in mind that negative harmonization in this field goes quickly to the core of the sovereignty of the Member States, which, it appears, does not always make it easy for the Court to present a consistent approach. This might limit the indicative value of this strand of case law when it comes to judging the question of whether national measures in other subject areas also concerned with the regulation of an ongoing business are discriminatory in their nature.

As regards national measures that establish a discriminatory regime, not for treatment of an ongoing business, but for first-time access to a Member State's market, within the Community it is difficult to envisage 'essential attributes' that would question the comparability of a domestic investment and an investment from another Member State *per se*; differences especially in economic development or tax, social, or labour politics are not an argument. The same applies not only to inbound but, *mutatis mutandis,* also to outward investments.

3. The Scope of Prohibition of Article 56(1) EC in a Third Country Context—Any Modification?

Having put forward a construction of the scope of prohibition of Art 56(1) EC in an intra-Community context above, in this section I shall consider whether this interpretation needs to be reassessed when it comes to third country capital movement. I shall therefore look for deviations from the intra-Community interpretation of Art 56(1) EC in jurisprudence and in academic writing. However, both the Court's case law[275] and the literature, as they present themselves to us today, at the beginning of their evolution, hardly provide more than a sketchy picture. Trying to identify possible future issues in the construction must, therefore, inevitably be to a certain degree prognostic in nature. Having said this, I predict that future discussion will evolve around three points. First, the persuasiveness of teleological considerations based on the argument of allegedly limited aims pursued by free capital movement in a third country context will probably be at the centre of debate.[276] Second, within the non-discrimination test, the question of 'comparability in principle' of domestic/intra-Community and third country investment could prove to be a crucial one. However, third, the aforementioned questions will only start to play a role if—and there is some indication given by the Court that this is a big 'if'[277]—the relationship

---

[275] Joined Cases C-163/94, C-165/94, and C-250/94 *Criminal proceedings against Lucas Emilio Sanz de Lera, Raimundo Díaz Jiménez and Figen Kapanoglu*; Case C-452/01 *Margarethe Ospelt and Schlössle Weissenberg Familienstiftung*; Case C-452/04 *Fidium Finanz AG*; Case C-374/04 *Test Claimants in Class IV of the ACT Group Litigation (Pirelli, Essilor and Sony), Test Claimants in Class IV of the ACT Group Litigation (BMW) v Commissioners of Inland Revenue*; Case C-446/04 *Test Claimants in the FII Group Litigation v Commissioners of Inland Revenue*; Case C-492/04 *Lasertec Gesellschaft für Stanzformen mbH (formerly Riess Laser Bandstahlschnitte GmbH) v Finanzamt Emmendingen*); Case C-524/04 *Test Claimants in the Thin Cap Group Litigation*; Case C-157/05 *Winfried Holböck v Finanzamt Salzburg-Land*; Case C-102/05 *Skatteverket v A and B*; Case C-101/05 *Skatteverket v A*; Case C-194/06 *Staatssecretaris von Financiën v Orange European Smallcap Fund NV*; Case C-201/05 *The Test Claimants in the CFC and Dividend Group Litigation v Commissioners of Inland Revenue*. Note also the Opinion of Advocate General Kokott in an intra-Community case, which, however, had third country relevance: Case C-319/02 (Opinion of AG Kokott) *Petri Manninen*.
[276] *Cf* recently Case C-101/05 *Skatteverket v A*, 69, 74 *et seq.*
[277] For a discussion of the relationship of free movement of capital and the freedom of establishment, see Chapter III.

already discussed between competing freedoms is resolved in favour of parallel applicability.

In this section I shall turn the spotlight on the first two issues mentioned. In the following section I shall first critically analyse and review the Court's evolving case law. As a second step, I shall scrutinize those arguments advanced by commentators who are of the opinion that Art 56(1) EC must be interpreted in a narrower sense when it comes to third country capital movement. The cases and the discussion in the literature have rarely focused particularly on direct investment. This fact is reflected in the following analysis, which is performed in a more general manner. Against the background of both the existing case law and the academic writing, I will develop my understanding of the scope of prohibition of Art 56(1) EC in a third country context. My hypothesis is that, in principle, both the non-discrimination and the non-hindrance tests, as developed in an intra-Community context, can be applied towards third country capital movement.

a. The Scope of Prohibition in a Third Country Context as reflected in the Emerging Case Law of the Court

The evolution of the Court's case law on third country capital movement began in the *Sanz de Lera* case,[278] a preliminary ruling in the course of criminal proceedings. This case was concerned with the unauthorized physical export of large quantities of banknotes by individuals from Member States to third countries. When looking at the facts presented, the national measure that made the physical transfer of money subject to prior declaration or authorization applied distinctly. While not distinguishing on the basis of currency, the measure did not apply to transfers within Spain but only to exports to other countries.[279]

The Advocate General noted that the case at hand was similar to that of *Bordessa*[280] and, thus, did not find it necessary to comment on the scope of application of Art 56(1) EC,[281] instead expanding on possible grounds of justification and the issue of the direct effect[282] of Art 56(1) EC.[283] The Court, also relying on its findings in *Bordessa*,[284] after having noted that the effect of prior authorization

---

[278] Joined Cases C-163/94, C-165/94, and C-250/94 *Criminal proceedings against Lucas Emilio Sanz de Lera, Raimundo Díaz Jiménez and Figen Kapanoglu*.
[279] Ibid, para 6.
[280] Joined Cases C-358/93 and C-416/93 *Criminal proceedings against Aldo Bordessa and Vicente Marí Mellado and Concepción Barbero Maestre*.
[281] Joined Cases C-163/94, C-165/94, and C-250/94 (Opinion of AG Tesauro) *Criminal proceedings against Lucas Emilio Sanz de Lera, Raimundo Díaz Jiménez and Figen Kapanoglu*, para 7.
[282] For a discussion of whether Art 56(1) EC has direct effect with respect to third countries, see Chapter V. 2.
[283] Joined Cases C-163/94, C-165/94, and C-250/94 *Criminal proceedings against Lucas Emilio Sanz de Lera, Raimundo Díaz Jiménez and Figen Kapanoglu*.
[284] Joined Cases C-358/93 and C-416/93 *Criminal proceedings against Aldo Bordessa and Vicente Marí Mellado and Concepción Barbero Maestre*.

'is to cause the exercise of the free movement of capital to be subject to the discretion of the administrative authorities and thus be such as to render that freedom illusory',[285] turned straight to the proportionality question within the ambit of Art 58(1) lit. b EC, the issue of applicability of the grandfathering clause of Art 57(1) EC,[286] and the problem of direct effect[287] of Art 56(1) EC in a third country context. The 'nonchalance' displayed in the treatment of the scope of prohibition of Art 56(1) EC in a third country context can be viewed as an indication that neither the Advocate General nor the Court intended to deal with this situation differently than in an intra-Community context.[288]

In the *Ospelt* case,[289] property under lease (farm land) situated in Austria, owned by a Liechtenstein national, was intended to be transferred to a Liechtenstein-based foundation. The Austrian authorities refused to grand prior authorization of this transfer mainly due to the fact that the transferee himself was not farming the land.[290] At first blush, this case appears to be a third country case, the Principality of Liechtenstein not being a Member State of the European Union. However, due to the effects of the EEA Agreement,[291] one could take the position that this case has only limited authority as to the scope of prohibition of Art 56(1) EC with respect to third countries. This study tends to disagree partly with such a proposition. While it is certainly true that in this case the EEA Agreement had a bearing on the permissible exceptions to Art 56(1) EC, notably the question of application of Art 57(1) EC,[292] it had only a limited effect on the scope of prohibition because both Art 56(1) EC and Art 40, in connection with Annex XII of the EEA Agreement, were found to be identical in substance regarding their scope of prohibition.[293] Having said this, one may note that the Court examined the national provision at issue both against the background of the non-discrimination[294] and the non-hindrance tests.[295] It appears that neither

---

[285] Joined Cases C-163/94, C-165/94, and C-250/94 *Criminal proceedings against Lucas Emilio Sanz de Lera, Raimundo Díaz Jiménez and Figen Kapanoglu*, para 25.
[286] Ibid, para 16 *et seq*.
[287] Ibid, para 40 *et seq*.
[288] See also FC de la Torre, 'Case Note Jointed Cases C-163/94, C-165/94 and C-250/94', 1071 *et seq*; Note S Mohamed, *Free Movement of Capital*, 219 *et seq* for different view on the *Sanz de Lera* case.
[289] Case C-452/01 *Margarethe Ospelt and Schlössle Weissenberg Familienstiftung*.
[290] For the detailed facts of the case, see ibid, para 17 *et seq*.
[291] EEA Agreement.   [292] See Chapter VII. 2.
[293] Case C-452/01 (Opinion of AG Geelhoed) *Margarethe Ospelt and Schlössle Weissenberg Familienstiftung*, para 70; Case C-452/01 *Margarethe Ospelt and Schlössle Weissenberg Familienstiftung*, para 32.
[294] Case C-452/01 *Margarethe Ospelt and Schlössle Weissenberg* Familienstiftung, para 35 *et seq*. Of course, it being the objective of the EEA Agreement to extend the Internal Market to the EFTA countries and thus to treat the EFTA countries, in practice, as if they were Member States [*cf* Case C-452/01 (Opinion of AG Geelhoed) *Margarethe Ospelt and Schlössle Weissenberg Familienstiftung*, para 67 *et seq*, 78], it would be more difficult to argue that a situation in an EC Member State and an EFTA Member State might *per se* not be comparable. See also Advocate General Kokott's '*obiter dicta*' in her Opinion on the *Manninen* case: Case C-319/02 (Opinion of AG Kokott) *Petri Manninen*, para 79.
[295] Case C-452/01 *Margarethe Ospelt and Schlössle Weissenberg Familienstiftung*, para 37.

The Scope of Prohibition of Article 56(1) EC in a Third Country Context 165

the Court nor the Advocate General suggested drawing any distinction between the construction of the scope of prohibition of Art 56(1) EC with respect to intra-Community and third country cases.[296]

The *van Hilten*[297] case was concerned with a Dutch regulation:

> under which the estate of a national of a Member State who dies within 10 years of ceasing to reside in that Member State is to be taxed as if that national had continued to reside in that Member State, even though benefiting from relief in respect of inheritance taxes levied by other States.[298]

Notably, Advocate General Léger, analysing in great detail the question of whether any restriction on the free movement of capital flows from the aforementioned regulation,[299] resorted for his argumentation to the case law developed within an intra-Community context. Thus, he appears to interpret the scope of prohibition of Art 56(1) EC in cases in which third country capital movements are involved no differently from those involving intra-Community capital movements.[300] The Court, having stated that Art 56(1) EC applies to non-member States as well, formulated in rather general wording that

> the measures prohibited by Article [56(1)] of the Treaty, ... include those which are *likely to discourage* non-residents from making investments in a Member State or to discourage that Member State's residents to do so in other States.[301]

Again, the Court in its interpretation did not deviate from its case law developed with respect to intra-Community capital movements.

The Opinion of Advocate General Stix-Hackl on *Fidium Finanz AG* provides another confirmative example for my hypothesis that the construction of

---

[296] *Cf* ibid, 34 *et seq*.
[297] Case C-513/03 *Heirs of M. E. A. van Hilten-van der Heijden v Inspecteur van de Belastingdienst/ Particulieren/Ondernemingen buitenland te Heerlen*.
[298] Ibid, para 27.
[299] He came to the conclusion that the Dutch tax regulation at issue does not discriminate between capital movements because it treats Dutch nationals who ceased to reside in the Netherlands in the same way as those who remained there. Moreover, by virtue of the aforementioned national regulation, the Member State does not place its own nationals who wish to take advantage of the fundamental freedoms in a less advantageous position than those who wish to remain in the country. According to the Advocate General, what Community law in the area of taxation does not require, as it stands today, is that a Member State actively place its own nationals who wish to take advantage of the fundamental freedoms in a better position than those who wish to remain in the country. [*Cf.* Case C-513/03 (Opinion of AG Léger) *Heirs of M. E. A. van Hilten-van der Heijden v Inspecteur van de Belastingdienst/Particulieren/Ondernemingen buitenland te Heerlen*, 65 *et seq*] For a critical view: D Hohenwarter and P Plansky, 'Anmerkung Schlussanträge Rs. van Hilten', 422 *et seq*, who state that the Court failed to consider the situation of whether equal treatment of unequal situations occurred. This criticism, however, is ultimately unconvincing. Even if the Court had considered this situation, it does not change the fact that the national measure does not place nationals that are willing to take advantage of the fundamental freedoms in a less favourable position than those who wish to remain within the country.
[300] More cautious but of the same view: A Schnitger, 'Kapitalverkehrsfreiheit', 493.
[301] [Emphasis added] Case C-513/03 *Heirs of M. E. A. van Hilten-van der Heijden v Inspecteur van de Belastingdienst/Particulieren/Ondernemingen buitenland te Heerlen*, para 44.

the scope of protection of Art 56(1) EC follows in principle the same lines in intra-Community and third country contexts. In contrast to the Court's subsequent judgment,[302] Advocate General Stix-Hackl proceeded from the assumption that the economic activity at issue in the case falls within the ambit of free movement of capital, that being the only freedom applicable in a third country context.[303] She applied both the non-discrimination and the non-hindrance tests contained in Art 56(1) EC towards the national measure at issue, drawing on the case law developed in an intra-Community context.[304] With regard to the national prior authorization requirement, acknowledging that it operates equally in law and in fact, she found, in accordance with the existing case law, that the mere existence of such a requirement in itself indicates the existence of a hindrance on free movement of capital.[305] Concerning the prerequisite of physical commercial presence in the country, the Advocate General concluded that '[t]his would entail considerable additional expenditure and might deter economic operations from pursuing such business'.[306] Looking again at the question of whether a difference in interpretation of the scope of application of Art 56(1) EC in a third country context in comparison with intra-Community cases can be witnessed, this must be answered in the negative.

In *Test Claimants in Class IV of the ACT Group Litigation*, concerned inter alia with the extension of benefits flowing from a double taxation treaty to non-beneficiaries, the Advocate General as well as the Court cited their own reasoning in the same case advanced with respect to the intra-Community situations when considering the third country question.[307]

In its recent judgment in *Holböck*, the Court limited itself to a short reference to its findings in *Lenz*. In *Lenz*, the ECJ had to deal with an almost identical situation, except for the fact that in *Holböck* the conflict arose in a third country context.[308] Hence, it transposed its jurisprudence developed in an intra-Community context, once again without distinction, to a third county situation.

---

[302] Case C-452/04 *Fidium Finanz AG*, paras 34, 43, 48. The Court in its judgment considered the commercial activity of granting credits as 'an unavoidable consequence of the restriction on the freedom to provide services' [Case C-452/04 *Fidium Finanz AG*, para 48] and, thus, concluded that 'it is not necessary to consider whether the rules are compatible with Article 56 EC et seq'. [Case C-452/04 *Fidium Finanz AG*, para 49]

[303] Case C-452/04 (Opinion of AG Stix-Hackl) *Fidium Finanz AG*, para 53.

[304] Ibid, para 109 *et seq*.

[305] Ibid, para 109 *et seq*. The Advocate General uses the language of 'restriction'. In order to be consistent with the terminology applied in this study, I refer to 'hindrance', which constitutes a subcategory of 'restriction'.

[306] Ibid, para 113.

[307] Case C-374/04 (Opinion of AG Geelhoed) *Test Claimants in Class IV of the ACT Group Litigation (Pirelli, Essilor and Sony), Test Claimants in Class IV of the ACT Group Litigation (BMW) v Commissioners of Inland Revenue*, para 97 *et seq*, esp. 99 *et seq*; Case C-374/04 *Test Claimants in Class IV of the ACT Group Litigation (Pirelli, Essilor and Sony), Test Claimants in Class IV of the ACT Group Litigation (BMW) v Commissioners of Inland Revenue*, para 75 *et seq*, esp. 89 *et seq*.

[308] Case C-157/05 *Winfried Holböck v Finanzamt Salzburg-Land*, para 30 '[A]s regards the provisions of the Treaty concerning the free movement of capital, it is true that the Court has, in paragraphs 20 to 22 of its judgment in Lenz, held that, insofar as the taxation of income from capital

The abovementioned cases might give rise to the impression that the way in which the non-discrimination and non-hindrance tests are applied in an intra-Community context is simply transferred to third country situations. However, this impression must be revised to a certain extent when considering the following jurisprudence highlighting the potential of the interpretative parameter 'comparability' within the non-discrimination test to limit the scope of application of free movements of capital in a third country context.

This facet of the whole picture first emerged in Advocate General Kokott's opinion on the *Manninen* case.[309] The dispute in this case arose out of different taxation by Finland of dividends paid to shareholders depending on the place of establishment of the distributing company. Without being in serious need—the dividends at issue in the proceedings originated from a Swedish company—the Advocate General speculated on the scope of application of Art 56(1) EC with regard to third countries.[310] She stated with respect to the non-discrimination test:

> The principle of the free movement of capital between Member States and third countries set out in Article 56(1) EC does not, however, lay down a binding requirement that corporation tax paid in third countries be offset in the same way as in situations involving two Member States. Here too, the rule is that equal treatment is required only if the situations are comparable.[311]

Whether and to what extent the principles, especially the *Schumacker*[312] case law with respect to direct taxation, developed in an intra-Community context can be transposed to a third country context was left open.

The suggestion of a different appreciation of the 'comparability issue' in intra-Community and third country capital movements re-emerged recently, inter alia, in Advocate General Geelhoed's opinion on *Test Claimants in the FII Group Litigation*.[313] In this case, the British advance corporation tax legislation put resident companies receiving a payment of non-nationally-sourced dividends in a worse position compared to resident companies receiving a payment of nationally-sourced dividends by granting to the latter a cash flow advantage. After considering the intra-Community situations, he turned to third-country-sourced dividends. The Advocate General observed meaningfully that 'different considerations may apply than is the case with purely

at a definitive tax rate of 25% or at a rate reduced by half is subject, under the national legislation, to a condition that the source of that income is in Austria, the legislation not only has the effect of deterring taxpayers living in Austria from investing their capital in companies established outside that Member State, but also produces a restrictive effect in relation to those companies, inasmuch as it constitutes an obstacle to their raising capital within Austria. According to the Court, such legislation constitutes a restriction on the free movement of capital which is, in principle, prohibited by Article 56(1) EC.'

[309] Case C-319/02 (Opinion of AG Kokott) *Petri Manninen*.
[310] Case C-319/02 *Petri Manninen*, para 79.
[311] Case C-319/02 (Opinion of AG Kokott) *Petri Manninen*, para 79.
[312] Case C-279/93 'Schumacker' *Finanzamt Köln-Altstadt v Roland Schumacker*.
[313] Case C-446/04 (Opinion of AG Geelhoed) *Test Claimants in the FII Group Litigation v Commissioners of Inland Revenue*, para 121.

intra-Community restrictions'.³¹⁴ The comment on the possible incomparability was made with respect to access of tax authorities to reliable information for the assessment of the taxes due and effective fiscal supervision. In the case at hand, however, he could not identify substantiated arguments as to why specific considerations were to apply to the third country context.³¹⁵

Advocate General Geelhoed's suggestion was basically reiterated in the Court's judgment on the respective case. It stated that

> the taxation by a Member State of economic activities having cross-border aspects which take place within the Community is *not always comparable* to that of economic activities involving relations between Member States and non-member countries.³¹⁶

The Court equally could not identify any reason that would justify the conclusion that domestic and third country capital movements would be incomparable in the situation at issue.³¹⁷

Having said this, I must limit myself for the moment to the assessment that the Court's case law is of an ambiguous nature. One strand of case law suggests that there is no difference in the scope of prohibition depending on whether intra-Community or third country capital movement is involved. The second strand, focusing on the non-discrimination test, suggests otherwise, although without clearly spelling out when certain differences would lead to incomparability of domestic/intra-Community and third country capital movement. Taking into account the evolving state of the jurisprudence, any conclusive evaluation would therefore be premature.

b. Making the Case for a Parallel Understanding of the Scope of Prohibition in a Third Country Context: A Critical Appraisal of Voices in the Literature

In this section I shall develop my understanding of the scope of prohibition of Art 56(1) EC in a third country context against the background of a critical review of the respective arguments advanced in legal writing. The Court's case law, as we have learned above, provides meaningful guidance in this respect only to a limited extent.

---

³¹⁴ Ibid.   ³¹⁵ Ibid.
³¹⁶ [Emphasis added] Case C-446/04 *Test Claimants in the FII Group Litigation v Commissioners of Inland Revenue*, para 170; Reiterated in: Case C-101/05 *Skatteverket v A*, para 37.
³¹⁷ Case C-446/04 *Test Claimants in the FII Group Litigation v Commissioners of Inland Revenue*, para 171. It is regrettable that both the Advocate General and the Court somewhat obfuscated the issue of whether possible differences in access to information necessary to effectively conduct fiscal supervision by national tax authorities—depending on whether another Member State or a third county is involved—would relate to the question of comparability within the non-discrimination test and/or to the level of grounds of justification. I shall discuss the issue in detail when turning to the construction of the non-discrimination test in a third country context. See also Case C-101/05 (Opinion of AG Bot) *Skatteverket v A*, 118 *et seq*; Advocate General Bot qualified the issue of effective fiscal supervision as one of the level of grounds of justification.

I shall begin my analysis with the wording of the provision. Later, I shall review those teleological and systematic arguments advanced by commentators who choose to interpret the scope of prohibition of Art 56(1) EC in a third country context more narrowly than in an intra-Community context. I will scrutinize and call into question the proposition that certain alleged preconditions for interpreting the scope of prohibition of Art 56(1) EC similarly in both intra-Community and third country contexts are still lacking. In particular, it is not a precondition for unilateral liberalization of capital movements *vis-à-vis* third countries that the EC Treaty was aiming at an optimized global capital allocation *per se,* and it is not *conditio sine qua non* that legal harmonization with third countries is brought about before capital movements are liberalized. Furthermore, the Community does not lack bargaining powers with respect to third countries in order to press for reciprocal market access and equal treatment within the third country market; nor is the EC ill-equipped to fend off possible abusive practices by third countries or third country market participants. Moreover, it creates a vicious circle to argue that the greater number of permissible restrictions on the freedom in a third country context suggests a respectively more restricted *telos* of Art 56(1) EC in such a situation. Finally, restricting the scope of prohibition of Art 56(1) EC in a third country context would not have the effect of meaningfully restricting the access of third country investors to the Common Market.

An entire section is devoted to the operation of the 'comparability issue' within the non-discrimination test. I shall argue that there are no such considerations ('essential attributes') that would suggest ruling out 'comparability' of domestic/intra-Community and third country capital movement *per se.*

This study will therefore suggest making no distinction in principle in the construction of the scope of prohibition of Art 56(1) EC depending on whether intra-Community or third country capital movement is concerned.[318]

It should be mentioned that the arguments reviewed in this section were mostly made in the context of taxation, but they are also valid and utilizable outside this situation. The discussion in legal writing has rarely revolved particularly around direct investment. This fact resonates in the following analysis, which is undertaken in a more general fashion.

---

[318] *Cf,* eg, A Honrath, *Kapitalverkehr*, 128; A Rohde, *Kapitalverkehr*, 181 *et seq*; JCW Müller, *Kapitalverkehrsfreiheit*, 99; HG Ruppe, 'Kapitalverkehrsfreiheit', 17; M Sedlaczek, 'Kapitalverkehrsfreiheit', 50 *et seq*; L Flynn, 'Coming of Age', 785; G Ress and J Ukrow, Art. 56 EC (2002), mn 52; U Haferkamp, *Kapitalverkehrsfreiheit*, 207 *et seq*; M Sedlaczek, Art. 58 EC (2003), 1 *et seq*; C Barnard, *Substantive Law*, 480; W Kessler, et al, 'Gesellschafter-Fremdfinanzierung', 327. But see C Ohler, 'Kapitalverkehrsfreiheit', 1808 (not applying Art. 56 *et seq.* to FDI); C Ohler, Art. 56 EC (2002), mn 139, 214 *et seq* (with the exception that in areas of overlap with the freedom of establishment the *erga omnes* rule shall not apply); S Weber, 'Kapitalverkehr', 564; W Schön, 'Kapitalverkehr mit Drittstaaten', 493, 505 (making the application of Art 56 EC *et seq* subject to an international agreement that grants reciprocal market access).

(1) *The Clear and Unambiguous Wording of Article 56(1) EC*

Any interpretation of a legal provision begins with the wording, but at the same time, also meets with its outer limits there.[319] Put clearly, Art 56(1) EC states that '[w]ithin the framework of the provisions set out in this chapter, all restrictions on the movement of capital between Member States and between Member States and third countries shall be prohibited.'[320] It unambiguously establishes one basic rule for capital movement within the Community and between the Community and third countries, suggesting that the scope of protection[321] of the freedom in the latter case is as far-reaching as in the former.[322] Although the wording hardly allows for any other reading of Art 56(1) EC besides that suggested above, nonetheless some commentators, based on teleological and systematic reasoning, maintain that Art 56(1) EC is to be interpreted differently[323] when it comes to third country capital movement. Their arguments will be discussed in the following section.

(2) *Keeping the Promise of Free Capital Movement* Erga Omnes? *Teleological and Contextual Arguments to Restrict the Scope of Prohibition in a Third Country Context*

(a) 'One Provision—Two Meanings? How to Split what Belongs together'

With reference to the ECJ opinion on the EEA Agreement[324] and certain rulings on free-trade agreements,[325] all of which are international treaties, some commentators are of the opinion that Art 56(1) EC can be, or even more strictly, must be, interpreted differently depending on whether intra-Community or third country capital movement is involved due to the different objectives allegedly pursued.[326] In its EEA opinion, the Court expressed the view that although some provisions of the EEA Agreement on free movement have the same wording as the corresponding provisions in the EC Treaty, this does not preclude the possibility

---

[319] F Müller and R Christensen, *Methodik*, 75.
[320] [Emphasis added]
[321] It is not disputed that at the level of grounds of justification, more restrictions are allowed in third country capital movement than in an intra-Community context.
[322] *Cf* also Case C-101/05 (Opinion of AG Bot) *Skatteverket v A*, para 74 *et seq*. Confirmed: Case C-101/05 *Skatteverket v A*, para 31.
[323] *Cf,* eg, R Smits, 'Payments and Capital', 250, 254: 'Yet, the scope of the actual liberalisation with respect to third countries is more limited than what the reader of Art. 73 B (1) [now, after amendment, Art 56(1) EC] is led to believe.' W Schön, 'Kapitalverkehr mit Drittstaaten', 493 *et seq*; K Ståhl, 'Movement of Capital', 50 *et seq*.
[324] Opinion 1/91 *Draft Agreement between the Community, on the one Hand, and the Countries of the European Free Trade Association, on the other, Relating to the Creation of the European Economic Area*.
[325] eg, Case 270/80 *Polydor Limited and RSO Records Inc. v Harlequin Records Shops Limited and Simons Records Limited*, para 15 *et seq*; Case C-312/91 *Procedural Issue relating to a Seizure of Goods belonging to Metalsa Srl*, para 11 *et seq*.
[326] K Ståhl, 'Movement of Capital', 51; see also R Smits, 'Payments and Capital', 254; S Mohamed, *Free Movement of Capital*, 230; W Schön, 'Kapitalverkehr mit Drittstaaten', 505.

of different interpretations of the respective provisions in light of differing objectives underlying the two Treaties.[327] Some of the proponents admit that the situation with respect to Art 56(1) EC is hardly comparable to the ones mentioned above. In the case of Art 56(1) EC, there is just one provision in one and the same EC Treaty; with respect to the EEA or free-trade agreements, there are always two treaties: one of those just mentioned and the EC Treaty. It is maintained that 'the provisions on the free movement of capital to and from third countries should be interpreted in light of their own purpose'.[328] While this study has problems seeing the relevance of the abovementioned opinion and judgments for the question, it certainly agrees with the proposition that the provisions on free capital movement in a third country context must be interpreted in the light of their own *telos* and in their textual as well as in historical context.

The *telos* of a provision has to be extracted from its wording, from the systematics, and from historical materials.[329] Here the aims of the Treaty, especially those referred to in Arts 2 and 3 EC, play a significant role. I have discussed above those aims that can possibly be pursued by a unilateral liberalization of capital movement *erga omnes*. This analysis concluded that those aims are served best if the freedom of capital movement is construed in a liberal and wide understanding, just as in the case of intra-Community capital movement.[330] Nevertheless, there are arguments advanced that suggest doing otherwise, allegedly speaking in favour of a restrictive interpretation of the scope of prohibition of Art 56(1) EC in a third country context. I will review these below, thereby proceeding on the basis that a prudent teleological interpretation meets its limits in the wording of a provision.[331]

(b) A Factual 'Domaine Réservé'?

A suggestion to restrict the scope of Art 56(1) EC, stipulated by Schön, goes some way towards creating a factual '*domaine réservé*' of the Member States for tax rules affecting third country capital movements.[332]

In cases where a restrictive effect originates in national tax legislation, there are only two situations where a third country participant in a cross-border capital movement will be entitled to rely on Art 56(1) EC. Either a third country to which the capital movement relates has concluded an international treaty with

---

[327] Opinion 1/91 *Draft Agreement between the Community, on the one Hand, and the Countries of the European Free Trade Association, on the Other, Relating to the Creation of the European Economic Area*, para 14.
[328] K Ståhl, 'Movement of Capital', 52.
[329] F Müller and R Christensen, *Methodik*, 76 *et seq* for further references.
[330] See Chapter I. 2. a. (1).
[331] F Müller and R Christensen, *Methodik*, 75 for further references.
[332] W Schön, 'Kapitalverkehr mit Drittstaaten', 502 *et seq*. See also C Peters and J Gooijer, 'Movement of Capital', 475, who state that if the provisions on free movement of capital in relation to third countries were to be applied in accordance with the existing ECJ case law on intra-Community capital movements, the budgetary consequences for the Member States would be incalculable.

the EC that provides for reciprocal liberalization of capital movements,[333] such as the EEA Agreement with the EFTA States,[334] or a national measure constitutes a restriction (discrimination and hindrance) of the 'technical access of capital to, or exit from, the EC market'. In consequence, in the absence of an international treaty, the only national tax rules subject to Art 56(1) EC are those that specifically burden the technical transfer of capital.[335] Discriminatory or otherwise, restrictive national measures that relate to the holding of capital or the earnings flowing from this capital shall be exempted from the scope of prohibition of Art 56(1) EC in third country relations.[336]

It is striking that this view departs considerably from the wording of Art 56(1) EC. The Treaty neither provides in its text for liberalization in third country relations to be conditioned on the existence of an international treaty, nor does it give the Member States *carte blanche* to discriminate or otherwise restrict the holding of or the profits generated from capital.[337] Thus, there must be profound teleological and systematic arguments in existence to justify such an evident deviation from the wording of Art 56(1) EC.

The arguments that I will outline in the following section were advanced with respect to taxation, as already mentioned. However, it appears that most of the arguments could also be advanced outside the ambit of taxation in favour of creating a factual '*domaine réservé*' for any national measure restricting third country capital movement. Thus, I have chosen to discuss them in a general fashion, making reference to the particular issue of taxation where appropriate.

i. Aiming at Optimized Global Capital Allocation per se *as a Precondition for Liberalizing Capital Movements* Erga Omnes? The first argument advanced in favour of the aforementioned view can be summarized as follows: only if the EC opened up its capital market unilaterally to the world for the benefit of an optimized global capital allocation *per se*—ie, making a contribution to a 'liberalized world capital market' without looking at the costs it might have to bear— would the *erga omnes* principle in Art 56(1) EC be justified. Due to the fact that the Community allegedly lacks the necessary powers to bring about regulatory harmonization with third countries apart from concluding international

---

[333] W Schön, 'Kapitalverkehr mit Drittstaaten', 505 *et seq*. The logic of the argument is probably the following: only if a certain degree of harmonization between two legal orders is in existence can the capital flow be freed between the two respective countries. In the international sphere, harmonization can only be brought about by international treaty; thus, it is only consequential under such premises to make the reliance on Art 56(1) EC subject to the conclusion of an international treaty, which provides for some degree of harmonization.

[334] The EEA Agreement [EEA Agreement] constitutes an association agreement in the sense of Art 310 EC.

[335] Metaphorically speaking, a tax shall be subject to Art 56(1) EC if it works like a 'duty' on technical transfer of capital across the external borders of the EC.

[336] W Schön, 'Kapitalverkehr mit Drittstaaten', 508 *et seq*.

[337] It is, however, not disputed that the Treaty provides for more justifications for restricting capital movement from and towards third countries than with respect to intra-Community flows.

treaties and is ill-equipped to protect the legitimate interests of the Member States against abusive practices by third countries, Schön doubts that the idea behind Art 56(1) EC was to further the establishment of a world capital market. This would supposedly justify a restrictive interpretation of the scope of prohibition of Art 56(1) EC.[338]

I am of the opinion that the argumentation just advanced is not compelling; I would suggest that it operates with several assumptions that must be questioned.

First, it is not clear why the intention to create a 'global capital market' would exclusively justify the *erga omnes* principle.[339] As I have already critically pointed

---

[338] W Schön, 'Kapitalverkehr mit Drittstaaten', 502 *et seq*; along similar lines: S Mohamed, *Free Movement of Capital*, 217 *et seq*; K Ståhl, 'Movement of Capital', 52., Schön points to the lack of harmonization, not only with respect to the capital markets but also in regard to economic and monetary policies. Due to the fact that third countries are not involved in the coordination of Economic and Monetary Union, he argues, there is no need to apply Art 56(1) EC to third countries in the same way that it applies to the Member States. It suffices to subject only the actual transfer to the freedom. [W Schön, 'Kapitalverkehr mit Drittstaaten', 510 *et seq*] Therefore, if one were to follow this view, what needs to be secured from and towards third countries is the pure act of free transfer of financial means but not equal treatment of EU and non-EU investment. It is purportedly sufficient to prevent Member States from applying different exchange control mechanisms, which could have distorting economic effects for the Community at large. [W Schön, 'Kapitalverkehr mit Drittstaaten', 506 *et seq*] This conclusion is supposedly supported by the predecessor provisions of Art 56(1) EC, ie, Art 70 EEC and Art 7(1) of Directive 88/361/EEC, which targeted only national exchange control provisions.

Again, I am of the opinion that coordination of economic and monetary policy with third countries may be desirable to a certain extent. However, it appears not to be a *conditio sine qua non* for the freedom of capital movement to be applied *erga omnes*. It should be recalled that increased coordination, while reducing currency fluctuations, merely masks existing economic imbalances and reduces the pressure on the political leadership to correct failed economic policy. Ultimately, drastic exchange rate adjustments with devastating overall economic effects might become unavoidable. [See JCW Müller, *Kapitalverkehrsfreiheit*, 105, fn 403] Regarding the historical argument, the content of predecessor provisions is usually not very enlightening in EC law for the interpretation of the current provision. [See for the value of the historical argument in interpreting EC law F Müller and R Christensen, *Methodik*, 57 *et seq*] This study proceeds from the assumption that the shift from the prohibition of exchange control to the prohibition of any restriction on free capital movement *erga omnes* was indeed intended by the Treaty makers. [*Cf* AFP Bakker, *Capital Movements*, 230 *et seq*]

Moreover, to build and maintain trust in the common currency, which is intended to aspire to be a world investment, financing, trade, and reserve currency [*cf* G Gomel, *Implications of the Euro*], it is not sufficient to guarantee the absence of exchange controls but to present the monetary area as open, liberal, and market driven. The possibility of the introduction of national measures capable of interfering arbitrarily with the market process of capital allocation would threaten and undermine the credibility of the currency. *Cf.* A Rohde, 'Freier Kapitalverkehr', 457 *et seq*; see also A Baines, 'Capital Mobility', 346, who mentions London's 'Big Bang' in the late 70s and early 80s, which opened up the domestic market for international competition as an example for a successful unilateral market liberalization]

[339] In this respect one could indeed debate whether this was one of the intentions of the Treaty makers. As I have already pointed out above (*cf* Chapter I. 2), the Treaty contains policies (Common Commercial Policy, *cf* Art 131 EC) that are to be pursued because, among other reasons, they are believed to serve the common good on a world scale, justifying putting the selfish interests of the Community, at least theoretically, in second place. While it is true that in the chapter on capital movements no provision similar to Art 131 EC can be found, one could deduce such an underlying intention from the wording of the provisions on capital movement. Article 56(1) EC sets out clearly the complete abolition of any restriction on capital movements, and Art 57(2) EC

out with respect to the Treaty aims that are pursued by a unilateral liberalization of capital movements,[340] Schön underrates the fact that the *erga omnes* liberalization of capital movements can generate real benefits for the Common Market; for example, in the form of intensified competition fuelling economic growth, in the form of increased freedom of choice, especially for European capital recipients, and in the form of increased pressure to maintain fiscal and tariffs discipline within the Member States, which can have overall stabilizing effects on the Common Market.[341]

Second, I see no conclusive evidence to suggest that regulatory harmonization is necessary before capital flows are freed; at most, it might be desirable. Schön is right to point out that, while regulatory powers to harmonize differing Member States' legislation (Arts 94 EC and 95 EC)—'replacing' the regulatory sovereignty of the Member States,[342]—vest in the Community in order to establish an internal legal framework, ie, the Internal Market on capital, the Community lacks such powers with regard to third countries due to fact that the latter cannot be bound by EC legislative acts.[343] Thus, harmonization, if one perceives it as necessary for an opening of the Common Market, has to be brought about by other means, ie, international treaty making. However, the crucial question that still awaits a reply is not whether international treaties are an equally as suitable and effective means

---

makes liberalization towards third countries easier than de-liberalization, thus intentionally erecting hurdles for the Community to pursue narrow-minded aims by means of restricting capital movements with respect to third countries. See W Schön, 'Kapitalverkehr mit Drittstaaten', 503 *et seq*, who states that if one were to proceed from the assumption that the *erga omnes* principle embodied in Art 56(1) EC aims at the optimal allocation of capital on a world scale, this would rule out such a factual '*domaine réservé*' of the Member States for tax measures. Note also A Schnitger, 'Kapitalverkehrsfreiheit', 493 and Recital (20) of Directive 2000/12/EC.

[340] See Chapter I. 2. b.

[341] That unilateral liberalization can be of real benefit for the domestic market can be illustrated by the unilateral liberalization of capital markets in the US, the UK, and all other major European countries in the 1970s and 1980s. [*Cf* A Baines, 'Capital Mobility', 346] However, it is worth mentioning that '...state policies have tended to converge on a more liberal, deregulatory approach because of the changing structural character of the international system...'. [PG Cerny, 'Financial Globalization', 321] See also C Daude and M Fratzscher, *Cross-Border Investment*, who advance the hypothesis that portfolio investment is generally more sensitive to the openness and development of the market and the quality of economic and political institutions than direct investment.

[342] One can cast doubt on the proposition that the loss of sovereignty by the Member States in the area of free movement of capital must be inversely coupled at a ratio of 1:1 with respective competences of the Community. If one holds the duty contained in Art 56(1) EC to be an unconditional obligation to completely liberalize capital movements, ie, to bring about a negative integration, then far-reaching and extensive Community competences, such as those within the ambit of the free movement of workers (*cf* Art 40 EC), freedom of establishment (*cf* Art 44 EC), and freedom to provide and receive services (*cf* Art 52 EC)—where integration is achieved more by active law-making (positive integration)—would not be necessary to the same extent due to the fact that obstacles are removed automatically by virtue of Art 56(1) EC and, furthermore, it would also contradict the underlying basic notion of liberalization.

[343] W Schön, 'Kapitalverkehr mit Drittstaaten', 504; Ståhl puts forward a rather similar argument, saying that the 'liberalisation is not accompanied by the institutional structure, the harmonisation of rules and the common legal system that characterises the EU collaboration and the EU's internal capital market'. [K Ståhl, 'Movement of Capital', 51]

as EC directives and regulations to bring about legal harmonization with third countries; it is whether such harmonization is indeed *conditio sine qua non* for free capital movement *erga omnes*. From an economic perspective—and this is the one that is decisive here if one is concerned about possible devastating economic effects on the Common Market due to a lack of harmonization—this study tends to follow the school of thought that does not regard harmonization in the case of the Community as a *conditio sine qua non*. The Common Market is sufficiently robust to absorb external shocks.[344] This, however, does not mean that harmonization with a view to liberalization is for economic reasons not desirable.[345] That this task has to be accomplished by the cumbersome but usual way of negotiating international agreements should not deter anybody from pursuing this path. Having said this, however, I am aware that I need to answer the question of how the Community should convince a third country to conclude a treaty with it in which the third country agrees to liberalize its capital market taking into consideration that the EC's Common Market, by virtue of Art 56(1) EC, has already been unilaterally opened to third country capital.

The Community neither lacks bargaining powers with respect to third countries to an extent that would justify the creation of a '*domaine réservé*' nor is the Community close to being a 'paper tiger', helpless against alleged destructive or impairing practices by third countries abusing the Community's unilateral freedom of capital movement towards them. This will lead me to my third point: the Community is not sufficiently 'equipped' with regulatory competence to handle the unilateral opening of its market.[346]

This study does not dispute the necessity of endowing the Community with powers to preserve and protect the interests of the Community and its Member States against any abusive or impairing practices of third countries, these powers being exercised with a view to implementing the freedom of capital movements to the greatest extent possible. However, the argument advanced by those who favour a narrow reading of Art 56(1) EC understates the regulatory powers of the Community to respond to abusive or impairing practices.

Article 57(2) EC, the most important EC competence within the chapter on free movement of capital and freedom of payments, explicitly provides for Community powers to set an autonomous regulatory agenda towards third countries with respect to direct investment and the other types of capital mentioned therein.[347] This power can also be employed when it comes to treaty negotiation

---

[344] See Chapter I. 2. a. (1).

[345] Similar or identical rules reduce the compliance costs for businesses. Such legal harmonization and coordination should be governed by the following principle: 'As much "market" as possible, as little "regulation and supervision" as necessary.' [*Cf* though stated in an intra-Community context, H Tietmeyer, 'Europäische Währung', 112]

[346] Concurring, albeit with a different reasoning: Case C-101/05 *Skatteverket v A*, para 38.

[347] For a discussion of the scope of competence flowing from Art 57(2), see Chapter VII. 3. b.; see also W Shan, 'Community Policy', 608 *et seq*; W Shan, *EU-China Investment Relations*, 59 *et seq*; J Karl, 'Competence', 415 *et seq*.

with third countries, for example, to push for reciprocal market access.[348] The Community could simply threaten a unilateral withdrawal from its commitment to guarantee free movement of capital towards those countries that seek the benefits of access to the EC market but are unwilling to open theirs for EC investors.[349] In this sense, the Community has reasonable bargaining powers with respect to third countries. It is also true that restrictive measures based upon Art 57(2) EC require a unanimous vote, which is sometimes difficult to achieve. However, this threshold is an expression of the liberal overall notion of the provisions on free movement of capital.[350]

Moreover, to the extent that a Community measure cannot be based on Art 57(2) EC, Arts 94 and 95 EC allow not only for the enactment of directives that are inward-looking, ie, directed at the Common Market, but also for

---

[348] *Cf* W Kiemel, Art. 57 EC (2003), mn 16; G Ress and J Ukrow, Art. 57 EC (2002), mn 16; J Bröhmer, Art. 57 EC (2002), mn 8; A Rohde, *Kapitalverkehr*, 182 *et seq*; see also Case C-101/05 *Skatteverket v A*, para 833.

[349] *Cf* J Karl, 'Competence', 415 *et seq*. In case a third country is unimpressed by this perspective, the question of whether an actual closing of the EC capital market for that country is desirable from an EC point of view must be judged on an individual basis. It should, however, be recalled that the Common Market can already benefit from one-sided free capital flow.

In the context of Art 57(2) EC, ECJ Opinion 1/94 should be mentioned. The Court stated that 'the *chapters on the right of establishment and on freedom to provide services* do not contain any provision expressly extending the competence of the Community to "relationships arising from international law". As has rightly been observed by the Council and most of the Member States that have submitted observations, the sole objective of those chapters is to secure the right of establishment and freedom to provide services for nationals of Member States. *They contain no provisions on the problem of the first establishment of nationals of non-member countries and the rules governing their access to self-employed activities.* One cannot therefore infer from those chapters that the Community has exclusive competence to conclude an agreement with non-member countries to liberalize first establishment and access to service markets, other than those which are the subject of cross-border supplies within the meaning of GATS, which are covered by Article 113.' [Emphasis added. Opinion 1/94 *Competence of the Community to Conclude International Agreements Concerning Services and the Protection of Intellectual Property*, para 81] The Court addressed here both internal (autonomous) law-making and the conclusion of international treaties. [P Eeckhout, *External Relations*, 77; A Dashwood, 'Attribution', 130]

Two remarks should be made with respect to this Opinion. First, the Court's statement in its scope clearly does not extend to the chapter on free movement of capital. Hence, the Court did not rule out that the Community can take autonomous actions regulating first establishment or access of market participants from non-Member States on the basis of Art 57(2) EC. [See in this respect also European Commission, 'Commission Staff Working Paper on CLS no. 6393/96 "Opinion of the Council's Legal Service as regards the Provisions of the EC Treaty applicable to Foreign Direct Investment and to Freedom of Establishment of Companies or Firms Owned or Controlled by Third-Country Natural or Legal Persons" [Title varying]' (SEC (97) 1428), para 4, 8]

Secondly, the Court confirmed in the same Opinion, some paragraphs further on, that competence vests in the Community on the basis of the chapters on the right of establishment and on freedom to provide services to enact autonomous acts relating to the treatment of non-Member State market participants. [Opinion 1/94 *Competence of the Community to Conclude International Agreements Concerning Services and the Protection of Intellectual Property*, para 90 *et seq*; *cf* also P Eeckhout, *External Relations*, 79 *et seq*; A Dashwood, 'Attribution', 130 *et seq*]

[350] As I have noted above, Art 57(2) EC also inherently carries the seed of liberalization. See footnote 339 of this Chapter.

directives establishing an autonomous Community-wide regime towards third countries.[351]

In exceptional cases where movements of capital to or from third countries cause, or threaten to cause, serious difficulties for the operation of Economic and Monetary Union, the EC can enact safeguard measures pursuant to Art 59 EC.[352] Article 60 EC allows for politically motivated derogations from the duty to liberalize (economic sanctions).[353]

With respect to the particular case of taxation, even if one is of the opinion that Art 57(2) EC does not provide a legal basis for tax-related legislative acts,[354] autonomous Community measures in this area directed at the establishment of a common regime towards third countries or in an internal context[355] can generally be based on Art 93 for indirect taxes and on Arts 94 EC, 95(2) EC, and 308 EC for direct taxes.[356] Admittedly, this requires the threshold of unanimity which is (politically) rather hard to overcome.[357] However, against this background it is an exaggeration of the situation when one alleges that the 'extensive loss of Member States' tax sovereignty'[358]—which is actually only the loss of 'sovereignty' to discriminate or restrict in an unjustifiable manner against third country capital—finds hardly any complement on the side of the Community with respect to third countries.

To recapitulate, neither the lack of institutional structure (ie, the non-convergence of rules and the absence of a common legal system; in short, the lack of harmonization towards third countries, which this study does not consider to be *conditio sine qua non*) nor the number and breadth of Community powers to defend the interests of the Community itself and its Member States justify

---

[351] S Leible, Art. 94 EC (2003), mn 10; see also W Shan, 'Community Policy', 610 ; W Shan, *EU-China Investment Relations*, 61 *et seq*; and see P Eeckhout, *External Relations*, 121 *et seq* with respect to goods.

[352] A Rohde, 'Freier Kapitalverkehr', 457 *et seq* notes that Art 59 EC provides a means to deal with unexpected economic turbulence. While it is true that Art 59 EC prioritizes the functioning of Economic and Monetary Union over third country capital movement liberalization 'in case of emergency', the narrow wording of the provision supports the interpretation that the basic emphasis is to be placed on maximally liberalized capital movement from and towards third countries. For an in-depth discussion of Art 59 EC, See Chapter VII. 4.

[353] For an in-depth discussion of this provision, See Chapter VII. 5.

[354] Schön argues that Art 57(2) EC does not form a sufficient legal basis to enact Community rules on cross-border taxation of capital due to the fact that it neither requires a unanimous vote nor provides for participation of the European Parliament in the legislative procedures; both are usually required (*cf*, eg, Arts 93 EC, 94 EC, 95(2) EC, and 175(2) lit. a) EC. [W Schön, 'Kapitalverkehr mit Drittstaaten', 504 *et seq*] See M Seidel, 'Kapitalmarkt', 770 *et seq*.

[355] S Leible, Art. 94 EC (2003), mn 10. Due to the fact that Art 93 EC is also directed at the Internal Market, ie, *lex specialis* to Art 94 EC [*cf* H-G Kamann, Art. 93 EC (2003), mn 11], the reasoning advanced by Leible with respect to Art 94 EC also applies, *mutatis mutandis,* to Art 93 EC.

[356] *Cf*, eg, B Terra and PJ Wattel, *European Tax Law*, 14 *et seq*.

[357] For example, liberal-minded Member States could refuse to vote in favour of a proposed Community measure that is more restrictive than its national regime towards a third country. See Chapter VII. 3.

[358] Translation by the author. See W Schön, 'Kapitalverkehr mit Drittstaaten', 505.

the teleological creation of a factual '*domaine réservé*' for tax rules or any other form of national measures. Instead of calling for an (overly) restrictive interpretation of Art 56(1) EC, one should rather start building consensus among the Member States to effectively employ the designated means on the Community level. Furthermore, all of the aforesaid also connotes that one cannot persist in an opinion which seeks to make reliance on Art 56(1) EC conditional upon the conclusion of an international agreement.[359]

ii. Free Capital Movement Erga Omnes *as a Mere 'Auxiliary Function'?* The second argument in support of a narrow construction of Art 56(1) EC, also advanced by Schön, proceeds from the basis that the *erga omnes* principle is to be seen exclusively as a mere 'auxiliary function' to the establishment of the Common Market.[360] The 'external component' of Art 56(1) EC has, according to this view, the function of securing the Common Market against possible distorting effects caused by different rules on access and exit of capital maintained by the Member States, which, moreover, are ineffective due to the fact that they are easily circumvented.[361]

If one were to attribute such an 'auxiliary function' to Art 56(1) EC in third country relations, it would consequently suffice, it is argued, to secure free 'technical' access and exit[362] to the Common Market by applying Art 56(1) EC merely to the actual transfer of capital. This would result in the establishment of a deregulated 'common border regime' prohibiting discrimination or hindrance of third country capital at the moment of technical access to or exit from the Common Market.[363] With respect to taxation, on which the proponent of this view has modelled his argument, only those national measures that specifically target the cross-border transfer of capital would be subject to Art 56(1) EC. However, in any other situation, eg, the treatment of foreign capital once it is put to any use within the Common Market, it would not be necessary to accord treatment free of discrimination or hindrance.

This finding is allegedly supported by a systematic comparison with the Customs Union, Art 23 EC *et seq*, which, according to this view, operates in the ambit of trade in a similar way to how it operates in the ambit of capital. The Customs Union does not aim to create a global market for goods, but rather free

---

[359] See footnote 333 of this Chapter.

[360] W Schön, 'Kapitalverkehr mit Drittstaaten', 506.

[361] Access to the Common Market can be sought through the country with the most liberal regime. See also Chapter IV. 3. b. (2) (d).

[362] Schön does not describe how he intends to distinguish those rules that restrict the 'technical' access to or exit from the market from those national measures that restrict the holding of capital.

[363] W Schön, 'Kapitalverkehr mit Drittstaaten', 506 *et seq*. Schön tries to support his view by stating that such a differentiation is already known to the EC legal order. Directive 69/335/EEC [Directive 69/335/EEC] differentiates between transfer (ie, increase) and the mere holding of capital or its earnings. However, the fact that such a distinction is known to secondary legislation is not a convincing argument for restricting the scope of application of Art 56(1) EC whatsoever.

movement of goods within the Community. The Customs Union requires the abolition of internal customs borders and, on the other hand, a uniform approach toward third countries in the form of the Common Customs Tariff. Different customs regimes of the Member States towards third countries are not reconcilable with the idea of the Customs Union, but destabilize the Common Market.[364] Article 90 EC establishes that taxes must operate non-discriminatorily for domestic goods and those originating from other Member States. Goods imported from third countries, which are not in free circulation within the meaning of Art 24 EC, can be subjected to discriminatory taxation.[365]

Schön's comparison of the Customs Union and free movement of capital, while superficially raising the impression that similarities might exist, cannot convince in substance. As a preliminary observation, there are difficulties in seeing the alleged similar effects caused by the Customs Union and Schön's interpretation of Art 56(1) EC, ie, applying the provision only to national measures specifically targeting the act of crossing the border. Following Schön's understanding of Art 56(1) EC, the access of third country capital to the Common Market would be, in principle, free of discrimination or hindrance, while the holding and use of it would be restrictable. The Customs Union seems to work differently. While access to the Common Market is restricted for third country goods, the flow of goods once within the Common Market is in principle free.[366]

Turning to a closer examination of the provisions shaping the Customs Union and those on the freedom of capital movement, doubts are hardly dissipated. In fact, it becomes apparent that within the provisions on the Customs Union, a distinction is established right from the outset: there are goods originating from other Member States (Art 23 EC) and those that came from third countries (Art 24 EC). Article 90 EC, though implicitly, differentiates between third country goods and those originating from other Member States. Only the former can be discriminated against until they are released into free circulation within the meaning of Art 24 EC.

In contrast, the fundamental provision within the chapter on free capital movement, Art 56(1) EC, explicitly does not establish different regimes for capital originating from third countries and capital coming from other Member States. Regarding the specific issue of taxation, a provision such as Art 90 EC is missing within the ambit of free movement of capital. It therefore remains to be explained how these explicit differences between the Customs Union and free movement of capital can lead to a claim of similarity, recalling that a prudent teleological or systematic construction should stop at the point where it turns into an 'amendment of the Treaties on which the Union is founded'.[367]

---

[364] W Schön, 'Kapitalverkehr mit Drittstaaten', 507 *et seq.*
[365] Case C-130/92 *OTO SpA v Ministero delle Finanze*; H-G Kamann, Art. 90 EC (2003), mn 7.
[366] *Cf* Arts 24 EC and 90 EC.
[367] Art 48 EU. See with respect to the limits of the teleological argument: F Müller and R Christensen, *Methodik*, 75.

Moreover, as already pointed out above, by reducing the freedom of capital movement in a third country context to a mere prohibition of exchange control, Schön forgoes the possible benefits for the Common Market in the form of stronger economic growth generated by increased competition and competitiveness and greater freedom of choice. Denying potential third country investors the guarantee of a level playing field will certainly discourage them from entering the EC market. In fact, such a restrictive interpretation runs counter to the idea of a non-protectionist, open market economy (*cf* Arts 4(1) EC, 98, 2nd sentence EC, and 105(1) 3rd sentence EC). It signals to the world that, while a third country investor is free to bring his capital into the Community, as soon as the investor dares to make use of it, eg, by trying to set up a company, a level playing field is no longer guaranteed.

(c) Does the Greater Number of Permissible Restrictions Lead to a Restricted *Telos* in a Third Country Context?

When looking at the Treaty chapter on free movement of capital, it is difficult not to recognize that the freedom with respect to third countries is more susceptible of restriction than in an intra-Community context. Beyond the 'general' grounds of justification contained in Art 58 EC, applicable to intra-Community and third country capital movement alike, the Treaty provides in Arts 57 EC, 59 EC, 60 EC, 119, and 120 EC for possible restrictions specifically applicable in third country relations.

An argument that draws from the mere existence of a larger number of permitted restrictions in third country capital movement,[368] the conclusion that the purpose pursued by Art 56(1) EC in a third country context 'is considerably *more limited* than the purpose that lies behind free capital movements within the EU'[369] is hardly convincing.[370] In fact, such an argument infers from the mere existence of a larger number of exceptions to the rule first that the purpose to be pursued by the rule must also be more limited and, consequently, that the scope of prohibition of the rule itself must be interpreted more narrowly. This appears to be a vicious circle. The mere fact that a freedom is more restrictable does not justify a restrictive reading of the scope of prohibition; at most it is the purpose that is pursued by those permitted restrictions that can help enlighten the purpose pursued by the freedom.[371]

---

[368] Also the argument that Declaration No 7 on Art 58(1) EC of the Intergovernmental Conference adopting the Maastricht Treaty [Maastricht Treaty—Final Act. Note that this declaration is only of a political nature, *cf* W Kiemel, Art. 58 EC (2003), mn 11 for further references, see also HG Ruppe, 'Kapitalverkehrsfreiheit', 23 *et seq*], allegedly supporting a narrower reading of Art 56(1) EC, can be grouped in this category. [See for such a view R Smits, 'Payments and Capital', 254] The Declaration stipulated that Member States shall refrain from introducing tax law provisions that distinguish between residence and place of investment in intra-Community capital movement.

[369] [Emphasis added] K Ståhl, 'Movement of Capital', 52.

[370] Along similar lines: Case C-101/05 (Opinion of AG Bot) *Skatteverket v A*, para 78 *et seq*.

[371] See Chapter IV. 3. b. (2) (b) i for Schön's view. He correctly does not make any inference from the mere existence of a greater number of grounds of justification in third country capital

Thus, it is anything but compelling that the mere existence of more exceptions to the freedom of capital movements in an extra- than an intra-Community context points to a more limited purpose with respect to the former. As stated above, this study is of the opinion that there is sufficient purpose to oppose any different reading of the scope of prohibition of Art 56(1) EC in a third country context. The purposes that lie behind the permitted exceptions to Art 56(1) EC do not run counter to this reading. The liberalization of third country capital movement operates in a different setting from capital movement within the Community. Thus, the former requires a different means of operation. Within the Community, the danger of abusive practice of the freedom is limited due to fact that any Member State is subject to one and the same binding and enforceable set of rules. In third country relations, where rules are considerably less harmonized and policies hardly coordinated, the Community needs to be equipped with other means, ie, those contained in Arts 57(2), 59, and 60 EC, to be able to respond to possible abusive practices by other States or unforeseeable turbulence on the international capital markets.

Hence, it is in fact the purpose pursued by those specific exemptions applicable only in third country contexts that suggests that Art 56(1) EC possesses the same scope in intra-Community and third Country contexts.[372]

In the end it is on a factual basis true that the liberalization of capital movements is more complete within the Community than towards third countries due to the fact that fewer exceptions to the rule are allowed by the Treaty. However, the larger number of permitted exceptions in a third country context has no bearing on the *telos* of Art 56(1) EC. I have outlined above that reaching a possibly complete liberalization *erga omnes* best serves the aims of the Community.[373] The existence of provisions allowing for restrictions on complete liberalization, partly to defend interests *vis-à-vis* third countries and partly the result of a political compromise reached in the Maastricht negotiations, cannot alter this finding.

(d) The 'Channel Phenomenon' Remedied by Evaporating the Scope of Prohibition of Article 56(1) EC to a Mere Ban of Exchange Controls?

Some commentators point towards 'the potentially enormous impact that the total liberalisation of capital movements towards third countries would have.'[374] It is feared that the freedom of establishment and the freedom to provide and receive services are indirectly extended, 'through the backdoor so to speak',[375] to third countries, which could not have been the intention of the Treaty makers. Preventing the aforesaid would allegedly justify confining Art 56(1) EC's

---

movement but refers in his argument— which in its ultimate reasoning I do not share—to the purpose of those grounds.

[372] Case C-101/05 (Opinion of AG Bot) *Skatteverket v A*, para 79; For a probably different view: Case C-101/05 *Skatteverket v A*, para 32.
[373] See Chapter I. 2. b.
[374] eg, K Ståhl, 'Movement of Capital', 52.   [375] Ibid.

applicability in a third country context to 'direct obstacles to the transfer of capital such as exchange restrictions'.[376] In all other situations, liberalization would be subject to positive Council action.[377] Those who seek to restrict the scope of prohibition to 'free movement of banknotes'[378] appear to be of the same view, though they arrive there by a partially different reasoning.[379]

Both of the interpretations above must be strongly contested. I do not see any evidence that a restrictive interpretation of Art 56(1) EC, in the sense of making further liberalizing steps dependent on Council action, could in any way remedy the phenomenon that liberal-minded Member States would function as a channel for third country investors into the Common Market. Even in the absence of free movement of capital *erga omnes*, the

> denial by one country would simply cause the prospective entrant to apply elsewhere and often subsequently penetrate the market of the original refusing state through exports or through affiliates gaining entry under the right of establishment.[380]

Thus, due to the existence of the rights of free movement of goods, the freedom to provide and receive services, and the freedom of establishment[381] within the Community, no single Member State is in a position to prevent entry of third country investors. Even worse, by refusing entry, the refusing State risks losing any direct or indirect control over the business activities of the foreign investor, who now operates from another, more liberal, Member State.[382]

This being said, it becomes apparent that it is not capital liberalization *erga omnes* that is the cause of the 'channel phenomenon', but basically the fundamental freedoms mentioned above. Thus, the 'channel phenomenon' cannot be

---

[376] Ibid, 54.
[377] Ibid, 53. Note that *Ståhl* towards the very end of her discussion—I think rightly—reverses her preliminary conclusion with reference to the wording of Art 56(1) EC and the case law of the Court. She finally notes that '[d]espite the fact that the purpose behind the provisions may speak against it, my conclusion is nevertheless that the majority of arguments support the view that tax restrictions can also, in fact, be examined. In this examination one must, however, still observe the purpose behind the Treaty rules.' [K Ståhl, 'Movement of Capital', 54]
[378] S Mohamed, *Free Movement of Capital*, 219 *et seq*.
[379] Mohamed suggests that the liberalization of capital movements referred to in Art 57(2) EC is subject to positive Council action, and thus, those categories of capital movements were to be excluded from the scope of Art 56(1) EC. [S Mohamed, *Free Movement of Capital*, 219 *et seq*] This reading, however, is hardly reconcilable with Art 57(1) EC, which would not make any sense if the categories of capital movements referred to in this provision were not covered by Art 56(1) EC. [*Cf* K Ståhl, 'Movement of Capital', 53]
[380] CD Wallace, *Multinational Enterprise*, 309.
[381] Having recourse to the nationality of those who control the enterprise is not permissible due to the clear wording of Art 48 EC. It therefore suffices, for example, that an enterprise is formed in accordance with the law of a Member State and has its registered office within the Community. [*Cf* P-C Müller-Graff, Art. 48 EC (2003), mn 10 *et seq*; A Schnitger, 'Geltung', 711 *et seq*; Case C-221/89 *R v Secretary of State for Transport, ex p Factortame Ltd and others*, para 30. Whether there is an additional unwritten criterion of a 'real and lasting connection' between the economy of the Member State and the enterprise at issue in order to rely on Arts 43 and 48 EC is disputed. For a brief discussion and further references see J Bröhmer, Art. 48 EC (2002), mn 7.
[382] CD Wallace, *Multinational Enterprise*, 309.

cured by means of restricting the scope of prohibition of the freedom of capital movement.

However, the 'phenomenon' could in theory be somewhat attenuated by introducing a common border (access and exit) regime for third country capital, possibly geared to the restrictive approach of the less liberal-minded Member States and based on Art 57(2) EC and/or Arts 94 EC, 95 EC, and 308 EC.[383] However, one must ask why a Member State with a liberal access/exit policy should vote in favour of such a regime. Such a Member State clearly benefits from its own open door policy, which makes it the base of operations of third country investments for the penetration of less liberal Member States' markets. It is therefore highly doubtful that the Member States could agree on a restrictive common border regime. From a Community perspective, such a regime would smooth capital allocation distortions caused by different access/exit rules. Against the background of the understanding advocated in this study, such a regime would only further the Treaty aims if shaped in the most liberal way possible. Due to the fact that, by virtue of Art 56(1) EC, a liberalized, ie, deregulated, common border regime is brought about 'automatically,' the harmonization measure of the Community was to be restricted in its function to accompanying measures, eg, establishing common procedures for handling access and exit of third country capital, laying out rules on how to tackle abusive practice of the freedom by third States or third State capital market participants, or abolishing grandfathered restrictions[384] on certain categories of capital movement still present in some Member States.

In summary, the arguments advanced so far in support of a restrictive interpretation of Art 56(1) EC are either not compelling or inconclusive in nature. Instead, it appears to us that no deviation should be allowed from the clear wording of the provision, which declares capital movements free not just in an intra-Community context but also with respect to third countries.

(3) The Operation of the Non-discrimination Test in a Third Country Context

In this section I shall discuss the operation of the non-discrimination test in a third country context. In particular, the 'issue of comparability' will become the centre of attention. I shall search in the case law and the available literature for

---

[383] However, it should not be forgotten that once an investment is admitted—even under a common border regime—it is difficult for a less liberal host State to accord discriminatory treatment to an ongoing direct investment with third country controlling participation. For example, it suffices that an enterprise is formed in accordance with the law of a Member State and has its registered office within the Community in order to benefit from the fundamental freedoms. Having recourse to the nationality of those who control the enterprise is not permissible due to the clear wording of Art 48 EC.

[384] Art 57(1) EC.

considerations that would fundamentally call into question the comparability of domestic/intra-Community and foreign direct investment.

However, before entering into the discussion of the 'comparability issue' I shall briefly comment on Art 58(1) lit. a, (3) EC, which, according to some commentators, allegedly carries constitutive functions in a third county context.

(a) General Exceptions from the Non-discrimination Test?—Article 58(1) lit. a EC

I have discussed above the question of whether Art 58(1) lit. a EC constitutes a general exception for national rules differentiating on the basis of residency and place of investment from the prohibition of discrimination contained in Art 56(1) EC. This study has concluded that, due to the development of the case law, Art 58(1) lit. a EC is only of a declaratory nature.[385] Hence, there is no *domaine réservé* for national rules employing the abovementioned distinguishing criteria.

Although a majority of commentators are prepared to accept that Art 58(1) lit. a EC carries only declaratory functions in an intra-Community context, some[386] choose to attribute constitutive meaning to the provision with respect to third countries. They argue that while in an intra-Community context the scope of application of Art 58(1) lit. a EC must be restricted in order to preserve the *aquis communautaire* already achieved, in a third country context no such *aquis* exists and, thus, the provision is in full effect.

Such a proposition, however, is called into question by the fact that the Treaty contains explicit third country exceptions. If the drafters wanted to exclude certain areas in a third country context from the duty to liberalize, they would have done so explicitly.[387] Moreover, as in an intra-Community context, the interpretation of Art 58(1) lit. a EC has to be conducted against the background of the existing case law in the relevant area. In the following section, it will be shown that principles developed within the intra-Community context have the same validity in a third country context.

Thus, in a third country context, no different understanding of Art 58(1) lit.a EC is indicated.[388]

(b) Comparability of Capital Movements in a Third Country Context

Within the process of examination as to whether a national measure is discriminatory in nature, the comparability of the contrasted situations or persons

---

[385] See Chapter IV. 2. b. (4) (a) iv.
[386] B Knobbe-Keuk, 'Ruding Committee Report', 30; AJ Martin-Jiménez, 'Limitation of Benefits', 80.
[387] M Peters, 'Taxation', 9; U Haferkamp, *Kapitalverkehrsfreiheit*, 142 *et seq.*
[388] Unclear: JA Usher, *Law of Money*, 58, 235 *et seq*, who seems to proceed from different presumptions, inter alia, that Art 58 (1) lit. a EC cannot authorize discrimination, which is also prohibited by other freedoms. [*Cf* JA Usher, *Law of Money*, 58] Moreover, he considers Declaration No 7 as binding upon the Member States [*cf* JA Usher, *Law of Money*, 56], a view this study does not share. Due to its mere political effect [*cf* above footnote 261 of this Chapter], it has no influence on the debate in a third country context.

constitutes—alongside the selection of comparison groups—the most important determinant. The comparability question can arise in a third country context, as already stated above,[389] in two different situations: first, in a national treatment context, and second, in a situation after the style of the most-favoured nation treatment principle. The former principle points towards the question of whether domestic and third country capital movement are comparable. The latter seeks to compare either a capital movement originating from or directed to a Member State and a third country capital movement or the treatment of two different third country capital movements.

When looking at the literature and the case law available, it quickly becomes apparent that the issue of comparability in a third country context has been explored, explained, and clarified to an even lesser extent than in situations related to intra-Community capital movement. The contributions in the literature and the available case law mainly deal (again) with the area of direct taxation. Thus, it does not come as a surprise that it was in a case on direct taxation that Advocate General Kokott pointed meaningfully to the potential inherent in the interpretative parameter 'comparability' for a flexible limitation of the scope of Art 56(1) EC in third country situations. She stated:

[p]articular problems may arise where third countries are involved. The principle of the free movement of capital between Member States and third countries set out in Article 56(1) EC does not, however, lay down a binding requirement that corporation tax paid in third countries be offset in the same way as in situations involving two Member States. Here too, the rule is that equal treatment is required only if the situations are comparable. In view of the facts in the dispute in the main proceedings, however, it is not necessary to decide to what extent the principles developed here can be transposed to cases involving third countries.[390]

Also, Advocate General Geelhoed, in his recent opinion on the *Test Claimants in the FII Group Litigation* case,[391] speculated on the question of comparability in a third country context. He asked:

whether the same considerations apply to the analysis of Article 56 EC as regards intra-Community capital movements as opposed to capital movements between Member States and third countries. In this regard, it is evident from the wording of Article 56(1) EC that restrictions on free movement of capital between Member States and third countries are, in principle, prohibited. Nonetheless, it is my view that, in analysing whether such restrictions are justified (whether under Article 58(1) EC *or under the discrimination*

---

[389] See Chapter IV. 2. b. (1).
[390] As mentioned (and left open) by AG Kokott: Case C-319/02 (Opinion of AG Kokott) *Petri Manninen*, para 79. The ECJ refused to comment on this hint: Case C-319/02 *Petri Manninen*, para 51.
[391] Case C-446/04 (Opinion of AG Geelhoed) *Test Claimants in the FII Group Litigation v Commissioners of Inland Revenue*; see especially para 30 *et seq*, 107 *et seq*.

analysis of Article 56 EC), different considerations may apply than is the case with purely intra-Community restrictions.[392]

I shall endeavour to trace those 'different considerations', which might apply to the analysis of comparability, in the following subsections.

In principle, as in the case of intra-Community capital movement, those 'different considerations,' or 'essential attributes,' must be identified on a case-by-case basis, taking into account primarily the actual circumstances and conditions against the background of the purpose and content of the respective national measure and under consideration of the value-based decisions stipulated by the Community legal order.[393]

In the following discussion, I shall direct my focus in particular on two arguments that allegedly call into question in fundamental terms the comparability of domestic/intra-Community and foreign direct investment. I shall first address the question of whether (sometimes significant) differences, eg, in the level of taxation, social contributions, labour costs, or disparities in the competitive structure and the development of the market in a third country, 'are of a greater concern'[394] than in an intra-Community context. The issue is discussed within the ambit of taxation by way of example. The second question to be addressed will revolve around the impact of intra-Community harmonization on comparability, whereby the impact of those Community measures that provide for mutual recognition will be the main concern. I shall deal with the question in the context of a market access regulation.

i. Comparability and Direct Taxation in a Third Country Context: Taking Differences in the Levels of Taxation into Account? Substantial evidence in jurisprudence for a possible different appreciation of the 'comparability issue' in the context of direct taxation is rare when it comes to third country capital movement. One could split the available jurisprudence into two groups. One group, which shall be disregarded in this context, relates to cases in which the Advocate General and the Court avoided expanding on the issue altogether by simply not applying Art 56(1) EC to the third country context.[395] The cases found in the other group,

---

[392] [Emphasis added] Ibid, para 121. Note that the Advocate General chose to apply the provisions on free movement of capital *only* in the case where the UK company holds a participation in a company resident in a third country that does not give the UK company decisive influence over this third country undertaking (portfolio investment). In other words, the Advocate General states that Art 56(1) EC does not apply to outbound foreign direct investment. See also Case C-101/05 *Skatteverket v A*, para 37.

[393] See Chapter IV. 2. b. (4).

[394] *Cf* Case C-374/04 (Opinion of AG Geelhoed) *Test Claimants in Class IV of the ACT Group Litigation (Pirelli, Essilor and Sony), Test Claimants in Class IV of the ACT Group Litigation (BMW) v Commissioners of Inland Revenue*, para 121.

[395] *Cf*, eg, Case C-524/04 *Test Claimants in the Thin Cap Group Litigation*; Case C-492/04 *Lasertec Gesellschaft für Stanzformen mbH (formerly Riess Laser Bandstahlschnitte GmbH) v Finanzamt Emmendingen)*; for a discussion of this approach, see Chapter III. 3. b. (3).

as already discussed above,[396] either simply have recourse to the existing case law relating to intra-Community situations,[397] or amount to nothing more than 'meaningful insinuations' that domestic/intra-Community and third country capital movements need not always be comparable.[398] However, those cases also ended up being treated in line with the respective intra-Community law.

Given that the current case law does not provide us with the hoped-for guidance, I turn now to the legal literature[399] in search of 'different considerations' specific to third country capital movement, which could possibly render domestic/intra-Community and third country capital movements, both subject to direct taxation, incomparable.

Arguments put forward which seek to negate comparability with respect to third countries are rarely based on the factual circumstances or the legal status[400] of a taxpayer set by the national laws, but rather on 'value-based decisions stipulated by the Community legal order'. In *Test Claimants in the FII Group Litigation*, for example, the UK government suggested that a 'drain of revenue' out of the Community due to third country movements is of greater concern than in an intra-Community context.[401] While an argument advanced in such an undifferentiated way would certainly not lead the ECJ to negate comparability of intra-Community and third country capital movement,[402] the statement points to the valid question of how to deal with differences in the level of taxation

---

[396] See Chapter IV. 3. a.

[397] *Cf* Case C-513/03 *Heirs of M. E. A. van Hilten-van der Heijden v Inspecteur van de Belastingdienst/Particulieren/Ondernemingen buitenland te Heerlen*; Case C-374/04 *Test Claimants in Class IV of the ACT Group Litigation (Pirelli, Essilor and Sony), Test Claimants in Class IV of the ACT Group Litigation (BMW) v Commissioners of Inland Revenue*; Case C-157/05 *Winfried Holböck v Finanzamt Salzburg-Land*. In *Saint-Gobain* [Case C-307/97 *Compagnie de Saint-Gobain, Zweigniederlassung Deutschland v Finanzamt Aachen-Innenstadt*] and *Gottardo* [Case C-55/00 *Elide Gottardo v Istituto nazionale della previdenza sociale (INPS)*], the former related to a double taxation treaty, the latter to a social security convention (old age benefits), the Court had the opportunity to decide on the question of whether international treaties concluded between Member States and third countries can in their effects be extended to residents of other Member States not party to the aforementioned Treaty. However, those cases are of no value when it comes to the question of comparability in a third country context. What was compared were residents and non-residents from different Member States.

[398] Case C-319/02 (Opinion of AG Kokott) *Petri Manninen*, para 79; Case C-446/04 (Opinion of AG Geelhoed) *Test Claimants in the FII Group Litigation v Commissioners of Inland Revenue*, para 121.

[399] *Cf*, eg, W Schön, 'Kapitalverkehr mit Drittstaaten'; A Schnitger, 'Kapitalverkehrsfreiheit'; R Lyal, *Free Movement of Capital*; note also M O'Brien, 'Third Country Dimension'; S Kingston, 'Direct Tax'; P Pistone, 'Direct Taxation'; JA Jones, 'European Int'l Tax Law'.

[400] As a factual observation, traditionally, the tax law of the Member States as well as international tax law—despite the question of whether this would be permissible—does not differentiate on the basis of legal, political, and economic relations with other Member States on the one hand, and third countries on the other. [W Schön, 'Kapitalverkehr mit Drittstaaten', 512]

[401] Case C-374/04 (Opinion of AG Geelhoed) *Test Claimants in Class IV of the ACT Group Litigation (Pirelli, Essilor and Sony), Test Claimants in Class IV of the ACT Group Litigation (BMW) v Commissioners of Inland Revenue*, para 121.

[402] Ibid.

(or social contributions, labour costs, etc) that undeniably exist between Member States and third countries.

While the very idea of the Common Market prohibits any countervailing duty for such differences in an intra-Community context, one must ask whether this is equally true with respect to third countries. In an intra-Community context, Advocate General Mischo states that:

> [o]ne can only share the Commission's opinion that accepting such justification 'would interfere with the foundations of the internal market. If differences in the direct taxation of undertakings could be "neutralised" by compensatory levies imposed by Member States on intra-Community movements of goods, services and capital, little would remain of those fundamental freedoms. Virtually all goods and services moving between Member States would be subject to one compensatory levy or another... Member States and undertakings must in principle accept differences in fiscal charges in the same way as differences in social charges or labour costs.'[403]

With third countries no Common Market exists, and one cannot rely on intra-Community aims pursued by the free movement of capital in interpreting Art 56(1) EC. From the aforesaid, some commentators draw the conclusion that differences in the level of direct taxation (the same would also be true for social contribution, labour costs, etc) can consequently be taken into account when it comes to third country capital movement. Schön, for example, seeks to negate comparability for tax havens with an extraordinarily low level of taxation.[404]

While there is an obvious need to secure stable tax revenues for the Member States and certainly a necessity to provide the Community and the Member State with meaningful policy space to deal with these tax shelters, it is doubtful whether the suggested method finds sufficient support in the argument advanced.

It is indisputably true that if one were to allow for countervailing duties to level differences in direct taxation (or social contribution, labour costs, etc) among the different Member States, then little would remain of the fundamental freedoms. However, one can also question what would remain of the stipulation in Art 56(1) EC promising free capital movement *erga omnes* when Member States are allowed to impose countervailing duties with respect to third countries on capital movements. Little, I suggest. Such a result would only be acceptable if the aims pursued by third country capital movement were considerably less far-reaching than in an intra-Community context and, thus, would allow for a restrictive interpretation of third country capital movements. This is precisely the unstated assumption with which the proponents of a restrictive interpretation operate. As discussed extensively above,[405] this study cannot find sufficient evidence for this

---

[403] Case C-294/97 (Opinion of AG Mischo) *Eurowings Luftverkehrs AG v Finanzamt Dortmund-Unna*, para 59; and just recently Case C-196/04 *Cadbury Schweppes and Cadbury Schweppes Overseas Ltd v Commissioners of Inland Revenue*, para 49.
[404] W Schön, 'Kapitalverkehr mit Drittstaaten', 512 *et seq*; see also A Schnitger, 'Kapitalverkehrsfreiheit', 498; R Lyal, *Free Movement of Capital*, 10 *et seq*.
[405] See Chapter I. 2.

assumption; quite the contrary, the aims pursued by third country capital movement point in the direction of a broad and liberal understanding.

Once more one can ask the question—with respect to direct taxation, but also in more general terms—whether the lack of harmonization, ie, the absence of a Common Market or Economic and Monetary Union, with third countries rules out the comparability of intra-Community capital movement and capital movement with a link to a third country. For example, Schön, with respect to direct taxation, argues that a restriction on the tax powers of the Member States leads automatically to a shift of possible tax revenues ['*Steuersubstrat*'] to a third country. Intra-Community mechanisms, such as those embodied in Arts 93–95 EC, 10 EC, and 158 EC *et seq*, that help to coordinate the fiscal interests of the Member State *vis-à-vis* the market participants, are missing with respect to third countries.[406]

Recapitulating the consequences of such argumentation, if one were to answer the above stated question in the affirmative, ie, negating comparability, then the promise given to the world in Art 56(1) EC, ie, the unilateral liberalization of capital movements *erga omnes,* which, for third country market participants, amounts to nothing less than a freedom to invest within the EC, would be rendered an empty phrase. Comparability of intra-Community and third country capital movements would need to be made conditional upon harmonization by means of international treaties on the basis of reciprocal market opening. However, as argued before, precisely such a condition cannot be derived from the Treaty. The Treaty accepts the challenges posed by a unilateral opening of the Common Market to the world because it serves the attainment of its aims.[407] The aforementioned should not be understood to mean that I am ignorant of the problem of tax havens in particular and a 'drain of revenue' in general. I suggest, however, that this problem is best dealt with on the level of grounds of justification, with its proportionality test, which allows for a more nuanced solution than the interpretative parameter comparability.

---

[406] W Schön, 'Kapitalverkehr mit Drittstaaten', 516; A Schnitger, 'Kapitalverkehrsfreiheit', 498. Note also Case C-446/04 *Test Claimants in the FII Group Litigation v Commissioners of Inland Revenue*, para 169 *et seq*, where the Court (in an outbound investment situation) states: 'The only argument specifically raised by that Government in relation to the free movement of capital is based on the fact that, where companies making distributions are established in non-member countries, it may be more difficult to determine the tax paid by those companies in the State in which they are resident than in a purely Community context. It is true that, because of the degree of legal integration that exists between Member States of the Union, in particular by reason of the presence of Community legislation which seeks to ensure cooperation between national tax authorities, such as Council Directive 77/799/EEC of 19 December 1977 concerning mutual assistance by the competent authorities of the Member States in the field of direct taxation (...), the taxation by a Member State of economic activities having cross-border aspects which take place within the Community is *not always comparable* to that of economic activities involving relations between Member States and non-member countries.' [Emphasis added]

[407] See Chapter I. 2. b and Chapter IV. 3. b. (2) (b) i.

Concerning the loss of possible tax revenues, which could also be termed 'adoption costs', if the Member States feel that they are not willing to bear those costs, they need to agree within the Council on a common approach towards third countries. Thus, the feared loss of possible revenues also has a positive aspect: it could potentially produce the necessary political will to agree on a common regime for direct taxes for the Common Market and its relations to third countries.

ii. *Comparability and Market Access and Exit Regulation*

(i) *Comparability and Market Access Regulation: Taking Community Harmonization into Account?* I have stated above,[408] that domestic direct investment and direct investment from another Member State are, in principle, in comparable situations with respect to market access regulations. The non-domestic origin of a direct investment itself can never lead to incomparability. This follows from the fact that the 'origin of capital' constitutes the prohibited distinguishing criterion within the non-discrimination test, which itself forms a 'non-essential attribute' in the process of comparison. The different nationality of the holder of the direct investment can likewise never result in incomparability. The same considerations apply with respect to foreign direct investments.

As already explained previously,[409] and equally true in the context of foreign direct investment, in many cases the regulatory questions posed by a direct investment are unrelated to the origin of the capital movement or the nationality of the owner of the capital, but are rooted in a conflict of private commercial interests and *Gemeinwohlinteressen* (issues of the public good).[410] Moreover, particularly in a third country context, it is worth stressing that a direct investment held by a private person and a direct investment held by a State are in principle comparable.

---

[408] See Chapter IV. 2. b. (4) (b).
[409] Ibid.
[410] For example, suppose that a Member State chooses to allow the setting-up of branches by an undertaking established within its own territory without authorization but requires such authorization in a case where an undertaking established in a third country wishes to do so. If a (host) Member State chooses to control the establishment of branches of third country undertakings by means of prior authorization and/or special requirements, it might do so with the intention of securing proper business practice of the branch with a view to maintaining trust in the proper functioning of the respective market and/or safeguard legitimate interests of market participants. Concerning the issue of comparability, it is obvious that a branch of a domestic undertaking and a branch of a foreign established undertaking can both fall well below the required proper business practice standard. The information on the branch activity necessary in order to prevent such incidence will be the same in both cases. Thus, both branches are in comparable circumstances.

However, even though the two branches are in comparable situations, the (host) Member State may feel that it is nevertheless necessary to treat the branch of a third country undertaking differently in order to secure proper business standards. In case of a domestic undertaking, the Member State can, for example, supervise the activities of the branch via its 'parent' organization, which will usually not be the case with respect to a branch of a third country undertaking. In such cases, the Member State may apply different means of supervision such as prior authorization, etc. However, this still constitutes a case of discrimination, although one that might be justifiable based on the argument of maintaining a proper business practice within the territory of the Member State.

While it cannot be ruled out that the latter could exploit its position as owner by pursuing political rather than commercial interests in the host State by means of its direct investment—take the example of *Gazprom* of Russia[411]—the pursuance of such political interests presupposes first and foremost respective market power. If one fears dependency from a certain investor, this calls for rigorous application of competition law in order to restrict this market power. The State ownership of the direct investment, though, plays no significant role in this respect.[412]

The considerations mentioned above have not yet touched upon the influence of intra-Community harmonization on the 'comparability issue'. I shall therefore now turn to a question that arises only with respect to third country cases. This is the question of whether intra-Community harmonization[413] has a bearing on the 'issue of comparability', and if answered in the affirmative, what the nature of this bearing might be. In doing so, I shall in particular focus on harmonizing measures providing for mutual recognition.[414]

Harmonization can be brought about in different ways. In some instances, harmonization is '*total*', ie, the Member States are completely prevented from regulating the subject matter. In other cases, national legislation is only pre-empted with respect to cross-border movements, which effectively leads to two sets of rules: one harmonized set for cross-border movements and another for pure domestic dealings. Such harmonization can be termed '*optional*' harmonization. In both cases, harmonization can be '*complete*' or '*partial*'. The former relates to the complete and comprehensive regulation of a subject area by Community law. The latter refers to the regulation of certain aspects within a subject area.[415] A different form of harmonization sets minimum standards only ('*minimum*' harmonization). Here, Member States are free to apply stricter standards.[416] Also, one means of harmonization is the requirement in secondary Community law to recognize the standards present in another Member State as sufficient ('*mutual recognition*'), with the consequence that the host Member State is prevented from implementing its own control mechanism for cross-border movements.

I shall first consider the effect of harmonization on comparability without the requirement of mutual recognition in a national treatment scenario. For a domestic direct investment, harmonization means that, depending on the form of harmonization, it has to conform with the respective access standards set either by

---

[411] The Russian Federation holds over 50 per cent of the shares in Gazprom.
[412] Sachverständigenrat zur Begutachtung der gesamtwirtschaftlichen Entwicklung, *Jahresgutachten 2007/08*, mn 634 *et seq*.
[413] This means that the harmonizing measure does not explicitly establish a special regime for the access of non-EC undertakings.
[414] Mutual recognition in this context is not to be confused with the 'Second Cassis Principle', which operates as a rebuttable presumption that a good, etc, lawfully produced and marketed in one of the Member States, can also be introduced in any other Member State. [*Cf* Case 120/78 *Rewe-Zentral AG v Bundesmonopolverwaltung für Branntwein ('Cassis de Dijon')*, para 14]
[415] A von Bogdandy, 'Außenaspekte', 377 *et seq*; D Chalmers, et al, *EU Law*, 475 *et seq*.
[416] A von Bogdandy, 'Außenaspekte', 378 *et seq*; D Chalmers, et al, *EU Law*, 478 *et seq*.

the Community (in case of 'total' harmonization, or in case the Member State has chosen not to go beyond 'minimum' harmonization) or by the Member State (in case of 'optional' harmonization, or in case the Member State has chosen to go beyond 'minimum' harmonization). The same is true for third country investments. Harmonization is assumed not to have a bearing on comparability. Intra-Community harmonization in this context sets only the market access standards for an investment.

Having discussed harmonized access rules without a mutual recognition requirement from the perspective of the national treatment standard, I shall now turn to those rules which provide for mutual recognition. I shall do so by employing a most-favoured-nation treatment scenario. In order to better visualize the situation, I shall consider the following example. Assume that the Community not only set standards on what qualifies for the taking-up of a certain business, what constitutes proper business practice, and how to supervise it, but a given directive provides for the mutual recognition of authorization of the business and, on the other hand, attributes in principle the powers of exercise of supervisory functions to the respective Member State in which the business is established ('home State supervision'). Branches of such businesses placed outside their home Member State do not require an additional authorization by the host Member State, and supervisory functions of the home Member State of the business also extend to a large degree to those branches. Broadly speaking, the conditions for the setting-up and pursuit of the respective economic activity through branches are determined by the home Member State, which is bound to the harmonized standards set by the respective directive.

Assume further, for the sake of argument, that only those branches benefit from the 'free pass', which belong to a business authorized and supervised by a Member State in pursuance of the provisions of the fictional directive mentioned above. Thus, the Member States, by virtue of the given directive, are not required to extend the 'free pass' to branches of non-EC businesses situated within their territory.

In this situation one might doubt whether a branch of a non-EC business is comparable to one of an EC business. Only if answered in the affirmative would a branch of a non-EC business be treated in a discriminatory fashion, if—in contrast to a branch of a EC business, which enjoys a 'free pass'—it were required by national legislation to apply for an additional authorization and to produce different documents in the process of supervision than a branch of an EC business.[417]

---

[417] This, for example, is precisely what the KWG (Germany) does. § 53 (1) Sentence 1 of the KWG (Germany) contains the order to treat branches of banks established abroad, for the purposes of the Act, as legally independent banks, with the consequence that they require authorization in pursuance of § 32 of the Act and are subject to full supervision by the *Bundesanstalt für Finanzdienstleistungsaufsicht (BaFin)* (Federal Financial Supervisory Authority). [For a more detailed explanation, refer to J Marwede, '§ 53', mn 4, 16] § 53b(1) Sentence 1 exempts branches of EC banks from the legal fiction contained in § 53(1) Sentence 1. Thus, the KWG (Germany) establishes a different regime, inter alia, for branches of banks established in a Member State and those

Comparing branches of EC businesses and those of non-EC businesses (MFN situation) could become relevant for a third country investor, in particular if a Member State were to choose to require authorization not only for branches of third country businesses but also for the setting-up of branches of domestic businesses, which, from the outset, would render any claim based on the national treatment standard impossible.

I suggest that intra-Community harmonization does not lead to a negation of comparability of the branches of EC and non-EC businesses only because the conditions for the setting-up of the former are determined by the respective home Member State of the EC business. Irrespective of whether a Community measure harmonizes a subject matter completely or sets minimum standards, the consequence is regularly that a direct investment from one Member State that complies with this standard has to be accepted by another Member State without further consideration because it is recognized as equivalent with its own standards.[418] With respect to the access of branches of an EC business, this means that the host Member State 'agreed' to admit an investment from another Member State on the conditions set by the latter. The home Member State conditions or standards must not fall below the harmonized Community standard.

The fact that a jurisdiction other than the host Member State sets the admission standards for access to the host Member State's market does yet not rule out comparability between a branch from another Member State and a branch from a third country. This fact touches only on the question of who in the first place sets the standards, but it does not alter the situation in which branches of EC and non-EC businesses are placed. The potential threat flowing from branch activities for the proper functioning of the host State's market is the same irrespective of where the parent undertaking is situated and at which standard a branch is admitted. The regulatory aim pursued by the Community measures with respect to branches of EC businesses and the national measures with respect to the branches of non-EC businesses is still the same. If the host Member State now applies stricter standards to branches of non-EC businesses than to those applied to branches of EC businesses[419]—the latter standards being the standards set

---

in a third country. In application of the interpretation of Art 56(1) EC suggested in this study, it follows that this discriminatory treatment needs to be justified; the respective discriminatory measures in particular must be proportionate. The attainment of the whole purpose—guaranteeing good business practice (qualitative supervision) and subjecting branches to capital and solvency regulations (quantitative supervision) with a view to protect creditors—pursued by the special regime for branches of non-EC banks can partially, ie, with respect to the quantitative supervision, be questioned. The purpose pursued becomes even more dubious against the background of the introduction to 'Basle II'. [See J Marwede, '§ 53', mn 17 *et seq*] If the stricter regime is, however, not capable of effectively protecting creditors, then the question of compatibility of § 53 of the KWG (Germany) with Art 56(1) EC appears at the horizon.

[418] A von Bogdandy, 'Außenaspekte', 370 *et seq*.
[419] This means in essence also that a third country investor can choose as a comparison the branch of an EC business, which enjoys the least strict standards by virtue of the laws of its home Member State, if EC harmonization was only directed at setting minimum standards.

by the respective home Member State of the business—then the host Member State attributes different, ie, less favourable, treatment to branches of non-EC businesses, although it aims at the prevention of one and the same threat to the common interest. Thus, the host State discriminates against branches of non-EC businesses, and this, in principle, is prohibited by Art 56(1) EC. If it were otherwise, Art 56(1) EC would be rendered meaningless in a third country context in all situations in which the Community has enacted harmonizing measures that provide for mutual recognition.[420]

The same principal considerations apply if a host Member State has agreed, by concluding an international agreement, to recognize the supervisory standards and activities of a non-EC country. If a business established in another non-EC country now intends to set up a branch in the respective Member State, it is entitled to treatment that is no less favourable than that accorded to the non-EC country with which the respective international agreement was concluded. In this connection, it should also be noted that a Member State is not entitled to apply to third country investors more favourable treatment than that accorded to investors from other Member States. This is inherent in the idea of the Common Market as a level playing field and can be deduced from Art 10 EC.

To encapsulate the aforesaid, in principle, direct investments originating from third countries are comparable to domestic investments as well as to those from other Member States with respect to access to a Member State's market. Of course, ultimately, the actual details of the case will decide the comparability question. However, it can be established that this study cannot identify 'value-based decisions stipulated by the Community legal order' of such a kind as to justify a negation of comparability.

(ii) Comparability and Market Exit Regulation for Direct Investment Directed to Third Countries In the same way as inbound foreign direct investments might be subject to discriminatory national measures, Member States may also apply different regulatory answers to outbound direct investments depending on the place where the prospective investments will be situated. While it is beyond doubt that '[a]s a general rule the EC Treaty assumes the equality of investments throughout the European Union',[421] again, when it comes to third countries, it appears that this 'unanimity' is quickly lost. While a domestic investment and an investment in another Member State are, in principle, comparable, and thus, any distinction based on the place of investment needs to be justified, such comparability is called into question with respect to third countries. Reviewing the arguments advanced in support of the stipulation of lacking comparability, we meet some 'old friends'. It is, for example, argued that an investment outside the EC only

---

[420] Advocate General Stix-Hackl also seems to share this view in her Opinion of *Fidium Finanz AG*, where she does not rule out 'comparability' with the argument that within the Community harmonization was carried out, but she tries to solve the issue at the level of grounds of justification. [*Cf* Case C-452/04 (Opinion of AG Stix-Hackl) *Fidium Finanz AG*, para 126 *et seq*]

[421] A Rust, 'National Report Germany', 277.

'indirectly furthers the development of the European Union;' the EC 'cannot hinder the third State to use the investment to the detriment of the European Union'[422] due to the fact that it cannot regulate the investment conditions. In essence, this translates into the following: first, free capital flow *erga omnes* does not really further the aims to be achieved by the Community; second, an opening of the market would require—as a *conditio sine qua non*—regulatory convergence with third countries; and third, the Community is ill-equipped to deal with potential abuse of the unilateral market opening.[423] Thus, the proponents of the aforesaid view come to the conclusion that Art 56(1) EC has to be interpreted strictly, ie, denying the 'comparability' of direct investments placed within and those situated outside the Community.

I have demonstrated above,[424] that precisely those three assumptions do not find sufficient support, either in the wording, in the systematics, or in the *telos* of Art 56(1) EC to be upheld. It is, nevertheless, worth stressing a particular point once more: the guarantee of, in principle, unrestricted outflow of direct investments—the negation of comparability of direct investment placed in another Member State and direct investment directed to a third country would be the opposite—is a vital instrument for maintaining trust in the 'European Union' investment area. Knowing that one can move one's capital out of the area whenever one deems it appropriate—barring the threat of becoming a prisoner of a protectionist national economic policy—often stimulates the decision to invest in the area in the first place. Moreover, the economic benefits for the European economies flowing from direct investments by their entrepreneurs in third countries not only indirectly further the development of the Community, but those investments are part of the reason why this area has experienced such prosperity in recent decades. The great majority of economic schools of thought—irrespective of the different rationales they advance—see the direct benefits of an economy that allows in principle for unrestricted outflow of foreign direct investment.[425] Therefore, generally denying comparability of an investment placed within the Community and an investment directed towards a third country does not

---

[422] Ibid. It should be noted that *Rust* advances those arguments with respect to direct taxation.
[423] It is surprising that, with respect to the second and third points, *Rust* [Ibid, 278] refers to the two Mutual Assistance Directives of the Community [Directive 77/799/EEC and Directive 76/308/EEC] to support his argument that investments placed in another Member State and those situated in a third country are not comparable, but at the same time acknowledges that the ECJ invokes the aforementioned Directives to reject possible justifications of discriminatory treatment by the Member States. This study, indeed, concurs with the idea that a lack of assistance by third countries with respect to the provision of information, etc—obviously, the two Directives do not apply to them—might lead to a justification of discriminatory treatment of third country direct investment that would otherwise, ie, in an intra-Community context, not be successful with a reference to those Directives. However, the mere non-applicability of these Directives in a third country context cannot lead to general denial of comparability due to the consequences that such a denial, as described above, would possibly have.
[424] See Chapter IV. 3. b. (2).
[425] For an account of the different schools of thought within the academic discipline of economics and their understandings of foreign direct investment, refer to R Gilpin, *Economy*, 278 *et seq*.

only mean applying the axe to the roots of European economic prosperity—its advancement being one of the Treaty's aims—but it means depriving Art 56(1) EC of most of its meaning with respect to third countries. The Treaty, by virtue of Art 56(1) EC, assumes not only in general the equality of investments throughout the European Union, but indeed *erga omnes*. From the point of view of practical experience, it should be noted that by the mid-1990s the Member States that are also members of the OECD had almost completely liberalized outward capital flows.[426]

While the Member States today maintain hardly any prohibitive restrictions on outward foreign direct investment besides the issue of less favourable tax treatment[427] of investments in third countries, Member States provide for a variety of measures that affect outward foreign direct investment by favouring direct investments differently, depending on the place of investment, by means of financial incentives[428] in the form of grants, loans, or equity participation for certain investment projects, investment insurance schemes[429] covering political risk in potential host countries, and also through targeted investment climate information programmes.[430] All of these measures of the Member States could come within the range of Art 56(1) EC if indeed operated discriminatorily.[431] Discrimination must then be justified by mandatory requirements, such as the protection of the environment or the promotion of development in the second and third world.

(c) Appraising 'Comparability'—A Hardly Effective Interpretative Parameter to Limit the Freedom's Scope

Denying 'comparability' of two direct investments has been described as one possible way to limit the scope of application of Art 56(1) EC, especially in a third

---

[426] UNCTAD, *Home Country Measures*, 7.
[427] See in this respect: Case C-101/05 *Skatteverket v A*.
[428] UNCTAD, *Home Country Measures*, 32 *et seq*. In this context it must be mentioned that many Member States also provide for incentives to attract foreign direct investment to their territories. Apart from classic financial incentives, the far-reaching activities of investment promotion agencies in particular must be noted. They range from the provision of information on the processing of applications or permits ('one stop shopping') to so-called after-care functions, which may even comprise schooling for children. [*Cf* S Young and N Hood, 'Inward Investment Policy', 492]
[429] UNCTAD, *Home Country Measures*, 37 *et seq*; for the German Scheme, refer to: PricewaterhouseCoopers Aktiengesellschaft Wirtschaftsprüfungsgesellschaft (PwC AG) and Euler Hermes Kreditversicherungs-AG, 'Investment Guarantees of the Federal Republic of Germany' (Website, Hamburg 2006).
[430] UNCTAD, *Home Country Measures*, 22 *et seq*.
[431] The abovementioned financial incentives and investment guarantee schemes, by their very concept, apply only to investments abroad and, thus, draw a distinction between domestic investment and investment in other Member States or third countries. Such regulation places those who do not wish to make use of the freedom in a less favourable position and, thus, would constitute so-called 'reverse discrimination,' which, in the current state of Community law, is not prohibited. However, seen from the most-favoured-nation treatment angle, different treatment of Member States on the one hand and third countries on the other, or different treatment of different third countries, could be discriminatory if not justifiable.

country context. A distinction has to be made, however, between considerations that are specific to the respective case, ie, the factual and legal situation in which the two compared investments are placed, and arguments that I have termed 'value-based decisions stipulated by the Community legal order'. While the former considerations can lead to the result that two investments are indeed incomparable, with respect to the latter the Community legal order does not contain any such value-based decisions, which would from the outset rule out the comparability of intra-Community investment and investment directed towards or originating from third countries. In particular, neither differences in the level of taxation, social contributions, or labour costs, nor intra-Community harmonization can justify the negation of 'comparability'. Consequences flowing from the opening of the Community capital market to the world have to be accepted in the same way as in an intra-Community context. This is based on the view that third country capital movement contributes to the attainment of the Treaty aims just as intra-Community capital movement does. This study cannot find sufficient evidence for a rebuttable presumption of incomparability. Quite the contrary, the aims of Treaty and the spirit and purpose of Art 56(1) EC *et seq.* suggest that intra-Community and third country investments are *per se* comparable. Otherwise, next to nothing would remain of Art 56(1) EC in a third country context.[432]

Meaningful case law that sheds light on the construction of free movement of capital in a third country context in general and on the issue of comparability in particular is just starting to evolve. Considering the Court's 'Centre of Gravity' approach in dealing with the relationship of free movement of capital and the freedom of establishment, one could be tempted to reason that this evolution is about to end before it has really started. Apart from this, it is doubtful whether 'interpretative parameter comparability', except for direct taxation cases, would play as significant a role in the Court's considerations. In intra-Community cases, the Court hardly ever has recourse to the non-discrimination test and the inherent question of 'comparability'. This assessment is only preliminary in nature given that virtually no cases[433] have been handed down.

c. Putting Together the Pieces: No Principal Differences in Construing the Scope of Protection in a Third Country Context

In conclusion, so far, the scope of prohibition of Art 56(1) EC in a third country context has to be interpreted along the same lines as developed for

---

[432] The ECJ—although not ruling out the possibility that in certain situations intra-Community and third country capital might not be comparable—has so far always accepted 'comparability' and solved the issue at the level of grounds of justification within the proportionality test. *Cf* for an outbound investment situation: Case C-446/04 (Opinion of AG Geelhoed) *Test Claimants in the FII Group Litigation v Commissioners of Inland Revenue*, para 169 *et seq*; Case C-101/05 *Skatteverket v A*, para 37 *et seq*. This approach is, on principle, delicate as it allows for appropriate differentiations without curtailing the freedom in a third country context.

[433] See, in particular, Case C-101/05 *Skatteverket v A*, para 37 *et seq*.

intra-Community capital movement. This conclusion is predominantly based on views in the legal literature. The Court's case law is of an ambiguous nature. Taking into account the evolving state of the jurisprudence, any conclusive evaluation would be premature.

To begin with, the wording of Art 56(1) EC[434] is a prime example of clarity speaking in favour of an understanding in a third country context that does not deviate from the one which is valid for intra-Community capital movement.

I have reviewed teleological and systematic arguments advanced by commentators who choose to interpret the scope of prohibition of Art 56(1) EC more narrowly in a third country context. This study could not establish any conclusive evidence that would support their view. To the contrary, this study has disproved the proposition that certain preconditions which, if they were fulfilled, would justify interpreting the scope of prohibition similarly in an intra-Community and a third country context, are still lacking.

First, the *erga omnes* principle within the ambit of free movement of capital not only makes sense if the Community wished to make an 'altruistic' contribution to the advancement of a liberalized world capital market at large—although there is evidence in the EC Treaty that the EC indeed indeed have wanted this—but the Community itself also benefits. Liberalized capital movement with third countries, for example, furthers economic growth within the EC by intensified competition, increased freedom of choice, especially for European capital recipients, and pressure on the Member States to maintain fiscal and tariffs discipline. Therefore, the unilateral liberalization of capital movements *erga omnes* advances those Treaty aims that are directed at the development of the Common Market.

Second, liberalizing capital movements in third country relations, economically speaking, requires—in the sense of a *conditio sine qua non*—neither the harmonization of third country and Common Market rules nor the coordination of monetary and economic policies between the EC and third countries. However, aiming at some degree of harmonization or coordination is desirable.

Third, this study suggests that the bargaining powers of the Community *vis-à-vis* third countries are sufficient to press for reciprocal market access and equal treatment of EC direct investments in third country markets. Thus, the configuration of the EC competences (esp. Arts 57(2) EC, 59 EC, 60 EC, 93 EC, and 94 EC together with Arts 95(2) EC and 308 EC) are not of such a kind as to describe the Community as insufficiently equipped to defend its and its Member States' interests. Protecting Community and Member State interests, therefore, does not require making liberalization of third county capital movement subject to reciprocity.

---

[434] The *erga omnes* principle in Art 56(1) EC can be seen as one of the clearest affirmations of the Community's commitment to a non-protectionist, open market economy, disapproving any notion of a 'Fortress Europe'.

Fourth, it is a vicious circle to argue that the greater number of permissible restrictions on the freedom in a third country context suggests a respectively more restricted *telos* of Art 56(1) EC in such a situation.

Fifth, restricting third country capital movement would not meaningfully prevent access of third country investors to the Common Market. The circumvention of restrictive access regimes in some Member States is possibly due to the so-called *'channel phenomenon'*. The 'channel phenomenon', ie, more liberal-minded Member States functioning as 'access channels' to the Common Market for third country capital movements that less liberal-minded Member States wished to have excluded or otherwise restricted, is caused by the way in which the other fundamental freedoms operate.

This having been said, this study submits that neither a *domaine réservé* for tax rules nor for any other type of national regulatory measure is justified on the basis of teleological or systematic considerations. Moreover, while I agree that Art 56(1) EC must apply to national measures that restrict the technical access of capital to and exit from the Common Market, I think there are profound reasons not to limit the scope of application to these instances.

I have already pointed out above the possible benefits that the unilateral liberalization of capital flows *erga omnes* can generate for the Common Market. Beyond that, liberalized capital movement *erga omnes* is also necessary in order to build up and maintain trust in the common currency, which is intended to aspire to be a world investment, financing, trade, and reserve currency. If one hopes to achieve this comprehensive end, it does not suffice to guarantee the absence of exchange controls; an equally comprehensive prohibition of any discrimination or hindrance of third country capital movements is also required.

In the discussion of the non-discrimination test, this study placed its focus on the 'comparability issue'. A distinction has to be made between case-specific considerations and those I termed 'value-based decisions stipulated by the Community legal order'. The former can always lead to a negation of comparability of domestic/intra-Community and third country direct investments. With respect to the latter, however, this study could not identify 'value-based decisions' that would suggest incomparability *per se*. In particular, arguments based on existing differences between a Member State and a third country in the level of taxation, social contributions, or labour costs, etc or the existence of intra-Community harmonization cannot form the basis for 'value-based decisions' and, thus, are unsuitable to justify the negation of 'comparability'.

Encapsulating all of the above leads to the conclusion that, in principle, both the non-discrimination and the non-hindrance tests as developed in an intra-Community context apply without alteration when it comes to third country capital movement. Thus, there is no difference in construction of the scope of prohibition of Art 56(1) EC depending on whether intra-Community or third country capital movement is involved. This interpretation leaves us with the following picture: the access, exit, and transit of third country capital must in principle be free of any restrictions. Once a third country investment is placed within the Common Market (inbound) or an investment originating from a Member State is established in a third country market (outbound), the Member States are not allowed to treat them less favourably than a comparable domestic investment or an investment from another State.

V
Personal Scope of Application

1. Introduction

This section will shed light on the personal scope of application of Art 56(1) EC. As this study has chosen to discuss the freedom from the perspective of a market participant, it will start by examining the personal scope of application, defining the group of beneficiaries who can rely on the freedom. Although Art 56(1) EC does not describe any characteristics to be met by those who wish to have recourse to the freedom, this does not mean that its personal scope is without any limitations.

Before setting out the group of beneficiaries, however, the preliminary issue of vertical direct effect must be considered. Such an effect is the precondition for the existence of any individual right based on a Community provision. Prima facie the fundamental freedoms display only an institutional dimension: they aim at the implementation of the Common Market. However, as early as *van Gend and Loos* in 1963, the Court transcended a purely objective view of the freedoms and cleared the way for an understanding of them as individual rights.[1] Subsequently, the Court has declared all but one freedom directly effective. For a long time, free movement of capital was far behind the other freedoms.[2] It was not until the entry into force of the Maastricht amendments that free movement of capital ultimately joined the other freedoms. It now equally confers individual rights upon those taking part in capital movements across national borders.[3]

After having discussed the group of beneficiaries, I will identify the group of addressees of the corresponding obligations flowing from Art 56(1) EC.

2. Vertical Direct Effect

An individual right based on a Community provision presupposes its direct effect.[4] The criteria a Treaty provision has to meet in order to be vertically directly

---

[1] Case 26/62 *NV Algemene Transport- en Expeditie Onderneming van Gend & Loos v Netherlands Inland Revenue Administration*.
[2] *Cf* Case 203/80 *Criminal proceedings against Guerrino Casati*.
[3] See with respect to Directive 88/361/EEC: Joined Cases C-358/93 and C-416/93 *Criminal proceedings against Aldo Bordessa and Vicente Marí Mellado and Concepción Barbero Maestre*, para 35.
[4] The terminology in this respect varies. One can also speak of 'direct applicability', which would be a direct translation from the German term 'unmittelbare Anwendbarkeit'. In the

effective are the following: (1) the content of the obligation embodied in the rule at issue must be sufficiently clear and precise, (2) the provision must be unconditional, and (3) it must leave no room for the exercise of discretion in implementation by Member States or the Community.[5]

It is settled case law[6] and undisputed in the literature[7] that Art 56(1) EC meets these criteria and is today[8] vertically directly effective in an intra-Community context, ie, the provision may be relied upon before national courts and may render inapplicable national rules inconsistent therewith.[9]

Having said that the issue of direct effect in an intra-Community context is resolved, the situation is somewhat more intricate with respect to third country capital movements. There is, to begin with, the opinion of Advocate General Tesauro in the *Sanz de Lera* case, the landmark case on direct effect of Art 56(1) EC. The case was concerned with capital movements to Turkey and Switzerland. He suggested that Art 56(1) EC has vertical direct effect with respect to third countries, except for direct investments.[10] Although the Advocate General's opinion is not completely clear on this point, it appears that he issued a caveat with respect to direct investment due to the reservation of certain powers for the Member States in Art 57(1) EC.[11] The ECJ, however, was of a different opinion. The Court found that the clear and unconditionally worded prohibition in Art 56(1) EC, which does not require further implementation despite the qualifications contained in Art 57(1) and Art 58 EC, possessed direct effect with regard to third countries.[12] From the wording of the judgment, it appears that the ECJ did not want to create a factual *domaine réservé* with respect to direct investment, but

English literature it is sometimes used differently; *cf* in this respect S Mohamed, *Free Movement of Capital*, 40.

[5] *Cf* Case 26/62 *NV Algemene Transport- en Expeditie Onderneming van Gend & Loos v Netherlands Inland Revenue Administration*; Case 57/65 *Alfons Lütticke GmbH v Hauptzollamt Sarrelouis*; note also J Steiner and L Woods, *EC Law*, 90 *et seq*, esp. 91.

[6] Implicitly since the Court's judgment in Joined Cases C-358/93 and C-416/93 *Criminal proceedings against Aldo Bordessa and Vicente Marí Mellado and Concepción Barbero Maestre*, paras 17, 33 *et seq*, which was based on the EC Capital Movements Directive.

[7] S Weber, 'Kapitalverkehr', 562; JA Usher, 'Capital Movements', 44; F Kimms, *Kapitalverkehrsfreiheit*, 135 *et seq*; R Smits, *ECB*, 59 *et seq*; R Smits, 'Payments and Capital', 252; A Honrath, *Kapitalverkehr*, 69; A Rohde, *Kapitalverkehr*, 135 *et seq*; JCW Müller, *Kapitalverkehrsfreiheit*, 140 *et seq*; A Glaesner, Art. 56 EC (2000), mn 4; F Roy, *Niederlassungsrecht und Kapitalverkehrsfreiheit*, 29; U Haferkamp, *Kapitalverkehrsfreiheit*, 60 *et seq*; C Ohler, Art. 56 EC (2002), mn 290 *et seq*; G Ress and J Ukrow, Art. 56 EC (2002), mn 70; W Kiemel, Art. 56 EC (2003), mn 35 *et seq*; M Dahlberg, *Direct Taxation*, 281; T Schürmann, Art. 56 EC (2006), mn 15.

[8] For a brief historical account, refer to J Lübke, *Kapitalverkehrs- und Niederlassungsfreiheit*, 147 *et seq*; for a very detailed historical and political study of the provisions on free movement of capital, see AFP Bakker, *Capital Movements*.

[9] *Cf* with respect to the legal effects: Case 6/64 *Flaminio Costa v E.N.E.L*; Case 106/77 *Amministrazione delle Finanze dello Stato v Simmenthal SpA*, para 17 *et seq*; see also C Ohler, Art. 56 EC (2002), mn 290 *et seq*.

[10] Joined Cases C-163/94, C-165/94, and C-250/94 (Opinion of AG Tesauro) *Criminal proceedings against Lucas Emilio Sanz de Lera, Raimundo Díaz Jiménez and Figen Kapanoglu*, para 20.

[11] Ibid, para 13 *et seq*.

[12] Joined Cases C-163/94, C-165/94, and C-250/94 *Criminal proceedings against Lucas Emilio Sanz de Lera, Raimundo Díaz Jiménez and Figen Kapanoglu*, para 40 *et seq*.

merely stated that as long as restrictive national or EC measures are in place they, by virtue of Art 57(1) EC,[13] are outside the prohibitive scope of Art 56(1) EC. Insofar, however, as none of the aforementioned measures restrict the freedom, 'Article 73b(1) [now, after amendment, Art 56(1)], in conjunction with Articles 73c [now, after amendment, Art 57] and 73d (1) (b) [now, after amendment, Art 58 (1) lit. b] of the Treaty, may be relied on before national courts and may render inapplicable national rules inconsistent therewith.'[14] In this sense, one can draw from this judgment that Art 56(1) EC was declared directly effective for any kind of capital movement.[15]

In the *Ospelt* case, Advocate General Geelhood concurred in this view and stated clearly—without any reservation—that third country nationals or legal persons can also rely on Art 56(1) EC before national courts.[16] In the Court's judgment, the issue of direct effect of Art 56(1) EC was not explicitly touched upon. However, by the mere fact of applying Art 56(1) EC to the facts of the case, it becomes evident that the provision must also have direct effect with respect to third country relations.

In the Opinion on *Fidium Finanz AG,* the Advocate General—presenting it as a matter of course—stated that an undertaking established outside the Community can rely on Art 56(1) EC.[17] The judgment of the Court in this case, as well as in subsequent cases concerned with third country capital movement, confirmed this view and has not left any room for doubt: Art 56(1) EC is also directly applicable in a third country context.[18]

Despite the clear rulings of the Court, some older comments on the Court's jurisprudence suggested that direct effect of Art 56(1) EC was to be considerably more limited in a third country context. Mohamed, for example, chooses to exclude the categories of capital mentioned in Art 57 EC from direct effect on the grounds that Art 57(2) EC allegedly 'requires the Council intervention

---

[13] See on the interpretation of Art 57(1) EC Chapter VII. 2.
[14] Joined Cases C-163/94, C-165/94, and C-250/94 *Criminal proceedings against Lucas Emilio Sanz de Lera, Raimundo Díaz Jiménez and Figen Kapanoglu*, para 48.
[15] A different view was held by Mohamed—S Mohamed, *Free Movement of Capital*, 219 *et seq*—who sought to interpret the judgment in the sense that only the physical import and export of money from and towards third countries was liberalized. I do not think this interpretation can reasonably be maintained.
[16] Case C-452/01 (Opinion of AG Geelhoed) *Margarethe Ospelt and Schlössle Weissenberg Familienstiftung*, para 45 *et seq*, esp. para 47: '[N]ationals of third countries and legal persons established in third countries may invoke the free movement of capital by virtue of the EC Treaty. If, in a specific case, Community law provides for an exception in relation to them, it is necessary to consider the extent to which that exception restricts a right which they enjoy in accordance with an obligation on the European Community under international law.'
[17] Case C-452/04 (Opinion of AG Stix-Hackl) *Fidium Finanz AG*, para 43.
[18] *Cf*, eg, Case C-452/04 *Fidium Finanz AG*; Case C-446/04 *Test Claimants in the FII Group Litigation v Commissioners of Inland Revenue*; Case C-524/04 *Test Claimants in the Thin Cap Group Litigation*; Case C-157/05 *Winfried Holböck v Finanzamt Salzburg-Land*. Recently: Case C-101/05 *Skatteverket v A*, para 27.

to liberalise capital movements'[19] with respect to those categories mentioned in this provision. However, in view of the Court's case law, which is now sufficiently clear on this point, such assertions seem to be outdated.[20] Apart from that, if one were of the opinion that the categories of capital mentioned within Art 57 EC are effectively excluded from liberalization by virtue of the second paragraph of the aforementioned provision, then one would also need to explain what function to attribute to Art 57(1) EC. Clearly, para (1) of Art 57 EC would not make much sense any more.[21]

In conclusion, Art 56(1) EC is vertically directly effective in intra-Community and third country contexts.[22]

3. The Irrelevance of Nationality and Habitual Residence for the Personal Scope of Application

Above, I have classified Art 56(1) EC as an object-related production factor freedom. I explained that although all fundamental freedoms have persons as beneficiaries, their guarantees are partially tied up to the movement of objects. That is inter alia the case for free movement of capital, which liberalizes an economic activity due to its object, not by reason of the persons involved.[23]

It is due to this nature that Art 56(1) EC does not specify or limit the group of beneficiaries. It extends in its guarantee—irrespective of nationality[24] and, in principle, also irrespective of place of habitual residence[25]—to all natural and legal persons.[26] The object orientation of Art 56(1) EC implies moreover

---

[19] S Mohamed, *Free Movement of Capital*, 221. Sharing this view: C Ohler, Art. 56 EC (2002), mn 270. Usher was surprised about the extension of direct effect to the third country context: JA Usher, 'Tax Discrimination', 272 *et seq*.
[20] C Peters and J Gooijer, 'Movement of Capital', 476.
[21] *Cf* K Ståhl, 'Movement of Capital', 53.
[22] Sharing this opinion: eg, F Kimms, *Kapitalverkehrsfreiheit*, 135 *et seq*; R Smits, *ECB*, 59 *et seq*; R Smits, 'Payments and Capital', 252 *et seq*; A Honrath, *Kapitalverkehr*, 69; A Rohde, *Kapitalverkehr*, 135 *et seq*; JCW Müller, *Kapitalverkehrsfreiheit*, 139 *et seq*; F Roy, *Niederlassungsrecht und Kapitalverkehrsfreiheit*, 29; G Ress and J Ukrow, Art. 56 EC (2002), mn 70; W Kiemel, Art. 56 EC (2003), mn 35 *et seq*; M Dahlberg, *Direct Taxation*, 281; W Schön, 'Kapitalverkehr mit Drittstaaten', 491 *et seq*; J Lübke, *Kapitalverkehrs- und Niederlassungsfreiheit*, 147 *et seq*, 154 *et seq*; A Cordewener, et al, 'Emerging Issues', 110 *et seq*. Expressly only in regard to intra-Community capital movement: S Weber, 'Kapitalverkehr', 562; A Glaesner, Art. 56 EC (2000), mn 4; U Haferkamp, *Kapitalverkehrsfreiheit*, 60 *et seq*; T Schürmann, Art. 56 EC (2006), mn 15.
[23] See Chapter II.
[24] For a different view: T Kingreen and R Störmer, 'Subjetiv-öffentlichen Rechte', 274 *et seq*; T Kingreen, *Struktur der Grundfreiheiten*, 78 *et seq*.
[25] For a different view: A Pajunk, *Mobiliarkreditsicherheiten*, 35.
[26] S Weber, 'Kapitalverkehr', 593; JCW Müller, *Kapitalverkehrsfreiheit*, 149; J Glöckner, 'Grundverkehrsbeschränkungen', 606; U Haferkamp, *Kapitalverkehrsfreiheit*, 104; G Ress and J Ukrow, Art. 56 EC (2002), mn 73; K-P Follak, 'Kapital- und Zahlungsverkehr', mn 5; W Kiemel, Art. 56 EC (2003), mn 24; J Lübke, *Kapitalverkehrs- und Niederlassungsfreiheit*, 156; T Schürmann, Art. 56 EC (2006), mn 14; probably also A Glaesner, Art. 56 EC (2000), mn 18; in principle also

that Art 56(1) EC does not require drawing a doctrinal distinction between an 'active' and a 'passive' freedom of capital movement;[27] a distinction drawn from the person-related freedoms, which prima facie focus on the person who actively performs a certain economic activity. Both transferor as well as transferee can rely on Art 56(1) EC without further ado.[28]

The (habitual) residence of the market participant also does not, in principle, constitute a formal condition to be met in order to have recourse to Art 56(1) EC.[29] Transferor and transferee, for example, need not be resident within the Community. However, residence is not completely irrelevant within the ambit of free movement of capital. As explained above, a capital movement, in order to be covered by Art 56(1) EC, must occur across a border[30] and display a 'sufficient link'[31] to a Member State. In order to localize meaningfully the transfer of intangible capital across borders, having recourse to its holder is inevitable. The holder is placed where its (habitual) residence is to be found. In this sense, the place of residence of the transferor or transferee can gain a certain relevance within the ambit of free movement of capital.

With respect to third country nationals, *Bröhmer* suggests attributing a more far-reaching significance to the criteria of nationality and residency than that just depicted.[32] Unfortunately, he does not go into detail with respect to his proposition.

C Ohler, Art. 56 EC (2002), mn 221 However, he seeks to attribute significance to the nationality of the market participant in cases in which an intra-Community economic activity is subject to more than one freedom, ie, it qualifies as establishment within the meaning of Art 43 EC or service as understood in Art 49 EC and as capital movement subject to Art 56(1) EC. In such cases, Ohler seeks to allow for the application of Art 56(1) EC only if the market participant who wants to rely on free movement of capital possesses the nationality of or has its registered office in a Member State. Otherwise, he believes, one would attribute primacy to Art 56(1) EC over the other freedoms. [*Cf.* C Ohler, Art. 56 EC (2002), mn 222 *et seq*] However, I have difficulties seeing why one would attribute primacy to Art 56(1) EC in such a case. Rather, it appears that 'importing' additional elements into the scope of application of Art 56(1) EC would mean disregarding the object orientation of free movement of capital [*cf* see above Chapter II] as well as attempting to restrict unreasonably the freedom's third country applicability.

[27] J Lübke, *Kapitalverkehrs- und Niederlassungsfreiheit*, 156. Drawing such a distinction: eg, U Haferkamp, *Kapitalverkehrsfreiheit*, 104 *et seq*; G Ress and J Ukrow, Art. 56 EC (2002), mn 36.

[28] *Cf*, eg, U Haferkamp, *Kapitalverkehrsfreiheit*, 104 *et seq*; PO Mülbert, 'Kapitalmarktrecht', 2089; U Wackerbart, 'Internationale Übernahmeangebote', 1749; J Lübke, *Kapitalverkehrs- und Niederlassungsfreiheit*, 156 *et seq*. For the Court see, eg, Case C-439/97 *Sandoz GmbH v Finanzlandesdirektion für Wien, Niederösterreich und Burgenland*; Case C-242/03 (Opinion of AG Kokott) *Ministre des Finances v Jean-Claude Weidert and Élisabeth Paulus*, para 13.

[29] G Ress and J Ukrow, Art. 56 EC (2002), mn 73; W Kiemel, Art. 56 EC (2003), mn 24; K-P Follak, 'Kapital- und Zahlungsverkehr', mn 5; J Lübke, *Kapitalverkehrs- und Niederlassungsfreiheit*, 156 *et seq*, 160; T Schürmann, Art. 56 EC (2006), mn 14; probably also A Glaesner, Art. 56 EC (2000), mn 18; but see C Ohler, Art. 56 EC (2002), 216 *et seq*, along similar lines: J Bröhmer, Art. 56 EC (2007), mn 7; A Pajunk, *Mobiliarkreditsicherheiten*, 35.

[30] See Chapter II. 3.   [31] See Chapter II. 4. c. (2).

[32] J Bröhmer, Art. 56 EC (2007), mn 7.

For the sake of argument, one possible approach to restricting the ambit of Art 56(1) EC with respect to third country capital movement is to restrict the personal scope of the freedom in such a way that Member State nationals could claim rights under Art 56(1) EC with regard to their investment in third countries, but third country nationals could not with respect to their investment within the territory of the EC.[33] However, such a suggestion is not convincing. To begin with, any evidence for such a suggestion within the wording of the provisions on free movement of capital is lacking. Moreover, due to the fact that free movement of capital protects both the transferor and the transferee, the distinction suggested above would not lead to an effective limitation of the scope of application, but merely to a monopolization of the right to initiate legal actions on the part of a Member State national.[34]

4. The Beneficiaries of the Freedom in Detail

Free movement of capital first and foremost entitles private market participants, natural and legal[35] persons alike.[36]

Concerning legal persons, following the general idea contained in Art 48(2) EC, free movement of capital also extends to those that were established on the basis of public law as long as they carry out economic activities for financial gain.[37] *A fortiori* profit-making enterprises organized on the basis of civil law that are 'merely' directly or indirectly owned by a Member State (or the Community or a third country[38]) must be able to rely on Art 56(1) EC.[39]

---

[33] Discussed but also disapproved by W Schön, 'Kapitalverkehr mit Drittstaaten', 495 *et seq*.
[34] Ibid, 497.
[35] The general notion inherent in Art 48(2) EC also applies to the ambit of free movement of capital.
[36] eg, JCW Müller, *Kapitalverkehrsfreiheit*, 149.
[37] C Ohler, Art. 56 EC (2002), mn 225; W Weiß, 'Öffentliche Unternehmen', 171; W Frenz, *Europarecht*, mn 233; J Lübke, *Kapitalverkehrs- und Niederlassungsfreiheit*, 157. Certainly, this view leads to the consequence that public undertakings can be both beneficiaries as well as addressees (*cf* Art 86(2) EC) of Art 56(1) EC. This, however, is not a problem due to the fact that the right exists *vis-à-vis* the Member State, but the duty is owed towards the other beneficiaries of Art 56(1) EC. [W Weiß, 'Öffentliche Unternehmen', 173 *et seq*; W Frenz, *Europarecht*, mn 233 *et seq*, esp. 240; J Lübke, *Kapitalverkehrs- und Niederlassungsfreiheit*, 157]
[38] Lately, as mentioned in the introduction to this study, the increasing activities of so-called 'sovereign wealth funds,' ie, special investment funds created or owned by governments to hold foreign assets for long-term purposes [International Monetary Fund, Global Financial Stability Report, 2007, 45], have led to calls on the Member States to restrict their activities. However, as long as they pursue economic activities for financial gain, there is no reason to exclude them from the personal scope of application of Art 56(1) EC.
[39] W Weiß, 'Kommunale Energieversorger', 567; W Frenz, *Europarecht*, mn 233.

Public undertakings not pursuing any economic activity for financial gain within the meaning of Art 48(2) EC are outside the personal scope of the freedom.[40] However, insofar as they deal with private persons, those undertakings participate indirectly in the protection flowing from the freedom, as a private market participant can rely on Art 56(1) EC in any event.[41]

In practice, the group of market participants is not limited to those mentioned above. The activities of the Member States, the EC, and their respective institutions[42] on the financial market reach a significant volume. Taking into consideration that the fundamental freedoms are predominantly individual rights to be protected from the State, as addressees of this very right it appears questionable whether the Member States and the Community can rely on the freedom.[43] Rather, the respective competences of the Community[44] and the Member States[45] in EC primary law constitute the legal basis to act in the private financial market. Article 10 EC obliges both the Community and the Member States not to restrict each other in their dealings.[46]

However, if a private person enters into dealings with a Member State (or the EC), purchasing, for example, government bonds, then he can rely on Art 56(1) EC.[47] In this way the Member States and the Community participate indirectly in the freedom's guarantee.[48]

Third countries cannot rely on Art 56(1) EC. The EC Treaty constitutes for them a *res inter alios acta*. They can derive neither rights nor duties from the EC Treaty, *cf* Art 34 of 1969 Vienna Convention on the Law of Treaties.[49]

---

[40] W Frenz, *Europarecht*, mn 246 *et seq*.
[41] *Cf* Case C-478/98 *Commission v Kingdom of Belgium (Re Loans issued abroad)*, para 16; see also W Frenz, *Europarecht*, mn 249.
[42] Concerning the European Investment Bank and the European Central Bank, they are not institutions of the Community, *cf* Art 7 EC. The European Investment Bank and the European Central Bank are empowered to act on the private financial market by virtue of their banks' statutes. Due to an analogous application of Art. 10 EC, the Member States are obliged not to restrict the operations of those banks. [C Ohler, Art. 56 EC (2002), mn 232 *et seq*] Private market participants entering into dealings with these banks can of course rely on Art 56(1) EC.
[43] *Cf* W Frenz, *Europarecht*, mn 252 *et seq*.
[44] R Scheibe, *Anleihekompetenzen*, 312 *et seq*, 362, 402; C Waldhoff, Art. 269 EC (2007), mn 14 *et seq*; S Magiera, Art. 269 EC (2006), mn 37; but see U Häde, *Finanzausgleich*, 463 *et seq*; U Häde, Art. 100 EC (2007), mn 5; U Häde, Art. 119 EC (2007), mn 12.
[45] *Cf* Arts 101 EC, 102 EC, and 104 EC.
[46] C Ohler, Art. 56 EC (2002), mn 229 *et seq*; AC Digel, 'Europäischer Finanzmarkt', Inaugural-Dissertation, Eberhard-Karls-Universität, 118 *et seq*.
[47] Case C-478/98 *Commission v Kingdom of Belgium (Re Loans issued abroad)*, para 16. The Court was more concerned with the question of whether the transaction in issue was occurring cross-border.
[48] C Ohler, Art. 56 EC (2002), para 227.
[49] Article 34 of the 1969 Vienna Convention on the Law of Treaties reads: '*A treaty does not create either obligations or rights for a third State without its consent.*' See also Z Bognar, *Währungsintegration*, 163 *et seq*; C Ohler, Art. 56 EC (2002), mn 234.

5. The Addressees of the Corresponding Obligations

a. Member States

Free movement of capital—in the same way as the other freedoms—is predominantly State-centric.[50] The obligations in Art 56(1) EC are therefore first and foremost addressed to the Member States.[51]

Whether certain conduct constitutes an action of a (Member) State is decided by the Court on a case-by-case basis, applying a different notion of 'State' depending on the Community law context to which the conduct relates.[52] However, the ECJ always perceives the notion as a dichotomic one: conduct that cannot be attributed to the State is private and *vice versa*.[53]

The notion of State in the context of the fundamental freedoms comprises, to begin with, the three 'classic' branches of power: legislature, executive authority, and judiciary. The notion applies to all organizational and territorial subdivisions: to the nation State itself, regional authorities, semi-public sector bodies, and private persons exercising public authority.[54]

Moreover, it does not constitute a difference for the purposes of Art 56(1) EC if a Member State chooses to act through the means of private law. Also, such measures must equally be comprised of the notion of '(Member) State' in order to prevent the circumvention of Art 56(1) EC by simply seeking refuge in private law. Any action based on private law, not only those with which the State performs public functions such as borrowing on the capital market for budgetary purposes, but also those that comprise economic activity for financial gain, is subject to the fundamental freedom.[55]

---

[50] The freedoms aim at the eradication of restrictions on free movement, which exist due to the existence of State borders. The perspective of the freedoms is evidenced by the existence of express exceptions for Member States to preserve or introduce restrictions on free movement. With respect to free movement of capital, these are Arts 57(1) EC, 58(1) EC, and 60(2) EC. [S Wernicke, *Privatwirkung*, 107; J Lübke, *Kapitalverkehrs- und Niederlassungsfreiheit*, 237]

[51] JCW Müller, *Kapitalverkehrsfreiheit*, 150; C Ohler, Art. 56 EC (2002), mn 235; G Ress and J Ukrow, Art. 56 EC (2002), mn 62; J Lübke, *Kapitalverkehrs- und Niederlassungsfreiheit*, 238.

[52] S Wernicke, *Privatwirkung*, 108.

[53] Case C-188/89 (Opinion of AG Van Gerven) *A. Foster and others v British Gas plc*, para 10.

[54] S Wernicke, *Privatwirkung*, 108 *et seq* for further references; see also JCW Müller, *Kapitalverkehrsfreiheit*, 150; J Lübke, *Kapitalverkehrs- und Niederlassungsfreiheit*, 240 *et seq*. The attribution of conduct of private persons exercising public authority to the respective Member State is carried out on the basis of national law measured against the principles of attribution found in public international law. [G Ress and J Ukrow, Art. 56 EC (2002), mn 62]

[55] Confirmed by the Court in: Joined Cases C-282/04 and C-283/04 (Opinion of AG Maduro) *Commission v Kingdom of the Netherlands (Re Golden Shares VI)*, para 20 *et seq*; see also JCW Müller, *Kapitalverkehrsfreiheit*, 150; G Ress and J Ukrow, Art. 56 EC (2002), mn 65; C Ohler, Art. 56 EC (2002), mn 236; J Lübke, *Kapitalverkehrs- und Niederlassungsfreiheit*, 253 *et seq*.

Additionally, the conduct of private entities in no way organizationally attached to a Member State can, under certain conditions,[56] be attributed to it.[57] A Member State not only has the duty to refrain from any restrictive conduct, but it is also under the positive obligation to prevent any private conduct restricting free capital movement.[58] In this respect, one can have recourse to the jurisprudence within the ambit of free movement of goods that *mutatis mutandis* also applies with respect to Art 56(1) EC.[59]

The Court held in this respect that:

the Member States [are] not merely [required] themselves to abstain from adopting measures or engaging in conduct liable to constitute an obstacle to trade but also, when read with Article 5 [now, after amendment, Art. 10 EC] of the Treaty, to take all necessary and appropriate measures to ensure that that fundamental freedom is respected on their territory.[60]

Public undertakings and undertakings to which Member States grant special or exclusive rights[61] within the meaning of Art 86(1) EC are not directly bound by the fundamental freedoms; rather, their conduct is attributed to the Member States. The latter are under the obligation to exercise their influence in order to prevent such undertakings from restricting free movement of capital.[62]

Undertakings entrusted with the operation of services of general economic interest or having the character of a revenue-producing monopoly as mentioned in Art 86(2) EC are by virtue of that provision directly bound to Art 56(1) EC.[63]

b. European Community

The group of addressees is not limited to the Member States. The Community and its institutions are also addressees of the obligations contained in Art 56(1)

---

[56] *Cf* Case C-265/95 *Commission v French Republic (Re Trade Barriers Resulting from Actions by Private Individuals)*, para 56.
[57] JCW Müller, *Kapitalverkehrsfreiheit*, 150.
[58] G Ress and J Ukrow, Art. 56 EC (2002), mn 63 *et seq*; C Ohler, Art. 56 EC (2002), mn 235.
[59] G Ress and J Ukrow, Art. 56 EC (2002), mn 63.
[60] Case C-265/95 *Commission v French Republic (Re Trade Barriers Resulting from Actions by Private Individuals)*, para 32. See also Case C-112/00 *Eugen Schmidberger, Internationale Transporte und Planzüge v Republik Österreich*, para 59.
[61] See for an account of those two notions: J Lübke, *Kapitalverkehrs- und Niederlassungsfreiheit*, 241 *et seq*.
[62] F von Burchard, Art. 86 EC (2000), mn 46 *et seq*; C Ohler, Art. 56 EC (2002), mn 240; J Lübke, *Kapitalverkehrs- und Niederlassungsfreiheit*, 240 *et seq*; for the ambit of free movement of goods: P-C Müller-Graff, Art. 28 EC (2003), mn 290; different view: W-H Roth, 'Drittwirkung', 1231; S Wernicke, *Privatwirkung*, 130; I Pernice and S Wernicke, Art. 86 EC (2003), mn 8; W Weiß, 'Öffentliche Unternehmen', 170 *et seq*. To the extent that private persons are bound by the Treaty, such undertakings can also be addressees of the obligations contained within the Treaty. [*Cf.* C Ohler, Art. 56 EC (2002), mn 240]
[63] C Ohler, Art. 56 EC (2002), mn 241.

EC.⁶⁴ This can be drawn—*argumentum e contrario*—from the existence of Arts 57(2) EC, 59 EC, and 60 EC, which grant powers to the Community for certain specific occasions on which it can restrict capital movements.⁶⁵ In situations other than those referred to in the aforementioned provisions, the Community may not restrict free movement of capital.

As a consequence of the aforesaid, secondary legislation must in principle be reconcilable with Art 56(1) EC.⁶⁶ However, the Court has been very reluctant to strictly scrutinize secondary legislation against the background of the fundamental freedoms. The Community enjoys considerably more discretion than the Member States when harmonizing national legislation and establishing a Community-wide standard.⁶⁷ Furthermore, subject to the aforementioned limitation, actions of the Community and its institutions on the basis of private law must also be subject to scrutiny on the basis of Art 56(1) EC.⁶⁸

c. Private Persons—Horizontal Direct Effect

Probably the most contentious issue within the discussion on the group of addressees of Art 56(1) EC is that of whether private persons are bound by the provisions. This is not a problem specific to Art 56(1) EC, but relates to the general controversy in Community law of whether the fundamental freedoms unfold (horizontal) direct effect among private persons.⁶⁹ This discussion is not about those national mandatory or optional rules that are applied by private persons in their dealings among each other, such as the provisions of the civil code. They are enacted by the Member States and can clearly be attributed to them.⁷⁰ Rather, the core discussion revolves around the question of whether party-autonomous actions must be measured against the fundamental freedoms in general and free movement of capital in particular.

The answers provided with respect to free movement of capital (but also in regards to the other freedoms) differ widely. Some commentators completely

---

⁶⁴ W Frenz, *Europarecht*, mn 309 *et seq*. HD Jarass, 'Dogmatik II', 715; JCW Müller, *Kapitalverkehrsfreiheit*, 150; G Ress and J Ukrow, Art. 56 EC (2002), mn 66; U Haferkamp, *Kapitalverkehrsfreiheit*, 108 *et seq* for further references.

⁶⁵ One can also refer to Art 230(2) EC in order to argue for the binding force of Art 56(1) EC with respect to the Community. [*Cf* C Ohler, Art. 56 EC (2002), mn 237] See also T Kingreen, 'Fundamental Freedoms', 577 *et seq*.

⁶⁶ B Matzka, *Freiheit des Kapitalverkehrs*, 53; G Ress and J Ukrow, Art. 56 EC (2002), mn 66.

⁶⁷ *Cf* Case C-233/94 *Federal Republic of Germany v European Parliament and Council (Re Directive on Deposit-guarantee Schemes)*, para 16 *et seq*; W Frenz, *Europarecht*, mn. 316 *et seq*; in detail: R-O Schwemer, *Bindung*.

⁶⁸ C Ohler, Art. 56 EC (2002), mn 238.

⁶⁹ *Cf*, eg, recently published monographs TO Ganten, *Drittwirkung*; S Wernicke, *Privatwirkung*; H Parpart, *Unmittelbare Bindung*; K Preedy, *Drittwirkung*; P Förster, *Unmittelbare Drittwirkung*.

⁷⁰ E Steindorff, *EG-Vertrag und Privatrecht*, 79; R Streinz and S Leible, 'Drittwirkung', 465; C Ohler, Art. 56 EC (2002), mn 243; R Streinz, *Europarecht*, mn 836 *et seq*; J Lübke, *Kapitalverkehrs- und Niederlassungsfreiheit*, 248 *et seq* for further references.

reject this concept;[71] others want to limit it to special situations.[72] Still others embrace it unreservedly.[73] The Court's case law is equally unclear on this point.[74] It appears that the ECJ differentiates between object-oriented and person-oriented freedoms and is more willing to embrace horizontal direct effect in the ambit of the latter freedoms.[75] With respect to person-related freedoms, the Court allowed in particular for horizontal direct effect *vis-à-vis* so-called 'intermediary powers',[76] which are private persons who due to their regulatory powers act in a State-like manner and are, hence, placed in between 'ordinary' private persons and the State.[77]

Although free movement of capital is an object-related freedom, it appears reasonable also to accept in its ambit horizontal direct effect as *ultima ratio* for the just depicted situation, ie, if party autonomous action appears State-like in a legal or factual sense.[78] While it is true that in principle, the EC rules on competition are designed to remove private restrictions on free movement, and the fundamental freedoms aim predominantly at restrictive State action, the existence of

---

[71] P Oliver, 'Free Movement of Capital', 413; W-H Roth, 'Drittwirkung', 1241; R Eckhoff, 'Kapital- und Zahlungsverkehr', mn 1770; R Streinz and S Leible, 'Drittwirkung', 464 *et seq*; AC Digel, 'Europäischer Finanzmarkt', Inaugural-Dissertation, Eberhard-Karls-Universität, 114 *et seq*; see also T Kingreen, 'Fundamental Freedoms', 578 *et seq* for an alternative concept of 'right to protection'.

[72] JA Usher, 'Capital Movements', 46; A Randelzhofer and U Forsthoff, Art. 39–55 EC (2001), mn 69 *et seq*, esp. 73 *et seq*; G Ress and J Ukrow, Art. 56 EC (2002), mn 67 *et seq*; C Ohler, Art. 56 EC (2002), mn 242 *et seq*; U Haferkamp, *Kapitalverkehrsfreiheit*, 111 *et seq*; J Lübke, *Kapitalverkehrs- und Niederlassungsfreiheit*, 256 *et seq*.

[73] P Vigneron and P Steinfeld, 'Circulation des Capitaux', 431. See also TO Ganten, *Drittwirkung*, 220.

[74] Judgments in favour of horizontal direct effect in the ambit of free movement of goods: Case 58/80 *Dansk Supermarked A/S v A/S Imerco*, para 17. For a sceptical view: Joined Cases 177 and 178/82 *Criminal proceedings against Jan van de Haar and Kaveka de Meern BV*, para 11 *et seq*; Case 311/85 *ASBL Vereniging van Vlaamse Reisbureaus v ASBL Sociale Dienst van de Plaatselijke en Gewestelijke Overheidsdiensten*, para 30. In favour of horizontal direct effect in the ambits of person-related freedoms in earlier case law: Case 36/74 *B.N.O. Walrave and L.J.N. Koch v Association Union cycliste internationale, Koninklijke Nederlandsche Wielren Unie et Federación Española Ciclismo*; Case 13/76 *Gaetano Donà v Mario Mantero*. More recently: Case C-415/93 *Union royale belge des sociétés de football association ASBL v Jean-Marc Bosman, Royal club liégeois SA v. Jean-Marc Bosman and others and Union des associations européennes de football (UEFA) v Jean-Marc Bosman)*, para 82 *et seq*, 95 *et seq*; Case C-281/98 *Roman Angonese v Cassa di Risparmio di Bolzano SpA*, para 30 *et seq*.

[75] K Preedy, *Drittwirkung*, 56 *et seq*; see also J Lübke, *Kapitalverkehrs- und Niederlassungsfreiheit*, 258.

[76] M Jaensch, *Unmittelbare Drittwirkung*, 263 *et seq*.

[77] W-H Roth, 'Drittwirkung', 1246 *et seq*.

[78] JA Usher, *Law of Money*, 25 *et seq*; C Ohler, Art. 56 EC (2002), mn 244; G Ress and J Ukrow, Art. 56 EC (2002), mn 69; F Kainer, *Unternehmensübernahmen*, 242 *et seq*; J Lübke, *Kapitalverkehrs- und Niederlassungsfreiheit*, 265; for a different view: A Glaesner, Art. 56 EC (2000), mn 17; indirect effect on private persons by the fact of the legislature's direct obligation to observe the Treaty: eg, R Eckhoff, 'Kapital- und Zahlungsverkehr', mn 1770; R Streinz and S Leible, 'Drittwirkung', 464 *et seq*; JCW Müller, *Kapitalverkehrsfreiheit*, 151; AC Digel, 'Europäischer Finanzmarkt', Inaugural-Dissertation, Eberhard-Karls-Universität, 114 *et seq*; G Ress and J Ukrow, Art. 56 EC (2002), mn 68 but also approving a limited horizontal direct effect of 'intermediary powers', *cf* G Ress and J Ukrow, Art. 56 EC (2002), mn 69.

these two systems has not *per se* led to the conclusion that they are mutually exclusive.[79] For cases in which private market participants unilaterally restrict party autonomy of the other private party participants without the latter having the chance to escape this situation, the application of the fundamental freedoms to this State-like restriction secures the optimal allocation of the resources in the Common Market.[80] Applying the fundamental freedoms to such narrowly defined situations averts the danger of depriving the competition rules of their scope of application.[81] Moreover, such a construction does not run counter to the underlying idea of Art 86(1) EC, which deals with undertakings governed by private law.[82] While the actions of those undertakings—even though they are governed by private law—are attributed to the State because they are subject to State influence, the horizontal direct effect is based on the notion of overwhelming dominance of a private market participant over others of their ilk. In Art 86(1) EC, the exercise of such overwhelming dominance by the undertaking is no precondition.[83] Hence, the concept of horizontal direct effect does not deprive Art 86(1) EC of its unique scope of application.

Certainly, a private person bound to the freedoms must have recourse to grounds of justification that can be envisaged in his Community fundamental rights, especially the general freedom to act.[84]

All in all, Art 56(1) EC is horizontally directly effective in cases in which a measure of a private person is State-like in the sense mentioned above. However, it is worth stressing once more that applying free movement of capital among private persons constitutes only the *ultima ratio*.

6. Summary so Far

Article 56(1) EC is vertically directly effective in intra-Community and third country contexts.

---

[79] F Kainer, *Unternehmensübernahmen*, 228 *et seq*, 231, *et seq*, 243 for further references.
[80] *Cf* K Preedy, *Drittwirkung*, 123 *et seq*.
[81] J Lübke, *Kapitalverkehrs- und Niederlassungsfreiheit*, 261 *et seq*. See also Case 229/83 *Association des Centres distributeurs Édouard Leclerc and others v SARL 'Au blé vert' and others*; E Steindorff, 'Drittwirkung', 583.
[82] For a different view: W-H Roth, 'Drittwirkung', 1243 *et seq*.
[83] J Lübke, *Kapitalverkehrs- und Niederlassungsfreiheit*, 262.
[84] K Vieweg and A Röthel, 'Verbandsautonomie und Grundfreiheiten', 24 *et seq*; A Randelzhofer and U Forsthoff, vor Art. 39–55 EC (2001), 81 *et seq*; C Ohler, Art. 56 EC (2002), mn 244; J Lübke, *Kapitalverkehrs- und Niederlassungsfreiheit*, 265; see also Case C-281/98 *Roman Angonese v Cassa di Risparmio di Bolzano SpA*, para 42 *et seq*, where the Court states that a private measure 'could be justified only if it were based on objective factors unrelated to the nationality of the persons concerned and if it were in proportion to the aim legitimately pursued'. For a consideration of the level of the scope of application: D Schaefer, *Unmittelbare Wirkung*, 210 *et seq*, 233 *et seq*; P-C Müller-Graff, Art. 28 EC (2003), mn 306; H Parpart, *Unmittelbare Bindung*, 361 *et seq*.

The freedom's guarantees are not bound to a particular nationality or place of habitual residence of the market participants. The place of residence, though, may gain significance for the purpose of identifying the cross-border link of a given transaction or in order to verify whether a transaction displays a sufficient link to the Community.

Any private market participant, natural and legal persons alike, can rely on the freedom. Following the gist of Art 48(2) EC, legal persons that were established on the basis of public law are also covered by the personal scope as long as they carry out economic activities for financial gain. The Member State, the Community, and their respective institutions, as well as third countries, cannot rely on the freedom. However, a private person who entered into dealings with those entities is covered by Art 56(1) EC.

The freedom is predominantly addressed to the Member States. Their measures are all-encompassingly covered irrespective of whether they act in a sovereign capacity or through the means of private law. A Member State is not only under the duty to refrain from any restrictive conduct, but is also under the positive obligation to prevent any private conduct restricting free capital movement.

The group of addressees extends to the Community and its institutions. Private persons can also be subject to Art 56(1) EC if their measures are State-like in the sense that they unilaterally restrict the party autonomy of other private market participants without the latter having the chance to escape this situation.

VI

Exceptions to the Freedom Applicable to Intra-Community and Third Country Situations

1. Introduction

In principle, Art 56(1) EC comprehensively liberalizes cross-border direct investment irrespective of whether it occurs in an intra-Community or third country context. It will, however, not come as a real surprise that this liberalization is not without exception. The EC Treaty allows for certain national or Community measures even though they might restrict cross-border direct investment. In this and the following chapter, those exceptions will be identified and discussed.

For systematic reasons, they will be split into two clusters: those exceptions applying to intra-Community and third country capital movements alike, and those that exclusively relate to third country capital movement. While the latter will be the concern of the following chapter,[1] here I will deal with those exceptions applicable in intra-Community and third country contexts alike.

The written exceptions applying to intra-Community and third country capital movements alike are basically enshrined in Art 58(1) lit. b EC. The first group of exceptions in Art 58(1) lit. b EC grants to the Member States the right to take the requisite measures to prevent infringement of national laws and regulations. The provision refers, by way of example, to measures in the area of taxation, which also constitutes the most important field of application. The inclusion of such a provision, unique among the fundamental freedoms, together with Art 58(1) lit. a, (3) EC, can be seen as the Member States' effort to respond to a development in the case law at the time when the Treaty of Maastricht was negotiated.[2] The Member States simply felt that their sovereignty was too curtailed by the Court, which started to dismantle restrictions on freedoms flowing from national tax regulations.[3]

---

[1] See Chapter VII.
[2] HG Ruppe, 'Kapitalverkehrsfreiheit', 19.
[3] *Cf* Case 270/83 *Commission v French Republic (Re Corporation Tax and Shareholders' Tax Credits: 'avoir fiscal'*; U Haferkamp, *Kapitalverkehrsfreiheit*, 114.

The second group of exceptions provided for in Art 58(1) lit. b EC—also only found in the chapter on capital movement—allows the Member States to restrict the fundamental freedom in order to run procedures for the declaration of capital movements for the purposes of administrative or statistical information.

The only 'common denominator' contained in similar form in every chapter on the fundamental freedoms, constitutes the classic *ordre public* formula embodied as the third group of exceptions in Art 58(1) lit. b EC.

The aforementioned provision is complemented by Art 58(2) EC, which makes reference to the exceptions accepted in the ambit of the freedom of establishment. Outside of the chapter on capital movement, exceptions might be found in Art 297 EC and, for individual Member States, in certain accession treaties. In contrast to some views in legal writing, which are shared by a number of Advocates General, Art 295 EC does not constitute an exception to the freedom.

Exceptions to the freedom that apply to both intra-Community and third county capital movement are not limited to those expressly stated in the Treaty. The Court firmly established that non-written grounds of justification may also be relied on by the Member States when restricting a freedom. In this study, I refer to this jurisprudence as the 'rule of reason', also commonly known as the 'first Cassis principle'.

The following discussion will by and large follow the structure discussed above. The focus will be on working out possible differences in construction depending on whether the exceptions operate with regards to an intra-Community or a third country direct investment.

2. Exceptions by virtue of Article 58 EC: Grounds of Justification and Reference Provision

Article 58 EC can be split into three characteristically distinct regulatory parts:

Paragraph (1) lit. b sets out the express grounds of justification within the Treaty chapter on free movement of capital (and freedom of payments), which apply to both intra-Community and third country situations. As a general rule of construction, grounds of justification are principally to be interpreted strictly.[4] Against this background, the seemingly 'open-ended list'[5] within this part of the provision—national measures aimed at the prevention of infringements of national law and regulations do not imperatively but only 'in particular' relate to the area of taxation or supervision of financial institutions—raises the question of the limits of Art 58(1) lit. b EC.

---

[4] C Ohler, Art. 58 EC (2002), mn 1.
[5] Ibid. JCW Müller, *Kapitalverkehrsfreiheit*, 181; for a different view: A Honrath, *Kapitalverkehr*, 77 *et seq*.

The second regulatory part of Art 58 EC is formed by para (1) lit. a and para (3), which, as previously argued,[6] must be read together. Article 58(1) lit. a EC states that Member States may apply relevant provisions of their tax law that distinguish between resident and non-resident[7] taxpayers and on the basis of the place where the capital is invested.[8] Moreover, Art 58(3) EC provides that 'the measures and procedures referred to in paragraphs 1 and 2 shall not constitute a means of arbitrary discrimination or a disguised restriction on the free movement of capital and payments as defined in Article 56'.

In respectful concurrence with Schön[9] and others, I have already set forth above[10] that Art 58(1) lit. a EC read together with para (3) and the settled case law neither constitutes a *domaine réservé* for tax rules nor grounds of justification that have an independent scope of application. With the Court's jurisprudence in mind, the situation can be depicted as follows: Art 56(1) EC prohibits, inter alia, any discrimination based on residence or the place of investment. Article 58(1) lit. a EC allows for continued application of national measures employing the aforementioned distinguishing criteria. In accordance with Art 58(3) EC, however, those measures must pursue a legitimate public interest and be proportionate. If all this is taken together, it becomes apparent that Art 58(1) lit. a EC, while probably thought by the drafters to be of a constitutive nature,[11] is superfluous today and will not be further discussed in this section.

The third and last regulatory part of Art 58 EC constitutes para (2); it does not establish grounds of justification in its own right, but is a reference provision. It mirrors Art 43(2) EC within the ambit of the freedom of establishment. As will be explained,[12] both provisions resolve a possible conflict of competing freedoms on the level of grounds of justification by allowing for justification of restrictive measures on grounds of either freedom. It suffices that a restriction serves a legitimate interest recognized within the ambit of either the freedom of establishment or free movement of capital.

a. Exceptions based on Article 58(1) lit. b EC: Intra-Community Context

Article 58(1) lit. b EC—containing three distinct groups of grounds of justification[13]—allows the Member States:

---

[6] See Chapter IV. 2. b. (4) (a) iv.
[7] For a discussion of the notion of 'place of residence', refer to footnote 245 of Chapter IV and Chapter IV. 2. b. (4) (a).
[8] For a discussion of the notion of 'place where the capital is invested', refer to footnote 246 of Chapter IV and Chapter IV. 2. b. (4) (a) iv.
[9] W Schön, 'Kapitalverkehrsfreiheit', 766 *et seq.*
[10] For a lengthy discussion, see Chapter IV. 2. b. (4) (a) iv.
[11] *Cf* HG Ruppe, 'Kapitalverkehrsfreiheit', 23.
[12] See Chapter VI. 2. c.
[13] The provision transferred Art 4 (1) of the EC Capital Movements Directive [Directive 88/361/EEC] into the Treaty (1st group and 2nd group) and, on the other hand, introduced an *ordre public*

to take all requisite measures to prevent infringements of national law and regulations, in particular in the field of taxation and the prudential supervision of financial institutions [1st group], or

to lay down procedures for the declaration of capital movements for purposes of administrative or statistical information [2nd group], or

to take measures which are justified on grounds of public policy or public security [3rd group].

Article 58(1) lit. b EC may not be (ab-)used by the Member States to disguise motivations of a purely economic nature.[14] As in the ambit of other freedoms, they do not constitute a valid consideration capable of justifying a restriction on the freedom.[15] Competition between the different economic systems of the Member States is inherent in the Treaty. The Member States, therefore, must prove that a given national measure serves in its aims and effect predominantly a non-economic legitimate public interest.[16] As long as one can objectively establish that such an interest is pursued, side-effects of an economic nature, even if they might be intended by the respective Member State, must be neglected.[17]

The following discussion will first address each group of grounds of justification separately with respect to its scope of application, predominantly giving attention to the first and third groups, which are the most relevant ones in practice. Within the first group, the focus is placed on national measures securing effective fiscal supervision and preventing tax evasion and avoidance. They carry great potential for protectionist interferences with direct investments, though not constituting a phenomenon specific to this economic activity. Moreover, also in the context of the first group of grounds of justification, I shall address the nature of this group, seemingly an open-ended list, which calls into question the need for a 'dual system' of grounds of justification—ie, written and unwritten—within the ambit of free movement of capital. The discussion in the context of the third group, referring to the *ordre public* exception, will revolve around the question of whether and to what degree it allows the Member States to self-judge public policy and public security requirements. The *ordre public* clause constitutes the most important potential legal basis for saving national measures aiming specifically at the restriction of cross-border direct investment.

---

exception of the kind already found in the ambit of other freedoms to that of capital movement (3rd group).

[14] G Ress and J Ukrow, Art. 58 EC (2002), mn 4; M Sedlaczek, 'Kapitalverkehrsfreiheit', 57; U Haferkamp, *Kapitalverkehrsfreiheit*, 115 *et seq*; A Honrath, *Kapitalverkehr*, 78 *et seq*.

[15] An exception from the generally excepted notion.

[16] For further references C Ohler, Art. 58 EC (2002), mn 3.

[17] U Haferkamp, *Kapitalverkehrsfreiheit*, 116 *et seq*. See A Cordewener, *Grundfreiheiten*, 134 *et seq*, with further references, for a very critical account of the interpretation of the notion of 'economic' in the case law of the Court.

As a second step, I shall elaborate on the application of the proportionality test within the ambit of Art 58(1) lit. b EC. It is the Court's rigorous application of this test—which is to be welcomed—that has caused most attempts to justify restrictive national measures on the basis of the abovementioned groups to be unsuccessful. Within this section, the discussion will in particular centre upon the permissibility of 'prior authorization regimes' and of additional burdens on cross-border direct investment due to alleged 'administrative difficulties' in supervising such activity.

(1) Preventing Infringements of National Law and Regulations

The first group of grounds of justification relates to the prevention of infringement of national law and regulations. The national legal orders of the Member States are subject to protection.[18] Given that it is the aim of the first group of grounds of justification to prevent the infringement or circumvention of national law and regulations, the national measures capable of justification under this heading must be preventive in nature and flank the enforcement of other national legislation.[19] It goes without saying that the national legislation to be protected must not directly aim to restrict free movement of capital. Rather, such national legislation could not realize its full effectiveness if the monitoring of its enforcement were to be prevented or interfered with due to freedom of capital movement.[20]

(a) National Measures in the Field of Taxation

Measures in the field of taxation are those which provide control mechanisms and sanctions for the effective enforcement of substantial tax law. Thus, the first group of grounds of justification constitutes the express basis[21] for national measures ensuring effective fiscal supervision and preventing tax evasion (fraud) or

---

[18] S Weber, 'Kapitalverkehr', 564; T Schürmann, Art. 58 EC (2006), mn 6. Due to the fact that the *ordre public* formula at the end of Art 58(1) lit. b EC, to which I refer as the 3rd group of grounds of justification, implicitly also serves, inter alia, the protection of the legal orders of the Member States. The 3rd group and the 1st group in theory could overlap in some areas. [F Kimms, *Kapitalverkehrsfreiheit*, 191; J Bröhmer, Art. 58 EC (2002), mn 10] This partial 'duplication' can be described as a 'congenital defect' of the provision, but a defect without significant bearing. This duplication becomes comprehensible by considering the drafting history of Art 58(1) lit. b EC. The first (as well as the second) group of grounds of justification contained in Art 58(1) lit. b EC originate from Art 4(1) of the EC Capital Movements Directive [Directive 88/361/EEC] as already mentioned. The inclusion of the *ordre public* formula as the third group of grounds of justification results from a desire to draft the fundamental freedoms as much as possible in parallel terms. [U Haferkamp, *Kapitalverkehrsfreiheit*, 128]

[19] S Weber, 'Kapitalverkehr', 564; G Ress and J Ukrow, Art. 58 EC (2002), mn 21.

[20] A Honrath, *Kapitalverkehr*, 96; J Bröhmer, Art. 58 EC (2002), mn 10.

[21] *Cf* Case C-478/98 *Commission v Kingdom of Belgium (Re Loans issued abroad)*, para 40 *et seq*; Case C-436/00 *X and Y v Riksskatteverket*, para 72; Case C-315/02 *Anneliese Lenz v Finanzlandesdirektion für Tirol*, para 44 *et seq*. See also G Ress and J Ukrow, Art. 56 EC (2002), mn 79.

avoidance (abuse);²² within the ambit of the other freedoms, they are based on the rule of reason.²³

The varying legal base for these grounds of justification is not without problems: Written grounds of justification apply both to national measures that constitute discrimination and to those that form a mere hindrance. Hence, national measures ensuring effective fiscal supervision and preventing tax evasion or avoidance can be justified within the ambit of free movement of capital even though they might be discriminatory.²⁴ We learned above that within the ambit of the other freedoms, national measures ensuring effective fiscal supervision and preventing tax evasion or avoidance can only be justified by reference to the 'rule of reason'. The 'rule of reason', which one can still frequently read in many standard texts on Community law but also in judgments of the Court,²⁵ purportedly applies only to measures that merely hinder market access but not to those that discriminate.

At first sight, this might lead to the view that within the ambit of free movement of capital, restrictive national measures can be justified more easily than within the scope of the other fundamental freedoms. However, this view could prove to be deceptive. Only if it is true that discriminatory national measures cannot be justified by the 'rule of reason' could one indeed speak of a disparity among the fundamental freedoms. This study respectfully disagrees with such an understanding of the 'rule of reason', as I will explain in more detail further below.²⁶ At this point in the discussion, it suffices to note that there is no disparity between free movement of capital and the other freedoms concerning the justification of national measures ensuring effective fiscal supervision and preventing tax evasion or avoidance.

I stated above that measures in the field of taxation are in particular those that ensure effective fiscal supervision and prevent tax evasion or avoidance. More specifically, effective fiscal supervision comprises the process of gathering the necessary information in order to calculate the taxes due, but must also extend

---

²² *Cf*, eg, Case C-439/97 *Sandoz GmbH v Finanzlandesdirektion für Wien, Niederösterreich und Burgenland*, para 37 *et seq*; Case C-478/98 *Commission v Kingdom of Belgium (Re Loans issued abroad)*, para 40 *et seq*; Case C-436/00 *X and Y v Riksskatteverket*, para 72; Case C-334/02 *Commission v French Republic (Re Tax on Income Arising from Investment)*, para 27; Case C-315/02 *Anneliese Lenz v Finanzlandesdirektion für Tirol*, para 44 *et seq*.

²³ For example, with respect to 'tax avoidance' *cf* Case C-264/96 *Imperial Chemical Industries plc (ICI) v Kenneth Hall Colmer (H.M. Inspector of Taxes)*, para 26. See also G Ress and J Ukrow, Art. 56 EC (2002), mn 79.

²⁴ *Cf*, eg, Case C-478/98 *Commission v Kingdom of Belgium (Re Loans issued abroad)*, para 39 *et seq*. Case C-302/97 *Klaus Konle v Republik Österreich*, para 43 *et seq*; Case C-439/97 *Sandoz GmbH v Finanzlandesdirektion für Wien, Niederösterreich und Burgenland*, para 33 *et seq*.

²⁵ *Cf*, eg, A Haratsch, et al, *Europarecht*, mn 916 *et seq*; G Ress and J Ukrow, Art. 56 EC (2002), mn 81 who cite S Leible, Art. 28 EC (2000), mn 19 *et seq*; Case C-367/98 *Commission v Portuguese Republic (Re Golden Shares I)*, para 49; see also M Sedlaczek, 'Kapitalverkehrsfreiheit', 57.

²⁶ See Chapter VI. 6. a.

to measures that seek to ensure that the established tax claim can be enforced in cross-border situations.[27] The category of measures aiming at prevention of tax evasion or avoidance constitutes a special subsection of 'effective fiscal supervision'.[28] National measures that seek to prevent tax evasion are those that aim to prevent intentional or negligent misrepresentations, or non-disclosure contrary to duty, of significant facts by the taxpayer at the expense of the tax authorities.[29] National measures directed against tax avoidance aim at the prevention of a different behaviour. Within an EC law context, one can speak about tax avoidance if someone resorts to certain cross-border tax planning arrangements in an attempt to utilize the different tax regimes of different States to reduce the amount of tax due by means that are in principle within the law. The decisive characteristics of such tax arrangements are that they are designed to conflict with or defeat the evident intention of the national tax legislation, and they are, therefore, considered harmful by the Member State (in particular by those that charge higher taxes).[30] In the first recital of Directive 77/799/EEC,[31] they are described as:

leading to budget losses and violations of the principle of fair taxation and are liable to bring about distortions of capital movements and of conditions of competition; whereas they therefore affect the operation of the common market.

Such a view is, however, not without problems. Taking advantage of the fundamental freedoms means, inter alia, also taking advantage of different jurisdictions; absent full Community harmonization, competition between different regulatory systems is inherent in the Common Market.[32]

Remaining true to the maxim of interpreting exceptions narrowly, the Court took a firm stance in applying this exception: attempts by the Member States to argue that respective national measures would be justified by reason of ensuring effective fiscal supervision or preventing tax evasion or avoidance were hardly successful within the ambit of free movement of capital or within the sphere of any other freedom. The *Sandoz* case[33] is a rare example of a national measure

---

[27] The enforcement problems are rooted in the general principle of international law that a State cannot enforce tax claims in the territory of another State. Thus, a State must develop mechanisms to ensure that it can enforce its tax claims as long as it can reach the taxpayer. However, national measures that, for example, require a non-resident to pay taxes in a lump sum in advance before the precise amount of taxes due is calculated, must be viewed with caution due to the fact that such regulations are coupled with the restrictive effect of a cash-flow disadvantage. [*Cf* for an in-depth account A Cordewener, *Grundfreiheiten*, 943 *et seq*]

[28] Ibid, 953.   [29] Ibid, 952 for further references.

[30] *Cf* Ibid, 950 *et seq* for further references.

[31] Directive 77/799/EEC.

[32] *Cf* Case 81/87 (Opinion of AG Darmon) *R v H.M. Treasury and Commissioners of Inland Revenue, ex p Daily Mail and General Trust plc*, para 12; see also Case C-196/04 *Cadbury Schweppes and Cadbury Schweppes Overseas Ltd v Commissioners of Inland Revenue*, para 49.

[33] Case C-439/97 *Sandoz GmbH v Finanzlandesdirektion für Wien, Niederösterreich und Burgenland*, para 24; for a discussion see, eg, F Rödler, 'Austrian Stamp Duty'; R Kilches, 'Auslandsdarlehen'; T Steinvorth, 'Sandoz', 24. See also, recently: Case C-446/03 *Marks & Spencer*

aiming to combat tax evasion/avoidance that could be justified on the basis of Art 58(1) lit. b EC (1st group). This lack of success was predominantly due to a rigorous application of the proportionality test, to which I shall turn in detail further below.[34]

(b) National Measures in the Field of Prudential Supervision of Financial Institutions

The inclusion of prudential supervision of financial institutions[35] as a subject of protection in Art 58(1) lit. b EC (1st group) serves first and foremost the functions of protecting investors and securing an overall sound financial system. Building and maintaining trust in financial institutions in particular and in the integrity of the financial system in general, recalling the possible devastating impact bankruptcies and market misconduct could have, is vital for the national economy as a whole.[36]

As with national measures in the field of taxation, in the area at hand it does not suffice to refer to the necessity of supervision in general.[37] The national measure must pursue legitimate public interests such as those already mentioned: investor protection[38] or maintaining stability[39] in or protecting the reputation[40] of the financial market. Moreover, the scope of application of this ground of justification is not only limited by the general consideration that exceptions must be construed narrowly but also by the fact that the autonomous regulatory powers of the Member States have to some degree been restricted by Community harmonization.[41]

---

plc v David Halsey (H.M. Inspector of Taxes), para 49 *et seq*, 57; criticizing the aforementioned judgment: M Lang, 'Marks & Spencer II', 7.

[34] See Chapter IV 2. a. (4).
[35] 'Financial institution' is defined in Annex I of Directive 88/361/EEC as 'banks, savings banks and institutions specializing in the provision of short-term, medium-term and long-term credit, and insurance companies, building societies, investment companies and other institutions of like character'. The aforementioned Directive can serve as a means of interpretation of the Treaty provisions on free movement of capital. See Chapter II. 2. a. See also Ohler, who has recourse to the definition in Art 4 No 1 of Regulation 3604/93/EC. [C Ohler, Art. 58 EC (2002), para 14] Ress/Ukrow seek to employ the definitions contained in Art 1 No 1 of Directive 2000/12/EC (credit institution) and Art 4 (1) No 1 of Directive 2004/39/EC (investment firm). [G Ress and J Ukrow, Art. 58 EC (2002), mn 24]
[36] U Haferkamp, *Kapitalverkehrsfreiheit*, 129 *et seq*.
[37] *Cf*, eg, Case C-254/97 *Société Baxter, B. Braun Médical SA, Société Fresenius France and Laboratoires Bristol-Myers-Squibb SA v Premier Ministre, Ministère du Travail et des Affaires sociales, Ministère de l'Economie et des Finances and Ministère de l'Agriculture, de la Pêche et de l'Alimentation*, para 19 *et seq*.
[38] K-P Follak, 'Banking Supervision', 389; P Royla, *Finanzmarktaufsicht*, 23 *et seq*.
[39] Ibid.
[40] Case C-384/93 *Alpine Investments BV v Minister van Financiën*, para 44. The protection of the reputation of the financial market served as a legitimate public interest for prohibiting so-called 'cold calling'. This idea is of general value. [*Cf* C Ohler, Art. 58 EC (2002), mn 22]
[41] Probably the most important EC regulatory measure in this respect is Directive 2006/48/EC 'Bank Directive (Recast)'. However, it is worth mentioning that, in principle, financial supervision remains on the national level. [G Ress and J Ukrow, Art. 56 EC (2002), mn 128] Art 105(5) EC

(c) National Measures in other Fields—A Gradual Changeover to the Rule of Reason

Article 58(1) lit. b EC (1st group) in its wording seems to provide for an 'open-ended' list ('in particular') of exceptions to free movement of capital. The Court in *Bordessa*—a judgment based on the equivalent provision found in Art 4 of Directive 88/361 EEC[42]—appears at first sight to confirm such a reading when stating that '[i]t follows that other measures [than the ones explicitly mentioned] are also permitted insofar as they are designed to prevent illegal activities of *comparable seriousness*'.[43] It enumerated for example money laundering, drug trafficking, or terrorism as comparable in their seriousness.[44] In *Konle,* the Court referred to the prevention of infringement of national legislation on secondary residences.[45]

Such an 'open-ended' list is a singular occurrence among the fundamental freedoms. It does not come as a surprise, therefore, that some commentators[46] cast doubt on the necessity of a 'dual system' of grounds of justification[47]—consisting

---

attributes only supporting functions—which do not go beyond consultation—to the European Central Bank. [*Cf* B Kempen, Art. 105 EC (2003), mn 16]. Furthermore, a transfer of more far-reaching competences in pursuance of Art 105(6) EC has not yet taken place. [B Kempen, Art. 105 EC (2003), mn 25] For further details on EC regulatory measures in the area of financial supervision, refer to G Ress and J Ukrow, Art. 56 EC (2002), mn 115 *et seq.*

[42] Directive 88/361/EEC.

[43] [Emphasis added] Joined Cases C-358/93 and C-416/93 *Criminal proceedings against Aldo Bordessa and Vicente Marí Mellado and Concepción Barbero Maestre*, para 21. See for a third country context: Joined Cases C-163/94, C-165/94, and C-250/94 *Criminal proceedings against Lucas Emilio Sanz de Lera, Raimundo Díaz Jiménez and Figen Kapanoglu*, para 24 *et seq*. See R Smits, 'Payments and Capital', 253 for a critical account of the *Bordessa* judgment. He states that he regrets 'the Court's decision to permit advance declaration of such [currency export] transactions as being within the range of measures which Art. 73 D [now, after amendment, Art. 58] permits. Applying different regimes to intra-State and inter-State [ie, intra-Community] transactions is . . . contrary to the letter as well as the spirit of the internal market.'

[44] Joined Cases C-358/93 and C-416/93 *Criminal proceedings against Aldo Bordessa and Vicente Marí Mellado and Concepción Barbero Maestre*, para 21. Article 4 of Directive 88/361/EEC did not contain the *ordre public* exception that is now contained in Art 58 (1) lit. b EC. Measures, eg, to prevent drug trafficking or terrorism would today probably be better placed under the heading of the *ordre public* exception. Joined Cases C-358/93 and C-416/93 *Criminal proceedings against Aldo Bordessa and Vicente Marí Mellado and Concepción Barbero Maestre*, para 22; A Honrath, *Kapitalverkehr*, 96 *et seq*; L Flynn, 'Coming of Age', 795; U Haferkamp, *Kapitalverkehrsfreiheit*, 131. Not differentiating: J Bröhmer, Art. 58 EC (2002), mn 9. Unclear: Joined Cases C-163/94, C-165/94, and C-250/94 *Criminal proceedings against Lucas Emilio Sanz de Lera, Raimundo Díaz Jiménez and Figen Kapanoglu*, para 22.

[45] Case C-302/97 *Klaus Konle v Republik Österreich*, para 43 *et seq.*

[46] Not seeing the need for the rule of reason within the ambit of free movement of capital: JCW Müller, *Kapitalverkehrsfreiheit*, 169 *et seq*, 181; R Eckhoff, 'Kapital- und Zahlungsverkehr', mn 1721.

[47] *Cf* Case 120/78 *Rewe-Zentral AG v Bundesmonopolverwaltung für Branntwein* ('Cassis de Dijon'), para 8. One could debate the power of persuasion of a doctrinal construction that interprets written grounds strictly and denies analogies, but on the other hand, introduces additional grounds, called mandatory requirements in the general interest, through the back door. However, such criticism would have to be advanced against the Court's interpretation of the freedoms in general and, therefore, will not be the concern of this study.

of explicit grounds on one side and the 'rule of reason' on the other—in the ambit of free movement of capital.

This study does not share those doubts, although it acknowledges that there is no sharp dividing line between the two groups, but a gradual changeover.[48] To begin with, in contrast to the proponents of a 'singular system' of grounds of justification, it is suggested that the 'open-ended' list is in fact not as open-ended as others would have us believe. While the applicability of this group is not limited to measures in the field of taxation and the supervision of financial institutions,[49] national measures must aim to prevent illicit activities in order to be covered. Thus, the 'open-ended' list is limited by an 'ancillary function' nexus between the 'anti-infringement rule' and the rule that enforcement shall be secured by the former.[50]

Looking at its more recent judgments, the Court also proceeds from the assumption that within the ambit of free movement of capital, a 'dual system' of grounds of justification applies, which also means that free capital movement follows the converging tendencies in the interpretation among the fundamental freedoms on the level of grounds of justification. This is well illustrated by the Court's judgment in *Commission v Portuguese Republic (Golden Shares I)*:

> The free movement of capital, as a fundamental principle of the Treaty, may be restricted only by national rules which are justified by *reasons referred to in Article 73d (1) of the Treaty* [now, after amendment, Art 58(1)] or by *overriding requirements of the general interest* and which are applicable to all persons and undertakings pursuing an activity in the territory of the host Member State. Furthermore, in order to be so justified, the national legislation must be suitable for securing the objective which it pursues and must not go beyond what is necessary in order to attain it, so as to accord with the principle of proportionality.[51]

Permitting free movement of capital to participate in the general system of construction of the fundamental freedoms allows for the accommodation of legitimate public interests that would otherwise be difficult to attain. It is true that within the ambit of free movement of capital there are legitimate public interests, such as effective fiscal supervision and the prevention of tax abuse and evasion, which—in contrast to other freedoms—are covered expressly by Art 58(1) lit. b EC.[52] However, limiting the grounds of justification to those set out within this

---

[48] Holding the same opinion, eg, A Cordewener, *Grundfreiheiten*, 928; G Ress and J Ukrow, Art. 56 EC (2002), mn 77.
[49] G Ress and J Ukrow, Art. 58 EC (2002), mn 13.
[50] M Sedlaczek, 'Kapitalverkehrsfreiheit', 59, esp. fn 121. See also the introductory remarks to Chapter VI. 2.
[51] [Emphases added] Case C-367/98 *Commission v Portuguese Republic (Re Golden Shares I)*, para 49. This jurisprudence can be described as established case law.
[52] *Cf* Case C-478/98 *Commission v Kingdom of Belgium (Re Loans issued abroad)*, para 40 *et seq*; Case C-436/00 *X and Y v Riksskatteverket*, para 72; Case C-315/02 *Anneliese Lenz v Finanzlandesdirektion für Tirol*, para 44 *et seq*. See also G Ress and J Ukrow, Art. 56 EC (2002), mn 79.

provision would lead to an exclusion from the possibility of justification of national measures serving likewise legitimate and accepted public interests.[53] Such legitimate public interests, for example, relate to the protection of the environment,[54] the preservation of viable small-scale agriculture,[55] town, country, and regional planning,[56] and cultural aspects,[57] but also to fiscal cohesion,[58] foreseeability and transparency of the mortgage system,[59] defence of the consumer,[60] or the fairness of commercial transactions.[61] One could indeed debate whether such concerns could not be dealt with by the *ordre public* exception instead, being based on the 'rule of reason'. This, however, is a different discussion, which questions the Court's doctrinal construction of the permissible exceptions to the freedoms in general and will, therefore, not be my concern here.

In sum, while there is a partial crossover of mandatory requirements in the public interest accepted under the 'rule of reason' and the subjects of protection of Art 58(1) lit. b EC, it appears that there is still sufficient room for the application of the 'First Cassis Principle' within the ambit of free movement of capital. An exclusion of those interests within this ambit would not only distinguish free capital movement from the other freedoms, for which this study cannot identify sufficient justification, but it runs counter to the converging

---

[53] U Haferkamp, *Kapitalverkehrsfreiheit*, 151; G Ress and J Ukrow, Art. 56 EC (2002), para 77.
[54] Case 302/86 *Commission v Kingdom of Denmark*, para 8 *et seq*.
[55] Case C-452/01 *Margarethe Ospelt and Schlössle Weissenberg Familienstiftung*, para 39 *et seq*. The public interest of protection of small-scale agriculture is to be distinguished from that of town or regional planning: *cf* Case C-452/01 (Opinion of AG Geelhoed) *Margarethe Ospelt and Schlössle Weissenberg Familienstiftung*, para 85 *et seq*.
[56] Case C-302/97 *Klaus Konle v Republik Österreich*, mn 40; Joined Cases C-515/99 and C-527/99 to C-540/99 and Joined Cases C-519/99 to C-524/99 and C-526/99 *Hans Reisch and Others v Bürgermeister der Landeshauptstadt Salzburg and Grundverkehrsbeauftragter des Landes Salzburg and Anton Lassacher and Others v Grundverkehrsbeauftragter des Landes Salzburg and Grundverkehrslandeskommission des Landes Salzburg*, mn 34.
[57] Case C-148/91 *Vereniging Veronica Omroep Organisatie v Commissariaat voor de Media*, mn 10.
[58] First mentioned in Case C-204/90 *Hanns-Martin Bachmann v The Belgian State*, para 21 *et seq*; Case C-300/90 *Commission v Kingdom of Belgium (Re Deduction of Insurance Contributions)*, para 14 *et seq*. This study is of the opinion that the ground of justification of fiscal cohesion does not fall within the scope of Art 58(1) lit. b EC (1st group), but it constitutes an accepted mandatory requirement in the general interest within the ambit of the rule of reason. Case law supporting this view: Case C-35/98 *Staatssecretaris van Financiën v B.G.M. Verkooijen*, para 49 *et seq*; Case C-478/98 *Commission v Kingdom of Belgium (Re Loans issued abroad)*, para 35 *et seq*; Case C-315/02 *Anneliese Lenz v Finanzlandesdirektion für Tirol*, para 34 *et seq*; Case C-319/02 *Petri Manninen*, para 40 *et seq*; Case C-242/03 *Ministre des Finances v Jean-Claude Weidert and Élisabeth Paulus*, para 20 *et seq*; probably suggesting otherwise: Case C-436/00 *X and Y v Riksskatteverket*, para 72; of the same opinion as the Court in the aforementioned judgment: M Dahlberg, *Direct Taxation*, 297.
[59] Case C-222/97 *Manfred Trummer and Peter Mayer*, para 29 *et seq*.
[60] First mentioned in Case 120/78 *Rewe-Zentral AG v Bundesmonopolverwaltung für Branntwein ('Cassis de Dijon')*, para 8.
[61] First mentioned ibid.

tendencies of construction of the fundamental freedoms.[62] The partial overlap can be explained by the 'delayed development' of free movement of capital into a full-fledged fundamental freedom until the Maastricht Treaty. In the context of the Maastricht revision, mandatory requirements, then only accepted as implied grounds of justification, found their way into the Treaty text.

(2) Procedures for the Declaration of Capital Movements for the Purpose of Administrative or Statistical Information

By virtue of Art 58(1) lit. b EC (2nd group), the Member States are authorized to install and maintain procedures with regard to capital movements for administrative or statistical information.[63] Measures covered by this exception, for example, relate to declaration procedures with respect to foreign direct investment for the purpose of compiling the balance of payments statistics of Member States[64] or to assorted statistics gathered by the central banks in the area of banking and finance. It already follows from the pursued aim of gathering information that an authorization regime would not be permissible under the heading of this Treaty exception, but a declaration procedure would suffice.[65] Recalling that reporting and declaration duties can place a heavy burden on capital movements and make them less attractive, a *laissez-faire* attitude towards national measures that impose such duties is therefore not appropriate. As in the ambit of all other groups within Art 58(1) lit. b EC, the exception must be interpreted strictly.

(3) Public Policy and Public Security—The Ordre Public Exception

The third group of grounds of justification contained in Art 58(1) lit. b EC relates to public policy and security. The *ordre public* exception within the ambit of free movement of capital echoes similar provisions in the ambit of other fundamental freedoms and, thus, exemplifies and confirms the converging tendencies among them. On the other hand, Art 58(1) lit. b EC (3rd group) is more narrowly defined than Art 30, 1st sentence EC, Art 46, 1st sentence EC, or Art 55 EC, which also have recourse to public morality, public health, or official authority. This difference in wording, however, seems not to strike the Court. The ECJ transposed its jurisprudence developed within the ambits of other freedoms to that of capital movement.[66] Within this jurisprudence, the Court has avoided providing a

---

[62] Also arguing along these lines: U Haferkamp, *Kapitalverkehrsfreiheit*, 151. See also C Ohler, Art. 58 EC (2002), mn 11, 19 *et seq.*
[63] In regard to other freedoms, no such competence exists. [L Flynn, 'Coming of Age', 796]
[64] See in this respect § 26(2) of AWG (Germany) in connection with §§ 58a and 58b of AWV (Germany) and the relevant decision of the Administrative Court of Munich: VG München, 21 May 1996, WM 1997, 286 *et seq.*
[65] Joined Cases C-163/94, C-165/94, and C-250/94 *Criminal proceedings against Lucas Emilio Sanz de Lera, Raimundo Díaz Jiménez and Figen Kapanoglu*, para 27 *et seq.*
[66] Case C-54/99 *Association Eglise de Scientologie de Paris and Scientology International Reserves Trust v The Prime Minister*. See also N Dautzenberg, 'Steuervorbehalt', 542, who states that the *ordre public* exception is of merely declaratory nature.

comprehensive general Community law definition of what constitutes 'public policy' or 'public security' beyond the rather expressionless statements that the former concept relates to established basic rules that touch upon the fundamental interests of society[67] and the latter to the fundamental interests of a Member State to maintain essential public services and to safeguard the functioning of its institutions.[68] The Court, therefore, identifies valid public policy or security interests in each individual case that allow the Court to respond to changing needs of the Member States in this area.[69] In the words of the ECJ, this reads as follows:

> [Although} the Member States are still, in principle, free to determine the requirements of public policy and public security in the light of their national needs [,]...their scope cannot be determined unilaterally by each Member State without any control by Community institutions.[70]

A holistic look at the case law shows that in the ambit of free movement of capital too, the *ordre public* exception has to be interpreted strictly[71] and the Member States may rely on it only 'if there is a genuine and sufficient serious threat to the fundamental interest of society'.[72] A mere reference by national legislation to public policy or public security, therefore, does not suffice. In the case of defence, for example, the Member State concerned has to show for each individual case that without the measure, military interests would be exposed to a real, specific, and serious risk, and no less restrictive means would suffice to remedy this risk.[73] It is worth mentioning that a differing view voiced by Advocate General Cosmos, who suggested that in case of defence only a low level review should be applied with respect to Art 58(1) lit. b EC (3rd group),[74] was rejected by the Court. Advocate General Cosmos suggested that a Member State merely needs to

---

[67] Recourse to the concept of public policy 'presupposes, in any event, the existence, in addition to the perturbation of the social order which any infringement of the law involves, of a genuine and sufficiently serious threat to the requirements of public policy affecting one of the *fundamental interests of society*.' [Emphasis added, Case 30/77 *R v Pierre Bouchereau*, para 35]

[68] Case 72/83 *Campus Oil Limited and others v Minister for Industry and Energy and others*, para 34.

[69] G Ress and J Ukrow, Art. 58 EC (2002), mn 34; U Haferkamp, *Kapitalverkehrsfreiheit*, 136. See to this effect: Case 41/74 *Yvonne van Duyn v Home Office*, para 18 *et seq*; Case 30/77 *R v Pierre Bouchereau*, para 31 *et seq*.

[70] Case C-54/99 *Association Eglise de Scientologie de Paris and Scientology International Reserves Trust v The Prime Minister*, para 17.

[71] Settled case law; first mentioned with respect to the concept of public policy in Case 41/74 *Yvonne van Duyn v Home Office*, para 18.

[72] Case C-54/99 *Association Eglise de Scientologie de Paris and Scientology International Reserves Trust v The Prime Minister*, para 17; Case C-483/99 *Commission v French Republic (Re Golden Shares II)*, para 48; Case C-503/99 *Commission v Kingdom of Belgium (Re Golden Shares III)*, para 47. See also C Bond, Art. 68 EEC (1999), § 68.03[2].

[73] Case C-423/98 *Alfredo Albore*, para 21 *et seq*. It is worth noting that the Court in its judgment, however, did not clearly distinguish between Art 58(1) lit. b EC (3rd group) and Art 297 EC.

[74] Case C-423/98 (Opinion of AG Cosmas) *Alfredo Albore,* para 53.

show a formal minimal motivation abiding by the rules of logic and the lessons of common sense.[75]

Having just mentioned the area of defence,[76] the Court also recognized that public security considerations, which can be summarized under the heading of 'ensuring continuity in public services',[77] include 'the objective of ensuring a minimum supply of petroleum products'[78] and electricity or a minimum level of telecommunications services at all times.[79] In this respect, it is important to point out that the activity of placing a direct investment itself does not constitute a sufficient serious threat to public policy or security of a Member State; only certain kinds of direct investments originating from abroad, such as those in the public services or defence sectors,[80] may amount to such a threat.[81]

Moreover, the notion of public policy and public security extends to activities such as combating terrorism[82] or drug trafficking,[83] but it can also cover the

---

[75] Ibid, para 54 *et seq*.
[76] Public security extends also to external security of a Member State: ibid, para 18.
[77] *Cf* Case C-463/00 *Commission v Kingdom of Spain (Re Golden Shares IV)*, para 70.
[78] Initially: Case 72/83 *Campus Oil Limited and others v Minister for Industry and Energy and others*, para 34 *et seq*; within the ambit of free movement of capital: Case C-483/99 *Commission v French Republic (Re Golden Shares II)*, para 47; Case C-503/99 *Commission v Kingdom of Belgium (Re Golden Shares III)*, para 46.
[79] Case C-463/00 *Commission v Kingdom of Spain (Re Golden Shares IV)*, para 71.
[80] German legislation (§ 7(1) and (2) No 5 of *AWG* [AWG (Germany)] in connection with § 52 *AWO* [AWV (Germany)]) provides for a declaration procedure with the option of *ex post facto* opposition against the legal transactions referring to the purchase of resident companies or acquisition of shares in such companies that produce or develop war weapons and other military equipment, or produce cryptographic systems admitted for the transmission of governmental classified information in order to guarantee the vital security interests of the Federal Republic of Germany; this applies in particular if the political and security interests of the Federal Republic of Germany or military security precautions would be endangered as a result of the purchase. § 7(1) and (2) No 5 of *AWG* in connection with § 52 *AWO* and respective Annexes clearly state the strategic assets covered by the legislation and the means available to the authorities. Recourse to the national courts can be had against any kind of restrictive negative decision by the administration. The provisions, moreover, restrict the possibility of prohibition of takeovers in full or in part (at least 25 per cent of the voting rights) to vital security, ie, non-economic, policy considerations, which are further specified by mentioning, by way of example, 'political and security interests of the Federal Republic' and 'military security precautions'. [For further detail on the relevant provisions of the German Foreign Trade and Payments Act, refer to J Bast, § 7 AWG (2006), mn 2, 3, 20 *et seq*; K Friedrich, § 52 AWV (2006); See also D Besse, 'German Foreign Trade Laws'] In this respect, however, it remains to be seen whether this phrase was drafted strictly enough in order to fulfil the requirements in terms of predictability and clarity set by the Court. [*Cf.* K Friedrich, § 52 AWV (2006), mn 45 *et seq*, who is of the opinion that the provisions are in conformity with Community law] In this context, it should be mentioned that currently a draft bill is under discussion that suggests introducing the option of *ex post facto* opposition for all kinds of industry related to the Security interests of Germany. [*Cf.* eg, B Benoit, 'German Call to Curb Foreign Buyers' *Financial Times.com* (12.07.2007); C Teichmann, 'Kapitalverkehrsfreiheit', 365; K Krolop, 'Staatliche Einlasskontrolle bei Staatsfonds und anderen ausländischen Investoren im Gefüge von Kapitalmarktregulierung, nationalem und internationalem Wirtschaftsrecht'; K Krolop, 'Staatsfonds']
[81] See Chapter IV. 2. a. (4).
[82] Note the recent judgment of the Court of First Instance in this respect: Case T-306/01 *Ahmed Ali Yusuf and Al Barakaat International Foundation v Council and Commission*, para 146.
[83] Refer to footnote 44 of this Chapter above.

prohibition of activities of political parties which are directed at overthrowing the constitutional order of a Member State.[84] However, aims of a purely economic nature may not be pursued by the Member States in any way.[85]

As with respect to the first group of grounds of justification, a defence of a restrictive national measure based on the *ordre public* exception barely succeeded due to a strict application of the proportionality test, which will be discussed in the next section.

(4) The Proportionality Test

The reason why most attempts to 'salvage' a restrictive national measure on the basis of Art 58(1) lit. b EC turned out to be fruitless is the rigorous application of the proportionality test in the ambit of this provision.

In this respect, what immediately catches one's attention is a peculiarity contained within the first group of Art 58(1) lit. b EC. The provision demands that all national measures that seek to be justified on the basis thereof must be '*requisite*'.[86] This formula constitutes not only an express reference to the general principle of proportionality but also confirms the general rule of interpretation to construe exceptions narrowly.[87] However, whether it goes beyond a mere declaratory meaning in the sense that within the ambit of free movement of capital an even stricter interpretation is required is unclear. The case law of the Court does not explicitly touch upon this point but transposes the jurisprudence developed with respect to other fundamental freedoms, where no such clause can be found, to the ambit of free movement of capital. This approach, as well as the general converging tendency in interpreting the fundamental freedoms, suggests that the criterion of 'requisite' has no constitutive meaning.[88]

Given that the term 'requisite' does not establish a special, ie, elevated, standard applied to the proportionality test, it is the general one which sets a high hurdle within the first group for national measures to overcome. In abstract terms, the proportionality test asks first whether the measure under scrutiny is suitable for securing the attainment of the objective that it purportedly pursues. Second, the Court requires that the measure at issue does not go beyond what is necessary.[89]

---

[84] G Ress and J Ukrow, Art. 58 EC (2002), mn 36.
[85] Case C-54/99 *Association Eglise de Scientologie de Paris and Scientology International Reserves Trust v The Prime Minister*, para 17; Case C-35/98 *Staatssecretaris van Financiën v B.G.M. Verkooijen*, para 48. See also T Schürmann, Art. 58 EC (2006), mn 8.
[86] See for a general account of the requirement of a measure being 'requisite': G Ress and J Ukrow, Art. 58 EC (2002), mn 15 *et seq*; W Kiemel, Art. 58 EC (2003), mn 19.
[87] G Ress and J Ukrow, Art. 58 EC (2002), mn 15.
[88] U Haferkamp, *Kapitalverkehrsfreiheit*, 131 *et seq*; probably of the same opinion J Bröhmer, Art. 58 EC (2002), mn 10. Ruppe is of the view that the threshold for the justification of restricting national measures is a higher one as compared to the 'usual' balancing of interests within the proportionality test, *cf* HG Ruppe, 'Kapitalverkehrsfreiheit', 20. Unclear: W Kiemel, Art. 58 EC (2003), mn 19; G Ress and J Ukrow, Art. 58 EC (2002), mn 15 *et seq*.
[89] eg, Case C-478/98 *Commission v Kingdom of Belgium (Re Loans issued abroad)*, para 41.

The criterion of 'suitability' or 'appropriateness' acts as a threshold control.[90] On several occasions, the Court has not hesitated to inform the Member States that their measures run 'counter to the objective pursued'[91] or are 'not apt to prevent fraud'.[92] Moreover, it made clear that 'a general presumption of tax evasion or tax fraud cannot justify a fiscal measure'.[93] In order to render the fundamental freedoms effective, one cannot help but concur with the statement that utilizing the fundamental freedoms embodied in the Treaty does not carry the presumption of abuse but the assumption of lawful use.[94] Therefore, the Member States have to prove that in the individual situation there is a real, tangible, and serious danger of infringement of national law and regulations.[95] With respect to measures aiming at the prevention of tax evasion or avoidance, the Court stated that the national measure at issue must specifically be drafted to exclude from a tax advantage only purely artificial schemes designed to circumvent tax law,[96] ie:

> the specific objective of such a restriction must be to prevent conduct involving the creation of wholly artificial arrangements which do not reflect economic reality, with a view to escaping the tax normally due on the profits generated by activities carried out on national territory.[97]

Application of the second test, ie, to prove objectively the absence of less restrictive measures to achieve the aims pursued, within the ambit of this provision

---

[90] L Flynn, 'Coming of Age', 801.

[91] Case C-439/97 *Sandoz GmbH v Finanzlandesdirektion für Wien, Niederösterreich und Burgenland*, para 34.

[92] Ibid, para 35. See also Case C-436/00 *X and Y v Riksskatteverket*, para 63 read in connection with para 72.

[93] Case C-28/95 *A. Leur-Bloem v Inspecteur der Belastingdienst/Ondernemingen Amsterdam 2*, para 44; Case C-264/96 *Imperial Chemical Industries plc (ICI) v Kenneth Hall Colmer (H.M. Inspector of Taxes)*, para 26; Case C-254/97 *Société Baxter, B. Braun Médical SA, Société Fresenius France and Laboratoires Bristol-Myers-Squibb SA v Premier Ministre, Ministère du Travail et des Affaires sociales, Ministère de l'Economie et des Finances and Ministère de l'Agriculture, de la Pêche et de l'Alimentation*, para 19; Case C-478/98 *Commission v Kingdom of Belgium (Re Loans issued abroad)*, para 45. See also Case C-436/00 *X and Y v Riksskatteverket*, para 62 read in connection with para 72.

[94] For the interpretation guiding the model of a 'freedom using, not abusing, market participant' refer to G Ress and J Ukrow, Art. 58 EC (2002), mn 25 *et seq*.

[95] J Bröhmer, Art. 58 EC (2002), mn 13.

[96] Case C-436/00 *X and Y v Riksskatteverket*, para 61 read in connection with para 72. Note lately, although not on the basis of Art 58(1) lit. b EC 1 (1st group): Case C-196/04 *Cadbury Schweppes and Cadbury Schweppes Overseas Ltd v Commissioners of Inland Revenue*, para 51 *et seq*; Case C-446/03 *Marks & Spencer plc v David Halsey (H.M. Inspector of Taxes)*, para 57. Critical with respect to the latter judgment: Case C-446/03 (Opinion of AG Maduro) *Marks & Spencer plc v David Halsey (H.M. Inspector of Taxes)*, 8, who envisages a tendency to possible softening of the strict interpretation of the formula's 'wholly artificial arrangements'. In the relevant case, the non-deducibility within the process of the tax assessment of the parent company of losses incurred in another Member State by a non-resident subsidiary was viewed as a measure necessary to prevent tax evasion.

[97] Case C-196/04 *Cadbury Schweppes and Cadbury Schweppes Overseas Ltd v Commissioners of Inland Revenue*, para 55.

can be exemplified by the evaluation of the permissibility of prior authorization regimes and the fruitlessness of the plea of 'administrative difficulties'.

The question of admissibility of prior authorization regimes was first discussed in *Bordessa*[98] and *Sanz de Lera;*[99] two cases concerned with national legislation aiming to prevent infringement of foreign exchange regulation. The Court held with respect to both intra-Community as well as third country currency export that a regime of prior authorization would go beyond what is necessary because it would render the freedom of capital movements illusory. A declaration procedure would in any way suffice.

While in the area of currency export, no such prior authorization procedure seems to be permissible, in the ambit of real property transfer and direct investment, such a procedure is in principle admissible. In *Konle,* the ECJ found that national measures may—in principle—require prior authorization in order to pursue a 'town and country planning objective such as maintaining, in the general interest, a permanent population and an economic activity independent of the tourist sector in certain regions'.[100] However, due to the fact that a system of prior authorization, although not *per se* contrary to Community law,[101] inherently carries the risk of discrimination and might make the free movement of capital illusory,[102] it is necessary to demonstrate that the system was proportionate, based on objective, non-discriminatory criteria known in advance to the persons concerned, and all affected by the restrictive measure had to have a legal remedy available to them.[103] While 'prior verification, in connection with the acquisition of property ownership, does not reflect merely a need for information', and, thus, mere prior declaration may not suffice to attain the aim of supervision of the proper execution of the rules on secondary residence, this still must not compellingly lead to the conclusion that prior authorization is permissible. There are still measures imaginable that are less restrictive:

---

[98] Joined Cases C-358/93 and C-416/93 *Criminal proceedings against Aldo Bordessa and Vicente Marí Mellado and Concepción Barbero Maestre.*

[99] Joined Cases C-163/94, C-165/94, and C-250/94 *Criminal proceedings against Lucas Emilio Sanz de Lera, Raimundo Díaz Jiménez and Figen Kapanoglu.*

[100] Case C-302/97 *Klaus Konle v Republik Österreich*, para 40 *et seq*, esp. 44 *et seq*.

[101] Case C-54/99 *Association Eglise de Scientologie de Paris and Scientology International Reserves Trust v The Prime Minister*, para 19.

[102] Joined Cases C-358/93 and C-416/93 *Criminal proceedings against Aldo Bordessa and Vicente Marí Mellado and Concepción Barbero Maestre*, para 24 *et seq*.

[103] Indicated in: Joined Cases C-163/94, C-165/94, and C-250/94 *Criminal proceedings against Lucas Emilio Sanz de Lera, Raimundo Díaz Jiménez and Figen Kapanoglu*, paras 23–28; expressly in: Case C-302/97 *Klaus Konle v Republik Österreich*, para 44. Confirmed in: Case C-367/98 *Commission v Portuguese Republic (Re Golden Shares I)*, para 50; Case C-483/99 *Commission v French Republic (Re Golden Shares II)*, para 46; Case C-463/00 *Commission v Kingdom of Spain (Re Golden Shares IV)*, para 69. Within the ambit of freedom to provide and receive services: Case C-205/99 *Asociación Profesional de Empresas Navieras de Líneas Regulares (Analir) and Others v Administración General del Estado*, para 35 *et seq*; see also F Möslein, 'Kapitalverkehrsfreiheit und Gesellschaftsrecht', 212.

an infringement of national legislation on secondary residences... may be *penalised by a fine*, by a *decision requiring* the acquirer *to terminate the unlawful use of the land* forthwith under penalty of its compulsory sale, or by a *declaration that the sale is void* resulting in the reinstatement in the land register of the entries prior to the acquisition of the property.[104]

Thus, while a prior authorization regime is not ruled out in principle with respect to the transfer of real property, the hurdle that the Member States would have to overcome is set rather high. Seen against the background of the aims pursued by the freedom of free capital movement, such a strict construction is to be welcomed. Eventually, it also exemplifies the general rule on interpretation to construe exceptions narrowly.

The Court seems to allow for equally little latitude on the side of the Member States with respect to direct investment. In *Église de Scientologie*, in a public policy/security exception context but in conceptual terms equally relevant here, the Court stated that:

In the case of direct foreign investments, the difficulty in identifying and blocking capital once it has entered a Member State may make it necessary to prevent, at the outset, transactions which would adversely affect public policy or public security. It follows that, in the case of direct foreign investments which constitute a genuine and sufficiently serious threat to public policy and public security, a system of prior declaration may prove to be inadequate to counter such a threat.[105]

In the respective case, the prior authorization regime could not be justified due to the fact that the national measure was lacking transparency, predictability, and a clear scope of application, which basically made the decision of whether a direct investment could go ahead without governmental interference dependent on the discretion of the administration.[106] While, again in principle, the Court does not wish to rule out the admissibility of prior authorization regimes—from the quoted paragraph of the judgment in *Église de Scientologie*, one could even gain the (misleading) impression that the Court would be more generous with respect to regulation of direct investments than in regard to real estate transfers—at the same time, it sets high standards for national legislation in terms of transparency, predictability, and legal protection against its administrative decisions. The national legislation at issue in *Commission v Belgium (Golden Shares III)*[107] can

---

[104] [Emphases added] Case C-302/97 *Klaus Konle v Republik Österreich*, para 47; confirmed in Joined Cases C-515/99 and C-527/99 to C-540/99 and Joined Cases C-519/99 to C-524/99 and C-526/99 *Hans Reisch and Others v Bürgermeister der Landeshauptstadt Salzburg and Grundverkehrsbeauftragter des Landes Salzburg and Anton Lassacher and Others v Grundverkehrsbeauftragter des Landes Salzburg and Grundverkehrslandeskommission des Landes Salzburg*, para 38.
[105] Case C-54/99 *Association Eglise de Scientologie de Paris and Scientology International Reserves Trust v The Prime Minister*, para 20.
[106] Ibid, para 21 *et seq*.
[107] Case C-503/99 *Commission v Kingdom of Belgium (Re Golden Shares III)*, para 50 *et seq*. For a specific account of the issues surrounding so-called 'Golden Shares' and the relevant

serve as an example of one that fulfilled the requirements set out by the Court: the national regime '*listed specifically the strategic assets* concerned and the *management decisions which could be challenged* in any given case'.[108] Furthermore, the possible administrative interventions were

strictly limited to cases in which the objectives of the energy policy were jeopardised. Any decision in that context had to be supported by a formal statement of reasons and was subject to an effective review by the [national] courts.[109]

It is important to note that the Belgian system was one of *ex post facto* opposition, which is less restrictive than a system of prior approval.[110] It is therefore reasonable to argue that in cases of prior approval, the requirements to be met by the national legislation in terms of predictability, transparency, legal remedies, etc would be even higher.

Not only must the national legislation in the ambit of direct investment that aims at the preservation of a certain degree of influence fulfil high standards in terms of 'due process', but it is also strictly confined to undertakings 'active in fields involving the provision of services in the public interest or strategic services'.[111] The branches of industry falling under this meaning must be set out expressly in national legislation, and they may comprise only the most essential strategic assets, such as undertakings in the defence sector or those that are active in the petroleum, telecommunications, postal, and electricity sectors 'safeguarding supplies of such products or the provision of such services within the Member State concerned in the event of a crisis'.[112] Against this background it is easily comprehensible that an undertaking which

produces tobacco, and...commercial banks which operate in the traditional banking sector and which are not claimed to carry out any of the functions of a central bank or similar body, are not undertakings whose objective is to provide public services.[113]

jurisprudence of the Court refer to: M Pießkalla, *Goldene Aktien*; J Bröhmer, 'Golden Shares'; S Pläster, 'Kapitalverkehrsfreiheit'.

[108] [Emphasis added] Case C-463/00 *Commission v Kingdom of Spain (Re Golden Shares IV)*, para 78; summarizing the findings in Case C-503/99 *Commission v Kingdom of Belgium (Re Golden Shares III)*.

[109] Case C-463/00 *Commission v Kingdom of Spain (Re Golden Shares IV)*, para 78; summarizing the findings in Case C-503/99 *Commission v Kingdom of Belgium (Re Golden Shares III)*; Very critical with respect to this finding, especially if contrasted with the judgment in Case C-483/99 *Commission v French Republic (Re Golden Shares II)*: Case C-463/00 and C-98/01 (Opinion of AG Colomer) *Commission v Kingdom of Spain and United Kingdom (Re Golden Shares IV and V)*, para 38 *et seq*.

[110] Case C-503/99 *Commission v Kingdom of Belgium (Re Golden Shares III)*, para 49, reiterated and summarized in Case C-463/00 *Commission v Kingdom of Spain (Re Golden Shares IV)*, para 78. Note in this context also J Oechsler, 'Golden Shares VI', 164 *et seq*.

[111] Case C-367/98 *Commission v Portuguese Republic (Re Golden Shares I)*, para 47; Case C-483/99 *Commission v French Republic (Re Golden Shares II)*, para 43; Case C-503/99 *Commission v Kingdom of Belgium (Re Golden Shares III)*, para 43.

[112] Case C-463/00 *Commission v Kingdom of Spain (Re Golden Shares IV)*, para 71; with respect to postal services, refer to Joined Cases C-282/04 and C-283/04 *Commission v Kingdom of the Netherlands (Re Golden Shares VI)*, para 38.

[113] Case C-463/00 *Commission v Kingdom of Spain (Re Golden Shares IV)*, para 70.

Exceptions by virtue of Article 58 EC 233

With respect to the question of whether it is proportionate to deprive non-residents of certain benefits just because the respective Member State faces '*administrative difficulties*' in accessing the eligibility due to the fact that a cross-border capital movement was involved, the Court had long provided a clear answer:

As regards effective fiscal supervision, the Commission has rightly referred to Council Directive 77/799/EEC of 19 December 1977 concerning mutual assistance by the competent authorities of the Member States in the field of direct taxation,[114] which can be invoked by a Member State in order to check whether payments have been made in another Member State, or to obtain all necessary information, where those payments and that information must be taken into account in determining the correct amount of income taxes.[115] Member States are free to resort to these arrangements when it appears appropriate to them to do so.[116]

Even if the directive should be ineffective in a particular situation, before denying the benefit at issue, the competent authority of the Member State must grant the person concerned the opportunity to provide the information himself.[117] 'In such a case it will nonetheless be necessary to ensure that those requirements do not exceed what is necessary in order to attain the objective of securing the information sought.'[118] Within this proportionality test, other available instruments of mutual assistance besides the cited Directive,[119] such as respective provisions contained in double taxation treaties concluded between Member States or within multinational mutual assistance treaties, should also be taken into account.[120]

---

[114] Directive 77/799/EEC.
[115] Case C-204/90 *Hanns-Martin Bachmann v The Belgian State*, para 18; Case C-55/98 *Skatteministeriet v Bent Vestergaard*, paras 26, 28.
[116] [References made by the Court to other cases were referred from the main body of the text to the footnotes] Case C-334/02 *Commission v French Republic (Re Tax on Income Arising from Investment)*, para 31; confirmed in, inter alia, Case C-315/02 *Anneliese Lenz v Finanzlandesdirektion für Tirol*, para 48; Case C-319/02 *Petri Manninen*, para 54. See for an account: A Cordewener, *Grundfreiheiten*, 937 *et seq*.
[117] Case C-334/02 *Commission v French Republic (Re Tax on Income Arising from Investment)*, para 32 with reference to Case C-300/90 *Commission v Kingdom of Belgium (Re Deduction of Insurance Contributions)*, para 13, which reads: '[T]he inability to request such collaboration cannot justify the non-deductibility of insurance contributions. There is nothing to prevent the Belgian tax authorities from requiring the person concerned to provide such proof as they may consider necessary and, where appropriate, from refusing to allow deduction where such proof is not forthcoming.' See also Case C-254/97 *Société Baxter, B. Braun Médical SA, Société Fresenius France and Laboratoires Bristol-Myers-Squibb SA v Premier Ministre, Ministère du Travail et des Affaires sociales, Ministère de l'Economie et des Finances and Ministère de l'Agriculture, de la Pêche et de l'Alimentation*, para 20; Case C-136/00 *Rolf Dieter Danner*, para 52; Case C-334/02 *Commission v French Republic (Re Tax on Income Arising from Investment)*, para 34 *et seq*.
[118] Case C-446/03 *Marks & Spencer plc v David Halsey (H.M. Inspector of Taxes)*, para 81.
[119] Directive 77/799/EEC is not an exclusive instrument. *Cf* Art. 11 of Directive 77/799/EEC, which provides 'The foregoing provisions shall not impede the fulfilment of any wider obligations to exchange information which might flow from other legal acts.'
[120] Refer to A Cordewener, *Grundfreiheiten*, 942 for further references.

However, recently the language of the Court has lost its clear and bright sound and turned into something like dissonance. Without bothering to provide any explanatory argument, the ECJ in *Marks & Spencer* 'forgot' about Council Directive 77/799/EEC—Advocate General Maduro in his Opinion was apparently more considerate and certainly more balanced on this point[121]— and required the market participant to 'demonstrate to the tax authorities that those conditions [under which cross-border group tax relief could be granted] are fulfilled'.[122] This new tendency is worrying in two respects. First, the Court does not (or does not wish to) take notice of the potential discrimination of cross-border capital movement inherent in such a duty to provide information. Information might be impossible to provide, or the market participant might compile it only with great delay.[123] In both cases, the administration can deny the benefits stemming from the fundamental freedoms. Requiring the taxpayer to produce certain evidence should therefore only be *ultima ratio*. Second, the Court seems not only to intend to reduce the pressure previously exercised on the Member States to find ways of dissolving the deadlock in terms of harmonization of direct taxation,[124] but it also discourages the Member States from compiling relevant information on their own, *ex officio* as it were, and from seeking effective methods of administrational cooperation among them.

(5) Summary so Far

Article 58(1) lit. b EC contains the only express grounds of justification, to be construed narrowly, within the chapter on free movement of capital. It can be subdivided into three groups: the first group relates to national measures preventing infringements of national law and regulations; this group itself can be split into three subcategories, ie, anti-infringement rules in the field of taxation, those in the field of prudential supervision of financial institutions, and anti-infringement rules in other fields. The second group within Art 58(1) lit. b EC allows for national declaration procedures for the purpose of administrative and statistical information. The third and last group constitutes a classic *ordre public* caveat.

---

[121] Advocate General Maduro, first, referred to the relevant Directive but also mentioned the possibility—on an equal footing—'that the Member State concerned may impose on a company claiming group relief a duty of information as to the tax situation of the group to which it belongs and in particular the possibility of dealing with the losses of the subsidiaries in the State in which they are established. In such a case it will nonetheless be necessary to ensure that those requirements do not exceed what is necessary in order to attain the objective of securing the information sought.' [Case C-446/03 (Opinion of AG Maduro) *Marks & Spencer plc v David Halsey (H.M. Inspector of Taxes)*, para 81 citing Case C-250/95 *Futura Participations SA and Singer v Administration des contributions*, para 36] See also A Cordewener, *Grundfreiheiten*, 941 for further references.

[122] Case C-446/03 *Marks & Spencer plc v David Halsey (H.M. Inspector of Taxes)*, para 56.

[123] See M Lang, 'Marks & Spencer II', 10 for the problems surrounding the provision of information with respect to British group tax relief regulations at issue in Case C-446/03 (Opinion of AG Maduro) *Marks & Spencer plc v David Halsey (H.M. Inspector of Taxes)*. Note also E Marschner, 'Dividenden', 87 *et seq*.

[124] Along similar lines: M Lang, 'Marks & Spencer II', 11.

Within the first group of grounds of justification, the subcategory of anti-infringement rules in the field of taxation appears to be the one that has attracted the most attention. Anti-infringement rules in the field of taxation are mainly those that ensure effective fiscal supervision and prevent tax evasion ('fraud') or avoidance ('abuse'). In order to avoid opening a loophole to the Member States for the enactment of protective measures, the Court requires that the Member States must show in the individual case that there is real, tangible, and serious danger of infringement of national laws and regulations. In case of alleged tax avoidance, only purely artificial tax schemes may be targeted. In particular, with respect to national anti-tax avoidance measures, a firm stance appears *conditio sine qua non* in order to avoid eroding the freedom. Taking advantage of the Common Market in the absence of harmonization must also mean utilizing the differences between the national tax systems for one's own advantage.

National measures preventing infringements of national law and regulations are not confined to the fields of taxation (and prudential supervision of financial institutions) in order to be justifiable; the provision extends to fields other than those explicitly mentioned. These measures must, however, aim at the prevention of illicit activities of comparable seriousness in order to be covered. The list— at first sight 'open-ended'—is limited by an 'ancillary function' nexus between the 'anti-infringement rule' and the rule that enforcement shall be secured by the former. From the open wording of the provision, it cannot be deduced that free movement of capital does not participate in the general system of construction of the fundamental freedoms; a 'dual system' of grounds of justification—the grounds mentioned explicitly in the Treaty on one side and the 'rule of reason' on the other—also applies here. However, one must acknowledge that a certain degree of overlap exists between the two categories of written and implied grounds of justification, which can be explained by the 'delayed development' of free movement of capital into a full-fledged fundamental freedom.

Although the Member States, in defence of their restrictive national measures, regularly refer to Art 58(1) lit. b EC (1st group) in their pleadings, the Court has rarely accepted their arguments. This is owing to a rigorous application of the proportionality principle, which this study welcomed. In this context it should be noted that the term 'requisite' found in Art 58(1) lit. b EC (1st group) has no constitutive meaning.

While the second group of grounds of justification within Art 58(1) lit. b EC does not play a significant role, the situation is different when turning to the third group, the *ordre public* exception. No meaningful all-embracing definition of what qualifies as a public policy or security consideration that may justify a restriction on free movement of capital is in existence, so this must be established on a case-by-case basis. For my purposes, it is particularly important to note that the activity of placing a direct investment itself does not constitute a sufficiently serious threat to public policy or security of a Member State; only certain kinds of direct investments originating from abroad, such as those in the public services or defence sectors, may amount to such. Even if the direct investment can be grouped into the aforementioned sectors, this does not automatically mean that a Member State can resort to restrictive measures. The Member State must demonstrate that, in the absence of the measures taken, its interests would be exposed to a real, specific, and serious risk, and no less restrictive measure would suffice.

The proportionality test within the ambit of Art 50(1) lit. b EC is to be applied in a rigorous manner. This can be exemplified by the Court's treatment of the issue of the admissibility of prior authorization regimes (aiming to prevent infringement of national law and regulations), which is essentially a question of 'necessity,' ie, no less restrictive measure can be identified in order to achieve the aim pursued. With respect to direct investment and purchase of land, the Court, while accepting in abstract terms the possibility of requiring prior authorization, places particular emphasis on the fact that an authorization regime adheres to very strict standards of transparency, especially clarity of the scope of application, predictability, and making legal remedies available to the market participant.

Furthermore, 'administrative difficulties' allegedly faced by the Member States in dealing with cross-border transactions should not be accepted as a justification of restrictive national measures. In particular, it appears that assessing tax liabilities in cross-border situations has never been a smooth undertaking for the competent authorities. Very often the fiscal authorities were faced with seemingly insurmountable 'administrative difficulties', especially with respect to the acquisition of reliable information. For a long time, 'administrative difficulties' in conducting cross-border tax assessments could not justify more restrictive measures by the Member States, but they were asked to cooperate among themselves in order to acquire the necessary information. Lately, the Court's pronouncement of this axiom has become fuzzier. It seems that the duty to provide information has passed on to the market participant in such situations, a tendency that must be met with scepticism recalling the potential burden for cross-border investments inherent in such an approach.

b. Exceptions based on Article 58(1) lit. b EC: Third Country Context

The applicability of Art 58(1) lit. b EC is not limited to intra-Community capital movements, but extends equally to third country situations.[125] This follows from the reference contained in Art 58(3) EC to Art 56 EC, the latter being applicable to third countries. 'If that were not so, more extensive restrictions would be permitted within the Community than in relations with third countries.'[126]

---

[125] *Cf* Joined Cases C-358/93 and C-416/93 *Criminal proceedings against Aldo Bordessa and Vicente Marí Mellado and Concepción Barbero Maestre*, para 19 *et seq*.

[126] Case C-452/04 (Opinion of AG Stix-Hackl) *Fidium Finanz AG*, para 126. Note, though, that the statement of the Advocate General disregards those exceptions that apply to third

Because Art 58(1) lit. b EC does not differentiate between intra-Community and third country capital movement and express exceptions exist for third country capital movements in Arts 57(1) EC, 59 EC, and 60 EC, some conclude that Art 58(1) lit. b EC is to be interpreted uniformly, ie, strictly, in both situations.[127] Others, however, who appear to perceive the *erga omnes* applicability of Art 56(1) EC as 'potentially harmful',[128] seeks to interpret the provision in a very broad sense in order to give the Member States more policy space in a third country context.

The structure of the following discussion will seize on the division of Art 58(1) lit. b EC into three groups of grounds of justification. First, linking to the focal point of my analysis in an intra-Community context, I shall answer the question of whether third country capital movement in general and foreign direct investment in particular pose an increased risk, or even have to be brought under general suspicion of infringement of national laws and regulations, which would allow for more restrictive national measures ensuring effective supervision and preventing tax evasion and avoidance in a third country context.

Second, I shall turn to measures that establish procedures for the gathering of administrative and statistical information and those that come under the *ordre public* exception, placing emphasis on the application of the latter group of grounds of justification. In this respect, I shall consider the question of whether foreign direct investment constitutes an increased risk to public policy or public security due merely to the fact that it originates from or is directed to a third country.

(1) National Measures to Prevent Infringements of National Laws and Regulations

We learned above that national measures that prevent infringement of national law and regulations are, inter alia, those that aim at effective fiscal supervision. For national measures securing effective fiscal supervision to be justified in an intra-Community context, the Court requires that in the individual situation there is a real, tangible, and serious danger of infringement of national law and regulations.[129]

With respect to third country capital movements, one might have the idea of giving the Member States more latitude by arguing that such capital movements

---

country capital movement only. See also W Frenz, *Europarecht*, mn 2822; J Bröhmer, Art. 58 EC (2007), mn 1.

[127] Along these lines: J Röhrbein and K Eicker, 'Verlustberücksichtigung', 470; U Haferkamp, *Kapitalverkehrsfreiheit*, 208. See also Unabhängiger Finanzsenat Außenstelle Linz (Austria), GZ. RV/0279-L/04 para 34 *et seq*. Note the contrasting decisions of the Swedish Coucil for Advance Tax Rulings (*Skatterättsnämnden*) mentioned by C Peters and J Gooijer, 'Movement of Capital', 479 and the Hessian Tax Court (*Hessisches Finanzgericht*) referred to by J Röhrbein and K Eicker, 'Verlustberücksichtigung', 471.

[128] See Chapter I. 2. b.   [129] See Chapter IV. 2. a. (4).

constitute a general danger of infringement of national law and regulations.[130] A general suspicion, however, appears neither convincing nor sensible. In legal terms, allowing for an across-the-board examination amounts to *carte blanche* for the Member States to considerably reduce the effectiveness of the freedom in a third country context. On a factual basis, to maintain that capital movements originating from the United States of America constitute on average a more serious danger of infringement of national law and regulation than—for the sake of the argument let us say—those from Romania is highly speculative, to say the least.

Wishing to operate on the basis of a general suspicion—for which no indication can be found in the wording of Art 58(1) lit. b EC, but quite the contrary—would presuppose teleological considerations of a compelling nature. Again, the ominous arguments of 'a limited purpose'[131] allegedly pursued by third country capital movement and the 'missing reciprocity'[132] of capital liberalization are put forward. In the course of the discussion above on the Treaty aims pursued by unilateral liberalization *erga omnes*,[133] as well as within the elaboration of possible systematic and teleological reasons that might speak in favour of a restrictive interpretation of the freedom,[134] I could neither find sufficient evidence to support the 'limited purpose argument' nor am I convinced that the 'missing reciprocity' towards third countries constitutes an argument that would allow for a restrictive interpretation of the freedom, or accordingly, for expansive construction of the exceptions to Art 56(1) EC in third country situations.

In order to achieve both ends, ie, keeping capital movements as unrestricted as possible and guaranteeing effective fiscal supervision, it is best to stick with the flexible approach of balancing free movement and effective fiscal supervision on a case-by-case basis. This balancing is done within the proportionality test.[135] In an intra-Community context, the Court clearly gives priority to the freedom and, therefore, applies a very strict test. A Member State's defence is regularly rejected by reference to the Council Directive Concerning Mutual Assistance by the Competent Authorities of the Member States in the Field of Direct Taxation and Taxation of Insurance Premiums.[136] The Court's argument is essentially that before enacting restrictive national measures on intra-Community capital movement, the Member States must resort to available means of inter-administrational cooperation. Even if no such means are available, the Member States must grant the market participant the opportunity to provide the information himself before restricting free movement.

---

[130] Leaning in this direction A Schnitger, 'Kapitalverkehrsfreiheit', 501.
[131] eg, K Ståhl, 'Movement of Capital', 54 *et seq*.
[132] eg, A Schnitger, 'Kapitalverkehrsfreiheit', 501.   [133] See Chapter I. 2. b.
[134] See Chapter IV. 3. b. (2) and Chapter IV. 3. b. (2) (b) ii.
[135] Concurring: Case C-101/05 *Skatteverket v A*, para 63.
[136] Directive 77/799/EEC.

Apparently, in a third country context the Court cannot structure its argument in the same way, the aforementioned Directive not being applicable.[137] However, recourse can be had to international treaties concluded between the respective Member State and third country.[138] What comes to mind first is that the great majority of the bilateral tax treaties concluded by the Member States with third countries contain provisions on exchange of information on tax matters.[139] Other agreements with less far-reaching commitments should also be taken into account;[140] Advocate General Stix-Hackl, in her seminal opinion on *Fidium Finanz AG,* speaks about 'a minimum degree of cooperation' that would be required.[141] Therefore, in order to keep capital movements between a Member State and a third country as unrestricted as possible, it should be determined in each individual case whether the substantial and procedural means provided within the international treaties applicable are sufficient to attain the aim of effective fiscal supervision.[142]

Some commentators point to the fact that the enforceability of the abovementioned Directive is guaranteed by way of referring the case to the ECJ, *cf* Art 227 EC. With respect to double taxation treaties and other international instruments, the situation is different. Their enforceability is neither subject to Community law nor are there any equally effective legal means available to the Member State to enforce the respective international instrument.[143]

While this is true, the lack of effectiveness should not be admitted as a general excuse for the Member States not to resort to those international instruments, but the application of the available international instruments in practice should be taken into account. Even if the means available under international law might prove in the individual case not to be sufficient, the taxpayer should first be given the opportunity—in the same way as the Court established for intra-Community capital movements—to provide the information by himself[144] before having

---

[137] A Schnitger, 'Kapitalverkehrsfreiheit', 494; A Rust, 'National Report Germany', 278; K Ståhl, 'Movement of Capital', 54 *et seq.*
[138] W Schön, 'Kapitalverkehr mit Drittstaaten', 517 *et seq.*
[139] *Cf,* though in a intra-Community context, Case C-196/04 *Cadbury Schweppes and Cadbury Schweppes Overseas Ltd v Commissioners of Inland Revenue,* 71.
[140] Art 76(2) 1st indent of EC–Russia PCA reads as follows: 'The Parties shall encourage the exchange of information and know-how, inter alia, in areas such as:... legal, administrative, technical, tax, financial and other conditions necessary for setting up and expansion of SMEs and for cross-border cooperation.'
[141] Case C-452/04 (Opinion of AG Stix-Hackl) *Fidium Finanz AG,* para 180.
[142] Ibid, para 175 *et seq*; along similar lines, but probably more restrictive: K Ståhl, 'Movement of Capital', 55.
[143] *Cf,* eg, K Ståhl, 'Movement of Capital', 55; D Hohenwarter, 'Vorlagebeschluss des VwGH', 228 *et seq*; M Lang, 'Wohin geht das Internationale Steuerrecht?' 296; A Schnitger, 'Kapitalverkehrsfreiheit', 494.
[144] A Schnitger, 'Kapitalverkehrsfreiheit', 494; K Ståhl, 'Movement of Capital', 55; the ECJ takes a different view: Case C-101/05 (Opinion of AG Bot) *Skatteverket v A,* para 135 *et seq.* Advocate General Bot, in his opinion on *Skaatteverket v A,* argues that the Court's jurisprudence which requires the Member States to allow the market participant to provide the required information first himself before applying national measures restricting capital movement cannot be

recourse to additional national restrictive measures. The Court seems to be willing to acquiesce in this rationale when it states:

> that, where the legislation of a Member State makes the grant of a tax advantage dependent on satisfying requirements, compliance with which can be verified only by obtaining information from the competent authorities of a third country, it is, in principle, legitimate for that Member State to refuse to grant that advantage if,..., it proves impossible to obtain such information from that country.[145]

Concerning measures aimed at the prevention of tax avoidance, the Court has made clear in an intra-Community context that only the prevention of purely artificial tax schemes can be justified under Art 58(1) lit. b EC (1st group), which is reasonable when seen against the background of the problematic character of this ground of justification.[146] Preventing the realization of advantages flowing

---

transferred to a third country context. He suggests: in an intra-Community capital movement, the Court required the Member States to allow a market participant to provide the information himself only in those cases in which the duty of mutual administrational assistance on the basis of Directive 77/799/EEC—due to its limited scope—does not apply. Because the duty of mutual administrational assistance does *per definitionem* not exist towards a third country in the first place, the Advocate General holds the view that the Court's jurisprudence cannot be applied to third countries. [Case C-101/05 (Opinion of AG Bot) *Skatteverket v A*, para 128 *et seq*]

However, this conclusion, it is respectfully submitted, is not compelling. As a matter of fact, it does not make a difference whether a Member State, although bound by a general duty of administrational cooperation, is not obliged to provide information because the duty is in some way limited or whether a State is not obliged to provide information at all. In both cases the State is simply not obliged to make information available. Why a market participant should be allowed to supply the much needed information in the former case but not in the latter remains unclear. Eventually in both cases there is the threat of abuse by the market participant. Hence, the market participant should, in an intra-Community as well as in a third country context, be allowed to supply the information himself. If that information does not fulfil the required standards in terms of credibility then it can still be refused as insufficient in the individual case. [Concurring: Case C-101/05 *Skatteverket v A*, para 63]

If the Advocate General, however, wanted to suggest that a market participant in a third country context may *per se* not receive the opportunity to provide the information himself simply because harmonization is lacking towards third countries [*cf* Case C-101/05 (Opinion of AG Bott) *Skatteverket v A*, paras 140, 152], then such an approach would provide the Member States with a dangerous role model for all sorts of measures restricting third country capital movement.

The Advocate General also mentioned that only by denying a market participant the opportunity to provide information himself in a third country context could non-Member States be motivated to conclude administrational cooperation agreements with the Community and the Member States. [Case C-101/05 (Opinion of AG Bot) *Skatteverket v A*, para 146 *et seq*] However, one must doubt whether this route will indeed lead to the result hoped for. The Advocate General's solution will probably only lead to the redirection of capital movements towards those Member States that are willing to accept information provided by the market participant. One must also wonder whether the relevant Member State would be motivated by the suggested ruling to conclude administrative cooperation agreements. I envisage therefore that the only meaningful approach in this respect lies in resorting to action on the Community level.

[145] [Emphasis added] Case C-101/05 *Skatteverket v A*, para 63.
[146] One could, though, consider classifying tax schemes that involve so-called offshore tax havens as 'purely artificial schemes'. *The Economist*, for example, tentatively adopted the following description: 'What...identifies an area as a tax haven is the existence of a composite tax structure established deliberately to take advantage of, and exploit, a worldwide demand for opportunities

from the competition between different regulatory systems appears as awkward in an intra-Community context as with respect to third country situations if one accepts the assumption that the Community wants to take up the challenge of competition not just among Member States but also *vis-à-vis* third counties.

Ståhl's suggestion—again based on the 'limited purpose' argument—is that it should 'be easier to justify rules that seek to counteract tax evasion and avoidance when these rules are examined against the provisions on free movement towards third countries'.[147] While in an intra-Community context, anti-tax avoidance rules of the Member States that operate too imprecisely and mechanically fail to meet the proportionality test[148] with respect to third country capital movement, Ståhl pleads that those national measures should stand the test. This study, however, cannot support such a view. Allowing for anti-tax avoidance rules that operate 'mechanically' or 'imprecisely' would inevitably lead to a restriction on those capital movements with third countries that can in no way be related to tax avoidance schemes. In other words, following Ståhl's suggestion means nothing other than accepting an across-the-board treatment of third country capital movements. This study, however, cannot find sustainable justification of a teleological or systematic nature, as explained above, for placing third country capital movements under a general suspicion of tax avoidance.[149] The same principal considerations apply *mutatis mutandis* with respect to measures serving the aim of preventing tax evasion.

(2) National Measures that Establish Procedures for the Gathering of Administrative and Statistical Information and the Ordre Public *Exception*

National measures applicable to third country capital movements and to be justified by reference to the second and third group of grounds of justification contained in Art 58(1) lit. b EC must in principle conform to the same requirements as those that were adopted in an intra-Community context.

In particular, across-the-board classifications of foreign direct investments as a general threat to public policy and public security will be unsuccessful for the reasons repeatedly advanced above.[150] While the Court recognized that public security concerns of the Member States in certain specific economic sectors such

---

to engage in tax avoidance.' C Doggart, *Tax Havens*; (in German C Doggart, *Steuerparadiese*). However, a generally accepted definition of 'tax haven' is still missing. The question of where to draw the boundary between legitimate tax planning and illegitimate tax avoidance demands an answer.

[147] K Ståhl, 'Movement of Capital', 55.
[148] *Cf* Case C-436/00 *X and Y v Riksskatteverket*, para 57 *et seq*; Case C-324/00 *Lankhorst-Hohorst GmbH v Finanzamt Steinfurt*, para 37 *et seq*.
[149] Also critical with respect to a general assumption of tax avoidance with respect to third countries: W Schön, 'Kapitalverkehr mit Drittstaaten', para 517.
[150] See Chapter VI. 2. a.

as energy, electricity, or telecommunications are indeed legitimate,[151] I cannot identify any substantial argument as to why those sectors should be extended in a third country context. For example, it appears highly unlikely that the Court would suddenly allow for national measures restricting the acquisition of or participation in casinos under the heading of the *ordre public* exception. Aims of a purely economic nature may also not be pursued by the Member States in a third country context.

The possible differences between intra-Community and third country capital movement are to be taken into account in the proportionality test. However, under the given conditions, it is unclear why the Court should forbear from the guidelines informing the application of the proportionality test developed in an intra-Community context. Even in the sectors in which the Court recognized the public security interests of the Member States, it is doubtful that it will in a third country context suddenly permit mechanical or imprecise national measures restricting foreign direct investment. Even national measures that establish only the possibility of *ex post facto* opposition with respect to certain management decisions in undertakings active in sectors relevant to public security—not to speak of prior authorization rules for takeovers or participations—must fulfil high standards in terms of predictability, transparency, and due process.[152] In most cases, measures restricting the market access of foreign direct investment will not be the least restrictive means available to the Member State. For example, the threat that a third country could interfere in or influence the politics of a Member State by way of foreign direct investment through undertakings in which the third country indirectly holds a share is more effectively faced by means of competition law, which aims at the eradication of undue market dominance.

(3) Appraisal: No Fundamental Differences

In principle, Art 58(1) lit. b EC must be interpreted in the same way irrespective of whether intra-Community or third country capital movements are involved. This reasoning is supported by the wording of the provision, which does not differentiate between the two kinds of capital movements. The existence of specific exceptions to third country capital movements in Arts 57(1) EC, 59 EC, and 60 EC underlines that the drafters of the Treaty chose to expressly indicate in which situations they wanted to differentiate between intra-Community and third country capital movement. The lack of persuasiveness of other teleological and systematic considerations, such as the purported 'limited purpose' of third country capital movements or missing harmonization with third countries, prohibits an across-the-board treatment of these capital movements which, if allowed, would amount to nothing less than *carte blanche* for the Member States to restrict the freedom in these situations. Therefore, possible differences between intra-Community and third country capital movements are best considered in

---

[151] See Chapter IV. 2. a. (3). [152] See Chapter VI. 2. a. (4).

the balancing process taking place within the proportionality test. However, this study could not identify a good reason why one should deviate from the guidelines developed by the Court to inform the application of the proportionality test in an intra-Community context.

In the context of the proportionality test, attention should also be directed towards the operation of the 'second Cassis principle' in a third country context. In an intra-Community context, the 'second Cassis principle',[153] also called the 'principle of mutual recognition' or the 'principle of functional parallelism',[154] gives rise to the rebuttable presumption within the proportionality test that once a capital movement has complied with the rules and regulations in one Member State, further measures by other Member States are not necessary to protect their interests.[155] Thus, a Member State recognizes the different regulations of another Member State as being equivalent to its own measures because they are functionally parallel.

Due to the applicability of the freedom of capital movements to third countries, the principle of 'functional parallelism' must in general also be valid in these situations with one self-evident modification: that the principle, like the freedom itself, applies only unilaterally. Thus, only a Member State must demonstrate that the regulatory measure at issue does not serve a functionally parallel purpose compared to the one pursued by the regulation in a third country.

Within the ambit of free movement of goods in which the principle was originally developed, it applies only if a good has been lawfully produced, ie, if it is in conformity with the regulations, manufactured using means that are fair and traditional in the exporting country, and sold within the country.[156] Such reasoning can also be transferred into the ambit of free movement of capital. The notion of 'fairness' could prove to be an especially useful tool to provide the Member States with some policy space.

c. The Relationship of Free Movement of Capital and Freedom of Establishment on the Level of Grounds of Justification: Article 58(2) EC

Article 58(2) EC provides that '[t]he provisions of this chapter [related to free movement of capital] shall be without prejudice to the applicability of restrictions on the right of establishment which are compatible with this Treaty.' The Treaty

---

[153] Initially Case 120/78 *Rewe-Zentral AG v Bundesmonopolverwaltung für Branntwein* ('*Cassis de Dijon*'), para 14. See for a broader perspective on this principle PP Craig and G de Búrca, *EU Law*, 668 *et seq*. Note also KJ Alter and S Meunier-Aitsahalia, 'Judicial Politics'.

[154] A Dashwood, 'Harmonisation'.

[155] *Cf* J Steiner, et al, *EU Law*, 307; PP Craig and G de Búrca, *EU Law*, 638; D Ehlers, 'Allgemeine Lehren', mn 96; W Frenz, *Europarecht*, mn 170; JHH Weiler, 'Evolution', 366 *et seq*.

[156] *Cf* European Commission, 'First Biennial Report on the Application of the Principle of Mutual Recognition In Product and Services Market' (SEC (1999) 1106), point 2.1.

chapter on establishment contains a mirror-inverted provision in Art 43(2) EC referencing the chapter on free movement of capital.

In the course of discussing the relationship of the two aforementioned freedoms on the level of the scope of application, in regard to the cross-sectional activity of direct investment, this study found that those provisions have no implication in this respect,[157] but relate to the level of grounds of justification. The understanding of the relationship of the two freedoms and, consequently, the reading of Arts 58(2) EC and 43(2) EC, again differ significantly among commentators.

Three major approaches lend themselves to an understanding of the relationship of the freedoms on the level of the grounds of justification. One could, to begin with, proceed from the assumption that a restriction on an economic activity that falls into the ambit of more than one freedom can be justified only by the grounds of justification of one of the freedoms, which would then take priority over the others.

This relationship of exclusivity can be termed absolute or partial. In the former case, a restriction falling into the scope of application of two freedoms may only be justified by grounds of justification of one specific pertinent freedom. If this fails, then the restriction is contrary to Community law. Which grounds of which freedom will ultimately apply will again be determined by one of the distinguishing criteria already suggested by proponents of an exclusive application of one of the freedoms on the level of the scope of application.[158]

The 'Partial exclusivity' approach[159] works differently. In principle, the grounds of justification of both freedoms apply. If the justification fails within the ambit of free movement of capital but serves legitimate interests recognized in the ambit of the freedom of establishment, then the restriction as a whole is nevertheless justified. The opposite way around, however—ie, the restriction is justified within the ambit of free movement of capital but not within the freedom of establishment—will not lead to an overall justification of the restriction. Hence, it would be contrary to Community law.

However, both exclusivity approaches, besides the fact that they are hardly reconcilable with the mutual references in Arts 43(2) EC and 58(2) EC, must be met with scepticism. The 'absolute exclusivity' approach encounters similar difficulties to those 'exclusivity theories' advanced with respect to the level of the scope of application of the freedoms.[160] They all create only the illusion of a logical and comprehensible delineation of the two freedoms in case of an economic cross-sectional activity. The view that favours 'partial exclusivity' of the freedom of establishment tries to substantiate its position, inter alia, by arguing that a

---

[157] See Chapter III. 3. a.   [158] See Chapter III. 3. c. (1).
[159] W Schön, 'Kapitalverkehrsfreiheit', 752; W Schön, 'Kapitalverkehr mit Drittstaaten', 500; U Haferkamp, *Kapitalverkehrsfreiheit*, 202 *et seq*, the latter with references in older literature; along similar lines: B Bachmann, 'Diskriminierungsverbote', 851; G Ress and J Ukrow, Art. 58 EC (2002), mn 44 *et seq*.
[160] See Chapter III. 3. c. (3).

person-oriented freedom must be superior to an object-oriented one.[161] Not only can no argumentative support for such a hypothesis be found,[162] but the approach unacceptably neglects the reference contained in Art 43(2) EC, which expressly refers to the chapter on free movement of capital and, hence, opens up the freedom of establishment to legitimate interests specifically recognized within the ambit of free movement of capital.

Turning to the second possible approach, it is equably plausible to perceive the relationship of the two freedoms—in the same way as with respect to the level of the scope of application—as being strictly parallel: a national measure that restricts two freedoms must be 'double' justified by the respective grounds of justification provided for within each ambit. If justification with respect to the restriction on one of the freedoms fails, then the whole national measure is contrary to Community law.

This seems to have been the position of the Court, at least until recently. In *Commission v Kingdom of Belgium*,[163] a case decided before the partial shift in jurisprudence,[164] the Court referred to the relationship with respect to the level of grounds of justification, albeit in an *obiter dicta*. The Court held that, due to the fact that the Treaty chapter on establishment also contained a public security exception, the national measure restricting the freedom of establishment would be justified for the same reasons as those advanced with respect to free movement of capital.[165] Thus, the Court seems to require that a national measure that constitutes a restriction on both freedoms needs to be justified in each case with the respective grounds of justification provided for in the respective chapter of the Treaty.

While one can certainly not deny that this understanding secures the maximum level of protection for the market participant,[166] the reading completely disregards Arts 43(2) EC and 58(2) EC and must, therefore, be rejected.[167]

As indicated above, the current status of the case law—after the English Group Litigation cases and the connected partial renunciation of the hitherto existing jurisprudence[168]—has become somewhat uncertain; it appears to be still in a state of flux. From the Court's observations in the *Test Claimants in the FII Group Litigation* case, one could conclude that—as long as the Court does not resolve the issue of competing freedoms on the level of the scope of application—it has

---

[161] Originally: RH Weber, Art. 73d ToM (1994), mn 9; later renounced: *cf* RH Weber, Art. 58 EC (2003), mn 9; critical with respect to Weber's original argument: W Schön, 'Kapitalverkehrsfreiheit', 752; U Haferkamp, *Kapitalverkehrsfreiheit*, 203.
[162] W Schön, 'Kapitalverkehrsfreiheit', 752; U Haferkamp, *Kapitalverkehrsfreiheit*, 203
[163] Case C-503/99 *Commission v Kingdom of Belgium (Re Golden Shares III)*.
[164] See for an account of this shift in jurisprudence Chapter III. 3. b. (3).
[165] Case C-503/99 *Commission v Kingdom of Belgium (Re Golden Shares III)*, para 59.
[166] Along similar lines: M Sedlaczek, 'Kapitalverkehrsfreiheit', 47.
[167] J Lübke, *Kapitalverkehrs- und Niederlassungsfreiheit*, 473; AC Digel, 'Europäischer Finanzmarkt', Inaugural-Dissertation, Eberhard-Karls-Universität, 188.
[168] See Chapter III. 3. b. (3).

so far not altered its jurisprudence and continues to treat the freedoms in strict parallelism on the level of grounds of justification.[169]

Another arguable approach—probably the predominant view in the literature[170]—on how to deal with the issue of competing freedoms is to allow for justification by the grounds of justification of either freedom. Consequently, it would suffice that a restriction serves a legitimate interest recognized within the ambit of free movement of capital or the freedom of establishment.[171] This interpretation appears to be the only one that takes sufficient account of the mutual references in Arts 58(2) EC and 43(3) EC. Moreover, in contrast to one commentator,[172] such a construction is not precluded by the principle of *'in dubio pro libertate'* due to the simple fact that there is no room for 'doubt'. The abovementioned Articles give evidence of the fact that no freedom shall annul the restrictions already permissible within the ambit of the respective other freedom.[173]

In summary, for a restriction to be justified it suffices that it serves, in the actual situation at issue, a legitimate interest recognized within the ambit of either of the freedoms. In this context, however, it is worth pointing out that in practice, the question of cumulative or alternative application of the grounds of justification will not play a significant role due to the fact that the recognized legitimate interests in each ambit, if one takes written and unwritten grounds together, have been shaped similarly by the Court to a very large degree.[174] Also within the proportionality test, in the process of balancing conflicting interests, differences between the freedoms may not be easily noticeable with respect to direct investment. Both require a similar degree of integration into the host country and, thus, the conflicting interests will probably be weighted in a similar way.[175]

Having discussed the relationship of the two freedoms in terms of principle, in the following paragraphs I shall put my finding to the test and elaborate on

---

[169] Case C-446/04 *Test Claimants in the FII Group Litigation v Commissioners of Inland Revenue*, paras 94, 98.

[170] *Cf* S Weber, 'Kapitalverkehr', 565; A Honrath, *Kapitalverkehr*, 110; A Rohde, *Kapitalverkehr*, 164; JCW Müller, *Kapitalverkehrsfreiheit*, 193; A Glaesner, Art. 58 EC (2000), mn 8; C Ohler, Art. 58 EC (2002), mn 44; P-C Müller-Graff, 'Einflußregulierungen', 934; W Kiemel, Art. 58 EC (2003), mn 29; J Lübke, *Kapitalverkehrs- und Niederlassungsfreiheit*, 472 *et seq*; J Bröhmer, Art. 58 EC (2007), mn 33 Along similar lines: B Matzka, *Freiheit des Kapitalverkehrs*, 52; JM Mössner and D Kellersmann, 'Kapitalverkehrsfreiheit', 509; F Kimms, *Kapitalverkehrsfreiheit*, 140 *et seq*. For a critical view: U Haferkamp, *Kapitalverkehrsfreiheit*, 200 *et seq*.

[171] eg, C Ohler, Art. 58 EC (2002), mn 44.

[172] U Haferkamp, *Kapitalverkehrsfreiheit*, 201.

[173] *Cf* P-C Müller-Graff, 'Einflußregulierungen', 934. The argument of Lübke runs along similar lines. He states that the teleological consideration advanced with respect to the level of the scope of application—ie, that each freedom exclusively protects a specific aspect of a certain economic activity and, therefore, cannot be masked out if one does not want to allow for 'loopholes' in the scope of protection of the fundamental freedoms—does not apply in the context of the level of grounds of justification due to the fact that the Treaty, by virtue of Arts 43(2) EC and 58(2) EC, explicitly derogates from this. [J Lübke, *Kapitalverkehrs- und Niederlassungsfreiheit*, 472 *et seq*]

[174] *Cf* U Haferkamp, *Kapitalverkehrsfreiheit*, 203.

[175] For a critical view: ibid.

its application in a third country situation. As a matter of course, in this context only free movement of capital can principally open up its ambit for grounds of justification exclusively to be found in the ambit of the freedom of establishment. It will not be the case, however, the other way around, due to the limited territorial scope of the freedom of establishment.

Suppose that the justification of a restrictive measure on the basis of the grounds provided for within the ambit of free movement of capital fails. This inevitably directs the focus to the question of what the effect of Art 58(2) EC in a third country context will be. One could take the view that the reference in Art 58(2) EC that presupposes '*restrictions* on the right of establishment which are compatible with the Treaty',[176] achieves nothing in such a situation by arguing that a national measure that is not subject to the freedom of establishment cannot constitute a restriction to it and, consequently, also does not need 'to be made compatible' with the Treaty, ie, to be justified.

Such an approach, however, could be too broad. Rather, one should differentiate between national measures that apply exclusively to third country situations, ie, establishing a special regime for foreign direct investment, and those applicable to intra-Community and third country contexts alike. With respect to the latter, the sketched interpretation would potentially lead to a surprising result. In a third country context, one and the same restrictive national measure could be based only on grounds of justification found to be within the ambit of free movement of capital. In an intra-Community context, however—both freedoms being applicable—the Member State could refer to the aforementioned grounds of justification and, by virtue of Art 58(2) EC, also to those provided for in the Treaty chapter on establishment. Hence, potentially more restrictions could be applied by the Member States in an intra-Community than in a third country context. However, the Treaty certainly does not seek to establish a more favourable regime for third country investors than for those from other Member States; it aims for a level playing field for both in the Common Market. Such a level playing field can only be achieved when the Member States are able to base their national measures on the same grounds of justification in both intra-Community and third country situations. Thus, if a national measure applies to intra-Community and third country investors alike, then the Member State can also invoke, by virtue of Art 58(2) EC, legitimate interests that are exclusively recognized within the Treaty chapter on establishment.

However, if a national measure applies exclusively to third country situations—ie, it establishes a special regime for third country direct investment—then Art 58(2) EC indeed, taking the words from above, achieves nothing due to the fact that there is no restriction whatsoever on intra-Community establishment to which it could be referred by virtue of Art 58(2) EC.

[176] [Emphasis added]

3. 'The System of Property Ownership' as a Ground of Justification?: Article 295 EC

Turning away from the narrow focus of the Treaty chapter on capital movement and the broader view in search of express grounds of justification applicable to intra-Community and third country capital movement alike, I shall turn my attention to Art 295 EC. This provision has repeatedly been cited by the Member States in an attempt to defend national measures restricting cross-border direct investment in previously privatized undertakings. Whether the Member States succeeded in their plea, and, more generally, whether Art 295 EC qualifies as a legal basis for national measures restricting direct investment in intra-Community and third country contexts will be answered in the following section.

Article 295 EC states 'in forceful and unconditional nature'[177] that the contents of the 'Treaty shall in no way prejudice the rules in Member States governing the system of property ownership'. However, despite the forceful and unconditional nature of its wording, the Court has not attributed any significant importance to this provision, which pledges the Community to neutrality *vis-à-vis* the Member States' property ownership systems.[178] The case law mirrors, in essence, an understanding of the provision as a mere competence rule, which is limited in its effect to stating that the Member States continue to have vested in them the competence[179] to shape their systems of property ownership.[180] It does not, however, comprise any significant material effect;[181] the individual rules of the respective property ownership system are subject to a comprehensive review against the background of Community law, in particular the fundamental freedoms and the competition rules.[182]

With respect to the transfer of real property the ECJ, in *Konle*, held in terse fashion, without bothering to provide any further enlightening argument:

[A]lthough the system of property ownership continues to be a matter for each Member State under Article 222 of the Treaty [now, after amendment, Art. 295], that provision

---

[177] Case C-367/98, C-483/99, and C-503/99 (Joined Opinion of AG Colomer) *Commission v Portuguese Republic, French Republic and Kingdom of Belgium (Re Golden Shares I-III)*, para 44.
[178] C Koenig and J Kühling, Art. 295 EC (2003), mn 1.
[179] However, this competency is not unqualified: see ibid, mn 2 for further references.
[180] Very critical with respect to such an interpretation: Case C-367/98, C-483/99, and C-503/99 (Joined Opinion of AG Colomer) *Commission v Portuguese Republic, French Republic and Kingdom of Belgium (Re Golden Shares I-III)*, para 63: 'It makes no sense for the EC Treaty to contain a provision whose sole aim is to state the obvious, namely that the Treaty does not affect the structure of property legislation in the Member States.'
[181] One of the rare instances in which Art 295 EC has material effects is with respect to nationalizations that are carried out in a non-discriminatory fashion, *cf* Case 182/83 *Robert Fearon & Company Limited v Irish Land Commission*.
[182] C Koenig and J Kühling, Art. 295 EC (2003), mn 2, 7.

does not have the effect of exempting such a system from the fundamental rules of the Treaty.[183]

Against this background it can, therefore, be reasonably established that with respect to transfer of real property, Art 295 EC has no limiting impact on the fundamental freedoms. In fact, '[a]ccess to ownership of immovable property is...implicit in the freedom[s] guaranteed by the Treaty'.[184]

When it comes to national rules encroaching upon property ownership in previously privatized undertakings, for example, by requiring authorization for acquiring shareholdings above a certain threshold, establishing administrative rights to object to certain management decisions, or by having a say in appointing the members of the board of directors, the Court adheres to its adopted interpretation of Art 295 EC.[185] However, the ECJ acknowledges that:

certain concerns may justify the retention by Member States of a degree of influence within undertakings that were initially public and subsequently privatised, where those undertakings are active in fields involving the provision of services in the public interest or strategic services[186]

It does not stop there, but instantly qualifies its statement by holding that:

those concerns cannot entitle Member States to plead their own systems of property ownership...by way of justification for obstacles, resulting from privileges attaching to their position as shareholder in a privatised undertaking, to the exercise of the freedoms provided for by the Treaty.... [Art. 295] does not have the effect of exempting the Member States' systems of property ownership from the fundamental rules of the Treaty.[187]

Thus, restrictions of the kind mentioned above on the freedom of capital movement cannot be justified by reference to Art 295 EC, but only 'by reasons referred to in Article 73d(1) of the Treaty [now, after amendment, Art 58 (1)] or by overriding requirements of the general interest'.[188] Again, the Court did not feel

---

[183] Case C-302/97 *Klaus Konle v Republik Österreich*, para 38 referring to Case 182/83 *Robert Fearon & Company Limited v Irish Land Commission*, para 7.
[184] Case C-302/97 (Opinion of AG La Pergola) *Klaus Konle v Republik Österreich*, para 14.
[185] *Cf* Case C-367/98 *Commission v Portuguese Republic (Re Golden Shares I)*; Case C-483/99 *Commission v French Republic (Re Golden Shares II)*; Case C-503/99 *Commission v Kingdom of Belgium (Re Golden Shares III)*; Case C-463/00 *Commission v Kingdom of Spain (Re Golden Shares IV)*; Case C-98/01 *Commission v United Kingdom (Re Golden Shares V)*; Joined Cases C-282/04 and C-283/04 *Commission v Kingdom of the Netherlands (Re Golden Shares VI)*; Case C-274/06 *Commission v Kingdom of Spain (Re Golden Shares VIII)*. See also with respect to Case C-112/05 (Opinion AG Colomer) *Commission v Germany (Re Golden Shares VII 'Volkswagengesetz')* the following appreciations: Kleinschmit, *Volkswagengesetz*; F Sander, 'Volkswagen'; M Weiss, 'VW-Gesetz'.
[186] Case C-367/98 *Commission v Portuguese Republic (Re Golden Shares I)*, para 47; reiterated in Case C-483/99 *Commission v French Republic (Re Golden Shares II)*, para 43; Case C-503/99 *Commission v Kingdom of Belgium (Re Golden Shares III)*, 43; and recently Joined Cases C-282/04 and C-283/04 *Commission v Kingdom of the Netherlands (Re Golden Shares VI)*, para 38.
[187] Case C-367/98 *Commission v Portuguese Republic (Re Golden Shares I)*, para 48.
[188] Ibid, para 49. Of the same opinion: S Grundmann and F Möslein, 'Goldene Aktie', 338 *et seq*; R Ruge, 'Goldene Aktien', 423; D Booß, Art. 295 EC (2006), mn 3; Criticizing: C Koenig and

obliged to provide any further argument for its reasoning and thus missed the chance to shed light on the nebulous scope of Art 295 EC.[189] It therefore comes as no real surprise that the Court's interpretation is not without opposition.[190] It is notable that with respect to the judgment restated above, the Court did not follow the Opinion[191] delivered by Advocate General Colomer and instead reached a contrarian solution. The Advocate General suggested adopting a broader understanding of Art 295 EC extending 'to any measure which, through intervention in the public sector, understood in the economic sense, allows the State to contribute to the organisation of the nation's financial activities'.[192] Thus, every rule that is capable of attributing economic titles with respect to an undertaking, ie, rules allowing the holder of such titles to exercise decisive influence on the control of economic activities, could fall within the scope of Art 295 EC. While, in the eyes of the Advocate General, Art 295 EC does not provide exemption from the application of the mandatory rules of the Treaty, such as the prohibition of discrimination, it creates a presumption in favour of a national measure restricting the economic influence over the use or fundamental aspects of the activity of the undertaking being compatible with the Treaty, 'unless it is proved otherwise'.[193] This presumption is limited to national measures that the Member State would have been able to adopt if it had retained public ownership

---

J Kühling, Art. 295 EC (2003), mn 13; Case C-463/00 and C-98/01 (Opinion of AG Colomer) *Commission v Kingdom of Spain and United Kingdom (Re Golden Shares IV and V)*, para 37 *et seq*.

[189] *Cf* Case C-463/00 and C-98/01 (Opinion of AG Colomer) *Commission v Kingdom of Spain and United Kingdom (Re Golden Shares IV and V)*, para 37.

[190] See, for an overview of the different views in the literature and further references, C Koenig and J Kühling, Art. 295 EC (2003), mn 9 *et seq*. The views in the literature can roughly be broken into two major 'camps'. One view maintains that Art 295 EC protects only the creation of different forms of property ownership and its subsequent allocation either to private or public holders within a Member State. The other opinion views Art 295 EC as referring to both the creation and exercise of property ownership rights. Not only in the literature but also within the Court, one can hardly speak of a 'monolithic' interpretation of the provision: on one side the ECJ, frequently cited above, supported by Joined Cases C-282/04 and C-283/04 (Opinion of AG Maduro) *Commission v Kingdom of the Netherlands (Re Golden Shares VI)*, para 28 *et seq*; on the other Cases C-367/98, C-483/99, and C-503/99 (Joined Opinion of AG Colomer) *Commission v Portuguese Republic, French Republic and Kingdom of Belgium (Re Golden Shares I-III)*; Cases C-463/00 and C-98/01 (Opinion of AG Colomer) *Commission v Kingdom of Spain and United Kingdom (Re Golden Shares IV and V)*.

[191] Cases C-367/98, C-483/99, and C-503/99 (Joined Opinion of AG Colomer) *Commission v Portuguese Republic, French Republic and Kingdom of Belgium (Re Golden Shares I-III)*; similar arguments were advanced again in Case C-463/00 and C-98/01 (Opinion of AG Colomer) *Commission v Kingdom of Spain and United Kingdom (Re Golden Shares IV and V)*, para 37 *et seq*, 54 *et seq*.

[192] Cases C-367/98, C-483/99, and C-503/99 (Joined Opinion of AG Colomer) *Commission v Portuguese Republic, French Republic and Kingdom of Belgium (Re Golden Shares I-III)*, para 56; recently Case C-112/05 (Opinion AG Colomer) *Commission v Germany (Re Golden Shares VII 'Volkswagengesetz')*, para 49.

[193] Cases C-367/98, C-483/99, and C-503/99 (Joined Opinion of AG Colomer) *Commission v Portuguese Republic, French Republic and Kingdom of Belgium (Re Golden Shares I–III)*, para 67; of the same opinion: C Koenig and J Kühling, Art. 295 EC (2003), mn 13; of the opposing view: T Kingreen, Art. 295 EC (2002), mn 12; M Pießkalla, *Goldene Aktien*, esp. 170 *et seq*.

in the previously privatized undertaking.¹⁹⁴ Thus, if a Member State reserves itself certain rights, such as those mentioned above, in a previously privatized undertaking (if it engages in gradual privatization, so to speak), then this process is perceived as attributing property ownership by means of distributing economic titles between public and private holders. If this process does not infringe fundamental principles of Community law, such as the prohibition of discrimination, then it is covered by the exception of Art 295 EC.

By pursuing this line of argument, the Advocate General automatically disapproved a view of the term 'system of property ownership' in Art 295 EC as including only the two opposing situations of public and private ownership, a view put forward by the Commission.¹⁹⁵ Such a 'reductionistic'¹⁹⁶ understanding of Art 295 EC, which merely has recourse to the identity of the shareholders, would lead to different treatment of two situations that, so he argues, produce identical effects with respect to the fundamental freedoms:

> on the one hand, that of an undertaking either wholly or mostly owned by a public authority [to which Art. 295 EC would apply]; and, on the other, that of a private undertaking subject to a general system of administrative supervision with respect to its decision [to which it would not apply].¹⁹⁷

Moreover, he argued that it would be against common sense to allow, by virtue of Art 295 EC, for nationalization,¹⁹⁸ but exclude private ownership subject to special powers, a less serious form of interference, from the scope of application.¹⁹⁹

In a nutshell, while the Court appears to be content to consider Art 295 EC only as a competence rule, which would then solely state the obvious, the aforementioned view of the Advocate General takes an economic perspective in which Art 295 EC covers all kinds of national measures attributing an economic title that allows for influence over the activities of an undertaking, irrespective of 'whether this influence stems from possession of securities, administrative authorisation, provisions in the articles of association or any other means allowed in private or public law'.²⁰⁰

Not wishing to enter into an overly lengthy discussion of the interpretation of Art 295 EC, the consequences of and also the objections against the interpretation of the Advocate General (and any other broader understanding of Art 295 EC) should not be overlooked; I shall limit myself, though, to a broad-brush account. While Advocate General *Colomer* chooses to give

---

[194] Cases C-367/98, C-483/99, and C-503/99 (Joined Opinion of AG Colomer) *Commission v Portuguese Republic, French Republic and Kingdom of Belgium (Re Golden Shares I-III)*, para 70.
[195] Ibid, para 42.
[196] Ibid.   [197] Ibid., para 64.
[198] *Cf* Case 182/83 *Robert Fearon & Company Limited v Irish Land Commission*, para 7.
[199] Cases C-367/98, C-483/99, and C-503/99 (Joined Opinion of AG Colomer) *Commission v Portuguese Republic, French Republic and Kingdom of Belgium (Re Golden Shares I-III)*, para 66.
[200] Ibid, para 65.

priority to the fundamental freedoms over Art 295 EC in cases in which national measures that aim at the retention of some degree of administrative influence operate in a discriminatory fashion, he seems to take the opposite view when it comes to national measures that merely hinder free capital movement. Such an approach provides great latitude for a national economic policy that aims at protectionism and preservation of powers[201] and, thus, runs counter to the aim of creation and maintenance of a Common Market since it would allow for market-partitioning rules, although they may not be discriminatory. These rules—and this is no new insight—can severely restrict access to a Member State's market and, thus, deprive Community law of much of its effectiveness. Although the Treaty allows for the maintainance of public ownership in certain undertakings, it does not entitle a Member State 'to curtail selectively the access of market operators to certain economic sectors once those sectors have been privatised'.[202] This follows from the requirement that when a Member State decides to privatize a certain sector of its economy, it must subsequently act in a consistent manner, not contradicting its previous decision. The requirement for consistency 'arises from the need to ensure that the State acts in conformity with either the market process or the political process'.[203]

Furthermore, it may be doubted whether Advocate General Colomer's interpretation of Art 295 EC takes sufficient account of the development of the fundamental freedoms in general and of free movement of capital in particular, which took them beyond the mere prohibition of discrimination to a comprehensive duty to liberalize, exemplified by the prohibition of any hindrance. As Community law stands today, it is reasonable to regard the prohibition of hindrance, in the same way as the prohibition of discrimination, as a mandatory rule of the Treaty that takes priority over Art 295 EC.[204]

Therefore, this study agrees with the conclusion reached by the Court even though it reduces the scope of Art 295 EC considerably. The Court's interpretation of Art 295 EC takes into account the development of the Common Market in general and the fundamental freedoms in particular. Article 295 EC as perceived by Advocate General Colomer would not only be alien but hostile to the level of integration and liberalization reached within the Common Market.

---

[201] M Pießkalla, *Goldene Aktien*, 173.

[202] Joined Cases C-282/04 and C-283/04 (Opinion of AG Maduro) *Commission v Kingdom of the Netherlands (Re Golden Shares VI)*, para 29.

[203] Ibid, para 28; citing Case C-205/03 P (Opinion of AG Maduro) *Federación Española de Empresas de Tecnología Sanitaria (FENIN), formerly Federación Nacional de Empresas, Instrumentación Científica, Médica, Técnica y Dental*, para 26 and Joined Cases C-94/04 and C-202/04 'Cipolla' (Opinion of AG Maduro) *Federico Cipolla v Rosaria Fazari, née Portolese and Stefano Macrino et Claudia Capoparte v Roberto Meloni*, para 31 *et seq*; indicated also by M Pießkalla, *Goldene Aktien*, 177.

[204] M Pießkalla, *Goldene Aktien*, 173 *et seq*.

4. The *'Ultima Ratio'* Defence and Security Exception: Article 297 EC

Another provision outside the chapter on capital movement on which the Member States might rely in order to restrict cross-border direct investment in intra-Community and third country contexts is Art 297 EC. It contains an *ordre public* safety valve for three extreme situations.[205] These relate, first, to serious internal disturbances affecting the maintenance of law and order, second to the event of war or serious international tension constituting a threat of war, or, third, to the carrying out of obligations a Member State has accepted for the purpose of maintaining peace and international security. The provision was at issue in *Albore,* where the Court explained that a mere reference to the requirements of defence of the national territory on the basis of Art 297 EC does not suffice to justify a restrictive measure[206] and transposed the strict interpretation developed within other ambits of the Treaty to that of capital movement. It implicitly confirmed that there is no 'general exception covering all measures taken for reasons of public security',[207] which include measures relating to the armed forces and national defence.[208] In principle

> situations falling within the scope of the special safeguard clauses of Art. 223 et seq of the EC Treaty [now, after amendment, Art. 296 et seq]... are justified only in the cases and under the conditions expressly provided for by Community legislature[209]

which are to be found, inter alia, in Art 58(1) lit. b EC (3rd group). Only in extreme situations, which presuppose the actual materialization of the events and circumstances mentioned within the provision, can recourse be had to Art 297 EC.[210] The provision constitutes the *ultima ratio* in the sense that its application is limited to cases in which no other Treaty provision can accommodate the legitimate security interests of the Member States, which carry the ultimate responsibility for the protection of their citizens.[211]

---

[205] For an account of Art 296 EC *et seq*, refer, inter alia, to: S Bohr, *Schutznormen*; K Wirbel, 'Ausnahmezustand', University of Bonn; W Hummer, 'Das griechische Embargo'; P Koutrakos, 'Reserve of Sovereignty'; M Trybus, 'European Defence Integration'; M Trybus, 'Article 297 EC'.

[206] Case C-423/98 (Opinion of AG Cosmas) *Alfredo Albore*, para 21.

[207] Case C-273/97 *Angela Maria Sirdar v The Army Board and Secretary of State for Defence*, para 16; first held in Case 222/84 *Marguerite Johnston v Chief Constable of the Royal Ulster Constabulary*, para 26.

[208] Case C-423/98 (Opinion of AG Cosmas) *Alfredo Albore*, para 16.

[209] As shown by ibid, para 19.

[210] Case C-423/98 *Alfredo Albore*, para 22.

[211] Case C-83/94 *Criminal proceedings against Peter Leifer, Reinhold Otto Krauskopf and Otto Holzer*, para 31; Case C-273/97 *Angela Maria Sirdar v The Army Board and Secretary of State for Defence*, para 27; see also, for further references, J Kokott, Art. 297 EC (2003), mn 3, 46; for a different view see Advocate General Cosmos, who is less cautious and suggests reviewing the narrow approach towards Art 296 EC *et seq*, esp. Art 297 EC, taken in earlier cases, *cf* Case C-423/98 (Opinion of AG Cosmas) *Alfredo Albore*, para 25 *et seq*.

5. Transitional Periods and Permanent Derogations from the Duty to Liberalize Capital Movements

a. Transitional Periods Granted to Accession Countries

A foreign direct investment can involve the purchase of property or cultivated land and forest. In the course of the accession negotiations of new Member States entering the European Union in 2004 and 2007,[212] transitional periods of varying lengths were agreed upon for governing the possibility of purchasing the aforesaid. The respective provisions are found under the heading 'free movement of capital' in the annexes to the treaties of accession.[213] Also, with respect to Member States that joined the European Union earlier, transitional periods for the abolition of restrictions on free movement of capital were included in the accession treaties; those, however, expired.[214]

b. Permanent Derogations Granted to Individual Member States

With respect to Denmark, Protocol No 1 of the Treaty on European Union stipulates that, notwithstanding the provisions of the Treaty on the free movement of capital, Denmark may maintain the existing legislation on the acquisition of second homes. However, the respective provisions may not discriminate.[215]

Protocol No 2 of the Finnish Accession Treaty provides for certain derogations from the provisions of the EC Treaty with respect to the Åland Islands, which, although under Finnish sovereignty, enjoy relative autonomy as negotiated through the League of Nations in 1921. The Åland Islands may maintain non-discriminatory national provisions in force on 1 January 1994 regarding,

---

[212] Those States which joined the EU in 2004 are: Cyprus, Estonia, Hungary, Latvia, Lithuania, Poland, the Czech Republic, Slovakia, Slovenia, and Malta; in 2007: Bulgaria and Romania.

[213] Treaty of Accession of the Czech Republic, Estonia, Cyprus, Latvia, Lithuania, Hungary, Malta, Poland, Slovenia and Slovakia—Annexes V to XIV; Act concerning the Conditions of Accession of the Czech Republic, the Republic of Estonia, the Republic of Cyprus, the Republic of Latvia, the Republic of Lithuania, the Republic of Hungary, the Republic of Malta, the Republic of Poland, the Republic of Slovenia and the Slovak Republic and the Adjustments to the Treaties on which the European Union is Founded—Protocol No. 6 on the Acquisition of Secondary Residences in Malta; Act concerning the Conditions of Accession of the Republic of Bulgaria and Romania and the Adjustments to the Treaties on which the European Union is Founded—Annex VI—List Referred to in Article 23 of the Act of Accession: Transitional Measures, Bulgaria; Act concerning the Conditions of Accession of the Republic of Bulgaria and Romania and the Adjustments to the Treaties on which the European Union is Founded—Annex VII: List Referred to in Article 23 of the Act of Accession: Transitional Measures, Romania. For an overview, refer to European Commission, 'Purchasing Property in Another Member State' (Website, European Commission, Brussels 2005).

[214] *Cf* W Kiemel, Art. 56 EC (2003), mn 33.

[215] Treaty on European Union—Protocol (No 1) on the Acquisition of Property in Denmark; see also W Kiemel, Art. 56 EC (2003), mn 32.

inter alia, restrictions on the right of natural and legal persons to acquire and hold real property without permission from the competent authorities of the Islands.[216]

6. The 'Rule of Reason' within the Ambit of Free Movement of Capital

In the introduction to this chapter,[217] it was stated that exceptions to the freedom are not limited to those expressly mentioned in the Treaty. They are complemented by unwritten ones. Unwritten grounds of justification were initially introduced in 1979 in the ambit of free movement of goods by the *Cassis de Dijon* judgment[218] as a response to two major problems from the foundation period. The 'Cassis jurisprudence' constituted an answer to the then-widening gap between the changed public sentiment in the late 1970s and early 1980s (eg, consumer or environmental protection, cultural policy, or fairness of commercial transaction) and the frozen balance between free trade and other competing values were cemented in the words of the Treaty of 1957. Furthermore, the formula also represents a partial qualification of the earlier overstretched expansion of the scope of the freedoms as a consequence of the *Dassonville*[219] judgment.[220]

Following the initial decision in *Cassis de Dijon*,[221] the formula over the years has gradually developed into a general rule of justification. Beyond the formal assimilation, ie, its applicability had been extended to other fundamental freedoms,[222] the 'rule of reason' has been converging in structure and function.[223] The 'rule of reason' is open as regards its content; national interests that must be accepted as mandatory and, thus, constitute an exception to the fundamental freedoms are identified and appreciated on a case-by-case basis.[224] Accepted mandatory requirements are not limited in their applicability to the fundamental freedom in the context of which they were first established, but are exchangeable

---

[216] Act concerning the Conditions of Accession of the Kingdom of Norway, the Republic of Austria, the Republic of Finland and the Kingdom of Sweden and the Adjustments to the Treaties on which the European Union is Founded—Protocol No 2 on the Åland Islands.
[217] See Chapter VI. 1.
[218] Case 120/78 *Rewe-Zentral AG v Bundesmonopolverwaltung für Branntwein ('Cassis de Dijon')*.
[219] Case 8/74 *Procureur du Roi v Benoît and Gustave Dassonville*.
[220] JHH Weiler, 'Evolution', 364 *et seq*.
[221] Case 120/78 *Rewe-Zentral AG v Bundesmonopolverwaltung für Branntwein ('Cassis de Dijon')*, para 8.
[222] Case C-76/90 *Manfred Säger v Dennemeyer & Co Ltd*, para 15; Case C-19/92 *Dieter Kraus v Land Baden-Württemberg)*, para 32; Case C-55/94 *Reinhard Gebhard v Consiglio dell'Ordine degli Avvocati e Procuratori di Milano*, para 39.
[223] A Cordewener, *Grundfreiheiten*, 132 *et seq*.
[224] A Arnull, et al, *European Union Law*, 352.

among all fundamental freedoms. The latter is in particular relevant for the freedom of capital movements, being the 'belated freedom'.[225]

Having said this, it does not come as a surprise that, in an effort to interpret all fundamental freedoms in a converging manner,[226] the Court extended the so-called '(first[227]) Cassis principle' or 'rule of reason' into the ambit of free capital movement.[228] The ECJ in its judgments today regularly states that the freedom may be restricted not only for the reasons expressly mentioned in the Treaty, but also by mandatory requirements of the general interest. Those mandatory requirements may not be of a purely economic nature.[229] Moreover, the Court, at first sight, seems to require—though it is far from doing so in a consistent manner[230]—that measures capable of being justified by mandatory requirements are such as to apply 'to all persons and undertakings pursuing an activity in a territory of the host Member State'.[231] It further holds—this time consistently—that 'in order to be justified, the national legislation must be suitable for securing the objective which it pursues and must not go beyond what is necessary in order to attain it, so as to accord with the principle of proportionality'.[232]

---

[225] *Cf* G Ress and J Ukrow, Art. 56 EC (2002), mn 75 *et seq*.

[226] The application of an increasingly consistent 'rule of reason' with an interpretation that does not significantly deviate depending on the individual freedom eases delineation problems, which undoubtedly exist at the level of the scope of application of the fundamental freedoms, at least for the level of grounds of justification. [*Cf.* A Cordewener, *Grundfreiheiten*, 139]

[227] Therefrom the so-called 'second Cassis principle' (principle of 'functional parallelism' or 'mutual recognition') needs to be distinguished. For an evolutionary account, refer to JHH Weiler, 'Evolution', 366 *et seq*, for further references at the end of the chapter.

[228] First indications in Case C-148/91 *Vereniging Veronica Omroep Organisatie v Commissariaat voor de Media*, para 9 *et seq*; Case C-302/97 *Klaus Konle v Republik Österreich*, para 40 *et seq*; Case C-222/97 *Manfred Trummer and Peter Mayer*, para 29 *et seq*; Case C-35/98 *Staatssecretaris van Financiën v B.G.M. Verkooijen*, para 43 *et seq*. Explicitly, for example, in Case C-367/98 *Commission v Portuguese Republic (Re Golden Shares I)*, para 49; more recently, for example, Case C-174/04 *Commission v Italian Republic (Re Automatic Suspension of Voting Rights in Privatised Undertaking)*, para 35; concurring: A Honrath, *Kapitalverkehr*, 71 *et seq*; A Rohde, *Kapitalverkehr*, 160 *et seq*; J Steiner, et al, *EU Law*, 350 *et seq*; W Frenz, *Europarecht*, mn 2732. Against the background of the aforementioned case law, voices in the literature [*cf*, eg, JCW Müller, *Kapitalverkehrsfreiheit*, 169 *et seq*; R Eckhoff, 'Kapital- und Zahlungsverkehr', mn 1721; M Seidel, 'Kapitalmarkt', 771], which doubt whether there is a need for the 'rule of reason' within the ambit of free movement of capital—usually referring to the allegedly 'open-ended' list in Art 58(1) lit. b EC that, as we learned above, can hardly be described as being 'open-ended' in the literal sense—are deprived of their persuasiveness. See Chapter VI. 2. a. (1) (c).

[229] Case C-367/98 *Commission v Portuguese Republic (Re Golden Shares I)*, para 52. The prerequisite that the mandatory requirements be of a non-economic nature, which has been stressed by the Court over decades, must be treated with cautious scepticism. The prerequisite is probably better understood as a 'marginal negative delineation' not excluding any national measure taken in the 'areas concerned with economic activities' but excluding only fiscal or protectionist considerations of the Member States. For a detailed account with further references, refer to A Cordewener, *Grundfreiheiten*, 134 *et seq*, esp. 136 *et seq*.

[230] For a discussion of the question of whether the 'rule of reason' applies to discriminatory national measures, see Chapter VI. 6. a.

[231] Case C-367/98 *Commission v Portuguese Republic (Re Golden Shares I)*, para 49.

[232] Ibid.

In the following section, I shall first set out the scope of the 'rule of reason' in the ambit of free movement of capital, thereby focusing on the question of whether the formula applies only to hindering or also to discriminatory national measures. Second, I shall elaborate on mandatory requirements accepted and refused by the Court. In doing so I shall pay particular attention to the recognized mandatory requirement of fiscal cohesion and the refused one of securing the tax base; both will play a significant role later, in the discussion on the operation of the rule of reason in a third country context.

a. The Scope of the 'Rule of Reason': Applicability to Discriminatory National Measures

This study conceives the 'rule of reason' as referring to the level of grounds of justification.[233] This formal[234] placement, however, does not answer the crucial question of whether the type of restriction, ie, either a hindrance of market access or direct or indirect discrimination, shall decide compellingly over the applicable grounds of justifications. Written grounds of justification can in principle save all kinds of national restrictions, whether they discriminate or merely hinder market access. However, for quite a long time it had commonly been thought that the 'rule of reason' applied to non-discriminatory national measures only.[235] The Court has frequently, though not consistently, reiterated in its judgments on fundamental freedoms that the formula is only relevant to national measures that apply 'to all persons and undertakings pursuing an activity in a territory of the host Member State.'[236]

---

[233] This view is favoured due to the fact that the 'rule of reason' contains a fully-fledged proportionality test: *cf* D Ehlers, 'Allgemeine Lehren', mn 63, 74; W Frenz, *Europarecht*, mn 2875, see also Case C-368/95 *Vereinigte Familiapress Zeitungsverlags- und vertriebs GmbH v. Heinrich Bauer Verlag*, para 18; Joined Cases C-34/95, C-35/95, and C-36/95 *Konsumentombudsmannen (KO) v De Agostini (Svenska) Förlag AB and TV-Shop i Sverige AB*, para 46. Of the same opinion, inter alia, A Epiney, *Umgekehrte Diskriminierungen*, 42; also G Hirsch, 'Warenverkehrsfreiheit', 511 *et seq*, who critically asks whether the question of where to locate the 'rule of reason' indeed constitutes a decisive question or rather a problem of legal '*Schubladendenken*' (stereotyped thinking) or a doctrinal glass bead game. Leaning towards the same view: JHH Weiler, 'Evolution', 366, who speaks of '*formalist sophistry*'. See also HD Jarass, 'Dogmatik II', 719. Of the opinion that the rule of reason relates to the level of the scope of application: eg, C Moench, 'Reinheitsgebot', 1109; T Schilling, 'Rechtsfragen', 52; M Ahlt, *Europarecht*, 91; T Jestaedt and F Kästle, 'Keck-Urteil', 27; M Hoffmann, *Abwehrrechte*, 111; G Ress and J Ukrow, Art. 56 EC (2002), mn 75.
[234] See, eg, Kingreen, who speaks of '*theoretical classification difficulties*'. [T Kingreen, 'Fundamental Freedoms', 573]
[235] 'Academic literature has for a long time understood this notion to mean that (overt or covert) discriminatory provisions may only be justified by means of the codified grounds.' Ibid, 574.
[236] Case C-367/98 *Commission v Portuguese Republic (Re Golden Shares I)*, para 49. For free movement of goods refer, for example, to Case 113/80 *Commission v Ireland (Re Irish Souvenirs)*, para 10; Case 59/82 *Schutzverband gegen Unwesen in der Wirtschaft v Weinvertriebs-GmbH*, para 11; Case 229/83 *Association des Centres distributeurs Édouard Leclerc and others v SARL 'Au blé vert' and others*, para 29 *et seq*. For the freedom to provide and receive services note, inter alia, Case 352/85 *Bond van Adverteerders and others v The Netherlands State*, para 32 *et seq*; Case C-353/89

I mentioned above that these statements might be delusive, to say the least. It appears that only the façade of this view has been (somewhat) preserved;[237] however, behind this façade, a major conversion has taken place.[238] The more recent jurisprudence on free movement of goods, the freedom to provide services, the freedom of establishment, and free movement of workers clearly reveals that the 'rule of reason' is not limited to mere hindrances, but provides valid grounds to justify national measures that constitute *indirect* discrimination.[239] If one wishes to take the converging interpretation of the fundamental freedoms seriously, then nothing else can be true with respect to free movement of capital.[240]

While the applicability of the 'rule of reason' in cases of indirect discrimination can be said to be widely accepted today[241]—a distinction between mere hindrance and indirect discrimination being hardly convincing to draw in practice[242]—the justification of *direct* discrimination by the 'rule of reason' still seems to cause some discomfort in the literature. Direct discrimination is viewed as the kind of restriction on free movement that impedes the most, and therefore, the respective Member State should not be rewarded with additional grounds of justification.[243] The Court, while certainly going to great pains not

Commission v Kingdom of the Netherlands (Re Television Advertising), para 15. For free movement of workers and the freedom of establishment see, eg, Case C-19/92 *Dieter Kraus v Land Baden-Württemberg)*, para 32.

[237] See for a recent judgment: Case C-367/98 *Commission v Portuguese Republic (Re Golden Shares I)*, para 49.

[238] A Cordewener, *Grundfreiheiten*, 143.

[239] For the freedom to provide services see, eg, Joined Cases 110 and 111/78 *Ministère public and 'Chambre syndicale des agents artistiques et impresarii de Belgique' ASBL v Willy van Wesemael and others*, para 27 *et seq*; Joined Cases 62 and 63/81 *Société anonyme de droit français Seco et Société anonyme de droit français Desquenne & Giral v Etablissement d'assurance contre la vieillesse et l'invalidité*, paras 8–10; Case C-360/89 *Commission v Italian Republic (Re Award of Public Works Contracts)*, para 11 *et seq*, 14; Case C-55/98 *Skatteministeriet v Bent Vestergaard*, para 22 *et seq*; for the ambits of free movement of workers and freedom of establishment see Case 270/83 *Commission v French Republic (Re Corporation Tax and Shareholders' Tax Credits: 'avoir fiscal'*, paras 19, 20 *et seq*; Case 175/88 *Klaus Biehl v Administration des contributions du grand-duché de Luxembourg*, para 13 *et seq*; Case C-204/90 *Hanns-Martin Bachmann v The Belgian State*, para 8 *et seq*; Case C-300/90 *Commission v Kingdom of Belgium (Re Deduction of Insurance Contributions)*, para 6 *et seq*; Case C-279/93 'Schumacker' *Finanzamt Köln-Altstadt v Roland Schumacker*, para 38 *et seq*; Case C-80/94 *G. H. E. J. Wielockx v Inspecteur der Directe Belastingen*, para 20 *et seq*; Case C-107/94 *P. H. Asscher v Staatssecretaris van Financiën*, para 20 *et seq*; Case C-237/94 *John O'Flynn v Adjudication Officer*, para 19, 24 *et seq*; Case C-254/97 *Société Baxter, B. Braun Médical SA, Société Fresenius France and Laboratoires Bristol-Myers-Squibb SA v Premier Ministre, Ministère du Travail et des Affaires sociales, Ministère de l'Economie et des Finances and Ministère de l'Agriculture, de la Pêche et de l'Alimentation*, para 18.

[240] Dissenting: A Haratsch, et al, *Europarecht*, mn 916; G Ress and J Ukrow, Art. 56 EC (2002), mn 81; M Sedlaczek, 'Kapitalverkehrsfreiheit', 57. Probably also: A Honrath, *Kapitalverkehr*, 73 *et seq*.

[241] Note A Cordewener, *Grundfreiheiten*, 163; dissenting, eg: M Sedlaczek, 'Kapitalverkehrsfreiheit', 57; A Haratsch, et al, *Europarecht*, mn 916; B Terra and PJ Wattel, *European Tax Law*, 43.

[242] *Cf* D Ehlers, 'Allgemeine Lehren', mn 90 for further references and A Arnull, et al, *European Union Law*, 355 *et seq*.

[243] D Ehlers, 'Allgemeine Lehren', mn 90.

to admit it openly,[244] recognized in its decisions on free movement of goods and workers, the freedom to provide services and the freedom of establishment, and also in regard to Arts 12 EC and 141 EC, that there are situations in which direct discrimination can be saved by the 'rule of reason'. In fact, although not settled conclusively, an increasing tendency can be shown towards the application of the rule of reason to national measures that constitute direct discrimination.[245]

In principle, such an approach appears to be sensible. It is difficult to comprehend why a national measure constituting indirect discrimination—a situation in which the restricting effect is disguised—should be easier to justify than direct discrimination.[246] Moreover, one must critically ask whether directly discriminating national measures exist which conceivably serve a mandatory requirement that outweighs free movement. This question must be answered in the affirmative if one considers the mandatory requirement of the protection of the

---

[244] *Cf* probably the best known judgment in this respect: Case C-2/90 *Commission v Kingdom of Belgium (Re Prohibition of Tipping Waste Originating in Another Member State)*. See also P Oliver, *Movement of Goods*, mn 6.76.

[245] On the free movement of goods see: implicitly in Case 113/80 *Commission v. Ireland (Re Irish Souvenirs)*, para 7 *et seq*, 14 *et seq*; maintaining the façade in Case C-2/90 *Commission v Kingdom of Belgium (Re Prohibition of Tipping Waste Originating in Another Member State)*, 29–31; Case C-389/96 *Aher-Waggon GmbH v Federal Republic of Germany*, para 14 *et seq*; note in this respect also the statement of Advocate General Jacobs on Case C-203/96 (Opinion of AG Jacobs) *Chemische Afvalstoffen Dusseldorp BV and Others v Minister van Volkshuisvesting, Ruimtelijke Ordening en Milieubeheer*, para 82 *et seq*, esp. para 89 *et seq*. More recently Joined Cases C-34/95, C-35/95, and C-36/95 *Konsumentombudsmannen (KO) v De Agostini (Svenska) Förlag AB and TV-Shop i Sverige AB*, para 44 *et seq*; see in this respect the interpretation of M Novak, 'De Agostini', esp. 2591, and see, moreover, Case C-203/96 *Chemische Afvalstoffen Dusseldorp BV and Others v Minister van Volkshuisvesting, Ruimtelijke Ordening en Milieubeheer*, para 39 *et seq*; Case C-379/98 *PreussenElektra AG v Schhleswag AG, in the presence of Windpark Reußenköge III GmbH and Land Schleswig-Holstein*, para 71 *et seq*. With respect to the judgment just mentioned see the striking analysis of Advocate General Jacobs: Case C-379/98 (Opinion of AG Jacobs) *PreussenElektra AG v Schhleswag AG, in the presence of Windpark Reußenköge III GmbH and Land Schleswig-Holstein*, para 220 *et seq*, esp. para 233; for a sharp-witted account of the earlier jurisprudence of the Court, refer to P von Wilmowsky, *Abfallwirtschaft*, 158 *et seq* for further references; for the freedom to provide services note: Case C-300/90 *Commission v Kingdom of Belgium (Re Deduction of Insurance Contributions)*, para 11; see also W-H Roth, 'Bachmann', 393; for a contradictory view: Case C-484/93 *Peter Svensson et Lena Gustavsson v Ministre du Logement et de l'Urbanisme*, para 12 *et seq*; Case C-101/94 *Commission v Italian Republic (Re Dealing in Transferable Securities)*, para 19 *et seq*, 29 *et seq*; for free movement of workers see: Case C-415/93 (Opinion of AG Lenz) *Union royale belge des sociétés de football association ASBL v Jean-Marc Bosman, Royal club liégeois SA v Jean-Marc Bosman and others and Union des associations européennes de football (UEFA) v Jean-Marc Bosman*, para 135; Case C-415/93 *Union royale belge des sociétés de football association ASBL v Jean-Marc Bosman, Royal club liégeois SA v Jean-Marc Bosman and others and Union des associations européennes de football (UEFA) v Jean-Marc Bosman*, para 127 *et seq*. Reiterating the 'old' view: eg, Case C-224/97 *Erich Ciola v Land Vorarlberg*, para 16; for a discussion of the aforementioned case law and on Arts 12 EC 141 EC, including further references, refer to A Cordewener, *Grundfreiheiten*, 150 *et seq*.

[246] JHH Weiler, 'Evolution', 366; T Kingreen, 'Fundamental Freedoms', 575 *et seq*.

260   *Exceptions Applicable to Intra-Community & Third Country Situations*

environment.²⁴⁷ An 'abusive' practice can be countered by setting respective high standards for the proportionality test.²⁴⁸

With the converging tendencies in interpreting the fundamental freedoms in mind, the same reasoning advanced above must also be true for free movement of capital.²⁴⁹ The case law, although not conclusively,²⁵⁰ shows indications of the application of the rule of reason to national measures constituting direct discrimination.²⁵¹ This converging interpretation has, moreover, the positive effect of avoiding the already mentioned potential disparity in treatment among the fundamental freedoms with respect to national measures ensuring effective fiscal supervision and preventing tax evasion or avoidance. While within the ambit of free movement of capital, such measures can be justified by having recourse to written grounds contained in Art 58(1) lit. b EC (1st group), in the sphere of the other fundamental freedoms, they can only be defended with reference to the 'rule of reason'.²⁵²

After having considered all of the above, one can conclude that the 'rule of reason' should be applied irrespective of whether a national measure constitutes

---

²⁴⁷ A Epiney, 'Freiheit des Warenverkehrs', 245; T Kingreen, 'Fundamental Freedoms', 576; note also the striking statement of Advocate General Jacobs in Case C-379/98 (Opinion of AG Jacobs) *PreussenElektra AG v Schhleswag AG, in the presence of Windpark Reußenköge III GmbH and Land Schleswig-Holstein*, para 233.
²⁴⁸ S Heselhaus, '*Rechtfertigung*', 648 *et seq*.
²⁴⁹ U Haferkamp, *Kapitalverkehrsfreiheit*, 155; dissenting: G Ress and J Ukrow, Art. 56 EC (2002), mn 81.
²⁵⁰ See in this respect the restrictive interpretation in the *Konle* judgment, where the Court held: 'discrimination is prohibited by Art. 73 b of the Treaty [now, after amendment, Art. 56(1) EC], unless it is justified on *grounds permitted by the Treaty*' [Emphasis added Case C-302/97 *Klaus Konle v Republik Österreich*, para 24] and '[t]o the extent that a Member State can justify its requirement of prior authorisation by relying on a town and country planning objective...the restrictive measure inherent in such a requirement can be accepted only *if it is not applied in a discriminatory manner* ...'. [Emphasis added. Case C-302/97 *Klaus Konle v Republik Österreich*, para 40] See also Case C-367/98 *Commission v Portuguese Republic (Re Golden Shares I)*, para 49.
²⁵¹ With respect to the mandatory requirement of 'fiscal cohesion', see Case C-35/98 *Staatssecretaris van Financiën v B.G.M. Verkooijen*, para 31; Case C-478/98 *Commission v Kingdom of Belgium (Re Loans issued abroad)*, para 17 *et seq*, para 32 *et seq*; Case C-319/02 (Opinion of AG Kokott) *Petri Manninen*, para 36 *et seq*, para 40 *et seq*; Case C-242/03 *Ministre des Finances v Jean-Claude Weidert and Élisabeth Paulus*, para 11 *et seq*, para 16 *et seq*; Case C-315/02 *Anneliese Lenz v Finanzlandesdirektion für Tirol*, para 20 *et seq*, para 34 *et seq*. Advocate La Pergola in his opinion on *Verkooijen* interprets the case law of the Court in a way suggesting that only the mandatory requirement of 'fiscal cohesion' is capable of justifying direct discriminations; other mandatory requirements, however, are limited to national measures that constitute a mere hindrance to market access. [Case C-35/98 (First Opinion of AG La Pergola) *Staatssecretaris van Financiën v B.G.M. Verkooijen*, paras 18, 23] However, an approach to introducing an abstract hierarchy of different mandatory requirements is not only doctrinally unconvincing, but his reading also seems to be outdated against the background of the more recent case law of the Court.
²⁵² See Chapter VI. 2. a. (1). See also Case C-242/03 (Opinion of AG Kokott) *Ministre des Finances v Jean-Claude Weidert and Élisabeth Paulus*, para 28.

direct or indirect discrimination or a mere hindrance.[253] This finding, however, cannot disguise the 'remaining tensions' inherent in the dual system of grounds of justification advocated by the Court. If one applies the 'rule of reason' to all kinds of restrictions—which, as explained above, I view as compelling—then it is open to question how to reconcile the Court's interpretive maxim of 'singularia non sunt extenda', ie, that written grounds of justification constitute a conclusive list of exceptions, not expandable and strictly construed, and the open-ended list of unwritten exceptions to the fundamental freedoms enshrined in the 'rule of reason'. An answer to this question may be envisaged in the rather more positivistic suggestion that 'all grounds for justification should be established where they are mentioned by the Treaty'.[254] The public policy clause—'the classic "security outlet for national interests" of international treaties'[255]—which can be found with respect to all fundamental freedoms could integrate all mandatory requirements now contained in the 'rule of reason.'[256]

However, while it is true that the present approach of the ECJ can hardly form the foundation of a consistent doctrinal approach,[257] it would go beyond the scope of this study to discuss this approach in sufficient depth. For the time being I therefore adhere to the traditional dual system of grounds of justification in the discussion of free movement of capital. For my purposes it is central but, at the same time, it also suffices to note that the 'rule of reason' applies to all kinds of national measures restricting free movement of capital.

b. Mandatory Requirements Established by the Court in an Intra-Community Context

As explained above, the list of possible mandatory requirements is in no way limited, but open to accommodating the changing needs of the Member States. The Court has, inter alia, accepted the following mandatory requirements as being capable of restricting free movement of capital: in *Trummer*, the Court held that national

---

[253] Concurring, eg, W Weiß, 'Niederlassungsfreiheit', 496 *et seq*; W-H Roth, 'Zwingenden Erfordernisse', 983 *et seq*; S Heselhaus, 'Rechtfertigung', 650; T Kingreen, 'Fundamental Freedoms', 576; more cautiously: A Cordewener, *Grundfreiheiten*, 150 *et seq*; dissenting, eg, A Arnull, et al, *European Union Law*, 356; W Frenz, *Europarecht*, mn 2640 *et seq*, esp. 2643 for further references; D Ehlers, 'Allgemeine Lehren', mn 90; M Burgi, 'Anmerkung zu C-234/03', 306.
[254] T Kingreen, 'Fundamental Freedoms', 576 *et seq*; of a different view but acknowledging the trend in the case law: S Leible, Art. 28 EC (2000), mn 20.
[255] T Kingreen, 'Fundamental Freedoms', 577, see also H Schneider, *Öffentliche Ordnung* 57 *et seq*; P Oliver, *Movement of Goods*, mn 6.77.
[256] T Kingreen, 'Fundamental Freedoms', 577; with respect to free movement of capital in principle concurring, though also applying a dual system in their analysis: A Rohde, *Kapitalverkehr*, 159 *et seq*; U Haferkamp, *Kapitalverkehrsfreiheit*, 155; for a 'single' approach see: JCW Müller, *Kapitalverkehrsfreiheit*, 169 *et seq*; W Frenz, *Europarecht*, mn 2876 *et seq*.
[257] Refer to T Kingreen, *Struktur der Grundfreiheiten*, 156 *et seq*; W-H Roth, 'Zwingenden Erfordernisse', 984; S Heselhaus, 'Rechtfertigung'; P-C Müller-Graff, Art. 30 EC (2003), mn 26 *et seq*; T Jürgensen and I Schlünder, 'EG-Grundrechtsschutz', 217. Note also A Cordewener, *Grundfreiheiten*, 162 *et seq*.

measures may ensure that 'the mortgage system clearly and transparently prescribes the respective rights of mortgagees inter se, as well as the rights of mortgagees as a whole vis-à-vis other creditors'.[258] In *Konle*, it was established that national measures may require prior authorization in order to pursue a 'town and country planning objective such as maintaining, in the general interest, a permanent population and an economic activity independent of the tourist sector in certain regions'.[259] Also, cultural policy objectives may constitute a mandatory requirement. In *Veronica*, the ECJ stated that the establishment and maintenance of a

> pluralistic and non-commercial broadcasting system... [which] forms part of a cultural policy intended to safeguard, in the audio-visual sector, the freedom of expression of the various (in particular social, cultural, religious and philosophical) components[260]

forms a legitimate public interest.

Within the ambit of free movement of capital is the mandatory requirement of the protection of the integrity of the national tax system—in short, fiscal cohesion—is of special interest. It aims in particular at the preservation of national regulatory systems that serve the realization of fiscal equality.[261] In systematic terms, the mandatory requirement is not to be located within Art 58(1) lit. b EC (1st group),[262] but within the 'rule of reason'.[263] This classification, however, has no practical bearing due to the fact that this study proceeds from the assumption that the 'rule of reason' can also be invoked for the justification of discriminatory national measures. The content and meaning of the mandatory requirement is said to be rather elusive.[264] However, while it is true that its scope depends very much on the individual case,[265] it is nevertheless possible to distil broad lines in a simplistic manner.

The mandatory requirement of fiscal cohesion was accepted for the first time in the *Bachmann* case.[266] In subsequent cases,[267] however, the scope of the mandatory requirement has steadily been reduced.

---

[258] Case C-222/97 *Manfred Trummer and Peter Mayer*, para 30; see also G Ress and J Ukrow, Art. 56 EC (2002), mn 78.
[259] Case C-302/97 *Klaus Konle v Republik Österreich*, para 40.
[260] Case C-148/91 *Vereniging Veronica Omroep Organisatie v Commissariaat voor de Media*, para 9.
[261] A Cordewener, *Grundfreiheiten*, 960 *et seq*; H Weber-Grellet, *Europäisches Steuerrecht*, § 8, mn 40; more broadly: C Staringer, 'Dividendenbesteuerung', 109; perceiving 'fiscal cohesion' as an 'empty phrase': eg, O Thömmes, 'Diskriminierungen', 831.
[262] For a similar view see, eg, R Eckhoff, 'Kapital- und Zahlungsverkehr', mn 1721.
[263] M Sedlaczek, 'Kapitalverkehrsfreiheit', 57.
[264] O Thömmes, 'Diskriminierungen', 826.
[265] A Cordewener, *Grundfreiheiten*, 958 *et seq*.
[266] Case C-204/90 *Hanns-Martin Bachmann v The Belgian State*, para 23 *et seq*; on the same day with similar facts: Case C-300/90 *Commission v Kingdom of Belgium (Re Deduction of Insurance Contributions)*; see, for a comprehensive discussion of the mandatory requirement of fiscal cohesion, A Cordewener, *Grundfreiheiten*, 956 *et seq*, 459 *et seq*. Its applicability is accepted throughout all fundamental freedoms. [A Cordewener, *Grundfreiheiten*, 958 *et seq* for further references]
[267] eg, Case C-204/90 *Hanns-Martin Bachmann v The Belgian State*; Case C-300/90 *Commission v Kingdom of Belgium (Re Deduction of Insurance Contributions)*; Case C-107/94

In the *Bachmann* case,[268] a German citizen, Bachmann, temporarily moved to Belgium in connection with employment there. A long time before he left Germany, he subscribed to sickness, disability, and life insurance policies with German insurance companies. While in Belgium, Bachmann continued to pay on those insurance policies. However, under Belgian tax law, those contributions were only deductible from his income generated in Belgium if they were paid to a Belgian insurance company. The Court found that such a national measure constitutes indirect discrimination for workers from other Member States and restricts the freedom to provide services for insurance companies located outside Belgium.[269] The Belgian government advanced three justifications: first, consumer protection; second, effectiveness of fiscal supervision; and, third, the need to maintain the cohesion of the national tax system.[270] While the first and second justifications were to no avail, the Court accepted the last one: fiscal cohesion. The Court's reasoning was colourfully summarized by *Terra* and *Wattel* as follows:

Under Belgian tax law, a direct link exists between deductibility on contributions and taxation of future benefits: deduction of contributions, then taxation of benefits; no deduction of contributions, then no taxation of benefits. In this system the loss of tax revenue due to deduction was offset by subsequent taxation of pensions, annuities and capital sums payable later.[271]

This direct link—the 'cohesion'—would have been disrupted if the Court had forced Belgium to allow for deductibility of contributions to foreign insurance companies because, under international law, Belgium neither has jurisdiction to subject foreign insurers to a withholding tax on the benefits paid, nor can Belgium tax payments by foreign insurers in the hands of the policy holders, like Bachmann, who by then had emigrated to another country.[272] Due to the fact that no less restrictive measures were available, the Court upheld the Belgian tax legislation.[273]

P. H. Asscher v Staatssecretaris van Financiën, para 58 *et seq*; Case C-251/98 *C Baars v Inspecteur der Belastingen Particulieren/Ondernemingen Gorinchem*, para 37 *et seq*; Joined Cases C-397/98 and C-410/98 *Metallgesellschaft Ltd and Others, Hoechst AG and Hoechst (UK) Ltd v Commissioners of Inland Revenue and H.M. Attorney General*, para 69 *et seq*; Case C-436/00 *X and Y v Riksskatteverket*, para ; Case C-319/02 *Petri Manninen*, para 40 *et seq*; Case C-315/02 *Anneliese Lenz v Finanzlandesdirektion für Tirol*, para 36; Case C-446/03 *Marks & Spencer plc v David Halsey (H.M. Inspector of Taxes)*; see for short summaries of the cases: M Dahlberg, *Direct Taxation*, 242 *et seq*.

[268] Case C-204/90 *Hanns-Martin Bachmann v The Belgian State*.
[269] Ibid, paras 13, 31.
[270] Ibid, para 14 *et seq*.
[271] B Terra and PJ Wattel, *European Tax Law*, 66; see Case C-204/90 *Hanns-Martin Bachmann v The Belgian State*, para 23 *et seq*.
[272] B Terra and PJ Wattel, *European Tax Law*, 66 *et seq*.
[273] A further reason why the *Bachmann* case is so important is because it seems to allow in principle for exit taxes (so-called 'macro clearing') upon emigration of the taxpayer and/or his assets to another jurisdiction if shaped in a proportionate manner [Of the same opinion: eg, ibid,

As mentioned above, the scope of the mandatory requirement was substantiated but also limited in later cases. What seems to be required in order to justify a national measure by the plea of fiscal cohesion is a direct link between deductibility and subsequent taxability. Thus, a macro-economic link between tax expenditure and tax revenue does not suffice. This was explained in *Svensson and Gustavsson*: Luxembourg subsidized mortgage interest payments of residents if the loan was taken out with a Luxembourg bank. Lenders who borrowed from a bank established in another country were thus denied the subsidy. The Court found that such a national measure constitutes a restriction on free movement of capital and the freedom to provide services.[274] It further held that such legislation was also not capable of justification on the basis of fiscal cohesion due to the fact that the subsidy was paid out of general tax revenue and, thus, the direct link between the subsidy and its financing was missing.[275]

The direct link was subsequently defined even more narrowly.[276] It must be present within the same tax and within the same taxpayer or even within the same contract. In *Verkooijen*, a Netherlands resident was denied dividend exemptions for dividends received from a company established in another Member State while such exemption was available for dividends distributed by Dutch companies. The Court found that such legislation constitutes a restriction on the free movement of capital[277] and proceeded to discuss possible grounds of justification. In this respect the Dutch government argued that there is cohesion between the corporate tax on the profits of a company and the exemption from individual income tax on dividends paid out of those profits.[278] The Court, however, was not like-minded. It stated that in *Bachmann* the granting of the tax advantage and the offsetting of that advantage by a fiscal levy related to the same tax, in

---

70 W Schön, 'Besteuerung im Binnenmarkt', 296 *et seq*; Case C-436/00 *X and Y v Riksskatteverket*, para 59; critical: M Lang, 'Wohin geht das Internationale Steuerrecht?' 292 *et seq*; opposing: eg European Commission, 'Taxation: Commission Requests Germany to End Exit Tax Rules' (IP/04/493); J Hey, 'Unternehmensbesteuerung', 199. See in this respect the judgment of the Court in Case C-9/02 *Hughes de Lasteyrie du Saillant v Ministère de l'Économie, des Finances et de l'Industrie*. For the application of the proportionality test, see in particular Case C-436/00 *X and Y v Riksskatteverket*, para 59] Exit tax rules aim at the recapturing of tax deferrals, which were granted under the assumption that the future benefits will be taxable, and taxation of uncrystallized capital gains that otherwise would be lost by the exit jurisdiction. [B Terra and PJ Wattel, *European Tax Law*, 67 *et seq*] The problem with exit taxes due at the moment of emigration is, however, that they require the payment of cash that is not there. The emigrating taxpayer does not sell any of its assets nor receive any pension or retirement payments but he merely changes jurisdiction. This constitutes a considerable hindrance to free movement [B Terra and PJ Wattel, *European Tax Law*, 67 *et seq*] that calls for a very strict application of the proportionality test.

[274] Case C-484/93 *Peter Svensson et Lena Gustavsson v Ministre du Logement et de l'Urbanisme*, para 10 *et seq*.
[275] Ibid, para 18 *et seq*.
[276] B Terra and PJ Wattel, *European Tax Law*, 71 *et seq*.
[277] Case C-35/98 *Staatssecretaris van Financiën v B.G.M. Verkooijen*, para 34 *et seq*.
[278] Ibid, para 49 *et seq*.

contrast to the situation present in *Verkooijen*.²⁷⁹ In the latter case there were two different taxes (corporate tax and personal income tax) levied on different taxpayers (the company distributing dividends and the person receiving dividends).²⁸⁰ The same conclusion was reached in the *Baars* case, decided upon the rules on the freedom of establishment.²⁸¹ It appears, therefore, that Member States must recognize foreign dividends as equivalent to domestic ones and foreign corporation tax as creditable as domestic corporation tax.²⁸²

The mandatory requirement of fiscal cohesion can also not be pleaded

if the Member State concerned concluded a tax treaty with the other State involved containing allocation rules which imply that fiscal cohesion at individual taxpayer's level was waived in return for fiscal cohesion at macro-economic level (interstate level).²⁸³

This was first held explicitly in *Wielockx*,²⁸⁴ while in earlier cases, especially in *Bachmann*, the Court did not seriously consider the impact of tax treaties.²⁸⁵ Despite all of this, it is important to note that after *Bachmann*²⁸⁶ and *Kommission v Belgium*,²⁸⁷ the Member States have not been successful in relying on the mandatory requirement of fiscal cohesion.²⁸⁸ Despite the fact that the mandatory requirement is frequently referred to, in all but one case—*Manninen*²⁸⁹—the Court could not even detect the 'direct link' as required by the *Bachmann* jurisprudence.

Besides the mandatory requirements explicitly discussed by the Court within the context of free movement of capital, recourse can also be had, as mentioned earlier, to mandatory requirements considered with respect to other fundamental freedoms. Thus, Member States may have recourse to mandatory requirements such as the protection of investors or the defence of consumers,²⁹⁰ the maintenance

---

²⁷⁹ Ibid, para 57.   ²⁸⁰ Ibid, para 58.
²⁸¹ Case C-251/98 *C Baars v Inspecteur der Belastingen Particulieren/Ondernemingen Gorinchem*. See, however, the reasoning of Advocate General *Kokott* in *Manninen*, where she argued that the criteria of 'within the same tax' and 'within the same taxpayer' need not be present cumulatively but are merely a strong indication of 'fiscal cohesion'. [Case C-319/02 (Opinion of AG Kokott) *Petri Manninen*, para 55] The Court's reasoning on this point is nebulous. [*Cf* Case C-265/04 *Margaretha Bouanich v Skatteverket*, para 45] See also G Kofler, 'Manninen', 585; G Kofler, 'Manninen II', 28; K Eicker and R Obser, 'Weidert', 445; M Lang, 'Wohin geht das Internationale Steuerrecht?'
²⁸² B Terra and PJ Wattel, *European Tax Law*, 73.
²⁸³ Ibid, 74; see also W Schön, 'Kapitalverkehrsfreiheit', 770 *et seq*.
²⁸⁴ Case C-80/94 *G. H. E. J. Wielockx v Inspecteur der Directe Belastingen*, para 24 *et seq*; for a critical account, note PJ Wattel, 'International Tax Law', 243 *et seq*; A Cordewener, *Grundfreiheiten*, 969 *et seq*.
²⁸⁵ For a critical account of the decision in *Bachmann*, see B Knobbe-Keuk, 'Discriminatory Tax Provisions', 79 *et seq*.
²⁸⁶ Case C-204/90 *Hanns-Martin Bachmann v The Belgian State*.
²⁸⁷ Case C-300/90 *Commission v Kingdom of Belgium (Re Deduction of Insurance Contributions)*.
²⁸⁸ See G Kofler, 'Manninen II', 27 for further references.
²⁸⁹ In *Manninen,* the national measure was not proportionate. See footnote 281 of this Chapter.
²⁹⁰ First mentioned in Case 120/78 *Rewe-Zentral AG v Bundesmonopolverwaltung für Branntwein ('Cassis de Dijon')*, para 8.

of stability in or protecting the reputation[291] of the financial market,[292] the fairness of commercial transactions,[293] the protection of the environment,[294] or the preservation of available small-scale agriculture.[295]

c. Mandatory Requirements Rejected by the Court in an Intra-Community Context

In the course of its jurisprudence, the Court considered a multitude of alleged mandatory requirements in the general interest suggested by the Member States that were ultimately rejected. The judgment in *'avoir fiscal'* offers a rich pool of such putative mandatory requirements: the Court discussed the effects of counterbalancing advantages, the voluntary submission to a disadvantageous tax regime by choice of a certain form of establishment, the lack of Community competence within the area of direct taxation, and a respective lack of harmonization.

The ECJ held—doctrinally actually not a question to be discussed on the level of grounds of justification[296] but relating to the issue of 'difference in treatment'— that a difference in (tax) treatment cannot be undone even if disadvantages in one area are compensated by various advantages in other areas.[297] The Court considers only the effects of the specific national measure with respect to its specific addressee in the specific situation and thus does not take into account other measures that might provide counterbalancing advantages for the person concerned.[298]

The Court also rejected the argument that voluntary submission to disadvantageous taxation by choice of a certain form of establishment would justify discriminatory treatment. Market participants are 'free to choose the appropriate legal form in which to pursue their activities in another member state and that freedom of choice must not be limited by discriminatory tax provisions'.[299]

Furthermore, the ECJ did not allow the Member States to plead the fact that the Community lacked competence in the area of direct taxation as a justification

---

[291] Case C-384/93 *Alpine Investments BV v Minister van Financiën*, para 44.
[292] F Kimms, *Kapitalverkehrsfreiheit*, 185; G Ress and J Ukrow, Art. 56 EC (2002), 77; U Haferkamp, *Kapitalverkehrsfreiheit*, 156 *et seq*.
[293] Case 120/78 *Rewe-Zentral AG v Bundesmonopolverwaltung für Branntwein ('Cassis de Dijon')*, para 8.
[294] Case 302/86 *Commission v Kingdom of Denmark*, para 8 *et seq*.
[295] Case C-452/01 *Margarethe Ospelt and Schlössle Weissenberg Familienstiftung*, para 39 *et seq*.
[296] A Cordewener, *Grundfreiheiten*, 933 *et seq*. The Court, nevertheless, speaks of justification: *cf* Case C-330/91 *R v Inland Revenue Commissioners, ex p Commerzbank AG*, para 19.
[297] eg, Case 270/83 *Commission v French Republic (Re Corporation tax and Shareholders' Tax Credits: 'avoir fiscal'*, para 17 *et seq*; Case C-330/91 *R v Inland Revenue Commissioners, ex p Commerzbank AG*, para 19; Case C-307/97 *Compagnie de Saint-Gobain, Zweigniederlassung Deutschland v Finanzamt Aachen-Innenstadt*, para 53.
[298] O Thömmes, 'Diskriminierungen', 819.
[299] Case 270/83 *Commission v French Republic (Re Corporation tax and Shareholders' Tax Credits: 'avoir fiscal'*, para 22.

for their restrictive national measures. With respect to double taxation treaties, the Court held that:

a Member State cannot make respect for [the fundamental freedoms contained in the EC Treaty] subject to the contents of an agreement concluded with another Member State. In particular, that does not permit those rights to be made subject to a condition of reciprocity imposed for the purpose of obtaining corresponding advantages in other Member States.[300]

Even if the Member States remain competent to divide and allocate tax powers among themselves and also towards third countries, 'as far as the exercise of the power of taxation so allocated is concerned, the Member States nevertheless may not disregard Community law'.[301] In this context the Member States also advanced the argument that an EC law-friendly design of their law on direct taxation stands subject to harmonization. The Court, however, rejected this plea and merely noted that the direct effects of the fundamental freedoms are not dependent on prior harmonization.[302]

The 'general purpose' of securing the tax base and preventing the loss of tax revenue has not been accepted by the Court as a mandatory requirement, which was confirmed in *ICI*,[303] *Saint-Gobain*,[304] *Metallgesellschaft*,[305] *Lankhorst-Hohorst*,[306] and other judgments.[307] This is understandable if seen in the wider context of the settled case law according to which purposes of a purely economic nature, such as budgetary interests or protectionist aims, cannot justify restrictive national measures.[308] However, while the Court continues to state that possible non-taxation of profits must be accepted as a consequence of the fact that harmonization of direct taxes is lacking and of the effect of the fundamental freedoms, in its recent judgments—most notably in *Marks & Spencer*—it seems to be of a different view

---

[300] Ibid, para 26.
[301] Case C-307/97 *Compagnie de Saint-Gobain, Zweigniederlassung Deutschland v Finanzamt Aachen-Innenstadt*, para 57.
[302] Case 270/83 *Commission v French Republic (Re Corporation Tax and Shareholders' Tax Credits: 'avoir fiscal'*, para 24.
[303] Case C-264/96 *Imperial Chemical Industries plc (ICI) v Kenneth Hall Colmer (H.M. Inspector of Taxes)*, para 28.
[304] Case C-307/97 *Compagnie de Saint-Gobain, Zweigniederlassung Deutschland v Finanzamt Aachen-Innenstadt*, para 49 et seq.
[305] Joined Cases C-397/98 and C-410/98 *Metallgesellschaft Ltd and Others, Hoechst AG and Hoechst (UK) Ltd v Commissioners of Inland Revenue and H.M. Attorney General*, para 59. The Court referred to this finding as settled case law.
[306] Case C-324/00 *Lankhorst-Hohorst GmbH v Finanzamt Steinfurt*, para 36.
[307] eg, Case C-9/02 *Hughes de Lasteyrie du Saillant v Ministère de l'Économie, des Finances et de l'Industrie*, para 60; Case C-35/98 *Staatssecretaris van Financiën v B.G.M. Verkooijen*, para 59; Case C-136/00 *Rolf Dieter Danner*, para 55 et seq; Case C-436/00 *X and Y v Riksskatteverket*, para 50.
[308] Case C-484/93 *Peter Svensson et Lena Gustavsson v Ministre du Logement et de l'Urbanisme*; cf A Cordewener, *Grundfreiheiten*, 936 et seq; for a different view see W Schön, 'Kapitalverkehr mit Drittstaaten', 515 et seq.

with respect to double tax relief for loss (incurred by a non-resident subsidiary).[309] The argument with which it seeks to justify its reasoning is surprising, to say the least: the Member State has insufficient means available to prevent double tax relief. From a political viewpoint one can certainly comprehend that the Court wished to counter the threat of double tax relief. From a doctrinal perspective, however, this reasoning contradicts its holding with respect to the non-taxation of profits in particular and the non-acceptance of the erosion of the tax basis as a mandatory requirement in general.[310]

d. Summary so Far

The 'rule of reason' has been firmly established within the ambit of free movement of capital. Its scope of application is not limited to national measures that cause a mere hindrance to free movement, but also extends to indirect and direct discrimination. The list of mandatory requirements is non-exhaustive. Of particular prominence within the ambit of free movement of capital is the rather vaguely defined mandatory requirement of fiscal cohesion, frequently pleaded by the Member States and almost as frequently rejected by the Court. Its basic idea is to preserve those national regulatory systems that serve the realization of fiscal equality, ie, to keep intact the direct link between a tax advantage that was granted under the assumption of subsequent taxability. By requiring, inter alia, that direct link to be present within the same tax and within the same taxpayer or even within the same contract, the mandatory requirement was stripped of most of its significance.

Alleged mandatory requirements such as 'the existence of counterbalancing advantages', 'the voluntary submission to disadvantageous tax regimes by choice of a certain form of establishment', 'the lack of competence of the Community in the area of direct taxation lack of harmonization', 'the general purposes of securing the tax base and preventing the loss of tax revenue' are, in accordance with the Court's case law, to be rejected.

e. The Operation of the 'Rule of Reason' in a Third Country Context

The applicability of the 'rule of reason' is not limited to national measures that restrict intra-Community capital movements; the formula applies equally to third country capital movements.[311] While the extension of the 'rule of reason' to

---

[309] Case C-446/03 *Marks & Spencer plc v David Halsey (H.M. Inspector of Taxes)*, para 45 *et seq*.
[310] M Lang, 'Marks & Spencer II', 7.
[311] Except for those who in general do not want to apply the 'rule of reason' in the ambit of free movement of capital—*cf* footnote 46 above—the extension of the formula to third country situations is not disputed. Refer, eg, to K Ståhl, 'Movement of Capital', 54 *et seq*; W Schön, 'Kapitalverkehr mit Drittstaaten', 515 *et seq*, 518 *et seq*; A Schnitger, 'Kapitalverkehrsfreiheit',

third country situations in principle is hardly disputed, this accord erodes quickly when one turns to the question of how the formula should operate in the actual situation.

In an intra-Community context, the Court accepted in principle a multitude of mandatory requirements, while at the same time it has consistently set challenging high standards for national measures in terms of proportionality.[312] As we have learned above, a government has hardly ever succeeded de facto in their plea. Recalling that an unrestricted free movement of capital best serves the attainment of the Treaty aims, I welcomed such an approach.

With respect to third country situations, the few available views in the literature range from an interpretation of the formula analogous to the one adopted for intra-Community capital movements[313] to a significant constructive expansion calling for a more generous application of accepted mandatory requirements and the acceptance of mandatory requirements that were rejected in an intra-Community context.[314] The accepted mandatory requirement (in an intra-Community context) of 'fiscal cohesion' and the rejected one of 'securing the tax base and preventing the loss of tax revenue' will be at the centre of the following discussion.

(1) The Mandatory Requirement of 'Fiscal Cohesion'—Reloaded?

The mandatory requirement of fiscal cohesion aims, as already mentioned above, at the preservation of the integrity of the national tax system. The Court, in an intra-Community context, took a tough stance and construed the mandatory requirement in a very narrow sense. This was greeted with considerable distaste by the Member States due to the fact that the Court's rulings not only caused tax shortfalls, but also forced them to reconsider certain legal constructions, such as imputation systems, in general terms. With respect to third countries, similar adoptions of the legal orders of the Member States might become necessary. However, there are commentators who think that the Member States can be saved from having to do so if only the Court could be convinced to deviate from its approach adopted in an intra-Community context.

Schön—not so much aiming at a different interpretation of 'fiscal cohesion' depending on whether intra-Community or third country capital movement is involved, but speaking in more general terms—suggests renouncing the requirement that a direct link must be present within one and the same tax and the same taxpayer. He wants to look at the overall tax situation, considering, for example,

---

494; M Lang, 'Wohin geht das Internationale Steuerrecht?' 296; J Röhrbein and K Eicker, 'Verlustberücksichtigung', 470.

[312] See Chapter VI. 6. b; note also K Ståhl, 'Movement of Capital', 54.
[313] eg, U Haferkamp, *Kapitalverkehrsfreiheit*, 207 *et seq*; J Röhrbein and K Eicker, 'Verlustberücksichtigung', 470; see also Unabhängiger Finanzsenat Außenstelle Linz (Austria), GZ. RV/0279-L/04 34 *et seq*.
[314] eg, K Ståhl, 'Movement of Capital', 54.

the overall tax burden of the company distributing dividends and the receiving shareholders. Such an interpretation would certainly ease the pressure on legal constructions such as thin-cap capitalization,[315] add-back taxation,[316] or imputation systems.[317]

Schnitger, discussing imputation systems, goes further when explaining that the logic behind the rejection of the 'fiscal cohesion' argument in many intra-Community cases is that the Member States must accept foreign corporation tax as being functionally equivalent to domestic corporation tax. A third country, however, is not obliged to do so, which could, Schnitger believes, erode the basis of the Court's argumentation and allow for a generous understanding of the 'direct link' mentioned above in a third country context.[318]

In terms of the ability-to-pay principle—an abbreviated notion of the principle of fiscal equality[319]—one can certainly debate the question of how broadly or narrowly to define the 'direct link' between tax allowance and taxation. This, however, is a debate that is relevant to intra-Community and third country capital movements alike. The crucial issue here is that of whether to interpret the mandatory requirement of fiscal cohesion differently depending on the geographical mapping of a capital movement: a narrow understanding of fiscal cohesion in an intra-Community context and a *laissez-faire* construction when it comes to third county capital movement.

While Schnitger's aforementioned analysis might be correct on a factual basis, this study has difficulties accepting the conclusion he reached. Ultimately, what Schnitger's argument comes down to is the missing reciprocity in third country capital movements. The diagnosis that third countries are not obliged to 'recognize' corporation taxes levied in the Member States is not really surprising since we are talking about a unilateral opening of the Common Market to the world. That 'lacking reciprocity' can, however, hardly be the argument for restricting the freedom in a third country context, as explained in detail elsewhere in this study.[320] I can only repeat myself by stating that by making free capital movement *erga omnes* dependent on the precondition of reciprocity, little would remain of the freedom. Furthermore, the argument that, in a third country situation, the Member States always suffer the loss of tax revenue is, although true, a short-sighted view completely ignoring the benefits flowing from unilateral opening of the market, which I identified above.[321]

---

[315] [*Gesellschafterfremdfinanzierung*]
[316] [*Hinzurechnungsbesteuerung*]
[317] *Cf* W Schön, 'Kapitalverkehr mit Drittstaaten', 519; see also Case C-319/02 (Opinion of AG Kokott) *Petri Manninen*, para 55.
[318] A Schnitger, 'Kapitalverkehrsfreiheit', 495; along similar lines: D Hohenwarter, 'Vorlagebeschluss des VwGH', 229; see J Brinkmann, *Unternehmensbesteuerung*, 104 *et seq* for a discussion of 'fiscal cohesion'.
[319] K Tipke, *Die Steuerrechtsordnung*, 480.
[320] See Chapter I. 2. b.   [321] See ibid.

Considering all of the above, it appears to the author of this study that the mandatory requirement of 'fiscal coherence' must in principle be interpreted in a third country context in the same way as with respect to intra-Community capital movement. In particular, I cannot see sufficient evidence to interpret the criterion of a 'direct link' variously depending on whether intra-Community or third country capital movement is involved, but this is an issue that must be resolved uniformly. This study would suggest to the Member States that they resort to tax regulations that operate in the first place in a non-discriminatory fashion with respect to third countries. Ultimately, instead of trying to develop legal constructions which aim to restrict the fundamental freedom of free movement of capital, and which are hardly reconcilable with the Treaty, the Member States should instead have recourse to the means available (Art 57(2) EC and Arts 94 EC, 95 EC, and 308 EC) and develop a common approach towards third countries.

(2) *The Mandatory Requirement of Securing the Tax Base and Preventing the Loss of Tax Revenue—Rebuilt?*

Some commentators[322] suggest that in third country capital movement, mandatory requirements such as the need to secure the national tax base and/or to prevent the loss of tax revenue should not be rejected outright in the same way as in an intra-Community context.

Schön, for example, is of the opinion that the measures that pursue the aim of securing the tax base and preventing the loss of tax revenue do not constitute measures aiming at a purely economic purpose, which, as we have learned above, cannot justify restrictive national measures. He makes the following distinction: while purely economic purposes are rejected because they would lead to protectionism, the rejection of the mandatory requirement of securing the tax base and preventing the loss of tax revenue allegedly relates to the Common Market model, which aims at efficient resource allocation within this market and, thus, prohibits discriminatory or restrictive fiscal measures that could distort this process.[323]

With respect to third countries, Schön believes that the situation would be different due to the fact that they are not part of the Common Market. He points out—which I view as a kind of a secondary argument—that unilateral renouncement of the tax sovereignty of a Member State would lead automatically to a gain in the hands of a third country. A so-called 'institutional counterbalance of legal

---

[322] W Schön, 'Kapitalverkehr mit Drittstaaten', 515 *et seq*; K Ståhl, 'Movement of Capital', 54; and along similar lines M Lang, 'Wohin geht das Internationale Steuerrecht?' 296.

[323] W Schön, 'Kapitalverkehr mit Drittstaaten', 515. Along similar lines, though based on the argument that free movement of capital in a third country context 'does not carry as much weight [...] as when it concerns the movement within the EU': K Ståhl, 'Movement of Capital', 54. With respect to the latter, I should stress that this study cannot embrace such reasoning. I did not find sufficient evidence that the purpose of free capital movement in a third country context is limited in a way that would allow for an expansive interpretation of the grounds of justification, but to the contrary, the well established rule of construction that exceptions are to be interpreted narrowly remains valid in a third country context.

harmonisation' on the basis of Arts 93–95 EC, which eventually leads to a balance of the different interests among the Member States, is missing in relation to third countries. Furthermore, mechanisms such as those contained in Art 158 EC *et seq*, the principle of solidarity embodied in Art 10 EC or the 'Maastricht criteria', etc are all non-binding on third countries. From the aforesaid, he concludes that measures that pursue the aim of securing the tax base and preventing the loss of tax revenue constitute a valid mandatory requirement.[324]

Considering the restrictive potential inherent in such a mandatory requirement—which basically serves budgetary purposes—this study cannot embrace Schön's suggestion. To begin with, this study has difficulties relating to Schön's distinction between measures that pursue purely economic purposes and those that encroach upon the effective allocation of resources. One must critically ask the question whether the prohibition of measures of a purely economic nature does not also rest on the idea that they run counter to the creation and maintenance of a Common Market, and, thus, relate equally to the Common Market model.[325] Furthermore, do protectionist measures not interfere with the free market processes and, as a consequence, disturb the effective allocation of resources? If this is true, then Schön's distinction between measures that pursue purely economic purposes and those that encroach upon the effective allocation of resources appears somewhat artificial.

Schön also puts forward the argument that an alleged 'institutional counterbalance of legal harmonisation' on the basis of Arts 93–95 EC eventually leads to a balancing of the different interests among the Member States. Such a counterbalance is not present with respect to third countries, which were to allow for the application of the mandatory requirement at hand. It is undeniably true that with respect to indirect taxation, the Community has endeavoured to bring about a high degree of legal harmonization.[326] However, concerning direct taxation, one can hardly speak of an 'institutional counterbalance of legal harmonisation' considering the very limited amount of secondary legislation in place.[327] Be that as it

---

[324] W Schön, 'Kapitalverkehr mit Drittstaaten', 516.

[325] W Frenz, *Europarecht*, 937.

[326] See for an account of the status quo of legal harmonization, with further references, in the area of indirect taxation: S Eilers, et al, Art. 93 EC (2003), mn 32 *et seq*; C Waldhoff, Art. 93 EC (2007), mn 9 *et seq*.

[327] A Schnitger, 'Kapitalverkehrsfreiheit', 494 *Cf* for secondary legislation on company taxation: Directive 90/435/EEC; Directive 90/434/EEC; Directive 88/361/EEC. See also Council and Representatives of the Governments of the Member States Meeting in the Council, 'Resolution on a Code of Conduct for Business Taxation'; European Commission, 'Communication to the Council, the European Parliament and the European Economic and Social Committee—An Internal Market without Company Tax Obstacles: Achievements, Ongoing Initiatives and Remaining Challenges' (COM (2003) 0726 final), for an appraisal of the aforementioned secondary legislation and further references, see S Eilers, et al, Vorb. zu den Art. 90 bis 93 EC (2003), mn 9 *et seq*; for secondary legislation on taxation of savings, see: Directive 2003/48/EC; Directive 2003/49/EC; for a Commission initiative on taxation of dividends, refer to: European Commission, 'Communication to the Council, The European Parliament and the European Economic and Social Committee: Dividend Taxation of Individuals in the Internal Market' (COM (2003) 810 final).

may, what Schön's argument really comes down to is again the lack of reciprocity with respect to third countries. The Member States 'give up' something for which the return is somewhat 'uncertain' or more difficult to display. This, however, is the very consequence of a unilateral liberalization of capital movements. I explained above,[328] that the unilateral liberalization is indeed meant to be unilateral and is not bound to any condition of reciprocity. I also referred to the benefits derived from a liberalization of capital movements *erga omnes* and found that the Treaty aims are indeed best served when one takes the wording of Art 56(1) EC seriously and interprets the freedom in a wide sense. In this respect, it should also be recalled that even if one were prepared to follow Schön's suggestion, it is questionable whether national measures restricting free movement of capital in the name of securing the tax base and preventing the loss of tax revenue in a third country context can achieve their aims. Such measures would still have the effect of distorting the efficient allocation of resources in the Common Market: third country investors would simply penetrate the market through Member States with less restrictive regimes. EC investors would channel capital out of the EC, again choosing the Member State with the least restrictive regulatory rules. In this sense, I suggest that such national measures would cause more harm than they would allegedly do good.

While this study can concur with the understanding that the notion of 'purely economic purposes' has turned into a mere 'marginal negative delineation',[329] it is difficult to comprehend that in a third country context, budgetary purposes[330] can suddenly serve as valid mandatory requirements. Ultimately, Schön's interpretation amounts to a *domaine réservé* for tax measures with respect to third countries.[331] I could not find sufficient evidence for such a reduction of the scope of the freedom in a third country context in the *telos* and systematics of the Treaty, as repeatedly stated above.[332] While a rejection of the mandatory requirements of securing the tax base and preventing the loss of tax revenue can indeed lead to unilateral loss of tax revenue, one should not try to justify an expansive interpretation of the grounds of justification—which, by the way, runs counter to the general rule of interpretation of exceptions—with reference to the power of the real,[333] but rather take recourse to the means provided for in the Treaty instead. If the Member States should indeed feel that the loss of tax revenue is of greater significance than what their economies gain from the unilateral liberalization of the capital markets, then they must resort to the procedures embodied in Arts 57(2) EC, 94 EC *et seq*, and 308 EC.

---

[328] See Chapter I. 2. b. and Chapter IV. 3. b. (2).
[329] A Cordewener, *Grundfreiheiten*, 137.
[330] Ibid, 137, esp. fn 129.
[331] A Schnitger, 'Kapitalverkehrsfreiheit', 494; D Hohenwarter, 'Vorlagebeschluss des VwGH', 229.
[332] See Chapter I. 2. b. and Chapter IV. 3. b. (2).
[333] *"Die normative Kraft des Faktischen"*.

(3) Appraisal: No Across-the-board Judgments but Careful Balancing on a Case-by-case Basis

The 'rule of reason' also applies in a third country context. Its interpretation should not vary depending on whether the capital movement relates to the Community or to a third country, but may follow the same lines drawn by the Court for intra-Community capital movements. Thus, no across-the-board judgments penalizing third country capital movements will be applied, but the mandatory requirement allegedly pursued by a national measure and the freedom must be carefully balanced on a case-by-case basis.[334] Furthermore, this study could not identify sufficient support for the view which seeks to interpret accepted mandatory requirements, such as 'fiscal cohesion', variously depending on the geographical mapping. This study, on the basis of the *telos* and systematics of the Treaty, perceives the unilateral liberalization of free movement of capital *erga omnes* as unconditional. Missing reciprocity is, therefore, no argument for a restriction of third country capital movement, but the very consequence of this unilateral act.

This having been said, it becomes clear that the introduction of mandatory requirements pursuing budgetary purposes also based on 'lacking reciprocity' in a third country context can equally not be accepted. Closely related to the 'lacking reciprocity' argument is that of 'lacking harmonization' in a third country context, which I have also identified as not being a valid plea to restrict third country capital movement. While 'lacking reciprocity' comes 'naturally' with a unilateral opening of the market, 'lacking harmonization' is the consequence of not being a Member State of the Community. If the freedom is to be effective with respect to third countries, then these two pleas must be rejected as an argument to restrict the fundamental freedom. If it were otherwise, Art 56(1) EC would be relegated to little more than a mere political declaration of intent.

---

[334] Note M Lang, 'Wohin geht das Internationale Steuerrecht?' 296.

VII

Exceptions to the Freedom Exclusively Applicable to Third Country Contexts

1. Introduction

The EC Treaty, by virtue of Art 56(1) EC, liberalizes capital movements *vis-à-vis* third countries[1] in a similar way to those in the Common Market. At the same time, it subjects the freedom in a third country context to a larger number of exceptions.

Those exceptions take account of the different conditions—in particular the lack of reciprocity harmonization—under which the freedom operates when it comes to capital movements originating from or directed to third countries. While the Community constitutes a mature financial market with the necessary breadth and depth to absorb possible economic turbulences and shocks,[2] nevertheless, the open-door approach and inevitable asymmetries with third countries, which are not at all obliged to open up their markets, must be 'managed'. Article 57(2) EC,[3] and Arts 59 and 60 EC equip the Community[4] with the necessary 'management tools' to develop and shape a coherent common approach to foreign direct investment and certain other important categories of capital movement with respect to third countries, as well as to effectively respond to economic and political crises or to situations at the brink of such crises.

On the other hand, those provisions providing for exceptions exclusively applicable to third country capital movement, in particular Art 57(1) EC, mirror the political compromise that had to be struck in order to establish free movement of capital *erga omnes* as the basic rule instead of the exception.[5] The complete renouncement of an element of reciprocity with respect to the

---

[1] For the notion of third country, refer to Chapter II. 4. c. (1).
[2] *Cf* European Commission, 'Responses to the Challenges of Globalisation—A Study on the International Monetary and Financial System and on Financing for Development' (SEC (2002) 186 final), 58 'The modest impact on EU financial markets of the 11 September attacks indicate that Member States with their move to a single currency have successfully reduced the vulnerability of their economies to external financial turbulences.'
[3] The 'management tool' of Art 57(2) EC is complemented by Arts 94 EC, 95 EC, and 308 EC.
[4] While Art 60 EC predominantly empowers the Community, Art 60(2) contains a residual Member State competence. See Chapter VII. 5.
[5] See Chapter I. 3 and Chapter IV. 3. b. (2) (c).

liberalization of third country capital movements could simply not be achieved during the Maastricht negotiations. The Member States wished to reserve policy space in view of certain categories of capital movement that touch upon sensitive common welfare issues.[6]

The discussion which follows will begin with an in-depth account of Art 57(1) EC. The provision contains a grandfathering clause for restrictive national and Community laws with respect to the categories of direct investment, including real estate, establishment, provision of financial services, and admission of securities to capital markets.

As regards Art 57(2)—empowering the Community to adopt measures involving the categories of capital movement mentioned above—I shall limit myself to a broad-brush depiction of the provision. Due to the chosen perspective of this study, a comprehensive analysis of the issue of Community competences on the regulation of foreign direct investment under the current Treaty[7] must be reserved for future examination.

Alongside Art 57 EC, there are two other provisions that provide for the possibility of restricting foreign direct investment. I shall therefore consider Arts 59 EC and 60 EC. Article 59 EC allows the Community to take temporary safeguard measures with regard to third countries if, in exceptional circumstances, movements of capital to or from third countries cause, or threaten to cause, serious difficulties for the operation of Economic and Monetary Union. Article 60 EC provides the EC, and on an interim basis also the Member States, in the framework of the Common Foreign and Security Policy (CFSP), with a tool to adopt economic sanctions—ie, actions to interrupt or to reduce, in part or completely, economic relations—against one or more third countries in the area of free movement of capital.

The discussion of the abovementioned exceptions will centre upon their effects on the standard of liberalization of foreign direct investment achieved by virtue of Art 56(1) EC.

2. The True Blind Spot on the Mirror of Free Movement of Capital *Erga Omnes*: The Grandfathering Clause of Article 57(1) EC

Article 57(1) EC provides that:

[t]he provisions of Article 56 shall be without prejudice to the application to third countries of any restrictions which exist on 31 December 1993 under national or Community law adopted in respect of the movement of capital to or from third countries involving

---

[6] C Ohler, Art. 57 EC (2002), mn 1; W Kiemel, Art. 57 EC (2003), mn 1.
[7] Note the changes possibly brought about by the Treaty of Lisbon.

direct investment—including in real estate—establishment, the provision of financial services or the admission of securities to capital markets.

As mentioned briefly above, the provision constitutes a grandfathering clause granting the Member States and the Community the capacity to maintain unreservedly and indefinitely certain restrictive laws in relation to third country capital movements beyond the date of entry into force of the second stage of the Economic and Monetary Union.[8]

Article 57(1) EC does not grandfather any national law restricting third country capital movement.[9] Rather, it singles out four categories of capital movement that are deemed of such economic (and political) importance that their liberalization is to be carried out under particular consideration of the general welfare.[10] These categories relate to:

- direct investment, including in real estate,
- establishment,
- the provision of financial services, and
- the admission of securities to capital markets.

The Member States are entitled to verify whether a given capital movement falls within one of these categories in order to render their national legislation, grandfathered by virtue of this provision, effective. However, ex-ante authorization procedures are not permissible under Art 57(1) EC.[11]

The predominant idea behind the inclusion of direct investment[12] in this list is to preserve a certain degree of Member State control on the system of property ownership in those States.[13] The Member States shall be entitled to continue applying their existing national legislation that prevents or restricts the acquisition or exercise of entrepreneurial control over undertakings situated in their territory by third country residents. Preserving the possibility of restricting outward foreign direct investment does not cause so much concern.[14]

Article 57(1) EC probably constitutes the most general and broad-based exception—not subject to any proportionality considerations—from the duty to

---

[8] C Bond, Art. 68 EEC (1999), § 68.02. Note, though, that with respect to Estonia and Hungary, this date varies, *cf* Art 57(1) 2nd sentence EC.

[9] It is, moreover, worth pointing out—although actually already clear from the wording of the provision—that Art 57(1) EC does not apply to measures restricting the freedom of payments. [Joined Cases C-163/94, C-165/94, and C-250/94 *Criminal proceedings against Lucas Emilio Sanz de Lera, Raimundo Díaz Jiménez and Figen Kapanoglu*, para 31 *et seq*; G Ress and J Ukrow, Art. 57 EC (2002), mn 5, 13; T Schürmann, Art. 57 EC (2006), mn 2]

[10] C Ohler, Art. 57 EC (2002), mn 1.

[11] Joined Cases C-163/94, C-165/94, and C-250/94 *Criminal proceedings against Lucas Emilio Sanz de Lera, Raimundo Diaz Jiménez and Figen Kapanoglu*, para 37; M Sedlaczek, Art. 57 EC (2003), mn 3; W Kiemel, Art. 57 EC (2003), mn 7; J Bröhmer, Art. 57 EC (2007), mn 3.

[12] Including direct investment in real estate.

[13] C Ohler, Art. 57 EC (2002), mn 1.

[14] For a negotiation history of this provision, refer to AFP Bakker, *Capital Movements*, 233 *et seq*.

liberalize all capital movements in relation to third countries.[15] Such provisions must be construed strictly.[16] As explained above, the fewer restrictions on free capital movement maintained in the categories mentioned by Art 57(1) EC, the better the Treaty aims are accommodated.[17] While the Member States are under no duty to carry out further liberalization with respect to the categories mentioned in Art 57(1) EC,[18] this could[19] and—to the extent that existing restrictions lead to unacceptable misallocations of capital, this study suggests—should be brought about by Community action based on Art 57(2) EC. Thus, not only can the respective Member State that enacted the restrictive measure later remove it, but the Community can also act on its own account.[20]

While these general considerations chiefly indicate the direction in which the interpretation of Art 57(1) EC should proceed, they must now be further specified when addressing the individual issues of construction that are posed by this provision.

In the discussion which follows, I shall deal with five groups of questions: first, the effect on Art 57(1) EC of the commitments of the Community under international law to engage in further-reaching liberalization of capital movements *vis-à-vis* third countries than is required under the EC Treaty will be discussed. Second, the meaning of 'restriction' within the ambit of Art 57(1) EC is set out. As a third step, I shall critically review the Court's broad interpretation of the notion of foreign direct investment in the context of a provision that provides an exception to the freedom. Fourth, I shall elaborate on the question of whether, in order to be covered by Art 57(1) EC, the restrictive 'national or Community law', must specifically relate to direct investment (or to one of the other categories mentioned) and exclusively apply to third country capital movement. Furthermore, Art 57(1) EC requires that a law, in order to be saved, must have existed up to a certain date. I shall therefore, as a fifth step, address the interpretive issue of from what moment one can speak of the existence of a law within the meaning of the provision.

---

[15] C Ohler, Art. 57 EC (2002), mn 14.
[16] G Ress and J Ukrow, Art. 57 EC (2002), mn 4; W Frenz, *Europarecht*, mn 2845; J Röhrbein and K Eicker, 'Verlustberücksichtigung', 470; for the opposite view: A Honrath, *Kapitalverkehr*, 137 *et seq*; N Wunderlich and C Blaschke, 'Kapitalverkehrsfreiheit in Bezug auf Drittstaaten', 759 *et seq*.
[17] See Chapter I. 2. b. See also W Kiemel, Art. 57 EC (2003), mn 10.
[18] G Ress and J Ukrow, Art. 57 EC (2002), mn 15; W Kiemel, Art. 57 EC (2003), mn 10; J Bröhmer, Art. 57 EC (2002), mn 6; see also Case C-452/01 (Opinion of AG Geelhoed) *Margarethe Ospelt and Schlössle Weissenberg Familienstiftung*, para 49.
[19] W Kiemel, Art. 57 EC (2003), mn 10, 16; M Seidel, 'Kapitalmarkt', 773; for an account of Art 57(2) EC, refer to W Kiemel, Art. 57 EC (2003), mn 16 *et seq*; G Ress and J Ukrow, Art. 57 EC (2002), mn 16 *et seq*; C Ohler, Art. 57 EC (2002), mn 16 *et seq*.
[20] T Schürmann, Art. 57 EC (2006), mn 4; J Bröhmer, Art. 57 EC (2007), mn 7; for the opposite view: A Glaesner, Art. 57 EC (2000), mn 6.

a. International Treaties and Article 57(1) EC

Insofar as international treaties concluded by the Community provide for more far-reaching duties to liberalize capital movements *vis-à-vis* third countries than the EC Treaty, the Member States cannot invoke Art 57(1) EC[21] in order to save their restrictive national measures.[22]

An example of such a situation is provided by the EEA Agreement,[23] which was the focus of attention in *Ospelt*.[24] The provisions on capital movements in the EEA Agreement (Art 40 *et seq.* and respective Annex) do not contain a grandfathering clause such as Art 57(1) EC: 'The standstill-clauses contained in Annex XII of the EEA Agreement—the annex which implements Art. 40 of the EEA Agreement—have a much more limited scope and period of validity.'[25] This leads to the rather peculiar and exceptional situation that the EEA Agreement grants rights that are not equally enjoyed under primary Community law.[26] In such an event, the Community and the Member States are under an obligation to ensure 'that the rights enjoyed by nationals of the EEA countries [by virtue of the EEA Agreement, which constitutes an association agreement within the meaning of Art 310 EC[27] and is an integral part of the Community legal order] can be exercised in the territory of the European Community'.[28] Interpreting the EC Treaty 'in accordance with an obligation on the European Community under international law',[29] Article 57(1) EC cannot be applied in such circumstances.[30]

At first sight—due to the somewhat abbreviated style of the judgment—one might wonder how the result reached by the Court might fit within the hierarchy of EC legal sources: primary Community law, including Art 57(1) EC, ranks above an international treaty concluded by the Community, *cf* Art 300(7) EC. Thus, restrictive national measures of Member States—by virtue of Art 57(1) EC—would take precedence over any international treaty concluded by the Community. However, the Community is empowered to abolish those restrictions on the basis of Art 57(2) EC, also by means of international treaties.[31]

---

[21] Note that Art 57(1) EC has merely a Community-internal effect and no influence on the binding force of an international agreement concluded by the Community and a third country. [C Ohler, Art. 57 EC (2002), mn 15. See also A Rohde, *Kapitalverkehr*, 201 *et seq*]

[22] W Kiemel, Art. 57 EC (2003), mn 6; see also W Kiemel, Art. 56 EC (2003), mn 48 *et seq*. For the reverse situation, in which it is argued that the EEA Agreement constitutes a 'Community law' within the meaning of Art 57(1) EC, see Chapter VI. 2. g.

[23] EEA Agreement.

[24] Case C-452/01 *Margarethe Ospelt and Schlössle Weissenberg Familienstiftung*.

[25] Case C-452/01 (Opinion of AG Geelhoed) *Margarethe Ospelt and Schlössle Weissenberg Familienstiftung*, para. 74.

[26] Ibid, para 78.   [27] Ibid, para 75.   [28] Ibid.   [29] Ibid, para 47.

[30] Case C-452/01 *Margarethe Ospelt and Schlössle Weissenberg Familienstiftung*, para 31; see also Case C-452/01 (Opinion of AG Geelhoed) *Margarethe Ospelt and Schlössle Weissenberg Familienstiftung*, para 76.

[31] See CF Schneider, 'Grundstückserwerb', 385, who advances an arguments which is similar in structure. Without further explanation, he refers, however, to Art 310 EC instead of Art 57(2)

Furthermore, the Member States are under the duty to fulfil the obligations accepted under international law by the Community, *cf* Art 300(7) EC. In this sense, it would indeed be contradictory to apply their restrictive national laws when endeavouring to give effect to an international agreement that seeks to liberalize capital movements.[32]

Situations similar to the one depicted above could also occur with respect to any other association agreement, but also, for example, in regard to the framework of the WTO-Agreements.[33]

b. The Notion of 'Restrictions'

Article 57(1) EC refers to 'restrictions' that the Member States or the Community may maintain with respect to third countries. This term is synonymous with the one used within Art 56(1) EC and, thus, covers national measures that constitute discrimination, as well as those referred to by this study as hindrances to free capital movement.[34]

c. The Notion of 'Foreign Direct Investment' within the Scope of Article 57(1) EC: Less is More!

While Art 57(1) EC covers four categories of capital movement,[35] the following discussion will be limited to the focus of this study—direct investment.

EC. It appears that he acts on the assumption that Art 310 EC constitutes a substantial competence. The proponents of such a reading base their argument, inter alia, on the Court's ruling in Case 12/86 *Meryem Demirel v Stadt Schwäbisch Gmünd*, para 9; Case C-192/89 *S. Z. Sevince v Staatssecretaris van Justitie*, para 8 *et seq*; Case C-237/91 *Kazim Kus v Landeshauptstadt Wiesbaden*, para 9. Thus, Art 310 EC grants treaty making power for all subject matters that are at least within the shared or parallel competence of the Community. [*Cf.* A Weber, Art. 310 EC (2004), mn 18]

Another possible reading of Art 310 EC is that the provision does not constitute a competence in its own right; rather each proviso in an association agreement has to be founded upon a specific legal basis in the Treaty, and each time the question of whether the Community enjoys exclusive treaty making power must be asked. It is worth pointing out that all association agreements, except those with Malta [Agreement Establishing an Association between the European Economic Community and Malta] and Cyprus [Agreement Establishing an Association between the European Economic Community and the Republic of Cyprus], were concluded in the form of a 'mixed agreement'. This position has never been legally challenged in Court by the Commission. [*Cf* R Mögele, Art. 310 EC (2003), mn 20]

For a concise but very instructive discussion of the two opinions, see A Weber, Art. 310 EC (2004), mn 12; see also P Eeckhout, *External Relations*, 103; R Mögele, Art. 310 EC (2003), mn 18.

[32] Concurring: CF Schneider, 'Grundstückserwerb', 385.
[33] W Kiemel, Art. 57 EC (2003), mn 6.
[34] *Cf* C Ohler, Art. 57 EC (2002), mn 3; Case C-446/04 *Test Claimants in the FII Group Litigation v Commissioners of Inland Revenue*, para 184.
[35] The catalogue of the categories of capital movement mentioned in Art 57(1) EC constitutes an exhaustive enumeration. [Joined Cases C-163/94, C-165/94, and C-250/94 *Criminal proceedings against Lucas Emilio Sanz de Lera, Raimundo Díaz Jiménez and Figen Kapanoglu*, para 44; G Ress and J Ukrow, Art. 57 EC (2002), para 44]

As we already know, the notion of direct investment is nowhere defined in the Treaty. Interpretive guidance[36] is, however, offered by the EC Capital Movements Directive,[37] which describes 'direct investment' in abstract terms as comprising:

[i]nvestments of all kinds by natural persons or commercial, industrial or financial undertakings, and which serve to establish or to maintain lasting and direct links between the person providing the capital and the entrepreneur to whom or the undertaking to which the capital is made available in order to carry on an economic activity.[38]

The Exemplary Notes of the Directive call for an application of the notion of direct investment 'in its widest sense'.[39] This, however, must not be misunderstood. I suggested earlier in this study that this interpretative instruction merely seeks to point out that the different varieties of direct investment mentioned under Heading I of the Directive are not comprehensive, but only examples. The call for a wide understanding, though, is not meant to lower the required threshold necessary to identify the 'lasting and direct links between the person providing the capital and the entrepreneur to whom or the undertaking to which the capital is made available in order to carry on an economic activity'. Rather, this link must be interpreted strictly, essentially in parallel terms to the 'definite influence test' required in Art 43 EC for the identification of an 'establishment'.[40] This suggestion was basically put forward in order to secure that the exception to the freedom is construed narrowly, which gives to the freedom itself a broad scope of application, as the Treaty aims suggest.[41]

The tendency in jurisprudence to perceive dividend payments as 'direct investment' is not without problems in this respect.[42] The foundations of this

---

[36] Concerning the methodology of construction, the notions mentioned in Art 57 EC are all to be interpreted autonomously from the perspective of EC law [G Ress and J Ukrow, Art. 56 EC (2002), mn 6; for a different view: A Rohde, *Kapitalverkehr*, 190, who pleads with respect to the definitions employed by the Member States merely for control of the absence of arbitrariness by the ECJ]; consequently, also the notion of 'direct investment'. The Court made clear in this respect that '[t]he exception provided for in Article 73c (1) of the Treaty [now, after amendment, Art. 57 (1)]... is precisely worded, with the result that *no latitude* is granted to the Member States or the Community legislature regarding... the categories of capital movements which may be subject to restrictions.' [Emphasis added. Joined Cases C-163/94, C-165/94, and C-250/94 *Criminal proceedings against Lucas Emilio Sanz de Lera, Raimundo Díaz Jiménez and Figen Kapanoglu*, para 44]

[37] Case C-446/04 *Test Claimants in the FII Group Litigation v Commissioners of Inland Revenue*, para 178 *et seq.*

[38] Annex I, Explanatory Notes Directive 88/361/EEC; for a more lengthy discussion, see Chapter II. 4. b.

[39] Annex I, Explanatory Notes, ibid.

[40] See Chapter III. 2. for a detailed discussion of whether the required 'link' present between the investor and the investment within the notion of 'direct investment' ('effective participation test') requires the same threshold as the 'definite influence test' for the finding of an 'establishment' within the meaning of Art 43 EC.

[41] For a detailed discussion, see Chapter II. 4. b. (1).

[42] Case C-446/04 *Test Claimants in the FII Group Litigation v Commissioners of Inland Revenue*, para 183; Case C-157/05 *Winfried Holböck v Finanzamt Salzburg-Land*, 36.

jurisprudence go back to the Court's judgment in *Verkooijen,* where it applied a global view to the initial transaction and considered the transfer of shares and the entitlement to participate in expected profits of the public company (dividends) as a unit; a distribution of dividends 'necessarily presupposes'[43] a transfer of shares. Hence, it seems that the shares, including the holding out of the prospect of future dividend payments, appeared to the Court as an initial transfer (performance) for which a certain amount of money was paid (counter performance). In this way it could qualify the restrictions on cross-border dividend payments as restrictions on capital movements.[44]

This line of case law was consistently continued in *Test Claimants in the FII Group Litigation*[45] and *Holböck*.[46] While in *Verkooijen,* the dividend payments were connected to a portfolio investment,[47] in the latter two cases the dividend payments in issue were derived from an investment that granted the shareholder the possibility of participating effectively in the management or control of that investment. Hence, the Court concluded that such dividend payments would constitute 'direct investment' within the meaning of Art 57(1) EC.

The problem with this approach is that it clearly shifts the demarcation line between free movement of capital and payment at the expense of the latter and, at the same time, subjects dividend payments to a greater number of possible restrictions permissible under the heading of 'capital movement.' For this reason, one view in the literature qualifies dividend distributions as being payments, ie, consideration in an economic sense for the entrepreneurial risk inherent in the participation in an undertaking and therefore seeks to apply Art 56(2) EC.[48]

Construing Art 57(1) EC strictly means also applying a restrictive understanding of the notion of 'foreign'. A great number of direct investments, although they originate from and are ultimately directed to a Member State, probably display a nexus to a third country somewhere along the chain of transactions necessary to close the deal. In order not to turn Art 57(1) EC into a gateway for unreasonable restriction of intra-Community direct investment, the foreign link is to be searched for in the individual transaction(s) with which one seeks to establish (or perpetuate) the possibility of control over an undertaking. In this context, any broad view based on economic considerations would therefore be misguided.[49]

---

[43] Case C-35/98 *Staatssecretaris van Financiën v B.G.M. Verkooijen*, para 28.
[44] Ibid, para 27 *et seq*.
[45] Case C-446/04 *Test Claimants in the FII Group Litigation v Commissioners of Inland Revenue*, para 183.
[46] Case C-157/05 *Winfried Holböck v Finanzamt Salzburg-Land*, para 36.
[47] Case C-35/98 *Staatssecretaris van Financiën v B.G.M. Verkooijen*, para 14.
[48] *Cf*, eg, A Glaesner, Art. 56 EC (2000), mn 9; U Haferkamp, *Kapitalverkehrsfreiheit*, 44 *et seq*; J Lübke, *Kapitalverkehrs- und Niederlassungsfreiheit*, 199.
[49] See Chapter II. 4. c. (3).

d. The Notion of 'National or Community Law': Don't Break the Link!

The strict construction of Art 57(1) EC must also be reflected in the requirements to be met by lawmakers concerning the configuration of their respective 'national or Community law' on which the restriction of third country capital movement is based.

Article 57(1) EC requires that a restriction on capital movement may not flow from any measure, but must originate from 'national or Community law'. A law is an abstract and general rule of conduct or action of a binding nature, established in a certain specific procedure and promulgated. While this also includes international treaties concluded by the Member States or the Community,[50] measures that merely form administrative customs, ie, procedures only internally binding on the administration or decisions on individual cases, are not covered by Art 57(1) EC.

This elevated standard in relation to the national measure encroaching on the economic freedom underscores the exceptional nature of Art 57(1) EC and also has the principle of predictability in mind.

Article 57(1) EC grandfathers only such laws as were 'adopted in respect of the movement of capital to or from third countries involving direct investment'.[51] This phrasing suggests that the respective law must specifically refer to both a third country context and direct investment. Any law that would non-specifically refer, for example, to direct and portfolio investments, or intra-Community and foreign direct investments, would fall outside the ambit of the grandfathering provision.[52]

---

[50] C Ohler, Art. 57 EC (2002), mn 4 citing P Vigneron and P Steinfeld, 'Circulation des Capitaux', 440. For the EEA Agreement, it is worth pointing out that it does not exclude non-EC parties to the Agreement from exercising the parallel-running rights contained in Art 56(1) EC and, hence, does not constitute a restrictive Community 'law' within the meaning of Art 57(1) EC. It is already doubtful whether the EEA Agreement would fulfil the temporal requirements of Art 57(1) EC since it entered into force on 1 January 1994. On the other hand, interpreting the EEA Agreement as a restrictive 'Community law' within the meaning of Art 57(1) EC would run counter to the very purpose of the EEA Agreement. The aim of the EEA Agreement is 'to provide for the fullest possible realisation of the free movement of goods, persons, services and capital within the whole European Economic Area, so that the internal market established within the European Union is extended to the EFTA States'. [Case C-452/01 *Margarethe Ospelt and Schlössle Weissenberg Familienstiftung*, para 29] With respect to the free movement of capital, the regulatory sprit and purpose for the conclusion of the EEA Agreement—but also of other association agreements [See for a categorization of the types of association agreements R Mögele, Art. 310 EC (2003), mn 4 *et seq*]—has not been to restrict access to the, in principle, open EC market but to secure, in a legally binding fashion, access to the market of association countries.

[51] [Emphasis added]

[52] B Matzka, *Freiheit des Kapitalverkehrs*, 71; C Ohler, Art. 57 EC (2002), mn 3; W Schön, 'Kapitalverkehr mit Drittstaaten', 494 *et seq*; J Röhrbein and K Eicker, 'Verlustberücksichtigung', 470; J Schönfeld, 'Anmerkung zu FG Hamburg vom 9.3.2004', 413; F Wassermeyer and J Schönfeld, 'Anmerkung zu BFH vom 14. 9. 2005', 413 *et seq*; H Rehm and J Nagler, 'Anmerkungen zum BFH-Urteil vom 9. 8. 2006', 859; this view was also held by the Court in its

A brief glance at other translations of the Treaty seems to support this view. The German version of the Treaty likewise displays a nexus between the given law and third country capital movement. The 'Rechtsvorschriften' must be '*für den Kapitalverkehr mit dritten Ländern im Zusammenhang mit Direktinvestitionen*'.[53] The French version also states that the law '*en ce qui concerne* les mouvements de capitaux à destination ou en provenance de pays tiers lorsqu'ils impliquent des investissements directs'.[54] Equally, the Italian text confirms that the law: '*per quanto concerne* i movimenti di capitali provenienti da paesi terzi o ad essi diretti, che implichino investimenti diretti'.[55]

The ECJ[56] and some voices in the literature,[57] however, wish to have recourse to the individual case. The scope of application of the law that causes the restriction on free capital movement in the respective case is irrelevant as long as the economic activity at hand alludes to one of the categories of capital movement mentioned in Art 57(1) EC and occurs in a third country context. Such an approach can be studied by way of example in the Court's *Holböck*[58] decision. Mr Holböck received dividends[59] from a Swiss company of which he held two thirds of all shares, which allowed him to participate effectively in the management or control of the distributing company. The rule on the basis of which the respective Member State applied a discriminatory tax regime towards Mr Holböck neither differentiated between direct and portfolio investment nor between intra-Community and third country capital movement.[60] Nevertheless, the respective national tax law was found to be covered by Art 57(1) EC.[61]

---

old case law: Joined Cases C-163/94, C-165/94, and C-250/94 (Opinion of AG Tesauro) *Criminal proceedings against Lucas Emilio Sanz de Lera, Raimundo Díaz Jiménez and Figen Kapanoglu*, para 31 *et seq*.

[53] [Emphasis added].   [54] [Emphasis added].
[55] [Emphasis added].
[56] Case C-446/04 *Test Claimants in the FII Group Litigation v Commissioners of Inland Revenue*, para 185; Case C-157/05 *Winfried Holböck v Finanzamt Salzburg-Land*, para 37; Joined Cases C-163/94, C-165/94, and C-250/94 *Criminal proceedings against Lucas Emilio Sanz de Lera, Raimundo Díaz Jiménez and Figen Kapanoglu*, para 14 *et seq*; however, in an earlier judgment, the Court took the opposite view: Joined Cases C-163/94, C-165/94, and C-250/94 *Criminal proceedings against Lucas Emilio Sanz de Lera, Raimundo Díaz Jiménez and Figen Kapanoglu*, para 31 *et seq*.
[57] A Schnitger, 'Wirkungsgrenzen der Grundfreiheiten', 635 *et seq*; W Kessler, et al, 'Schweiz', 666; probably also D Hohenwarter, 'Vorlagebeschluss des VwGH', 232.
[58] Case C-157/05 *Winfried Holböck v Finanzamt Salzburg-Land*.
[59] The Courts perceived them as 'direct investment'. [Ibid, para 36; and earlier: Case C-446/04 *Test Claimants in the FII Group Litigation v Commissioners of Inland Revenue*, para 183]
[60] Case C-157/05 *Winfried Holböck v Finanzamt Salzburg-Land*, para 3 *et seq*.
[61] Ibid, para 37 *et seq*. In an earlier judgment, the identical tax provision, applied in an intra-Community context, was declared irreconcilable with EC law. [Case C-315/02 *Anneliese Lenz v Finanzlandesdirektion für Tirol*] The same, it can be assumed, would have happened if Mr Holböck had only placed a portfolio investment in the Swiss distributing company.

Although the Court's approach appears at least as a syllogism and stringent continuation of its understanding of the relationship of the freedoms of establishment and free movement of capital, this, unfortunately, neither makes the ECJ's treatment of Art 57(1) EC nor its view of the relationship of Arts 43 EC and 56(1) EC any more convincing. As discussed earlier,[62] the Court perceives national measures that apply only to direct investment as falling exclusively within the ambit of the freedom of establishment. Hence, it is impossible for the Court to apply in relation to Art 57(1) EC a perspective that looks at the abstract scope of the respective law. Laws that apply exclusively to foreign direct investment are—in the eyes of the Court—outside the scope of the EC Treaty because in such a situation Art 56(1) EC is superseded by Art 43 EC. Left with only one choice, the Court must have recourse in its interpretation of Art 57(1) EC to the actual economic activity; in doing so, it neglects the wording of the provision.

However, not only the wording of Art 57(1) EC calls the Court's approach into question. Teleological considerations too suggest having recourse to the abstract scope of application of the respective law instead of considering the economic activity in the individual case for the purposes of interpreting Art 57(1) EC.

If one were to allow for an 'individual case perspective', thereby lending Art 57(1) EC a broad scope, one would increase the danger that restrictive national laws would lead to misallocation of capital within the Common Market without these laws even effectively achieving their aim. A Member State usually wishes to reserve control over certain economic activities for its own nationals, or it intends to strengthen its bargaining powers by such laws in order to push for reciprocal concessions from third countries.

However, a Member State applying such a restrictive policy cannot prevent a liberal-minded Member State from functioning as a channel for third country investors into the Common Market. The

> denial by one country would simply cause the prospective entrant to apply elsewhere and often subsequently penetrate the market of the original refusing state through exports or through affiliates gaining entry under the right of establishment.[63]

Thus, due to the existence of the fundamental freedoms, within the Community no single Member State is in a position to effectively prevent entry of third country investors.[64] Art 57(1) EC can only have a meaningful restrictive effect in case of a 'Community law'. Only in this situation can a 'channel effect' not be exploited by third country investors.

Summing up the above, for a law to be covered by Art 57(1) EC, it must first be an abstract and general rule of conduct or action of a binding nature, established according to a certain specific procedure and promulgated. Secondly, it must

---

[62] See Chapter III. 3. b. (3).
[63] CD Wallace, *Multinational Enterprise*, 309.
[64] See, for a more detailed account, Chapter IV. 3. b. (2) (d).

specifically apply to both a third country context and direct investment (or one of the other categories mentioned in the provision). This certainly reduces the scope of Art 57(1) EC significantly, which corresponds to its nature as an exception to the freedom in particular and to the purpose and spirit of the provisions on free movement of capital in general.[65] This interpretation will also exclude most of the Member States' tax rules from the scope of the provision, since they only rarely distinguish between Member States and third countries.[66]

e. Determining the Crucial Date: Effectiveness of a Law

Article 57(1) 1st sentence EC applies only to restrictions flowing from a national or Community law 'which exist on 31 December 1993'. Some uncertainty surrounded the question of when one can speak of 'existence' within the meaning of the provision in issue.

Considering first national laws, the earliest point in time to which one could refer is the date on which the law was enacted.[67] At that moment, a bill turns into a law and thus comes into being. Another point which could be taken is the date of entry into force.[68] The latest possible moment at which one could speak of 'existence' is the date on which the law becomes 'effective'.[69] By a law becoming 'effective', I mean that sometimes it is provided with respect to a certain law that its material effects come into operation at a later moment in time than the law itself entered into force. It should, however, be mentioned that in practice, the date of entry into force and the date of becoming effective usually coincide.[70]

---

[65] For the aims pursued by the provisions on free movement of capital, see Chapter I. 2.
[66] W Kessler, et al, 'Schweiz', 666. Also, double taxation treaties concluded pre-1994, modelled on Art 23 of 2005 OECD Articles of the Model Convention with respect to Taxes on Income and on Capital, would not be covered by Art 57(1) EC. [*Cf.* J Röhrbein and K Eicker, 'Verlustberücksichtigung', 470]
[67] Of the opinion that the date in Art 57(1) EC refers to the enactment: M Sedlaczek, *Besteuerung in- und ausländischer Investmentfonds*, 19 cited by D Hohenwarter, 'Vorlagebeschluss des VwGH', 231, fn 46; M Sedlaczek, Art. 57 EC (2003), mn 3; probably also T Schürmann, Art. 57 EC (2006), 4, who states that the law must be 'Bestandteil der mitgliedschaftlichen Rechtsordnung' (part of the national legal order), as well as G Ress and J Ukrow, Art. 57 EC (2002), mn 15.
[68] Probably C Ohler, Art. 57 EC (2002), mn 5.
[69] Of the opinion that the date in Art 57(1) EC refers to the date on which a law becomes 'effective': W Kiemel, Art. 57 EC (2003), mn 8; W Kessler, et al, 'Schweiz', 667; N Dautzenberg, 'Lankhorst-Hohorst', 194; U Prinz, 'Lankhorst-Hohorst-Entscheidung', 650; C Spengel and M Golücke, 'Gesellschafter-Fremdfinanzierung', 339; W Kessler, et al, 'Gesellschafter-Fremdfinanzierung', 327 *et seq*; A Schnitger, 'Wirkungsgrenzen der Grundfreiheiten', 636; U Prinz, 'Anmerkung zu FG Baden-Württemberg, Beschl. v. 14.10.2004 - 3 K 62/99', 371; F Wassermeyer and J Schönfeld, 'Anmerkung zu BFH vom 14. 9. 2005', 413.
[70] An example of a law for which these two dates do not coincide is provided by § 8a of KStG (Germany) in the version that was at issue in Case C-492/04 *Lasertec Gesellschaft für Stanzformen mbH (formerly Riess Laser Bandstahlschnitte GmbH) v Finanzamt Emmendingen)*. [For an account of the judgment see H Schießl, 'Rangverhältnis'] However, due to the Court's view of the relationship of free movement of capital and the freedom of establishment, it did not have to elaborate on this issue. But see Case C-415/06 *Stahlwerk Ergste Westig GmbH v Finanzamt Düsseldorf-Mettmann*.

If one considers that Art 57(1) 1st sentence EC refers in its wording to '*restrictions* which *exist*'[71] instead of '*laws* that *exist*,' then the literal interpretation of the provision suggests that it is the moment at which the law begins its legal restrictive effect on the market participant—not potentially[72] but actually—that is the crucial date. Such a reading supercharges the fundamental freedom with the greatest possible effectiveness and, at the same time, interprets the exception contained in Art 57(1) 1st sentence EC narrowly.[73] Therefore, with respect to national laws, the decisive date is in principle that on which it becomes effective.[74]

Article 57(1) 1st sentence EC is not limited to national but extends also to Community 'laws'.[75] For an EC regulation, it can be said that the same reasoning as is advanced in relation to national laws applies *mutatis mutandis*.[76]

The question arises of when an EC directive becomes effective within the meaning of Art 57(1) 1st sentence EC, recalling that it is not directed towards the individual, but to the Member States. If one is prepared to regard the moment at which the EC directive has an effect on the market participant as the decisive one then it appears that in the case of an EC directive, the crucial date is the date of transposition. This is the latest date by which the Member States must give effect to the restrictive provisions in their national jurisdictions.

While this detached assessment of an EC directive appears to be comprehensible, it quickly becomes apparent that it is the interaction between directive and national law that brings up the critical questions. Two situations in this respect deserve closer elaboration.

In the first situation, a directive that contains restrictions on free movement of capital *vis-à-vis* third countries entered into force some time before 1 January 1994. Its transposition into national law was, however, not due until 1 July 1995.

---

[71] [Emphasis added].
[72] 'Potential effects' are those that occur when market participants change their behaviour, awaiting the time at which a certain law becomes effective in the future.
[73] This construction is also in line with the Court's interpretation of the transition periods contained in the different accession treaties. *Cf* for example, Case 77/82 *Anastasia Peskeloglou v Bundesanstalt für Arbeit*, para 11 *et seq*.
[74] The Court had the opportunity to answer this question conclusively in Case C-492/04 *Lasertec Gesellschaft für Stanzformen mbH (formerly Riess Laser Bandstahlschnitte GmbH) v Finanzamt Emmendingen)* but did not do so due to its view of the relationship of Arts 56(1) EC and 43 EC.
[75] It is undoubtedly true that secondary Community law must not run counter to primary Community law. This already follows from Arts 7(1), 2nd sentence EC, 192(1) EC, 202 EC, 211 EC, 230 EC, and 249(1) EC. [See M Nettesheim, 'Normenhierarchien', 746 for further references] However, it must also be stressed that the Court has taken a very rigid approach towards measuring secondary Community law against primary. [*Cf.* For a very critical view of this approach: D Ehlers, 'Allgemeine Lehren', mn 7; see also M Nettesheim, 'Normenhierarchien', 746 *et seq*] It is, therefore, open to question whether the Court would declare restrictive secondary Community measures in the area of third country capital movement void if these cannot be saved by taking recourse to Art 57(1) EC.
[76] *Cf* Art 249(2) EC: an EC regulation—on cursory inspection—can be best compared to a national law in its function and effect.

It could happen that one Member State (effectively) implemented the respective directive before 1 January 1994, and another Member State chose to do so after this date.

In such a situation, it is suggested that the EC directive be distinguished from the national laws. With respect to the EC directive, recourse is had to the date on which it had to be transposed into national laws, because this is latest date at which the restrictive effect began to affect all market participants. If the EC has chosen to allow for implementation after 31 December 1993, then it cannot save its restrictive directive by reference to Art 57(1) 1st sentence EC. Moreover, if a directive restricting third country capital movement cannot be saved by reference to any other exception to the fundamental freedoms—which in practice appears not very likely[77]—then it is void or at least can be declared void.[78]

Turning to the national laws, if one considers the date on which they become effective as the decisive one, then this leads to the conclusion that the respective law would be grandfathered by Art 57(1) 1st sentence EC in one Member State, but not in the other. At first sight, it appears that such an interpretation would allow for fragmentation of EC law, which would run counter to the very idea of legislating on the Community level. This solution seems nevertheless to be convincing and in line with the spirit of Art 57(1) 1st sentence EC if one considers that the Member State that enacted the respective law before 1 January 1994 could also have chosen to enact a restrictive law on its own account. Thus, fragmentation of the legal orders of the Member States is in any case sanctioned before 1 January 1994.

In the second situation, which I shall examine more closely, an EC directive entered into force and had to be transformed into national law well before 1 January 1994. One Member State, however, failed to meet the transformation deadline and implemented the directive after 31 December 1993.

With respect to the EC directive, Art 57(1) 1st sentence EC indisputably applies. One could, however, doubt whether in the situation at hand the effect of the grandfathering clause extends to the national law, having stated above that the crucial date is the one on which the national law becomes effective. In such a situation, it is suggested that one should not refer to the national law, but should have recourse to the transposition date of the EC directive. Such an exception is necessary in order to prevent the fragmentation of EC law. Otherwise, a Member State would be barred from implementing the restrictive EC Directive into national law if the measures restricting third country capital movement could only be saved by virtue of Art 57(1) 1st sentence EC.

In summary, the crucial date to which Art 57(1) 1st sentence EC refers is in principle the date on which the respective 'national or Community law' becomes effective.

---

[77] Refer to footnote 75 of this Chapter.
[78] See for a discussion of the possible effect of a conflict of secondary Community law with primary Community law: M Nettesheim, 'Normenhierarchien', 748 *et seq.*

With respect to Member States that joined the Community at a later point, in the absence of any express derogation in the respective accession treaty,[79] the relevant date remains the one mentioned in Art 57(1) 1st sentence EC. By joining the EC, those countries accepted the *aquis communautaire* of which the aforementioned provision forms a part.[80] Hungary and Estonia, however, succeeded in accession negotiations to have included in Art 57(1) EC a second sentence that sets the date with respect to their restrictive national laws to 31 December 1999.

Furthermore, the impact of subsequent changes to laws that originally became effective before 1 January 1994 or 2000, respectively, also deserves examination. Restrictions on third country capital movement contained in Community laws can be abolished, in part, progressively or in full, by respective legislation. However, the Community may also decide to erect further restrictions. Both must be based on Art 57(2) EC.[81]

Concerning national laws, following the gist of the fundamental freedoms, the Member States can always ease certain capital movement restrictions introduced before the deadline[82] as long as they do not alter the basic ideas underlying the respective national law. They may do so in full but also in part or progressively: 'The greater power will usually include the lesser.'[83] Further restrictions, on the other hand, are prohibited, except for the case in which the Member States were especially empowered by secondary Community law.[84] This does not mean that any alteration of the laws is forbidden.[85] In the literature, it is suggested that only 'fundamental' changes to restrictive national provisions, which bring about an aggravation of the existing restrictions, are ruled out.[86] It appears, however, that for the Court it suffices for the establishment of a 'fundamental' change—facilitating the jurisprudence on face-out clauses in accession treaties[87]—if the newly adopted legislation is 'based on an approach which differs from that of the previous law and establishes new procedures'.[88] Although the Court states in *Konle* and subsequent case law that it meets its requirements if the new law is identical in

---

[79] The Treaty on European Union—Protocol (No. 1) on the Acquisition of Property in Denmark is of limited relevance in this respect.
[80] W Kessler, et al, 'Schweiz', 665, fn 90; left open in Case C-452/01 *Margarethe Ospelt and Schlössle Weissenberg Familienstiftung*, para 31.
[81] C Ohler, Art. 57 EC (2002), mn 6.
[82] Case C-302/97 *Klaus Konle v Republik Österreich*, para 52.
[83] Case C-452/01 (Opinion of AG Geelhoed) *Margarethe Ospelt and Schlössle Weissenberg Familienstiftung*, para 53.
[84] C Ohler, Art. 57 EC (2002), mn 6.
[85] Therefore, this study speaks of grandfathering instead of the stand-still clause. See also ibid.
[86] N Dautzenberg, 'Fürstentum Liechtenstein II', 1127; W Schön, 'Kapitalverkehr mit Drittstaaten', 494; C Ohler, Art. 57 EC (2002), mn 6.
[87] A Schnitger, 'Kapitalverkehrsfreiheit', 503; W Kessler, et al, 'Schweiz', 665.
[88] Case C-302/97 *Klaus Konle v Republik Österreich*, para 53; confirmed in Case C-446/04 (Opinion of AG Geelhoed) *Test Claimants in the FII Group Litigation v Commissioners of Inland Revenue*, para 192; Case C-157/05 *Winfried Holböck v Finanzamt Salzburg-Land*, para 41. Note that the national law must have formed part of the legal order of the Member State concerned *continuously* since 31 December 2008. [*Cf* Case C-101/05 *Skatteverket v A*, para 49]

substance to the previous law,[89] the ECJ seems to focus on the question of whether the change improved the treatment of market participants rather than whether the law brought about no aggravation of the situation of the market participant.[90]

In a nutshell, one can note that 'Member States are empowered to adapt existing legislation by virtue of the stand still[91] clause without altering the existing legal situation.'[92]

f. Appraisal and Summary: A Gateway for Unreasonable Restriction of Intra-Community and Third Country Capital Movement?

Article 57(1) EC constitutes a temporally unlimited carve-out from the duty to liberalize for certain categories of capital movement. These carve-outs may be provided for in national and 'Community law'. 'Community laws' covered by Article 57(1) EC are rare and, as yet, have not truly given any cause for concern in terms of undue restrictions on free movement of capital. The situation is, however, different if one turns to national laws.

Not being subject to any proportionality test, national laws covered by the grandfathering provision constitute true blind spots on the mirror of free movement of capital *erga omnes*. Depending on the breadth accorded to Art 57(1) EC, these blind spots can either quickly turn into black holes of protectionism, or they can provide the Member States with some reasonable room to manoeuvre to slowly shift economic policy from a protectionist to a more liberal attitude and phase out their restrictive laws.

The Court seems to be willing to lend a broad reading to the Article,[93] thereby turning itself into an accomplice of the Member States' protectionist sentiments, which they seek to defend by reliance on Art 57(1) EC.

The ECJ applies a wide understanding of the notion of 'direct investment', extending it, eg, to dividend payments. Moreover, it widens the scope of the provision by extending the group of capital movements that are considered 'third country'. That not being enough, instead of requiring—in accordance with the

---

[89] Case C-302/97 *Klaus Konle v Republik Österreich*, para 52; confirmed in Case C-446/04 (Opinion of AG Geelhoed) *Test Claimants in the FII Group Litigation v Commissioners of Inland Revenue*, para 192; Case C-157/05 *Winfried Holböck v Finanzamt Salzburg-Land*, para 41.

[90] Case C-302/97 *Klaus Konle v Republik Österreich*, para 53; recently: Case C-446/04 *Test Claimants in the FII Group Litigation v Commissioners of Inland Revenue*, para 193. Compare Case C-452/01 *Margarethe Ospelt and Schlössle Weissenberg Familienstiftung*, para 53, in which it is sought to include existing administrative practice in the evaluation.

[91] [Footnote added] Instead of 'stand-still clause,' the term 'grandfathering clause' would be better, *cf* footnote 85 of this Chapter.

[92] Case C-452/01 (Opinion of AG Geelhoed) *Margarethe Ospelt and Schlössle Weissenberg Familienstiftung*, para 53.

[93] Reaching the same conclusion: A Cordewener, et al, 'Outer Boundaries', 375.

wording of Art 57(1) EC—that the law that causes the restriction on free movement of capital specifically refer to direct investment and apply to third countries only, the ECJ asks whether the economic activity in the individual case amounts to foreign direct investment, disregarding the abstract scope of the national law. This approach surely brings many national tax rules within the scope of Art 57(1) EC, since they rarely differentiate between intra-Community and third country capital movement.

Overall, contrary to the general rule of construction to interpret exceptions narrowly and contrary to the purpose and spirit of the freedom of free movement of capital as a whole, the Court intransigently pursues its not-truly-hidden agenda to reduce the scope of the freedom in a third country context to a minimum, thereby turning itself from the pacemaker of liberalization into the brake pedal in this subject area.

This study proceeds from a fundamentally different basis. As I perceive free movement of capital *erga omnes* as clearly contributing to the attainment of the Treaty aims, Art 56(1) EC must be interpreted in a liberal and wide sense, both in an intra-Community and in a third country context. In contrast, restrictions, such as that contained in Art 57(1) EC, are construed narrowly in the way suggested above in order to give the freedom the greatest possible effectiveness.

Therefore, I suggested that the notion of direct investment must be construed strictly. The 'lasting and direct links between the person providing the capital and the entrepreneur to whom or the undertaking to which the capital is made available in order to carry on an economic activity' must be understood essentially in parallel terms to the 'definite influence test' required in Art 43 EC for the identification of an 'establishment'.

In order not to turn Art 57(1) EC into a gateway for unreasonable restriction of intra-Community direct investment, the 'foreign link' is to be sought in the individual transaction(s) with which one seeks to establish (or perpetuate) the possibility of control over an undertaking. The law within the meaning of this provision must specifically refer to a third country context and to direct investment (or one of the other categories mentioned in the provision). Furthermore, a law, in order to be covered by Art 57(1) EC, must in principle have become effective, ie, have its legal restrictive effect on the market participant, before 1 January 1994 or 2000, respectively. Subsequent changes of national laws are allowed as long as the change improves the position of the market participant.

g. Incursus: National and Community Laws Restricting Third Country Capital

(1) Identifying National Laws Restricting Third Country Capital Movements

The most self-evident way of identifying national laws restricting foreign direct investment and/or the other categories of capital movements mentioned in Art 57(1) EC would be to enter into the analysis of the 27 legal orders of the Member States. This not being the most feasible solution, it might be more useful, in order to gain an overview of the sectors and matters possibly affected by discriminatory treatment, to look at the reservations registered in the lists of Annex B and E of the OECD Code of Liberalisation of Capital Movements[94] and the Annex on Article II Exemptions[95] and Schedules of Specific Commitments with respect to supply of services through commercial presence (so-called 'Mode III,' Art I:2c GATS) of the General Agreement on Trade in Services.

(a) OECD Code of Liberalisation of Capital Movements

Concerning inward foreign direct investment as defined in Annex A, List A, Section I of the Code of Liberalisation of Capital Movements[96] reservations were lodged with respect to the following sectors or matters: agriculture,[97] fishing,[98] mining,[99] auditing,[100] accountancy services;[101] banking,[102] legal services,[103] engineering and architectural services,[104] energy,[105] different kinds of transport (mainly air transport),[106] gambling and lotteries;[107] publishing;[108] radio and television broadcasting,[109] audio-visual communications,[110] telecommunications,[111] flour milling activities,[112] travel agencies,[113] real estate (including agricultural and forestry land),[114] acquisition of ships (including those for fishing purposes),[115] and the establishment of branches in general.[116] With respect to outward foreign direct investment, only Portugal has noted a reservation for the banking sector. Moreover, all parties to the agreement subject certain sectors or matters—inter alia, insurance, banking, minerals/hydrocarbons/fuels, transport, travel agencies and publishing[117]—to reciprocity considerations, which are listed in Annex E of the Code.

---

[94] 1961 OECD Code of Liberalisation of Capital Movements (as amended 01.11.2007).
[95] *Cf* Art XXIX.
[96] 1961 OECD Code of Liberalisation of Capital Movements (as amended 01.11.2007).
[97] France.   [98] Denmark; Sweden.   [99] Greece; Spain.
[100] Austria; Finland.
[101] Austria; Belgium; Denmark; Greece; Sweden.
[102] Czech Republic; Germany; Greece; Hungary; Poland; Portugal.
[103] Austria; Belgium; Denmark; Finland; Greece; Spain; Sweden.
[104] Austria; Greece.   [105] Austria; Finland; Slovak Republic.
[106] Austria; Czech Republic; Denmark; Finland; France; Germany; Greece; Hungary; Ireland; Italy; The Netherlands; Poland; Portugal; Slovak Republic; Spain; Sweden; United Kingdom.
[107] Czech Republic; Poland; Slovak Republic; Spain.   [108] Italy.
[109] Germany; Greece; Italy; Poland; Portugal; Spain; United Kingdom.
[110] Italy; Sweden.   [111] Portugal; Spain; Sweden.
[112] Ireland.   [113] Portugal.
[114] Austria; Czech Republic; Finland; Greece; Ireland; Poland.
[115] Austria; Belgium; Denmark; Finland; France; Germany; Greece; Hungary; Ireland; Italy; The Netherlands; Poland; Sweden; United Kingdom.
[116] Finland.
[117] Note that the United Kingdom also names mergers and takeovers in general.

It is, however, worth noting that the explanatory value is limited in several aspects. To begin with, only 19 out of 27 Member States[118] are party to the Code and thus, noted the respective reservations they wished to apply towards other parties. Moreover, an authorization requirement for the conclusion or execution of transactions and transfers to which the Code is applicable does not itself constitute discrimination, *cf* Art 2(a) of the Code. Possible reservations that would stem from public order and security interests of the parties do not even appear in the Annex B lists due to the broad public order and security exception (on a self-judging basis) to the whole Code contained in Art 3 thereof. Last but not least, reservations are broadly defined, not mentioning respective laws and regulations in force and, thus, may be no more than an indication in which subject area of law a foreign investor has to start his research.

(b) WTO GATS: Annex on Article II Exemptions and Schedules of Specific Commitments

The General Agreement of Trade in Services sets out in Art I:2c GATS that one of the ways in which services can be supplied is through commercial presence, ie, the provision of services is preceded by direct investment (so-called 'Mode III provision of services').[119] The Agreement contains in Art II:1 GATS the general commitment to accord most-favoured-nation treatment to service providers and the services supplied, including such services provided by way of Mode III. The principle of most-favoured-nation treatment in Art II:1 GATS, however, does not extend to market access. Access to a party's market and, moreover, national treatment and other additional commitments are, in principle, subject to further negotiations with a view to advancing liberalization progressively (Art XIX GATS).[120]

The GATS provides for the possibility of lodging reservations to the general commitment of most-favoured-nation treatment (Art II:2 GATS). They are contained in the Annex on Article II Exemptions,[121] which follows a negative list approach, ie, sectors or matters mentioned therein are exempted from the commitment.[122] In contrast, the specific commitments (*cf* Art XIX GATS) in principle follow a positive list approach, ie, the schedules state for the different service sectors[123] the specific commitments with respect to market access,

---

[118] Member States that are not party to the Code are as follows: Cyprus, Estonia, Latvia, Lithuania, Malta, Slovenia, Bulgaria, and Romania.

[119] See, for further references, C Ohler, '§ 18', mn 842.

[120] See, for further references, ibid, mn 858.

[121] *Cf* Art XXIX.

[122] See for the relevant reservations: WTO, 'Services Commitments : Schedules of Commitments and Lists of Article II Exemptions' (Website, WTO, Geneva 2006).

[123] The schedules of specific commitments are divided into two broad groups, ie, horizontal commitments, a general part applying to all sectors, and sector-specific commitments. The sector categorization follows the GATT Secretariat classification; see WTO, 'Service Sectoral Classification List' (MTN.GNS/W/120).

national treatment, etc which a party has accepted (Art XX GATS). Although the parties endeavour to use standardized terminology[124] when compiling their national schedules, explanatory notes or restrictions are often added or formulated, in contrast to the original idea, in a negative list approach, simply stating the exceptions to the liberalization of a certain sector.[125]

In order to identify sectors or matters in which laws of the Member States could possibly discriminate against foreign direct investment, one is confronted with the task of reading both abovementioned lists with a holistic view. Difficulties may arise from the fact that Member States—or the Community on behalf of the Member States[126] (or in its own right)—have not always properly notified their specific commitments or exceptions. Nevertheless, the lists maintained by the GATS List of Art II Exceptions and the Schedules of specific commitments are considerably more detailed and probably more carefully compiled than the Annex B lists containing the reservations to the OECD Code and, thus, are of exemplary value when it comes to the identification of possible sources of discrimination against foreign direct investment.

Due to the fact that virtually all Member States have lodged reservations to one of the sectors mentioned in the Annex or Schedules with respect to most-favoured nation-treatment, market access, national treatment, etc, not to mention the restrictions on horizontal commitments, this study refrains from spelling them out.[127]

Instead, in the following section I shall briefly discuss three prominent examples of Community laws restricting third country capital movement that (at least partially) could fall within the scope of Art 57(1) EC. They relate to the areas of financial institutions, non-life and life insurers, and transport.

(2) Selected Examples for Restrictive Laws

(a) Credit Institutions ('Banks'), Investment Firms, Management and Investment Companies

The respective EC directives in the finance sector,[128] by and large, do not establish a special regime for third country investors for authorization to take up the

---

[124] WTO, 'Guide to Reading the GATS Schedules of Specific Commitments and the List of Article II (MFN) Exemptions' (Website, WTO, Geneva 2006). See also C Ohler, '§ 18', mn 872 et seq.
[125] C Ohler, '§ 18', mn 875.
[126] Commitments and exemptions of European Union members are found under 'European Communities', except for the 1993–1995 commitments of Austria, Finland, and Sweden, who joined the EU in 1995, the accession countries that joined the EU in 2004, and Romania and Bulgaria, which followed in 2007.
[127] In lieu thereof, refer to WTO, 'Services Commitments: Schedules of Commitments and Lists of Article II Exemptions' (Website, WTO, Geneva 2006).
[128] eg, Directive 2000/12/EC; Directive 2000/39/EC; Directive 85/611/ECC.

business of credit institution,[129] investment firm,[130] management company, or investment company[131] by primary establishment or subsidiary.

However, it is worth pointing out that this principle is not consequently adhered to. The respective directives provide that authorization of the aforementioned undertakings must be refused

if the laws, regulations or administrative provisions of a non-member country governing one or more natural or legal persons with which the [financial institution] has close links, or *difficulties involved in their enforcement*, prevent the effective exercise of their supervisory functions.[132]

'Enforcement difficulties' are no ground of refusal in case the natural or legal persons with which the financial institution has close links are governed by a Member State's jurisdiction since it is probably assumed that the aforementioned problems will not occur in an intra-Community context. Prima facie, financial institutions to be established within the EC and controlled by EC nationals that have dealings with third country natural or legal persons are equally subject to this provision. Financial institutions to be established within the EC and controlled by third country persons, however, are much more likely to have close links to persons governed by a third country jurisdiction. Yet, this restriction on free movement of capital cannot be saved by Art 57(1) EC, inter alia, due to the fact that the respective provisions were introduced later than 31 December 1993.[133]

Entering a Member State's market through the particular form of establishment of a branch does not require (additional) authorization for those branches of the respective credit institution,[134] investment firm,[135] or management company[136] authorized in another Member State. The directives, however, are silent on the establishment of branches by undertakings authorized in a third country. Thus, the possibility of requiring (additional) authorization for a branch of the aforementioned undertakings established in a third country is left to the respective Member State. If the Member States have chosen to adopt such restrict-

---

[129] Art 4 *et seq.* of Directive 2000/12/EC. Note that this Directive represents only a consolidated version of various directives, eg, Directive 77/780/EEC; Directive 89/646/EEC, dating back to a time before 31 December 1993. *Cf* European Commission, 'The Taking-up and Pursuit of the Business of Credit Institutions' (Website, Brussels 2006).

[130] Art 5 *et seq* of Directive 2004/39/EC.

[131] Art 5 *et seq* and 12 *et seq* of Directive 85/611/ECC, respectively.

[132] [Emphasis added] Art 7(3) 2nd subparagraph of Directive 2000/12/EC; now Art 12(3) 2nd subparagraph of Directive 2006/48/EC 'Bank Directive (Recast)', Art 10(2) of Directive 2004/39/EC, Art 5a(2) 2nd subparagraph, 13a(1) 3rd subparagraph of Directive 85/611/ECC, respectively.

[133] *Cf* Art 2(2) of Directive 95/26/EC; Art 1 of Directive 2001/107/EC.

[134] Art 13 of Directive 2000/12/EC; now Art 16 of Directive 2006/48/EC 'Bank Directive (Recast)'.

[135] Art 32(1) of Directive 2004/39/EC.

[136] Art 6(2) of Directive 85/611/ECC.

ive authorization procedures, those can in principle be saved if they were effectively introduced in national law before 31 December 1993.[137]

Having already mentioned above—'[a]s the Community intends to keep its financial markets open to the rest of the word'[138]—it had not until recently itself established active restrictions on direct investments originating from third countries.[139] Instead, Community legislation in the area of financial institutions operated with reciprocity clauses.

By way of example, Arts 23–24 of the now repealed Directive 2000/12/EC on credit institutions[140] established two systems, one of notification of all authorizations by the Member States of subsidiaries, holdings, and branches[141] of third country credit institutions,[142] and another of monitoring and 'stepped response' towards third countries depending on the treatment accorded to Community credit institutions in those third countries as regards establishment and the carrying on of banking activities and the acquisition of holdings in third country credit institutions.[143]

Whenever it appeared to the Commission that a third country did not grant effective market access comparable to that granted by the Community to credit institutions from that third country, the Commission could seek a mandate from the Council for negotiations with a view to obtaining comparable competitive opportunities for Community credit institutions (Art 23(4)).[144]

If a third country, in the view of the Commission, failed to grant effective market access and national treatment offering the same competitive opportunities as are available to domestic credit institutions, the Commission could initiate negotiations on its own account (Art 23(5.1)).[145] In the aforementioned circumstances, even simultaneously with negotiations, the Commission in a committee procedure could decide that the Member States must limit or suspend pending authorization procedures[146] and decisions

---

[137] *Cf*, eg, § 53 of KWG (Germany).
[138] Recital (20) of Directive 2000/12/EC.
[139] Disregarding such provisions as those mentioned above, in which a restrictive effect might flow from certain requirements in authorization procedures, which could potentially weigh more heavily on third country than EC financial institutions.
[140] Directive 2000/12/EC; formerly Arts 8 and 9 of Directive 89/646/EEC and Art 9 of Directive 77/780/EEC.
[141] Only branches of credit institutions authorized in another Member State may not require authorization, Art 13 of Directive 2000/12/EC.
[142] Arts 23(1) and 24(2) of ibid.   [143] Art 23(2)–(7) EC.
[144] Formerly Art 9 of Directive 89/646/EEC.
[145] Formerly Art 9 of ibid.
[146] The suspension option 'does not apply to the opening by a non-EU bank of a branch rather than a subsidiary in a Member State. The opening of a branch does not confer a single licence and is therefore a purely bilateral matter between the Member State and the third country concerned.' M Fowle and A Smith, 'European Union Single Banking and Finance Market', 81. While the wording of Art 23(5.2) and (5.3) of the Directive could possibly also accommodate another system of reasoning, systematic and teleological reasoning seem to confirm the aforementioned view. *Cf* Recital (20) of Directive 2000/12/EC.

regarding the acquisition of holdings or future requests for such by third country investors for a maximum period of three months. If, in the mean time, negotiations conducted with the respective third country had not produced the desired outcome, the Commission could propose to the Council, which decided on the basis of a qualified majority, that the measures taken should be continued.

The option of restricting or preventing the access of third country investors active in the sector of credit institutions to the Common Market provided the Community with both the necessary bargaining tool in international negotiations to demand reciprocal treatment of Community capital institutions on third country markets[147] and a defence instrument against protective or abusive practices by third countries.[148] However, the aforementioned provisions in principle also amounted to a restriction on free movement of capital *vis-à-vis* third countries within the meaning of Art 56(1) EC, which could in principle be saved by reference to Art 57(1) EC.

However, the recently adopted Directive 2006/48/EC (Recast) on credit institutions abolished this approach. Article 38(3) now reads as follows:

…the Community may, through agreements concluded with one or more third countries, agree to apply provisions which accord to branches of a credit institution having its head office outside the Community identical treatment throughout the territory of the Community.

Capital movement restrictions similar to those in the repealed Directive 2000/12/EC are found in the area of the establishment and pursuit of the business of an investment firm[149] and of management and investment companies.[150] Those provisions, however, relate to a time period after 31 December 1993 and thus would not fall within the scope of Art 57(1) EC.

(b) Non-Life and Life Insurers

Within the insurance sector, in principle, the authorization of a primary establishment or a subsidiary also does not depend on the origin of the direct investment. However, as in the finance sector, Community law requires that the competent authority shall refuse authorization

if the laws, regulations or administrative provisions of a non-member country governing one or more natural or legal persons with which the undertaking has close links, or *difficulties involved in their enforcement*, prevent the effective exercise of their supervisory functions.[151]

---

[147] W Kiemel, Art. 57 EC (2003), mn 16.   [148] Ibid, mn 13.
[149] Art 15 of Directive 2000/39/EC; formerly Art 7 of Directive 93/22/EEC.
[150] Art 5c of Directive 85/611/ECC, introduced by Directive 2001/107/EC.
[151] [Emphasis added] Art 8(1) 3rd subparagraph of Directive 73/239/EEC; Art 6(2) 2nd subparagraph of Directive 2002/83/EC.

Since the restriction was first introduced in 1995, it is not covered by Art 57(1) EC.[152] Restrictions that could, however, fall within the scope of Art 57(1) EC are those relating to the establishment of branches and agencies. While Directive 73/239/EEC[153] in Art 23 *et seq* provides for market access, at the same time it establishes a special regime for the taking up and pursuit of the business of direct insurance other than life insurance by means of a branch or agency by any undertaking whose head office is outside the Community. Similar provisions are contained in Art 51 *et seq* of Directive 2002/83/EC concerning life assurance,[154] which to a large extent consolidated older directives in the subject area.[155]

As in the finance sector, Directives 73/239/EEC and 2002/83/EC also contain reciprocity clauses and rules that allow for restricting or preventing the access of third country investors in the insurance sector.[156]

(c) **Transport**

Direct investments in the European air transport market are practically reserved for EC nationals or EC undertakings. Regulation 2407/92 requires, in order to be granted an operation licence, that

> the undertaking shall be owned and continued to be owned directly or through majority ownership by Member States and/or nationals of Member States. It shall at all times be effectively controlled by such States or such nationals.[157]

Moreover, the air carriers may use only aircraft that are registered within the Member State granting the licence or within the Community.[158]

In relation to Art 57(1) EC, if the potential acquirer of an 'EC air carrier' is habitually resident within one of the Member States but holds the nationality of a third country, the purchase would—in the view of the author of this study—qualify as an intra-Community transaction.[159] Hence, as the respective provision of the regulation at hand does not exclusively apply to third country capital movement, it cannot be saved by reference to Art 57(1) EC.

Within the sector of transport of goods or persons by inland waterway between the Member States, Community law provides, inter alia, that the carrier has to

---

[152] Art 2(2) of Directive 95/26/EC.
[153] Directive 73/239/EEC.   [154] Directive 2002/83/EC.
[155] With respect to branches of third country undertakings, Art 31 of Directive 79/267/EEC is of particular relevance.
[156] For direct insurance other than life assurance, refer to Arts 29a and 29b of Directive 73/239/EEC; introduced by Art 4 of Directive 90/618/EEC; for life assurance, see Arts 58 and 59 of Directive 2002/83/EC; introduced by Art 9 of Directive 90/619/EEC.
[157] Art 4(2) of Regulation 2407/92/EEC. Even direct investment through an undertaking registered in a third country but fully owned by an EC national is not permissible, *cf* Art 4(1) lit. a of Regulation 2407/92/EEC.
[158] Art 8(2) lit. a of Regulation 2407/92/EEC.
[159] See Chapter II. 4. c. (3).

be established within a Member State,[160] and it may be permitted to carry out cabotage only if it

use[s] for this purpose only vessels whose owner or owners are:
(a) natural persons domiciled in a Member State and who are Member States nationals; or
(b) legal persons:
  (i) which have their registered place of business in a Member State; and
  (ii) the majority holding in which or majority of which belongs to Member State nationals.[161]

Such regulations severely curtail direct investment from third countries. For example, a third country investor would in principle not be allowed to own the means of work, but he would be forced to rent or lease vessels from an EC natural or legal person if he wished to carry out the business within the Community. Hence, a 'simple' takeover of an EC carrier that owns vessels would require an unbundling of the ownership of the undertaking and the ownership of the vessels before carrying out business activities. Such preconditions might make the whole deal less attractive.[162]

Concerning the question of whether such a regulation can be saved by reference to Art 57(1) EC, the same reasoning as advanced above with respect to air transport applies here *mutatis mutandis*.

3. A Liberalization and Bargaining Tool: Article 57(2) EC

a. Underlying Liberal Notion

Article 57(2) EC empowers the Community to adopt measures on capital movement to and from third countries involving the categories of capital movement mentioned therein. The Community must exercise these powers with a view to 'endeavouring to achieve the objective of free movement of capital between Member States and third countries to the greatest extent possible'. Against the background of this programmatic commitment[163] to maximum freedom as well as the abovementioned interpretive direction set by the Treaty aims,[164] the spirit and purpose of this provision can be described as follows: it gives the Community the power—though not the duty[165]—to remove the remaining national restrictions on free movement of capital grandfathered by

---

[160] Art 1 of Regulation 3921/91/EEC.
[161] Art 2 of ibid; see also Regulation 1356/96/EC.
[162] It should be noted, however, that a Member State may exceptionally provide for derogations. *Cf* Art 2(2) of Regulation 3921/91/EEC.
[163] C Ohler, Art. 57 EC (2002), mn 16 mentions in this respect that the Community has a wide margin of appreciation in implementing these aims.
[164] See Chapter I. 2.   [165] C Ohler, Art. 57 EC (2002), mn 24.

virtue of Art 57(1) EC.[166] On the other hand, it forms the legal basis and source of the bargaining power of the Community that is necessary in order to negotiate with third countries with a view to achieving unrestricted access to third country markets and treatment of EC investors within these markets comparable to that attributed to third country investors active within the EC.[167] These negotiations, of course, can lead to the conclusion that at a certain point in time it is advisable to unilaterally restrict capital movements originating from a given third country in order to motivate it to allow free access to and equal treatment of EC investors in its market.[168] However, recalling that the Treaty aims are best served if capital can flow in as unrestricted a way as possible, the Council must take into consideration in such situations the possible long-term benefits of the option of leaving the Common Market open unilaterally even if the third country should continue to resist according similar treatment to EC investors.

The underlying liberal notion[169] of Art 57(2) EC is confirmed and backed up by the procedural requirements stipulated by the provision. In order to remove existing restrictions on free movement of capital, only a qualified majority is required. Erecting new hurdles to the free flow of capital presupposes a unanimous vote in the Council.[170] Whether a measure taken by the Council constitutes such a hurdle, or in the words of the provision, forms a 'step back in Community law as regards the liberalisation of the movement of capital to or from third countries' must be judged by the direct and indirect, factual and potential effect of the Community measure at issue on the standard of liberalization already achieved.[171]

The point of reference for the 'standard of liberalisation already achieved' is not completely undisputed. One commentator wants to take recourse to the majority of the Member States.[172] One could also take as the decisive test the standard within the most liberal Member State since any Community measure more restrictive than this standard would negatively affect capital movement between this Member State and third countries. If, however, one wishes to take seriously the wording of Art 57(2) EC, which refers to a 'step back in

---

[166] A Rohde, *Kapitalverkehr*, 191; W Kiemel, Art. 57 EC (2003), mn 20; see also J Karl, 'Competence', 415 *et seq*, 434; W Shan, 'Community Policy', 609; W Shan, *EU-China Investment Relations*, 59 *et seq*; JA Usher, *Law of Money*, 232.

[167] W Kiemel, Art. 57 EC (2003), mn 16; J Bröhmer, Art. 57 EC (2007), mn 8; For a discussion of the breadth of an EC treaty making competence in the area of foreign direct investment, refer to: W Shan, 'Community Policy'; J Karl, 'Competence'; J Ceyssens, 'Common Foreign Investment Policy'; N Maydell, 'Minimum Platform on Investment'.

[168] Such an approach has been chosen, for example, with respect to credit institutions, *cf* Arts 23–24 of Directive 2000/12/EC.

[169] A Rohde, *Kapitalverkehr*, 212; W Kiemel, Art. 57 EC (2003), mn 18, 20; different view A Honrath, *Kapitalverkehr*, 137.

[170] The European Parliament is not involved.

[171] R Molzahn, *Kapitalverkehrsfreiheit und Währungsunion*, 178; A Glaesner, Art. 57 EC (2000), mn 6; G Ress and J Ukrow, Art. 57 EC (2002), mn 16; W Kiemel, Art. 57 EC (2003), mn 16.

[172] Along similar lines: W Kiemel, Art. 57 EC (2003), mn 20.

Community law',[173] then it becomes apparent that the correct point of reference is the standard already achieved on the Community level in regard to the categories of capital mentioned within Art 57 EC.[174]

b. Competence

Article 57(2) EC *a priori* contains an internal competence of the Community to take autonomous secondary measures.[175] Whether this competence is concurrent or exclusive is not ultimately settled. Those who advocate an exclusive competence argue that any action towards third countries is only meaningful and effective (*cf* the channel phenomenon[176]) if taken by the Community.[177] However, (foreign) direct investment constitutes a cross-sectional activity, which poses regulatory questions in diverse areas of law such as the law of property, company law, consumer and investor protection law, the law on administrative supervision, and tax law. Hence, the competence is better perceived as concurrent.[178]

In practice, the Community has frequently referred to Art 57(2) EC for the purpose of concluding jointly with the Member States a number of Partnership and Cooperation Agreements[179] and WTO-related agreements,[180] as well as the Energy Charter Treaty and Protocol,[181] although Art 57(2) EC does not mention expressly any competences under international law. This, however, does

---

[173] [Emphasis added].
[174] C Ohler, Art. 57 EC (2002), mn 22; the point of reference extends to secondary (as in Art 57(1) EC) but also to primary Community law. This distinction can be drawn on the basis of the argument that the first section of Art 57 EC speaks of '…Community law *adopted*…' but the second section refers to 'Community law' without any such addendum. Hence, apart from the areas covered by restrictive grandfathered laws, the standard of liberalization achieved on the Community level is in principle the one established by virtue of Art 56(1) EC.
[175] The only known autonomous secondary act based on Art 57(2) EC (in concert with other provisions) is Regulation 2271/96/EC. Digel states that the main field of application of Art 57(2) EC are so-called 'reciprocity clauses' in secondary community law, such as Art 15 of Directive 2000/39/EC, Art 5c of Directive 85/611/ECC, Arts 29a and 29b of Directive 73/239/EEC, and Arts 58 and 59 of Directive 2002/83/EC. However, it is worth noting that none of those clauses have ever legally been based on Art 57(2) EC.
[176] See 5. c. (5) (d).
[177] Along similar lines: A Glaesner, Art. 57 EC (2000), mn; R Smits, 'Payments and Capital', 256; P Eeckhout, *External Relations*, 124; see also the related discussion in the context of the Constitutional Treaty summarized at J Ceyssens, 'Common Foreign Investment Policy', 269 *et seq*.
[178] S Weber, 'Kapitalverkehr', 566; JCW Müller, *Kapitalverkehrsfreiheit*, 187; C Ohler, Art. 57 EC (2002), mn 17; W Kiemel, Art. 57 EC (2003), mn 18; T Schürmann, Art. 57 EC (2006), mn 5; AC Digel, 'Europäischer Finanzmarkt', Inaugural Dissertation, Eberhard-Karls-Universität, 156 *et seq*; probably also A Rohde, *Kapitalverkehr*, 191.
[179] Decision 2007/548/EC; Decision 2007/547/EC; Decision 2007/546/EC; Decision 2007/541/EC, Euratom; Decision 2007/376/EC; Decision 2007/318/EC; Decision 2007/251/EC; Decision 1999/491/EC, ECSC, Euratom; Decision 1999/490/EC, ECSC, Euratom; Decision 98/401/EC, ECSC, Euratom; Decision 98/149/EC, ECSC, Euratom; Decision 97/800/EC, ECSC, Euratom.
[180] Decision 96/412/EC; Decision 1999/61/EC.
[181] Decision 94/998/EC; Decision 98/181/EC, ECSC, Euratom.

not mean that such competences do not vest in the Community. External competences do not necessarily need to be given expressly in a certain provision of the Treaty or secondary legislation.[182] They may also arise by implication from the system of the EC Treaty or from provisions that prima facie confer internal competences only[183] ('principle of implication'). According to the Court, there are two occasions when external competences can be construed in the absence of express conferment. Either the Community adopted secondary legislation and the operation of those rules might be affected[184] by concurrent Member State actions ((1) 'AETR principle'),[185] or, whenever the exercise of an external competence significantly improves the chances of effectuating the objectives of the Treaty, for which explicit internal competences capable of extending to relationships arising from international law have been granted[186] to the Community ((2) 'complementarity principle'[187] or often (falsely) referred to as the 'principle of parallelism'[188]).

---

[182] See in regard to 'self-empowerment' by secondary legislation, R Geiger, 'Vertragsschlußkompetenzen', 980 *et seq*.

[183] Case 22/70 *Commission v Council (Re European Agreement on Road Transport: 'AETR')*, para 15 reads as follows: 'To determine in a particular case the Community's authority to enter into international agreements, regard must be had to the *whole scheme of the treaty* no less than to its *substantive provisions*.' [Emphases added]

[184] The concurrent Member State action at issue has to fall, in a formal sense, within the scope of application of the secondary legislation. [B Fassbender, 'Völkerrechtssubjektivität', 37, 34]

[185] Case 22/70 *Commission v Council (Re European Agreement on Road Transport: 'AETR')*, paras 17, 22; reiterated in Joined Cases 3, 4, and 6/76 *Cornelis Kramer and others*, paras 17–20.

[186] It is not necessary for the Community to have first laid down internal measures. [A Dashwood and J Heliskoski, 'Classic Authorities', 11 *et seq*; Opinion 1/76 *Draft Agreement Establishing a European Laying-up Fund for Inland Waterway Vessels*, para 3 *et seq*].

[187] Indicated in Joined Cases 3, 4, and 6/76 *Cornelis Kramer and others*, para 30 *et seq*; explicitly in Opinion 1/76 *Draft Agreement Establishing a European Laying-up Fund for Inland Waterway Vessels*, para 4; clarified in Opinion 2/91 *Convention No 170 of the International Labour Organization concerning Safety in the Use of Chemicals at Work*, para 7 as a principle of a general nature detached from the special circumstances in Opinion 1/76 *Draft Agreement Establishing a European Laying-up Fund for Inland Waterway Vessels*. What was made clear in Opinion 1/94 *Competence of the Community to Conclude International Agreements Concerning Services and the Protection of Intellectual Property*, para 81 was that the internal Community rules need to be capable of 'extend[ing] to relationships arising from international law', or in other words, they need to have an external dimension that, for example, the rules on the provision of services and freedom of establishment, targeted on internal objectives, are lacking. In contrast, open rules might be found in the fields of agriculture, fisheries, transport, capital and payments, and social policy and the rules on the relationship with third countries. [A Dashwood, 'Attribution', 129 *et seq*]

[188] The author of this study agrees with the suggestion of *Dashwood* and *Heliskoski*, who view the labeling '*principle of parallelism*' as misleading. 'Things which are parallel...run alongside each other without ever meeting: manifestly this does not convey the relationship between express internal and implied external competence.' [A Dashwood and J Heliskoski, 'Classic Authorities', 12 *et seq*] The idea of parallelism, ie, every attribution of substantive internal power automatically confers, by implication, external power upon the Community, was strongly advocated by the Commission [*cf* Opinion 1/94 *Competence of the Community to Conclude International Agreements Concerning Services and the Protection of Intellectual Property*, para 74] and seems to be rejected by the Court in the same instance [*cf* ibid, paras 75, 81]—otherwise the EC would have been competent to conclude the agreement in question (GATS), since internal competences covering the subject matter of the international agreement were available within the EC Treaty (note Arts 43

Moreover, to the extent that the Community has completely or almost completely covered a subject area by autonomous acts, it holds exclusive external competence[189] in this area.[190]

c. Limits on the Competence

In accordance with what was said with respect to Art 57(1) EC, in order to fall within the ambit of Art 57(2) EC, Community measures must, first, establish a special regime that may apply only to third county capital movement and, second, relate to one of the categories of capital movements mentioned therein.[191] Community measures that do not distinguish between intra-Community and third country capital movement and/or between, for example, portfolio and direct investment cannot (solely) be based on this Article.

Moreover, the competence contained in Art 57(2) EC is 'without prejudice to the other chapters of this Treaty'. This reference, first and foremost, points to the

---

EC *et seq* and 49 EC *et seq*). Thus, not every internal competence automatically generates an external one. [A Dashwood, 'Attribution', 129 *et seq*]

Concurring: M Bothe, 'Umweltabkommen', 688 *et seq*; S Griller and K Gamharter, 'Competences', 74; TC Hartley, *EU Law*, 277 *et seq*, esp. 231; W Heintschel von Heinegg, 'Internationale Organisationen', mn 20; J Heliskoski, *Mixed Agreements*, 30; W Kilian, *Europäisches Wirtschaftsrecht*, mn 128; I MacLeod, et al, *External Relations*, 51 *et seq*.

Interpreting the case law as giving way to 'parallelism' of internal and external competence in the sense of *'in foro interno in foro externo'* and thereby reducing the importance of 'necessity', in the process of establishing an implied external power, to mere marginality: S Breier, 'Vertragsschlusskompetenz', 349; M Cremona, 'External Competence', 138 *et seq*; A Epiney and D Gross, 'Außenkompetenzen', 32; A Epiney and D Gross, 'Völkerrechtliche Verträge', 4; A Epiney, 'Außenbeziehungen', 442; W Frenz, *Außenkompetenzen*, 42 *et seq*; R Frid, *International Organizations*, 80 *et seq*; M Nettesheim, 'Kompetenzen', 436 with a critical appraisal of the concept of parallelism against the background of the present case law; C Tomuschat, Art. 281 EC (2004), mn 5. See also A Proelß, 'Mixed Agreements'.

[189] M Sedlaczek, Art. 57 EC (2003), mn 5; *cf* Case 22/70 *Commission v Council (Re European Agreement on Road Transport: 'AETR')*, para 17 *et seq*. See also D O'Keeffe, 'Exclusive, Concurrent and Shared Competence', 182. The rationale for this doctrine is to prevent Member States from taking unilateral or collective actions that would undermine or conflict with internal EC measures. It is an expression of the principle of loyalty embodied in Art 10 EC. [D O'Keeffe, 'Exclusive, Concurrent and Shared Competence', 182; see also for a discussion of the role of Art 10 EC within the external competences of the Community: A Epiney, 'Außenbeziehungen', 442; A von Bogdandy, Art. 10 EC (2002), mn 67 *et seq*] In order to rely on the AETR doctrine, internal community rules need to regulate a particular area completely or exhaustively. [Opinion 1/94 *Competence of the Community to Conclude International Agreements Concerning Services and the Protection of Intellectual Property*, para 96; Opinion 2/92 *Competence of the Community or one of its Institutions to Participate in the Third Revised Decision of the OECD on National Treatment: 'OECD'*; Case C-476/98 *Commission v Federal Republic of Germany (Re 'Open Skies' Agreement)*, para 110. [D O'Keeffe, 'Exclusive, Concurrent and Shared Competence', 185. Internally, this is described as 'pre-emption'; externally it gives rise to exclusive EC competence. [D O'Keeffe, 'Exclusive, Concurrent and Shared Competence', 183]

[190] *Cf* J Karl, 'Competence', 415 *et seq*; see also N Maydell, 'Minimum Platform on Investment'.

[191] Probably also W Kiemel, Art. 57 EC (2003), mn 16, who speaks of a 'connection' between the Community measure and the categories of capital movement mentioned in Art 57(2) EC.

principle of proportionality (cf Art 5(3) EC)[192] and subsidiarity (Art 5(2) EC),[193] but also to the fundamental rights.[194]

Constraints on competence may also flow from international agreements concluded by the Community or by the Member States. While, for example, Art 40 of the EEA Agreement[195] directly obliges the Community to abolish all restrictions on free movement of capital with respect to the other parties to the agreement, Arts 10 EC, 307 EC, and 304 EC require the Community to take into consideration Member States' obligations under international law and to cooperate with respective international organizations of which the Member States are members.[196]

d. Means of Action

The Community may choose its means of action; the Treaty does not stipulate any restriction in this respect.[197] Hence it can have recourse in particular to regulations (Art 249(2) EC), directives (Art 249(3) EC), or decisions (Art 249(4) EC).

e. Appraisal: The Sleeping Beauty yet to be Woken?

Although Art 57(2) EC also provides for the possibility of restricting free movement of capital in a third country context, it is liberal in its underlying notion. The precise restrictive or liberalizing effect of Art 57(2) EC is very much dependent on the legislative activity of the Community taken on the basis of this provision. So far, only a very limited number of legislative acts have solely or in conjunction with other competences been based on Art 57(2) EC.

It has neither been used to remove existing protectionist national provisions grandfathered by virtue of Art 57(1) EC, nor has it been employed to restrict third country capital movement. This leaves us with a 'mixed performance':

---

[192] C Ohler, Art. 57 EC (2002), mn 24; U Haferkamp, *Kapitalverkehrsfreiheit*, 213; S Lütke, *CFC-Legislation*, 102; but: A Honrath, *Kapitalverkehr*, 139, who points out—though with the questionable argument that the Community is not bound by the fundamental freedoms—that the principle of proportionality applies only in a constricted fashion to Community measures. See for the issue of whether the Community is (also) an addressee of the fundamental freedoms: T Kingreen, 'Fundamental Freedoms', 577 *et seq*. For more recent case law, see: Case 15/83 *Denkavit Nederland BV v Hoofdproduktschap voor Akkerbouwprodukten*, para 15 *et seq*; Case C-51/93 *Meyhui NV v Schott Zwiesel Glaswerke AG*, para 11 *et seq*; Case C-114/96 *Criminal proceedings against René Kieffer and Romain Thill*, para 29 *et seq*.
[193] S Weber, 'Kapitalverkehr', 566; A Honrath, *Kapitalverkehr*, 138; JCW Müller, *Kapitalverkehrsfreiheit*, 187; U Haferkamp, *Kapitalverkehrsfreiheit*, 212 *et seq*; T Schürmann, Art. 57 EC (2006), mn 5; different view: R Smits, 'Payments and Capital', 256, who does not see any room for the application of the principle of subsidiarity due to the fact that Art 57(2) EC contains an exclusive competence of the Community; concurring A Glaesner, Art. 57 EC (2000), mn 6.
[194] J Lübke, *Kapitalverkehrs- und Niederlassungsfreiheit*, 432.
[195] EEA Agreement.   [196] C Ohler, Art. 57 EC (2002), mn 25 *et seq*.
[197] Ibid, mn 23; more cautiously: A Honrath, *Kapitalverkehr*, 138 *et seq*.

the Member States have resisted further liberalization; on the other hand, the Community and the Commission in particular have refrained from treading the protectionist path. The latter might be an expression of the predominant liberal ideology found in the Commission.

However, in view of an expected dramatic increase in inward foreign direct investment in economic areas of strategic interest, such as energy supplies or telecommunications, from third country owned or controlled investment funds, the balance just referred to might shift towards a more protectionist sentiment.[198] Whether Art 57(2) EC will be used in this context as competence for the enactment of restrictive measures has to be seen.

4. Managing Situations of Economic Emergency: Article 59 EC

Article 59 EC provides that:

[w]here, in exceptional circumstances, movements of capital to or from third countries cause, or threaten to cause, serious difficulties for the operation of economic and monetary union, the Council, acting by a qualified majority on a proposal from the Commission and after consulting the ECB, may take safeguard measures with regard to third countries for a period not exceeding six months if such measures are strictly necessary.

The provision forms an economic exception to—or rather a temporal step backwards from—the duty to liberalize capital movements and is intended to provide the Community with a necessary tool to manage the *erga omnes* applicability of the freedom.

The purpose of Article 59 is to allow the Council to take short-term emergency measures where large influxes or outflows of capital affect the interest rates set by the European Central Bank, thus damaging the Euro-zone economies.[199]

---

[198] *Cf* European Commission, 'Proposal for a Directive amending Directive 2003/54/EC of 26 June 2003 concerning Common Rules for the Internal Market in Electricity, for a Directive amending Directive 2003/55/EC of 26 June 2003 concerning Common Rules for the Internal Market in Natural Gas, for a Regulation establishing an Agency for the Cooperation of Energy Regulators, for a Regulation amending Regulation (EC) No 1228/2003 and for a Regulation amending Regulation (EC) No 1775/2005—Explanatory Memorandum' (Explanatory Memorandum of the 3rd Energy Package), 7; see in this respect: J Dempsey, 'EU Considers Adding Protectionist Measures to Energy Policy' *International Herald Tribune* (18.9.2007); see also: International Institute for Sustainable Development, 'EU FTAs'; International Institute for Sustainable Development, 'Commission's Investment Negotiating Ideas'; European Council, 'Minimum Platform on Investment for EU FTAs' (15375/06); European Commission, 'Minimum Platform on Investment for EU FTAs—Provisions on Establishment in Template for a Title on "Establishment, Trade in Services and E-commerce"' (D (2006) 9219); European Commission, 'Issues Paper: Upgrading the EU Investment Policy'; B Benoit and M Schieritz, 'Berlin Looks to Vet Foreign Funds Deals' *Financial Times.com* (26.06.2007); B Benoit, 'German Call to Curb Foreign Buyers' *Financial Times.com* (12.07.2007); H Williamson, 'EU "Should Vet State-funded Bids"' *Financial Times.com* (18.07.2007).

[199] PR Vergano, Art. 59 EC (2005), § 139.03; see also R Molzahn, *Kapitalverkehrsfreiheit und Währungsunion*, 186 *et seq*.

The provision—although applicable to any category of capital movement—unfolds its practical relevance especially with respect to capital imports and exports on short notice, which refers in particular to the category of portfolio investments. Such investments are usually of a highly speculative nature.[200]

Commensurate with this emergency character, the safeguard clause is strictly defined and limited in several ways. On the side of the scope of application, first, only capital movements to or from a third country[201] are subject to the provision. Second, 'exceptional circumstances' must cause or threaten to cause 'serious difficulties' for the operation of the EMU. In order to be able to respond swiftly to a danger or threat of danger—in contrast to Art 57(2) EC—the provision at hand demands 'merely' a qualified majority.[202] The mandatory consultation of the ECB stresses the 'interlocking' of economic and monetary policy, with the latter independently conducted by the ECB, cf Art 105 EC et seq.

With respect to the legal consequence, first, the safeguard measures are limited to a maximum period of six months. Second, those measures must be 'strictly necessary'.

Speaking in terms of competence, Art 59 EC establishes the exclusive power of the Community to take safeguard measures out of economic considerations.[203] The power, however, cannot be used for political reasons such as to press for reciprocity in the treatment of capital movements by third countries.[204]

a. Preconditions for Resorting to Safeguard Measures

Article 59 EC requires the existence of 'exceptional circumstances'. What is made clear by this phrase is that the provision must be construed narrowly and applied with caution.[205] What amounts to exceptional circumstances—an exceptionally large amount of capital transferred in a short period of time certainly constitutes one important criterion of determination[206]—cannot be answered across the board, but must be judged on an individual basis, probably best by a comparison to and differentiation from 'normal economic fluctuation'.[207] In doing so, the Council enjoys a considerable degree of discretion that will hardly be litigable.[208]

---

[200] U Haferkamp, *Kapitalverkehrsfreiheit*, 214.
[201] Non-introduction of the Euro does not place a Member State in the category of a 'third country' within the meaning of Art 59 EC. [G Ress and J Ukrow, Art. 59 EC (2002), mn 7]
[202] PR Vergano, Art. 59 EC (2005), § 139.03.
[203] A Rohde, 'Freier Kapitalverkehr', 457; G Ress and J Ukrow, Art. 59 EC (2002), mn 2; W Kiemel, Art. 59 EC (2003), mn 5.
[204] W Kiemel, Art. 59 EC (2003), mn 2.
[205] The Court already held in one of its earlier judgments that safeguard clauses must be interpreted restrictively, cf Joined Cases 286/82 and 26/83 *Graziana Luisi and Giuseppe Carbone v Ministero del Tesoro*.
[206] Cf Art 3 of Directive 88/361/EEC; see also R Molzahn, *Kapitalverkehrsfreiheit und Währungsunion*, 179; W Kiemel, Art. 59 EC (2003), mn 6; T Schürmann, Art. 59 EC (2006), mn 1.
[207] C Ohler, Art. 59 EC (2002), mn 2.
[208] Cf T Schürmann, Art. 59 EC (2006), mn 3; R Molzahn, *Kapitalverkehrsfreiheit und Währungsunion*, 83.

'Serious difficulties' or the threat of serious difficulties for the operation of the EMU are those that manifest themselves in a disruption or threat of disruption of the permanent convergence among the Member States, in particular with respect to price stability, government deficits, exchange rate stability, and long-term interest rates. One may also speak of such difficulties or threat of difficulties if capital movements undermine or threaten to undermine the Common Monetary Policy.[209] The situation just mentioned also includes that in which the transition to the Third Stage of the EMU is restricted for Member States that are still 'outside' of it.[210] Difficulties or the threat thereof are 'serious' if they cannot be remedied by 'ordinary means' of monetary and exchange policy.[211]

Although Art 59 EC does not mention economic determinants that refer to a situation in a Member State, Honrath, Molzahn and others are of the opinion that serious fiscal difficulties within one Member State suffice to activate Art 59 EC. After the entry into force of the third stage of the EMU, the coordination of the Common Economic Policy among the Member States has reached a level in which serious fiscal difficulties in one Member State 'automatically' cause a threat of serious difficulties for long-term convergence among all other Member States.[212]

Although it is quite possible that serious fiscal difficulties in one Member State can severely affect the functioning of the EMU, this study suggests refraining from making such general statements and argues in favour of a comprehensive analysis of the overall economic situation in the individual case of the Member States as a whole, preventing any automatism in enacting safeguard measures. Only in this way can one give sufficient consideration to the character of the provision as a temporary exception to free movement of capital *erga omnes*.[213]

Since the provision does not require the materialization of difficulties, it also allows for precautionary measures to be taken. However, in this case the threat

---

[209] R Molzahn, *Kapitalverkehrsfreiheit und Währungsunion*, 178; G Ress and J Ukrow, Art. 59 EC (2002), mn 4; U Haferkamp, *Kapitalverkehrsfreiheit*, 214; W Kiemel, Art. 59 EC (2003), mn 7; for a somewhat broader view: A Rohde, *Kapitalverkehr*, 193; Note C Ohler, Art. 59 EC (2002), mn 6 *et seq*, who seeks to decide whether there are 'difficulties' by having recourse to a change in the balance of payments only.
[210] G Ress and J Ukrow, Art. 59 EC (2002), mn 4; note, however, that institutional problems are not covered by Art 59 EC. [A Honrath, *Kapitalverkehr*, 215 *et seq*]
[211] In more detail: R Molzahn, *Kapitalverkehrsfreiheit und Währungsunion*, 179 *et seq*; see also W Kiemel, Art. 59 EC (2003), mn 7.
[212] A Honrath, *Kapitalverkehr*, 226; R Molzahn, *Kapitalverkehrsfreiheit und Währungsunion*, 83; of the same opinion: U Haferkamp, *Kapitalverkehrsfreiheit*, 214.
[213] For an even stricter view: A Honrath, *Kapitalverkehr*, 217 *et seq*, who notes that 'excessive government deficits' within the meaning of Art 104(1) EC or other 'critical' developments in the 'budgetary situation' and the 'stock of government debt', *cf* Art 104(2) EC—which lead to serious difficulties in the operation of the EMU or the threat thereof—do not justify capital and payments restrictions *vis-à-vis* third countries due to the fact that cross errors in the aforementioned areas cannot be remedied by capital and payments restrictions. Of the same opinion: G Ress and J Ukrow, Art. 59 EC (2002), mn 4; C Ohler, Art. 59 EC (2002), mn 4. While I can concur with the aforesaid, this study suggests that the debate is better located within the proportionality test.

must be real, ie, very likely, and not just based on allegations; the mere possibility of difficulties does not suffice because otherwise the provision would be deprived of its 'ultima ratio character'.[214]

b. Which Form of 'Safeguard Measures'?

Article 59 EC contains no further specification of what form the safeguard measure may take. The Council is therefore free to choose the appropriate means of restricting free movement of capital and payments.[215] However, the provision requires that those means must be 'strictly necessary', which suggests applying an elevated standard to the proportionality test.[216] This elevated standard is relativized, though, by the Council's discretion, which is only litigable to a limited extent.[217]

Among commentators, the question of whether Art 59 EC allows only for safeguard measures that take effect in those Member States which are part of the Euro-zone or whether the scope of the provision extends to all Member States is not completely settled. Vergano, for example, without advancing further explanation, states that Art 59 EC 'is designed to apply to those Member States in the Euro-zone'.[218] This, however, is not convincing. In order for a safeguard measure to have the greatest effectiveness, it must also apply to those Member States that are not part of the Euro-zone.[219] Otherwise, those measures could easily be circumvented by entering the Common Market by passing through a Member State that is not part of the Euro-zone; capital movements between the Member

---

[214] A Honrath, *Kapitalverkehr*, 225 *et seq*; S Mohamed, *Free Movement of Capital*, 225; See also G Ress and J Ukrow, Art. 59 EC (2002), mn 6, who suggest that the threat must come close to being instant, overwhelming and leave no choice of means, and no moment of deliberation. ('Caroline-formula'—constituting the traditional definition of the right of self-defence in customary international law, *cf* MN Shaw, *Int'l Law*, 1024 *et seq* for further references).

[215] A Honrath, *Kapitalverkehr*, 231; G Ress and J Ukrow, Art. 59 EC (2002), mn 2. While the difficulties for the operation of the EMU must flow from capital movements only, the provision is silent with respect to whether restrictions enacted to remedy those difficulties may also be applied on free movement of payments. This has to be answered in the affirmative, at least for payments that are connected to capital movements. *Cf* C Ohler, Art. 59 EC (2002), mn 9; J Bröhmer, Art. 59 EC (2007), mn 2; for a more critical view: W Kiemel, Art. 59 EC (2003), mn 9; A Rohde, *Kapitalverkehr*, 194.

[216] U Haferkamp, *Kapitalverkehrsfreiheit*, 214; but note R Molzahn, *Kapitalverkehrsfreiheit und Währungsunion*, 83, who states that this phrase cannot disguise the fact that the Council enjoys a considerable degree of discretion.

[217] A Honrath, *Kapitalverkehr*, 232 *et seq*; R Molzahn, *Kapitalverkehrsfreiheit und Währungsunion*, 83.

[218] PR Vergano, Art. 59 EC (2005), § 139.02. It remains somewhat unclear whether his statement also applies to the voting procedure. Of the same opinion, but more cautiously: M Sedlaczek, Art. 59 EC (2003), mn 2, probably also JA Usher, *Law of Money*, 203. Along similar lines: C Ohler, Art. 59 EC (2002), mn 3, who seeks to exclude those Member States that do not prepare for the Third Stage of the EMU from the scope of Art 59 EC.

[219] A Honrath, *Kapitalverkehr*, 229 *et seq*; U Haferkamp, *Kapitalverkehrsfreiheit*, 215; along similar lines: S Mohamed, *Free Movement of Capital*, 225, fn 52.

States *de lege lata* cannot be restricted for reasons mentioned in Art 59 EC.[220] With respect to Member States outside the Euro-zone, in the event of serious difficulties or the threat of serious difficulties or crises regarding their balance of payments, safeguard measures can be taken on the basis of Art 119 EC *et seq*, which also apply to intra-Community capital movements.[221]

Safeguard measures may not exceed the maximum period of six months. If necessary they can be renewed;[222] not, however, without a constantly increasing burden of justification by the Council.[223] In this context, it should be stressed that having (repeated) recourse to the safeguard clause is not without problems because it considerably damages the image of the Common Market and the Euro.

When taking safeguard measures on the basis of Art 59 EC, the prohibition of discrimination contained in Art 12 EC, the general principle of protection of confidence, fundamental rights,[224] and international commitments *vis-à-vis* third countries must all be observed.[225]

c. Voting in a 'Diminished Council'?

Article 59 EC requires a qualified majority vote on a proposal of the Commission after consulting the ECB.[226]

---

[220] *Cf* R Molzahn, *Kapitalverkehrsfreiheit und Währungsunion*, 183, who, however, advances this argument with respect to the opposite situation: a national currency runs into trouble, and it is open to question whether the safeguard measures shall be limited to this Member State or must extend to all Member States, including those that are part of the Euro-zone, even though the Euro is not directly affected. The underlying issue is that any safeguard measure applied damages the image of the common currency. Molzahn opts, therefore, for a regional application of Art 59 EC in this situation. [R Molzahn, *Kapitalverkehrsfreiheit und Währungsunion*, 188 *et seq*] He must, however, admit that this leads again to the 'circumvention problem', which he can only solve by suggesting an amendment to the EC Treaty. See also A Honrath, *Kapitalverkehr*, 230 *et seq*.

[221] *Cf* Art 122(6) EC. See also PR Vergano, Art. 59 EC (2005), § 139.02; W Kiemel, Art. 56 EC (2003), mn 39 *et seq*; C Ohler, Art. 59 EC (2002), mn 14; R Smits, 'Payments and Capital', 250 *et seq*. Note Regulation 332/2002/EC, which spells out what is meant by 'mutual assistance' within the meaning of Art 119(2) EC. It should be pointed out that in terms of market integration, these safeguard clauses are not without problems, *cf* M Seidel, 'Kapitalmarkt', 768 *et seq*; AFP Bakker, *Capital Movements*, 231 *et seq*. For a short account of Art 119 EC *et seq*, with further references, refer to B Kempen, 'Art. 119 EC'; B Kempen, 'Art. 120 EC'; R Bandilla, Art. 119 EC (2004); R Bandilla, Art. 120 EC (2004).

[222] R Smits, *ECB*, 62; R Smits, 'Payments and Capital', 257; G Ress and J Ukrow, Art. 59 EC (2002), mn 11; T Schürmann, Art. 59 EC (2006), mn 4.

[223] G Ress and J Ukrow, Art. 59 EC (2002), mn 8.

[224] For more details, refer to A Honrath, *Kapitalverkehr*, 233 *et seq*.

[225] Ibid, 236 *et seq*; G Ress and J Ukrow, Art. 59 EC (2002), mn 14; W Kiemel, Art. 59 EC (2003), mn 15 *et seq*; T Schürmann, Art. 59 EC (2006), mn 5. In this respect it is worth pointing out that safeguard clauses, eg, in Art 7 lit. c of 1961 OECD Code of Liberalisation of Capital Movements (as amended 01.11.2007), Art. 7 lit. c of 1961 OECD Code of Liberalisation of Current Invisible Operations (as amended 19.02.2008), Art XII GATT and Art XII of 1994 WTO General Agreement on Trade in Services, Art VIII section 2 of 1944 Agreement of the International Monetary Fund (as amended, effective 1969, 1978, 1992), are not identical to Art 59 EC.

[226] For a discussion of the question of who will take part in the ECB's internal decision processes, refer to R Molzahn, *Kapitalverkehrsfreiheit und Währungsunion*, 183 *et seq*.

Insofar as the difficulties affect the operation of the monetary—in contrast to the economic—union, it is open to question whether only those Member States that actually joined the Euro-zone[227] or all Member States[228] can vote within the Council on temporary safeguard measures. The wording of Art 59 EC, however, does not support the view that argues in favour of voting in a 'diminished Council'. The provision at hand speaks simply of 'the Council, acting by a qualified majority on a proposal from the Commission'. Article 205(2) EC, which specifies the voting procedure, does not provide for different voting rules in regard to monetary union matters. Furthermore, Art 122 EC, which sets out the special rules for those Member States that have not joined the common currency, does not provide any indication in favour of an allegedly specific voting procedure within the ambit of Art 59 EC.[229] Beyond these formal considerations, one must take into account that in most cases it will hardly be possible to differentiate between difficulties in the operation of the monetary union and difficulties in the operation of the economic union; with respect to the latter, all Member States are entitled to vote. Both parts are closely interrelated and will affect each other.[230]

Furthermore, as explained above, safeguard measures also take effect with respect to those Member States that are not part of the Euro-zone. Thus, if those Member States have to bear the consequences, then they must also have a say; after all, every Member State is, in pursuance of Arts 2 EC and 4 EC, obliged to facilitate the operation of Economic and Monetary Union.[231]

In sum, all Member States vote in the Council irrespective of whether they are part of the Euro-zone.

d. Appraisal: Setback in the Standard of Liberalization?

Overall, Art 59 EC cannot be viewed as a general derogation from the *erga omnes* liberalization of capital movements. Opening up the EC capital market unilaterally cannot be successfully accomplished without having 'ready at hand' the relevant managing tools that are required to respond appropriately to the challenges such an opening potentially holds. The quorum of a qualified majority enables the Council to act more swiftly in case of emergency instead of entering into the tedious and time-consuming process of negotiations in order to secure a unanimous vote.

---

[227] So, eg, M Seidel, 'Kapitalmarkt', 776; J Welcker and C Nerge, *Die Maastrichter Verträge—zum Scheitern verurteilt?*, 61; but see R Molzahn, *Kapitalverkehrsfreiheit und Währungsunion*, 180 *et seq*, who convincingly rebuts *Seidel*'s arguments in great detail.
[228] eg, R Molzahn, *Kapitalverkehrsfreiheit und Währungsunion*, 180 *et seq*; G Ress and J Ukrow, Art. 59 EC (2002), mn 13; U Haferkamp, *Kapitalverkehrsfreiheit*, 215.
[229] R Molzahn, *Kapitalverkehrsfreiheit und Währungsunion*, 181.
[230] U Haferkamp, *Kapitalverkehrsfreiheit*, 215.
[231] A Honrath, *Kapitalverkehr*, 229 *et seq*; R Molzahn, *Kapitalverkehrsfreiheit und Währungsunion*, 181.

Although the Council enjoys considerable discretion in its decisions, the rather narrowly defined scope of the provision and the temporal limitation of a measure ensure that that the liberalization standard achieved will be undercut only in a state of economic emergency and only for a limited period of time.[232]

5. Responding to Situations of Political Crisis: Article 60 EC

Above, it was stated that Art 59 EC constitutes a temporal exception to the duty to liberalize capital movements *vis-à-vis* third countries for economic reasons. Article 60 EC, in contrast, concerns politically motivated derogations from the already achieved standard of liberalization. While Art 59 EC empowers only the Community, Art 60 EC contains both a 'primary' empowerment of the Community in the first paragraph and a 'residual' one for the Member States in para (2). Article 60 EC reads as follows:

1. If, in the cases envisaged in Article 301, action by the Community is deemed necessary, the Council may, in accordance with the procedure provided for in Article 301, take the necessary urgent measures on the movement of capital and on payments as regards the third countries concerned.
2. Without prejudice to Article 297 and as long as the Council has not taken measures pursuant to paragraph 1, a Member State may, for serious political reasons and on grounds of urgency, take unilateral measures against a third country with regard to capital movements and payments. The Commission and the other Member States shall be informed of such measures by the date of their entry into force at the latest.

The Council may, acting by a qualified majority on a proposal from the Commission, decide that the Member State concerned shall amend or abolish such measures. The President of the Council shall inform the European Parliament of any such decision taken by the Council.

a. Community Measures: Article 60(1) EC

The first paragraph of Art 60 EC authorizes the Community to impose restrictions on free movement of capital (and on payments) *vis-à-vis* third countries within the broader context of adopting economic sanctions[233] against third countries on the basis of Art 301 EC[234] in connection with a common position or a joint action under the Common Foreign and Security Policy (CFSP). These

---

[232] G Ress and J Ukrow, Art. 59 EC (2002), mn 8; W Kiemel, Art. 59 EC (2003), mn 14; U Haferkamp, *Kapitalverkehrsfreiheit*, 216; for a different view: M Seidel, 'Kapitalmarkt', 775 *et seq*; J Welcker and C Nerge, *Die Maastrichter Verträge—zum Scheitern verurteilt?*, 60.

[233] For a brief but catchy account of the regulation of sanctions in the course of European integration, refer to P Koutrakos, *EU Int'l Relations Law*, 428 *et seq*.

[234] Art 301 EC refers to 'economic sanctions', which is the more general term compared to 'financial sanctions'. Art 60(1) EC merely clarifies that those economic sanctions extend to financial ones, although free movement of capital, as the only freedom, extends also to third countries

restrictions, more appropriately termed 'financial sanctions', 'imposed pursuant to Article 60 and 301 EC... may [, for example,] prohibit investments, the transfer of certain or any financial assets or freeze the assets of the targets'[235] and are either adopted by the Community on the basis of autonomous political considerations or in fulfilment of international obligations of the Member States, in particular those arising from decisions of the United Nations Security Council (UNSC) that are, by virtue of Arts 25 and 48 UN Charter, binding upon the member States of the United Nations (UN).[236]

Article 60 EC intertwines the 'pillar architecture' of the EU by linking the intergovernmental 'second pillar' (CFSP) to the supranational first one (EC) with a view to 'strengthen the position of the EU to adopt measures to impose economic sanctions against third countries'[237] and, thus, the provision 'has indirectly facilitated the Union's ambitious plans to adopt a Common Foreign and Security Policy'.[238] This intertwining is, however, not without problems. In particular, the EU implementation of UN sanctions directed against individuals, mostly adopted within the broader context of the international effort to combat terrorism, brought up the question of the standard of protection of human rights in the European Union.[239] A multitude of intensive academic debates has revolved around issues of 'due process,' especially transparency and participation, and 'legal remedies'.[240] Lately the discussion has also expanded to the challenges the UNSC sanction policy poses to the very architecture of EU governance.[241]

In the following discussion, this study neither seeks to place the abovementioned 'human rights issues'—ie, the balancing of the conflicting aims of protecting individual rights and the effectiveness of the fight against international terrorism—nor the EC governance debate at the centre of the discussion, but rather seeks to narrow down its focus in the process of elaboration of Art 60 EC to the provision's character as a limitation on the fundamental freedom of free movement of capital with regard to third countries.

---

and, thus, liberalizes all capital movements *vis-à-vis* those countries. [*Cf* M Sedlaczek, Art. 60 EC (2003), mn 4; P Gilsdorf and B Brandtner, Art. 301EC (2004), mn 18]

[235] P Koutrakos, *EU Int'l Relations Law*, 432.

[236] For a current, consolidated list of financial sanctions applied by the EU/EC, refer to the so-called 'EU terrorism list': Common Position 2001/931/CFSP; implemented through Regulation 2580/2001/EC; note also: European Commission, 'Consolidated List of Persons, Groups and Entities Subject to EU Financial Sanctions' (Website, European Commission, Brussels 2007).

[237] S Mohamed, *Free Movement of Capital*, 227.

[238] Ibid, 226.

[239] It should be mentioned that this debate is not limited to the EU level, but similar controversies exist on the UN as well as nation State levels.

[240] eg, C Tomuschat, 'Yusuf and Kadi'; S Hörmann, 'Resolutionen'; A von Arnauld, 'UN-Sanktionen'; S Steinbarth, 'Individualrechtsschutz'; K Schmalenbach, 'Vorrang'; M Kotzur, 'Yusuf'; S Schmahl, 'Targeted Sanctions'; C Möllers, 'EuG konstitutionalisiert'; L Harings, 'Rechtsgemeinschaft'; S Bartelt and HE Zeitler, 'Intelligente Sanktionen'.

[241] See M Nettesheim, 'UN Sanctions', 569.

(1) Admissibility of Restrictive Measures Taken by the EC under International Law: A Brief Overview

It is important to distinguish between the EC-internal attribution of competences described above and the admissibility of the restrictive measures taken *vis-à-vis* third countries under international law.[242] The most important questions that arise under general public international law and the limits for the application of the EC competence flowing from it are outlined in the following section, whereby a general distinction will be drawn between the implementation of UNSC resolutions by the European Union and European Community and autonomous action by them.

Even though the Community is not a member of the UN, there can be hardly any doubt about the admissibility of the implementation of UN sanction regimes through the Community. Concerning the admissibility *vis-à-vis* the UN, not only the UN practice evidenced by several UNSC resolutions, which have regularly called upon international organizations to act in conformity with them, but also Art 48(2) UN Charter, from which it can be deduced that the member States of the UN are not obliged to fulfil their obligations *in personam*, support this viewpoint.[243] With respect to the admissibility *vis-à-vis* the addressee of the sanctions, international organizations are, in pursuance of Art 48(2) EC and Art 53 UN Charter integrated in the enforcement of UN sanction regimes and, thus, member States of the UN must acquiesce in the implementation of such regimes by an international organization on behalf of its members.[244]

A different, still unsettled question is that of whether the Community is legally obliged under international law to implement a UNSC resolution, recalling that Art 25 UN Charter declares those resolutions only binding upon States. Article 48(2) UN Charter provides merely for the possibility but not for a duty binding upon the international organization to implement UN sanction regimes on behalf of its member States.[245]

In this respect, this study follows the decision reached in the legally not undisputed[246] judgment of the Court of First Instance (CFI) in *Yusuf*. The CFI, first, rightly confirmed that:

> unlike its Member States, the Community as such is not directly bound by the Charter of the United Nations and that it is not therefore required, as an obligation of general public international law, to accept and carry out the decisions of the Security Council in accordance with Article 25 of that Charter.[247]

---

[242] Note G Ress and J Ukrow, Art. 60 EC (2002), mn 3, who, however, use the 'old' term of 'reprisal'.
[243] K Osteneck, *Umsetzung von UN-Wirtschaftssanktionen*, 68 *et seq*.
[244] Ibid, 69 *et seq*.   [245] U Brandl, 'Sanktionsresolutionen', 394.
[246] *Cf*, eg, M Nettesheim, 'UN Sanctions', 586; different view: C Tomuschat, 'Yusuf and Kadi', 540 *et seq*, esp. 543.
[247] Case T-306/01 *Ahmed Ali Yusuf and Al Barakaat International Foundation v Council and Commission*, para 242.

However, the CFI continued 'its deliberations by demonstrating...that...the EC Treaty itself acknowledges the primacy of the UN Charter.'[248] It referred to Art 307 EC, which recognizes that the UN Charter commitments of the Member States remain unaffected,[249] and pointed to Art 297 EC, which was introduced to enable the Member States to discharge their duties under the UN Charter.[250] Even though the aforesaid might already provide an indirect answer to the question of whether UNSC resolutions are binding on the EC, the CFI chose to elaborate expressly on this issue, stating that to the extent that the Community has assumed powers formerly exercised by the Member States in the subject areas governed by the UN Charter, those powers were acquired together with the restrictions or obligations to which these powers were already subjected, ie, first and foremost the obligations under Art 25 UN Charter.[251] Thus, the competences assumed by the Community by virtue of including Art 301 EC and Art 60 EC within the EC Treaty were already 'burdened with' the obligations of the Member States *vis-à-vis* the UN. From this, the CFI draws the conclusion that 'the Community must be considered to be bound by the obligations under the Charter of the United Nations in the same way as its Member States, *by virtue of the Treaty establishing it*'.[252]

While in doctrinal terms doubts exist about whether the judgment rests on firm ground

[t]he efficiency of sanctions and the political coherence of the EU indeed provide good reasons for this step. And from a viewpoint of the EU competences, such an interpretation of the EU's action is certainly permissible.[253]

Outside a UN Security Council authorization to take restrictive measures,[254] economic sanctions in the area of capital movements against other countries will usually[255] be legally defended by subsuming them under the concepts of either 'countermeasure' or 'retorsion'.[256] Ambitions of less and least developed countries, as well as the former block of socialist States, to outlaw economic sanctions as a prohibited category of 'force' within the meaning of Art 2(4) UN Charter—although still not completely and definitely settled[257]—can, in agreement with

---

[248] C Tomuschat, 'Yusuf and Kadi', 541.
[249] Case T-306/01 *Ahmed Ali Yusuf and Al Barakaat International Foundation v Council and Commission*, para 235 *et seq*.
[250] Ibid, para 238.   [251] Ibid, para 253.
[252] [Emphasis added] Ibid, paras 243, 254.
[253] M Nettesheim, 'UN Sanctions', 586; see also C Tomuschat, 'Yusuf and Kadi', 551, who embraces the judgment as a 'courageous step forward in acknowledging the primacy of the UN system over the Community legal order'.
[254] *Cf* G Garçon, *Handelsembargen*, 226 *et seq*.
[255] One could, of course, also think of having recourse to the defence of collective self-defence: K Osteneck, *Umsetzung von UN-Wirtschaftssanktionen*, 111 *et seq*.
[256] *Cf* M Schröder, 'Verantwortlichkeit', mn 116.
[257] eg, MN Shaw, *Int'l Law*, 1019 *et seq*, who describes the current state as 'dubious'.

the majority view, be regarded as successfully frustrated.[258] Equally, financial sanctions, in almost any case, will neither amount to a violation of the principle of non-intervention[259] nor does the EC require an authorization by the UNSC in order to resort to restrictive measures outside a UNSC sanction regime.[260]

A countermeasure within the meaning of the ILC Articles on Responsibility of States for Internationally Wrongful Acts (hereafter: 'ILC Articles on State Responsibility')[261] refers to a *per se* unlawful act to which an injured State is entitled to resort as a reaction to a previously unlawful act of another State with a view to induce the latter State to comply with its obligations owed to the injured State.[262] No doubt exists about the entitlement in principle of the Community as a subject of international law to take countermeasures. However, the taking of countermeasures involves certain preconditions and limitations, which can be summarized as follows: before resorting to countermeasures, an injured State (or an injured international organization) shall call on the responsible State to fulfil its obligations, notify the latter in advance of any decision to take countermeasures, and offer to negotiate with that State, *cf* Art 52 ILC Articles on State Responsibility. Furthermore, countermeasures shall be terminated as soon as the responsible State has complied with its obligations, *cf* Art 53 ILC Articles on State Responsibility. Countermeasures are subject to the principle of proportionality, *cf* Art 51 ILC Articles on State Responsibility, and shall, inter alia, not affect the obligation to refrain from the threat or use of force, the obligation to protect fundamental human rights, or other obligations under peremptory norms of general international law, *cf* Art 50(1) Articles on State Responsibility.[263]

In principle, countermeasures may only be taken by the injured State or injured international organization, respectively,[264] as the law on countermeasures is characterized by the principle of reciprocity.[265] Thus, the Community may resort to countermeasures in cases in which the third country violates an international obligation owed to the EC. Countermeasures of the Community against the violation of international obligations owed *erga omnes*, such as gross

---

[258] M Schröder, 'Verantwortlichkeit', mn 116; K Osteneck, *Umsetzung von UN-Wirtschaftssanktionen*, 75 *et seq*; E-U Petersmann, 'Wirtschaftssanktionen', 8 *et seq*; for a comprehensive evaluation of trade sanctions in the form of embargos against the background of Art 2(4) UN Charter, refer to G Garçon, *Handelsembargen*, 154 *et seq*, esp. 165.

[259] K Osteneck, *Umsetzung von UN-Wirtschaftssanktionen*, 78 *et seq*. See also G Garçon, *Handelsembargen*, 165 *et seq*, esp. 178 *et seq*, although he writes on trade sanctions.

[260] K Osteneck, *Umsetzung von UN-Wirtschaftssanktionen*, 72 *et seq*.

[261] 2001 UN General Assembly Resolution A/RES/56/83 of 12.12.2001 on ILC Draft Articles on Responsibility of States for Internationally Wrongful Acts.

[262] Art 22 together with Part III, Chapter II of ILC Articles on State Responsibility.

[263] For a more detailed account, refer to T Stein and C von Buttlar, *Völkerrecht*, mn. 1150 *et seq*; A Cassese, *Int'l Law*, 302 *et seq*; M Schröder, 'Verantwortlichkeit', mn. 111 *et seq*; K Osteneck, *Umsetzung von UN-Wirtschaftssanktionen*, 75 *et seq*.

[264] M Schröder, 'Verantwortlichkeit', mn 113; G Ress and J Ukrow, Art. 60 EC (2002), mn 3.

[265] K Osteneck, *Umsetzung von UN-Wirtschaftssanktionen*, 101.

violations of human rights or the breach of the prohibition of the use of force, without being directly affected, can only be the *ultima ratio* due to the fact that such situations are usually characterized by both a high degree of legal uncertainty as to the existence of a violation of an obligation owed *erga omnes*, as well as the danger of an overreaction.[266] An even more critical question is whether the Community may take countermeasures in reaction to a violation of an international obligation by a third State owed not to itself, but to a Member State or a group of Member States. Bleckmann characterizes a countermeasure as being similar to an 'act of defence of others' as a subcategory of the right of self-defence under national law and thus seeks to grant the right to respond to a violation of an international obligation owed to a Member State or a group of them by means of countermeasures of both the unaffected Member States and the Community.[267] However, the alleged similarity between the two legal concepts on which Bleckmann's argument is based is not persuasive due to the fact that the countermeasure is an active means of law enforcement, but 'defence of others' as a subcategory of the right to self-defence is mainly characterized as a tool for preventing and averting a danger. Furthermore, an interpretation such as that advanced by Bleckmann would lead to an almost complete disregard of the principle of reciprocity.[268] More convincing, therefore, would be the view that aims to grant to the Community the right to resort to countermeasures in the situation at hand if the third country that breached an international obligation owed to a Member State has recognized, expressly or implicitly, the Community as a subject of international law.[269] The argument runs as follows: The legal personality of an international organization is limited to the competences, usually set out in the charter of the organization,[270] transferred to it by its member States[271] and exists only between its members and towards those third States that have recognized it.[272] The act of recognition by a third country of the international

---

[266] Generally on countermeasures as a reaction to an alleged violation of an obligation owed *erga omnes*: M Schröder, 'Verantwortlichkeit', mn 113, with further references; T Stein and C von Buttlar, *Völkerrecht*, mn 1152 *et seq*; see also A Cassese, *Int'l Law*, 306 *et seq*. With respect to the Community, not critical on the admissibility of countermeasures taken by the Community in such a situation: G Ress and J Ukrow, Art. 60 EC (2002), mn 3; see also K Osteneck, *Umsetzung von UN-Wirtschaftssanktionen*, 101 *et seq*, 106; G Garçon, *Handelsembargen*, 220 *et seq*.

[267] A Bleckmann, *Rechtmäßigkeit der EG-Sanktionen*, 16.

[268] G Garçon, *Handelsembargen*, 218 *et seq*.

[269] W Meng, 'Kompetenz', 796; T Stein, *Außen- und Sicherheitspolitik*, 17; R Arnold, 'Außenhandelsrecht', mn 111; T Stein, 'Sanktionen', 1139; F Kimms, *Kapitalverkehrsfreiheit*, 200; G Garçon, *Handelsembargen*, 218 *et seq*; G Ress and J Ukrow, Art. 60 EC (2002), mn 3. Note that the EC measures in response to the Argentinian attack on the British Falkland Islands were already justified in terms of international law on the basis of a violation of the *erga omnes* rule of the prohibition of the use of force. [W Meng, 'Kompetenz', 796; K Osteneck, *Umsetzung von UN-Wirtschaftssanktionen*, 107]

[270] A Cassese, *Int'l Law*, 137.

[271] ICJ, *Advisory Opinion on Legality of the Use by a State of Nuclear Weapons in Armed Conflict*, para 25. See also A Cassese, *Int'l Law*, 137 *et seq*.

[272] V Epping, 'Internationale Organisationen', mn 5; V Epping, 'Grundlagen', mn 38.

organization logically comprises the competences contained in its charter. Due to the fact that Art 60(1) EC, as part of the EC's 'charter', sets out the competence of the Community to apply financial sanctions *vis-à-vis* third countries, the latter must accept that the Community rather than the injured Member State has recourse to countermeasures for the violation of international obligations owed to the Member State.[273]

While a countermeasure itself constitutes an international wrong as an answer to another international wrong, a retorsion

embraces any retaliatory act by which a State responds, by an unfriendly act not amounting to a violation of international law, to either (a) a breach of international law or (b) an unfriendly act, by another State.[274]

The Community can readily have recourse to this means.[275] Such means need neither be proportionate nor must the EC notify the addressee in advance. The EC, moreover, also need not be the 'victim' of the wrongful or unfriendly act in order to resort to a retorsion.[276] Within the area of financial sanctions, a retorsion may, for example, comprise the discontinuance or reduction of investment or the non-conclusion or non-extension of treaties. In general terms, the Community can revoke any unilateral concession voluntarily granted in the area of free movement of capital to a third country as long as it does not violate any international obligation. In the latter case, the restrictive measure must fulfil the requirements of a countermeasure.

(2) Procedure

Community action on the basis of Arts 60 EC and 301 EC presupposes a common position, *cf* Art 15 EU, or a joint action, *cf* Art 14 EU, under the Common Foreign and Security Policy.[277] In this sense, the CFSP measure 'pre-programmes' the EC measure.[278] The CFSP measure usually explains the legal and political context that made the imposition of sanctions necessary and provides in broad terms[279] for the regime to be adopted by the Council under Arts 60 EC and 301 EC.[280]

---

[273] G Garçon, *Handelsembargen*, 219; W Meng, 'Kompetenz', 796; R Arnold, 'Außenhandelsrecht', mn 111. The principles of legal certainty and protection of legitimate expectations cannot alter this finding. *Cf* G Garçon, *Handelsembargen*, 220.

[274] A Cassese, *Int'l Law*, 310.

[275] K Osteneck, *Umsetzung von UN-Wirtschaftssanktionen*, 100.

[276] Ibid; of the same opinion but in general terms: H Fischer, 'Friedenssicherung', mn 44; probably also A Verdross and B Simma, *Universelles Völkerrecht*, § 66. Opting for a generous application of the principle of proportionality when having recourse to a retorsion: R Arnold, 'Außenhandelsrecht', mn 109. Of the opinion that a retorsion must be proportionate in gravity as well as being discontinued as soon as the unfriendly or wrongful behaviour of the third country that gave rise to the retorsion is ceased: A Cassese, *Int'l Law*, 310; K Doehring, *Völkerrecht*, mn 1026.

[277] G Ress and J Ukrow, Art. 60 EC (2002), mn 5; W Kiemel, Art. 60 EC (2003), mn 5.

[278] P Gilsdorf and B Brandtner, Art. 301EC (2004), mn 6.

[279] The CFSP measure may not provide for the EC measure in any detail. Otherwise the 'proposal monopoly' of the Commission as well as the powers of the EC Council would be eroded. [Ibid, mn 7]

[280] P Koutrakos, *EU Int'l Relations Law*, 432.

The Community takes 'urgent measures' on this basis.[281] This phrase is not to be misunderstood as 'provisional measures' but refers to the pressing need, in a temporal sense, to act.[282] The Member States—as long as a Community action is absent—may resort to such 'provisional measures' on the basis of Art 60(2) EC.

The Council decides by a qualified majority on a proposal from the Commission (Art 301 EC). In case the CFSP measure implements a UNSC resolution, any possible scope of discretion with respect to the 'if' of a measure taken under Arts 60 EC and 301 EC is reduced to zero. Discretion exists—at most—with respect to the 'how' of the implementation, which is also limited by the pre-setting contained in the UNSC resolution. This follows from the fact that the EC, by virtue of its own Treaty, is bound by the UNSC resolution, as explained above.

However—even in the absence of any UNSC resolution—if the measures taken within the framework of the CFSP provide for action within the supranational EC, then the Council is not free to decide whether or not to implement those on the basis of Arts 301 EC and 60(1) EC.[283] The wording of Art 60(1) EC, which states that the Council 'may' take measures—in contrast to Art 301 EC, where such language is not provided for—is to some extent misleading. The difference in wording of the former provision appears to be the result of a lack of coordination while drafting the Treaty.[284] Both provisions are to be interpreted in the same way.[285] Discretionary powers with respect to Arts 60 EC and 301 EC must therefore be exercised with a view to ensuring coherence among the different pillars, ie, balancing the different aims pursued by the intergovernmental pillar of the CFSP and the supranational one of the EC.[286] In a comprehensive balancing process the Commission would, for example, have to refrain from submitting any proposal in situations in which the CFSP measure violates general principles of Community law or even public international law, or it must submit a moderating proposal in cases in which the CFSP measure might partly infringe Community as international law.[287]

---

[281] Those measures, usually taking the form of Council regulations, commonly attribute certain tasks—inter alia the determination of penalties for violations of the restrictive Community measures, the granting of exemptions, receiving information from, and cooperating with, economic operators (including financial institutions), and reporting upon their implementation to the Commission—to the Member States. [*Cf.* Ibid]

[282] G Ress and J Ukrow, Art. 60 EC (2002), mn 7 *et seq*; J Bröhmer, Art. 60 EC (2007), mn 5; M Sedlaczek, Art. 60 EC (2003), mn 6.

[283] Along similar lines but stricter: J Bröhmer, Art. 60 EC (2007), mn 2; probably with a different view: W Kiemel, Art. 60 EC (2003), mn 5.

[284] With a different view: G Ress and J Ukrow, Art. 60 EC (2002), mn 11.

[285] P Gilsdorf and B Brandtner, Art. 301 EC (2004), mn 18; M Sedlaczek, Art. 60 EC (2003), mn 10.

[286] Such a view is not undisputed: *cf*, eg, P Gilsdorf and B Brandtner, Art. 301 EC (2004), mn 6 *et seq*. with further references. Note also S Sick, *Wirtschaftssanktionen*. In particular Art 47 EU, which obliges the European Union to preserve the *acquis communautaire*, and Art 3 EU, seeking to ensure coherence among the different pillars, must be observed.

[287] P Gilsdorf and B Brandtner, Art. 301EC (2004), mn 7.

The word 'necessary' in Art 60(1) EC denotes the principle of proportionality.[288] While countermeasures, under public international law, are already bound by the principle of proportionality, retorsions are not, as stated above. Community law, however, also provides compellingly for the application of the principle in the latter case. However, it should be pointed out that the discretion on the question of what it considers proportionate is in any case broadly defined,[289] although restricted by the 'pre-programming' contained in the CFSP measure. Outside the sphere in which the EC resorts to sanctions autonomously, the significance of the principle of proportionality is considerably reduced by the duty to implement the UNSC resolutions.[290]

(3) Sanction Addressees—'As Regards the Third Countries Concerned'

In recent years, UN sanction regimes have shifted more and more frequently towards targeting specific persons, groups, and entities responsible for objectionable policies or behaviour (so-called 'smart sanctions') instead of nation States:

> Those sanctions replace classic general...embargos aimed at a country with targeted and selective measures, so as to reduce the suffering endured by the civilian population of the country concerned, while none the less imposing genuine sanctions on the targeted regime and those in charge of it.[291]

In cases in which the Community implements UNSC resolutions, but also in situations in which the Community should decide to resort to autonomous measures, this paradigm shift creates problems in regard to due process and judicial protection of individuals and also poses tangible doctrinal questions within the ambit of Art 60(1) EC.

Art 60(1) EC provides that the Council may take urgent measures 'as regards the third countries concerned'. This clause prompts a twofold question: First, one must ask whether only State actors or also non-State actors, such as international organizations, 'regimes', individuals, or groups of individuals can be addressees of restrictive measures by the Community on the basis of this provision. Second, the question must be answered as to whether the measure must be directed solely against third State addressees or whether a measure can also target Member State addressees, 'provided that such measures are intended to interrupt or reduce, in part or completely, economic relations with one or more third countries'.[292]

---

[288] See, for example, Case T-306/01 *Ahmed Ali Yusuf and Al Barakaat International Foundation v Council and Commission*, para 122 *et seq* for a review of the application of the principle of proportionality within the ambit of Arts 60 EC and 301 EC, which, however, does not provide much guidance.
[289] A Glaesner, Art. 60 EC (2000), mn 2; G Ress and J Ukrow, Art. 60 EC (2002), mn 9.
[290] J Bröhmer, Art. 60 EC (2007), mn 4; M Sedlaczek, Art. 60 EC (2003), mn 7.
[291] Case T-315/01 *Yassin Abdullah Kadi v Council and Commission)*, para 90; note: Joint Cases C-402/05 P and C-415/05 P *Yassin Abdullah Kadi and Al Barakaat International Foundation v Council and Commission*.
[292] Case T-306/01 *Ahmed Ali Yusuf and Al Barakaat International Foundation v Council and Commission*, para 85; proposition of the Council in the aforementioned case.

In regard to sanctions targeted at individuals connected to a regime, the Court of First Instance in *Yusuf*, dealing with the legality of the Community measures implementing UNSC 'smart sanctions' against the *Taliban* of Afghanistan and *Osama bin Laden*, provided some guidance.[293] It stated quite bluntly:

> that nothing in the wording of those provisions [i.e., Art 60 EC and Art 301 EC] makes it possible to exclude the adoption of restrictive measures directly affecting individuals or organisations, whether or not established in the Community, in so far as such measures actually seek to reduce, in part or completely, economic relations with one or more third countries.[294]

The CFI added that 'the fact that the measure at issue also affected transactions having no cross-border element is not relevant'[295] due to the fact that only in this way could funding of international terrorism effectively be prevented. These findings were supported—one might wonder which rule of construction the CFI is actually applying—with reference to the 'realities', citing the Council's recent practice, which developed parallel to the practice within the UN, to adopt restrictive measures on the basis of Arts 60 EC and 301 EC not against third countries, but against

> entities which or persons who physically controlled part of the territory of a third country (…) and against entities which or persons who effectively controlled the government apparatus of a third country and also against persons and entities associated with them and who or which provided them with financial support (…).[296]

Further reinforcing its interpretation of Arts 60 EC and 301 EC, the Court of First Instance—without feeling the need to go into any detail—referred nebulously to 'considerations of effectiveness' and 'humanitarian concerns'.[297]

With respect to the link that must expressly be established between the individual at which sanctions are directly aimed and the territory and governing regime of a third country ultimately hit by the sanction, it must, in the words of the CFI, be 'sufficient'.[298] By way of example, the Court explained what it would consider a 'sufficient link':

---

[293] Ibid, appealed: Joint Cases C-402/05 P and C-415/05 P *Yassin Abdullah Kadi and Al Barakaat International Foundation v Council and Commission*; see also the following cases in which the CFI reiterated the position it had taken in the aforementioned case: Case T-315/01 *Yassin Abdullah Kadi v Council and Commission)*; Case T-253/02 'Ayadi' *Chafiq Ayadi v Council*, appealed on 27 September 2006, Case T-362/04 *Leonid Minin v Commission*.

[294] Case T-306/01 *Ahmed Ali Yusuf and Al Barakaat International Foundation v Council and Commission*, para 112; see also Case T-315/01 *Yassin Abdullah Kadi v Council and Commission)*, para 89.

[295] Case T-306/01 *Ahmed Ali Yusuf and Al Barakaat International Foundation v Council and Commission*, para 123.

[296] Ibid, para 114.

[297] Ibid, para 116; see also Case T-315/01 *Yassin Abdullah Kadi v Council and Commission)*, para 91.

[298] Case T-306/01 *Ahmed Ali Yusuf and Al Barakaat International Foundation v Council and Commission*, paras 115, 127; note, though, that the link within the ambit of Art 57(1) EC is a different one. See Chapter VII. 2. c.

In so far as the applicants complained that Regulation No. 467/2001 was directed at Usama bin Laden and not the Taliban regime, the Council has added that Usama bin Laden was in fact the head and 'éminence grise' of the Taliban and that he wielded the real power in Afghanistan. His temporal and spiritual titles of 'Sheikh' (head) and 'Emir' (prince, governor or commander) and the rank he held beside the other Taliban religious dignitaries can leave little doubt on that score. Moreover, even before 11 September 2001, Usama bin Laden had sworn an oath of allegiance ('Bay'a') making a formal religious bond between him and the Taliban theocracy. He was thus in a situation comparable to that of Mr. Milosevic and the members of the Yugoslav Government at the time of the economic and financial sanctions taken by the Council against the Federal Republic of Yugoslavia (see paragraph 114 above). With regard to Al-Qaeda, the Council has observed that it was common knowledge that it had many military training camps in Afghanistan and that thousands of its members had fought beside the Taliban between October 2001 and January 2002, during the intervention of the international coalition.

As soon as this link between the individual at which sanctions are directly aimed and the territory and governing regime of a third country breaks down, for example, by a collapse of the regime, as happened to the Taliban of Afghanistan, Arts 60 EC and 301 EC no longer provide a sufficient legal basis for sanctions.[299] '[F]or the sake of the requirement of consistency laid down in Article 3 of the Treaty on European Union',[300] however, measures lacking this link can be based on Arts 60 EC and 301 EC, supplemented by the additional legal basis of Art 308 EC, because otherwise the Community would lack 'the power necessary, in the field of economic and financial sanctions, to act for the purpose of attaining the objective pursued by the Union and its Member States under the CFSP'.[301]

---

[299] Ibid, para 127 *et seq*, esp. 132 *et seq*; see also Case T-315/01 *Yassin Abdullah Kadi v Council and Commission)*, para 93 *et seq*.

[300] Case T-306/01 *Ahmed Ali Yusuf and Al Barakaat International Foundation v Council and Commission*, para 164.

[301] Ibid; see also Case T-315/01 *Yassin Abdullah Kadi v Council and Commission*, para 122 *et seq*; The ECJ in its appeal decision, as a result, upheld the conclusions of the CFI in respect of the legal foundations of the relevant Community Measure. It held, however, that 'while it is correct to consider, as did the Court of First Instance, that a bridge has been constructed between the actions of the Community involving economic measures under Articles 60 EC and 301 EC and the objectives of the EU Treaty in the sphere of external relations, including the CFSP, neither the wording of the provisions of the EC Treaty nor the structure of the latter provides any foundation for the view that that bridge extends to other provisions of the EC Treaty, in particular to Article 308 EC. . . . [I]f the position of the Court of First Instance were to be accepted, that provision would allow, in the special context of Articles 60 EC and 301 EC, the adoption of Community measures concerning not one of the objectives of the Community but one of the *objectives under the EU Treaty* in the sphere of external relations, including the CFSP.' [Emphasis added; Joint Cases C-402/05 P and C-415/05 P *Yassin Abdullah Kadi and Al Barakaat International Foundation v Council and Commission*, para 197 *et seq*] Consequently: '[t]he objective pursued by the contested regulation may be made to refer to one of the objectives of the *Community* for the purpose of Article 308 EC'. [Emphasis added; Joint Cases C-402/05 P and C-415/05 P *Yassin Abdullah Kadi and Al Barakaat International Foundation v Council and Commission*, para 225] This having been said, the ECJ discovered that 'Articles 60 EC and 301 EC are the expression of an *implicit underlying objective*, namely, that of making it possible to adopt such measures through the efficient use of a Community instrument. That objective may be regarded as constituting an objective of the Community for the purpose of

In sum, Arts 60 EC and 301 EC cover sanctions against individuals as long as a significant link can be evidenced between the individual directly targeted and a third country or a 'regime' effectively controlling parts of a third country. If such a link is missing, then the aforementioned provisions in isolation do not constitute a sufficient legal basis.[302]

A more hypothetical question is that of whether sanctions may be targeted at international organizations due to the fact that hardly any international organization exists that has vested competences in the area of free movement of capital and to which, thus, sanction-triggering behaviour can be allocated. Although the wording suggests that sanctions can be targeted only against State actors, but not international organizations, there is no apparent reason why the former should be treated differently from the latter.[303] The argument in this context that exceptions are to be interpreted narrowly is not convincing due to the fact that the scope of the provision is not broadened by including international organizations as targets of sanctions. In any case, sanctions could be directed at the member States 'behind' the international organization.

b. Member State Measures: Article 60(2) EC

Article 60(2) EC constitutes the only remaining (residual) competence of the Member States—besides Art 119 EC *et seq*—to introduce new capital movements restrictions.[304] It is worth stressing that it is this (residual) Member State competence that distinguishes the legal regime of financial sanctions from that of (general) economic sanctions regulated by Art 301 EC.[305] In the latter case, it is only the Community that is competent to resort to sanctions. The residual competence of the Member States in the area of financial sanctions is to be explained by the speed at which large capital flows can be redirected, which requires the possibility of rapid action.

Mohamed rightly points out that:

[t]he danger in allocating such unilateral competence [to the Member States to enact financial sanctions] is that in the event of a Member State invoking this provision in an indiscriminate manner, it will bring into disrepute not only the Member State concerned, but also the EU as a whole in the context of its international relations.[306]

Article 308 EC. [Emphasis added; Joint Cases C-402/05 P and C-415/05 P *Yassin Abdullah Kadi and Al Barakaat International Foundation v Council and Commission*, para 226 *et seq*]

[302] P Gilsdorf and B Brandtner, Art. 301EC (2004), mn 4.

[303] G Ress and J Ukrow, Art. 60 EC (2002), mn 6; P Gilsdorf and B Brandtner, Art. 301EC (2004), mn 4; opposing sanctions directly targeting international organizations: J Bröhmer, Art. 60 EC (2007), mn 2; M Sedlaczek, Art. 60 EC (2003), mn 2.

[304] G Ress and J Ukrow, Art. 60 EC (2002), mn 14.

[305] See on the relationship between Arts 60 EC and 301 EC: P Gilsdorf and B Brandtner, Art. 301EC (2004), mn 18.

[306] S Mohamed, *Free Movement of Capital*, 228.

It is, however, not only the damage to the 'political capital' of the European Union in international relations, but also the negative impact of financial sanction regimes that differ from Member State to Member State on the attainment of the economic aims of the EC Treaty which highlight the problematic nature of this competence. If one considers, moreover, that the possible effectiveness of unilateral measures taken by one or a group of Member States against a third country within the framework of the Common Market is rather limited by the fact that the third county against which the unilateral restrictive measure was taken could simply penetrate the EC through another friendly-minded Member State,[307] then it becomes comprehensible that Art 60(2) EC must be construed in the narrowest sense in order to avert these consequences.[308]

(1) The Relationship of Article 297 EC and Article 60(2) EC

Article 60(2) EC grants the competence to resort to financial sanctions '[w]ithout prejudice to Article 297 [EC]', which requires a delineation of the two provisions.

Article 297 EC is, with respect to its preconditions to be fulfilled in order to activate the emergency competence, considerably more narrowly defined than Art 60(2) EC[309] (*lex specialis*). Recourse to the legal basis of Art 297 EC presupposes

> the event of serious internal disturbances affecting the maintenance of law and order, in the event of war, serious international tension constituting a threat of war, or in order to carry out obligations it has accepted for the purpose of maintaining peace and international security.

In contrast, Art 60(2) EC demands 'merely' 'serious political reasons', which is the broader term. From the fact that Art 297 EC is allegedly limited to military or forceful threats and thus excludes economic and social crises, Ress and Ukrow draw the conclusion that in the event of the latter crisis, Art 60(2) EC must be applicable. However, such a conclusion—at least with respect to an economic crisis—is not only not compelling, but inherently carries the danger that the Member States could resort to Art 60(2) EC for protective reasons. One can clearly deduce from Art 59 EC that economic considerations will not play a role within Art 60 EC.[310]

On the other hand, Art 297 EC in regard to its legal consequences is broader than Art 60(2) EC. While the latter allows only for measures in the area of free

---

[307] *Cf* Ibid. [308] *Cf* M Seidel, 'Kapitalmarkt', 774.
[309] G Ress and J Ukrow, Art. 60 EC (2002), mn 15; W Kiemel, Art. 60 EC (2003), mn 11; for a different, not readily comprehensible, view see: PR Vergano, Art. 60 EC (2005), § 140.03 [2], who states: 'Since Article 60 (2) [EC] is subject to the requirements of Article 297 [EC], it appears unlikely that unilateral measures adopted in circumstances other than those outlined in Art. 297 [EC] would be acceptable.'
[310] In his conclusion of the same opinion: JA Usher, *Law of Money*, 235.

movement of capital (and payments), the former does not restrict the areas in which the Member States may become active.

(2) 'Serious Political Reasons'

I explained above that the term 'serious political reasons'—although covering a broader spectrum of situations of political crisis than those envisaged in Art 297 EC and requiring a lower degree of tension or crisis[311]—does not relate to economic reasons. Furthermore, in order to prevent excessive misallocation and redirection of capital flows and severe damage to the reputation of the European Union in international relations, the 'political reasons' of a Member State for resorting to unilateral financial sanctions targeted at a third country must connect to a de facto situation of serious international tension or crisis. The Member State must face an imminent threat of being severely affected by this tension or crisis that renders it unacceptable to wait[312] for Council action on the basis of Art 60(1) EC.[313]

Once these conditions are fulfilled, the Member State is under a duty to inform the Commission and the other Member States about the restrictive measure by the date of the entry into force at the latest.[314]

The Member States must lift their financial sanctions as soon as the conditions mentioned above no longer exist or are changed in such a way that the sanctions no longer appear proportionate.

(3) 'Council Intervention': Community Sanctions on the Basis of Article 60(1) EC and Amendment or Abolishment of Autonomous Member State Measures by virtue of Article 60(2) Subparagraph 2 EC

Article 60(2) subparagraph 1, 1st sentence EC provides for an autonomous Member State competence 'as long as the Council has not taken measures'. It is open to debate whether the residual competence of the Member States exists as long as the Council has reached a positive decision on the basis of Art 60(1) EC or whether the Member States' competence also ceases in other situations. If the Council has explicitly stated, for example, in its procedure on the basis of Art 301 EC that it does not want to take financial sanctions on the basis of Art 60(1) EC, then this statement is also binding upon the Member States and excludes autonomous measures by the latter on the basis of Art 60(2)

---

[311] G Ress and J Ukrow, Art. 60 EC (2002), mn 15; with a different view: PR Vergano, Art. 60 EC (2005), § 140.03 [2]; probably also S Mohamed, *Free Movement of Capital*, 228.

[312] ie, the autonomous Member State measure must constitute the *ultima ratio*. [G Ress and J Ukrow, Art. 60 EC (2002), mn 15]

[313] For the interpretation of the term 'urgency', refer to ibid. It is obvious that political expediency and urgency must coexist. [S Mohamed, *Free Movement of Capital*, 228]

[314] G Ress and J Ukrow, Art. 60 EC (2002), mn 17. Without giving a further reason, being of the view that the Member State in question must inform before the entry into force: S Mohamed, *Free Movement of Capital*, 228.

EC. In favour of the latter position, one can advance the view that if follows from Art 60(2) subparagraph 2 EC that the Council has vested in it the 'ultimate authority' to decide on financial sanctions, and this competence would be eroded if some Member States could maintain their unilaterally enacted restrictions on third country capital movement.[315]

A similar argument could be put forward if the Council votes on possible financial sanctions, but fails to reach the majority required by Art 60(1) EC[316] in connection with Art 301 EC; the vote would clearly show that the Community opposes the introduction of financial sanctions *vis-à-vis* a third country. If in such a situation the Member States were allowed to maintain or introduce autonomous financial sanctions, then the Council's 'ultimate authority' to decide on financial sanctions would be eroded too.[317] However, at least with respect to the situation just mentioned, this result does not appear compelling. The wording of Art 60(2) subparagraph 2 EC, on which the argument of the 'ultimate authority' of the Council is based, could also be read as suggesting that a positive action—instead of just a failed vote—of the Council is required in order to bring to an end the residual competence of the Member States to enact and apply unilateral restrictive measures. The competence of the Council contained in Art 60(2) subparagraph 2 EC to amend or abolish autonomous Member State measures could be regarded as in any case sufficient to safeguard the Community interests.[318]

However, in order to prevent the adverse effects explained above, which such a patchwork sanctions regime would inevitably have, this study opts for the interpretation first presented.

c. Appraisal: Too much Leeway for the Member States?

In sum, Art 60 EC provides the Community and, on a residual basis, the Member States with the competence to restrict capital movements *vis-à-vis* third countries for political reasons, ie, to enable the Community in the first place to impose financial sanctions on third countries out of autonomous considerations or on the basis of UN Security Council decisions. In this sense, the provision constitutes an important instrument in implementing a Common Foreign and Security Policy.

When imposing sanctions upon third countries, the Community (as well as the Member States acting on their own account) must observe public international law. The rules on countermeasures provide some very modest limitations—take the principle of reciprocity, the duty to lift sanctions as soon as the addressee complies with its obligations under international law and the principle of proportionality—on the powers to restrict third country capital movements.

---

[315] G Ress and J Ukrow, Art. 56 EC (2002), mn 16; along similar lines: A Glaesner, Art. 60 EC (2000), mn 5.
[316] *Cf* J Bröhmer, Art. 60 EC (2007), mn 7.
[317] Along similar lines: G Ress and J Ukrow, Art. 56 EC (2002), mn 16.
[318] *Cf* J Bröhmer, Art. 60 EC (2007), mn 7.

Moreover, financial sanctions enacted on the basis of Arts 60 EC and 301 EC need not be directly targeted at a nation State, but may aim at individuals as long as they possess a 'significant link' to a third country or a 'regime' effectively in power in part of a third country. This development enables the EC to apply its capital movement restrictions more specifically and, thus, appears to reduce the negative impact of such restrictive measures on free movement of capital in a third country context.

Regrettably, measures on the basis of Art 60 EC are—in contrast to Art 59 EC—not expressly limited to a certain period of time, but merely by the principle of proportionality, which provides a weak corrective when considering the great latitude in evaluating the political situation enjoyed by the Community and Member States, respectively.

The residual Member State competence contained in Art 60(2) EC is problematic in two ways: Member States may impose sanctions which are non-simultaneous and of different intensity on third countries, which must inevitably lead to considerable distortions of capital flows. Because of this, together with the fact that unilateral sanctions are rather easily circumvented by playing one Member State against another by gaining access to the Common Market through the 'friendliest' Member State, the Member State's competence must be interpreted in the strictest sense possible. Therefore, the residual Member State competence must cease as soon as the Community will shows that an action at the EC level is not desired, for example by a failed vote on the basis of Art 60(1) EC. Arguing in terms of *de lege ferenda,* it would be more sensible to strengthen the decision-making process on the Community level in order to secure a homogenous approach of sanction regimes towards third countries.

Perspectives—'Anxiety is the Dizziness of Freedom'*

'Free movement of capital *erga omnes*'—if one is prepared to accept the doctrinal analysis of the Treaty provisions on free movement of capital put forward in this study, then this slogan amounts with respect to the European Community to more than a programmatic statement. It is a unilateral legally binding commitment. It is an effectively enforceable individual right to market access and to a level playing field in each of the 27 Member States for third country direct investments.

The endowment of market participants with such a powerful tool is the logical consequence of the realization that unilaterally liberalized capital movement from and towards third countries is of extraordinary importance for the overall development of the European Community. The comprehensive prohibition of restrictions on third country capital movement not only facilitates but partially constitutes a precondition for the successful attainment of a multitude of (socio-) economic Treaty aims. It fosters in particular economic growth in the Common Market, overall stabilization of the European economy, and the implementation of Economic and Monetary Union. In the end it is the European citizens themselves who benefit from economic prosperity through an elevated standard of living.

By comprehensively prohibiting restrictions on third country capital movement and providing the most effective mechanisms to market participants to enforce their rights to market access and a level playing field, the European Community sends a signal to the world that can hardly be overstated. It underlines that the Community is committed to a liberal economic constitution based on competition and open markets, and it creates much-needed trust in a stable regulatory environment by protecting market participants against sudden single-handed attempts by Member States to revert to protectionist ideas.

However, such a liberal reading of third country capital movement has prominent challengers among the Member States that appear to favour a different view of the freedom. How otherwise could a Member State propose a bill that, for example, provides that any inbound cross-border direct investment, irrespective of the economic sector, exceeding 25 per cent of the capital of an undertaking

---

* S Kierkegaard, *The Concept of Anxiety*.

would become subject to ministerial veto if found to be a (not further specified) 'threat to public order or security'?[1]

Apart from a vague reference to security interests in the preamble to such a bill, one can only speculate about the more concrete motivations of the respective proposal. Much more instructive, therefore, is a view on the present economic and political situation. This situation is—as mentioned in the introduction to this study—characterized by a changing environment for national security, increased challenges to protect technologies considered vital for national sovereignty and competitiveness, growing concerns among the population about the (socio-)economic effects of cross-border mergers and acquisitions, steadily intensifying activities of investors from developing and emerging market countries, and the sudden prominence of so-called sovereign wealth funds whose total assets could grow to € 8.4 trn = US$ 12 trn by 2015.[2]

Furthermore, one must realize that the EC Treaty provisions liberalizing third country capital movement bear harshly on the sovereignty of the Member States. They aggravate the already extremely sensitive issue of taxation. Free movement of capital *erga omnes* in principle means renouncing discriminatory tax practices not only with respect to intra-Community, but also in regard to third country direct investment, the latter on a unilateral basis. Equally problematic is the fact that Member States are no longer completely free to negotiate treaties on capital movement with third countries. They must bring their treaties in line with Art 56 EC *et seq.* and, on the other hand, would in many cases need to negotiate so-called mixed agreements together with the Community.

While the surrender of sovereignty is certainly justified by the (socio-)economic advantages brought about by free movement of capital and the ineffectiveness of national capital control measures in times of a Common Market and a globalized world, one should not be under the illusion that Member States would simply acquiesce in this rationale.

The Court equally seems to be committed to restricting the scope of the freedom of capital movement in third country situations. For that reason it became entangled, for example, in doubtful attempts to delineate free movement of capital and the freedom of establishment at the cost of the former.[3] It interpreted the grandfathering clause of Art 57(1) EC in a broad instead of a narrow way by lending a wide understanding to the notion of 'movement of capital to or from third countries involving direct investment'.[4] It also made it more difficult for third country investors to benefit from the freedom simply by restricting

---

[1] *Cf* Bundesministerium für Wirtschaft und Technologie, 'Entwurf eines Dreizehnten Gesetzes zur Änderung des Außenwirtschaftsgesetzes und der Außenwirtschaftsverordnung' (2007), Status: Referentenentwurf.
[2] For further references, see the Introduction to this study.
[3] See Chapter III. 3. b.   [4] See Chapter VII. 2. c.

the option that information necessary to correctly assess the taxes due can be provided by the respective market participant on its own account.[5]

It is difficult to avoid the impression that the Court is anxious to give more leeway to the Member States. One can certainly debate splendidly on whether the Court's interpretation of the provisions on free movement of capital in a third country context are still in the spirit of the drafters or whether it follows somewhat too closely the Member States' current political pre-setting. If one were to come to the conclusion that it is the latter, then the Court would be in remarkable concordance with its interpretative approach to the freedom applied throughout the development of the Treaty provisions on free movement of capital. As observed by Bakker, this jurisprudence reflects a tendency 'to merely follow the political agreement reached elsewhere on the pace of liberalisation in the Community'.[6]

The current position of the Commission—as guardian of the Treaty—is unclear with respect to third country capital movement. Instead of developing and shaping a visible and coherent policy, it is hiding. Instead of publicly formulating its position on third country capital movement—as it did with regard to the intra-Community context—it basically leaves the field to the Member States and a cautious, drifting Court.[7] An unresolved conflict between the Council and Member States on the one hand and the Commission on the other, simmering now for over 10 years, with respect to the interpretation of the scope of the freedom of capital movement and autonomous and treaty making competences on foreign direct investment might provide one reason for the Commission's self-restraint.[8] The resolution of this conflict is further complicated by the inextricably connected question of the limits of the Member States' powers to apply discriminatory (direct) tax regimes with respect to foreign investment.

Today it is not the struggle for an even more comprehensive liberalization of capital movement that seems to be urgently needed. It is that which has already been achieved that is increasingly put at risk. Present political sentiment in and legislative activities of some Member States seem to diverge from the compromise carved in stone with the adoption of the Maastricht Treaty. In fact, Member States are currently testing the outer boundaries of the framework permissible within policy adjustments. In some cases, political sentiment seems to be so strong that Member States would risk the consequence of crossing the outer boundaries of the framework set by Art 56 EC *et seq.*, ie, unduly restricting foreign direct investment.

In such a situation, retreating to the rather formal position that the very idea of concluding a treaty is to prevent such a crossing can only be a cold comfort if nobody currently appears to be seriously willing and able to stop that defection. Rather, it is more fruitful to turn one's attention to those driving motivations that

---

[5] See Chapter VI. 6. e. (1).
[6] AFP Bakker, *Capital Movements*, 47.
[7] See the Introduction to this study.
[8] Ibid.

might have induced modifications in foreign direct investment policy. A critical examination and better understanding of the driving forces might sensitize a wider audience and prevent us from prematurely sacrificing free movement of capital *erga omnes* and the related benefits for the Community and its citizens for ends that might possibly be better achieved by other means. In this respect, further academic research and effective communication of those findings can make a valuable contribution.

In-depth research on the scope of the Community's autonomous and treaty-making competence with respect to foreign direct investment would significantly reduce existing insecurities in the area and probably facilitate a more public and rational debate. Such research would not only have to deal with the direct taxation issue,[9] but also with the relationship of international investment instruments used by the Member States, such as bilateral investment treaties, and Community law.

Public policy and public security reasons are frequently cited in order to restrict foreign direct investment. However, the concept usually remains very vague and, hence, contributes to considerable legal uncertainty for investors. An inquiry into the different national, European, and international views of 'public policy and public security' with respect to capital movement will expose common denominators, but also differences among the Member States and might in this way reveal possible lines of compromise in order to formulate a common approach.

The increasing activities of investors from developing and emerging market countries is a source of considerable unease in some Member States. This scepticism increases, or sometimes becomes irrational blunt hostility, if the investment is placed by a so-called sovereign wealth fund headquartered in a developing or emerging market country. The dramatic growth in number, size and, ultimately, importance of these funds over the last few years has led to an urgent need to better understand their structure, function, and status under national, European, and international law. Research in this area is still in its infancy. Consolidated findings would certainly help to structure the current discussion in a more rational way.

Free movement of capital is the latecomer among the freedoms. It appears that it still suffers for this, as it meets difficulties in finding its place in the group of the fundamental freedoms as an emancipated, fully-fledged equal. One of

---

[9] In particular, the conflict between Member States' tax powers and the non-discrimination obligations enshrined in EC law should not be solved by cannibalizing the freedom of capital movement. Everything else would mean putting the cart before the horse. The amendment to Art 57 EC provided for in the Treaty of Lisbon tells a different story. It reads as follows: 'In the absence of measures pursuant to Article 57(3) [currently Art. 57 (2) EC], the Commission or, in the absence of a Commission decision within three months from the request of the Member State concerned, the Council, may adopt a decision stating that restrictive tax measures adopted by a Member State concerning one or more third countries are to be considered compatible with the Treaties insofar as they are justified by one of the objectives of the Union and compatible with the proper functioning of the internal market. The Council shall act unanimously on application by a Member State.'

many reasons might be that no study on a general theory of the fundamental freedoms exists that sufficiently takes into account free movement of capital. Due to this lack, such theories hardly look beyond the Common Market. The question of whether and in what way free movement of capital, with its third country applicability, blends into a general theory of the fundamental freedoms and to what degree such a theory might have to be extended is therefore a worthwhile area of research.

For the future of free capital movement, not only the research findings in the areas indicated above but also recognition and appreciation of already existing research by a wider audience will be of help in scrutinizing Member States' activities and their advanced justifications. Free movement of capital in general and foreign direct investment in particular can today easily be held responsible for scarcely related disadvantageous (socio-)economic effects or situations within a Member State without attracting much critical attention. The concern, for example, that a foreign investor, by way of cross-border merger or acquisition, could acquire overwhelming market power in a Member State cannot effectively be remedied by generally restricting foreign takeovers, but only by an active competition policy. In many cases, a careful and more rational cause-and-effect analysis would cut the ground from under national resentment, economic protectionism, and mercantilist-state capitalist theories. Free movement of capital *erga omnes* is objectively too important for the (socio-)economic development of the European Community and the welfare of its citizens to let it fall victim to subjective blindness.

Annex

Summary: Position Statements

1. Preparing the Ground: Economic Rationale of the Liberalization of Capital Movements and the Art of Political Compromise

1. The (socio-)economic aims of the EC Treaty are best served if free movement of capital is construed in a liberal and wide understanding, meaning the complete liberalization of all cross-border capital movements, including cross-border direct investment, within the Community. As the EC Treaty recognizes a diversity of interests, it is, however, conceivable that, in the individual case, measures are permissible even though they restrict free movement of capital.

1.1. Free, ie, unrestricted, capital movements can—if certain institutional preconditions, eg, first and foremost a stable banking and supervision system, free competition, and a functioning tax and legal system, are met—contribute in particular to the Treaty aims of price stability, equalization of the balance of payments, and economic growth.

1.2. Free movement of capital is the prerequisite for the attainment of the aim of Economic and Monetary Union.

1.3. A complete liberalization of capital movements is a precondition of the implementation of the other freedoms.

1.4. Free movement of capital makes possible and furthers the aim of undistorted competition as an essential element of the Common Market.

2. The aims pursued by the freedom of capital movement do not suggest a narrower interpretation of Art 56(1) EC, but they favour free, ie, liberalized, capital movement, including cross-border direct investment, between the Member States and non-EC countries.

2.1. The 'outrageous' act of unilateralism in which capital movements were liberalized in EC–third country relations is neither an editorial mistake of the Treaty drafters nor a huge political and economic error.

2.1.1. If one is prepared to perceive the Community as a non-protectionist, open market economy (*cf* Arts 4(1) EC, 98, 2nd sentence EC, and 105(1) 3rd sentence EC), disproving the notion of a 'Fortress Europe', then those arguments that speak in favour of a complete liberalization of capital movements within the Community can also be utilized in a third country context.

2.1.2. The unilateral liberalization of capital movements *erga omnes* does not—even in the absence of a level regulatory playing field (eg, no extension of Common Market, no Economic and Monetary Union, no other arrangement)—endanger the harmonious development of the Community's internal financial market.

2.1.2.1. From an economic viewpoint, formal policy coordination is to a certain extent desirable, but not actually required to allow for free capital movement.

2.1.2.2. By unilaterally opening up the EC market to third countries, the Community does not give away its bargaining powers to press for third country market access and regulatory convergence, but has the necessary management tools, in particular by virtue of Arts 57(2) EC, 94 EC, 95 EC, and 308 EC, ready to hand. The opening up of the EC market, therefore, need not be based from the outset upon the condition of reciprocity.

3. The genesis of the rules on free movement of capital indicates a drive to (almost) complete liberalization of capital movement. It can hardly be doubted that the current provisions bear the hallmarks of the 'economist camp' and embrace a liberal undercurrent both in an intra-Community and a third country context.

2. Material Scope of Application of Article 56(1) EC

a. What Constitutes a 'Movement of Capital'

4. The notion of 'capital' employed in Art 56(1) EC comprises both financial and real capital as understood in economics. However, not all of what qualifies as capital also amounts to a 'movement of capital'. Especially with respect to movable capital goods (real capital)—at the crossroads of free movement of capital and goods—a careful analysis is indicated.

5. No conclusive and exhaustive general definition of the term 'movements of capital' is in existence. A typified understanding—a useful basis from which the evaluation of a transaction in the individual case can start—refers to 'movement of capital' within the meaning of Art 56(1) EC as encompassing all unilateral financial operations between two Member States or one Member State and a third country essentially concerned with the investment of the funds in question rather than remuneration for service, goods, and the provision of capital.

6. The EC Capital Movements Directive—still of indicative value—reveals by way of example the scope of the freedom. The Court, using this directive as an 'ancilla of construction', has refrained from providing a general definition.
7. A given transaction must therefore be judged against the background of all available factual and legal circumstances on an individual basis. In particular, the economic purpose pursued by the transaction, the intended legal consequence in private law, the Treaty aims and system, as well as the function of the fundamental freedoms, shall guide the evaluation.
7.1. In order to achieve the end of an optimized capital allocation to the greatest extent possible and, hence, to endow the freedom with the greatest effectiveness (*'effet utile'*), a broad understanding of the term 'movement of capital' is indicated. Thus, the notion of 'movement of capital' does not only comprise the 'actual transfer', but also activities in the run-up to it, as well as follow-up activities.
8. Concerning the relationship of free movement of capital and payments, both freedoms being mutually exclusive, in case of doubt as to whether a certain transaction is remuneration for goods, etc or indeed capital, free movement of capital applies.

b. Capital Movements beyond National Boundaries

9. A cross-border element is present in a given capital movement if either the capital is actually crossing the border or, seen from an economic perspective, if a capital movement appears as a cross-border investment. This is the case when the return on investment is determined by the conditions present in that other country.
10. The location of capital depends on its type. Real property and moveable capital goods are located where they are situated. Intangible capital requires having recourse to the holder of that capital. The latter is placed where his habitual residence is to be found.

c. The Notions of 'Direct Investment' and 'Foreign Direct Investment' within the Ambit of Free Movement of Capital

11. An economic understanding constitutes the starting point for any meaningful evaluation of the notion of 'direct investment'. Speaking in economic terms, a direct investment occurs when an investor acquires managing control over economic activities. The distinctive feature is that the investor is placed in a position to pursue entrepreneurial aims.
12. 'Direct investment' in legal terms forms a sub-category of 'movement of capital' as mentioned in Art 56(1) EC and is, hence, within the material scope of application of the freedom.

12.1. This can be drawn—*argumentum e contrario*—from its mention in Art 57(1) EC, as well as from the reference in the Nomenclature of the EC Capital Movements Directive, which still carries indicative value for the construction of the notion of 'movement of capital'.

13. 'Direct investment' in abstract terms must be understood as covering '[i]nvestments of all kinds by natural persons or commercial, industrial or financial undertakings, and which serve to establish or to maintain lasting and direct links between the person providing the capital and the entrepreneur to whom or the undertaking to which the capital is made available in order to carry on an economic activity'.[1]

13.1. The notion of 'direct investment' must be interpreted, in particular with respect to the 'lasting and direct link', in a strict sense in the whole ambit of free movement of capital.

13.1.1. The call in the Exemplary Notes of the EC Capital Movements Directive for an understanding 'in its widest sense' is misleading. This interpretive guidance was given with a view to liberalizing capital movements within the Community. The current provisions on free movement of capital have created a completely different situation with the consequence that a wide interpretation of the notion of 'direct investment' would lead to the opposite result as the notion is today used in Art 57(1) EC in the context of restricting the freedom. In essence, one would turn a definition drafted with a view to liberalizing to the greatest extent possible into one that restricts the freedom to the greatest extent possible. Such a construction is, however, at odds with the basic axiom of construction to interpret exceptions strictly. Hence, the interpretive guidance in the Directive is to be understood in such a way that the varieties of direct investment mentioned therein under Heading I do not represent a conclusive enumeration.

13.2. The distinctive feature of the notion of 'direct investment'—in economics as well as in EC law—is that the investor is placed in a position to exercise control over entrepreneurial activities in such a way that major or important entrepreneurial decisions cannot be reached without his consent. This is also what is basically meant by the phrase of 'lasting and direct links' between investor and investment. In order to assess whether the investor is in the aforementioned position, recourse must be had to the actual circumstances in the individual case.

14. 'Foreign direct investment'—a set term not used in the EC Treaty, which instead speaks of 'movement of capital to or from third countries involving direct investment'—in this study refers to direct investment directed to or originating from non-EC countries. Hence, 'foreign' in this study, except where otherwise stated, deviates from the common understanding and denotes transactions that occur between a Member State and a non-EC country.

---

[1] Annex I, Explanatory Notes of Directive 88/361/EEC.

14.1. Third countries within the meaning of the EC Treaty are all those States to which it does not apply.
15. The scope of the freedom does not extent to direct investments that display no connection at all to the Community.
15.1. A transaction displays a 'sufficient link' to the Community if either of the two parties to the transaction is resident within the Community or the return on investment is determined by the economic conditions found in at least one Member State.
16. The Treaty requires drawing a distinction between intra-Community and foreign direct investment, *cf* Arts 57–60 EC.
16.1. The third country link is to be sought in the actual transfer that establishes (or perpetuates) control over the investment. Taking any wide 'global perspective' with respect to assessing the link of a transaction to a third country is in this situation—in contrast to the Court's view—not indicated due to the fact that it would impermissibly restrict intra-Community direct investment.
16.2. Foreign direct investment is on hand if either of the two parties to the transaction is resident within a third country or, although the two parties involved are resident within the Community, the return on investment is determined by the economic conditions present in a third country or *vice versa*.

d. The Influence of Competing Freedoms: The Relationship of Free Movement of Capital and the Freedom of Establishment

17. Direct investment constitutes an economic cross-sectional activity potentially within the scope of both the freedom of establishment and free movement of capital. It forms a (sub-)category of 'movement of capital' within the meaning of Art 56(1) EC, and it qualifies as 'establishment' for the purposes of Art 43 EC.
17.1. Establishment is the actual pursuit of an economic activity through a fixed establishment in another Member State for an indefinite period. It is not necessary that the economic activity be pursed in the manner of a sole trader. It suffices that an entrepreneur is in a position to exercise definite influence over the company's decisions and to determine the company's activities ('definite influence' test). This is the case when major or important entrepreneurial decisions (eg, influence on the composition of the management body) cannot be reached without the approval of the respective stockholder. In this regard, the number of voting rights or stocks has an indicative but not conclusive value.
17.2. The 'effective participation test', developed for the identification of direct investment with respect to holdings mentioned in Annex I, Heading I.2 to the EC Capital Movements Directive, requires essentially the same

threshold as the Court's 'definite influence test'. Hence, the notions of establishment and direct investment are perceived by this study as to a very great extent overlapping.

18. The relationship of free movement of capital and freedom of establishment on the level of the scope of application is of a parallel nature. The freedom of establishment does not supersede free movement of capital. Thus, competing freedoms do not have an influence on the scope of application of Art 56(1) EC in such a way that foreign direct investment would be excluded from it.

18.1. Articles 43(2) EC and 58(2) EC do not apply to the scope of application, but only to the level of grounds of justification, and therefore do not have the effect of establishing primacy of one freedom over the other on the level of the scope of application.

18.2. The Court, in principle, accepts parallel applicability of the provisions on free movement of capital and freedom of establishment with respect to direct investment. However, this affirmation is only half-hearted: cases in which the market participant is restricted in his economic activity by national measures applying only to undertakings over which definite control is exercised are subjected exclusively to the freedom of establishment ('centre of gravity' approach). This has fatal consequences for foreign direct investment. As soon as the national measure is phrased in the aforementioned fashion, it is completely exempted from scrutiny in the light of the fundamental freedoms. However, neither the way in which the Court delineates the freedoms from each other nor the achieved outcome is convincing.

18.3. The more convincing arguments in the literature speak in favour of a parallel application of Arts 43 EC and 56(1) EC.

18.3.1. Free movement of capital and the freedom of establishment are inextricably linked to each other with respect to the cross-sectional activity of direct investment. The different aspects of the economic activity cannot be separated in a comprehensible and clear-cut fashion. Only the parallel application of the freedoms can prevent an economic aspect of the activity being exposed to potentially unjustified discrimination or hindrance. Only in this way is it guaranteed that the freedoms are not deprived of their effectiveness in a situation in which an economic activity falls potentially into the ambit of more than one freedom.

e. **Which Level of Protection?—The Scope of the Prohibition of Restriction: Equal Treatment and Market Access**

19. Article 56(1) EC prohibits 'all restrictions on the movement of capital'. As in the case of the other fundamental freedoms, this prohibition equally breaks up into two complementary rights: equal treatment on the market and access to the market.

19.1. As regards the terminology used in this study, this study perceives the 'prohibition of restrictions' as a 'genus' that embraces two 'species' or tests: the prohibition of discrimination, referring to measures distinctly applicable, and the prohibition of hindrance, denoting measures operating indistinctly which have an adverse effect on cross-border capital movements.

(1) Intra-Community Context

(a) Non-hindrance Test

20. Free movement of capital takes part in the broader context of converging tendencies of construction among the fundamental freedoms. Article 56(1) EC contains, besides a prohibition of discrimination, also one of hindrance, which reads as follows: 'A national measure is subject to Art. 56(1) EC, even though the rules in issue may not give rise to unequal treatment, if they are capable of impeding cross-border capital movements and dissuading investors from investing.'

20.1. In the context of free movement of capital, no distinction is drawn between import and export of capital.

21. In order to prevent a potential overreach of the non-hindrance test as well as to remain true to 'market integration' as the central idea inherent in the fundamental freedoms, a *Keck*-style formula is applied to the freedom of capital movement. It can be sketched as follows: 'A national measure is not subject to Art 56(1) EC if it does not substantially impede capital movements across borders and, at the same time, if it applies indistinctly in law and in fact.'

21.1. The inherent weaknesses of the *Keck* formula are not of such a nature as to object in principle to an application of it to free movement of capital.

21.2. The seemingly non-exhaustive character of Art 58(1) lit. b EC does not render unnecessary the application of a *Keck*-style formula to the ambit of the freedom of capital movement.

21.3. The necessary degree of impediment in order to amount to a 'substantial impediment' is a question that cannot ultimately be answered in abstract terms, but must be left to clarification by the Court. It requires striking a balance between the gist of Art 56(1) EC, ie, to liberalize the movement of capital to the greatest extent possible, and the preservation of a coherent general legal framework within the Member State.

(b) Non-discrimination Test

22. The prohibition of discrimination contained in Art 56(1) EC not only requires that domestic and cross-border direct investments are treated equally in comparable circumstances, but also that different cross-border direct investments are not discriminated among themselves. The former prohibition resembles the international economic law principle of national treatment, the latter that of most-favoured-nation treatment.

22.1. In case of free movement of capital, an object-related freedom, the 'expressly' prohibited distinguishing criterion is the place of origin/destination of a capital movement. A measure that discriminates expressly on the basis of this criterion constitutes so-called direct discrimination.

22.2. Nationality and residence do not constitute additional expressly prohibited distinguishing criteria alongside the origin/destination of a capital movement.

22.2.1. Discrimination on the basis of the place of residence of a participant in a capital movement is, however, functionally equivalent to discrimination on the basis of origin/destination of a capital movement in case of intangible capital due to the fact that this capital is found—figuratively speaking—where its holder resides.

22.3. Indirect discrimination can be established if the national measure does not expressly refer to the origin/destination of a capital movement, but employs a surrogate criterion that 'in fact leads to the same results' as a distinction based on the expressly prohibited criterion.

22.4. So-called reverse discrimination, ie, national measures that operate solely to the detriment of domestic capital movement, is in principle outside the scope of the freedom.

23. The ECJ, while certainly acknowledging that national measures that differentiate on the basis of nationality, residence, etc. can constitute discrimination, fails to put forward reasoning of a more doctrinal nature on what constitutes direct and what indirect discrimination. It also has not made serious attempts to clearly delineate the 'non-discrimination test' from the 'non-hindrance test'.

24. Judging comparability of two situations has to be done on a case-by-case basis, taking into account actual circumstances against the background of the purpose and content of the respective national measure and under consideration of the value-based decisions stipulated by the Community legal order.

24.1. No consistent picture has so far emerged from the cases on national direct taxation legislation, ie, legislation that essentially encroaches upon ongoing direct investments, concerning comparability. What is clear, however, is that no general exception from the prohibition of discrimination in the area of taxation can be derived from the Treaty, especially not by reference to Art 58(1) lit. a, (3) EC.

24.1.1. The indicative value of the strand of case law on direct taxation, when it comes to judging the question of whether national measures in other subject areas also concerned with the regulation of an ongoing business discriminate, is limited. This is due to the fact that negative harmonization in this field goes quickly to the core of sovereignty of the Member States which, it appears, does not always make it easy for the Court to present a consistent approach.

24.2. Concerning national measures that establish a discriminatory regime for first-time access to or exit from a Member State's market, within the Community it is difficult to envisage 'essential attributes' that *per se* would question the comparability of domestic and cross-border direct investment. The regulatory questions posed by placing a direct investment do not vary depending on its origin or destination. Differences, especially in economic development or taxation, social, or labour politics, do not constitute 'essential attributes' to question comparability.

(2) Third Country Context

25. The scope of prohibition of Art 56(1) EC in a third country context has to be interpreted along the same lines as developed for intra-Community capital movement.

25.1. The wording of Art 56(1) EC is a prime example of clarity speaking in favour of an understanding in a third country context that does not deviate from the one valid for intra-Community capital movement.

25.2. Teleological and systematic arguments advanced by commentators who want to interpret the scope of prohibition of Art 56(1) EC more narrowly in a third country context are not convincing. The proposition that certain preconditions are still lacking, which, if they were fulfilled, would justify interpreting the scope of prohibition similarly in an intra-Community and a third country context, cannot be upheld.

25.2.1. The *erga omnes* principle within the ambit of free movement of capital would not only be justified if the Community wanted to make an 'altruistic' contribution to the advancement of a liberalized world capital market at large—although there is evidence in the EC Treaty that the EC could indeed have wanted this—but it already finds its justification in the socio-economic benefits the Community derives from a unilateral opening of its capital market.

25.2.1.1. Liberalized capital movement with third countries, for example, furthers economic growth within the EC by intensified competition, increased freedom of choice, especially for European capital recipients, and pressure on the Member States to maintain fiscal and tariffs discipline. Therefore, the unilateral liberalization of capital movements *erga omnes* advances those Treaty aims that are directed at the development of the Common Market.

25.2.2. Liberalizing capital movements in third country relations, economically speaking, neither requires—in the sense of a *conditio sine qua non*—the harmonization of third country and Common Market rules nor the coordination of monetary and economic policies between the EC and third countries. However, aiming at some degree of harmonization or coordination is desirable.

25.2.3. The bargaining powers of the Community *vis-à-vis* third countries are sufficient to press for reciprocal market access and equal treatment of EC direct investments in third country markets. Thus, the configuration of the EC competences (esp. Arts 57(2) EC, 59 EC, 60 EC, 93 EC, and 94 EC together with Arts 95(2) EC and 308 EC) are not of such a kind as to describe the Community as not sufficiently equipped to defend its and its Member States' interests. Protecting Community and Member State interests, therefore, does not require making liberalization of third county capital movement subject to reciprocity.

25.2.4. It is a vicious circle to argue that the greater number of permissible restrictions on the freedom in a third country context suggests a respectively more restricted *telos* of Art 56(1) EC in such situations.

25.2.5. Restricting third country capital movement would not meaningfully prevent the access of third country investors to the Common Market, but the circumvention of restrictive access regimes in some Member States is caused by the so-called 'channel phenomenon'. The 'channel phenomenon', ie, more liberal-minded Member States functioning as 'access channels' to the Common Market for third country capital movements that less liberal-minded Member States wished to have excluded or otherwise restricted, is caused by the way in which the other fundamental freedoms operate.

25.2.6. Neither a *domaine réservé* for tax rules nor for any other type of national regulatory measures is justified on the basis of teleological or systematic considerations.

25.2.7. While one can agree that Art 56(1) EC must apply to national measures that restrict the technical access of capital to and exit from the Common Market, there are profound reasons not to limit the scope of application to these instances.

25.2.7.1. Liberalized capital movement with third countries, for example, furthers economic growth within the EC by intensified competition, increased freedom of choice, especially for European capital recipients, and pressure on the Member States to maintain fiscal and tariffs discipline.

25.2.7.2. Liberalized capital movement *erga omnes* is also necessary in order to build up and maintain trust in the common currency, which is intended to aspire to be a world investment, financing, trade, and reserve currency.

25.2.7.3. The *erga omnes* principle can be seen as one of the clearest affirmations of the Community's commitment to a non-protectionist, open market economy, disproving any notion of a 'Fortress Europe'.

25.3. Concerning the non-discrimination test, a distinction has to be made between case-specific considerations and those that I have termed 'value-based decisions stipulated by the Community legal order'. The former can always lead to a negation of the comparability of domestic/intra-Community and third country direct investments. With respect to the latter, however, I could not identify 'value-based decisions' that would suggest incomparability *per se*.

25.3.1. Arguments based on existing differences between a Member State and a third country on the level of taxation, social contributions, or labour costs, etc or the existence of intra-Community harmonization cannot form the basis for 'value-based decisions' and are thus unsuitable to justify the negation of 'comparability'.

25.3.2. Consequences springing from the unilateral opening of the Community capital market to the world have to be borne in the same way as in an intra-Community context.

26. This interpretation leaves us with the following picture: the access, exit, and transit of third country capital must in principle be free of any restrictions. Once a third country investment is placed within the Common Market (inbound) or an investment originating from a Member State is established in a third country market (outbound), the Member States are not allowed to treat them less favourably than a comparable domestic investment or an investment from another State.

3. Direct Effect and Personal Scope

27. Article 56(1) EC is vertically directly effective in intra-Community and third country contexts.
28. Any private market participant, natural and legal persons alike, can rely on the freedom.
28.1. The freedom's guarantees are not bound to a certain nationality or place of habitual residence of the market participants.
28.1.1. The place of residence, though, may gain significance for the purpose of identifying the cross-border link of a given transaction or in order to verify whether a transaction displays a sufficient link to the Community.
29. Following the gist of Art 48(2) EC, such legal persons as were established on the basis of public law are also covered by the personal scope as long as they carry out economic activities for financial gain. The Member State, the Community and their respective institutions, as well as third countries, cannot rely on the freedom. However, a private person who entered into dealings with those entities is covered by Art 56(1) EC.
30. The freedom is predominantly addressed to the Member States.
30.1. Their measures are all-embracingly covered irrespective of whether they act in a sovereign capacity or by means of private law.

30.2. A Member State is not only under the duty to refrain from any restrictive conduct, but is also under the positive obligation to prevent any private conduct restricting free capital movement.
31. The group of addressees extends to the Community and its institutions.
32. Private persons can also be subject to Art 56(1) EC if their measures are state-like in the sense that they restrict unilaterally the party autonomy of other private party participants without the latter having the chance to escape this situation.

4. Exceptions to Free Movement of Capital

a. Exceptions Applicable to Intra-Community and Third Country Situations

(1) Article 58(1) lit. b EC

(a) Intra-Community Context

33. Article 58(1) lit. b EC contains the only express grounds of justification, to be construed narrowly, within the chapter on free movement of capital.
33.1. It can be subdivided into three groups:
33.1.1. The first group relates to national measures preventing infringements of national law and regulations, which itself can be split into three subcategories, ie, national measures in the field of taxation, those in the field of prudential supervision of financial institutions, and national measures in other fields.
33.1.1.1. National measures in the field of taxation are in particular those that ensure effective fiscal supervision and prevent tax evasion ('fraud') or avoidance ('abuse').
33.1.1.1.1. In order not to open up to the Member States a loophole for the enactment of protective national tax measures, the Member States must show in the individual case that there is a real, tangible, and serious danger of infringement of national laws and regulations.
33.1.1.1.1.1. In case of alleged tax avoidance, only purely artificial tax schemas may be targeted.
33.1.1.1.1.2. Taking advantage of the Common Market must also mean, in the absence of harmonization, utilizing the differences between the national tax systems to one's own advantage.
33.1.1.2. National measures preventing infringements of national law and regulations are not confined to the fields of taxation (and prudential supervision of financial institutions) in order to be justifiable, but

the provision also extends to other fields besides those mentioned explicitly within the first group.

33.1.1.2.1. Those measures must aim at the prevention of illicit activities of comparable seriousness in order to be covered.

33.1.1.2.2. The list—at first sight 'open-ended'—is limited by an 'ancillary function' nexus between the 'anti-infringement rule' and the rule that enforcement shall be secured by the former.

33.1.1.2.3. It cannot be deduced from the open wording of the provision that free movement of capital does not participate in the general system of construction of the fundamental freedoms. A 'dual system' of grounds of justification—on one hand, the grounds mentioned explicitly in the Treaty and, on the other, the 'rule of reason'—also applies here.

33.1.2. The second group within Art 58(1) lit. b EC allows for national declaration procedures for the purpose of administrational and statistical information.

33.1.3. The third group constitutes a classic *ordre public* caveat.

33.1.3.1. There is no meaningful all-embracing definition of what qualifies as a public policy or security consideration that may justify a restriction on free movement of capital. This must be established on a case-by-case basis.

33.1.3.2. The economic activity of cross-border direct investment does not in itself constitute a threat to public policy or public security.

33.1.3.2.1. The Member State has to demonstrate that in absence of the measure restricting cross-border direct investment, their legitimate interests would be exposed to a real, specific, and serious risk.

33.1.3.2.1.1. Besides the defence sector, legitimate public interests include the objective of ensuring a minimum supply of petroleum products, electricity, or a minimum level of telecommunications services at all times.

i. *The Proportionality Test*

33.2. The general principle of proportionality is, in accordance with the ECJ, to be applied rigorously.

33.2.1. The term 'requisite' found in Art 58(1) lit. b EC (1st group) has no constitutive meaning.

33.2.2. The admissibility of prior authorization regimes (aiming to prevent infringement of national law and regulations) is essentially a question of 'necessity,' ie, no less restrictive measure can be identified in order to achieve the aim pursued.

33.2.2.1. With respect to direct investment and purchase of land, while accepting in abstract terms the possibility of requiring prior authorization, emphasis is particularly placed on the fact that an authorization regime adheres to very strict standards of transparency, especially clarity of the scope of application, predictability, and making legal remedies available to the market participant.

33.2.3. Alleged 'administrational difficulties' in gaining reliable information for administrative supervisory purposes in dealing with cross-border transactions, which the Member States purportedly face, are in principle not to be accepted as justifying restrictions on cross-border direct investment.

33.2.3.1. Member States are first required to resort to means of inter-administrative cooperation as enshrined in the Council Directive Concerning Mutual Assistance by the Competent Authorities of the Member States in the Field of Direct Taxation and Taxation of Insurance Premiums. Even if the Directive should not be applicable in the individual case, the Member State must first provide the opportunity to the market participant himself to provide the information needed before restricting the freedom.

(b) Third Country Context

34. Supported by the wording and the existence of specific exceptions to third country capital movements by which the Treaty drafters expressly indicated in which situations they wished to make a distinction between intra-Community and third country capital movement, Art 58(1) lit. b EC must in principle be interpreted in the same way irrespective of whether intra-Community third country capital movements are involved.

34.1. The lack of persuasiveness of teleological and systematic considerations, such as the purported 'limited purpose' pursued by the liberalization of third country capital movements or missing harmonization with third countries, prohibit an across-the-board treatment of such capital movements within the ambit of this provision.

34.1.1. Third country capital movement does not constitute a general danger of infringement of national rules and regulations.

34.1.2. The economic activity of direct investment in a third country context does not *per se* constitute a threat to public policy or public security. The economic sectors in which public security concerns were recognized by the Court as legitimate are identical in an intra-Community and third country context.

35. Possible differences between intra-Community and third country capital movements are best considered in the balancing process taking place within the proportionality test. However, under the given conditions it is unclear why the Court should significantly deviate from the guidelines informing the application of the proportionality test developed in an intra-Community context.

35.1. Concerning effective fiscal supervision, the Member States must resort first to international treaties concluded between the respective Member State and a third country in order to gain the information needed before restricting the freedom.
35.2. Even if the means available under international law prove insufficient in the individual case, the market participant should first be given the opportunity to provide the information himself before recourse is had to additional national restrictive measures.
35.3. National measures that restrict foreign direct investment on the basis of the *ordre public* exception must fulfil the same high standards in terms of predictability, transparency, and due process as are applicable in an intra-Community context.
36. Due to the applicability of the freedom of capital movements to third countries, the 'second Cassis principle' (also called 'principle of mutual recognition' or 'principle of functional parallelism') must in general also be valid in such situations, but with one self-evident modification, ie, that the principle, like the freedom itself, applies only 'unilaterally'.
36.1. A Member State must demonstrate that the regulatory measure at issue does not serve a functionally parallel purpose compared to the one pursued by the regulation of a third country.

(2) Article 58(2) EC—The Relationship of Free Movement of Capital and Freedom of Establishment on the Level of Grounds of Justification

37. In principle, it suffices for a restriction to be justified that it serves, in the actual situation at issue, a legitimate interest recognized within the ambit of either freedom.
37.1. This interpretation is the only one that takes sufficient account of the mutual references in Arts 58(2) EC and 43(3) EC.
37.2. The Court's approach, which requires that a national measure that constitutes a restriction on both freedoms be justified in each case with the respective grounds of justification provided for in the respective chapter of the Treaty, while certainly securing the maximum protection for the market participant, completely disregards Arts 43(2) EC and 58(2) EC.
37.3. Exclusivity approaches at the level of the grounds of justification are subject to the same criticism as advanced above with respect to exclusivity approaches at the level of the scope of application.
37.4. In practice, the question of cumulative or alternative application of the grounds of justification will not play a significant role due to the fact that the recognized legitimate interests within each ambit, if one takes together written and unwritten grounds, have been similarly shaped to a very large degree by the Court. Also, within the proportionality test, in the process of balancing conflicting interests, differences between the freedoms may not be easily noticeable with respect to direct investment.

38. In a third country situation, only in the ambit of free movement of capital, but not in that of freedom of establishment, grounds of justification contained in the Treaty chapter of the respective other freedom can on principle be applied by virtue of Art 58(2) EC.
38.1. In this context one must differentiate between national measures that apply exclusively to third country situations, ie, that establish a special regime for foreign direct investment, and those that are applicable to intra-Community and third country contexts alike.
38.1.1. With respect to the former, Art 58(2) EC achieves nothing due to the fact that there are no 'restrictions on the right of establishment which are compatible with the Treaty' whatsoever to which it could be referred by virtue of the provision.
38.1.2. Regarding the latter, Art 58(2) EC refers to the grounds of justification exclusively to be found in the ambit of the freedom of establishment.

(3) Article 295 EC—The System of Property Ownership as Ground of Justification?

39. Article 295 EC does not constitute an exception to the freedom of capital movement on which national measures restricting cross-border direct investment could be based.
39.1. The provision is a rule of competence that is limited in its effect to stating that the Member States continue to have vested in them the competence to shape their systems of property ownership. However, it does not have any significant material effect; the individual rules of the respective property ownership system are subject to a comprehensive review against the background of Community law; in particular, the fundamental freedoms and the competition rules.

(4) Article 297 EC—The Ultima Ratio Defence and Security Exception

40. Only in extreme situations, which presuppose the actual materialization of the events and circumstances mentioned within the provision, can recourse be had to Art 297 EC.
41. The provision constitutes the *ultima ratio* in the sense that its application is limited to cases in which no other Treaty provision can accommodate the legitimate security interests of the Member States, which carry the ultimate responsibility for the protection of their citizens.

(5) Transitional Periods and Permanent Derogations from the Duty to Liberalize Capital Movements

42. In the course of the accession negotiations of new Member States entering the European Union in 2004 and 2007, transitional periods of varying lengths were agreed upon governing the possibility of purchasing property, cultivated land, or forest.

43. With respect to Denmark, Protocol No 1 of the Treaty on European Union stipulates that, notwithstanding the provisions of the Treaty on the free movement of capital, Denmark may maintain the existing legislation on the acquisition of second homes. However, the respective provisions may not discriminate.
44. Protocol No 2 of the Finnish Accession Treaty provides for certain derogations from the provisions of the EC Treaty with respect to the Åland Islands, which may maintain non-discriminatory national provisions in force on 1 January 1994 regarding, inter alia, restrictions on the right of natural and legal persons to acquire and hold real property without permission by the competent authorities of the Islands.

(6) Rule of Reason
(a) Intra-Community Context

45. The 'rule of reason' has been firmly established within the ambit of free movement of capital.
46. Its scope of application is not limited to national measures that cause a mere hindrance to free movement, but also extends to indirect and direct discrimination.
47. The list of mandatory requirements is non-exhaustive.
47.1. Of particular prominence within the ambit of free movement of capital is the rather vaguely defined mandatory requirement of fiscal cohesion.
47.1.1. The basic idea behind this mandatory requirement is to preserve those national regulatory systems that serve the realization of fiscal equality, ie, that keep intact the direct link between a tax advantage that was granted today and subsequent taxability.
47.1.2. By requiring, inter alia, that the direct link must be present within the same tax and within the same taxpayer or even within the same contract, the mandatory requirement is stripped of most of its significance.
47.2. Besides the mandatory requirements explicitly discussed by the Court within the context of free movement of capital, recourse can also be had to mandatory requirements considered with respect to other fundamental freedoms.
47.2.1. Member States may have recourse to mandatory requirements such as the protection of investors or the defence of consumers, the maintenance of stability in or protection of the reputation of the financial market, the fairness of commercial transactions, the protection of the environment, or the preservation of available small-scale agriculture.
47.3. Alleged mandatory requirements pleaded by the Member States such as the existence of counterbalancing advantages, the voluntary submission to disadvantageous tax regimes by choice of a certain form of establishment, the lack of competence of the Community in the area of direct taxation and a respective lack of harmonization, the general purpose of

securing the tax base and preventing the loss of tax revenue are, in accordance with the Court's case law, to be rejected.

(b) Third Country Context
48. The 'rule of reason' also applies in a third country context.
49. Its interpretation does not vary depending on whether the capital movement relates to another Member State or to a third country, but may follow in a third country context the same lines that have been drawn by the Court for intra-Community capital movement.
49.1. No across-the-board judgments penalizing third country capital movements shall be applied, but the mandatory requirement pursued by a national measure and the freedom of capital movements have to be balanced carefully on a case-by-case basis.
49.2. Sufficient argumentative support for the view which suggested interpreting accepted mandatory requirements, such as 'fiscal cohesion', variously depending on the geographical mapping cannot be identified as missing reciprocity in third country capital movement is no valid argument.
49.3. On the basis of the *telos* and systematics of the Treaty, the unilateral liberalization of free movement of capital *erga omnes* is to be perceived as unconditional. Missing reciprocity is not an argument for a restriction of third country capital movement, but the very consequence of this unilateral act.
49.4. The introduction of mandatory requirements pursuing budgetary purposes also based on 'lacking reciprocity' in a third country context must be rejected. Closely related to the 'lacking reciprocity' argument is that of 'lacking harmonization' in a third country context, which also cannot form a valid plea to restrict third country capital movement.

b. Exceptions Applicable Exclusively to Third Countries

(1) Article 57(1) EC
50. Article 57(1) EC constitutes a temporally unlimited carve-out from the duty to liberalize with respect to certain categories of capital movement deemed of such economic and political importance that their liberalization is to be carried out under particular consideration of general welfare. Restrictive measures may be found in national and Community law.
51. Insofar as international treaties concluded by the Community provide for more far-reaching duties to liberalize capital movements *vis-à-vis* third countries than the EC Treaty, the Member States cannot invoke Art 57(1) EC in order to save their restrictive national measures.
52. In any other case, Art 57(1) EC is to be construed strictly.
52.1. The notion of foreign direct investment is to be interpreted narrowly.

52.1.1. The 'lasting and direct links between the person providing the capital and the entrepreneur to whom or the undertaking to which the capital is made available in order to carry on an economic activity' must be understood essentially in parallel terms to the 'definite influence test' required in Art 43 EC for the identification of an 'establishment'.

52.1.2. In order not to turn Art 57(1) EC into a gateway for the unreasonable restriction of intra-Community direct investment, the 'foreign link' is to be sought in the individual transaction(s) with which one seeks to establish (or perpetuate) the possibility of control over an undertaking.

52.2. A law within the meaning of this provision must specifically apply to a third country context, as well as to direct investment (or one of the other categories mentioned in the provision).

52.3. A law, in order to be covered by Art 57(1) EC, must in principle have become effective, ie, has its legal restrictive effect on the market participant, before 1 January 1994 or 2000, respectively.

52.3.1. Subsequent changes of national laws are allowed as long as the change improves the position of the market participant.

53. The Court's broad reading of Art 57(1) EC is contrary to the general rule of construction to interpret exceptions narrowly, contrary to the purpose and spirit of the freedom and in partial contradiction to the wording of Art 57(1) EC.

(2) Article 57(2) EC

54. Although Art 57(2) EC also provides for the possibility to restrict the freedom in a third country context, the provision is liberal in its underlying notion.

55. Art 57(2) EC *a priori* contains a concurrent internal competence of the Community to resort to autonomous secondary measures. The competence flowing from the provision may by implication also extend to measures under international law.

56. The competence is limited by the fact that a measure based on Art 57(2) EC must first establish a special regime that may apply only to third county capital movement and, second, relate to one of the categories of capital movements mentioned therein. It is further limited by the principles of proportionality (*cf* Art 5(3) EC) and subsidiarity (Art 5(2) EC), but also by the fundamental rights. Constraints may also flow from international treaties concluded by the Community or the Member States.

57. The Community may choose its means of action (*cf* Art 249 EC).

58. The precise restrictive or liberalizing effect of Art 57(2) EC is very much dependent on the legislative activity of the Community taken on the basis of this provision.

58.1. So far only a very limited number of legislative acts have solely or in conjunction with other competences been based on Art 57(2) EC.
58.2. The Member States have resisted further liberalization, but on the other hand, the Community and the Commission in particular have refrained from treading the protectionist path by restricting third country capital movement.

(3) Article 59 EC

59. Article 59 EC, allowing for short-term emergency measures by the Community in case of serious difficulties or the threat thereof for the operation of the EMU, cannot be viewed as a general derogation from the *erga omnes* liberalization of capital movement.
59.1. Opening up the EC capital market unilaterally cannot be successfully accomplished without having the relevant 'managing tools' ready at hand, which are required to respond appropriately to the challenges such an opening potentially holds. Article 59 EC constitutes one of these 'tools'.
59.2. The quorum of a qualified majority contained in the provision enables the Council to act swiftly instead of entering into the tedious and time-consuming process of negotiations in order to secure a unanimous vote.
59.3. Although the Council enjoys considerable discretion in its decisions, the narrowly defined scope of the provision as well as the temporal limitation of a measure ensures that the liberalization standard achieved will be undercut only in a state of economic emergency and only for a limited period of time.

(4) Article 60 EC

60. The underlying notion of Art 60 EC is not liberal. However, its restrictive potential on free movement of capital in a third country context is limited.
60.1. Article 60 EC, provides the Community and, on a residual basis, the Member States with the competence to restrict capital movements *vis-à-vis* third countries for political reasons, ie, to enable the Community to first and foremost impose financial sanctions on third countries out of autonomous considerations or on the basis of UN Security Council decisions.
60.2. When imposing sanctions, the Community (as well as the Member States acting on their own account) must observe public international law.
60.2.1. The rules on countermeasures provide very modest restrictions on the powers to restrict third country capital movements.

60.3. Financial sanctions enacted on the basis of Arts 60 EC and 301 EC need not be directly targeted at a nation State, but may aim at individuals as long as they possess a 'significant link' to a third country or a 'regime' effectively in power in part of a third country ('political link'). In this way the sanctions can be targeted more specifically, and negative impacts of restrictive measures on free movement of capital can be reduced.

60.4. The principle of proportionality does not provide a strong corrective when considering the great latitude enjoyed by the Community and Member States, respectively, in evaluating a given political situation.

61. The residual Member State competence in Art 60(2) EC must be interpreted in the strictest sense possible.

61.1. The residual Member State competence contained in Art 60(2) EC is problematic in two ways.

61.1.1. Member States may impose sanctions at different times and of different intensity on third countries, which must inevitably lead to considerable distortions of capital flows.

61.1.2. Unilateral sanctions are rather easily circumvented by playing one Member State against another, gaining access to the Common Market through the 'friendliest' Member State.

61.2. The residual Member State competence must cease as soon as the Community shows that an action at the EC level is not desired, for example, by a failed vote on the basis of Art 60(1) EC.

61.3. Arguing in terms of *de lege ferenda,* it would be more sensible to strengthen the decision-making process on the Community level in order to secure a homogenous approach of sanction regimes towards third countries.

Bibliography

LITERATURE

Abs, Hermann J, 'Capital Movements and Investment in the European Communities' (1961) 26 Law & Contemp. Probs. 508.

Adler, Michael, and Philippe Jorion, 'Foreign Portfolio Investment' in Peter Newman, Murray Milgate and John Eatwell (eds), *The New Palgrave Dictionary of Money & Finance*, 172 (vol 2, Macmillan Press, London 1992).

Ahlt, Michael, *Europarecht : Examenskurs für Rechtsreferendare* (2nd edn C.H. Beck, München 1996).

Alexy, Robert, *Theorie der Grundrechte* (5th edn Suhrkamp, Frankfurt am Main 2006).

Alter, Karen J, and Sophie Meunier-Aitsahalia, 'Judicial Politics in the European Community: European Integration and the Pathbreaking Cassis de Dijon Decision' (1994) 26 Comparative Political Studies 535.

Altmann, Jörn, *Volkswirtschaftslehre: Einführende Theorie mit praktischen Bezügen* (UTB für Wissenschaft: Uni-Taschenbücher, Lucius & Lucius, Stuttgart 2003).

Anweiler, Jochen, *Die Auslegungsmethoden des Gerichtshofs der Europäischen Gemeinschaften* (Schriften zum internationalen und zum öffentlichen Recht, Lang, Frankfurt am Main [et al] 1997).

Arnold, Rainer, 'Außenhandelsrecht' in Manfred A. Dauses (ed), *Handbuch des EU-Wirtschaftsrechts*, loose-leaf; chapter K.I. (vol 2, Beck, München 1994).

Arnull, Anthony, et al, *Wyatt and Dashwood's European Union Law* (4th edn Sweet & Maxwell, London [et al] 2000).

Artis, Mike, and Frederick Nixson (eds), *The Economics of the European Union* (3th edn Oxford University Press, Oxford [et al] 2001).

Bachlechner, Markus, 'Liegenschaftserwerb und Kapitalverkehrsfreiheit' (1998) 1 ZEuS 519.

Bachmann, Birgit, 'Diskriminierungsverbote bei direkten Steuern im Regelungsbereich des EG Vertages' (1994) RIW 849.

Badura, Peter, and Rupert Scholz (eds), *Wege und Verfahren des Verfassungslebens : Festschrift für Peter Lerche zum 65. Geburtstag* (Beck, München 1993).

Baines, Adam, 'Capital Mobility and European Financial and Monetary Integration' (2002) 28 RIS 337.

Bakker, Age F P, *The Liberalization of Capital Movements in Europe—The Monetary Committee and Financial Integration, 1958–1994* (Financial and Monetary Policy Studies, Kluwer, Dordrecht [et al] 1996).

Bandilla, Rüdiger, in Eberhard Grabitz and Meinhard Hilf (eds), *Das Recht der Europäischen Union: Kommentar*, Art. 119 EC (vol 2, C.H. Beck, München 2004).

——in Eberhard Grabitz and Meinhard Hilf (eds), *Das Recht der Europäischen Union: Kommentar*, Art. 120 EC (vol 2, C.H. Beck, München 2004).

Baquero Cruz, Julio, *Between Competition and Free Movement: The Economic Constitutional Law of the European Community* (Hart, Oxford [et al] 2002).

Barnard, Catherine, 'Fitting the Remaining Pieces into the Goods and Persons Jigsaw?' (2001) 26 ELR 35.

——*The Substantive Law of the EU: The Four Freedoms* (Oxford University Press, Oxford [et al] 2004).

Bartelt, Sandra, and Helge Elisabeth Zeitler, '"Intelligente Sanktionen" zur Terrorismusbekämpfung in der EU' (2003) 14 EuZW 712.

Basedow, Jürgen, *Von der deutschen zur europäischen Wirtschaftsverfassung: erweiterte Fassung eines Vortrages, gehalten auf Einladung des Walter-Eucken-Instituts am 28. Januar 1992 in Freiburg im Breisgau* (Vorträge und Aufsätze Walter-Eucken-Institut, Mohr Siebeck, Tübingen 1992).

Bast, Joachim, in Ernst Hocke, et al (eds), *Außenwirtschaftsrecht: Gesetze, Verordnungen und Erlasse zum Außenwirtschaftsrecht mit Kommentar*, § 7 AWG (vol 1, R. v. Decker, Heidelberg 2006).

Behrens, Peter, 'Das wirtschaftsverfassungsrechtliche Profil des Konventsentwurfs eines Vertrags über eine Verfassung für Europa' in Andreas Fuchs (ed), *Wirtschafts- und Privatrecht im Spannungsfeld von Privatautonomie, Wettbewerb und Regulierung: Festschrift für Ulrich Immenga zum 70. Geburtstag*, 21 (Beck, München 2004).

Benoit, Bertrand, 'German Call to Curb Foreign Buyers' *Financial Times.com* (12.07.2007).

Benoit, Bertrand, and Mark Schieritz, 'Berlin Looks to Vet Foreign Funds Deals' *Financial Times.com* (26.06.2007).

Bernard, Nicolas, 'Discrimination and Free Movement in EC Law' (1996) 45 ICLQ 82.

Besse, Dirk, 'New German Foreign Trade Laws Could Hit Defence Sector Investment' (2005) Janes Defence Industry 5.

Beyerlin, Ulrich, and Max-Planck-Institut für Ausländisches Öffentliches Recht und Völkerrecht Heidelberg (eds), *Recht zwischen Umbruch und Bewahrung : Völkerrecht, Europarecht, Staatsrecht; Festschrift für Rudolf Bernhardt* (Springer, Berlin [et al] 1995).

Bieneck, Klaus (ed), *Handbuch des Außenwirtschaftsrechts mit Kriegswaffenkontrollrecht* (2nd edn Aschendorff, Münster 2005).

Blaurock, Uwe (ed), *Das Bankwesen in der Gemeinschaft* (Nomos, Baden-Baden 1981).

Bleckmann, Albert (ed), *Europarecht: Das Recht der Europäischen Union und der Europäischen Gemeinschaften* (6th edn Heymanns, Köln [et al] 1997).

Bleckmann, Albert, *Zur Rechtmäßigkeit der EG-Sanktionen gegen Argentinien nach allgemeinem Völkerrecht und dem Recht der Europäischen Gemeinschaft: Vortrag vor dem Europa-Institut der Universität des Saarlandes, Saarbrücken, 24. Mai 1982* (Vorträge, Reden und Berichte aus dem Europa-Institut, Universität des Saarlandes, Saarbrücken 1982).

Blitz, James, and Stefan Wagstyl, 'Gazprom Block over Centrica Ruled out' *Financial Times* (26.04.2006).

Bognar, Zoltan, *Europäische Währungsintegration und Außenwirtschaftsbeziehungen: eine Analyse des gemeinschafts- und völkerrechtlichen Rahmens der europäischen Außenwährungsbeziehungen* (Schriftenreihe des Europa-Kollegs Hamburg zur Integrationsforschung, Nomos, Baden-Baden 1997).

Bohr, Sebastian, *Schutznormen im Recht der Europäischen Gemeinschaften: Zuständigkeit der Mitgliedstaaten zu autonomem Handeln gem. Art. 224 EWG-Vertrag* (Europarecht-Völkerrecht, VVF, München 1994).

Bond, Christopher, in Dennis Campbell (ed), *The Law of the European Community: A Commentary on the EEC Treaty*, Article 67 EEC (vol 2, Bender, New York 1999).

——in Dennis Campbell (ed), *The Law of the European Community: A Commentary on the EEC Treaty*, Article 68 EEC (vol 2, Bender, New York 1999).

Boos, Karl-Heinz, Reinfrid Fischer, and Hermann Schulte-Mattler (eds), *Kreditwesengesetz: Kommentar zu KWG und Ausführungsvorschriften* (2nd edn C.H. Beck, München 2004).

Booß, Dierk, in Carl Otto Lenz and Klaus-Dieter Borchert (eds), *EU- und EG Vertrag—Kommentar zu dem Vertrag über die Europäische Union und zu dem Vertrag zur Gründung der Europäischen Gemeinschaft, jeweils in der durch den Vertrag von Nizza geänderten Fassung*, Art. 295 EC (4th edn Bundesanzeiger, Helbing & Lichtenhahn, Linde, Köln, [et al] 2006).

Borchardt, Klaus-Dieter, *Die rechtlichen Grundlagen der Europäischen Union: eine systematische Darstellung für Studium und Praxis* (3th edn C.F. Müller, Heidelberg 2006).

Borchert, Manfred, *Basic Issues in International Monetary Economics* (Schriften zu internationalen Wirtschaftsfragen, vol 8, Duncker & Humblot, Berlin 1988).

Borchert, Manfred, *Außenwirtschaftslehre: Theorie und Politik* (6th edn Gabler, Wiesbaden 1999).

Börner, Bodo, 'Die fünfte Freiheit des Gemeinsamen Marktes: Der freie Zahlungsverkehr' in Walter Hallstein (ed), *Zur Integration Europas: Festschrift für Carl Friedrich Ophüls aus Anlaß seines siebzigsten Geburtstages* (C.F. Müller, Karlsruhe 1965).

Bothe, Michael, 'Die EU in Internationalen Umweltabkommen' in Charlotte Gaitanides, Stefan Kadelbach and Gil Carlos Rodriguez Iglesias (eds), *Europa und seine Verfassung: Festschrift für Manfred Zuleeg zum siebzigsten Geburtstag* (Nomos, Baden-Baden 2005), 688.

Bradlow, Daniel D, and Alfred Escher (eds), *Legal Aspects of Foreign Direct Investment* (Kluwer, The Hague [et al] 1999).

Brandl, Ulrike, 'Die Umsetzung der Sanktionsresolutionen des Sicherheitsrats in der EU' (2000) AVR 376.

Breier, Siegfried, 'Die völkerrechtliche Vertragsschlusskompetenz der Europäischen Gemeinschaft und ihrer Mitgliedstaaten im Bereich des Umweltschutzes' (1993) 28 EuR 340.

Brewer, Thomas L., and Stephen Young, 'European Union Policies and the Problems of Multinational Enterprises' (1995) 29 JWT 33.

Brinkmann, Jan, *Der Einfluß des europäischen Rechts auf die Unternehmensbesteuerung* (Nomos-Universitätsschriften, Nomos, Baden-Baden 1996).

Bröhmer, Jürgen (ed), *Internationale Gemeinschaft und Menschenrechte: Festschrift für Georg Ress zum 70. Geburtstag am 21. Januar 2005* (Heymanns, Köln [et al] 2005).

Bröhmer, Jürgen, in Christian Calliess and Matthias Ruffert (eds), *Kommentar des Vertrages über die Europäische Union und des Vertrages zur Gründung der Europäischen Gemeinschaft—EUV/EGV*, Art. 48 EC (2nd edn Luchterhand, Neuwied [et al] 2002).

——in Christian Calliess and Matthias Ruffert (eds), *Kommentar des Vertrages über die Europäische Union und des Vertrages zur Gründung der Europäischen Gemeinschaft—EUV/EGV*, Art. 56 EC (2nd edn Luchterhand, Neuwied [et al] 2002).

——in Christian Calliess and Matthias Ruffert (eds), *Kommentar des Vertrages über die Europäische Union und des Vertrages zur Gründung der Europäischen Gemeinschaft—EUV/EGV*, Art. 57 EC (2nd edn Luchterhand, Neuwied [et al] 2002).

Bröhmer, Jürgen, in Christian Calliess and Matthias Ruffert (eds), *Kommentar des Vertrages über die Europäische Union und des Vertrages zur Gründung der Europäischen Gemeinschaft - EUV/EGV*, Art. 58 EC (2nd edn Luchterhand, Neuwied [et al] 2002).
—— in Christian Calliess and Matthias Ruffert (eds), *EUV· EGV—Kommentar*, Art. 56 EC (3rd edn C.H. Beck, München 2007).
—— in Christian Calliess and Matthias Ruffert (eds), *EUV· EGV—Kommentar*, Art. 57 EC (3rd edn C.H. Beck, München 2007).
—— in Christian Calliess and Matthias Ruffert (eds), *EUV· EGV—Kommentar*, Art. 58 EC (3rd edn C.H. Beck, München 2007).
—— in Christian Calliess and Matthias Ruffert (eds), *EUV· EGV—Kommentar*, Art. 59 EC (3rd edn C.H. Beck, München 2007).
—— in Christian Calliess and Matthias Ruffert (eds), *EUV· EGV—Kommentar*, Art. 60 EC (3rd edn C.H. Beck, München 2007).
—— 'The Free Movement of Capital in the European Union and the Problem of "Golden Shares" and Similar Instruments' (2008) 25 Law in Context 144.
Brown, Catherine, and Martha O'Brien, 'National Report Canada' in Michael Lang and Pasquale Pistone (eds), *The EU and Third Countries: Direct Taxation* (Linde, Wien 2007), 683.
Buckley, Neil, Rebecca Bream, and Lina Saigol, 'Gazprom Warned on Centrica Interest' *Financial Times.com* (03.02.2006).
Bundesverband der deutschen Industrie e.V., and Freshfields Bruckhaus Deringer, *Mehr Schutz vor ausländischen Investoren?—Wirtschaftliche und EU-rechtliche Aspekte der geplanten Beschränkung ausländischer Beteiligungen an deutschen Unternehmen*, Study, (Berlin 2008).
Burgi, Martin, 'Anmerkung zu C-234/03 (Re Contse SA and others v. Instituto Nacional de Gestión Sanitaria (Ingesa), formerly Instituto Nacional de la Salud (Insalud))' (2006) JZ 305.
Cadosch, Roger M., et al, 'The 2006 Leiden Forum on Taxation of Cross-Border Dividends in Europe and The Relation with Third Countries: the Cases Pending Before the European Court of Justice' (2006) 34 Intertax 622.
Calliess, Christian, and Matthias Ruffert (eds), *Kommentar des Vertrages über die Europäische Union und des Vertrages zur Gründung der Europäischen Gemeinschaft— EUV/EGV* (2nd edn Luchterhand, Neuwied [et al] 2002).
—— (eds), *EUV· EGV—Kommentar* (3rd edn C.H. Beck, München 2007).
Campbell, Dennis (ed), *The Law of the European Community: A Commentary on the EEC Treaty* (Bender, New York 1999).
Cassese, Antonio, *International Law* (2nd edn Oxford University Press, Oxford [et al] 2005).
Center for International Legal Studies, et al (eds), *Smit & Herzog on The Law of the European Union* (LexisNexis Bender, New York 2005).
Cerny, Philip G, 'The Dynamics of Financial Globalization: Technology, Market Structure, and Policy Response' (1994) 27 Policy Sciences 319.
Ceyssens, Jan, 'Towards a Common Foreign Investment Policy?—Foreign Investment in the European Union' (2005) 32 LIEI 259.
Chalmers, Damian, et al, *European Union Law: Text and Materials* (Cambridge University Press, Cambridge [et al] 2006).
Chirathivat, Suthiphand, et al (eds), *European Union and ASEAN: Historical Dimensions, Comparative Analysis and Politico-Economic Dynamics* (Springer, Berlin [et al] 2005).

Classen, Claus Dieter, 'Auf dem Weg zu einer einheitlichen Dogmatik der EG-Grundfreiheiten?' (1995) EWS 97.
Coing, Helmut, Heinrich Kronstein, and Ernst-Joachim Mestmäcker (eds), *Wirtschaftsordnung und Rechtsordnung: Festschrift zum 70. Geburtstag von Franz Böhm am 16. Februar 1965* (C.F. Müller, Karlsruhe 1965).
Cordewener, Axel, *Europäische Grundfreiheiten und nationales Steuerrecht: 'Konvergenz' des Gemeinschaftsrechts und 'Kohärenz' der direkten Steuern in der Rechtsprechung des EuGH* (O. Schmidt, Köln 2002).
Cordewener, Axel, Georg Kofler, and Clemens Philipp Schindler, 'Free Movement of Capital, Third Country Relationships and National Tax Law: An Emerging Issue before the ECJ' (2007) 47 ET 107.
——'Free Movement of Capital and Third Countries: Exploring the Outer Boundaries with Lasertec, A and B and Holböck' (2007) 47 ET 371.
Craig, Paul P and Gráine de Búrca (eds), *The Evolution of EU Law* (Oxford University Press, Oxford [et al] 1999).
Craig, Paul P and Gráinne de Búrca, *EU Law: Text, Cases, and Materials* (3rd edn Oxford University Press, Oxford [et al] 2003).
——*EU Law: Text, Cases, and Materials* (4th edn Oxford University Press, Oxford [et al] 2008).
Cranston, Ross (ed), *The Single Market and the Law of Banking* (2nd edn Lloyd's of London Press, London [et al] 1995).
Cremona, Marise, 'External Relations and External Competence: The Emergence of an Integrated Policy' in Paul P Craig and Gráine de Búrca (eds), *The Evolution of EU Law* (Oxford University Press, Oxford [et al] 1999), 137.
Dahlberg, Mattias, *Direct Taxation in Relation to the Freedom of Establishment and the Free Movement of Capital* (EUCOTAX Series on European Taxation, Kluwer, The Hague 2005).
Dashwood, Alan, 'Hastening Slowly: The Community's Path Towards Harmonisation' in Helen Wallace, William Wallace and Mark A Pollack (eds), *Policy Making in the European Community* (2nd edn Wiley, Chichester 1983), 177.
——'The Attribution of External Relations Competence' in Alan Dashwood, Christophe Hillion and Centre for European Legal Studies Cambridge (eds), *The General Law of E.C. External Relations* (Sweet & Maxwell, London [et al] 2000), 115.
Dashwood, Alan and Joni Heliskoski, 'The Classic Authorities Revisited' in Alan Dashwood, Christophe Hillion and Centre for European Legal Studies Cambridge (eds), *The General Law of E.C. External Relations* (Sweet & Maxwell, London [et al] 2000), 3.
Dashwood, Alan, Christophe Hillion, and Centre for European Legal Studies Cambridge (eds), *The General Law of E.C. External Relations* (Sweet & Maxwell, London [et al] 2000).
Daude, Christian, and Marcel Fratzscher, *The Pecking Order of Cross-Border Investment, No. 590, Feb. 2006* (ECB Working Paper Series, 2006).
Dauses, Manfred A (ed), *Handbuch des EU-Wirtschaftsrechts* (C.H. Beck, München loose-leaf: October 2007).
——*Rechtliche Grundlagen der Europäischen Wirtschafts- und Währungsunion* (Europäisches Wirtschaftsrecht, Beck, München 2003).
Dautzenberg, Norbert, 'Die Ertragsbesteuerung des Kapitaleinkommens in der EU: Zur Bestimmung des Begriffs "Kapitalanlageort" in Art. 73 d EGV' (1997) EWS 379.

Dautzenberg, Norbert, 'Die Wegzugsbesteuerung des § 6 AStG im Lichte des EG-Rechts' (1997) 52 BB 180.
——'2. Anmerkung zu BFH, Beschluß v. 17.12.1997, I B 108/97' (1998) IStR 301.
——'Die Bedeutung des EG-Vertrages für die Erbschaftssteuer' (1998) EWS 86.
——'Die Kapitalverkehrsfreiheit des EG-Vertrages, der Steuervorbehalt des Art. 73d EGV und die Folgen für die Besteuerung' (1998) RIW 537.
——'Die Kapitalverkehrsfreiheit des EG-Vertrags und die direkten Steuern: Auswirkungen aus dem Grundsatzurteil des EuGH vom 6.6.2000 in der Rechtssache Verkooijen' (2000) StuB 720.
——'Anmerkung zu EuGH, Urteil vom 12.12.2002—Rs. C-324/00; Lankhorst-Hohorst GmbH gegen FA Steinfurt' (2003) 58 BB 193.
——'Der steuerliche Status Liechtensteins in Europa' (2003) StuB 1126.
de Bont, Guido, 'Taxation and the Free Movement of Capital and Payments' (1995) 4 EC Tax Review 136.
De Ceulaer, Stefaan, 'Community Most-Favoured-Nation Treatment: One Step Closer to the Multilateralisation of Income Tax Treaties in the European Union' (2003) 57 BIFD 493.
de la Torre, Fernando Castillo, 'Joined Cases C-163/94, C-165/94 and C-250/94, Criminal Proceedings against L.E. Sanz de Lera, R. Díaz Jiménez and F. Kapanoglu, Judgment of 14 December 1995, [1995] ECR I-4821' (1996) 33 CMLR 1065.
Dempsey, Judy, 'EU Considers Adding Protectionist Measures to Energy Policy' *International Herald Tribune* (18.09.2007).
Dichtl, Erwin, and Otmar Issing (eds), *Vahlens Großes Wirtschaftslexikon* (vol 1, 2nd edn C.H. Beck / Franz Vahlen, München 1993).
Digel, Andreas Clemens, 'Die primärrechtlichen Grundlagen des Europäischen Finanzmarktes' (Inaugural-Dissertation, Eberhard-Karls-Universität 2006).
Doehring, Karl, *Völkerrecht* (2nd edn C.F. Müller, Heidelberg 2004).
Doggart, Caroline, *Steuerparadiese—und wie man sie nutzt* (4th edn Schaeffer-Poeschel, Stuttgart 2002).
——*Tax Havens and Their Uses* (4th edn Economist Intelligence Unit, London 2002).
Dölker, Angelika, and Martin Ribbrock, 'Die Kapitalverkehrsfreiheit im Verhältnis zu Drittstaaten—nunmehr gefestigte EuGH-Rechtsprechung?!' (2007) 62 BB 1928.
Dolzer, Rudolf, 'Wirtschaft und Kultur im Völkerrecht' in Wolfgang Graf Vitzthum (ed), *Völkerrecht* (4th edn de Gruyter, Berlin 2007), 491.
Dougherty, Carter, 'Europe Looks at Controls on State-owned Investors' *International Herald Tribune* (13.07.2007).
Dreher, Meinrad, and André Görner, 'Art. 49 EG 1/07' (2007) 23 EWiR 43.
Drewes, Detlef, 'Prosche ja, Gasprom nein' *Spiegel Online* (23.10.2007).
Due, Ole, Marcus Lutter, and Jürgen Schwarze (eds), *Festschrift für Ulrich Everling* (Nomos, Baden-Baden 1995).
Eberhartinger, Michael, 'Konvergenz und Neustrukturierung der Grundfreiheiten' (1997) EWS 43.
Eckhoff, Rolf, 'Die Freiheit des Kapital- und Zahlungsverkehrs' in Albert Bleckmann (ed), *Europarecht: Das Recht der Europäischen Union und der Europäischen Gemeinschaften* (6th edn Heymanns, Köln [et al] 1997), 617.
Eeckhout, Piet, *External Relations of the European Union: Legal and Constitutional Foundations* (Oxford University Press, Oxford [et al] 2004).

Ehlers, Dirk (ed), *Europäische Grundrechte und Grundfreiheiten* (2nd edn de Gruyter, Berlin 2005).
Ehlers, Dirk, 'Allgemeine Lehren' in Dirk Ehlers (ed), *Europäische Grundrechte und Grundfreiheiten*, 177 (2nd edn de Gruyter, Berlin 2005).
Eicker, Klaus, and Ralph Obser, 'Die Kapitalverkehrsfreiheit bekommt Konturen—zugleich Anmerkung zu den Schlussanträgen in den Rechtssachen Weidert und Paulus, Manninen und Lenz' (2004) 13 IStR 443.
Eilers, Stephan, Jochen Bahns, and Michael Sedlaczek, in Hans von der Groeben and Jürgen Schwarze (eds), *Kommentar zum Vertrag über die Europäische Union und zur Gründung der Europäischen Gemeinschaft*, Vorb. zu den Art. 90 bis 93 EC (vol 2, 6th edn Nomos, Baden-Baden 2003).
——in Hans von der Groeben and Jürgen Schwarze (eds), *Kommentar zum Vertrag über die Europäische Union und zur Gründung der Europäischen Gemeinschaft*, Art. 93 EC (vol 2, 6th edn Nomos, Baden-Baden 2003)
Epiney, Astrid, in Christian Calliess and Matthias Ruffert (eds), *Kommentar des Vertrages über die Europäische Union und des Vertrages zur Gründung der Europäischen Gemeinschaft - EUV/EGV*, Art. 12 EC (2nd edn Luchterhand, Neuwied [et al] 2002).
——'Freiheit des Warenverkehrs' in Dirk Ehlers (ed), *Europäische Grundrechte und Grundfreiheiten* (2nd edn de Gruyter, Berlin 2005), 227.
——*Umgekehrte Diskriminierungen: Zulässigkeit und Grenzen der discrimination à rebours nach europäischem Gemeinschaftsrecht und nationalem Verfassungsrecht* (Völkerrecht, Europarecht, Staatsrecht, Heymanns, Köln [et al] 1995).
——'Zur Tragweite des Art. 10 EGV im Bereich der Außenbeziehungen' in Jürgen Bröhmer (ed), *Internationale Gemeinschaft und Menschenrechte: Festschrift für Georg Ress zum 70. Geburtstag am 21. Januar 2005* (Heymanns, Köln [et al] 2005), 441.
Epiney, Astrid, and Dominique Gross, 'Zur Abgrenzung der Außenkompetenzen von Gemeinschaft und Mitgliedstaaten im Umweltrecht' (2004) JbUmweltTechnR 27.
——'Zur Abgrenzung der Kompetenzen zwischen der Gemeinschaft und den Mitgliedstaaten bei der Durchführung völkerrechtlicher Verträge' (2004) 1 EurUP 2.
Epping, Volker, '§ 6 Völkerrechtssubjekte : Internationale Organisationen' in Knut Ipsen (ed), *Völkerrecht*, 83 (5th edn C.H. Beck, München 2004).
——'§ 31 Internationale Organisationen : Grundlagen' in Knut Ipsen (ed), *Völkerrecht* (5th edn C.H. Beck, München 2004), 444.
Everling, Ulrich, in Ernst Wohlfarth, et al (eds), *Die Europäische Wirtschaftsgemeinschaft: Kommentar zum Vertrag*, Art. 67 EEC (Vahlen, Berlin 1960).
Fassbender, Bardo, 'Die Völkerrechtssubjektivität der Europäischen Union' (2004) 42 AVR 26.
Fischer, Anne, 'Die Kapitalverkehrsfreiheit in der Rechtsprechung des EuGH—Entscheidungen 'Trummer & Mayer' vom 16. März 1999 und 'Konle/Österreich' vom 1. Juni 1999' (2000) 3 ZEuS 391.
Fischer, Bernhard, and Helmut Reisen, *Zum Abbau von Kapitalverkehrskontrollen: ein Liberalisierungs-Fahrplan* (Veröffentlichungen des HWWA-Institut für Wirtschaftsforschung Hamburg, Weltarchiv, Hamburg 1992).
Fischer, Horst, '§ 59 Friedenssicherung und friedliche Streitbeilegung: Gewaltverbot, Selbstverteidigungsrecht und Intervention im gegenwärtigen Völkerrecht' in Knut Ipsen (ed), *Völkerrecht*, 1065 (5th edn C.H. Beck, München 2004).

Fleischer, Holger, 'Die Haftung des Verkäufers von Gesellschaftsanteilen' (1998) WM 849.
Flynn, Leo, 'Coming of Age: the Free Movement of Capital Case Law 1993–2002' (2002) 39 CMLR 773.
Follak, Klaus-Peter, 'International Harmonization of Banking Supervision and Regulation' in Albrecht Weber and Ludwig Gramlich (eds), *Währung und Wirtschaft: das Geld im Recht: Festschrift für Prof. Dr. Hugo J. Hahn zum 70. Geburtstag* (Nomos, Baden-Baden 1997), 379.
Follak, Klaus-Peter, 'Kapital- und Zahlungsverkehr' in Manfred A Dauses (ed), *Handbuch des EU-Wirtschaftsrechts*, loose-leaf; chapter F. II (vol 1, Beck, München 2002).
Förster, Philipp, *Die unmittelbare Drittwirkung der Grundfreiheiten: zur Dogmatik des Adressatenkreises von Pflichten aus EG-Grundfreiheiten* (Schriften zum deutschen und europäischen öffentlichen Recht, Lang, Frankfurt am Main [et al] 2007).
Fowle, Michael, and Alan Smith, 'The European Union Single Banking and Finance Market: Its Impact on European Banks, Their Structure, Operations and Accounts' in Ross Cranston (ed), *The Single Market and the Law of Banking* (2nd edn Lloyd's of London Press, London [et. al.] 1995), 75.
Freitag, Robert, 'Mitgliedstaatliche Beschränkungen des Kapitalverkehrs und Europäisches Gemeinschaftsrecht' (1997) 8 EWS 186.
——'§ 8a KStG 1/07' (2007) 23 EWiR 571.
Frenz, Walter, *Außenkompetenzen der Europäischen Gemeinschaften und der Mitgliedstaaten im Umweltbereich: Reichweite und Wahrnehmung* (Schriften zum europäischen Recht, Duncker & Humblot, Berlin 2001).
——*Handbuch Europarecht* (vol 1, Springer, Berlin [et al] 2004).
Frid, Rachel, *The Relations between the EC and International Organizations: Legal Theory and Practice* (Legal Aspects of International Organization, Kluwer, The Hague [et al] 1995).
Friedrich, Klaus, in Ernst Hocke, et al (eds), *Außenwirtschaftsrecht: Gesetze, Verordnungen und Erlasse zum Außenwirtschaftsrecht mit Kommentar*, § 52 AWV (vol 1, R. v. Decker, Heidelberg 2006).
Fröhlich, Hans-Peter, *Freier Kapitalverkehr in Europa* (Beiträge zur Wirtschafts- und Sozialpolitik, Dt. Inst.-Verlag., Köln 1990).
Fuchs, Andreas (ed), *Wirtschafts- und Privatrecht im Spannungsfeld von Privatautonomie, Wettbewerb und Regulierung: Festschrift für Ulrich Immenga zum 70. Geburtstag* (Beck, München 2004).
Fuller, Thomas, 'French Fear Eye of 'Ogre' is on Danone' *International Herald Tribune* (21.07.2005).
Gabler Wirtschaftslexikon (vol 1 (A–D), 15th edn Gabler, Wiesbaden 2000).
Gabler Wirtschaftslexikon (vol 3 (K–R), 15th edn Gabler, Wiesbaden 2000).
Ganten, Ted Oliver, *Die Drittwirkung der Grundfreiheiten: die EG-Grundfreiheiten als Grenze der Handlungs- und Vertragsfreiheit im Verhältnis zwischen Privaten* (Untersuchungen zum europäischen Privatrecht, Duncker & Humblot, Berlin 2000).
Garçon, Gérardine, *Handelsembargen der Europäischen Union auf dem Gebiet des Warenverkehrs gegenüber Drittländern: im Lichte der Änderungen durch den Maastrichter Vertrag und des Völkerrechts* (Saarbrücker Studien zum internationalen Recht, Nomos, Baden-Baden 1997).
'Gazprom kreuzt die Klinge mit Brüssel: Russlands Gasgigant will expandieren und stößt dabei auf Widerstand' *Handelsblatt* (26.04.2006).

Geiger, Rudolf, *EUV, EGV: Vertrag über die Europäische Union und Vertrag zur Gründung der Europäischen Gemeinschaft* (4th edn C.H. Beck, München 2004).

——'Vertragsschlußkompetenzen der Europäischen Gemeinschaft und auswärtige Gewalt der Mitgliedstaaten' (1995) 50 JZ 973.

Georgiadou, Afroditi-Sofia, *The Regulation of Foreign Direct Investments under International, European and Greek Law, with a Special Reference to Financial Services' Investments* (Sakkoulas, Athens 2004).

Geurts, Matthias, 'Das Konkurrenzverhältnis der EU-Grundfreiheiten: Zugleich eine Anmerkung zu EuGH Baars Rs. C 251/98' (2000) 9 IStR 572.

Gilpin, Robert, *Global Political Economy: Understanding the International Economic Order* (Princeton University Press, Princeton 2001).

Gilsdorf, Peter, and Barbara Brandtner, in Hans von der Groeben and Jürgen Schwarze (eds), *Kommentar zum Vertrag über die Europäische Union und zur Gründung der Europäischen Gemeinschaft*, Art. 301 EC (vol 4, 6th edn Nomos, Baden-Baden 2004).

Glaesner, Adrian, in Jürgen Schwarze (ed), *EU-Kommentar*, Art. 56 EC (Nomos, Baden-Baden 2000).

——in Jürgen Schwarze (ed), *EU-Kommentar*, Art. 57 EC (Nomos, Baden-Baden 2000).

——in Jürgen Schwarze (ed), *EU-Kommentar*, Art. 58 EC (Nomos, Baden-Baden 2000).

——in Jürgen Schwarze (ed), *EU-Kommentar*, Art. 60 EC (Nomos, Baden-Baden 2000).

Glöckner, Jochen, 'Grundverkehrsbeschränkungen und Europarecht' (2000) 35 EuR 592.

Gocke, Rudolf, Dietmar Gosch, and Michael Lang (eds), *Festschrift für Franz Wassermeyer* (C.H. Beck, München 2005).

Golub, Stephen S., 'Measures of Restrictions on Inward Foreign Direct Investment for OECD Countries' (Online Working Paper, OECD, Paris 2003) <http://www.olis.oecd.org/olis/2003doc.nsf/809a2d78518a8277c125685d005300b2/499a6d0cfebef77bc1256d390039ce23/$FILE/JT00145291.PDF> accessed 21.10.2007.

Gomel, Giorgio, *Implications of the Euro for International Monetary Relations: A Pole of Attraction in Europe and in the Mediterranean Basin, RSC No. 2001/34* (EUI Working Papers, 2001).

Grabitz, Eberhard, Armin von Bogdandy, and Martin Nettesheim (eds), *Europäisches Außenwirtschaftsrecht* (C.H. Beck, München 1994).

Grabitz, Eberhard, 'Das Recht auf Zugang zum Markt nach dem EWG-Vertrag' in Rolf Stödter (ed), *Hamburg, Deutschland, Europa: Beiträge zum deutschen und europäischen Verfassungs-, Verwaltungs- und Wirtschaftsrecht; Festschrift für Hans Peter Ipsen zum 70. Geburtstag* (Mohr Siebeck, Tübingen 1977), 645.

Graf Vitzthum, Wolfgang (ed), *Völkerrecht* (4th edn de Gruyter, Berlin 2007).

Graf Vitzthum, Wolfgang, Rostane Mehdi, and Catherine Prieto (eds), *Europe et mondialisation : actes du colloque de la Faculté de Droit et Science Politique d'Aix-Marseille et de la Faculté de Droit de l'Université de Tübingen (Aix-en-Provence 21–22 octobre 2004)* (Presses Universitaires d'Aix-Marseille, Aix-en-Provence 2006).

Graham, Edward M, 'Foreign Direct Investment' in Peter Newman, Murray Milgate, and John Eatwell (eds), *The New Palgrave Dictionary of Money & Finance* (vol 2, Macmillan Press, London 1992), 147.

Greider, William, *One World, Ready or Not: The Manic Logic of Global Capitalism* (Simon & Schuster, New York 1997).
Griller, Stefan, and Birgit Weidel (eds), *External Economic Relations and Foreign Policy in the European Union* (Springer, Wien 2002).
Griller, Stefan, and Katharina Gamharter, 'External Trade: Is there a Path Through the Maze of Competences?' in Stefan Griller and Birgit Weidel (eds), *External Economic Relations and Foreign Policy in the European Union* (Springer, Wien 2002), 65.
Groß, Wolfgang, *Direktinvestitionen und europäische Integration dargestellt am Beispiel der Bundesrepublik Deutschland* (Konstanzer Schriften zur Rechtswissenschaft, Hartung-Gorre, Konstanz 1989).
Grundmann, Stefan, and Florian Möslein, 'Die Goldene Aktie: Staatskontrolle in Europarecht und wirtschaftspolitischer Bewertung' (2003) ZGR 317.
Gutmann, Daniel, 'The Marks & Spencer Case: Proposals for an Alternative Way of Reasoning' (2003) 12 EC Tax Review 154.
Haasis, Heinrich, 'Sollten sensible Schlüsselindustrien vor der Übernahme durch ausländische Staatsfonds geschützt werden?' (2008) 61 Kreditwesen 14.
Habersack, Mathias, et al (eds), *Festschrift für Peter Ulmer zum 70. Geburtstag am 2. Januar 2003* (de Gruyter, Berlin 2003).
Häde, Ulrich, *Finanzausgleich: die Verteilung der Aufgaben, Ausgaben und Einnahmen im Recht der Bundesrepublik Deutschland und der Europäischen Union* (Jus publicum, Mohr Siebeck, Tübingen 1996).
——in Christian Calliess and Matthias Ruffert (eds), *EUV · EGV—Kommentar*, Art. 100 EC (3rd edn C.H. Beck, München 2007).
——, in Christian Calliess and Matthias Ruffert (eds), *EUV · EGV—Kommentar*, Art. 119 EC (3. edn C.H. Beck, München 2007).
Haferkamp, Ute, *Die Kapitalverkehrsfreiheit im System der Grundfreiheiten des EG-Vertrages* (Nomos, Baden-Baden 2003).
Hahn, Hartmut, *Die Vereinbarkeit von Normen des deutschen internationalen Steuerrechts mit EG-Recht* (IFSt-Schriften, vol 378, Institut 'Finanzen und Steuern' e.V., Bonn 1999).
——'Von Spartanern und Athenern—zum Beschluss des BFH vom 17.12.1997 zur Vereinbarkeit des § 6 AStG mit dem EGV, zu seinen Kritikern und zugleich ein Beitrag zur Dogmatik der Grundfreiheiten des EGV' (2000) DStZ 14.
Hallstein, Walter (ed), *Zur Integration Europas: Festschrift für Carl Friedrich Ophüls aus Anlaß seines siebzigsten Geburtstages* (C.F. Müller, Karlsruhe 1965).
Haltern, Ulrich, 'Pathos and Patina: The Failure and Promise of Constitutionalism in the European Imagination' (2003) 9 ELJ 14.
Haratsch, Andreas, Christian Koenig, and Matthias Pechstein, *Europarecht* (5th edn Mohr Siebeck, Tübingen 2006).
Harings, Lothar, 'Die EG als Rechtsgemeinschaft (?)—EuG versagt Individualrechtsschutz' (2005) 16 EuZW 705.
Hartley, Trevor Clayton, *European Union Law in a Global Context* (Cambridge University Press, Cambridge [et al] 2004).
Harz, Annegret, *Die Schutzklauseln des Kapital- und Zahlungsverkehrs im EWG-Vertrag* (Studien zum internationalen Wirtschaftsrecht und Atomenergierecht, Heymanns, Köln [et al] 1985).
Hasse, Rolf, and Joachim Starbatty (eds), *Wirtschafts- und Währungsunion auf dem Prüfstand: Schritte zur weiteren Integration Europas* (Lucius & Lucius, Stuttgart 1997).

Hasse, Rolf, and Joachim Starbatty, 'Überlegungen und Empfehlungen der Aktionsgemeinschaft Soziale Marktwirtschaft zur Währungsunion' in Rolf Hasse and Joachim Starbatty (eds), *Wirtschafts- und Währungsunion auf dem Prüfstand: Schritte zur weiteren Integration Europas* (Lucius & Lucius, Stuttgart 1997), 121.

Hatje, Armin, 'Wirtschaftsverfassung' in Armin von Bogdandy (ed), *Europäisches Verfassungsrecht: Theoretische und dogmatische Grundzüge* (Springer, Berlin [et al] 2003), 683.

Heintschel von Heinegg, Wolff, 'EG im Verhältnis zu internationalen Organisationen und Einrichtungen' in Hans-Werner Rengeling (ed), *Handbuch zum europäischen und deutschen Umweltrecht: eine systematische Darstellung des europäischen Umweltrechts mit seinen Auswirkungen auf das deutsche Recht und mit rechtspolitischen Perspektiven*, § 22 (vol 1, 2nd edn Heymanns, Köln [et al] 2003).

Heliskoski, Joni, *Mixed Agreements as a Technique for Organizing the International Relations of the European Community and its Member States* (The Erik Castrén Institute Monographs on International Law and Human Rights, Kluwer, The Hague [et al] 2001).

Hennes, Markus, 'Luxemburg hilft Arcelor im Kampf gegen Mittal' *Handelsblatt* (16.03.2006).

Henrichsmeyer, Wilhelm, Oskar Gans, and Ingo Evers, *Einführung in die Volkswirtschaftslehre* (UTB für Wissenschaft: Uni-Taschenbücher, 10th edn Ulmer, Stuttgart 1993).

Herzig, Norbert, and Norbert Dautzenberg, 'Der EWG-Vertrag und die Doppelbesteuerungsabkommen—Rechtsfragen im Verhältnis zwischen Doppelbesteuerungsabkommen und den Diskriminierungsverboten des EWGV' (1992) 45 DB 2519.

Heselhaus, Sebastian, 'Rechtfertigung unmittelbar diskriminierender Eingriffe in die Warenverkehrsfreiheit' (2001) 12 EuZW 645.

Hey, Johanna, 'Perspektiven der Unternehmensbesteuerung in Europa' (2004) StuW 193.

Heydt, Volker, 'Der Funktionswandel der EG-Grundfreiheiten infolge der Verwirklichung des Binnenmarktes' (1993) 4 EuZW 105.

Hindelang, Steffen, 'The EC Treaty's Freedom of Capital Movement as an Instrument of International Investment Law?—The Scope of Article 56(1) TEC in a Third Country Context and the Influence of Competing Freedoms' in August Reinisch and Christina Knahr (eds), *International Investment Law in Context* (Eleven International Publishing, Utrecht 2007), 43.

——'Wie viel Freiheit wagen?: Das Verhältnis von EG Kapitalverkehrs- und Niederlassungsfreiheit und die Reglementierung von Direktinvestitionen in und aus Drittstaaten' in August Reinisch and Christina Knahr (eds), *Aktuelle Probleme und Entwicklungen im Internationalen Investitionsrecht* (Boorberg, Stuttgart 2008), 83.

Hinnekens, Luc, 'Compatibility of Bilateral Tax Treaties with European Community Law—Application of the Rules' (1995) 4 EC Tax Review 202.

Hintersteininger, Margit, *Binnenmarkt und Diskriminierungsverbot: unter besonderer Berücksichtigung der Situation nicht-staatlicher Handlungseinheiten* (Schriften zum europäischen Recht, Duncker & Humblot, Berlin 1999).

Hirsch, Günter, 'Die aktuelle Rechtsprechung des EuGH zur Warenverkehrsfreiheit' (1999) 2 ZEuS 503.

Hocke, Ernst, et al (eds), *Außenwirtschaftsrecht : Gesetze, Verordnungen und Erlasse zum Außenwirtschaftsrecht mit Kommentar* (R. v. Decker, Heidelberg loose-leaf: April 2008).

Hoffmann, Bernd von, *Internationales Privatrecht einschließlich der Grundzüge des internationalen Zivilverfahrensrechts* (6th edn C.H. Beck, München 2000).
Hoffmann, Michael, *Die Grundfreiheiten des EG-Vertrags als koordinationsrechtliche und gleichheitsrechtliche Abwehrrechte* (Schriftenreihe Europäisches Recht, Politik und Wirtschaft, Nomos, Baden-Baden 2000).
Hohenwarter, Daniela, and Patrick Plansky, 'Besteuerung von Erbschaften nach Wegzug in einen Drittstaat im Gemeinschaftsrecht—Schlussanträge des GA Léger in der Rs. van Hilten-van der Heijden' (2005) 15 SWI 417.
Hohenwarter, Daniela, 'Vorlagebeschluss des VwGH zur Kapitalverkehrsfreiheit im Verhältnis zu Drittstaaten' (2005) 15 SWI 225.
Honrath, Alexander, *Umfang und Grenzen der Freiheit des Kapitalverkehrs: die Möglichkeiten zur Einführung einer Devisenzwangsbewirtschaftung in der Europäischen Union* (Schriften des Europa-Instituts der Universität des Saarlandes—Rechtswissenschaft, vol 18, Nomos, Baden-Baden 1998).
Hörmann, Saskia, 'Völkerrecht bricht Rechtsgemeinschaftsrecht? Zu den rechtlichen Folgen einer Umsetzung von Resolutionen des UN-Sicherheitsrats durch die EG' (2006) 44 AVR 267.
Horn, Norbert, 'Die Freiheit des Kapitalverkehrs in der EWG und der einheitliche Kapitalmarkt' in Uwe Blaurock (ed), *Das Bankwesen in der Gemeinschaft* (Nomos, Baden-Baden 1981), 47.
Hummel, Detlev, and Rolf-E Breuer (eds), *Handbuch Europäischer Kapitalmarkt* (Gabler, Wiesbaden 2001).
Hummer, Waldemar, 'Das griechische Embargo' in Ole Due, Marcus Lutter, and Jürgen Schwarze (eds), *Festschrift für Ulrich Everling* (vol 1, Nomos, Baden-Baden 1995), 511.
Hymer, Stephen Herbert, *The International Operations of National Firms: A Study of Direct Foreign Investment* (M.I.T. Monographs in Economics, MIT-Press, Cambridge 1976).
'Industrie will keinen Schutzzaun gegen Investoren—Verstoß gegen EU-Recht beklagt/"Die jetzigen Regeln reichen aus"' *Frankfurter Allgemeine Zeitung* (05.08.2008).
International Institute for Sustainable Development, 'EU Governments Debate Euro Commission's Investment Negotiating Ideas' [2006] ITN <http://www.iisd.org/> accessed 12.12.2005.
International Institute for Sustainable Development, 'European Govts Remain Split over Extent of Investment Provisions in EU FTAs' [2007] ITN <http://www.iisd.org/> accessed 16.03.2007.
Ipsen, Hans Peter, *Europäisches Gemeinschaftsrecht* (Mohr Siebeck, Tübingen 1972).
Ipsen, Knut (ed), *Völkerrecht* (5th edn C.H. Beck, München 2004).
Jaensch, Michael, *Die unmittelbare Drittwirkung der Grundfreiheiten: Untersuchung der Verpflichtung von Privatpersonen durch Art. 30, 48, 52, 59, 73b EGV* (Nomos-Universitätsschriften, Nomos, Baden-Baden 1997).
Jarass, Hans D, 'Elemente einer Dogmatik der Grundfreiheiten' (1995) 30 EuR 202.
——'Elemente einer Dogmatik der Grundfreiheiten II' (2000) 35 EuR 705.
Jen, Stephen, 'How Big Could Sovereign Wealth Funds Be by 2015?' (Morgan Stanley Research, London 2007).
Jestaedt, Thomas, and Florian Kästle, 'Kehrtwende oder Rückbesinnung in der Anwendung von Art. 30 EGV: Das Keck-Urteil' (1994) EWS 26.

Jones, Avery J. F., 'Carry On Discriminating' (1996) 36 ET 46.
Jones, John A., 'Flows of Capital between the EU and third Countries and the Consequences of Disharmony in European International Tax Law' (1998) 7 EC Tax Review 95.
Jung, Alexander, Matthias Schepp, and Benjamin Triebe, 'Märchenhafter Reichtum' *Der Spiegel*, 176 (31.03.2008).
Jürgensen, Thomas, and Irene Schlünder, 'EG-Grundrechtsschutz gegenüber Maßnahmen der Mitgliedstaaten' (1996) AöR 200.
Kaass, Jan, *Europäische Grundfreiheiten und deutsche Erbschaftsteuer: zur erbschaftsteuerlichen Behandlung grenzüberschreitender Sachverhalte* (Lang, Frankfurt am Main [et al] 2000).
Kainer, Friedemann, *Unternehmensübernahmen im Binnenmarktrecht: zugleich ein Beitrag zur Privatrechtswirkung der Grundfreiheiten* (Heidelberger Schriften zum Wirtschaftsrecht und Europarecht, Nomos, Baden-Baden 2004).
Kamann, Hans-Georg, in Rudolf Streinz (ed), *EUV/EGV: Vertrag über die Europäische Union und Vertrag zur Gründung der Europäischen Gemeinschaft*, Art. 90 EC (Beck, München 2003).
——in Rudolf Streinz (ed), *EUV/EGV: Vertrag über die Europäische Union und Vertrag zur Gründung der Europäischen Gemeinschaft*, Art. 93 EC (Beck, München 2003).
Karl, Joachim, 'The Competence for Foreign Direct Investment: New Powers for the European Union' (2004) 5 JWIT 413.
Kekic, Laza, 'Global Foreign Direct Investment to 2011' in The Economist Intelligence Unit (ed), *World Investment Prospects to 2011: Foreign Direct Investment and the Challenge of Political Risk* (The Economist Intelligence Unit, London 2007), 18.
Kempen, Bernhard, in Rudolf Streinz (ed), *EUV/EGV: Vertrag über die Europäische Union und Vertrag zur Gründung der Europäischen Gemeinschaft*, Art. 105 EC (C.H. Beck, München 2003).
——in Rudolf Streinz (ed), *EUV/EGV: Vertrag über die Europäische Union und Vertrag zur Gründung der Europäischen Gemeinschaft*, Art. 119 EC (C.H. Beck, München 2003).
——in Rudolf Streinz (ed), *EUV/EGV: Vertrag über die Europäische Union und Vertrag zur Gründung der Europäischen Gemeinschaft*, Art. 120 EC (C.H. Beck, München 2003).
Kessler, Wolfgang, Klaus Eicker, and Ralph Obser, 'Die Gesellschafter-Fremdfinanzierung im Lichte der Kapitalverkehrsfreiheit' (2004) 13 IStR 325.
——'Die Schweiz und das Europäische Steuerrecht—Der Einfluß des Europäischen Gemeinschaftsrechts auf das Recht der direkten Steuern im Verhältnis zu Drittstaaten am Beispiel der Schweiz' (2005) 14 IStR 658.
Kiemel, Wolfgang, in Hans von der Groeben, Jochen Thiesing and Claus-Dieter Ehlermann (eds), *Kommentar zum EWG-Vertrag*, Art. 67 EEC (vol 1, 4th edn Nomos, Baden-Baden 1991).
——in Hans von der Groeben, Jochen Thiesing, and Claus-Dieter Ehlermann (eds), *Kommentar zum EWG-Vertrag*, Vorbemerkungen zu den Artikeln 67 bis 73 EEC (vol 1, 4th edn Nomos, Baden-Baden 1991).
——in Hans von der Groeben and Jürgen Schwarze (eds), *Kommentar zum Vertrag über die Europäische Union und zur Gründung der Europäischen Gemeinschaft*, Art. 56 EC (vol 1, 6th edn Nomos, Baden-Baden 2003).

Kiemel, Wolfgang, in Hans von der Groeben and Jürgen Schwarze (eds), *Kommentar zum Vertrag über die Europäische Union und zur Gründung der Europäischen Gemeinschaft*, Art. 57 EC (vol 1, 6th edn Nomos, Baden-Baden 2003).
—— in Hans von der Groeben and Jürgen Schwarze (eds), *Kommentar zum Vertrag über die Europäische Union und zur Gründung der Europäischen Gemeinschaft*, Art. 58 EC (vol 1, 6th edn Nomos, Baden-Baden 2003).
—— in Hans von der Groeben and Jürgen Schwarze (eds), *Kommentar zum Vertrag über die Europäische Union und zur Gründung der Europäischen Gemeinschaft*, Art. 59 EC (vol 1, 6th edn Nomos, Baden-Baden 2003).
—— in Hans von der Groeben and Jürgen Schwarze (eds), *Kommentar zum Vertrag über die Europäische Union und zur Gründung der Europäischen Gemeinschaft*, Art. 60 EC (vol 1, 6th edn Nomos, Baden-Baden 2003).
—— in Hans von der Groeben and Jürgen Schwarze (eds), *Kommentar zum Vertrag über die Europäische Union und zur Gründung der Europäischen Gemeinschaft*, Vorbem. zu den Artikeln 56 bis 60 EC (vol 1, 6th edn Nomos, Baden-Baden 2003).
Kierkegaard, Søren, *The Concept of Anxiety* (Kierkegaard's Writings, vol 8, Princeton University Press, Princeton 1981).
Kilches, Ralph, 'Ersatzbeurkundungstatbestand bei Auslandsdarlehen gemeinschaftsrechtswidrig!' (1999) Ecolex 571.
Kilian, Wolfgang, *Europäisches Wirtschaftsrecht* (2nd edn Beck, München 2003).
Kimms, Frank, *Die Kapitalverkehrsfreiheit im Recht der europäischen Union* (Lang, Frankfurt am Main [et al] 1996).
Kindleberger, Charles P, 'The Pros and Cons of an International Capital Market' (1967) 123 ZGesStW 600.
Kingreen, Thorsten, *Die Struktur der Grundfreiheiten des Europäischen Gemeinschaftsrechts* (Schriften zum europäischen Recht, Duncker & Humblot, Berlin 1999).
—— in Christian Calliess and Matthias Ruffert (eds), *Kommentar des Vertrages über die Europäische Union und des Vertrages zur Gründung der Europäischen Gemeinschaft—EUV/EGV*, Art. 295 EC (2nd edn Luchterhand, Neuwied [et al] 2002).
—— 'Fundamental Freedoms' in Armin von Bogdandy and Jürgen Bast (eds), *Principles of European Constitutional Law* (Hart, Oxford [et al] 2005), 549.
Kingreen, Thorsten, and Rainer Störmer, 'Die subjetiv-öffentlichen Rechte des primären Gemeinschaftsrechts' (1998) 33 EuR 263.
Kingston, Suzanne, 'A Light in the Darkness: Recent Developments in the ECJ's Direct Tax Jurisprudence' (2007) 44 CMLR 1321.
Kirchhoff, Wolfgang, 'Die 'Festung Europa'—begründete Angst unserer Handelspartner oder politisches Schlagwort?: Ein Überblick zum Außenwirtschaftsrecht der EG im Hinblick auf 1993' (1991) 37 RIW 533.
Kirkpatrick, Betty, *Roget's Thesaurus of English Words & Phrases* (7th edn Penguin Books, London [et al] 1998).
Kleinschmit, *Deutsches Volkswagengesetz und Europäische Kapitalverkehrsfreiheit: Zur Auslegung einer Grundfreiheit unter besonderer Berücksichtigung der 'Goldene Aktien'-Judikatur des EuGH* (Cuvillier Verlag, Göttingen 2004).
Knapp, Andreas, 'Diskriminierende Grunderwerbsbeschränkungen' (1999) EWS 409.
Knobbe-Keuk, Brigitte, 'Restrictions on the Fundamental Freedoms Enshrined in the EC Treaty by Discriminatory Tax Provisions—Ban and Justification' (1994) EC Tax Review 74.

——'The Ruding Committee Report—An Impressive Vision of European Company Taxation for the Year 2000' (1992) 1 EC Tax Review 22.
Koenig, Christian, and Andreas Haratsch, *Europarecht* (4th edn Mohr Siebeck, Tübingen 2003).
Koenig, Christian, and Jürgen Kühling, in Rudolf Streinz (ed), *EUV/EGV: Vertrag über die Europäische Union und Vertrag zur Gründung der Europäischen Gemeinschaft*, Art. 295 EC (C.H. Beck, München 2003).
Kofler, Georg, 'Hughes de Lasteyrie Du Saillant: Wegzugsbesteuerung verstößt gegen die Niederlassungsfreiheit' (2003) ÖStZ 262.
——'Manninen: Kapitalverkehrsfreiheit verpflichtet zur grenzüberschreitenden Anrechnung ausländischer Körperschaftssteuer' (2004) ÖStZ 582.
——'Most-Favoured-Nation Treatment in Direct Taxation: Does EC Law Provide for Community MFN in Bilateral Double Taxation Treaties?' (2005) 5 Hous. J. Int'l L. 1.
——'Einige Überlegungen zur steuerlichen Kohärenz nach dem Urteil des EuGH in der Rs Manninen' (2005) ÖStZ 26.
——'Treaty Override, juristische Doppelbesteuerung und Gemeinschaftsrecht' (2006) SWI 62.
Kofler, Georg, and Clemens Philipp Schindler, ' "Dancing with Mr. D": The ECJ's Denial of Most-Favoured-Nation Treatment in the "D" Case' (2005) 45 ET 530.
Köhler, Stefan, and Martina Tippelhofer, 'Kapitalverkehrsfreiheit auch in Drittstaatenfällen? Zugleich Anmerkung zu den Entscheidungen des EuGH in den Rechtssachen Lasertec (C-492/04) und Holböck (C-157/05) sowie zum BMF-Schreiben v. 21.3.2007 (IV B 7 - G 1421/0)' (2007) 16 IStR 645.
Kokott, Juliane, in Rudolf Streinz (ed), *EUV/EGV: Vertrag über die Europäische Union und Vertrag zur Gründung der Europäischen Gemeinschaft*, Art. 297 EC (C.H. Beck, München 2003).
——in Rudolf Streinz (ed), *EUV/EGV: Vertrag über die Europäische Union und Vertrag zur Gründung der Europäischen Gemeinschaft*, Art. 299 EC (C.H. Beck, München 2003).
Kotzur, Markus, 'Eine Bewährungsprobe für die Europäische Grundrechtsgemeinschaft/ Zur Entscheidung des EuG in der Rs. Yusuf u.a. gegen Rat, EuGRZ 2005, S. 592ff.' (2006) EuGRZ 19.
Koutrakos, Panos, 'Is Article 297 EC a "Reserve of Sovereignty"?' (2000) 37 CMLR 1339.
——*EU International Relations Law* (Modern Studies in European Law, Hart, Oxford [et al] 2006).
Koyama, Takeshi, and Stephen S Golub, 'OECD's FDI Regulatory Restrictiveness Index: Revision and Extension to More Economies' (Online Working Paper, OECD, Paris 2006) <http://www.oecd.org/dataoecd/4/36/37818075.pdf> accessed 22.10.2007.
Kröger, Michael, and Associated Press, 'Ausländische Investoren sollen um Genehmigung bitten' *Spiegel Online* (30.10.2007).
Krolop, Kaspar, 'Schutz vor Staatsfonds und anderen ausländischen Kapitalmarktakteuren unter Ausblendung des Kapitalmarktrechts?' (2008) 41 ZRP 40.
——'Staatliche Einlasskontrolle bei Staatsfonds und anderen ausländischen Investoren im Gefüge von Kapitalmarktregulierung, nationalem und internationalem Wirtschaftsrecht' [2008] 13 Humboldt Forum Recht <http://www.humboldt-forum-recht.de/druckansicht/druckansicht.php?artikelid=170> accessed 21.05.2008.

Krugman, Paul R, and Maurice Obstfeld, *International Economics: Theory and Policy* (The Addison-Wesley series in economics, 6th edn Addison Wesley, Boston, Mass. [et al] 2003).

Kuczynski, Michael, 'Foreign Investment' in Peter Newman, Murray Milgate, and John Eatwell (eds), *The New Palgrave Dictionary of Money & Finance* (vol 2, Macmillan Press, London 1992) 166.

Kuwait Investment Authority, 'Kuwait Investment Authority' (Website, Kuwait City 2007) <http://www.kia.gov.kw/kia> accessed 02.11.2007.

Landsmeer, Arie, 'Movement of Capital and other Freedoms' (2001) 28 LIEI 57.

Lang, John Temple, 'The Right of Establishment of Companies and Free Movement of Capital in the European Economic Community' (1965) 65 University of Illinois Law Forum 684.

Lang, Michael, 'Kapitalverkehrsfreiheit und Doppelbesteuerungsabkommen' in Eduard Lechner, Claus Staringer, and Michael Tumpel (eds), *Kapitalverkehrsfreiheit und Steuerrecht—Eine Analyse des österreichischen Steuerrechts vor dem Hintergrund der Kapitalverkehrsfreiheit des EG-Rechts* (Linde, Wien 2000), 181.

——'Das EuGH-Urteil in der Rechtssache D.—Gerät der Motor der Steuerharmonisierung ins Stottern?' (2005) SWI 365.

——'Ist die Schumacker-Rechtsprechung am Ende?' (2005) RIW 336.

——'Marks & Spencer und die Auswirkungen auf das Steuerrecht der Mitgliedstaaten' (2005) SWI 255.

——'Marks & Spencer—Eine erste Analyse des EuGH Urteils' (2006) SWI 3.

——'Wohin geht das Internationale Steuerrecht?' (2005) 14 IStR 289.

Lang, Michael, et al (eds), *CFC Legislation: Domestic Provisions, Tax Treaties and EC Law* (Linde, Wien 2004).

Lang, Michael, and Pasquale Pistone (eds), *The EU and Third Countries: Direct Taxation* (Linde, Wien 2007).

Lehner, Moris (ed), *Grundfreiheiten im Steuerrecht der EU-Staaten* (C.H. Beck, München 2000).

Leible, Stefan, in Eberhard Grabitz and Meinhard Hilf (eds), *Das Recht der Europäischen Union: Kommentar*, Art. 28 EC (vol 1, C.H. Beck, München 2000).

——in Rudolf Streinz (ed), *EUV/EGV: Vertrag über die Europäische Union und Vertrag zur Gründung der Europäischen Gemeinschaft*, Art. 14 EC (C.H. Beck, München 2003).

——in Rudolf Streinz (ed), *EUV/EGV: Vertrag über die Europäische Union und Vertrag zur Gründung der Europäischen Gemeinschaft*, Art. 94 EC (C.H. Beck, München 2003).

Lenaerts, Koen, and Piet Van Nuffel, *Constitutional Law of the European Union* (2nd edn Sweet & Maxwell, London [et al] 2005).

Lenz, Carl Otto (ed), *EG-Vertrag: Kommentar zu dem Vertrag zur Gründung der Europäischen Gemeinschaften* (Bundesanzeiger, Köln 1994).

Lenz, Carl Otto, and Klaus-Dieter Borchert (eds), *EU- und EG Vertrag—Kommentar zu dem Vertrag über die Europäische Union und zu dem Vertrag zur Gründung der Europäischen Gemeinschaft, jeweils in der durch den Vertrag von Nizza geänderten Fassung* (4th edn Bundesanzeiger, Helbing & Lichtenhahn, Linde, Köln, [et al] 2006).

Lenz, Carl Otto, in Carl Otto Lenz and Klaus-Dieter Borchert (eds), *EU- und EG Vertrag—Kommentar zu dem Vertrag über die Europäische Union und zu dem Vertrag* zur Gründung der Europäischen Gemeinschaft, jeweils in der durch den Vertrag von Nizza geänderten Fassung, Art. 12 EC (3th edn Bundesanzeiger, Helbing & Lichtenhahn, Ueberreuter, Köln, [et al] 2003).

Leßmann, Herbert (ed), *Festschrift für Rudolf Lukes: zum 65. Geburtstag* (Heymanns, Köln [et al] 1989).

Lübke, Julia, *Der Erwerb von Gesellschaftsanteilen zwischen Kapitalverkehrs- und Niederlassungsfreiheit* (Heidelberger Schriften zum Wirtschaftsrecht und Europarecht, Nomos, Baden-Baden 2006).

Lüdicke, Jürgen, 'Die Besteuerung Nichtansässiger im Spannungsverhältnis zwischen Gemeinschaftsrecht und Doppelbesteuerungsabkommen' in Wolfgang Schön (ed), *Gedächtnisschrift für Brigitte Knobbe-Keuk in Zusammenarbeit mit Werner Flume und Horst Heinrich Jakobs, Eduard Picker, Jan Wilhelm*, 729 (O. Schmidt, Köln 1997).

Lütke, Stefan, *Die CFC-Legislation (Hinzurechnungsbesteuerung) im Spannungsfeld zwischen europäischer Kapitalverkehrsfreiheit und weltweiter Kapitalliberalisierung (WTO): Eine Analyse der Grenzen der europäischen Kapitalverkehrsfreiheit sowie der Steuerordnung der WTO in Hinblick auf Auswirkungen für Ausgleichsmaßnahmen im internationalen Steuerwettbewerb* (Beiträge zum Europäischen Wirtschaftsrecht, Duncker & Humblot, Berlin 2006).

Lyal, Richard, 'Free Movement of Capital and Non-member Countries—Consequences for Direct Taxation', The Influence of European Law on Direct Taxation. Recent and Future Developments Amsterdam (24.11.2006) <http://european-tax-adviser.com/wordpress/wp-content/uploads/2007/08/ac2006_lyal.pdf> accessed 22.12.2007.

Lynn, Matthew, 'Investing: France's "Don't Do that Here" Folly' *International Herald Tribune* (10.01.2006).

Lyons, Gerard, 'State Capitalism: The Rise of Sovereign Wealth Funds' (2008) 14 L. & Bus. Rev. Am. 179.

MacLeod, Iain, I D Hendry, and Stephen Hyett, *The External Relations of the European Communities: A Manual of Law and Practice* (Clarendon Press [et al], Oxford [et al] 1996).

Maduro, Miguel Poiares, *We the Court: The European Court of Justice and the European Economic Constitution; A Critical Reading of Art. 30 of the EC Treaty* (Hart, Oxford [et al] 1999).

Magiera, Siegfried, in Eberhard Grabitz and Meinhard Hilf (eds), *Das Recht der Europäischen Union: Kommentar*, Art. 269 EC (vol 3, C.H. Beck, München 2006).

Marschner, Ernst, 'Rechtsprechung des EuGH zu "Inbound"- und "Outbound"-Dividenden und seine Auswirkungen auf Österreich' (2007) FJ 86.

Martin-Jiménez, Adolfo J., 'EC Law and Clauses on 'Limitation of Benefits' in Treaties with the US after Maastricht and the US-Netherlands Tax Treaty' (1995) 4 EC Tax Review 78.

Marwede, Jan, '§ 53: Zweigstellen von Unternehmen mit Sitz im Ausland' in Karl-Heinz Boos, Reinfrid Fischer, and Hermann Schulte-Mattler (eds), *Kreditwesengesetz: Kommentar zu KWG und Ausführungsvorschriften* (2nd edn Beck, München 2004).

Mattsson, Nils, 'Does the European Court of Justice Understand the Policy behind Tax Benefits Based on Personal and Family Circumstances?' (2003) 43 ET 186.

Matzka, Bettina, *Das österreichische Steuerrecht im Lichte der Freiheit des Kapitalverkehrs* (Linde, Wien 1998).

Maxwell, Winston, 'France Criticised for New Foreign Investment Rules' (2006) 25 IFLR 44.
Maydell, Niklas, 'The European Community's Minimum Platform on Investment or the Trojan Horse of Investment Competence' in August Reinisch and Christina Knahr (eds), *International Investment Law in Context* (Eleven International Publishing, Utrecht 2007), 73.
—— 'The European Community's Competence to Conclude International Agreements on Investment: Revealing the Inconvenient Truth' (PhD Dissertation, University of Vienna Law School 2008).
Meng, Werner, 'Die Kompetenz der EWG zur Verhängung von Wirtschaftssanktionen gegen Drittländer' (1982) 42 ZaöRV 780.
Mestmäcker, Ernst-Joachim (ed), *Wirtschaft und Verfassung in der Europäischen Union: Beiträge zu Recht, Theorie und Politik der europäischen Integration* (Nomos, Baden-Baden 2003).
Mestmäcker, Ernst-Joachim, 'Offene Märkte im System unverfälschten Wettbewerbs in der Europäischen Wirtschaftsgemeinschaft' in Helmut Coing, Heinrich Kronstein, and Ernst-Joachim Mestmäcker (eds), *Wirtschaftsordnung und Rechtsordnung: Festschrift zum 70. Geburtstag von Franz Böhm am 16. Februar 1965*, 345 (C.F. Müller, Karlsruhe 1965).
—— 'Zur Wirtschaftsverfassung in der Europäischen Union' in Ernst-Joachim Mestmäcker (ed), *Wirtschaft und Verfassung in der Europäischen Union: Beiträge zu Recht, Theorie und Politik der europäischen Integration* (Nomos, Baden-Baden 2003), 507.
Mihm, Andreas, 'Investoren sollen Regierung informieren' *Frankfurter Allgemeine Zeitung* (30.10.2007).
Moench, Christoph, 'Reinheitsgebot für Bier—Zum Urteil des EuGH vom 12.3.1987, NJW 1987, 1133' (1987) NJW 1109.
Mögele, Rudolf, in Rudolf Streinz (ed), *EUV/EGV: Vertrag über die Europäische Union und Vertrag zur Gründung der Europäischen Gemeinschaft*, Art. 310 EC (C.H. Beck, München 2003).
Mohamed, Sideek, *European Community Law on the Free Movement of Capital and the EMU* (Stockholm studies in law, Norstedts Juridik [et al], Stockholm [et al] 1999).
Mohn, Astrid Sybille, *Der Gleichheitssatz im Gemeinschaftsrecht: Differenzierungen im europäischen Gemeinschaftsrecht und ihre Vereinbarkeit mit dem Gleichheitssatz* (Schriftenreihe Europa-Forschung, Engel, Kehl am Rhein 1990).
Möllers, Christoph, 'Das EuG konstitutionalisiert die Vereinten Nationen' (2006) 41 EuR 426.
Molzahn, Ralf, *Die normativen Verknüpfungen von Kapitalverkehrsfreiheit und Währungsunion im EG-Vertrag* (Springer, Heidelberg [et al] 1999).
More, Gillian, 'The Principle of Equal Treatment: From Market Unifier to Fundamental Right?' in Paul P Craig and Gráinne De Búrca (eds), *The Evolution of EU Law* (Oxford University Press, Oxford [et al] 1999), 517.
Möslein, Florian, 'Kapitalverkehrsfreiheit und Gesellschaftsrecht' (2007) 28 ZIP 208.
Mössner, Jörg M, and Dietrich Kellersmann, 'Freiheit des Kapitalverkehrs in der EU und das deutsche Körperschaftssteueranrechnungsverfahren' (1999) 87 DStZ 505.
Muchlinski, Peter, *Multinational Enterprises and the Law* (Blackwell, Oxford [et al] 1995).

Mülbert, Peter O, 'Konzeption des europäischen Kapitalmarktrechts für Wertpapierdienstleistungen' (2001) 55 WM 2085.
Müller, Friedrich, and Ralph Christensen, *Juristische Methodik: Europarecht* (vol 2, Duncker & Humblot, Berlin 2003).
Müller, Johannes C W, *Kapitalverkehrsfreiheit in der Europäischen Union: Bedeutung, Inhalt und Umfang, Weiterentwicklung, Auswirkung auf Völkerrecht und nationales Recht* (Beiträge zum europäischen Wirtschaftsrecht Duncker & Humblot, Berlin 2000).
Müller, Welf, 'EU-Grundfreiheiten und Doppelbesteuerungsrecht' (2007) Status: Recht 119.
Müller-Etienne, Daniel, *Die Europarechtswidrigkeit des Erbschaftsteuerrechts: das deutsche internationale Erbschaft- und Schenkungsteuerrecht auf dem Prüfstand des EG-Vertrages und der Europäischen Menschenrechtskonvention (EMRK)* (Schriften des Instituts für Ausländisches und Internationales Finanz- und Steuerwesen der Universität Hamburg, Nomos, Baden-Baden 2003).
Müller-Graff, Peter-Christian, and Manfred Zuleeg (eds), *Staat und Wirtschaft in der EG: Kolloquium zum 65. Geburtstag von Prof. Dr. Bodo Börner* (Nomos, Baden-Baden 1987).
——'Einflußregulierungen in Gesellschaften zwischen Binnenmarktrecht und Eigentumsordnung' in Mathias Habersack, et al (eds), *Festschrift für Peter Ulmer zum 70. Geburtstag am 2. Januar 2003* (de Gruyter, Berlin 2003), 929.
——in Hans von der Groeben and Jürgen Schwarze (eds), *Kommentar zum Vertrag über die Europäische Union und zur Gründung der Europäischen Gemeinschaft*, Art. 28 EC (vol 1, 6th edn Nomos, Baden-Baden 2003).
——in Hans von der Groeben and Jürgen Schwarze (eds), *Kommentar zum Vertrag über die Europäische Union und zur Gründung der Europäischen Gemeinschaft*, Art. 30 EC (vol 1, 6th edn Nomos, Baden-Baden 2003).
——in Rudolf Streinz (ed), *EUV/EGV: Vertrag über die Europäische Union und Vertrag zur Gründung der Europäischen Gemeinschaft*, Art. 43 EC (C.H. Beck, München 2003).
——in Rudolf Streinz (ed), *EUV/EGV: Vertrag über die Europäische Union und Vertrag zur Gründung der Europäischen Gemeinschaft*, Art. 48 EC (C.H. Beck, München 2003).
——in Rudolf Streinz (ed), *EUV/EGV: Vertrag über die Europäische Union und Vertrag zur Gründung der Europäischen Gemeinschaft*, Art. 49 EC (C.H. Beck, München 2003).
Nettesheim, Martin (ed), *Eberhard Grabitz und Meinhard Hilf: Das Recht der Europäischen Union: Kommentar* (C.H. Beck, München, looseleaf: January 2008).
Nettesheim, Martin, 'Kompetenzen' in Armin von Bogdandy (ed), *Europäisches Verfassungsrecht: Theoretische und dogmatische Grundzüge* (Springer, Berlin [et al] 2003), 415.
——'Einleitung III: Der Rahmen des Telekommunikationsrechts——Die europarechtliche und grundgesetzliche Wirtschaftsverfassung' in Franz-Jürgen Säcker (ed), *Berliner Kommentar zum Telekommunikationsrecht* (Recht und Wirtschaft, Frankfurt am Main 2006), 93.
——*Grundfreiheiten und Grundrechte in der Europäischen Union—Auf dem Weg zur Verschmelzung?* (Rechtsfragen der Europäischen Integration, vol 153, Universität Bonn, Bonn 2006).

Nettesheim, Martin, 'Normenhierarchien im EU-Recht' (2006) 41 EuR 737.

——'UN Sanctions against Individuals—A Challenge to the Architecture of the European Union Governance' (2007) 44 CMLR 567.

——'Unternehmensübernahmen durch Staatsfonds: Europarechtliche Vorgaben und Schranken' (2008) 172 ZHR 729.

Nettesheim, Martin, and Johann Ludwig Duvigneau, 'Art. 131 EC' in Rudolf Streinz (ed), *EUV/EGV: Vertrag über die Europäische Union und Vertrag zur Gründung der Europäischen Gemeinschaft* (C.H. Beck, München 2003).

Neumann, Manfred, *Theoretische Volkswirtschaftslehre: Makroökonomische Theorie: Beschäftigung, Inflation und Zahlungsbilanz* (Wirtschaftstheorie und Wirtschaftspolitik vol 1, 5th edn Vahlen, München 1996).

Newman, Peter, Murray Milgate, and John Eatwell (eds), *The New Palgrave Dictionary of Money & Finance* (Macmillan Press, London 1992).

Norges Bank, 'Statens pensjonsfond—Utland' (Website, Oslo 2007) <http://www.norges-bank.no/Pages/Article_____41137.aspx> accessed 01.11.2007.

Novak, Meinhard, 'Ungleichbehandlung von ausländischen Produkten oder Dienstleistungen—Einheitliche Rechtfertigungstatbestände im EG-Vertrag—Zugleich Urteilsanmerkung zu EuGH vom 9.7.1997, DB 1997 S. 2219 "De Agostini"' (1997) DB 2589.

O'Brien, Martha, 'Note: Case C-452/04, Fidium Finanz AG v. Bundesanstalt für Finanzdienstleistungsaufsicht, Judgment of the Court of Justice (Grand Chamber) of 3 October 2006, [2006] ECR I-9521' (2007) 44 CMLR 1483.

——'Taxation and the Third Country Dimension of Free Movement of Capital in EU Law: the ECJ's Rulings and the Unresolved Issues' (2008) B.T.R. 628.

Oechsler, Jürgen, 'Erlaubte Gestaltungen im Anwendungsbereich des Art. 56 I EG—Zugleich zur Entscheidung EuGH, NZW 2006, 942—Golden Shares VI' (2007) 10 NZG 161.

OGEL, 'Free Movement of Capital: Infringement Procedures against Denmark, Austria, Finland and Sweden concerning Bilateral Investment Treaties with Non-EU Countries' [2004] 2 OGEL <http://www.ogel.org/> accessed 12.12.2004.

Ohler, Christoph, 'Die Kapitalverkehrsfreiheit und ihre Schranken' (1996) WM 1801.

——'EuGH: Salzburger Grundverkehrsbeschränkungen des Zweitwohnungserwerbs (Anmerkung)' (2002) 13 EuZW 251.

——*Europäische Kapital- und Zahlungsverkehrsfreiheit Kommentar zu den Artikeln 56 bis 60 EGV, der Geldwäscherichtlinie und Überweisungsrichtlinie*, Art. 56 EC (Springer, Berlin [et al] 2002).

——*Europäische Kapital- und Zahlungsverkehrsfreiheit Kommentar zu den Artikeln 56 bis 60 EGV, der Geldwäscherichtlinie und Überweisungsrichtlinie*, Art. 57 EC (Springer, Berlin [et al] 2002).

——*Europäische Kapital- und Zahlungsverkehrsfreiheit Kommentar zu den Artikeln 56 bis 60 EGV, der Geldwäscherichtlinie und Überweisungsrichtlinie*, Art. 58 EC (Springer, Berlin [et al] 2002).

——*Europäische Kapital- und Zahlungsverkehrsfreiheit Kommentar zu den Artikeln 56 bis 60 EGV, der Geldwäscherichtlinie und Überweisungsrichtlinie*, Art. 59 EC (Springer, Berlin [et al] 2002).

——'§ 18 Handel mit Dienstleistungen' in Wolfgang Weiß and Christoph Herrmann (eds), *Welthandelsrecht* (C.H. Beck, München 2003), 345.

—— 'Zulässige Versagung der Erlaubnis zur gewerbsmäßigen Kreditvergabe: Anmerkung zu EuGH, Urteil vom 03.10.2006—C-452/04 (Fidium Finanz AG/Bundesanstalt für Finanzdienstleistungsaufsicht)' (2006) 17 EuZW 691.

O'Keeffe, David, 'Exclusive, Concurrent and Shared Competence' in Alan Dashwood, Christophe Hillion, and Centre for European Legal Studies Cambridge (eds), *The General Law of E.C. External Relations* (Sweet & Maxwell, London [et al] 2000), 179.

Oliver, Peter, 'Free Movement of Capital Between Member States: Article 67(1) EEC and the Implementing Directives' (1984) 9 ELRev. 401.

—— *Free Movement of Goods in the European Community: Under Articles 30 to 36 of the Rome Treaty* (3rd edn Sweet & Maxwell, London [et al] 1996).

Oliver, Peter, and Jean-Pierre Baché, 'Free Movement of Capital between the Member States: Recent Developments' (1989) 26 CMLR 61.

Oppermann, Thomas, 'Europäische Wirtschaftsverfassung nach der Einheitlichen Europäischen Akte' in Peter-Christian Müller-Graff and Manfred Zuleeg (eds), *Staat und Wirtschaft in der EG: Kolloquium zum 65. Geburtstag von Prof. Dr. Bodo Börner* (Nomos, Baden-Baden 1987), 53.

—— *Europarecht* (3rd edn Beck, München 2005).

Osteneck, Kathrin, *Die Umsetzung von UN-Wirtschaftssanktionen durch die Europäische Gemeinschaft: völker- und europarechtliche Rahmenbedingungen für ein Tätigwerden der Europäischen Gemeinschaft im Bereich von UN-Wirtschaftssanktionsregimen unter besonderer Berücksichtigung der Umsetzungspraxis der EG-Organe* (Beiträge zum ausländischen öffentlichen Recht und Völkerrecht, Springer, Berlin [et al] 2004).

Oxelheim, Lars, and Pervez N Ghauri (eds), *European Union and The Race for Foreign Direct Investment in Europe* (International Business & Management, Elsevier, Amsterdam [et al] 2004).

Pajunk, Axel, *Die Bedeutung und Reichweite der Kapitalverkehrs- und Dienstleistungsfreiheit des EG-Vertrages: die gegenseitige Anerkennung von Privatrechtsinstituten am Beispiel der englischen Mobiliarkreditsicherheiten* (Studien zum europäischen Privat- und Prozeßrecht, Lang, Frankfurt am Main [et al] 1999).

Pannier, Matthias, *Harmonisierung der Aktionärsrechte in Europa: insbesondere der Verwaltungsrechte* (Beiträge zum Europäischen Wirtschaftsrecht, Duncker & Humblot, Berlin 2003).

Pappers, Lars, 'National Report Netherlands' in Michael Lang and Pasquale Pistone (eds), *The EU and Third Countries: Direct Taxation* (Linde, Wien 2007), 393.

Parpart, Heike, *Die unmittelbare Bindung Privater an die Personenverkehrsfreiheiten im europäischen Gemeinschaftsrecht: eine Darstellung der Arbeitnehmerfreizügigkeit, Niederlassungs- und Dienstleistungsfreiheit* (Schriften des Instituts für Arbeits- und Wirtschaftsrecht der Universität zu Köln, C.H. Beck, München 2003).

Peers, Steve, 'Free Movement of Capital: Learning Lessons or Slipping on Spilt Milk?' in Catherine Barnard and Joanne Scott (eds), *The Law of the Single European Market: Unpacking the Premises* (Hart, Oxford [et al] 2002), 333.

Pernice, Ingolf, and Stephan Wernicke, in Eberhard Grabitz and Meinhard Hilf (eds), *Das Recht der Europäischen Union: Kommentar*, Art. 86 EC (vol 1, C.H. Beck, München 2003).

Peters, Cees, and Jan Gooijer, 'The Free Movement of Capital and Third Countries: Some Observations' (2005) 45 ET 475.

Peters, Martine, 'Capital Movements and Taxation in the EC' (1998) 7 EC Tax Review 4.

Petersmann, Ernst-Ulrich, 'Internationale Wirtschaftssanktionen als Problem des Völkerrechts und des Europarechts' (1981) 80 ZVglRWiss 1.

Pfeil, Werner, 'Freier Kapitalverkehr und § 110 I Nr. 2 BewG' (1996) RIW 788.

Phaturos, Argyres A (ed), *Transnational Corporations: The International Legal Framework* (The United Nations library on transnational corporations, vol 20, Routledge, London [et al] 1994).

Pießkalla, Michael, *Goldene Aktien aus EG-rechtlicher Sicht: Eine Untersuchung staatlicher und privater Sonderrechte in Wirtschaftsgesellschaften unter besonderer Berücksichtigung der Kapitalverkehrsfreiheit* (Studien zum Völker- und Europarecht, Verlag Dr. Kovač, Hamburg 2006).

——' "Lex Mol"—Ungarisches Parlament verabschiedet Gesetz zum Schutz strategisch bedeutsamer Unternehmen' (2008) 9 WiRO 48.

Pipkorn, Jörn, Angela Bardenhewer-Rating, and Hans Claudius Taschner, in Hans von der Groeben and Jürgen Schwarze (eds), *Kommentar zum Vertrag über die Europäische Union und zur Gründung der Europäischen Gemeinschaft*, Art. 14 EC (vol 1, 6th edn Nomos, Baden-Baden 2003).

Pistone, Pasquale, 'The Impact of European Law on the Relations with Third Countries in the Field of Direct Taxation' (2006) 34 Intertax 234.

Pläster, Sebastian, 'Nach VW und Golden Shares VII: Ein Krake namens Kapitalverkehrsfreiheit?' (2008) EWS 173.

Plötscher, Stefan, *Der Begriff der Diskriminierung im Europäischen Gemeinschaftsrecht: Zugleich ein Beitrag zur einheitlichen Dogmatik der Grundfreiheiten des EG-Vertrages* (Schriften zum europäischen Recht, Duncker & Humblot, Berlin 2003).

Preedy, Kara, *Die Bindung Privater an die europäischen Grundfreiheiten: zur sogenannten Drittwirkung im Europarecht* (Schriften zum europäischen Recht, Duncker & Humblot, Berlin 2005).

PricewaterhouseCoopers Aktiengesellschaft Wirtschaftsprüfungsgesellschaft (PwC AG), and Euler Hermes Kreditversicherungs-AG, 'Investment Guarantees of the Federal Republic of Germany' (Website, Hamburg 2006) <http://www.agaportal.de/en/dia/index.html> accessed 10.11.2006.

Prinz, Ulrich, 'Schnelle Reaktion der Finanzverwaltung auf die Lankhorst-Hohorst-Entscheidung des EuGH zur Europarechtswidrigkeit des § 8a KStG' (2003) FR 649.

——'Verstößt der "alte" § 8a KStG gegen die europäische Kapitalverkehrsfreiheit (Art. 56 EG) (Anmerkung zu FG Baden-Württemberg, Beschl. v. 14.10.2004 - 3 K 62/99)' (2005) FR 370.

Proelß, Alexander, 'The Intra-Community Effects of Mixed Agreements: Uniform Status versus Division of Competence' in Suthiphand Chirathivat, et al (eds), *European Union and ASEAN: Historical Dimensions, Comparative Analysis and Politico-Economic Dynamics* (Springer, Berlin [et al] 2005), 251.

Radu, Anca, 'Foreign Investors in the EU—Which "Best Treatment"? Interactions between Bilateral Investment Treaties and EU Law' (2008) 14 ELJ 237.

Rainer, Anno, 'Anmerkung I zu EuGH, Urteil vom 13.3.2007—C-524/04 (Test Claimants in the Thin Cap Group Litigation/Commissioners of Inland Revenue)' (2007) 16 IStR 259.

Randelzhofer, Albrecht, and Ulrich Forsthoff, in Eberhard Grabitz and Meinhard Hilf (eds), *Das Recht der Europäischen Union: Kommentar*, Art. 43 EC (vol 1, Beck, München 2001).

——in Eberhard Grabitz and Meinhard Hilf (eds), *Das Recht der Europäischen Union: Kommentar*, vor Art. 39–55 EC (vol 1, Beck, München 2001).
Randelzhofer, Albrecht, Rupert Scholz, and Dieter Wilke (eds), *Gedächtnisschrift für Eberhard Grabitz* (C.H. Beck, München 1995).
Redaktion der 'Zeitschrift für das gesamte Kreditwesen', and Jörg E Cramer (eds), *Knapps enzyklopädisches Lexikon des Geld-, Bank- und Börsenwesens* (vol 1 (A-I), 4th edn Knapp, Frankfurt am Main 1999).
——(eds), *Knapps enzyklopädisches Lexikon des Geld-, Bank- und Börsenwesens* (vol 2 (J-Z), 4th edn Knapp, Frankfurt am Main 1999).
'Regierungspläne: Schutz vor ausländischen Käufern' *Manager-Magazin.de* (30.06.2007).
Rehm, Helmut, and Jürgen Nagler, 'Verbietet die Kapitalverkehrsfreiheit nach 1993 eingeführte Ausländerungleichbehandlung?—Anmerkungen zum BFH-Urteil vom 9. 8. 2006, I R 95/05, IStR 2006, 864' (2006) 15 IStR 859.
Reich, Norbert, 'The 'November Revolution' of the European Court of Justice: Keck, Meng and Audi Revisited' (1994) 31 CMLR 459.
Reimer, Ekkehart, 'Die Auswirkungen der Grundfreiheiten auf das Ertragssteuerrecht der Bunderrepublik Deutschland—Eine Bestandsaufnahme' in Moris Lehner (ed), *Grundfreiheiten im Steuerrecht der EU-Staaten*, 39 (C.H. Beck, München 2000).
Reinisch, August, and Christina Knahr (eds), *Aktuelle Probleme und Entwicklungen im Internationalen Investitionsrecht* (Boorberg, Stuttgart 2008).
——(eds), *International Investment Law in Context* (Eleven International Publishing, Utrecht 2007).
Rengeling, Hans-Werner (ed), *Handbuch zum europäischen und deutschen Umweltrecht: eine systematische Darstellung des europäischen Umweltrechts mit seinen Auswirkungen auf das deutsche Recht und mit rechtspolitischen Perspektiven* (2nd edn Heymanns, Köln [et al] 2003).
Ress, Georg, and Jörg Ukrow, *Kapitalverkehrsfreiheit und Steuergerechtigkeit: Art. 73b ff. EGV und die Annahme des Anfangsverdachts einer Steuerhinterziehung bei der Unterhaltung eines Bankkontos im Ausland* (Schriften des Europa-Instituts der Universität des Saarlandes—Rechtswissenschaft, vol 16, Nomos, Baden-Baden 1997).
——in Eberhard Grabitz and Meinhard Hilf (eds), *Das Recht der Europäischen Union: Kommentar*, Art. 56 EC (vol 1, C.H. Beck, München 2002).
——in Eberhard Grabitz and Meinhard Hilf (eds), *Das Recht der Europäischen Union: Kommentar*, Art. 57 EC (vol 1, Beck, München 2002).
——in Eberhard Grabitz and Meinhard Hilf (eds), *Das Recht der Europäischen Union: Kommentar*, Art. 58 EC (vol 1, C.H. Beck, München 2002).
——in Eberhard Grabitz and Meinhard Hilf (eds), *Das Recht der Europäischen Union: Kommentar*, Art. 59 EC (vol 1, C.H. Beck, München 2002).
——in Eberhard Grabitz and Meinhard Hilf (eds), *Das Recht der Europäischen Union: Kommentar*, Art. 60 EC (vol 1, C.H. Beck, München 2002).
Ress, Hans-Konrad, 'Anmerkung zu EuGH Verb. Rs. C-358/93 and C-416/93 (Re Bordessa), Slg. 1995, I-361' (1995) JZ 1008.
Rödder, Thomas, and Jens Schönfeld, 'Meistbegünstigung und EG-Recht: Anmerkung zu EuGH vom 5.7.2005, C-376/03 ('D'), IStR 2005, 483' (2005) 14 IStR 523.
Rödler, Friedrich, 'European Court of Justice Holds Austrian Stamp Duty Rules on Inbound Loan Agreements Are Discriminatory' (1999) TNI 1695.

Rohde, Andreas, *Freier Kapitalverkehr in der Europäischen Gemeinschaft* (Studien und Materialien zum öffentlichen Recht, Lang, Frankfurt am Main [et al] 1999).
——'Wirtschafts- und Währungsunion und freier Kapitalverkehr' (1999) EWS 453.
Röhrbein, Jens, and Klaus Eicker, 'Verlustberücksichtigung über die Grenze—Aktuelle Rechtslage' (2005) 60 BB 465.
Rose, Klaus, and Karlhans Sauernheimer, *Theorie der Außenwirtschaft* (14th edn Vahlen, München 2006).
Roth, Wulf-Henning, 'Case C-204/90, Hanns-Martin Bachmann v. Belgian State, Judgment of 28 January 1992, not yet published' (1993) 30 CMLR 387.
——'Casenote on Keck and Hünermund' (1994) 31 CMLR 845.
——'Die Niederlassungsfreiheit zwischen Beschränkungs- und Diskriminierungsverbot' in Wolfgang Schön (ed), *Gedächtnisschrift für Brigitte Knobbe-Keuk in Zusammenarbeit mit Werner Flume und Horst Heinrich Jakobs, Eduard Picker, Jan Wilhelm* (O. Schmidt, Köln 1997), 729.
——'Diskriminierende Regelungen des Warenverkehrs und Rechtfertigung durch die 'zwingenden Erfordernisse' des Allgemeininteresses' (2000) WRP 979.
——'Drittwirkung der Grundfreiheiten?' in Ole Due, Marcus Lutter and Jürgen Schwarze (eds), *Festschrift für Ulrich Everling* (vol 2, Nomos, Baden-Baden 1995), 1231.
Roy, Friedemann, *Niederlassungsrecht und Kapitalverkehrsfreiheit in Polen, Tschechien und Ungarn: die Auswirkungen der Europa-Abkommen auf die Tätigkeit der Kreditinstitute* (DUV : Wirtschaftswissenschaft, Dt. Univ.-verlag, Wiesbaden 2002).
Royla, Pascal, *Grenzüberschreitende Finanzmarktaufsicht in der EG* (Münsterische Beiträge zur Rechtswissenschaft, vol 132, Duncker & Humblot, Berlin 2000).
Rudanko, Matti, and Pekka Timonen (eds), *European Financial Area: Proceedings of Closing Seminar of the Research Project of KATTI* (Institute of International Economic Law (KATTI), Helsinki 1998).
Ruge, Reinhard, 'Goldene Aktien und EG Recht' (2002) 13 EuZW 421.
Rupp, Hans Heinrich, *Grundgesetz und 'Wirtschaftsverfassung'* (Vorträge und Aufsätze Walter-Eucken-Institut, Mohr Siebeck, Tübingen 1974).
Ruppe, Hans Georg, 'Die Bedeutung der Kapitalverkehrsfreiheit für das Steuerrecht' in Eduard Lechner, Claus Staringer, and Michael Tumpel (eds), *Kapitalverkehrsfreiheit und Steuerrecht—Eine Analyse des österreichischen Steuerrechts vor dem Hintergrund der Kapitalverkehrsfreiheit des EG-Rechts* (Linde, Wien 2000), 9.
Rust, Alexander, 'National Report Germany' in Michael Lang, et al (eds), *CFC Legislation: Domestic Provisions, Tax Treaties and EC Law* (Linde, Wien 2004).
Sachs, Michael, '§ 77 Der Gewährleistungsgehalt der Grundrechte' in Klaus Stern (ed), *Das Staatsrecht der Bundesrepublik Deutschland* (vol III.2, C.H. Beck, München 1994).
Sachverständigenrat zur Begutachtung der gesamtwirtschaftlichen Entwicklung, *Das Erreichte nicht verspielen: Jahresgutachten 2007/08* (Statistisches Bundesamt, Wiesbaden 2007).
Säcker, Franz-Jürgen (ed), *Berliner Kommentar zum Telekommunikationsrecht* (Recht und Wirtschaft, Frankfurt am Main 2006).
Samuelson, Paul Anthony, and William D Nordhaus, *Economics* (18th edn McGraw-Hill, Boston 2005).
Sander, Florian, 'Volkswagen vor dem EuGH—der Schutz der Kapitalverkehrsfreiheit am Scheideweg' (2005) 16 EuZW 106.

——'Höchststimmrechte und Kapitalverkehrsfreiheit nach der VW-Gesetz-Entscheidung—Psychologisiert der EuGH den Schutzbereich des Art. 56 EG?' (2008) 19 EuZW 33.

Sass, Gert, 'Zur Rechtsprechung des EuGH und einigen Folgerungen für das deutsche Steuerrecht' (1998) FR 1.

Sauvant, Karl P., 'Regulatory Risk and the Growth of FDI' in The Economist Intelligence Unit (ed), *World Investment Prospects to 2011: Foreign Direct Investment and the Challenge of Political Risk* (The Economist Intelligence Unit, London 2007), 67.

——'The FDI Recession Has Begun' (Pdf-file, The Vale Columbia Center on Sustainable International Investment, New York 2008) <http://www.vcc.columbia.edu/documents/KPSPerspective-FDIrecessionhasbegun_000.pdf> accessed 20.12.2008.

Schaefer, Detlef, *Die unmittelbare Wirkung des Verbots der nichttarifären Handelshemmnisse, Art. 30 EWGV, in den Rechtsbeziehungen zwischen Privaten* (Europäische Hochschulschriften, Lang, Frankfurt am Main [et al] 1987).

Schaumburg, Harald, *Internationales Steuerrecht: Außensteuerrecht, Doppelbesteuerungsrecht* (2nd edn O. Schmidt, Köln 1998).

Scheibe, Roland, *Die Anleihekompetenzen der Gemeinschaftsorgane nach dem EWG-Vertrag: zu den Möglichkeiten und Grenzen der Kreditfinanzierung der EWG, zugleich ein Beitrag zur Finanzverfassung der EWG sowie zur 'Allgemeinen Ermächtigungsklausel' des Art. 235 EWGV* (Schriften des Instituts für Ausländisches und Internationales Finanz- und Steuerwesen der Universität Hamburg, Nomos, Baden-Baden 1988).

Scherer, Thomas, *Doppelbesteuerung und Europäisches Gemeinschaftsrecht—Auswirkungen des Gemeinschaftsrechts auf die Anwendung der Doppelbesteuerungsabkommen und des Außenwirtschaftsrechts* (C.H. Beck, München 1995).

Schießl, Harald, 'Neues zum Rangverhältnis zwischen Niederlassungsfreiheit und dem freien Kapitalverkehr' (2007) 9 StuB 584.

Schilling, Theodor, 'Rechtsfragen zu Art. 30 EGV—Zugleich eine Anmerkung zum EuGH-Urteil vom 24.11.1993 in den verbundenen Rechtssachen C-267 und 268/91' (1994) 29 EuR 50.

Schlag, Martin, in Jürgen Schwarze (ed), *EU-Kommentar*, Art. 43 EC (Nomos, Baden-Baden 2000).

Schleper, Norbert, *Auf dem Weg zu einer einheitlichen Dogmatik der Grundfreiheiten?, Nr. 16* (Göttingen e-Working Papers on European Law, 2004).

Schmahl, Stefanie, 'Effektiver Rechtsschutz gegen "targeted sanctions" des UN-Sicherheitsrats?' (2006) 41 EuR 566.

Schmalenbach, Kirsten, 'Normentheorie vs. Terrorismus: Der Vorrang des UN-Rechts vor EU-Recht' (2006) 61 JZ 349.

Schneider, Christian F, 'Kapitalverkehrsfreiheit für EWR-Bürger und Beschränkungen für den Grundstückserwerb' (2003) ELRep. 380.

Schneider, Hartmut, *Die öffentliche Ordnung als Schranke der Grundfreiheiten im EG-Vertrag* (Schriftenreihe Europäisches Recht, Politik und Wirtschaft, Nomos, Baden-Baden 1998).

Schnitger, Arne, 'Geltung der Grundfreiheiten des EGV für Drittstaatsangehörige im Steuerrecht' (2002) 11 IStR 711.

——'Mögliche Wirkungsgrenzen der Grundfreiheiten des EG-Vertrages am Beispiel des § 8a KStG—Zugleich Anmerkung zu dem Beitrag von Kessler/Eicker/Obser, IStR 2004, 325fff' (2004) 13 IStR 635.

Schnitger, Arne, 'Die Kapitalverkehrsfreiheit im Verhältnis zu Drittstaaten: Vorabentscheidungsersuchen in den Rs. van Hilten, Fidium Finanz AG und Lasertec' (2005) 14 IStR 493.

Schön, Wolfgang (ed), *Gedächtnisschrift für Brigitte Knobbe-Keuk in Zusammenarbeit mit Werner Flume und Horst Heinrich Jakobs, Eduard Picker, Jan Wilhelm* (O. Schmidt, Köln 1997).

Schön, Wolfgang, 'Europäische Kapitalverkehrsfreiheit und nationales Steuerrecht' in Wolfgang Schön (ed), *Gedächtnisschrift für Brigitte Knobbe-Keuk in Zusammenarbeit mit Werner Flume und Horst Heinrich Jakobs, Eduard Picker, Jan Wilhelm* (O. Schmidt, Köln 1997), 743.

——'Das Bild des Gesellschafters im Europäischen Gesellschaftsrecht' (2000) 64 RabelsZ 1.

——'Besteuerung im Binnenmarkt—die Rechtsprechung des EuGH zu den direkten Steuern' (2004) 13 IStR 289.

——'Der Kapitalverkehr mit Drittstaaten und das Internationale Steuerrecht' in Rudolf Gocke, Dietmar Gosch and Michael Lang (eds), *Festschrift für Franz Wassermeyer*, 489 (C.H. Beck, München 2005).

Schönfeld, Jens, 'Die Fortbestandsgarantie des Art. 57 Abs. 1 EG im Steuerrecht: Anmerkung zu FG Hamburg vom 9.3.2004, VI 279/01, EFG 2004, 1573' (2005) 14 IStR 410.

——'EuGH konkretisiert Anwendung der Kapitalverkehrsfreiheit im Verhältnis zu Drittstaaten: Mögliche Konsequenzen und offene Fragen aus steuerlicher Sicht: Zugleich Anmerkung zu EuGH-Urteil vom 03.10.2006 - Rs. C-452/04, Fidium Finanz AG' (2007) 60 DB 80.

——'Anmerkung II zu EuGH, Urteil vom 13.3.2007—C-524/04 (Test Claimants in the Thin Cap Group Litigation/Commissioners of Inland Revenue)' (2007) 16 IStR 260.

——'EuGH, Urteil vom 24.5.2007—C-157/05 (Winfried Holböck/FA Salzburg-Land): Anmerkung' (2007) 16 IStR 443.

Schraufl, Martin, 'Die Auswirkungen der Konkurrenz zwischen Niederlassungs- und Kapitalverkehrsfreiheit auf Drittstaatensachverhalte im Steuerrecht: Zugleich Anmerkung zum EuGH-Beschluss vom 10.5.2007, RIW 2007, 632 - Lasertec' (2007) RIW 603.

Schröder, Meinhard, 'Verantwortlichkeit, Völkerstrafrecht, Streitbeilegung und Sanktionen' in Wolfgang Graf Vitzthum (ed), *Völkerrecht*, 535 (3rd edn de Gruyter, Berlin 2004).

Schürmann, Thomas, in Carl Otto Lenz and Klaus-Dieter Borchert (eds), *EU- und EG Vertrag—Kommentar zu dem Vertrag über die Europäische Union und zu dem Vertrag zur Gründung der Europäischen Gemeinschaft, jeweils in der durch den Vertrag von Nizza geänderten Fassung*, Art. 56 EC (4th edn Bundesanzeiger, Helbing & Lichtenhahn, Linde, Köln, [et al] 2006).

——in Carl Otto Lenz and Klaus-Dieter Borchert (eds), *EU- und EG Vertrag—Kommentar zu dem Vertrag über die Europäische Union und zu dem Vertrag zur Gründung der Europäischen Gemeinschaft, jeweils in der durch den Vertrag von Nizza geänderten Fassung*, Art. 57 EC (4th edn Bundesanzeiger, Helbing & Lichtenhahn, Linde, Köln, [et al] 2006).

——in Carl Otto Lenz and Klaus-Dieter Borchert (eds), *EU- und EG Vertrag—Kommentar zu dem Vertrag über die Europäische Union und zu dem Vertrag zur*

Gründung der Europäischen Gemeinschaft, jeweils in der durch den Vertrag von Nizza geänderten Fassung, Art. 58 EC (4th edn Bundesanzeiger, Helbing & Lichtenhahn, Linde, Köln, [et al] 2006).

——in Carl Otto Lenz and Klaus-Dieter Borchert (eds), *EU- und EG Vertrag— Kommentar zu dem Vertrag über die Europäische Union und zu dem Vertrag zur Gründung der Europäischen Gemeinschaft, jeweils in der durch den Vertrag von Nizza geänderten Fassung*, Art. 59 EC (4th edn Bundesanzeiger, Helbing & Lichtenhahn, Linde, Köln, [et al] 2006).

Schwarz, Günter Christian, *Europäisches Gesellschaftsrecht* (Nomos, Baden-Baden 2000).

Schwarze, Jürgen (ed), *EU-Kommentar* (Nomos, Baden-Baden 2000).

Schwarze, Jürgen, *Europäisches Verwaltungsrecht: Entstehung und Entwicklung im Rahmen der Europäischen Gemeinschaft* (2nd edn Nomos, Baden-Baden 2005).

Schweitzer, Michael, and Waldemar Hummer, *Europarecht: das Recht der Europäischen Union; das Recht der Europäischen Gemeinschaften EGKS, EWG, EAG—mit Schwerpunkt EWG* (5th edn Luchterhand, Neuwied [et al] 1996).

Schwemer, Rolf-Oliver, *Die Bindung des Gemeinschaftsgesetzgebers an die Grundfreiheiten* (Schriften zum internationalen und zum öffentlichen Recht, vol 9, Lang, Frankfurt am Main [et al] 1995).

Schwenke, Michael, 'Die Kapitalverkehrsfreiheit im Wandel?—Eine erste Analyse neuer Entwicklungen in der Rechtsprechung des EuGH' (2006) 15 IStR 748.

Sedemund, Jan, 'Die mittelbare Wirkung der Grundfreiheiten für in Drittstaaten ansässige Unternehmen nach den EuGH-Urteilen Fidium Finanz AG und Cadbury Schweppes' (2006) 61 BB 2781.

Sedlaczek, Michael, *Die EG-Rechtsverträglichkeit der unterschiedlichen Besteuerung in- und ausländischer Investmentfonds* (Schriftenreihe der Steuer- und Wirtschaftskartei, Linde, Wien 1998).

——'Der Begriff der Diskriminierung und Beschränkung—Die Kapitalverkehrsfreiheit als konvergente Grundfreiheit des EG-Vertrages' in Eduard Lechner, Claus Staringer, and Michael Tumpel (eds), *Kapitalverkehrsfreiheit und Steuerrecht—Eine Analyse des österreichischen Steuerrechts vor dem Hintergrund der Kapitalverkehrsfreiheit des EG-Rechts* (Linde, Wien 2000), 27.

——in Rudolf Streinz (ed), *EUV/EGV: Vertrag über die Europäische Union und Vertrag zur Gründung der Europäischen Gemeinschaft*, Art. 56 EC (C.H. Beck, München 2003).

——in Rudolf Streinz (ed), *EUV/EGV: Vertrag über die Europäische Union und Vertrag zur Gründung der Europäischen Gemeinschaft*, Art. 57 EC (C.H. Beck, München 2003).

——in Rudolf Streinz (ed), *EUV/EGV: Vertrag über die Europäische Union und Vertrag zur Gründung der Europäischen Gemeinschaft*, Art. 58 EC (C.H. Beck, München 2003).

——in Rudolf Streinz (ed), *EUV/EGV: Vertrag über die Europäische Union und Vertrag zur Gründung der Europäischen Gemeinschaft*, Art. 59 EC (C.H. Beck, München 2003).

——in Rudolf Streinz (ed), *EUV/EGV: Vertrag über die Europäische Union und Vertrag zur Gründung der Europäischen Gemeinschaft*, Art. 60 EC (C.H. Beck, München 2003).

Seidel, Martin, 'Rechtliche Grundlagen eines einheitlichen Kapitalmarktes der Europäischen Gemeinschaft' in Herbert Leßmann (ed), *Festschrift für Rudolf Lukes: zum 65. Geburtstag* (Heymanns, Köln [et al] 1989), 575.

Seidel, Martin, 'Recht und Verfassung des Kapitalmarktes als Grundlage der Währungsunion' in Albrecht Randelzhofer, Rupert Scholz and Dieter Wilke (eds), *Gedächtnisschrift für Eberhard Grabitz* (C.H. Beck, München 1995), 763.

Shan, Wenhua, 'EU Enlargement and the Legal Framework of EU-China Investment Relations' (2005) 6 JWIT 237.

—— 'Towards a Common European Community Policy on Investment Issues' (2001) 2 JWIT 603.

—— *The Legal Framework of EU-China Investment Relations: A Critical Appraisal* (China and International Economic Law Series, Hart, Oxford [et al] 2005).

Shaw, Malcolm N, *International Law* (5th edn Cambridge University Press, Cambridge [et al] 2003).

Sick, Sebastian, *Das Kohärenzgebot bei Wirtschaftssanktionen der EU: zum Verhältnis zwischen gemeinsamer Außen- und Sicherheitspolitik und gemeinschaftlicher Handelspolitik* (Schriften des Europa-Instituts der Universität des Saarlandes—Rechtswissenschaft, Nomos, Baden-Baden 2001).

'Siemens: Staatsfonds willkommen' *manager-magazin.de* (28.08.2008).

Smit, Daniël S., 'The Relationship between the Free Movement of Capital and the other EC Treaty Freedoms in Third Country Relationships in the Field of Direct Taxation: a Question of Exclusivity, Parallelism or Causality?' (2007) 16 EC Tax Review 252.

Smits, René, 'Freedom of Payments and Capital Movements under EMU' in Albrecht Weber and Ludwig Gramlich (eds), *Währung und Wirtschaft: das Geld im Recht: Festschrift für Prof. Dr. Hugo J. Hahn zum 70. Geburtstag*, 245 (Nomos, Baden-Baden 1997).

—— *The European Central Bank: Institutional Aspects* (International banking and finance law, Kluwer, The Hague [et al] 1997).

Soanes, Catherine, and Agnus Stevenson, *Concise Oxford English Dictionary* (7th edn Oxford University Press, Oxford [et al] 2006).

Sørensen, Karsten Engsig, 'The Most-Favoured-Nation Principle in the EU' (2007) 34 LIEI 315.

Sornarajah, M, *The International Law on Foreign Investment* (2nd edn Cambridge University Press, Cambridge [et al] 2004).

Spengel, Christoph, and Martin Golücke, 'Gesellschafter-Fremdfinanzierung: Implikationen der EG-Rechtswidrigkeit von § 8a KStG für die Praxis und den Gesetzgeber' (2003) 49 RIW 333.

'Staatsfonds: Politiker verlangen Schutz vor Ausverkauf' *Manager Magazin.de* (08.07.2007).

Ståhl, Kristina, 'Dividend Taxation in a Free Capital Market' (1997) 6 EC Tax Review 227.

—— 'Free Movement of Capital between Member States and Third Countries' (2004) 13 EC Tax Review 47.

Staringer, Claus, 'Dividendenbesteuerung und Kapitalverkehrsfreiheit' in Eduard Lechner, Claus Staringer, and Michael Tumpel (eds), *Kapitalverkehrsfreiheit und Steuerrecht—Eine Analyse des österreichischen Steuerrechts vor dem Hintergrund der Kapitalverkehrsfreiheit des EG-Rechts* (Linde, Wien 2000), 93.

Statistisches Bundesamt, *Datenreport 2006: Zahlen und Fakten über die Bundesrepublik Deutschland* (Schriftenreihe, vol 544, Bundeszentrale für politische Bildung, Bonn 2006).

Stein, Torsten, *Die gemeinsame Außen- und Sicherheitspolitik der Union unter besonderer Berücksichtigung der Sanktionsproblematik* (Schriftenreihe des Forschungsinstitutes für Europarecht der Karl-Franzens-Universität Graz, Universität Graz, Graz 1993).

——'Außenpolitisch motivierte (Wirtschafts-)Sanktionen der Europäischen Union—nach wie vor eine rechtliche Grauzone?' in Ulrich Beyerlin and Max-Planck-Institut für Ausländisches Öffentliches Recht und Völkerrecht Heidelberg (eds), *Recht zwischen Umbruch und Bewahrung: Völkerrecht, Europarecht, Staatsrecht; Festschrift für Rudolf Bernhardt* (Springer, Berlin [et al] 1995), 1129.

Stein, Torsten, and Christian von Buttlar, *Völkerrecht* (11th edn Heymanns, Köln [et al] 2005).

Steinbarth, Sebastian, 'Individualrechtsschutz gegen Maßnahmen der EG zur Bekämpfung des internationalen Terrorismus: Die Entscheidungen des EuG in den Rs. „Yusuf u.a." sowie „Kadi"' (2006) 9 ZEuS 269.

Steinberg, Philipp, 'Zur Konvergenz der Grundfreiheiten auf Tatbestands- und Rechtfertigungsebene' (2002) EuGRZ 13.

Steinbrück, Peer, 'Schlüsselindustrien und ausländische Staatsfonds—die Sicht der Bundesregierung' (2008) 61 Kreditwesen 11.

Steindorff, Ernst, 'Drittwirkung der Grundfreiheiten im europäischen Gemeinschaftsrecht' in Peter Badura and Rupert Scholz (eds), *Wege und Verfahren des Verfassungslebens: Festschrift für Peter Lerche zum 65. Geburtstag* (Beck, München 1993), 575.

——*EG-Vertrag und Privatrecht* (Schriftenreihe Europäisches Recht, Politik und Wirtschaft, Nomos, Baden-Baden 1996).

Steiner, Josephine, Lorna Woods, and Christian Twigg-Flesner, *EU Law* (9th edn Oxford University Press, Oxford [et al] 2006).

Steinvorth, Till, 'Besteuerung von Darlehen und freier Kapitalverkehr (Sandoz/Finanzlandesdirektion für Wien, Niederösterreich und Burgenland, EuGH vom 14. Oktober 1999, C-439/97)' (2000) ELRep. 21.

Stern, Klaus (ed), *Das Staatsrecht der Bundesrepublik Deutschland* (vol III.2, C.H. Beck, München 1994).

Stödter, Rolf (ed), *Hamburg, Deutschland, Europa: Beiträge zum deutschen und europäischen Verfassungs-, Verwaltungs- und Wirtschaftsrecht; Festschrift für Hans Peter Ipsen zum 70. Geburtstag* (Mohr Siebeck, Tübingen 1977).

Story, Jonathan, and Ingo Walter, *Political Economy of Financial Integration in Europe: the Battle of the Systems* (Manchester University Press, Manchester 1997).

Streinz, Rudolf (ed), *EUV/EGV: Vertrag über die Europäische Union und Vertrag zur Gründung der Europäischen Gemeinschaft* (C.H. Beck, München 2003).

Streinz, Rudolf, *Europarecht* (7th edn C.F. Müller, Heidelberg 2005).

——in Rudolf Streinz (ed), *EUV/EGV: Vertrag über die Europäische Union und Vertrag zur Gründung der Europäischen Gemeinschaft*, Art. 2 EC (C.H. Beck, München 2003).

——in Rudolf Streinz (ed), *EUV/EGV: Vertrag über die Europäische Union und Vertrag zur Gründung der Europäischen Gemeinschaft*, Art. 3 EC (C.H. Beck, München 2003).

——in Rudolf Streinz (ed), *EUV/EGV: Vertrag über die Europäische Union und Vertrag zur Gründung der Europäischen Gemeinschaft*, Art. 12 EC (C.H. Beck, München 2003).

Streinz, Rudolf, and Stefan Leible, 'Die unmittelbare Drittwirkung der Grundfreiheiten—Überlegungen aus Anlass von EuGH, EuZW, 468—Angonese' (2000) 11 EuZW 459.

Streitz, Matthias, Christian Reiermann, and ddp, 'Union schmiedet Abwehrwaffen gegen Firmenaufkäufer' *Spiegel Online* (16.10.2007).

Teichmann, Christoph, 'Schutz vor ausländischen Investoren, Bahnprivatisierung und VW-Gesetz: Europäische Kapitalverkehrsfreiheit setzt dem deutschen Gesetzgeber Grenzen' (2007) Status: Recht 365.

Terra, Ben, and Peter J Wattel, *European Tax Law* (3rd edn Kluwer, London 2001).

The Economist Intelligence Unit (ed), *World Investment Prospects to 2011: Foreign Direct Investment and the Challenge of Political Risk* (The Economist Intelligence Unit, London 2007).

'The World's Most Expensive Club' *The Economist* (24.05.2007).

Thömmes, Otmar, 'Tatbestandsmäßigkeit und Rechtfertigung steuerlicher Diskriminierungen nach EG-Recht' in Wolfgang Schön (ed), *Gedächtnisschrift für Brigitte Knobbe-Keuk in Zusammenarbeit mit Werner Flume und Horst Heinrich Jakobs, Eduard Picker, Jan Wilhelm* (O. Schmidt, Köln 1997), 795.

Tiedje, Jürgen, and Peter Troberg, in Hans von der Groeben and Jürgen Schwarze (eds), *Kommentar zum Vertrag über die Europäische Union und zur Gründung der Europäischen Gemeinschaft*, Art. 43 EC (vol 1, 6th edn Nomos, Baden-Baden 2003).

——in Hans von der Groeben and Jürgen Schwarze (eds), *Kommentar zum Vertrag über die Europäische Union und zur Gründung der Europäischen Gemeinschaft*, Art. 48 EC (vol 1, 6th edn Nomos, Baden-Baden 2003).

Tietje, Christian, 'Die Meistbegünstigungspflicht im Gemeinschaftsrecht' (1995) 30 EuR 398.

——'Niederlassungsfreiheit' in Dirk Ehlers (ed), *Europäische Grundrechte und Grundfreiheiten* (2nd edn de Gruyter, Berlin 2005), 284.

——*Beschränkungen ausländischer Unternehmensbeteiligungen zum Schutz vor 'Staatsfonds'—Rechtliche Grenzen eines neuen Interventionismus* (Transnational Economic Law Research Center, 2007) <http://www2.jura.uni-halle.de/telc/PolicyPaper26.pdf> accessed 12.12.2008.

Tietmeyer, Hans, 'Europäische Währung und europäischer Kapitalmarkt', *Kapitalmärkte im europäischen Prozeß*, 101 (vol 34, Fritz Knapp Verlag, Frankfurt a. M. 1992).

Tipke, Klaus, *Die Steuerrechtsordnung* (vol 1, 2nd edn O. Schmidt, Köln 2000).

Tomuschat, Christian, in Hans von der Groeben and Jürgen Schwarze (eds), *Kommentar zum Vertrag über die Europäische Union und zur Gründung der Europäischen Gemeinschaft*, Art. 281 EC (vol 4, 6th edn Nomos, Baden-Baden 2004).

——'Case Note on Case T-306/01 Ahmed Ali Yusuf and Al Barakaat International Foundation v. Council and Commission, Judgment of the Court of First Instance of 21 September 2005; Case T-315/01, Yassin Abdullah Kadi v. Council and Commission, Judgment of the Court of First Instance of 21 September 2005' (2006) 43 CMLR 537.

Torrent, Ramón, 'The Legal Toolbox for Regional Integration: A Legal Analysis from an Interdisciplinary Perspective', Fifth Annual Conference of the Euro-Latin Study Network on Integration and Trade (ELSNIT) Barcelona (26–27.10.2007) <http://www.iadb.org.uy/intal/aplicaciones/uploads/ponencias/i_foro_ELSNIT_10_02_Ramon_Torrent.PDF> accessed 05.02.2008.

Tridimas, Takis, and Paolisa Nebbia (eds), *EU Law for the 21st Century: Rethinking the New Legal Order* (Hart, Oxford [et al] 2004).

Troberg, Peter, in Hans von der Groeben, Jochen Thiesing, and Claus-Dieter Ehlermann (eds), *Kommentar zum EU-/EG-Vertrag*, Art. 52 ToM (vol 1, 5th edn Nomos, Baden-Baden 1997).

Trüten, Dirk, *Die Mobilität von Gesellschaften in der Europäischen Gemeinschaft* (Schulthess, Zurich 2005).

Trybus, Martin, 'The EC Treaty as an Instrument of European Defence Integration: Judicial Scrutiny of Defence and Security Exceptions' (2002) 39 CMLR 1347.

——'At the Borderline Between Community and Member State Competence: the Triple-exceptional Character of Article 297 EC' in Takis Tridimas and Paolisa Nebbia (eds), *EU Law for the 21st Century: Rethinking the New Legal Order*, 137 (vol 2, Hart, Oxford [et al] 2004).

Usher, John A., 'Capital Movements and the Treaty on European Union' (1992) 12 YEL 35.

——'Tax Discrimination under the New Capital Movement Provisions and the Basic Treaty Freedoms' in Matti Rudanko and Pekka Timonen (eds), *European Financial Area: Proceedings of Closing Seminar of the Research Project of KATTI* (vol 31, Institute of International Economic Law (KATTI), Helsinki 1998), 259.

——*The Law of Money and Financial Services in the European Community* (Oxford European Community Law Series, 2nd edn Clarendon Press, Oxford 2000).

——'Financial Services: Some Taxing Problems' (2001) 4 ZEuS 247.

Verdross, Alfred, and Bruno Simma, *Universelles Völkerrecht: Theorie und Praxis* (3rd edn Duncker & Humblot, Berlin 1984).

Vergano, Paolo R, in Center for International Legal Studies, et al (eds), *Smit & Herzog on The Law of the European Union*, Art. 57 EC (vol 1, LexisNexis Bender, New York 2005).

——in Center for International Legal Studies, et al (eds), *Smit & Herzog on The Law of the European Union*, Art. 59 EC (vol 1, LexisNexis Bender, New York 2005).

——in Center for International Legal Studies, et al (eds), *Smit & Herzog on The Law of the European Union*, Art. 60 EC (vol 1, LexisNexis Bender, New York 2005).

Vermeend, Willem, 'The Court of Justice of the European Communities and Direct Taxes: "Est-ce que la justice est de ce monde"?' (1996) 5 EC Tax Review 54.

Vieweg, Klaus, and Anne Röthel, 'Verbandsautonomie und Grundfreiheiten' (2002) 166 ZHR 6.

Vigneron, Philippe, and Philippe Steinfeld, 'La Communauté Européenne et la Libre Circulation des Capitaux: Les Nouvelles Dispositions et leurs Implications' (1996) 32 C.D.E. 401.

von Arnauld, Andreas, 'UN-Sanktionen und gemeinschaftsrechtlicher Grundrechtsschutz' (2006) 44 AVR 201.

von Bogdandy, Armin (ed), *Europäisches Verfassungsrecht: Theoretische und dogmatische Grundzüge* (Springer, Berlin [et al] 2003).

von Bogdandy, Armin, '3. Teil, I. "Außenaspekte der binnenmarktbezogenen Rechtsangleichung—Allgemeine Charakteristika und systematische Aspekte"' in Eberhard Grabitz, Armin von Bogdandy and Martin Nettesheim (eds), *Europäisches Außenwirtschaftsrecht* (C.H. Beck, München 1994), 367.

——in Eberhard Grabitz and Meinhard Hilf (eds), *Das Recht der Europäischen Union: Kommentar*, Art. 10 EC (vol 1, C.H. Beck, München 2002).

——in Eberhard Grabitz and Meinhard Hilf (eds), *Das Recht der Europäischen Union: Kommentar*, Art. 12 EC (vol 1, C.H. Beck, München 2002).

von Bogdandy, Armin, and Jürgen Bast (eds), *Principles of European Constitutional Law* (Hart, Oxford [et al] 2005).
von Burchard, Friedrich, in Jürgen Schwarze (ed), *EU-Kommentar*, Art. 86 EC (Nomos, Baden-Baden 2000).
von der Groeben, Hans, Jochen Thiesing, and Claus-Dieter Ehlermann (eds), *Kommentar zum EWG-Vertrag* (vol 1, 4th edn Nomos, Baden-Baden 1991).
von der Groeben, Hans, and Jürgen Schwarze (eds), *Kommentar zum Vertrag über die Europäische Union und zur Gründung der Europäischen Gemeinschaft* (vol 2, 6th edn Nomos, Baden-Baden 2003).
von der Groeben, Hans, and Jürgen Schwarze (eds), *Kommentar zum Vertrag über die Europäische Union und zur Gründung der Europäischen Gemeinschaft* (vol 4, 6th edn Nomos, Baden-Baden 2004).
von der Groeben, Hans, Jochen Thiesing, and Claus-Dieter Ehlermann (eds), *Kommentar zum EU-/EG-Vertrag* (vol 1, 5th edn Nomos, Baden-Baden 1997).
von Hippel, Thomas, 'Fremdnützige Vermögenstransfers—ein Anwendungsfall der Kapitalverkehrsfreiheit?' (2005) 16 EuZW 7.
von Wilmowsky, Peter, *Abfallwirtschaft im Binnenmarkt: europäische Probleme und amerikanische Erfahrungen* (Umweltrechtliche Studien, Werner, Düsseldorf 1990).
——'Ausnahmebereiche gegenüber EG-Grundfreiheiten?' (1996) 31 EuR 362.
——*Europäisches Kreditsicherungsrecht: Sachenrecht und Insolvenzrecht unter dem EG-Vertrag* (Beiträge zum ausländischen und internationalen Privatrecht, vol 60, Mohr Siebeck, Tübingen 1996).
——'Freiheit des Kapital- und Zahlungsverkehrs' in Dirk Ehlers (ed), *Europäische Grundrechte und Grundfreiheiten* (2nd edn de Gruyter, Berlin 2005), 343.
Wackerbart, Ulrich, 'Von golden shares und poison pills: Waffengleichheit bei internationalen Übernahmeangeboten' (2001) 55 WM 1741.
Waldhoff, Christian, in Christian Calliess and Matthias Ruffert (eds), *EUV · EGV—Kommentar*, Art. 93 EC (3rd edn C.H. Beck, München 2007).
——in Christian Calliess and Matthias Ruffert (eds), *EUV · EGV—Kommentar*, Art. 269 EC (3rd edn C.H. Beck, München 2007).
Wallace, Cynthia Day, *The Multinational Enterprise and Legal Control: Host State Sovereignty in an Era of Economic Globalization* (2nd edn Nijhoff, The Hague [et al] 2002).
Wallace, Helen, William Wallace, and Mark A. Pollack (eds), *Policy Making in the European Community* (2nd edn Wiley, Chichester 1983).
Wassermeyer, Franz, and Jens Schönfeld, '§ 18 Abs. 3 Satz 4 AuslInvestmG und EG-Drittstaaten: Überlegungen zur Fortbestandsgarantie des Art. 57 Abs. 1 EG sowie zum Verhältnis der Vorlageverfahren nach Art. 100 GG und Art. 234 EG—Anmerkung zu BFH vom 14. 9. 2005, VIII B 40/05, IStR 2006, 173' (2006) 15 IStR 411.
Watrin, Christian, 'Währungsunion und supranationale Staatlichkeit' in Rolf Hasse and Joachim Starbatty (eds), *Wirtschafts- und Währungsunion auf dem Prüfstand: Schritte zur weiteren Integration Europas* (Lucius & Lucius, Stuttgart 1997), 31.
Wattel, Peter J, 'The EC Court's Attempts to Reconcile the Treaty Freedoms with International Tax Law' (1996) 33 CMLR 223.
——'The Schumacker Legacy—Taxing Non-Resident Employees: Coping with Schumacker' (1995) 35 ET 347.

——'Progressive Taxation of Non-Residents and Intra-EC Allocation of Personal Tax Allowances: Why Schumacker, Asscher, Gilly and Gschwind Do not Suffice' (2000) 40 ET 210.
Weatherill, Stephen, 'After Keck: Some Thoughts on How to Clarify the Clarification' (1996) 33 CMLR 887.
Weber, Albrecht, and Ludwig Gramlich (eds), *Währung und Wirtschaft: das Geld im Recht: Festschrift für Prof. Dr. Hugo J. Hahn zum 70. Geburtstag* (Nomos, Baden-Baden 1997).
Weber, Albrecht, in Hans von der Groeben and Jürgen Schwarze (eds), *Kommentar zum Vertrag über die Europäische Union und zur Gründung der Europäischen Gemeinschaft*, Art. 310 EC (vol 4, 6th edn Nomos, Baden-Baden 2004).
Weber, Rolf H., in Carl Otto Lenz (ed), *EG-Vertrag: Kommentar zu dem Vertrag zur Gründung der Europäischen Gemeinschaften*, Art. 73d ToM (Bundesanzeiger, Köln 1994).
——in Carl Otto Lenz and Klaus-Dieter Borchert (eds), *EU- und EG Vertrag—Kommentar zu dem Vertrag über die Europäische Union und zu dem Vertrag zur Gründung der Europäischen Gemeinschaft, jeweils in der durch den Vertrag von Nizza geänderten Fassung*, Art. 58 EC (3rd edn Bundesanzeiger, Helbing & Lichtenhahn, Ueberreuter, Köln, [et al] 2003).
——in Carl Otto Lenz and Klaus-Dieter Borchert (eds), *EU- und EG Vertrag—Kommentar zu dem Vertrag über die Europäische Union und zu dem Vertrag zur Gründung der Europäischen Gemeinschaft, jeweils in der durch den Vertrag von Nizza geänderten Fassung*, Vorb. Art. 56–60 EC (3rd edn Bundesanzeiger, Helbing & Lichtenhahn, Ueberreuter, Köln, [et al] 2003).
Weber, Stefan, 'Kapitalverkehr und Kapitalmärkte im Vertrag über die Europäische Union' (1992) 3 EuZW 561.
Weber-Grellet, Heinrich, *Europäisches Steuerrecht* (Beck, München 2005).
Weiler, Joseph H H, 'The Constitution of the Common Market Place: Text and Context in the Evolution of the Free Movement of Goods' in Paul P Craig and Gráinne de Búrca (eds), *The Evolution of EU Law* (Oxford University Press, Oxford [et al] 1999), 349.
Weiss, Michael, 'Staatlicher Schutz vor Investitionen nach dem Urteil zum VW-Gesetz' (2008) 19 EWS 13.
Weiß, Wolfgang, 'Nationales Steuerrecht und Niederlassungsfreiheit' (1999) 10 EuZW 493.
——'Kommunale Energieversorger und EG-Recht: Fordert das EG-Recht die Beseitigung der Beschränkungen für die kommunale Wirtschaft? Ein Beitrag zum Grundfreiheitsstatus öffentlicher Unternehmen' (2003) 118 DVBl. 564.
——'Öffentliche Unternehmen und EGV' (2003) 38 EuR 165.
Weiß, Wolfgang, and Christoph Herrmann (eds), *Welthandelsrecht* (C.H. Beck, München 2003).
Welcker, Johannes, and Carsten Nerge, *Die Maastrichter Verträge—zum Scheitern verurteilt?* (Verlag Moderne Industrie, Landsberg 1992).
Wellens, Andreas, 'Nichtabziehbare Betriebsausgaben bei Drittlandsdividenden—Kapitalverkehrsfreiheit contra Niederlassungsfreiheit' (2007) 45 DStR 1852.
Weniger, Lothar *Kapitalverkehrskontrollen im europäischen Währungssystem* (Europäische Hochschulschriften: Reihe 5, Volks- und Betriebswirtschaft, vol 905, Lang, Frankfurt am Main [et al] 1988).

Werner, Horst, *Die Kontrolle internationaler Kapitalbewegungen* (Untersuchungen/Institut für Wirtschaftspolitik an der Universität zu Köln, Institut für Wirtschaftspolitik, Köln 1976).

Wernicke, Stephan, *Die Privatwirkung im Europäischen Gemeinschaftsrecht: Strukturen und Kategorien der Pflichtenstellungen Privater aus dem primären Gemeinschaftsrecht unter besonderer Berücksichtigung der Privatisierungsfolgen* (Schriftenreihe Europäisches Verfassungsrecht, Nomos, Baden-Baden 2002).

Wernsmann, Rainer, 'Steuerliche Diskriminierung und ihre Rechtfertigung durch die Kohärenz des nationalen Rechts—Zur Dogmatik der Schranken der Grundfreiheiten' (1999) 34 EuR 754.

Williamson, Hugh, 'EU "Should Vet State-funded Bids"' *Financial Times.com* (18.07.2007).

Wirbel, Klaus, 'Der Ausnahmezustand im Gemeinschaftsrecht: zu Inhalt und Grenzen des Art. 224 EG-Vertrag' (University of Bonn 1994).

Wohlfarth, Ernst, et al (eds), *Die Europäische Wirtschaftsgemeinschaft: Kommentar zum Vertrag* (Vahlen, Berlin 1960).

Woll, Artur, *Allgemeine Volkswirtschaftslehre* (Vahlens Handbücher der Wirtschafts- und Sozialwissenschaften, 14th edn Vahlen, München 2003).

Wruuck, Patricia, 'Economic Patriotism: New Game in Industrial Policy' (Online Research Paper, Deutsche Bank, Frankfurt 2006) <http://www.dbresearch.com/PROD/DBR_INTERNET_EN-PROD/PROD0000000000199989.pdf> accessed 10.11.2007.

Wunderlich, Nina, and Christoph Blaschke, 'Die Gewährleistung der Kapitalverkehrsfreiheit in Bezug auf Drittstaaten—Neuere Entwicklungen in der Rechtsprechung des EuGH' (2008) IStR 754.

Young, Alasdair, 'The Adoption of European Foreign Economic Policy: From Rome to Seattle' (2000) 38 JCMS 93.

Young, Stephen, and Neil Hood, 'Inward Investment Policy in the European Community on the 1990s' (1993) 2 TCJ 35.

Zuleeg, Manfred, in Hans von der Groeben and Jürgen Schwarze (eds), *Kommentar zum Vertrag über die Europäische Union und zur Gründung der Europäischen Gemeinschaft*, Art. 2 EC (vol 1, 6th edn Nomos, Baden-Baden 2003).

——in Hans von der Groeben and Jürgen Schwarze (eds), *Kommentar zum Vertrag über die Europäische Union und zur Gründung der Europäischen Gemeinschaft*, Art. 12 EC (vol 1, 6th edn Nomos, Baden-Baden 2003).

OFFICIAL AND SEMI-OFFICIAL PUBLICATIONS AND DOCUMENTS OF THE INSTITUTIONS AND BODIES OF EUROPEAN COMMUNITY/UNION, NATIONAL GOVERNMENTS, AND INTERNATIONAL ORGANIZATIONS

European Community/Union (Chronological)

European Parliament, 'Resolution on the Deposit on Imports into Italy' (Brussels 18.06.1982), OJ C182 of 19.07.1982, 114 *et seq*.

——'Communication on 'A Level Playing Field for Direct Investment World Wide'' (COM (95) 42 final, Brussels 01.03.1995).

——'Resolution on the Communication from the Commission Entitled: "A Level Playing Field for Direct Investment World Wide"' (COM (95) 42, Brussels), OJ C17 of 22.01.1996, 175 *et seq.*
European Council, 'CLS no. 6393/96 "Opinion of the Council's Legal Service as regards the Provisions of the EC Treaty applicable to Foreign Direct Investment and to Freedom of Establishment of Companies or Firms Owned or Controlled by Third-Country Natural or Legal Persons" [Title varying]' (CLS no 6393/96, Brussels 10.04.1996).
——'CLS no. 6554/97 "Contribution of the Council's Legal Service to the Proceedings of the Ad Hoc Working Party on the Multinational Investment Agreement with regard to the On-going OECD Negotiations for the Conclusion of a Multilateral Investment Agreement (MAI)"' (CLS no 6554/96, Brussels 13.03.1997).
——'Minimum Platform on Investment for EU FTAs' (15375/06, Brussels 27.11.2006).
Council and Representatives of the Governments of the Member States Meeting in the Council, 'Resolution on a Code of Conduct for Business Taxation' (Brussels 01.12.1997), OJ C2 of 06.01.1998, 2 *et seq.*
European Commission, 'Allgemeines Programm zur Aufhebung der Beschränkungen der Niederlassungsfreiheit' (18.12.1961), OJ Nr. 2 of 15.01.1962, 36.
——*Der Aufbau eines Europäischen Kapitalmarktes* (Office for Official Publications of the European Communities Brussels 1966).
——'Need for Community Action to Encourage European Investment in Developing Countries and Guidelines for such Action' (COM (78) 23 final, Brussels 30.01.1978).
——'Investment Promotion and Protection Clauses in Agreements between the Community and Various Categories of Developing Countries: Achievements to Date and Guidelines for Joint Action' (COM (80) 204 final, Brussels 08.05.1980).
——*Vollendung des Binnenmarktes: Weißbuch d. Kommission an d. Europäischen Rat* (Office for Official Publications of the European Communities, Luxembourg 1985).
——'Completing the Internal Market. White Paper from the Commission to the European Council (Milan, 28–29 June 1985)' (COM (85) 310 final, Brussels 14.06.1985).
——'Commission Staff Working Paper on CLS no. 6393/96 "Opinion of the Council's Legal Service as regards the Provisions of the EC Treaty applicable to Foreign Direct Investment and to Freedom of Establishment of Companies or Firms Owned or Controlled by Third-Country Natural or Legal Persons" [Title varying]' (SEC (97) 1428, Brussels 10.07.1997).
——'Communication on "Certain Legal Aspects concerning Intra-EU Investment"' (Brussels 19.07.1997) C220 of 19.07.1997, 15.
——'First Biennial Report on the Application of the Principle of Mutual Recognition in Product and Services Market' (SEC (1999) 1106, Brussels 13.07.1999).
——'Responses to the Challenges of Globalisation—A Study on the International Monetary and Financial System and on Financing for Development' (SEC (2002) 186 final, Brussels 14.02.2002).
——'European Commission, Eight Acceding Countries and US Sign Bilateral Investment Understanding' (Website, Brussels 2003) <http://europa.eu.int/comm/trade/issues/bilateral/countries/usa/pr230903_en.htm> accessed 12.12.2005.
——'Communication to the Council, the European Parliament and the European Economic and Social Committee—An Internal Market without Company Tax

obstacles: Achievements, Ongoing Initiatives and Remaining Challenges' (COM (2003) 726 final, Brussels 24.11.2003).
——'Communication to the Council, The European Parliament and the European Economic and Social Committee: Dividend Taxation of Individuals in the Internal Market' (COM (2003) 810 final, Brussels 19.12.2003).
——'European Economy No. 6/2003: The EU Economy: 2003 Review' (European Commission, Brussels 2004).
——'Taxation: Commission Requests Germany to End Exit Tax Rules' (IP/04/493, Brussels 19.04.2004).
——'Provisions on Capital Movements in Multilateral & Bilateral Agreements of the European Union with Third Countries' (Pdf-file, European Commission, 2005) <http://europa.eu.int/comm/internal_market/capital/docs/multi-bilateral-agreements_en.pdf> accessed 12.03.2006.
——'Purchasing Property in Another Member State' (Website, European Commission, Brussels 2005) <http://europa.eu/scadplus/leg/en/lvb/l24404.htm> accessed 23.03.2007.
——'Internal Market: infringement cases against the UK, Portugal, Denmark, Austria, Sweden and Finland' (IP/05/352, Brussels 22.03.2005).
——'Commission Staff Working Document on "Special Rights in Privatised Companies in the Enlarged Union—A Decade Full of Developments"' (Brussels 22.07.2005).
——'Internal Market: infringement proceedings against Austria, Finland, France, Italy, Greece, Portugal and Sweden' (IP/05/1288, Brussels 17.10.2005).
——'Communication on Intra-EU Investment in the Financial Services' Sector' (Brussels), OJ C293 of 21.11.2005, 2.
——'Issues Paper: Upgrading the EU Investment Policy' (Brussels 30.05.2006).
——'Minimum Platform on Investment for EU FTAs—Provisions on Establishment in Template for a Title on "Establishment, Trade in Services and E-commerce"' (D (2006) 9219, Brussels 28.07.2006).
——'The Taking-up and Pursuit of the Business of Credit Institutions' (Website, Brussels 2006) <http://europa.eu/scadplus/leg/en/lvb/l24234.htm> accessed 18.08.2006.
——'Consolidated List of Persons, Groups and Entities Subject to EU Financial Sanctions' (Website, European Commission, Brussels 2007) <http://ec.europa.eu/comm/external_relations/cfsp/sanctions/list/consol-list.htm> accessed 17.03.2007.
——'Commission Staff Working Document on "The External Dimension of the Single Market Review—Accompanying Document to the Communication from the Commission to the European Parliament, the Council, the European Economic and Social Committee and the Committee of the Regions"' (SEC (2007) 1519, Brussels 20.11.2007).
——'A Common European Approach to Sovereign Wealth Funds' (COM (2008) 115 final, Brussels 27.02.2008).
——'Sovereign Wealth Funds—Frequently Asked Questions' (MEMO/08/126, Brussels 27.02.2008).
EUROSTAT, *European Union Foreign Direct Investment Yearbook 2007: Data 2001–2005* (Office for Official Publications of the European Communities, Luxembourg 2007).
——*European Union Foreign Direct Investment Yearbook 2008: Data 2001–2006* (Office for Official Publications of the European Communities, Luxembourg 2008).

European Economic and Social Committee, 'Opinion of the Economic and Social Committee on the "Global Harmonisation of Direct Investment Regulations"' (96/C153/16, Brussels), OJ C153 of 28.05.1996, 55 *et seq.*

Germany

Deutscher Bundestag, 'Europarechtliche Beurteilung der geplanten Änderungen des Außenwirtschaftsgesetzes: Antwort der Bundesregierung auf eine Kleine Anfrage der Abgeordneten Rainer Brüderle, Frank Schäffler, Dr. Karl Addicks, weiterer Abgeordneter und der Fraktion der FDP' (Berlin 03.01.2008) Drucksache 16/3258.

International Monetary Fund (Alphabetical)

International Monetary Fund, *Balance of Payments Manual* (5th edn International Monetary Fund, Washington, DC 1993).
——*Global Financial Stability Report: Financial Market Turbulence: Causes, Consequences, and Policies* (World Economic and Financial Surveys, International Monetary Fund, Washington, DC 2007).

Organisation for Economic Co-operation and Development (Alphabetical)

OECD, *International Investment Perspectives 2007: Freedom of Investment in a Changing World* (OECD, Paris 2007).
——OECD Articles of the Model Convention with respect to Taxes on Income and on Capital (adopted 15.07.2005) <http://www.oecd.org/dataoecd/50/49/35363840.pdf> accessed 22.07.2006.
——*OECD Benchmark Definition of Foreign Direct Investment* (3rd edn OECD, Paris 1996).
——*Sovereign Wealth Funds and Recipient Country Policies* (OECD, Paris 2008).

United Nations Conference on Trade and Development (Alphabetical)

UNCTAD, *Admission and Establishment* (UNCTAD Series on Issues in International Investment Agreements, United Nations, New York and Geneva 1999).
——*Home Country Measures* (UNCTAD Series on Issues in International Investment Agreements, United Nations, New York and Geneva 2001).
——*International Investment Agreements: Key Issues* (vol 1, United Nations, New York and Geneva 2004).
——*World Investment Report 2003: FDI Policies for Development: National and International Perspectives* (United Nations, New York and Geneva 2003).
——*World Investment Report 2006: FDI from Developing and Transition Economies: Implications for Development* (United Nations, New York and Geneva 2006).

United States of America (Alphabetical)

US Foreign Commercial Service, and US Department of State, 'Doing Business in the European Union: A Commercial Guide for the U.S. Companies' (U.S. State Department, Washington, DC 2007) <http://www.buyusa.gov/europeanunion/two_zero_zero_seven_ccg.pdf> accessed 10.10.2007.
US Mission to the European Union, 'U.S. Welcomes Bilateral Investment Treaty Understanding' (Brussels 03.09.2003).

US Mission to the European Union, 'U.S., EC Sign Bilateral Investment Understanding for Accession Countries' (Brussels 22.09.2003).

US Trade Representative, '2007 National Trade Estimate Report on Foreign Trade Barriers' (United States Trade Representative, Washington, DC 2007).

World Trade Organisation (Alphabetical)

WTO, 'Guide to Reading the GATS Schedules of Specific Commitments and the List of Article II (MFN) Exemptions' (Website, WTO, Geneva 2006) <http://www.wto.org/english/tratop_e/serv_e/guide1_e.htm> accessed 22.10.2006.

——'Service Sectoral Classification List' (MTN.GNS/W/120).

——'Services Commitments: Schedules of Commitments and Lists of Article II Exemptions' (Website, WTO, Geneva 2006) <http://www.wto.org/english/tratop_e/serv_e/serv_commitments_e.htm> accessed 22.10.2006.

Index

Administration and statistics
   intra-Community capital movements 225
   third country capital
      movements 241–242
***'Anxiety is the Dizziness of
      Freedom'*** 327–331

Balance of payments equalization 19–21
Banks 294–297

Capital
   'movement of capital' defined
      economic usage 45–46
      focus on 'movement' 48–57
      holistic interpretation of EC
         Treaty 43–45
      legal treatment 46–48
      summary 57–58
   position statement 333–334
'Centre of gravity' approach 96–108
'Channel phenomenon' 181–183
Common Market
   equal treatment and market access
      non-discrimination test within
         EC 129–162
      non-hindrance test 116–129
      third country capital
         movements 162–200
   rationale for liberalization of capital
      movements 24
Comparability
   comparison groups 131–135
   direct taxation
      EC Treaty 146–147
      international law 146
      introduction 145–146
      third country capital
         movements 186–190
      treatment of fully taxable
         residents 152–157
      treatment of non-residents by host
         State 147–152
   foreign direct investments 157–160
   summary and appraisal 160–162
   third country capital movements
      direct taxation 186–190
      foreign direct investment 194–196
      harmonization 190–196

      ineffective interpretation 196–197
      introduction 184–186
Competence
   Art 57(2)EC as basis for Community
      bargaining power
      limits on competence 303–304
      secondary measures 301–303
   Community treaty-making powers 330
   economic emergencies 305
   financial sanctions by Member
      States 322–323
Competition *see* **Free and fair competition**
Credit institutions 294–297
Cross-border capital movements
   see also **foreign direct investment**
   material scope of Art 56 (1)EC
      cross-border element 60–63
      localizing capital 58–59
   non-discrimination test within EC
      case law on 'non-discrimination'
         and non-hindrance' tests 140–143
      comparison groups 131–135
      introduction 129–131
      issue of comparability 143–160
      relevant criteria for distinguishing direct
         and indirect discrimination 135–140
      summary and appraisal 160–161

Derogations 254–255
Direct discrimination
   expressly prohibited
      distinguishing criteria
      nationality and residence 140
      origin/destination of capital
         movements 137–139
   indirect discrimination
      distinguished 140–143
   meaning 135–137
   position statement 339
Direct effect
   horizontal direct effect 210–212
   position statement 342–343
   vertical direct effect 201–204
Direct investment *see* **foreign direct
   investment**
Direct taxation
   EC Treaty 146–147
   international law 146

Direct taxation (*cont.*)
  introduction 145–146
  position statement 339
  third country capital movements 186–190, 186–190
  treatment of fully taxable residents 152–157
  treatment of non-residents by host State 147–152
Discrimination *see* Non-discrimination test
'*domaine réservé*' 171–172, 341

EC Treaty
  discriminatory direct taxation 146–147
  material scope of Art 56 (1)EC
    equal treatment and market access 115–200
    'movement of capital' defined 43–58
    relationship with freedom of establishment 81–114
  personal scope
    addressees of corresponding obligations 208–212
    beneficiaries of the freedom 206–208
    introduction 201
    irrelevance of nationality and residence 204–206
    summary 212–213
    vertical direct effect 201–204
  policy changes towards liberalization
    erga omnes capital movements 37–39
    establishment of EEC 32–34
    new policy twist with SEA 35–37
  rationale for liberalization of capital movements
    balance of payments equalization 19–21
    Common Market economic constitution 24
    conclusions 31
    economic and monetary union 21–22
    economic growth 19–21
    free and fair competition 23
    free movement of goods and services 23
    free movement of persons 23
    one of four fundamental freedoms 18–19
    position statement 332–333
    price stability 19–21
  reference sources 10
Economic activity
  failure to liberalize third party capital movements 24–30
  rationale for liberalization of capital movements
    balance of payments equalization 19–21
    Common Market economic constitution 24
    economic and monetary union 21–22
    economic growth 19–21
    free and fair competition 23
    free movement of goods and services 23
    free movement of persons 23
    one of four fundamental freedoms 18–19
    position statement 332–333
    price stability 19–21
    relationship with justifications under Art 58(2) EC 244–245
Economic and monetary union
  grounds for liberalizing third party capital movements 28–29
  rationale for liberalization of capital movements 21–22
Economic emergencies
  Commission approval 309–310
  form of 'safeguard measures' 308–309
  preconditions 306–308
  setback to liberalization 310–311
  Treaty provisions and scope 305–306
Emergencies *see* Economic emergencies
Equal treatment and market access
  introduction 115–116
  non-discrimination test within EC
    case law on 'non-discrimination' and non-hindrance' tests 140–143
    comparison groups 131–135
    introduction 129–131
    issue of comparability 143–160
    relevant criteria for distinguishing direct and indirect discrimination 135–140
    summary and appraisal 160–161
  non-hindrance test
    conclusions 129
    inbound and outbound capital movements 119–122
    prohibition of discrimination not enough 117–118
    readjustment of interpretative approach 122–123
    uncertainties of interpretation 116–117
  position statement
    meaning and scope 337–338
    non-discrimination test 338–342
    non-hindrance test 338
  'substantial impediment' test
    justification 128–129
    tendency towards new approach 123–128
  third country capital movements
    conclusion and appraisal 197–200
    critical review of legal writing 168–182
    introduction 162–163
    non-discrimination test 183–197
    scope reflected in case law 163–168

Index

Erga omnes capital movements
  'Anxiety is the Dizziness of Freedom' 327–331
  failure to liberalize third party capital movements 25–27
  material scope in third country context 178–180
  policy shit towards deregulation 37–39
  rationale for liberalization of capital movements 332–333
  third country capital movements 170–171, 340–341

European Commission
  economic emergencies 309–310
  policy changes towards liberalization
    loss of momentum by mid-1970s 34–35
    new policy twist with SEA 35–37
  reference sources 10–13
  third country capital movements 329

European Community (EC)
see also **Member States**
  addressee of corresponding obligations 209–210
  largest recipient of foreign direct investment 2–4
  unilateral promise not to interfere 8

European Court of Justice (ECJ)
  commitment to restrictions 328–329
  freedom of establishment
    'centre of gravity' approach 96–108
    introduction 89–90
    'not knowing' approach 90–92
    'not necessary' approach 92–96
  mandatory requirements in intra-Community context 261–266
  material scope in third country context 163–168
  re-adjustment of non-hindrance test 122–123

Exceptions to free movement of capital
  intra-Community and third countries situations
    intra-Community national measures 216–236
    introduction 214–215
    overview of Art 58 EC 215–216
    permanent derogations 254–255
    'property ownership' 248–252
    relationship of Art 58 with freedom of establishment 243–247
    third country national measures 236–243
    transitional periods 254
    '*ultimo ratio*' defence 253
    unwritten grounds based on 'rule of reason' 255–274
  position statements
    intra-Community and third countries situations 343–349
    third country capital movements only 349–352
  third countries situations only
    economic emergencies 305–311
    'grandfathering clauses' 276–299
    introduction 275–276
    liberalization of policy 299–305
    political crises 311–326
  third country capital movements 184

Exchange rates 29

Exclusivity
  appraisal 110–113
  ECJ case law
    'centre of gravity' approach 96–108
    introduction 89–90
    'not knowing' approach 90–92
    'not necessary' approach 92–96
  literary views 108–110

Financial institutions 221

Financial sanctions against third countries
  Community measures
    admissibility in international law 313–317
    procedure 317–319
    sanction addressees 319–322
    scope 311–312
    Treaty provisions 311
  Member States
    competence 322–323
    'Council intervention' 324–325
    importance 325–326
    relationship between Art 297EC and Art 60(2)EC 323–324
    'serious political reasons' 323–324
  position statement 349–352

Financial services 277
Financial transfers 52–53

Foreign direct investment
  comparability questions
    intra-Community capital movements 157–160
    third country capital movements 194–196
  course of this study 15–16
  EC approach 8
  EC's share 2–4
  effect of 'grandfathering clauses' on liberalization 280–282
  'grandfathering clauses' 277
  material scope of Art 56 (1)EC
    economic impregnation 64–66
    interpretation 'in its widest sense' 66–70
    introduction 63–64
    'lasting and direct links' 70–74

394 Index

Foreign direct investment (*cont.*)
  position statement 334–336
  summary 79–80
  third countries defined 74–78
  purpose of this study 13–15
  reference sources 8–13
  relationship with freedom of
    establishment 82–88
Free and fair competition
  grounds for liberalizing third party capital
    movements 27–28
  rationale for liberalization of capital
    movements 23, 332–333
Free movement of capital
  course of this study 15–16
  material scope of Art 56 (1)EC
    capital movements beyond national
      boundaries 58–63
    'foreign direct investment'
      defined 63–80
    introduction 42–43
    'movement of capital' defined 43–58
  purpose of this study 13–15
  reference sources 8–13
  restrained approach to government
    interference 1–2
Free movement of goods and services 23
Free movement of persons 23
Freedom of establishment
  ECJ approach 89–108
  ECJ case law
    'centre of gravity' approach 96–108
    introduction 89–90
    'not knowing' approach 90–92
    'not necessary' approach 92–96
  foreign direct investments as
    cross-sectional activity 82–88
  'grandfathering clauses' 277
  introduction 81–82
  literary views 108–113
    exclusivity approach 108–110
    parallelism 110
  position statement 346–347
  relationship with justifications
    under Art 58(2) EC 243–247
  summary 113–114
  Treaty provisions 88–89, 88–89

Global capital allocation 172–178
'Grandfathering clauses'
  appraisal of parallelism 113
  effect of Art 57(1) on liberalization
    of capital movements
    applicability to international
      treaties 279–280
    direct investment defined 280–282
    effectiveness of a law 286–290

  examples of restrictive laws 294–299
  a gateway for unreasonable
    restrictions 290–291
  identification of national laws 291–294
  role of national or community
    law 283–286
  scope of 'restrictions' 280
  overview 276–278

Habitual residence 204–205
Harmonization
  comparability of third country capital
    payments 190–196
  failure to liberalize third party capital
    movements 26–27, 29
Horizontal direct effect 210–212

Indirect discrimination
  direct discrimination
    distinguished 140–143
  meaning 135–137
  position statement 339
Insurers 297–298
Intra-Community capital movements
  comparability questions 157–160
  restrictions applicable to intra-Community
    and third country situations
    intra-Community national
      measures 216–236
    introduction 214–215
    overview of Art 58 EC 215–216
    permanent derogations 254–255
    'property ownership' 248–252
    relationship of Art 58 with freedom of
      establishment 243–247
    third country national
      measures 236–243
    transitional periods 254
    '*ultimo ratio*' defence 253
    unwritten grounds based on
      'rule of reason' 255–274
Investments
  see also **Foreign direct investment**
  examples for restrictive laws 294–297
  'movement of capital' defined 53–57
Investors 330

Justifications *see* Exceptions to
  free movement of capital

Liberalization of capital
  movements
  see also ***Erga omnes*** **capital movements**
  '*Anxiety is the Dizziness of Freedom*' 327–331
  Art 57(2)EC as basis for Community bar-
    gaining power
    choice of means of action 304

Index

competence to take secondary
    measures 301–303
  increasing future use 304–305
  limits on competence 303–304
  underlying notion 299–301
attainment of EC Treaty aims
  balance of payments equalization 19–21
  Common Market economic
    constitution 24
  economic and monetary union 21–22
  economic growth 19–21
  free and fair competition 23
  free movement of goods and services 23
  free movement of persons 23
  one of four fundamental
    freedoms 18–19
  price stability 19–21
central questions 7–8
conclusions 31
economic emergencies 310–311
effect of 'grandfathering clauses'
  applicability to international
    treaties 279–280
  direct investment defined 280–282
  effectiveness of a law 286–290
  examples of restrictive laws 294–299
  a gateway for unreasonable
    restrictions 290–291
  identification of national laws 291–294
  role of national or community
    law 283–286
  scope of 'restrictions' 280
introduction 17–18
lack of aims for third party capital
  movements 24–30
policy changes
  comprehensive multilateral agreements
    resulting in deregulation 39–41
  erga omnes capital movements 37–39
  establishment of EEC 32–34
  loss of momentum by mid-1970s 34–35
  new policy twist with SEA 35–37
  significant shift over time 31–32
purpose of this study 14–15
Loans 87

**Management and investment
    companies** 294–297
Market access *see* **Equal treatment
    and market access**
Material scope of Art 56 (1)EC
  capital movements beyond national
    boundaries
    cross-border element 60–63
    localizing capital 58–59
  equal treatment and market access
    introduction 115–116, 115–116

non-discrimination test
    within EC 129–162
  non-hindrance test 116–129
  third country capital
    movements 162–200
'foreign direct investment' defined
  economic impregnation 64–66
  interpretation 'in its widest sense' 66–70
  introduction 63–64
  'lasting and direct links' 70–74
  summary 79–80
  third countries defined 74–78
introduction 42–43
'movement of capital' defined
  economic usage 45–46
  focus on 'movement' 48–57
  holistic interpretation of EC
    Treaty 43–45
  legal treatment 46–48
  summary 57–58
position statement
  equal treatment and market
    access 337–342
  foreign direct investment 334–336
  freedom of establishment 336–337
  'movement of capital' 333–334
relationship with freedom of
    establishment
  ECJ approach 89–108
  foreign direct investments as
    cross-sectional activity 82–88
  introduction 81–82
  literary views 108–113
  summary 113–114
  Treaty provisions 88–89
Member States
  addressees of corresponding
    obligations 208–209
  challenges to liberalization 327–328
  derogations 254–255
  financial sanctions against third countries
    competence 322–323
    'Council intervention' 324–325
    importance 325–326
    relationship between Art 297EC and Art
      60(2)EC 323–324
    'serious political reasons' 323–324
  policy changes
    comprehensive multilateral agreements
      resulting in deregulation 39–41
    erga omnes capital movements 37–39
    establishment of EEC 32–34
    loss of momentum by mid-1970s 34–35
    new policy twist with SEA 35–37
    significant shift over time 31–32
  restrained approach to government
    interference 1–2

Member States (*cont.*)
    restrictions applicable to intra-Community and third country situations
        intra-Community national measures 216–236
        introduction 214–215
        overview of Art 58 EC 215–216
        permanent derogations 254–255
        'property ownership' 248–252
        relationship of Art 58 with freedom of establishment 243–247
        third country national measures 236–243
        transitional periods 254
        '*ultimo ratio*' defence 253
        unwritten grounds based on 'rule of reason' 255–274

Monetary union *see* **Economic and monetary union**

Movement of capital
    economic usage 45–46
    focus on 'movement'
        financial transfers 52–53
        investments 53–57
        prevailing view 48–49, 48–49
        unilateral transactions 49–52
    holistic interpretation of EC Treaty 43–45
    legal treatment 46–48
    position statement 333–334
    summary 57–58

National measures
    applicability of 'rule of reason' to discriminatory national measures 257–261
    Art 57(2)EC as basis for Community bargaining power
        choice of means of action 304
        competence to take secondary measures 301–303
        increasing future use 304–305
        limits on competence 303–304
        underlying notion 299–301
    effect of 'grandfathering clauses' on liberalization
        applicability to international treaties 279–280
        direct investment defined 280–282
        effectiveness of a law 286–290
        examples of restrictive laws 294–299
        a gateway for unreasonable restrictions 290–291
        identification of national laws 291–294
        role of national or community law 283–286
        scope of 'restrictions' 280

intra-Community capital movements
    administration and statistics 225
    extension of applicable fields of activity 222–225
    ordre public exception 225–228
    overview 216–218
    proportionality test 228–234
    summary 234–236
    supervision of financial institutions 221
    taxation 218–221
introduction 215–216
justifications based on property ownership 248–253
position statement 340
    proportionality test 344–345
position statements
    intra-Community capital movements 343–345
    third country capital movements 345–346
relationship with freedom of establishment 243–247
third country capital movements
    administration and statistics 241–242
    appraisal 242–243
    introduction 236–237
    national laws and regulations 237–241
    ordre public exception 241–242
    public policy 241–242
third country justifications 237–241

National security and safety
see also **Financial sanctions against third countries**
    justifications for national measures 253
    position statement 347

Nationality
    irrelevance to personal scope 205–206
    prohibition of direct discrimination 140

Non-discrimination test
    comparability for foreign direct investments 157–160
    comparison groups 131–135
    direct discrimination
        expressly prohibited distinguishing criteria 137–140
        indirect discrimination distinguished 140–143
        meaning 135–137
    indirect discrimination
        direct discrimination distinguished 140–143
        meaning 135–137
    introduction 129–131
    issue of comparability

Index

direct taxation 145–157
  essential precondition 143–145
  position statement 338–342
  third country capital movements
    comparability 184–196
    general exceptions 184
    introduction 183–184

Non-hindrance test
  conclusions 129
  direct and indirect discrimination
    distinguished 140–143
  inbound and outbound capital
    movements 119–122
  position statement 338
  prohibition of discrimination not
    enough 117–118
  readjustment of interpretative
    approach 122–123
  uncertainties of interpretation 116–117

'**Not knowing' approach** 90–92
'**Not necessary' approach** 92–96

OECD Code of Liberalization 292–293

Ordre public **exception**
  intra-Community capital
    movements 225–228
  position statement 344
  third country capital
    movements 241–242

Parallelism
  appraisal 110–113
  ECJ case law
    'centre of gravity' approach 96–108
    introduction 89–90
    'not knowing' approach 90–92
    'not necessary' approach 92–96
  literary views 110

Personal scope
  addressees of corresponding
    obligations 208–212
    European Community (EC), 209–210
    Member States 208–209
  beneficiaries of the freedom 206–208, 206–208
  introduction 201
  irrelevance of nationality and
    residence 204–206
  position statement 343
  summary 212–213
  vertical direct effect 201–204

Political policies
  see also **Financial sanctions against third countries**
  comprehensive multilateral agreements
    resulting in deregulation 39–41

erga omnes capital movements 37–39
establishment of EEC 32–34
loss of momentum by mid-1970s 34–35
new policy twist with SEA 35–37
significant shift over time 31–32
strength of debate leading to
  restrictions 5–7

Position statements
  direct effect 342–343
  equal treatment and market access
    meaning and scope 337–338
    non-discrimination test 338–342
    non-hindrance test 338
  exceptions to free movement of capital
    intra-Community and third countries
      situations 343–349
    third country capital movements
      only 349–352
  material scope of Art 56 (1)EC
    equal treatment and market
      access 337–342
    foreign direct investment 334–336
    freedom of establishment 336–337
    movement of capital 333–334
  personal scope 343
  rationale for liberalization of capital
    movements 332–333

Price stability 19–21

'**Property ownership**'
  freedom of establishment 87–88
  justifications for national
    measures 248–253
  position statement 347

Proportionality test
  'grandfathering clauses' 290
  intra-Community capital
    movements 228–234
  position statement 344–345

Public policy
  intra-Community capital
    movements 225–228
  position statement 344
  third country capital
    movements 241–242

Reference sources 8–13

Residence
  discriminatory direct taxation
    prohibition of direct
      discrimination 140
    treatment of fully taxable
      residents 152–157
    treatment of non-residents by host
      State 147–152
  irrelevance to personal scope 204–205
  position statement 339

Restrictive measures
see also **National measures; Exceptions to free movement of capital**
  financial sanctions against third countries
    admissibility in international law 313–317
    procedure 317–319
    sanction addressees 319–322
    scope 311–312
    Treaty provisions 311
  Member States
    competence 322–323
    'Council intervention' 324–325
    importance 325–326
    relationship between Art 297EC and Art 60(2)EC 323–324
    'serious political reasons' 323–324

Reverse discrimination 131, 339

'Rule of reason' exceptions
  applicability to discriminatory national measures 257–261
  appraisal 274
  mandatory requirements in intra-Community context
    established by court 261–266
    rejected by court 286–288
    summary 268
  overview 255–257
  position statement 348–349
  third country capital movements
    mandatory requirements 269–274
    overview 268–269

Sanctions *see* **Financial sanctions against third countries**

Scope of regulation
  material scope of Art 56 (1)EC
    equal treatment and market access 115–200
    'movement of capital' defined 43–58
    position statement 333–342
    relationship with freedom of establishment 81–114
  personal scope
    addressees of corresponding obligations 208–212
    beneficiaries of the freedom 206–208
    introduction 201
    irrelevance of nationality and residence 204–206
    position statement 343
    summary 212–213
    vertical direct effect 201–204

Securities 277

Statistics
  intra-Community capital movements 225
  third country capital movements 241–242

'Substantial impediment' test
  justification 128–129
  tendency towards new approach 123–128

Taxation
  'Anxiety is the Dizziness of Freedom' 328
  discriminatory direct taxation
    EC Treaty 146–147
    international law 146
    introduction 145–146
    position statement 339, 341
    treatment of fully taxable residents 152–157
    treatment of non-residents by host State 147–152
  economic emergencies 307
  national measures 218–221
  'rule of reason' exceptions
    'fiscal cohesion' 269–271
    securing tax base 271–273
  third country capital movements 186–190

Third country capital movements
see also **foreign direct investment**
  'Anxiety is the Dizziness of Freedom' 327–328
  course of this study 15–16
  equal treatment and market access
    conclusion and appraisal 197–200
    critical review of legal writing 168–182
    introduction 162–163
    non-discrimination test 183–197
    position statement 340–342
    scope reflected in case law 163–168
  lack of aims for liberalization 24–30
  material scope of Art 56 (1)EC 74–78
  personal scope 207
  purpose of this study 13–15
  reference sources 11
  restrictions applicable to intra-Community and third country situations
    intra-Community national measures 216–236
    introduction 214–215
    overview of Art 58 EC 215–216
    permanent derogations 254–255
    'property ownership' 248–252
    relationship of Art 58 with freedom of establishment 243–247
    third country national measures 236–243
    transitional periods 254
    'ultimo ratio' defence 253
    unwritten grounds based on 'rule of reason' 255–274

restrictions applicable to third country situations only
  economic emergencies 305–311
  'grandfathering clauses' 276–299
  introduction 275–276
  liberalization of policy 299–305
  political crises 311–326
Transitional periods 254, 347–348
Transport 298–299

'*ultimo ratio*' **defence**
  position statement 347
  third country capital movements 253
Unilateral transactions 49–52

Vertical direct effect 201–204

World Trade Organization (WTO) 293–294

Die Rechtssache X Holding BV – das endgültige Ende der Hoffnungen auf ein vom EuGH postuliertes europäisches Gruppenbesteuerungssystem, *von Dr. Sven Pache/Max Englert* 448

Praxisforum

Besonderheiten bei der Vermögensbindung eines Fördervereins: Gemeinnützigkeit von ausländischen Körperschaften öffentlichen Rechts, *von Torsten Wohltmann* 453

Rechtsprechung

Gemeinsames Steuersystem für Fusionen, Spaltungen, die Einbringung von Unternehmensteilen und den Austausch von Anteilen, die Gesellschaften verschiedener Mitgliedstaaten betreffen (EuGH v. 20. 5. 2010, *Modehuis A. Zwijnenburg BV/Staatssecretaris van Financiën*) 455

Teilvorbezug aus Schweizer Wohneigentumsförderung als Altersrente aus gesetzlicher Rentenversicherung (BFH v. 25. 3. 2010) 458

Verwaltungsanweisung

DBA Schweiz: Besteuerungsrecht von Abfindungen an Arbeitnehmer (BMF v. 25. 3. 2010) 460

12/10

Herausgeber: Prof. Dr. Dr. h. c. Franz Wassermeyer, Prof. Dr. Detlev Jürgen Piltz, Prof. Dr. Jürgen Lüdicke, Prof. Dr. Dr. h. c. Wolfgang Schön

Verlag C. H. Beck
München · Frankfurt a. M.

S. 413 bis 460 · 17. Juni 2010 · 19. Jahrgang
www.istr.de